LEARNING
ABOUT
LEARNING
DISABILITIES

LEARNING ABOUT LEARNING DISABILITIES

Edited by
Bernice Y. L. Wong
Faculty of Education
Simon Fraser University
Burnaby, British Columbia, Canada

Academic Press, Inc.
Harcourt Brace Jovanovich, Publishers
San Diego   New York   Boston
London   Sydney   Tokyo   Toronto

Copyright © 1991 by ACADEMIC PRESS, INC.

All Rights Reserved.

No part of this publication may be reproduced or transmitted in any form or by any means, electronic or mechanical, including photocopy, recording, or any information storage and retrieval system, without permission in writing from the publisher.

Academic Press, Inc.
San Diego, California 92101

United Kingdom Edition published by
Academic Press Limited
24–28 Oval Road, London NW1 7DX

Library of Congress Cataloging-in-Publication Data

Learning about learning disabilities / [edited by] Bernice Y.L. Wong.
    p. cm.
  Includes bibliographical references and index.
  ISBN 0-12-762530-5
  1. Learning disabilities. 2. Learning disabled children--Education. 3. Learning disabled youth--Education. I. Wong, Bernice Y. L.
LC4704.L376 1991
371.9--dc20   90-28812
                                        CIP

PRINTED IN THE UNITED STATES OF AMERICA
91 92 93 94   9 8 7 6 5 4 3 2 1

This book is dedicated with love to my husband, Rod,
and my daughter, Kristi.

Contents

5. Language Problems: A Key to Early Reading Problems
Virginia Mann

6. Visual Processes in Learning Disabilities
Dale M. Willows

7. Social Problems and Learning Disabilities
Tanis Bryan

8. The Relevance of Metacognition to Learning Disabilities
Bernice Y. L. Wong

Section II

Assessment and Instructional Aspects of Learning Disabilities

9. Early Reading and Instruction
Lynn M. Gelzheiser and Diana Brewster Clark

10. Reading Comprehension Failure in Children
Ruth Garner, Patricia A. Alexander, and Victoria Chou Hare

11. Writing Instruction
Steve Graham, Karen R. Harris, Charles MacArthur, and Shirley Schwartz

Section III

Understanding Learning Disabilities through a Life-Span Approach

Contributors

Numbers in parentheses indicate the pages on which the authors' contributions begin.

Pamela B. Adelman (563)
Department of Education
Barat College
Lake Forest, Illinois 60045

Patricia A. Alexander (283)
Department of Educational Psychology
Texas A&M University
College Station, Texas 77843

Bob Algozzine (39)
Department of Teaching Specialties
The University of North Carolina at
   Charlotte
Charlotte, North Carolina 28223

Tanis Bryan (195)
College of Education
University of Illinois at Chicago
Chicago, Illinois 60680

JoAnne Caldwell (375)
Cardinal Stritch College
Milwaukee, Wisconsin 53217

Diana Brewster Clark (261)
Department of Special Education
Teachers College
Columbia University
New York, New York 10027

Richard Conte (59)
The Calgary Learning Centre and
   Department of Psychology
University of Calgary
Calgary, Alberta, Canada T2N 4N9

John B. Cooney (103)
Department of Educational Psychology
Division of Research Evaluation and
   Development
University of Northern Colorado
Greeley, Colorado 80639

Edwin S. Ellis (505)
Program for Exceptional Children
Department of Educational Psychology
University of South Carolina
Columbia, South Carolina 29208

Patricia Friend (505)
Department of Educational Psychology
University of South Carolina
Columbia, South Carolina 29208

Ruth Garner (283)
Washington State University
Vancouver, Washington 98663

Lynn M. Gelzheiser (261)
Department of Educational Psychology and
   Statistics
State University of New York at Albany
Albany, New York 12203

Steve Graham (309)
Department of Special Education
University of Maryland
College Park, Maryland 20740

Victoria Chou Hare (283)
Department of Education
University of Illinois at Chicago
Chicago, Illinois 60680

Karen R. Harris (309)
Department of Special Education
University of Maryland
College Park, Maryland 20740

James M. Kauffman (465)
Department of Special Education
University of Virginia
Charlottesville, Virginia 22903

Barbara K. Keogh (485)
Graduate School of Education
University of California
Los Angeles, California 90024

G. Reid Lyon (375)
Department of Education
Johnson State College
Johnson, Vermont 05656

Charles MacArthur (309)
Department of Special Education
University of Maryland
College Park, Maryland 20740

Virginia Mann (129)
Department of Cognitive Sciences
University of California
Irvine, California 92717

Robert E. Newby (375)
Medical College of Wisconsin
Milwaukee, Wisconsin 53226

Donna Recht (375)
Cardinal Stritch College
Milwaukee, Wisconsin 53217

Diane P. Rivera (345)
Department of Special Education
Florida Atlantic University
Boca Raton, Florida 33432

Suzanne M. Robinson (441)
Department of Special Education

University of Kansas
Lawrence, Kansas 66054

Shirley Schwartz (309)
Department of Special Education
University of California
Riverside, California 92521

Sue Sears (485)
Department of Special Education
California State University
Northridge, California 91330

Deborah D. Smith (345)
Department of Special Education
College of Education
University of New Mexico
Albuquerque, New Mexico 87131

H. Lee Swanson[1] (103)
University of California
Riverside, California 92521

Joseph K. Torgesen (3)
Department of Psychology
Florida State University
Tallahassee, Florida 32306

Stanley C. Trent (465)
Department of Special Education
University of Virginia
Charlottesville, Virginia 22903

Sharon Vaughn (407)
School of Education
University of Miami
Coral Gables, Florida 33124

Susan A. Vogel (563)
Department of Psychology, Counseling,
   and Special Education
Northern Illinois University
DeKalb, Illinois 60015

---

[1] Present address: Department of Educational Psychology, Faculty of Education, University of British Columbia, Vancouver, B.C., Canada V6T 155

Dale M. Willows (163)
Department of Instruction and Special
    Education
Ontario Institute for Studies in Education
Toronto, Ontario, Canada M5S 1V6

Bernice Y. L. Wong (231)
Faculty of Education
Simon Fraser University
Burnaby, B.C., Canada V5A 1S6

Preface

Learning disabilities is an unusual discipline in that it contains two contrasting aspects: one intellectual and the other practical. In my view, neither one suffices in the training of a learning disabilities professional. This is because on the one hand, one needs to understand fully the historical, conceptual, and definitional issues in learning disabilities, as well as the research on the characteristics of learning disabilities. On the other hand, one needs to learn about various ways of assessing and remediating academic problems in students with learning disabilities.

If students are only taught the intellectual aspects of learning disabilities, devoid of any practical experiences in testing and teaching a learning-disabled child or adolescent, they emerge from the course work with a very shallow knowledge about learning disabilities because their knowledge is strictly from book learning. And if they were to speak on the topic, they would be operating at the arm chair level. To understand genuinely the phenomenon of learning disabilities and to raise relevant questions for research, students must have some interactive *human* encounters, since learning disabilities are embodied in the children, adolescents, and adults with such disorders. Students need some minimal experience, such as involvement in a research project with learning-disabled subjects or a semester-long practicum in testing and teaching children or adolescents with learning disabilities, in order to understand how learning disabilities impede cognitive functions.

The reverse is equally unsatisfactory vis-à-vis proper training of learning disabilities professionals. If students receive training only in the practical aspect of learning disabilities, they emerge from the course work at a loss when confronted with questions such as: "Why do you insist on calling this student learning disabled rather than simply a poor reader?"

Clearly I have laid bare my own bias in student training. I firmly believe that to produce competent professionals in learning disabilities, whether researchers or teachers, we should attend to training them in these twin aspects of our discipline both at the undergraduate and graduate levels. We need to provide students with a firm and balanced foundation in learning disabilities, especially at the undergraduate level, so that they can build on it in subsequent years of work experience and future academic pursuits.

My particular view on training in learning disabilities explains why I have chosen to produce this book. In my undergraduate teaching, I have long been frustrated with the available textbooks on the market because, with rare exception (I can only think of one or two), they tend to focus heavily on the practical aspect of learning disabilities while touching superficially on the conceptual and research issues and research in learning disabilities. I had tried to avoid the task of producing an undergraduate textbook on learning disabilities. But there came a time when I could no longer ignore the need for an undergraduate learning disabilities text that has a balanced focus on intellectual and practical issues. I need it for my own teaching.

To write an undergraduate text in learning disabilities that covers the twin foci of intellectual and practical aspects of the discipline is an enormous undertaking. I was unwilling to take it on solely by myself simply because I do not possess the range and depth of knowledge to cover all the necessary topics. Hence, I called upon my esteemed colleagues for help.

I am indeed blessed to have so many friends who were willing to contribute their time and energy in writing the scholarly chapters in this book. Each has drawn upon his or her area of expertise and thoughtfully produced chapters that are stimulating and instructive. I cannot thank them enough for their contributions.

There are three persons to whom I extend special thanks: J. K. Torgesen for consistently and patiently hearing me out every time I've been seized by a wild idea and transported by enthusiasm for it. I thank him for sound advice and good feedback. Thanks also to Tanis Bryan, who is always supportive, warm, and encouraging, and with whom Guru (Jim Bryan) and I share many a good laugh. I also thank Barbara Keogh, my esteemed senior colleague. In times of need, Barbara always gives a well-considered, timely piece of advice. Often her words stay in my mind and are vindicated as I age in academia!

At Simon Fraser University, there is one special person who greatly facilitates my writing. This is Eileen Mallory. She cheerfully word processes all my manuscripts and sundry writing. I am always delighted with her speed, ingenuity in formatting papers, and ability to produce marvelously clear tables out of complex webs of data! Truly, she is one person to whom I owe a great deal.

Last but not least, I thank my husband, Rod Wong, for his tacit and unwarranted faith in me regarding this book and other intellectual ventures, his terrific sense of humor, his reflective objectivity (i.e., Judge Wong never hesitates to be my best critic or point out the right path), and his loving support.

Bernice Y.L. Wong

To the Student

You are not likely to come across another textbook in learning disabilities that has such a careful balance between the intellectual (psychological) and practical (meat and potato) aspects of learning disabilities. The chapters in this book contain rich stores of knowledge for you to master. As well, they contain provocative issues that challenge your thinking skills.

But to master this body of knowledge, and to resolve the issues posed for your thinking, you need to have the *will* to learn, as Scott Paris puts it. You need to expend effort in learning and thinking.

This book is for those who genuinely seek to understand the complexities of learning disabilities, to be fully informed of the serious conceptual problems and the state-of-the-art status and issues of research and interventions in learning disabilities, and are prepared to work hard — think hard. For such students or professionals, this book should be satisfying.

To facilitate student readers, I have written an introduction for each chapter called "Editor's Notes." Here I highlight the themes in the chapters to ensure that you do not miss the big picture, so to speak. I shall be working on a student's study guide to accompany the text to promote thorough understanding of the contents of each chapter. I explain the focus of each section of the book as follows.

Section I focuses on conceptual and assessment issues and research in various areas of learning disabilities. Section II focuses on practical aspects in learning disabilities. Topics range from academic interventions to social skills enhancement, neuropsychological assessment of learning disabilities and consultation skills to issues in service delivery.

Section III contains three chapters. The first addresses issues in early identification and prediction involving young children at risk for the development of learning disabilities; the second is about the adolescent with learning disabilities; and the third reviews the adult with learning disabilities. These chapters represent the need to use a life-span approach to understand fully the phenomenon of learning disabilities. This section is unique in that to date, no textbook in learning disabilities has provided explicitly and systematically a life-span perspective to understanding learning disabilities.

As a final note, I would like to address the issue of language and style in this volume. As teachers, the contributors and I encourage the use of the term "student with a learning disability," rather than the abbreviated form "LD student" or even "student with LD." However, as writers, our desire for succinctness sometimes overrode our desire for correct terminology. Please bear with any inconsistencies among and within chapters. We are well aware of our responsibilities as educators to influence public perception of people with learning disabilities. We always wish to put people first and their disabilities second.

LEARNING
ABOUT
LEARNING
DISABILITIES

Conceptual, Historical, and Research Aspects of Learning Disabilities

CHAPTER 1

Learning Disabilities: Historical and Conceptual Issues

Joseph K. Torgesen

Editor's Notes

This introductory chapter provides an overview of the field of learning disabilities. Hopefully, this overview will be useful as a context within which the information and ideas discussed in the following chapters on more specific topics can be placed. The major elements of this chapter include (1) a description of the current status of the field designed to show its extent and strength, (2) a brief historical perspective focusing on development of the guiding assumptions of the field, and (3) a discussion of issues that provide present and continuing challenges for the future.

I. CURRENT STATUS OF THE FIELD

The strength and extent of the field of learning disabilities (LDs) can be appreciated by considering its achievements in four areas.

A. Largest Field of Special Education

First, more children are currently being served in learning disabilities programs than in any other area of special education. According to the 11th Annual Report to Congress prepared by the Office of Special Education Programs (1988) in the United States, 47% of all children identified for special services in the schools are classified as learning-disabled (LD). During the

1987–1988 school year, approximately 1.9 million students were identified as LD in the United States, while about 600,000 were identified as mentally retarded, and 370,000 as emotionally handicapped.

In addition to being the largest field of special education, over the last 11 years it has also been the fastest growing. Since the 1976–1977 school year, the number of LD students identified in the public schools has increased by 156%! During this same time period, programs for emotionally handicapped children increased by 32%, while children and youth identified as mentally retarded actually decreased by 40%. The most rapid period of growth in the numbers of students identified as LD occurred in the 6 years following the passage of legislation requiring schools to provide services to students with learning disabilities. For example, from 1976 to 1982, numbers of LD children served in the schools grew by 130%, while the next 5 years saw only an 11% increase.

Of all children currently enrolled in the public schools, 5% are identified as LD. However, prevalence rates do vary considerably from state to state. For example, one Northeastern state identified 9.6% of its children as LD, while one state in the South identified only 2.4% of its school population as LD. While these figures from the United States amply document the importance of learning disabilities as a field within special education, formal programs for LD children are not restricted to the United States. Canada has an extensive system of services for LD children, as do most of the countries of Western Europe.

B. Legal Status within the Law

The extensive services for children and youth with learning disabilities in the United States are the result of the field's firm status within the law. Beginning with P.L. 94-142 (The Education of the Handicapped Act of 1975), all school districts are required to provide free and appropriate education to children identified as LD. The law, and federal regulations developed to implement it, specified a wide range of practices that were to be followed in delivering services to LD children. The essential provisions of P.L. 94-142 were reaffirmed in P.L. 98-199 (The Education of the Handicapped Act of 1983), which also contained some provision for expansion of services at preschool, secondary, and postsecondary levels.

C. Professional Associations

A third indication of the current status of the learning disabilities field is found in the number of associations that have been formed to advocate on behalf of LD children, support professional development, and provide a forum for discussion of research. Currently, six major organizations focus exclusively on the interests of LD children and professionals. The largest of these organizations is the Learning Disabilities Association of America (LDA), which until 1989 was known as the Association for Children and Adults with Learning Disabilities. This organization has 60,000 members and is concerned primarily with advocacy for LD children at the state and federal level, parental issues, and the communication of information about educational programs and practices. The Division for Learning Disabilities (DLD) within the Council for Exceptional Children has about 13,000 members and is focused on enhancement of professional practices in the field. The Council for Learning Disabilities (CLD) is an independent organization of 4,000 members and has goals similar to those of the DLD. The oldest professional organization in the field is the Orton Dyslexia Society (ODS). It was formed in 1949, currently numbers about 8,600 members, and contributes primarily to professional development and communication of research about children with specific reading disabilities. The National Joint Committee on Learning Disabilities (NJCLD) is a small organization composed of appointed representatives from the major LD associations and other groups that have an interest in learning disabilities. Its purpose is to provide a forum for communication among associations and interdisciplinary consideration of many of the issues confronting the field. This organization periodically issues position statements on many of these issues. The NJCLD is in a uniquely influential position because its member organizations represent such a large portion of the entire learning disabilities community. The most recently formed organization is the International Academy for Research in Learning Disabilities (IARLD). Membership in this group is by invitation and consists mainly of active researchers. Its purpose is to provide a means for international communication about research on learning disabilities.

These organizations play a very important role in contributing to the development and continuing visibility of the field. They all hold at least annual meetings at the national level, and several of them publish professional journals on a monthly or quarterly basis. Their large and growing membership attests to the high level of concern for children with learning disabilities manifest by parents, educators, and researchers.

D. Active Area of Research

A final indicator of the current status of the learning disabilities field is found in the level of interest in the topic among researchers: It is a very active area of research. Within the last decade, many professionals from fields other than those traditionally associated with learning disabilities (i.e., special education) have shown increased interest in the topic. In particular, well-trained researchers from the fields of psychology, medicine, and linguistics promise to make important new contributions to knowledge about learning disabilities. In the United States, the National Institute of Mental Health recently sponsored a national conference on learning disabilities (Kavanagh and Truss, 1988) designed to provide guidance about further funding of research in the area. As an outgrowth of that conference, a number of large inter-disciplinary projects to study reading disabilities have been funded.

Communication about research and professional issues in learning disabilities is aided by the publication of six journals devoted exclusively to the topic. The most widely circulated of these is the *Journal of Learning Disabilities* (published by PRO-ED, Inc.). Others include *Learning Disabilities Quarterly* (published by the CLD), *Learning Disabilities Research* and *Practice* (published by the DLD), *Learning Disabilities* (published by the LDA), and *Annals of Dyslexia* (published by the ODS). The IARLD also publishes two or three monographs a year on topics related to learning disabilities. In addition to these outlets devoted exclusively to topics on learning disabilities, research related to learning disabilities is also frequently published in journals such as the *Journal of Educational Psychology, Reading Research Quarterly, Brain and Behavior, Developmental Medicine and Child Neurology*, and the *Journal of Applied Behavior Analysis*, all of which accept articles on a variety of topics.

E. Areas of Controversy

Although learning disabilities is solidly established as an important category of exceptionality in both research and educational practice, it is also an area full of controversy. As one writer recently suggested, "It seems as though the field is constantly getting into scrapes, is always on probation, is never really secure" (Stanovich, 1989a). Despite the field's solid accomplishments in establishing educational programs and services for LD children, controversy continues about many important issues. Some of these issues go to the very heart of the concept, while others involve difficult and relatively esoteric research–conceptual issues. Issues that potentially threaten the existence of the field as a continuing political–educational entity include (1) disagreements about basic definitions of LD children, (2) problems in diagnostically differentiating LD children from other types of children who show a variety of achievement and adjustment problems in school, and (3) difficulties in establishing that LD children either have a different prognosis or require fundamentally different educational treatments than children with other kinds of learning problems. Issues that continue to be primarily a focus of research and theoretical controversy include (1) challenges to the assumption that learning disabilities result from inherent, or biological, impairment in specific brain function, and (2) difficulties dealing with the heterogeneity of the LD school population—the central problem here is to find ways to adequately conceptualize, and empirically classify, the different types of learning problems that are assumed to be covered under the LD label. Although these latter two issues do not impinge as directly on the viability of learning disabilities as an educational entity, solutions, or firmer evidence in these areas, would undoubtedly place the whole field on firmer footing. Each of these issues is discussed in more detail later in this chapter.

II. A HISTORICAL PERSPECTIVE

When considering the history of the field of learning disabilities, it is helpful from the outset to make a distinction between learning disabilities as an applied field of special education and learning disabilities as an area of research on individual differences in learning and performance. In the former sense, the field shares many attributes with other political–social movements, while in the latter sense it is a loosely jointed, interdisciplinary area of scientific inquiry. A central point of this chapter is that confusion and occasional conflict between these two aspects of the field has created many problems over the course of its history and continues to be a source of many difficulties for the field. It is also true that, although both aspects have some elements of history in common, the primary impetus for learning disabilities as a political–social movement has a narrower historical base than the field as a whole. In this discussion, the broad history of ideas about individuals with specific learning difficulty is outlined as well as the special historical antecedents of the field as a movement. This discussion will be brief, but more detailed information about many historical points is available in other sources (Coles, 1987; Doris, 1986; Hallahan and Cruickshank, 1973; Hallahan et al., 1985; Kavale and Forness, 1985; Myers and Hammill, 1990; Wiederholt, 1974).

A. Early Developments

Interest in the possible causes and consequences of individual differences in mental functioning extends back at least as far as early Greek civilization (Mann, 1979); however, the beginning of scientific work of immediate relevance to learning disabilities was probably that of Joseph Gall at the beginning of the nineteenth century (Wiederholt, 1974). Gall described a number of cases in which specific loss of mental function in adults occurred as a result of brain damage. His description of one of his patients is interesting because it shows his concern with establishing that the patient's loss of functioning was isolated to one particular ability:

> In consequence of an attack of apoplexy a soldier found it impossible to express in spoken language his feelings and ideas. His face bore no signs of a deranged intellect. His mind (espirit) found the

answer to questions addressed to him and he carried out all he was told to do; shown an armchair and asked if he knew what it was, he answered by seating himself in it. He could not articulate on the spot a word pronounced for him to repeat; but a few moments later the word escaped from his lips as if involuntarily.... It was not his tongue which was embarrassed; for he moved it with great agility and could pronounce quite well a large number of isolated words. His memory was not at fault, for he signified his anger at being unable to express himself concerning many things which he wished to communicate. It was the faculty of speech alone which was abolished. (Head, 1926; 11)

Over the next century, many clinical studies of speech and language disorders were reported; among the best known are those of Bouillaud, Broca, Jackson, Wernicke, and Head (Wiederholt, 1974). The major goals of this work were to document the specific loss of various speech and language functions in adults who had previously shown these abilities and to identify the types of brain damage associated with the different kinds of functional disturbance. Of relevance to the study of learning disabilities, this work did establish the fact that very specific types of mental impairment can occur as a result of damage to isolated regions of the brain.

The first systematic clinical studies of specific reading disability were reported in 1917 by James Hinshelwood, a Scottish ophthalmologist. Hinshelwood (1917) examined a number of cases in which adults suddenly lost the ability to read while other areas of mental functioning remained intact. As with cases of sudden loss of oral language facility, the loss of reading ability was attributed to damage to specific areas of the brain, a fact Hinshelwood felt was frequently supported by the patient's history or postmortem examination.

In addition to his work on loss of function with adults, Hinshelwood also saw cases of children who had extreme difficulties acquiring reading skills. In his descriptions of these cases, Hinshelwood was careful to document that their reading difficulties occurred alongside quite normal abilities in other intellectual skills. For example, in his description of one 10-yr-old boy with severe reading problems, he states:

... The boy had been at school three years, and had got on well with every subject except reading. He was apparently a bright, and in every respect an intelligent boy. He had been learning music for a year, and had made good progress in it.... In all departments of his studies where the instruction was oral he had made good progress, showing that his auditory memory was good.... He performs simple sums quite correctly, and his progress in arithmetic has been regarded as quite satisfactory. He has no difficulty in learning to write. His visual acuity is good. (Hinshelwood, 1917: 46–47)

Hinshelwood attributed the boy's problems to a condition that he called "congenital word blindness" resulting from damage to a specific area of the brain that stored visual memories for words and letters. Given the similarities in symptoms between his cases of developmental reading problems and those of the adults he had observed, as well as his medical orientation, it is easy to see how Hinshelwood arrived at his explanation for specific reading disability in children. However, recent analysis of several of his cases suggests that he may have overlooked a number of environmental influences that could also have explained the reading problems of children he studied (Coles, 1987). Whatever the ultimate cause of the reading problems he studied, Hinshelwood clearly showed that severe reading problems could exist in children with average or superior intellectual abilities in other areas. He also believed that cases of true "word blindness" were very rare, with an incidence of less than 1/1,000.

Following Hinshelwood, the next major figure to report clinical studies of children with reading disabilities was Samual Orton, an American child neurologist. Based on his clinical examinations of children over a 10-year period, Orton (1937) developed an explanation for reading disability that was quite different from Hinshelwood's. Rather than proposing that children with specific reading disabilities had actual damage to a localized area of their brains, he proposed that the difficulty was caused by delay, or failure, in establishing dominance for language in the left hemisphere of the brain. He used the term "strephosymbolia," or twisted symbols, to refer to the fact that reading-disabled children, as he observed them, frequently had special difficulties reading reversible words (saw and was, not and ton) or letters (b and d, p and q) correctly. His theory explained reversals as resulting from confusions between the visual images of these stimuli projected on the two different brain hemispheres. Because, according to his theory, these projections were mirror images of one another, and because neither hemispheric image was consistently dominant, sometimes the child saw the stimulus as "b," and sometimes as "d."

Neither Orton's particular neurological theories of dyslexia (reading disability) nor his ideas that reversals are especially symptomatic of the disorder have stood the test of subsequent research (Liberman et al., 1971). However, his broad emphasis on dysfunction in the language-related areas of the brain as a cause of specific developmental dyslexia is consistent with important current theories in the field (Galaburda, 1988; Shankweiler and Liberman, 1989).

Orton's work did have a broader contemporary impact than Hinshelwood's, principally in the stimulation of research and the founding of several special schools and clinics to serve children with reading disabilities. The special educational techniques he developed for helping reading-disabled children were particularly influential, and, in 1949, the ODS was formed in partial recognition of his contributions. It is interesting that the educational programs developed by Orton and Hinshelwood were similar: They both recommended systematic instruction combined with intensive, skill-building practice in using letter–sound relationships (phonics) to recognize words. In their emphasis on direct instruction and practice in skills required for reading, these educational programs were quite different from the "process training" approaches that many educators advocated 30 years later, once the field of learning disabilities was officially established.

Although Orton's work did have an impact on the treatment of reading disorders in a number of isolated special schools and clinics, neither his nor Hinshelwood's theories about the neurological basis for reading disorders was widely assimilated in scientific and educational circles as an explanation for individual differences in reading ability (Doris, 1986). Educators and psychologists who dealt with the vast majority of reading disability cases in the public schools attributed reading problems to a variety of environmental, attitudinal, and educational problems. Texts on the diagnosis and remediation of reading problems published during the 1940s (Durrell, 1940) and 1950s (Vernon, 1957) generally discredited these theories and suggested that, at best, inherent brain dysfunction accounted for only a very small proportion of reading failure.

B. Immediate Precursors to the Field of Learning Disabilities

The work described thus far is part of the overall history of ideas concerning specific learning disabilities in children. However, the research and clinical activity that led most directly to the initial establishment of a formally organized field of learning disabilities was conducted by Heinz Werner and Alfred Strauss at the Wayne County Training School in Northville, Michigan. In fact, the historical threads between the work of Hinshelwood and Orton and the development of the learning disabilities movement in special education are quite tenuous. In retrospect, it seems that their work has assumed greater historical importance with the developing recognition that the vast majority of LD children have reading as their primary academic problem (Lyon, 1985) and as scientific interest in specific reading disabilities has increased over the last several years (Stanovich, 1990).

The work of Werner and Strauss was fundamentally different from that of Hinshelwood and Orton in that they sought to describe deficient general learning processes rather than to describe and explain failure on a specific academic task. Their work was interpreted as establishing the existence of a subgroup of children who, presumably because of mild brain damage, experienced specific limitations in their ability to process certain kinds of information. Werner and Strauss' work placed much more emphasis on deficient learning processes themselves (which were presumed to affect learning powerfully in many different situations) than on the specific academic tasks that were affected.

What were these deficient learning processes? They centered mostly on what today would be called distractibility, hyperactivity, and visual–perceptual and perceptual–motor problems. Werner and Strauss were influenced heavily by the work of Kurt Goldstein, who had studied the behavior of soldiers with head wounds during World War I. Goldstein observed that a number of behavioral characteristics were reliably found in many of his patients: inability to inhibit responding to certain external stimuli, figure–background confusions, hyperactivity, meticulosity, and extreme emotional lability.

Werner and Strauss sought to document the presence of similar behavioral–cognitive difficulties in a subgroup of children at their school. These children were presumed to have brain damage because of their medical histories and other aspects of their behavior. They compared the behavior of these "brain-damaged" children with that of other mentally retarded children who were presumed not to be brain damaged. Their general conclusions were that the brain-damaged children showed specific difficulties in attention (distractibility) and perception. These findings were coupled with other observations (Kephart and Strauss, 1940) that the subgroup identified as brain damaged did not profit from the educational curriculum at the Wayne County School as much as other children. Specifically, while the IQs of the non-brain-damaged children tended to increase over several years at the school, the IQs of the brain-damaged children declined.

From these observations, Werner and Strauss concluded that the brain-damaged children needed special educational interventions designed to overcome the weaknesses their research had identified (Strauss, 1943). In Strauss' words, "... the erratic behavior of brain-injured children in perceptual tasks might be explained by a figure–ground deficiency, and an approach to remedy such deficiency should be directed toward strengthening the figure–ground perception" (Strauss and Lehtinen, 1947: 50). Strauss's educational orientation was toward interventions that focused on either remediation of deficient learning processes (primarily perceptual in nature) or educational adjustments (eliminating distracting stimuli in the classroom) that sought to minimize the impact of these deficient processes. In the classic volumes "Psychopathology and Education of the Brain-Injured Child" (Strauss and Lehtinen, 1947) and "Psychopathology and Education of the Brain-Injured Child: Progress in Theory and Clinic," Vol. 2 (Strauss and Kephart, 1955), Strauss and his colleagues developed an extensive set of educational recommendations that became very influential in the education of mentally retarded and brain-injured children.

As Hallahan and Cruickshank (1973) have pointed out, Werner and Strauss' influence on the future learning disabilities field was profound. Not only did they develop specific educational recommendations that focused on a special set of deficient learning abilities, but they provided a general orientation that became very influential on the education of exceptional children. The elements of this general orientation were the following:

1. Individual differences in learning should be understood by examining the different ways that children approached learning tasks (the processes that aided or interfered with learning).
2. Educational procedures should be tailored to patterns of processing strengths and weaknesses in the individual child.
3. Children with deficient learning processes might be helped to learn normally if those processes are strengthened, or if teaching methods that did not stress weak areas could be developed.

As the learning disabilities movement began to gather strength after its initial inception in 1963, these three concepts were repeatedly used to provide a rationale for its development as a separate entity from other fields of education. They provided the core of what was "unique" about educational programming for LD children.

In retrospect, it is interesting to note that the scientific support for Werner and Strauss' ideas about unique processing disabilities in brain-damaged children was exceedingly weak. As far back as 1949, Sarason (1949) attacked their work because of the way they formed their groups of children with and without brain damage. Werner and Strauss sometimes assigned children to the brain-damaged group on the basis of behavior alone, even in the absence of direct evidence from neurological tests or medical history. Unfortunately, some of the behaviors that led to selection of children as brain damaged were very similar to those that were studied in the experiments. The circular reasoning involved in attributing experimental differences between groups to brain damage is obvious.

Apart from the problems of interpretation caused by weaknesses in their experimental design, it also turns out that the actual differences between groups in distractibility and perceptual–motor problems were not very large. For example, Kavale and Forness (1985) reported a meta-analysis of 26 studies conducted by Werner, Strauss, and their colleagues comparing "brain-damaged" with non-brain-damaged children. When all measures are combined, the overall difference between groups was 0.104 standard deviations! When the results were examined for different dependent variables (perceptual–motor, cognition, language, behavior, and intelligence), none of the estimates of effect size were statistically significant. Kavale and Forness concluded that "... this meta-analytic synthesis offered little empirical support for the alleged behavioral differences between exogenous (brain-injured) and endogenous (non-brain-injured) mentally retarded children" (Kavale and Forness, 1985: 57).

Although the scientific work of Werner and Strauss on learning deficiencies resulting from brain damage does not stand up well to close scrutiny, their ideas strongly influenced a number of colleagues who carried their work forward. William Cruickshank, for example, showed that cerebral-palsied children of normal intelligence exhibited some of the same intellectual characteristics as the "brain-damaged" retardates in earlier studies (Cruickshank *et al.*, 1957). Cruickshank also extended the teaching methods advocated by Werner and Strauss to children of normal intelligence, and his extensive evaluation of these techniques is reported in "A Teaching Method for Brain-Injured and Hyperactive Children" (Cruickshank *et al.*, 1961).

At about this same time, another former staff member at the Wayne County Training School, Newell Kephart, wrote "The Slow Learner in the Classroom" (1960). In this work, he embellished a theory first proposed by Werner and Strauss: that perceptual–motor development is the basis for all higher mental development, such as conceptual learning. A suggestion derived from this theory was that training in perceptual–motor skills should be helpful to many children experiencing learning difficulties in school. In his book, which was to be very helpful in providing "unique" educational procedures for learning disabilities classrooms, he detailed a number of procedures that teachers could use to enhance the perceptual–motor development of their students.

It should be emphasized that all during the 1940s and 1950s, and into the early 1960s, there was no field of learning disabilities per se. Instead, researchers and clinicians were observing a variety of problems in children of normal intelligence that seemed to interfere with learning. Children manifesting these difficulties went by a variety of labels including minimally brain damaged, perceptually impaired, aphasic, or neurologically impaired. In addition to perceptual–motor-processing difficulties, a variety of disorders with auditory and language processes were also being studied. Helmer Mykelbust, who had extensive experience working with the deaf, became interested in children who had more subtle problems in auditory and linguistic processing. In his words:

> ... children who have auditory verbal comprehension disabilities resulting from central nervous system dysfunction hear but do not understand what is said. ... Language disabilities of this type have been described in both children and adults and have been designated as receptive aphasia, sensory aphasia, auditory verbal agnosia, or word deafness. ... these disabilities should be differentiated from the

language deficits resulting from deafness or mental retardation. Frequently such a distinction is not easy to make in those who have serious impairments, but it is essential in planning an adequate educational program. (Johnson and Mykelbust, 1967: 74)

Language disabilities were also emphasized in the work of Samual Kirk, who had served for a brief time as a staff member at the Wayne County Training School with Werner and Strauss. In 1961, he published the experimental version of the "Illinois Test of Psycholinguistic Abilities" (McCarthy and Kirk, 1961). The purpose of this instrument was to examine a child's strengths and weaknesses in the area of language processing. It stimulated the development of a number of educational programs that specified unique interventions for children with different patterns of disabilities (Bush and Giles, 1969; Kirk and Kirk, 1971) and, thus, was used in a way consistent with the original educational ideas of Werner and Strauss.

Although many other important researchers and teachers were concerned with specific learning disorders during this time, the major themes of the period are represented in the work already described. Concern was being focused on children who appeared normal in many intellectual skills but who also displayed a variety of cognitive limitations that seemed to interfere with their ability to learn in the regular classroom. Not only were educational and mental health professionals concerned about these children, but also the concerns of parent's groups were becoming more focused and mobilized.

C. Formal Beginnings of the Learning Disabilities Movement

In 1963, at the Conference on Exploration into Problems of the Perceptually Handicapped Child, which was sponsored by the Fund for Perceptually Handicapped Children, Inc., Samual Kirk proposed the term "learning disabilities" as a descriptive title for the kind of children being generally discussed at the conference. In his words:

... I have used the term "learning disabilities" to describe a group of children who have disorders in development in language, speech, reading, and associated communication skills needed for social interaction. In this group I do not include children who have sensory handicaps such as blindness or deafness, because we have methods of managing and training the deaf and the blind, I also exclude from this group children who have generalized mental retardation. (Kirk, 1963: 2–3)

This speech served as a catalyst to focus the concern of many of those in attendance, and that evening they voted to form the Association for Children with Learning Disabilities (ACLD). The establishment of the ACLD represents the formal beginnings of the learning disabilities movement as a social–political–educational movement. It was primarily an organization for parents. Its professional advisory board was formed from many of the leading professionals of the day (i.e., Kirk, Cruickshank, Kephart, Frostig, Lehtinen, Mykelbust), but its Board of Directors was composed of parents and leaders from other segments of society. As the leader of a movement, its goal was to mobilize social and political concern for the plight of LD children and to create public sector services for them. The material presented in the beginning of this chapter attests to the enormous impact that the ACLD and associated organizations have had on education over the past 25 years.

At its inception, the movement faced three major challenges. First, it had to establish a clear sense of its identity as a field separate from existing special and remedial education areas. Second, it had to develop a broad base of support for publicly funded educational programs for LD children. Third, it had to encourage training efforts to prepare a large group of professionals for service in the field.

The learning disabilities movement approached the first challenge by selecting and promoting ideas about LD children that emphasized their differences from other children currently receiving services in the schools. The centerpiece of the distinction between LD and other children having trouble in school was that their learning problems were the result of inherent and specific difficulties in performing some of the psychological processes required for learning. This was a powerful idea in that it implied these children were genuinely handicapped through no fault of their own, their parents, or their teachers. The idea was also appealing because it was optimistic: If the right remediation for deficient processes were prescribed, these children's achievements in school might become consistent with their generally "normal" abilities in other areas.

The research and theories of Werner and Strauss were instrumental in providing support for these foundational assumptions about learning disabilities. For example, the focus of the new field on remediation of disabilities in fundamental learning processes separated it from the fields of remedial reading and remedial math, both by making it more general and by giving the impression that it was attacking educational difficulties in a more basic and powerful way (Hartman and Hartman, 1973). Professional fields are characterized by the "special" knowledge and expertise they possess. Claims about special knowledge in the diagnosis and treatment of specific processing disorders were instrumental in helping the learning disabilities movement establish an identity of its own.

It was also important for the young field to establish that its clients, and the services to be provided them, were distinct from those of the existing fields of mental retardation and emotional–behavior disorders. Here, an emphasis on the generally "normal" academic potential of LD children, and on the specific and probably short-term interventions they would require, were helpful in distinguishing between LD and mentally retarded children. In differentiating LD children from those with behavior disorders, the idea that LD children's learning problems are inherent (caused by brain dysfunction), and not the result of environmental influences, was also important.

As we shall see, some of the ideas that helped support the formation of the new field of LD were soon questioned by professionals within the field itself (Mann and Phillips, 1967; Hammill, 1972). Furthermore, *all* of the basic assumptions about learning disabilities that were so strongly advocated in the early days have been seriously challenged in recent research (Coles, 1987; Stanovich, 1986; Siegel, 1989; Torgesen, 1986). Original support for these ideas had come primarily from the clinical experience of the field's founders with a broad variety of unusual children. These clinically unique children thus provided the basis for what became a very broad social movement. At least part of the power of this movement came from the strength and certainty with which it generalized its assumptions about learning disabilities to relatively larger groups of children in the public schools. As Gerald Senf (1986) has pointed out, the young field had strong motives to include as many children under the learning disabilities umbrella as possible.

Although one certainly cannot blame those who provided impetus for the original movement (they were attempting to develop public support for their clients and their children), their very success in publicizing the concept of learning disabilities has created problems for the science of learning disabilities. Research attempting to verify foundational assumptions about learning disabilities using samples of LD children being served in the public schools frequently obtains negative results (Ysseldyke, 1983). However, as Stanovich (1990) has shown in his model of reading disabilities, these negative results are the likely product of overgeneralization of the LD label in current practice. Thus, the political success of the learning disabilities movement, in generating funds for services to very large numbers of children, has created inevitable ambiguities in the learning disability concept. The resolution of these ambiguities can only come through a more carefully disciplined use of the LD label in research and practice.

Historical developments with regard to public programs for LD children and training of learning disabilities professionals are closely entertwined and shall be reported together. Involvement of the U.S. government in activities that supported development of the field began as a series of Task Force reports between 1966 and 1969. These reports reviewed a variety of topics including characteristics of LD children, extent of current services, methods of treatment, and estimates of prevalence. The report of Task Force III (Chalfant and Scheffelin, 1969) described how little was actually known about assessing and remediating psychological processing disorders.

The first major legislative success came in 1969 with the passage of the Children with Learning Disabilities Act, which authorized the U.S. Office of Education to establish programs for LD students. The government also sponsored an institute in which plans for the training of learning disabilities professionals were discussed (Kass, 1970). In 1971, the Bureau of Education of the Handicapped initiated a program to fund Child Service Demonstration Projects to be conducted in the different states. These demonstration projects were to directly serve children with learning disabilities as well as provide a means for developing professional expertise in the area. Further support for professional development came through the Leadership Training Institute in Learning Disabilities at the University of Arizona, which was funded for 2 years beginning in 1971. In 1975, the learning disabilities field achieved a firm basis in law with the passage of P.L. 94–142, which required all states to provide an appropriate public education for children with learning disabilities. The passage of this law stimulated the enormous growth in the field that has occurred since that time.

D. Role of Psychological Processes in Learning Disabilities

As mentioned earlier, at least part of the learning disabilities field's claims for a unique professional identity came from its focus on identifying and remediating the specific psychological processing difficulties of LD children. A number of tests to identify specific processing disorders were developed such as the "The Marianne Frostig Developmental Test of Visual Perception" (Frostig *et al.*, 1964) and the "Illinois Test of Psycholinguistic Abilities" (McCarthy and Kirk, 1961), and various programs to remediate specific deficits in these processes were published. Popular activities in many learning disabilities classrooms during the 1960s and 1970s included practice in various visual–motor, auditory sequencing, visual–perceptual, or cross-modality training exercises. The rationale for these exercises was that improvement in deficient underlying learning processes would allow children to achieve their full potential in learning academic skills such as reading and math. Because many of the leading professionals at the time placed an emphasis on visual–perceptual-and visual–motor-processing difficulties as a fundamental cause of learning disabilities, many of the training activities had a decided emphasis on visual–perceptual processes (Hallahan and Cruickshank, 1973).

The first published attacks on this approach to the education of LD children came from Lester Mann (Mann and Phillips, 1967; Mann, 1971), who criticized the approach on theoretical and philosophical grounds. Shortly thereafter, a number of empirical investigations of the efficacy of perceptual–motor process training began to appear, and many of these were summarized and commented on by Donald Hammill and his colleagues (Hammill, 1972; Hammill *et al.*, 1974; Wiederholt and Hammill, 1971). Criticism of process training soon spread to psycholinguistic processes (Hammill and Larsen, 1974; Newcomer and Hammill, 1975), with the research reviews generally demonstrating that process training did not generalize to improvements in learning academic skills.

These initial reviews sparked a period of intense controversy within the learning disabilities movement for almost a decade. It is not surprising that the scientific questions at issue became politicized, with discussions sometimes containing more personal acrimony than reasoned debate (Hammill, 1990), because these criticisms were directed at one of the foundational pillars of the learning disabilities movement. It seems natural that the learning disabilities movement, with its political–social aims, would strongly resist a weakening of any aspect of its *raison d'etre*. When further evidence (Arter and Jenkins, 1977; Vellutino *et al.*, 1977; Ysseldyke, 1973) effectively closed the case against process training as a means for treating learning disabilities, the field turned to direct instruction of academic skills as its dominant mode of intervention. In Hammill's words: "Learning disabilities needed an approach with a better data base for its foundation; at the time, the principles of direct instruction satisfied this purpose" (Myers and Hammill, 1990: p. 42)

By 1977, dissatisfaction with the processing orientation to diagnosis and remediation of learning disabilities had become so widespread that the federal regulations implementing P.L. 94–142 did not require assessment of psychological processes as part of procedures to identify LD children for public school programs. Although learning disabilities were still defined as resulting from deficiencies in the basic psychological processes required for learning, LD children were to be diagnosed primarily in terms of a discrepancy between general measures of intelligence and measures of achievement in specific areas of learning.

Both the lack of positive criteria for the identification of learning disabilities (it was identified as underachievement not explicable in terms of physical, cultural, or environmental handicap) and the adoption of direct instruction as the treatment of choice undermine the rationale for learning disabilities as a distinct field within remedial and special education. Although direct instruction in academic skills may be effective with LD children, these procedures do not provide a foundation for learning disabilities *as a distinct field of professional expertise in education*. Rather, as Hallahan *et al.* (1985) suggest, the striking similarities in educational procedures across various remedial and special education programs seriously undermine the educational placement of LD children in programs separate from those of other children experiencing academic problems.

There are at least two possible explanations for the failure of the learning disabilities movement to document the utility of process oriented approaches to identification and treatment of LD children. The first is to concede that the fundamental assumptions are simply wrong. Coles (1987), for example, maintains that insufficient evidence indicates that LD children actually have inherent limitations in the ability to process specific kinds of information. Others (Hammill, 1990; Mann, 1979) suggest that no evidence suggests training in "hypothetical processes" can be more effective than direct instruction in academic skills as an intervention for LD children.

In contrast to these views, Torgesen (1979, 1986) suggested that the learning disabilities field's problems with psychological processes arose because it was an idea ahead of its time; i.e., approaches to identifying and training deficient processes in LD children were pressed into service when our understanding of mental processing operations and their relationships to learning academic tasks were at only a rudimentary stage of development. Since the 1960s, we have learned an enormous amount about how to measure mental processing operations, and many of our fundamental conceptualizations about them have changed (Butterfield and Ferretti, 1987; Brown and Campione, 1986). For example, we now recognize that processing operations are much more context-sensitive than previously supposed, which makes the problem of generalization of training particularly important. Furthermore, we have a much better understanding of how differences in background knowledge can influence performance on tasks supposedly measuring processing differences (Ceci and Baker, 1990). Finally, we have come to appreciate the enormous influence that differences in cognitive strategies can play on many different kinds of tasks (Butterfield and Ferretti, 1987). All of these improvements in understanding suggest that future developments in cognitively oriented training of psychological processes as an aid to academic improvement will look very different from that used in the past. In fact, there are some preliminary indications that cognitively oriented training programs in reading comprehension strategies (Brown and Palincsar, 1987), phonological awareness (Lundberg et al., 1988), and general study strategies (Ellis et al., 1987) can be quite effective in raising academic achievement in school. However, whether or not any of these interventions will prove uniquely useful to LD children, as opposed to other types of poor learners, remains to be demonstrated.

III. CURRENT AND FUTURE ISSUES

This section contains very brief discussions of several issues that are crucial either to the continued existence of learning disabilities as a unique category in special education or to the continued development of knowledge in the area. Issues that do not threaten the existence of the category, but may affect aspects of service delivery, such as those posed by the Regular Education Initiative (REI), are explicitly left out of this section. As Hammill (1990) points out, the REI is important because it may seriously impact the number of children identified as LD and may affect the general quality of services provided these children, but it does not threaten the existence of the field itself. Because all of the issues discussed here are very complex, they cannot be represented fully in the brief space allotted; rather, this section will state the essential questions in each area, suggest why they are important to the field, and provide a very limited exposure to current work in the area.

A. The Problem of Definition

Definitions, such as those proposed for learning disabilities, are offered to specify a particular type of condition or individual. They are valid as long as they apply to at least one individual. Definitions of learning disabilities are frequently critiqued because they almost universally state that neurological impairment is the presumed cause of the problem. However, even the most severe critics of the learning disabilities concept (cf. Coles, 1987) agree that at least a few children may have specific neurological impairment that interferes with school learning. The important question for these critics is how many of the 5% of school children currently identified as LD are adequately described by current definitions? Answers to this question may affect the numbers of children legitimately served under current law, but they do not threaten the validity of the concept.

The definition of learning disabilities accepted by the majority of persons in the field has changed in subtle ways since it was first formalized in 1967 by the National Advisory Committee on Handicapped Children (the definition later incorporated in P.L. 94–142). Most of the changes reflect additions to our knowledge about learning disabilities derived from research and practice. That first formal definition stated:

> "Specific learning disability" means a disorder in one or more of the basic psychological processes involved in understanding or in using language, spoken or written, which may manifest itself in an imperfect ability to listen, think, speak, read, write, spell, or to do mathematical calculations. The term includes such conditions as perceptual handicaps, brain injury, minimal brain dysfunction, dyslexia, and developmental aphasia. The term does not include children who have learning problems which are primarily the result of visual, hearing, or motor handicaps, of mental retardation, of emotional disturbance, or of environmental, cultural, or economic disadvantage.

A recent interagency report to the U.S. Congress (Interagency Committee on Learning Disabilities, 1987) identified at least four problems with this definition that have become apparent since it was proposed:

1. It does not indicate clearly enough that learning disabilities are a heterogeneous group of disorders.
2. It fails to recognize that learning disabilities frequently persist and are manifest in adults as well as in children.
3. It does not clearly specify that, whatever the cause of learning disabilities, the "final common path" is inherent alterations in the way information is processed.
4. It does not adequately recognize that persons with other handicapping or environmental limitations may have a learning disability *concurrently* with these conditions.

Newer definitions, such as those proposed by NJCLD in 1981 and revised in 1988 or that proposed by the ACLD in 1986 attempt to incorporate this new information in their definitions.

An interesting current controversy was stimulated by the definition proposed in the interagency committee's report to Congress (1987). Recognizing research findings on the problems LD children show in many social interactions, this definition added deficits in social skills as a type of learning disability. This proposal was explicitly rejected by the U.S. Department of Education. NJCLD's new definition, given below, also specifically excludes problems in social interaction as a defining characteristic of children with learning disabilities:

Learning disabilities is a general term that refers to a heterogeneous group of disorders manifested by significant difficulties in the acquisition and use of listening, speaking, reading, writing, reasoning, or mathematical abilities. These disorders are intrinsic to the individual, presumed to be due to central nervous system dysfunction, and may occur across the life span.

Problems in self-regulatory behaviors, social perception, and social interaction may exist with learning disabilities but do not by themselves constitute a learning disability.

Although learning disabilities may occur concomitantly with other handicapping conditions (for example, sensory impairment, mental retardation, serious emotional disturbance) or with extrinsic influences (such as cultural differences, insufficient or inappropriate instruction), they are not the result of those conditions or influences. (NJCLD Memorandum, 1988).

In a recent article in the *Journal of Learning Disabilities*, Hammill (1990) has argued strongly that the NJCLD definition represents the broadest current consensus in the field.

Although it is clearly important for learning disabilities as an educational–political movement to obtain relatively wide acceptance of a single broad definition of LD to provide a respectable coherence to the field, the utility of these definitions for researchers is less clear. The basic problem is that the definitions are so broad, they allow study of a great variety of children under the learning disabilities label (Wong, 1986). When researchers attempt to compare findings across studies that have used broad definitions as a guide to sample selection, they often find, not surprisingly, that they have obtained different results. As argued elsewhere (Torgesen, 1987), researchers need to adopt more restrictive definitions for their research samples than those used to identify children for services in the schools. Although researchers studying learning disabilities should not study children who fall outside the general definitions, they clearly need to go beyond these definitions to more narrowly define their specific population of interest.

B. Etiology

As mentioned earlier, the concept of learning disabilities is not threatened by our inability to show that every school-identified LD child has a processing disability resulting from neurological impairment. However, if only a miniscule percentage of children being served as LD actually fit the definition, this would clearly create problems for the learning disabilities movement. The fundamental assumption about learning disabilities at present is that they result from neurological impairment affecting specific brain functions. This is why it is given special status as a handicapping condition.

Learning disabilities as a movement has not been strongly concerned with questions about etiology (preferring to focus instead on problem description and intervention); however, its ultimate integrity as a separate field of education depends on finding answers to questions about the extent of brain pathology in the population it serves. At present, we may be satisfied with the presumption of brain dysfunction (given that we have "ruled out" environmental factors as a cause of the problem), but as the methodology for studying brain function improves, we must eventually be able to verify central nervous system dysfunction in a significant portion of children who fit our definition of learning disabilities.

Gerald Coles (1987) has recently mounted an extensive attack on the "neurological explanation" for learning disabilities. He correctly shows that all of our evidence for brain damage as a cause of learning disabilities is correlational, which does not necessarily imply causation. Furthermore, because of relatively weak technologies for examining brain function available in the past, even the correlational evidence is equivocal (Kavale and Forness, 1985).

In place of the "neurological explanation," Coles (1987) offers the "interactivity theory" to explain the learning problems of most learning disabled children. This theory suggests that learning disabilities arise in the context of a complex interplay of social interactions that build knowledge and create attitudes, values, and motivation critical for school success. These interactions occur in both the family and the school. The theory suggests that learning disabilities arise from an experiential base; many children's patterns of interaction with their environment (primarily social) have not prepared them to perform successfully the tasks required to learn in school.

The most obvious criticism of this theory is that it is a better explanation of general learning problems than specific learning disabilities (Stanovich, 1989b). That is, Coles does not provide convincing arguments linking causal factors in his theory to the kinds of discrepancies between general learning ability (general intelligence) and specific learning achievement demanded by current definitions of LD. The kinds of social–environmental variables invoked as causal agents in his theory seem more likely to have a mild, but pervasive, influence on intellectual development and academic achievement, rather than a highly focused one.

However, empirical research (Stanovich, 1986) has raised the possibility that many children currently being served as LD actually do have mild but pervasive learning deficits, rather than highly specific ones. It is also widely acknowledged (Kistner and Torgesen, 1987) that LD children frequently have motivational and attitudinal characteristics that can interfere with learning. Furthermore, most recommendations for intervention with LD children include special techniques for enhancing motivation to learn (Ellis *et al.*, 1987; Hallahan *et al.*, 1985). Finally, it is also true that procedures to "rule out" the influence of environmental factors in the diagnosis of learning disabilities are rudimentary at best (Kavale and Forness, 1985). Given all these facts, it does seem probable that Coles has identified a likely explanation for the learning problems of many children currently identified as LD. However, this does not necessarily imply that current conceptualizations of LD are invalid but, rather, that the concept is almost certainly overgeneralized in the public schools, with the result that it subsumes students who are underachieving but not LD.

Currently, the most viable link between neurology and learning disabilities has been established for developmental anomalies in the left temporal region of the brain as a cause of phonological processing disabilities that produce problems in learning to read. First, convincing evidence (Shankweiler and Liberman, 1989; Stanovich, 1990; Torgesen, in press; Wagner and Torgesen, 1987) indicates that deficits in the ability to process the phonological features of language lead to specific difficulties in acquiring reading skills. This type of processing skill is usually located in the left temporal region of the brain (Damasio and Geschwind, 1984). Furthermore, a series of surgical studies of the brains of deceased dyslexics has shown developmental anomalies in this same area of the brain (Galaburda, 1988). Theories of brain development suggest that these particular anomalies arise very early in development and, thus, could not be the result, rather than the cause, of reading problems. Finally, studies involving measurement of regional cerebral blood flow during reading have also verified that this same temporal region of the brain is differentially affected in dyslexics than in normal readers (Flowers et al., 1989). These converging sources of evidence, involving careful examination of a basic psycholinguistic-processing disability and two types of neurological study converge to indicate that many children may indeed have an inherent limitation in their ability to process certain kinds of information necessary for reading. It is also interesting that genetic studies (Olsen et al., 1989) have shown that limitations in phonological processing ability are highly heritable.

C. Differentiation of LDs from Other Conditions

The issue of etiology is important to the field of learning disabilities because it provides a basis for establishing that the learning problems of LD children are fundamentally different from those experienced by other types of poor learners. Another way to address the question of differences between LD and other poor learners is in terms of their cognitive or behavioral characteristics. Differences at this level are important to reliably differentiate between LD and other poor learners during the assessment–diagnostic process.

This issue has been most forcibly raised through the research of James Ysseldyke and his colleagues at the Minnesota Institute for the Study of Learning Disabilities. For example, Ysseldyke summarized over 5 years of research on assessment issues by stating that it was not possible, using current procedures, to reliably differentiate LD from other low achievers (Ysseldyke, 1983). In support of this contention, they reported data in several studies showing a large degree of overlap in test scores, and test score patterns, between groups of school-identified LD children and nonidentified slow learners (Ysseldyke et al., 1982; Shinn et al., 1982). Furthermore, they also showed that a sample of school psychologists and resource room teachers could not reliably classify children as LD or slow learners using clinical judgment applied to test data (Epps et al., 1981). Other investigators have found similarly high degrees of communality on cognitive, affective, and demographic variables among samples of LD, educable mentally retarded, and behaviorally disturbed children in the public schools (Gajar, 1980; Webster and Schenck, 1978).

Although these findings are potentially troublesome to the learning disabilities movement because they suggest that public monies are being selectively channeled to support a group of children (LD) who are not being reliably differentiated from other poor learners, they are irrelevant to basic scientific and conceptual issues. They say more about the social–political process of identification in the public schools than they do about the scientific validity of the concept of learning disabilities (Senf, 1986). While these findings may suggest that the concept has been overextended in practice, or that factors other than data about the child's psychological characteristics are important to placement decisions (Ysseldyke, 1983), they do not address basic scientific questions about the uniqueness of LD children.

Such questions are addressed, however, in research that directly compares carefully selected samples of children who have specific learning disabilities with other children who have more general learning problems. Research to date has focused on children who manifest specific disabilities in reading, and it has produced equivocal results. The usual method in such research is to contrast the performance of "garden-variety" (Gough and Tunmer, 1986) poor readers (children with below-average general learning skill) with that of specifically reading-disabled children who have a large discrepancy between their general learning ability (intelligence) and their reading achievement.

A pioneering study of this type was reported by Rutter and Yule (1975), who found a variety of reliable cognitive and neuropsychological differences between their samples of children with specific or general disabilities. Since that time, a number of other studies have reported differences in cognitive profile between samples of specifically disabled and garden-variety poor readers (Aaron, 1987; Ellis and Large, 1987; Jorm et al., 1986; Silva et al., 1985). In contrast to these studies, several other investigators found no appreciable differences in reading-related cognitive processes between similar comparison groups (Fredman and Stevenson, 1988; Siegel, 1989; Taylor et al., 1979).

One possible explanation for the differences in findings between these studies lies in the range of abilities on which they contrasted the groups. Those that found differences between garden-variety and specifically reading-disabled children tended to find them for skills that are not closely tied to reading decoding skill, such as those found on nonverbal (i.e., assembling puzzles, solving picture–word problems, reasoning tasks like Raven's matrices) or verbal–conceptual (i.e., vocabulary, abstract verbal reasoning) measures of intelligence. In contrast, the studies that reported few differences between groups tended to use measures of phonological skills or actual reading skills themselves. Thus, although children with specific reading disabilities have been shown to possess a broad variety of cognitive skills that are limited in garden-variety poor readers, we currently do not have good evidence that their actual reading processes, or abilities central to the attainment of basic reading skills, are different.

What can one conclude from all this? Probably the most important conclusion for the learning disabilities movement is that current standards for the identification of LD children in the schools do not reliably identify a group of children whose learning problems are fundamentally different from those of other poor achievers. It seems clear that we have overgeneralized the concept, and that it has been adulterated further by political–social forces at work during the diagnostic–placement process. In solving this problem, which is central to the continuing integrity of the learning disabilities movement, numbers may be very important; i.e., to identify a reliably different group of children as LD, we may have to adopt much more stringent placement criteria. Increasing the required discrepancy between general ability and intelligence or requiring firm evidence of a specific processing disorder would be two ways to increase the stringency of our criteria. Any such modifications to the criteria should, of course, reduce the numbers of children currently being served as LD.

Others have argued (Shepard, 1983) that simply altering the technical procedures or criteria for placement in learning disabilities classes will not solve the problem of overgeneralization. The basic problem is that these services are currently viewed as the most attractive educational solution for children with almost any kind of special educational need. Until effective educational services are available for the full range of learning problems manifest in schools, enrollment pressure on learning disabilities classrooms will continue to be enormous. This pressure will continue to produce placements based on the simple need for extra educational help rather than fulfillment of specific diagnostic criteria.

For the science of learning disabilities, the conclusions from research comparing LD children with other poor learners are less clear. Certainly, the failure to identify differences in reading-related cognitive processes among supposedly different kinds of poor readers is troublesome for those who want to maintain categorical distinctions between children with "specific" and "general" disabilities. These results have, in fact, led some researchers to conclude "if there is no clear distinction between the groups in terms of how they read, then the practice of identifying a special group of poor readers for special attention may no longer be necessary" (Fredman and Stevenson, 1988: 105). However, the differences between these children in other areas of cognitive functioning may have an impact on their response to treatment or their ultimate prognosis, either of which would provide justification for separate educational treatment. We turn now to a consideration of issues related to treatment and prognosis.

D. Specific Treatment–Prognostic Indications

With the demise of the process orientation to diagnosis and remediation of learning disabilities, and the adoption of direct instruction as the treatment of choice, one of the major distinctions between the learning disabilities field and other fields of special education disappeared. Most educational texts on learning disabilities at present advocate a mixture of remedial approaches that are not critically different from those used with remedial readers, the mentally retarded, or behaviorally impaired children (Hallahan et al., 1985; Myers and Hammill, 1990). Such procedures as drill and overlearning of component skills, increasing the structure of classroom procedures, programmatic use of incentives and rewards, presentation of material in multiple formats, use of concrete and manipulable materials, and frequent examination of learning progress are all good educational procedures that are helpful for all types of children with learning difficulties. Even the newer process-oriented instruction in learning strategies (Deshler et al., 1984a,b; Ryan et al., 1986) is very similar to the kinds of instruction being advocated for mentally retarded children (Campione and Brown, 1977; Pressley and Levin, 1987).

If differences do not exist in the *type* of special instruction required by LD children, perhaps some differences exist from other groups in terms of the intensity of instruction required, or in prognosis. For example, Rutter and Yule (1975) found that garden-variety poor readers made more progress in reading during their school years than did a sample of children with specific reading disability whose overall intelligence was higher; however, the dyslexic poor readers made more progress in math. Torgesen (in press) has recently obtained preliminary findings documenting that LD children with a particular type of processing disability (phonological coding) also made strikingly slower progress in acquiring basic reading skills than did another group of LD children of the same general intelligence level. Between ages 9 and 19, children with severe phonological coding problems improved only 1.3 grade levels in their basic word-reading skills, while other LD children in the same classrooms improved 6.3 grade levels. In contrast to this differential pattern in reading, the groups made equivalent progress in math. Both of these studies imply that children with certain types of specific disabilities may require more intensive instruction than other poor learners to master beginning reading skills. However, several other studies examining growth rates in reading have failed to report special learning problems for specifically disabled children (Labuda and DeFries, 1989; McKinney, 1987; Share et al., 1987). One possible reason for the differences in outcome between these two groups of studies is that the former studies apparently used more stringently selected samples of specifically disabled readers. This would suggest that future research on this issue needs to exercise particular care in selecting samples of reading-disabled children who do, in fact, show a specific and severe impairment in reading skill.

Although we do have some evidence about differential prognosis for children with specific impairments in early reading skills, no clear evidence at present indicates that LD children require different types of instruction from other categories of exceptional children. Both of these issues are very complex, and they are difficult to address in controlled research. It may be possible, for example, that children with specific reading disabilities will show slower progress in the attainment of basic reading skills (decoding), but that once their decoding difficulties are overcome, they may be able to comprehend a wider variety of material than children with more generalized cognitive limitations (Stanovich, 1989a). For example, Torgesen *et al.* (1987) showed that adolescents with specific reading disability were better able to profit from a comprehension-enhancement technique using recorded textbooks than were students whose IQ was more consistent with their reading level.

At present, the idea that LD children should be placed in special programs because they require either more or a different type of instruction from other poor learners must remain an undocumented assumption. In speaking of a similar issue with regard to specific reading disabilities, Stanovich comments:

> Until convincing data on such issues as differential response to treatment are provided the utility of the concept of dyslexia will continue to be challenged because the reading disabilities field will have no rebuttal to assertions that it is more educationally and clinically relevant to define reading disability without reference to IQ discrepancy. ... No amount of clinical evidence, case studies, or anecdotal reports will substitute for the large-scale experimental demonstrations that, compared to groups of garden-variety poor readers, discrepancy-defined poor readers show differential response to treatment and prognosis—and for further evidence that the reading-related cognitive profiles of these two groups are reliably different." (Stanovich, 1989a: 16).

Stanovich's comments indicate the pressing need for more research on these complex issues.

E. Subgroups and the Problem of Heterogeneity

It is now commonplace to recognize that LD children are a heterogeneous, or highly variable, group (Fletcher and Morris, 1986). No one would seriously argue that learning disabilities have a single cause or that they are manifest in only one way. It is also commonplace to recognize that the heterogeneity of samples of LD children has created serious problems for research. For example, variability among LD children leads to problems in comparing findings among studies, it frequently produces weak experimental results, and it makes applying research findings to practice difficult (Doehring, 1983; Lyon, 1987). In the view of many (Lyon, 1987; Fletcher and Morris, 1986;

McKinney, 1984; Torgesen, 1987), developing ways to more adequately identify and conceptualize the full range of disorders covered under the general LD label is crucial to further advancement of scientific knowledge in the field. Because teachers need to have a better sense of the type of children to which specific research results apply, better specification of types *within* learning disabilities will also help in applying research to practice.

Researchers have approached the problem of heterogeneity in a variety of ways (Boder, 1973; Kinsbourne and Warrington, 1966; Torgesen, 1982), but the most systematic methods have involved the use of sophisticated statistical techniques to identify children similar to one another in performance on large batteries of tests. This approach promises to help us better understand the variability within groups of LD children (McKinney, 1984), but there is currently no consensus about any particular classification scheme; however, a number of consistencies are found among several studies, and some particular subtypes have been studied extensively.

A finding common to many studies is that there is a subgroup of LD children who manifest deficits primarily in the verbal area (Doehring *et al.*, 1979; Petrauskas and Rourke, 1979; Satz and Morris, 1981; Lyon and Watson, 1981). Some studies have further subdivided the group with verbal deficiencies into those with general verbal problems and those with more specific (phonological) processing difficulties (Doehring *et al.*, 1979; Lyon and Watson, 1981; Speece, 1987). Classification studies also usually report a group of children with cognitive difficulties in the nonverbal realm (Rourke and Fisk, 1988; Satz and Morris, 1981; Lyon and Watson, 1981). In addition to these subgroups with relatively specific problems on a narrow range of tasks, studies almost always identify another group of children with difficulties in several areas.

Although most studies have attempted to classify children in terms of their performance on academic, neuropsychological, or cognitive tasks, McKinney and his colleagues have grouped children in terms of their overt behavior in classroom settings (McKinney, 1984, 1990). They identified six different behavior patterns in a group of 63 LD children whom they studied over a period of 3 years. The groups they identified were characterized primarily by (1) attention deficit, (2) conduct problems, (3) withdrawn behavior, (4) low positive behavior, (5) global behavior problems, and (6) normal behavior patterns. Over the 3-year period, the groups with attentional and classroom management problems showed a declining pattern of school achievement in comparison with the groups with normal or withdrawn behavior patterns.

The goal of classification research is to identify types of LD children that may then be studied more extensively. For example, Rourke and his colleagues (Rourke *et al.*, 1989) have conducted extensive research on children with nonverbal learning disabilities (NLD). These children show specific

academic difficulties in computational mathematics accompanied by tactile–
perceptual deficits, deficiencies in visual–spatial organization, and problems
in nonverbal problem-solving. They are also at particular risk for development of social–behavioral difficulties and have a higher-than-normal risk for
suicide. In contrast to this group, Torgesen (1988) has systematically studied
a group of LD children characterized by extreme problems in phonological
coding of verbal information. This group can perform normally on many
language comprehension tasks and is relatively unaffected in the attainment
of math skills, but has extreme difficulties acquiring basic word-identification
skills in reading. A recent follow-up study (Torgesen, in press) indicated that
children with extreme disabilities in this area made almost no progress between fourth grade and age 19 in improving their word-reading skills, despite
being in public school programs for LD children.

     To summarize, we are at only the beginning stages of understanding the
enormous variability in the LD population. Research in this area must
overcome a number of difficult theoretical and methodological problems
(Lyon, 1987) to move significantly beyond our current level of understanding.
We will never identify completely homogeneous subgroups of children,
because all the characteristics that contribute to learning disabilities are
almost certainly distributed continuously rather than in clusters. (Stanovich,
1990; Olsen *et al.*, 1985). While different types of learning disabilities clearly
exist, we should not expect the boundaries between the different subtypes to be
naturally defined, nor should we expect there to be little important variability
among children in a given subtype. Even with these problems, however,
continued efforts to understand the major ways that LD children differ from
one another seem crucial to the further development of the field.

IV. CONCLUDING COMMENTS

The field of learning disabilities is presently a strong and vital force within the
larger special and regular education communities. Its services, which are
mandated by law, are offered to vast numbers of children with a variety of very
difficult and unusual educational problems. Professionals in the field have
organized themselves into strong associations that provide adequate means
for communication about research and professional issues. Research in the
area is growing and becoming more diverse, and many new research initiatives
are being supported by governmental agencies.

     However, a number of recent developments in both the political–social
sector and the scientific community make it difficult to offer firm predictions
about the continued development of the field. Science is raising fundamental
questions about the nature of learning disabilities, and educational politics are

challenging current methods of service delivery. If ideas within the REI are validated, we could see an enormous reduction in the numbers of children identified as LD. Although such reductions could have a serious impact on the political power of the learning disabilities movement, they may actually help to support the integrity of the field in the long run. One of the most serious challenges to that integrity comes from demonstrations that many school-identified LD children are not demonstrably different from other children with learning problems who are not identified as LD. This situation, as many acknowledge, arises from the likely overutilization of the LD label to provide services to a wide variety of children for whom special services are not otherwise available. Unless the learning disabilities field chooses to broaden its base of concern to include all types of learning problems in school, it seems inevitable that we must find ways to exercise greater discipline in identifying children as specifically LD.

It is also difficult to predict the outcome that current research efforts will have on the field. Because much of the recent research is addressing the foundational assumptions of the field, the concept of learning disabilities itself is being placed at risk in these studies. While good evidence apparently indicates that very specific forms of brain dysfunction can produce processing disorders that have specific effects on achievement in some children, we have no firm ideas of how widespread these types of disabilities might be.

Although clear thinking and good communication are desirable attributes at any time, it seems that there was never a time in the history of our field in which they are so much in demand as now. Educational politics and scientific concerns have become very complex, and we have many thorny questions facing us. The only firm prediction I can offer is that the coming decade should prove very interesting indeed.

References

Aaron, P. G. (1987). Developmental dyslexia: Is it different from other forms of reading disability? *Ann. Dyslexia* **37,** 109–125.

Arter, J. A., and Jenkins, J. R. (1979). Differential diagnosis–perscriptive teaching: A critical appraisal. *Rev. Educ. Res.* **49,** 517–555.

Boder, E. (1973). Developmental dyslexia: A diagnostic approach based on three atypical reading–spelling patterns. *Dev. Med. Child Neurol.* **15,** 663–687.

Brown, A. L., and Campione, J. C. (1986). Psychological theory and the study of learning disabilities. *Am. Psychol.* **14,** 1059–1068.

Brown, A. L., and Palincsar, A. S. (1987). Reciprocal teaching of comprehension strategies: A natural history of one program for enhancing learning. *In* "Intelligence and Exceptionality: New Directions for Theory, Assessment, and Instructional Practices" (L. Borkowski and L. D. Day, eds.), pp. 81–132. Ablex, New York.

Bush, W. J., and Giles, M. T. (1969). "Aids to Psycholinguistics Teaching." Merrill, Columbus, Ohio.

Butterfield, E. D., and Ferretti, R. P. (1987). Toward a theoretical integration of cognitive hypotheses about intellectual differences among children. *In* "Cognition in Special Children: Comparative Approaches to Retardation, Learning Disabilities, and Giftedness" (L. Borkowski and L. D. Day, eds.), pp. 195–234. Ablex, New York.

Campione, J. C., and Brown, A. L. (1977). Memory and metamemory development in educable retarded children. *In* "Perspectives on the Development of Memory and Cognition" (R. V. Kail and J. W. Hagen, eds.). pp. 367–406. Lawrence Earlbaum, Hillsdale, New Jersey.

Ceci, S. J. and Baker, J. G. (1990). On learning ... more or less: A knowledge × process × context view of learning disabilities. *In* "Cognitive and Behavioral Characteristics of Children with Learning Disabilities" (J. K. Torgesen, ed.). pp. 159–178. PRO-ED, Austin, Texas.

Chalfant, J. C., and Scheffelin, M. A. (1969). "Central Processing Dysfunctions in Children: A Review of Research, Phase Three of a Three Phase Project." *NINDS Monogr.*, U.S. Department of Health, Education, and Welfare, Bethesda, Maryland.

Coles, G. S. (1987). "The Learning Mystique: A Critical Look at Learning Disabilities." Pantheon, New York.

Cruickshank, W. M., Bice, H. V., and Wallen, N. E. (1957). "Perception and Cerebral Palsy." Syracuse University Press, Syracuse, New York.

Cruickshank, W. M., Bentzen, F. A., Ratzeburg, F. H., and Tannhauser, M. T. (1961). "A Teaching Method for Brain-Injured and Hyperactive Children." Syracuse University Press, Syracuse, New York.

Damasio, A. R., and Geschwind, N. (1984). The neural basis of language. *Annu. Rev. Neurosci.* **7**, 127–147.

Deshler, D. D., Schumaker, J. B., and Lenz, B. K. (1984a). Academic and cognitive interventions for LD adolescents: Part I. *J. Learn. Disabil.* **17**, 108–117.

Deshler, D. D., Schumaker, J. B., Lenz, B. K., and Ellis, E. (1984b). Academic and cognitive interventions for LD adolescents: Part II, *J. Learn. Disabil.* **17**, 170–187.

Doehring, D. G. (1983). What do we know about reading disabilities? Closing the gap between research and practice. *Ann. Dyslexia* **23**, 175–183.

Doehring, D. G., Hoshko, I. M., and Bryans, B. N. (1979). Statistical classification of children with reading problems. *J. Clin. Neuropsychol.* **1**, 5–16.

Doris, J. (1986). Learning disabilities. *In* "Handbook of Cognitive, Social, and Neuropsychological Aspects of Learning Disabilities" (S. J. Ceci, ed.), pp. 3–53. Lawrence Erlbaum, Hillsdale, New Jersey.

Durrell, D. D. (1940). "Improvement of Basic Reading Abilities." World Book Company, New York.

Ellis, E. S., Lenz, B. K., and Sabornie, E. J. (1987). Generalization and adaptation of learning strategies to natural environments: Part 2: Research into practice. *Remed. Special Educ.* **8**, 6–23.

Ellis, N., and Large, B. (1987). The development of reading: As you seek so shall you find. *Br. J. Psychol.* **78**, 1–28.

Epps, S., Ysseldyke, J. E., and McGue, M. (1981). "Differentiating LD and non-LD students: I know one when I see one." Institute for Research on Learning Disabilities, Minneapolis, Minnesota.

Fletcher, J. M., and Morris, R. D. (1986). Classification of disabled learners: Beyond exclusionary definitions. *In* "Handbook of Cognitive, Social, and Neuropsychological Aspects of Learning Disabilities" (S. Ceci, ed.), pp. 55–80. Lawrence Erlbaum, Hillsdale, New Jersey.

Flowers, L., Wood, F. B., and Naylor, C. E. (1989). "Regional Cerebral Blood Flow in Adults Diagnosed as Reading Disabled in Childhood." Unpublished manuscript, Bowman-Gray School of Medicine, Winston-Salem, North Carolina.

Fredman, G., and Stevenson, J. (1988). Reading processes in specific reading retarded and reading backward 13-year-olds. *Br. J. Dev. Psychol.* **6,** 97–108.

Frostig, M., Lefever, D. W., and Whittlesey, J. R. B. (1964). "The Marianne Frostig Developmental Test of Visual Perception." Consulting Psychology Press, Palo Alto, California.

Gajar, A. H. (1980). Characteristics across exceptional categories: EMR, LD, and ED. *J. Special Educ.* **14,** 165–173.

Galaburda, A. M. (1988). The pathogenesis of childhood dyslexia. *In* "Language, Communication, and the Brain" (F. Plum, ed.), pp. 127–137. Raven Press, New York.

Gough, P., and Tunmer, W. (1986). Decoding, reading, and reading disability. *Remed. Special Educ.* **7,** 6–10.

Hallahan, D. P., and Cruickshank, W. M. (1973). "Psycho-Educational Foundations of Learning Disabilities." Prentice-Hall, Englewood Cliffs, New Jersey.

Hallahan, D. P., Kauffman, J. M., and Lloyd, J. W. (1985). "Introduction to Learning Disabilities." Prentice-Hall, Englewood Cliffs, New Jersey.

Hammill, D. D. (1972). Training visual perceptual processes. *J. Learn. Disabil.* **5,** 552–559.

Hammill, D. D. (1990). On defining learning disabilities: An emerging consensus. *J. Learn. Disabil.* **23,** 74–84.

Hammill, D. D., and Larsen, S. C. (1974). The efficacy of psycholinguistic training. *Excep. Children* **41,** 5–14.

Hammill, D. D., Goodman, L., and Wiederholt, J. L. (1974). Visual-motor processes: What success have we had in training them? *Read. Teacher* **27,** 469–478.

Hartman, N. C., and Hartman, R. K. (1973). Perceptual handicap or reading disability? *Read. Teacher* **26,** 684–695.

Head, H. (1926). *Aphasia and Kindred Disorders of Speech.* London: Cambridge University Press.

Hinshelwood, J. (1917). "Congenital Word Blindness." H. K. Lewis, London.

Interagency Committee on Learning Disabilities. (1987). "Learning Disabilities: A Report to the U.S. Congress." National Institutes of Health, Bethesda, Maryland.

Johnson, D. J., and Mykelbust, H. R. (1967). "Learning Disabilities: Educational Principles and Practices." Grune & Stratton, New York.

Jorm, A., Share, D., Maclean, R., and Matthews, R. (1986). Cognitive factors at school entry predictive of specific reading retardation and general reading backwardness: A research note. *J. Child Psychol. Psych.* **27,** 45–54.

Kass, C. E. (1970). "Final Report: Advanced Institute for Leadership Personnel in Learning Disabilities." Department of Education, University of Arizona, Tucson.

Kavale, K., and Forness, S. R. (1985). "The Science of Learning Disabilities." College-Hill Press, San Diego.

Kavanagh, J. F., and Truss, T. J. (1988). "Learning Disabilities: Proceedings of the National Conference." York Press, Parkton, Maryland.

Kephart, N. C. (1960). "The Slow Learner in the Classroom." Charles E. Merrill, Columbus, Ohio.

Kephart, N. C., and Strauss, A. A. (1940). A clinical factor influencing variations in IQ. *Am. J. Orthopsych.* **10,** 345–350.

Kinsbourne, M., and Warrington, E. K. (1966). Developmental factors in reading and writing backwardness. *In* "The Disabled Reader: Education of the Dyslexic Child" (J. Money, ed.). pp. 265–272. Johns Hopkins Press, Baltimore.

Kirk, S. A. (1963). Behavioral diagnosis and remediation of learning disabilities. *Proc. Conf. Explor. Probs. Perpet. Hndicpp. Child.* **1,** 1–23.

Kirk, S. A., and Kirk, W. D. (1971). "Psycholinguistic Learning Disabilities: Diagnosis and Remediation." University of Illinois Press, Chicago.

Kistner, J., and Torgesen, J. K. (1987). Motivational and cognitive aspects of learning disabilities. *In* "Advances in Clinical Child Psychology" (A. E. Kasdin and B. B. Lahey, eds.). Plenum Press, New York.

Labuda, M., and DeFries, J. C. (1989). Differential prognosis of reading-disabled children as a function of gender, socioeconomic status, IQ, and severity: A longitudinal study. *Read. Writ.: Interdiscip. J.* **1,** 25–26.

Liberman, I. Y., Shankweiler, D., Orlando, C., Harris, K. S., and Berti, F. B. (1971). Letter confusions and reversals of sequence in the beginning reader: Implications for Ortons's Theory of Developmental Dyslexia. *Cortex* **7,** 127–142.

Lundberg, I., Frost, J., and Peterson, O. (1988). Effects of an extensive program for stimulating phonological awareness in pre-school children. *Read. Res. Q.* **23,** 263–284.

Lyon, G. R. (1985). Identification and remediation of learning disability subtypes: Preliminary findings. *Learn. Disabil. Focus* **1,** 21–35.

Lyon, G. R. (1987). Learning disabilities research: False starts and broken promises. *In* "Research in Learning Disabilities" (S. Vaughn and C. S. Bos, eds.), pp. 69–80. College-Hill Press, San Diego.

Lyon, R., and Watson, B. (1981). Empirically derived subgroups of learning disabled readers: Diagnostic characteristics. *J. Learn. Disabil.* **14,** 256–261.

Mann, L. (1971). Psychometric phenology and the new faculty psychology: The case against ability assessment and training. *J. Special Educ.* **5,** 3–14.

Mann, L. (1979). "On the Trail of Process." Grune & Stratton, New York.

Mann, L., and Phillips, W. A. (1967). Fractional practices in special education: A critique. *Excep. Children* **33,** 311–317.

McCarthy, J. J., and Kirk, S. A. (1961). "Illinois Test of Psycholinguistic Abilities: Experimental Version." University of Illinois Press, Urbana.

McKinney, J. D. (1984). The search for subtypes of specific learning disability. *J. Learn. Disabil.* **17,** 43–50.

McKinney, J. D. (1987). Research on the identification of learning-disabled children: Perspectives on changes in educational policy. *In* "Research in Learning Disabilities" (S. Vaughn and C. Bos, eds.), pp. 215–233. College-Hill Press, San Diego.

McKinney, J. D. (1990). Longitudinal research on the behavioral characteristics of children with learning disabilities. *In* "Cognitive and Behavioral Characteristics of Children with Learning Disabilities" (J. Torgesen, ed.). pp. 115–138. PRO-ED, Austin, Texas.

Myers, P., and Hammill, D. D. (1990). "Learning Disabilities: Basic Concepts, Assessment Practices, and Instructional Strategies." PRO-ED, Austin, Texas.

Newcomer, P. L., and Hammill, D. D. (1975). ITPA and academic achievement. *Read. Teacher* **28**, 731–741.

Office of Special Education Programs, (1988). "Eleventh Annual Report to Congress on the Implementation of Public Law 94-142: The Education for All Handicapped Children Act." U.S. Department of Education, Washington, D.C.

Olsen, R., Kliegl, R. Davidson, B., and Foltz, G. (1985). Individual and developmental differences in reading disability. *In* "Reading Research: Advances in Theory and Practice," Vol. 4 (T. Waller, ed.), pp. 1–64. Academic Press, London.

Olsen, R., Wise, B., Conners, F., Rack, J., and Fulker, D. (1989). Specific deficits in component reading and language skills: Genetic and environmental influences. *J. Learn. Disabil.* **22**, 339–348.

Petrauskas, R., and Rourke, B. (1979). Identification of subgroups of retarded readers: A neuropsychological multivariate approach. *J. Clin. Neuropsychol.* **1**, 17–37.

Pressley, M., and Levin, J. R. (1987). Elaborative learning strategies for the inefficient learner. *In* "Handbook of Cognitive, Social, and Neuropsychological Aspects of Learning Disabilities," Vol. 2 (S. J. Ceci, ed.), pp. 175–212. Lawrence Erlbaum, Hillsdale, New Jersey.

Rourke, B. P., and Fisk, J. L. (1988). Subtypes of learning-disabled children: Implications for a neurodevelopmental model of differential hemispheric processing. *In* "Brain Lateralization in Children: Developmental Implications" (D. L. Molfese and S. J. Segalowitz, eds.), pp. 547–565. Guilford Press, New York.

Rourke, B. P., Young, G. C., and Leenaars, A. A. (1989). A childhood learning disability that predisposes those afflicted to adolescent and adult depression and suicide risk. *J. Learn. Disabil.* **22**, 169–175.

Rutter, M., and Yule, W. (1975). The concept of specific reading retardation. *J. Child Psychol. Psych.* **16**, 181–197.

Ryan, E. B., Weed, K. A., and Short, E. J. (1986). Cognitive behavior modification: Promoting active, self-regulatory learning styles. *In* "Psychological and Educational Perspectives on Learning Disabilities" (J. Torgesen and B. Y. L. Wong, eds.), Academic Press, New York.

Sarason, S. B. (1949). "Psychological Problems in Mental Deficiency." Harper, New York.

Satz, P., and Morris, R. (1981). Learning disability subtypes: A review. *In* "Neuropsychological and Cognitive Processes in Reading" (F. J. Pirozzalo and M. C. Wittrock, eds.), pp. 172–197. Academic Press, New York.

Senf, G. M. (1986). LD research in sociological and scientific perspective. *In* "Psychological and Educational Perspectives on Learning Disabilities" (J. K. Torgesen and B. Y. L. Wong, eds.). pp. 27–54. Academic Press, New York.

Shankweiler, D., and Liberman, I. Y. (1989). "Phonology and Reading Disability." University of Michigan Press, Ann Arbor.

Share, D. L., McGee, R., McKenzie, D., Williams, S., and Silva, P. A. (1987). Further evidence relating to the distinction between specific reading retardation and general reading backwardness. *Br. J. Dev. Psychol.* **5**, 35–44.

Shepard, L. (1983). The role of measurement in educational policy: Lessons from the identification of learning disabilities. *Educ. Measure.: Issues Prac.* **2**, 4–8.

Shinn, M. R., Ysseldyke, J., Deno, S., and Tindal, G. (1982). "A Comparison of Psychometric and Functional Differences between Students Labeled Learning Disabled and Low Achieving." Research report no. 71, Institute for Research on Learning Disabilities, University of Minnesota, Minneapolis.

Siegel, L. S. (1989). IQ is irrelevant to the definition of learning disabilities. *J. Learn. Disabil.* **22**, 469–479.

Silva, P. A., McGee, R., and Williams, S. (1985). Some characteristics of 9-year-old boys with general reading backwardness or specific reading retardation. *J. Child Psychol. Psych.* **26**, 407–421.

Speece, D. L. (1987). Information processing subtypes of learning disabled readers. *Learn. Disabil. Res.* **2**, 91–102.

Stanovich, K. E. (1986). Cognitive processes and the reading problems of learning-disabled children: Evaluating the assumption of specificity. *In* "Psychological and Educational Perspectives on Learning Disabilities" (J. K. Torgesen and B. Y. L. Wong, eds.). pp. 87–132. Academic Press, New York.

Stanovich, K. E. (1989a). 'Discrepancy Definitions of Reading Disability: Has Intelligence Led Us Astray?" Address presented at the Joint Conference on Learning Disabilities, Ann Arbor, Michigan, June.

Stanovich, K. E. (1989b). Learning disabilities in broader context. *J. Learn. Disabil.* **22**, 287–297.

Stanovich, K. E. (1990). Explaining the differences between the dyslexic and the garden-variety poor reader: The phonological-core variable-difference model. *In* "Cognitive and Behavioral Characteristics of Children with Learning Disabilities" (J. Torgesen, ed.). PRO-ED, Austin, Texas.

Strauss, A. A. (1943). Diagnosis and education of the cripple-brained, deficient child. *J. Excep. Children* **9**, 163–168.

Strauss, A. A., and Kephart, N. C. (1955. "Psychopathology and Education of the Brain-Injured Child: Progress in Theory and Clinic," Vol. 2. Grune and Stratton, New York.

Strauss, A. A., and Lehtinen, L. E. (1947). "Psychopathology and Education of the Brain Injured Child." Grune & Stratton, New York.

Taylor, H. G., Staz, P., and Friel, J. (1979). Developmental dyslexia in relation to other childhood reading disorders: Significance and clinical utility. *Read. Res. Q.* **15**, 84–101.

Torgesen, J. K. (1979). What shall we do with psychological processes? *J. Learn. Disabil.* **12**, 514–521.

Torgesen, J. K. (1982). The use of rationally defined subgroups in research on learning disabilities. *In* "Theory, and Research in Learning Disabilities" (J. P. Das, R. F. Mulcahy, and A. E. Wells, eds.), pp. 111–132. Plenum Press, New York.

Torgesen, J. K. (1986). Learning disabilities theory: Its current state and future prospects. *J. Learn. Disabil.* **19**, 399–407.

Torgesen, J. K. (1987). Thinking about the future by distinguishing between issues that have answers and those that do not. *In* "Issues and Future Directions for Research in Learning Disabilities" (S. T. Vaughn and C. S. Bos, eds.), pp. 55–64. San Diego: College Hill.

Torgesen, J. K. (1988). Studies of children with learning disabilities who perform poorly on memory span tasks. *J. Learn. Disabil.* **21**, 605–612.

Torgesen, J. K. Cross-age consistency in phonological processing. *In* "Phonological Processes in Literacy" (S. Bradey and D. Shankweiler, eds.). Lawrence Earlbaum, Hillsdale, New Jersey. (in press).

Torgesen, J. K., Dahlem, W. E., and Greenstein, J. (1987). Using verbatim text recordings to enhance reading comprehension in learning disabled adolescents. *Learn. Disabil. Focus* **3**, 30–38.

Vellutino, F. R., Steger, B. M., Moyer, S. C., Hardin, C. J., and Niles, J. A. (1977). Has the perceptual deficit hypothesis led us astray? *J. Learn. Disabil.* **10**, 375–385.

Vernon, M. D. (1957). "Backwardness in Reading." Cambridge University Press, London.

Wagner, R. K., and Torgesen, J. K. (1987). The nature of phonological processing and its causal role in the acquisition of reading skills. *Psycholog. Bull.* **101**, 192–212.

Webster, R. E., and Schenck, S. J. (1978). Diagnostic test pattern differences among LD, ED, EMH, and multi-handicapped students. *J. Educ. Res.* **72**, 75–80.

Wiederholt, J. L. (1974). Historical perspectives on the education of the learning disabled. *In* "The Second Review of Special Education" (L. Mann and D. A. Sabatino, eds.), pp. 103–152. PRO-ED, Austin, Texas.

Wiederholt, J. L., and Hammill, D. D. (1971). Use of the Frostig-Horne Visual Perceptual Program in the urban school. *Psychol. Schools* **8**, 268–274.

Wong, B. Y. L. (1986). Problems and issues in the definition of learning disabilities. *In* "Psychological and Educational Perspectives on Learning Disabilities" (J. K. Torgesen and B. Y. L. Wong, eds.) pp. 1–25. Academic Press, San Diego.

Ysseldyke, J. E. (1973). Diagnostic–prescriptive teaching: The search for aptitude–treatment interactions. *In* "The First Review of Special Education" (L. Mann and D. Sabatino, eds.). pp. 37–61. PRO-ED, Austin, Texas.

Ysseldyke, J. E. (1983). Current practices in making psycho-educational decisions about learning disabled students. *J. Learn. Disabil.* **16**, 209–219.

Ysseldyke, J. E., Algozzine, B., Shinn, M., and McGue, M. (1982). Similarities and differences between underachievers and students labeled learning disabled. *J. Special Educ.* **16**, 73–85.

CHAPTER 2

Decision Making and Curriculum-Based Assessment

Bob Algozzine

Editor's Notes

Following Torgesen's historical and conceptual overview, it is apropos to examine the topic of assessment of learning-disabled students, which Algozzine tackles deftly. Two themes underlie Algozzine's chapter. The first is that referral practices directly and seriously affect assessments for the purpose of classifying learning-disabled students. He highlights three problem areas in referral that affect the reliability in assessment, which in turn affects diagnosis–classification of learning disabilities. These three problem areas include (1) teachers' reasons for referral, (2) high rates in referral and the consequent problems this creates, and (3) what happens to students who have been referred.

The second theme is the solution to a common problem in assessment. Once diagnosis–classification of learning disabilities is made, the issue of instruction follows. However, assessment for the purpose of classification rarely leads to instructional planning and practice. Algozzine focuses on one recent development in assessment that attempts to redress the problem, namely, curriculum-based assessment. He explicates the assumption, nature, and procedures in curriculum-based assessment in the rest of the chapter.

Learning about Learning Disabilities

I. WHO ARE STUDENTS WITH LEARNING DISABILITIES?

More than 4 million students received special education services during recent school years. More than 40% of these students were classified based on "hidden handicaps" that were not even recognized as important when the earliest special education programs were established. In fact, recent government figures indicate that more learning-disabled (LD) students are receiving special education than any other group of exceptional students (United States Department of Education [USDE], 1989). Who are these students and where do they all come from?

Students who fail to profit from the menu of experiences provided in schools have always been a part of the American educational system (cf. Ysseldyke and Algozzine, 1982). For professionals trying to meet these students' needs, problems first surfaced when they tried to classify them into groups based on the causes of their failure. For example, Horn (1924) observed that $\frac{1}{4}$ to $\frac{1}{3}$ (25–33%) of the students finishing first grade failed to master the content presented. He provided the following classification scheme and suggested that differentiated education be provided based on differences in students:

Children who are exceptional for reasons primarily mental.
    The highly endowed
    The poorly endowed
Children who are exceptional for reasons primarily temperamental.
    The incorrigibles and truants
    The speech defectives
Children who are exceptional for reasons primarily physical.
    The deaf
    The blind
    The crippled

Similarities between this first classification system and that in use today are obvious. In fact, if Horn lived today, his classification system might look something like this:

Children who are exceptional for reasons primarily mental.
    The highly endowed—gifted and talented (GT)
    The poorly endowed—mentally retarded (MR)
    (The adequately endowed)—learning disabled (LD)
Children who are exceptional for reasons primarily temperamental.
    The incorrigibles and truants—emotionally handicapped (EH)
    The speech defectives—speech impaired (SI)
    (The perceptual deviants/chronically immature) (LD)

Children who are exceptional for reasons primarily physical.
   The deaf—deaf/hearing impaired (D/H)
   The blind—blind visually impaired (B/VI)
   The crippled—physically handicapped/multi-handicapped
      (PH/MH)
   (The learning disabled) (LD)

Learning disabilities is the most prevalent category of special education. About 5% of the school-aged population has been classified as LD; from 28 to 64% of the students receiving special education in recent years were identified as LD (Ysseldyke and Algozzine 1990). In most states, more students are classified as LD than any other category; in some states, these differences are very large (e.g., at least three to four times as great in Hawaii, North Carolina, and South Carolina) (USDE, 1989).

Most states base classification practices on definitions of exceptional conditions (Ysseldyke and Algozzine, 1990). A specific definition and related guidelines published in the *Federal Register* (December 2, 1977) are the basis for making decisions about students with learning disabilities in many states. According to that definition,

"children with learning disabilities" means those children who have a disorder in one or more of the basic psychological processes involved in understanding or in using language, spoken or written, which disorder may manifest itself in imperfect ability to listen, think, speak, read, write, spell, or to do mathematical calculations. Such disorders include such conditions as perceptual handicaps, brain injury, minimal brain dysfunction, dyslexia, and developmental aphasia. Such terms do not include children who have learning problems which are primarily the result of visual, hearing, or motor handicaps, of mental retardation, of emotional disturbance, or of environmental, cultural, or economic disadvantage. (p. 65803)

Criteria to be used in identifying students with learning disabilities were also provided in the *Federal Register*. They included the following:

   1. A team may determine that a child has a specific learning disability if:
      a. The child does not achieve commensurate with his or her age and ability levels in one or more of the following areas when provided with learning experiences appropriate for the child's age and ability levels: oral expression, listening comprehension, written expression, basic reading skill, reading comprehension, mathematics calculation, or mathematics reasoning.

    b. The team finds that a child has a severe discrepancy between achievement and intellectual ability in one or more of the same areas listed in the preceding statement.

  2. The team may not identify a child as having a specific learning disability if the severe discrepancy between ability and achievement is primarily the result of:

    a. a visual, hearing, or motor handicap

    b. mental retardation

    c. emotional disturbance

    d. environmental, cultural, or economic disadvantage. (p. 65803)

Despite efforts to make the concept of learning disabilities and process of finding it sophisticated and complex, this category of special education is largely composed of students who have earned reasonably high scores on intelligence tests and relatively low scores on a least one academic achievement test or subtest (Kavale and Forness, 1987; Lerner, 1989; Sleeter, 1986; Ysseldyke and Algozzine, 1990). Because of the relative ease with which this criterion (and others related to it) can be met, large numbers of students with learning disabilities are identified each year:

> The number of learning disabled students has risen consistently since 1977. The percentage increase from 1976–77 to 1986–87 was 141.6 and the rate of increase was the greatest between 1976–77 and 1982–83 when the average percentage increase was about 12 percent per annum. (USDE, 1988)

The rise in numbers of students classified as LD has not gone unexplained or unnoticed. Among reasons for the increases, Singer and Butler (1987) included the desire not to stigmatize children with other labels, the need to reclassify previously labeled mentally retarded students, and the desire to obtain supplementary educational services. When the results of research on assessment are compiled and reviewed, problems in referral and classification surface as exposition as well. These problems are briefly summarized below.

A. Problems in Referral

There are three problem areas in student referral. The first concerns teachers' reasons for referral. Student characteristics, the abilities, behaviors, or skills that students exhibit, interact with teachers' beliefs or characteristics to influence who is referred for special education placement. Individual differences among teachers, in the beliefs, expectations, or skill in dealing with specific kinds of problems, also influence decisions to refer students for evaluation; a teacher's sense of efficacy (or the beliefs one holds about professional competence) is at stake when a student "fails." Referral decisions are also influenced by instructional goals and the availability of specific kinds of strategies and materials, and teachers' decisions to refer students are also influenced by institutional constraints and external pressures. For example, new "standards for excellence" or desire to provide access to recently developed programs increase the likelihood that low-performing students will be referred. Also, teachers refer students when parents, teachers, and other professionals insist on referral of those students; they may not refer students when other people are opposed to referral. Similarly, the presence or absence of advocacy groups (such as the Association for Retarded Citizens or the Association for Children and Adults with Learning Disabilities) and the perceived or actual clout of those organizations can influence referral. Finally, many teachers refer students because the process previously resulted in removal of difficult student from their classroom (Skiba, 1989).

The second problem area in student referrals is rate of referral. Recently, as much as 6% of the school-aged population was referred each year. On the average, in a school system of 15,000 students between 450 and 900 students would be referred to specialists each year (Heller *et al.*, 1982). Little variation exists in who is referred in different regions and in different types of school systems (Algozzine *et al.*, 1982).

High rates of referral create problems for school personnel because most states have regulations mandating the maximum time that can lapse between referral and completion of evaluation. For example, in some states, evaluations must be completed within 30 days of referral, and failure to do so gives parents the right to enroll their child in a private facility for handicapped students, with the state responsible for paying the tuition.

High rates also create problems because people who conduct individualized assessments and special education teachers are in short supply. Recent government figures indicate that approximately 37% of the anticipated special services (e.g., counseling, transportation, work evaluations) needed by exceptional students were required by students with learning disabilities (USDE, 1989). Similarly, the greatest need to fill teaching positions was for teachers of the LD (i.e., almost 40% of total new teachers needed); and school psychologists as well as other diagnostic personnel continue to be in high demand and relatively short supply (USDE, 1988).

The third problem area in student referrals concerns what happens to referred students. A survey of special education directors indicated that 92% of referred students were tested and that this aspect of referral practices varied among school districts (Algozzine *et al.*, 1982). For example, as few as 39% of referred students were tested in some school districts, but in others every referred student was tested. In some schools, elaborate procedures are in place and teacher assistance teams review information on referred students before they receive additional testing. In other districts, informal procedures operate and teachers refer students simply by talking to school psychologists or other professionals.

Given that large numbers of students are referred for evaluation and that most referred students are tested, the probability that tested students will actually be declared eligible for and receive special education services is of interest. Seventy-three percent of tested students reported by directors of special education (cf. Algozzine *et al.*, 1982) were declared eligible for and received special education services; most of them probably were classified as LD. The probability is very high that students who are referred by their classroom teachers will be tested and declared eligible for special education services. The process is characterized by what Sarason and Doris (1979) call a "search for pathology." The task becomes finding out what is wrong with students who are referred by teachers, and this creates a tremendous need to find problems and use special education teachers and services to solve them.

Clearly, referral practices directly and seriously affect assessments for the purpose of classifying LD students. The flawed referral process creates problems in assessment, which in turn create reliability problems in the subsequent classification process. Although problematic, assessment for the purpose of classification is necessary. Current practice appears to involve a discrepancy between measured "intelligence" achievement (see definition and related guidelines in the *Federal Register*, December 29, 1977).

Once classification or the diagnosis of learning disabilities in a child or adolescent is made, the important issue of instruction follows. Typically, assessment done for the purpose of classification–diagnosis rarely leads directly and easily into instructional planning and practice. A new development in assessment aims to redress the preceding problem. This new assessment is the curriculum-based approach.

B. Promise of Curriculum-Based Methods of Assessment

Ysseldyke and Algozzine (1990) have suggested the following assumptions are among those that should be made in efforts to improve assessment practices: (1) there is no one way to assess students, (2) the primary goal of assessment should be improved instruction, (3) assessment should concentrate on relevant variables and occur often during teaching, and (4) assessment should occur where problem behaviors occur. Recent efforts to use the local curriculum as the basis for measuring educational progress address these assumptions and offer promising methods for improving current assessment practices.

Curriculum-based assessment (CBA) is "a procedure for determining the instructional needs of a student based on the student's ongoing performance within existing course content" (Gickling and Havertape, 1981; (55). According to Tucker:

> There is nothing new about curriculum-based assessment. In many respects it is like coming home to traditional classroom instruction. Under the rubric of curriculum-based assessment, some novel ideas are being proposed and reported, and several practical tools have emerged, but the basic idea is as old as education itself. It is unfortunate that good practice in education is often cast with the framework of "new" theories and "new" terms used to describe what has become a tried-and-true approach to teaching since the dawn of education. (Tucker, 1985: 199)

CBA includes (1) direct observation and analysis of the learning environment, (2) analysis of the processes used by students in approaching tasks, (3) examination of pupil products, and (4) control and arrangement of tasks for the student.

1. Observation of the Learning Environment

In CBA, the teacher or diagnostic specialist evaluates the learning environment in several ways. One of these involves looking specifically at the kinds of instructional materials being used with the student as well as the basis for selection and use of those materials. It also includes looking at ways in which instruction is organized and at the sequencing of both content and concepts within the curriculum. Teachers or diagnostic specialists look for pitfalls that may be contributing to interference with the student learning the content of the curriculum. They also examine how information is presented; that is, the methods used (lecture, workbook, programmed instruction) to convey information to the student are analyzed. In CBA, considerable effort is devoted to systematic analysis of several situational variables. For example, the ways in which groups are used to facilitate instruction are evaluated, as is the involvement of students in instructing peers. The ways in which volunteer personnel are used to work with individual students is evaluated, and considerable emphasis is placed on evaluating the structure of the school day. In this latter instance, diagnostic personnel systematically analyze the amount of time allocated to instruction and the amount of time the pupil is actually engaged in responding to academic material.

2. Evaluating Task Approach Strategies

Rather than immediately assuming that students who perform poorly do so because something is wrong with them, the teacher doing a CBA begins by looking at ways in which students approach tasks. The teacher evaluates student demeanor, student attention to task, and the extent to which students read and follow instructions.

3. Evaluating the Products of Instruction

Teachers regularly examine student products in CBAs. They do this to examine instances in which students are going wrong. Students regularly produce products in the form of written essays, completed worksheets, and tests or quizzes. Analysis of these products involves systematic examination of the performance and error analysis. For example, teachers may examine math worksheets, not only to find out how many problems students solved correctly, but also to identify specific error patterns.

4. Control and Arrangement of Tasks

This part of CBA often is called diagnostic teaching. Teachers and diagnostic personnel have an opportunity to manipulate systematically the ways in which materials are presented, the ways in which concepts are presented, and feedback strategies. They may observe the influence of such modifications on student performance and use the results of these observations to plan future instruction.

C. Curriculum-Based Methods of Assessment

Arguing that special education exists because generalized education programs fail to educate a portion of the students assigned to them, Deno (1989) presented a model for improving current practices using curriculum-based methods of assessment. During the problem identification (screening–referral) step, observations and performance records are gathered in educationally relevant domains (e.g., basal readers, district-wide mathematics textbooks). Deciding if discrepancies between expected and actual performance are important enough to require special education is central to the problem definition (eligibility–classification) step. During the problem resolution (intervention planning) step, treatment alternatives, probable performance improvements, and costs associated with them are identified. Deciding if attempted interventions should be continued or modified is central to the problem monitoring (progress monitoring) step. During the problem solution (program monitoring) step, differences between expected and actual performance are evaluated and decisions are made related to continuing an intervention program.

1. Problem Identification–Definition

A number of investigations have demonstrated that curriculum-based procedures are effective when making screening, referral, and classification decisions (Deno, 1985, 1986; Deno *et al.*, 1983; Marston, 1989; Shinn and Marston, 1985; Shinn *et al.*, 1986, 1987). According to Shinn (1989: 92), "when screening and/or eligibility decisions are made, the academic performance of any particular student of concern is indexed against local normative performance in the curriculum" and local norms can be developed at classroom, school, and district levels of complexity. To develop local norms, school district personnel must identify a representative sample of curriculum materials for each grade level, establish a sampling plan, train people to gather assessment information, and collect, score, and summarize performances. Local norms developed in a large metropolitan school district using the Ginn 720 Rainbow Series (Clymer and Bissett, 1980) as the basic reading curriculum are presented in Table 2.1.

Shinn (1989) points out that single-step or multiple-step identification models can be adapted and successfully used with curriculum-based measurement practices. After teams identify the specific nature of referral problems, gather necessary assessment information, and determine if additional intervention is necessary, curriculum-based decision-making takes one of two general forms.

For example, in single-step models, referred students are compared with local grade-level norms on appropriate curricular materials. In some districts, discrepancy ratios (Deno and Mirkin, 1977; Howell and Kaplan, 1980) are calculated by dividing normative performance by referred student's performance, and decisions are made based on cutoff scores established by local

Table 2.1

Means and Standard Deviations for Total Words Written on a Written Expression Task

Grade level	Assessment time frame		
	Fall	Winter	Spring
2	11.7	16.7	24.7
	(7.3)	(10.0)	(11.5)
3	22.9	27.8	33.8
	(10.3)	(11.9)	(12.4)
4	32.7	36.4	41.4
	(12.9)	(12.4)	(12.9)
5	40.3	44.6	46.4
	(14.5)	(13.7)	(13.6)
5	47.4	47.5	53.3
	(13.8)	(14.3)	(15.4)

Adapted from Table 4.6 (p. 112) in Shinn, M. (ed.) (1989), "Curriculum-Based Measurement: Assessing Special Students." Guilford Press, New York.

personnel (e.g., -2.0 or greater discrepancy ratio). In other districts, percentile scores derived from local norms are used in establishing cutoff scores and making eligibility decisions (Shinn, 1989).

In multiple-step models, several stages characterize the identification process. First, regular teachers or parents must refer a student. Next, evidence must illustrate performance outside the range of regular classroom peers. Third, performance of referred students must be outside the range that realistically can be accommodated in regular classrooms. This approach closely approximates the decision-making process described by Salvia and Ysseldyke (1985) and others (Loeber *et al.*, 1984; Shinn, 1989; Ysseldyke and Algozzine, 1990).

In traditional assessment practices, activities related to identification–classification take considerable time and often are seen as the primary reasons for gathering information about students. Of course, when the goal of assessment is simply identifying what to call a student, special educational experiences probably will not be exemplary. The most important decisions made about referred students are those related to deciding how to create instructional experiences to meet special learning needs identified during problem resolution–intervention planning stages of the assessment process.

2. Problem Resolution

Fuchs and Shinn (1989) identified two categories of problems associated with using traditional (i.e., non-curriculum-based) assessment methods to plan instructional programs. First, individualized education program (IEP) goals developed from them are typically vague and global (e.g., will improve one year in reading) or overly specific, covering small details outlining instructional programs students will receive. Second, most of the IEP goals are written so that substantive and procedural compliance with federal requirement related to evaluation procedures is difficult. Fuchs and Shinn (1989) suggest that instructional planning can be improved by writing curriculum-based IEP objectives; the process involves selecting goal structures, formulating objective, and writing objectives with and without local norms.

a. Selecting Goal Structures IEP goals can be written using long-term and short-term approaches. With the long-term approach, goals and a large pool of related measurement items are specified. For example, all of the new reading vocabulary presented in several basal readers might represent the pool of relevant items used to formulate goals for a second grade student in a learning disabilities resource program. With the short-time approach, goals correspond to steps in a curriculum. For example, goals related to phonetic patterns or word families within the new basel reader vocabulary would be appropriate short-term objectives. Fuchs and Shinn (1989) point out that assessment information is more closely linked to instructional material when using the short-term goal approach, but relations between long-term goals and traditional achievement tests are higher. They recommend long-term goal statements, because using them "tends to focus measurement on the 'terminal' or true expected outcome behavior and, relatedly, to produce growth on the type of out-come measure of greater importance to the generalizable functioning of students" (p. 134).

  b. *Formulating Objectives* Model objectives specify (1) the conditions under which performance is obtained, (2) the behavior being performed, and (3) the criterion for success (Mager, 1962). Deno (1986) described a three-step process for formulating curriculum-based IEP objectives. First, current performance data are collected. Next, a level of the curriculum is specified, measurement specifies (i.e., conditions and behavior) are identified, and a date for review is established. Finally, a criterion for success is specified based on local normative information or individual performance records. Having done this, the process of actually writing objectives is straightforward.

  c. *Writing Objectives* A format for curriculum-based IEP objectives is presented in Table 2.2. Fuchs and Shinn (1989) suggest that they can be written

Table 2.2

Format for Individualized Education Program Objectives in Selected Academic Content Areas

Content area	Condition	Behavior	Criterion
Reading	In (*no. of weeks to annual review*), when given a randomly selected passage from (*level and name of reading series*),	student will read aloud	at (*no. of words per minute correct/no. of errors*).
Math	In (*no. of weeks to annual review*), when given randomly selected problems from (*level and name of math series*) for 2 min,	student will write	(*no. of correct digits*).
Writing	In (*no. of weeks to annual review*), when given a story starter or topic sentence and 3 min in which to write,	student will write	a total of (*no. of words or letter sequences*).
Spelling	In (*no. of weeks to annual review*), when dictated randomly selected words from (*level and name of spelling series*) for 2 min,	student will write	(*no. of correct letter sequences*).

Source: Fuchs, L. S., and Shinn, M. R. (1989), Writing IEP objectives. *In* "Curriculum-Based Measurement: Assessing Special Children (M. Shinn, ed.), pp. 130–152. Guilford Press, New York.

without local norms, using expert judgment, instructional placement standards, and empirical standards when formulating measurement specifics and criteria for success. When local norms are available, same-grade peers or cross-grade methods are used.

3. Problem Monitoring

The process of using curriculum-based measures to monitor problems involves routinely checking levels of performance in materials targeted for year-end proficiency. When such assessment indicates student progress is inadequate, teachers modify instructional programs and re-evaluate performance. Fuchs (1989) provides an example of how curriculum-based measurement principles are used to monitor progress and revise intervention plans; steps illustrated in the example included deciding what to measure, deciding how to measure, and deciding how to use the data. Deciding what to measure involves selecting appropriate target behaviors and appropriate curriculum materials. Deciding how to measure involves selecting a method for gathering and scoring assessment information and deciding how long and how frequently to use it. Selecting methods of recording and making judgments about data are part of deciding how to use information gathered during curriculum-based problem monitoring.

4. Problem Solution

Concern has been expressed that much of traditional special education represents a "refer, classify, place, and forget" perspective on delivery of services to students with special learning needs (1986; Algozzine *et al.*, 1980; Ysseldyke and Algozzine, 1982, 1984). Curriculum-based measurement practices offer considerable promise in periodic and annual reviews used to decide whether to continue or terminate special education services (Allen, 1989; Marston and Magnusson, 1985; Shinn, 1986). Assessment activities for periodic and annual reviews are similar; annual reviews tend to be more thorough and typically are documented with a formal written report (Allen, 1989). The focus of these activities is assessing the general benefits of special education services and deciding whether to continue or modify current levels of service to meet special learning needs.

In determining benefits of special education, teachers make curriculum-based comparisons of student performances before and after entering special programs. Data gathered during the identification, resolution, and monitoring stages of curriculum-based decision-making are used during the problem solution stage.

Figure 2.1 illustrates typical data available after participation in curriculum-based special programming. Harry was placed in special education because his reading performance was sufficiently discrepant from that

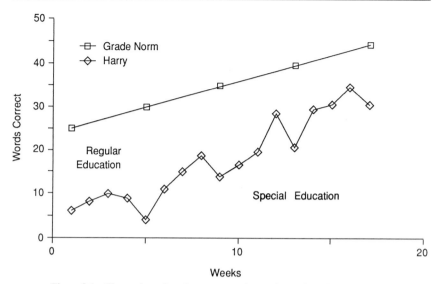

Figure 2.1   Illustration of student progress in regular and special education.

of his regular classroom peers. Data gathered during special class instruction reflect steady improvement, even though he is still not performing at levels commensurate with grade-level norms.

Comparisons of special education and regular education performance are used in deciding when to terminate special programs. If a student's performance falls within the average range of performance for grade-level peers (e.g., within 1 standard deviation above or below their mean), return to regular class placement would seem appropriate (Allen, 1989), albeit often too strict a criterion for mainstreaming (Marston, 1989). Performance of other low-achieving students may be a more appropriate standard (Allen, 1989; Gerber and Semmel, 1984).

Figure 2.2 illustrates a special education student's writing performance in relation to grade-level and low-achieving group norms. Fred improved steadily while participating in special education. His performance was consistently similar to that of other low-achieving students in the mainstream classroom and often exceeded that of the grade-level norm group. Placement of Fred in the mainstream classroom would be appropriate based on this assessment of his current levels of performance in special education.

Curriculum-based methods of assessment are not the answer to problems facing professionals trying to improve assessment practices; it does offer a number of advantages over traditional psychometric practices. First, gathering performance indicators in classroom-based curriculum materials and

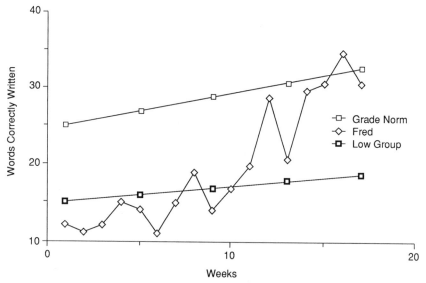

Figure 2.2 Comparison of writing performance for a student in special education.

comparing them with similar scores obtained by local peers clearly goes a long way in making assessment relevant for instruction. Too often, items on standardized tests and performances related to them bear little relation to curricula guiding daily classroom activities (Good and Salvia, 1987; Jenkins and Pany, 1978). Similarly, using simple, direct measures for problem identification, definition, resolution, monitoring, and solution provides clear benefits in addressing problems (e.g., limits of gain-score analysis, test–retest reliabilities, alternate forms) associated with using traditional, standardized test for these purposes. Finally, curriculum-based methods are particularly relevant in assessment of students with learning disabilities because the condition is an achievement–discrepancy-based "disability."

II. A PERSPECTIVE ON ASSESSMENT

Special educators have spent too much time answering the wrong questions and questioning the wrong answers. The penchant for finding the right definition, the right combination of test scores, and the right intervention for the right type of students is obvious. The results are less than impressive. Recently, professionals became embroiled in arguments about where to and who should deliver special education (e.g., Braaten *et al.*, 1988; Gerber, 1988;

J. Learning Disabil., January, 1988; Reynolds, 1988). Most of the time, "professional dialogue" surrounding issues such as the efficacy of ability-training, the appropriateness of this or that definition, finding the "real" LD student, or measuring pros and cons of vaguely conceptualized movements such as the regular education initiative, merely represents breastbeating that is a patent waste of time. Time spent looking for definitions, tests, or criteria is not time spent teaching students. Time spent arguing that category-specific interventions justify the existence of categorical distinctions among students is time spent depriving students with special needs of interventions that work.

Referral rates for special education are very high. Once referred, students stand a very good chance of being declared handicapped and eligible for special education services. Assessment teams operate, too often, simply to verify the existence of a problem that the classroom teacher says exists. Such efforts can be characterized as a "search for pathology" in students. When the emphasis is on declaring students eligible for services rather than on identifying, as best one can, the most appropriate instructional program for a student, the practice of special education (i.e., meeting the special learning needs of students being served) suffers. It suffers because the accuracy of decisions is questionable at best and assessment has been drastically over-sophisticated. Some tests can be used to assess nearly any characteristic, behavior, trait, or skill (Ysseldyke and Algozzine, 1990). Other tests are designed to pinpoint specifically the alleged cause of a youngster's difficulties, even if nothing can be done about it. Because the technical adequacy of many of these tests is poor, professionals sometimes find problems when none really exist.

Assessment is simply a process of collecting data for the purpose of making decisions about individuals. Tests do not indicate what decisions to make, they simply provide data. Yet, to read many test manuals and accounts of what tests will do and to listen to some professionals talk about how they use tests, one would think that tests perform miracles. It is time to take the mystique out of testing and to recognize tests for what they are—samples of behavior. The most appropriate samples of behavior are those gathered using curriculum materials used in classrooms where instruction is being delivered.

New tests, new procedures, new labels, and new initiatives are not the answer. We have enough tests, procedures, labels, and initiatives to make better assessment decisions; we know enough to make better assessment decisions. In doing it, we must recognize the social, political, and economic nature of the decisions we are making. Then, we simply have to do it better with what we have. Some argue that the best minds must be applied to the solution of the problems that plague decision-making in the area of learning disabilities. Frankly, the best minds have been doing this, and we are the best minds.

References

Algozzine, B., and Morsink, C. V. (1989). "Analysis of Instruction in Self-Contained Special Education Classrooms: Final Report." Department of Special Education, University of Florida, Gainesville, Florida.

Algozzine, B., and Ysseldyke, J. E. (1981). Special education services for normal children: Better safe than sorry. *Excep. Children* **48,** 238–243.

Algozzine, B., and Ysseldyke, J. E. (1982). Classification decisions in learning disabilities. *Educ. Psycholog. Measur.* **2(2),** 117–129.

Algozzine, B., and Ysseldyke, J. E. (1983). Learning disabilities as a subset of school failure: The oversophistication of a concept. *Excep. Children* **50,** 242–246.

Algozzine, B., and Ysseldyke, J. E. (1986). The future of the LD field: Screening and diagnosis. *J. Learn. Disabil.* **19,** 394–398.

Algozzine, B., Christenson, S., and Ysseldyke, J. E. (1982). Probabilities associated with the referral to placement process. *Teacher Educ. Special Educ.* **5,** 19–23.

Algozzine, B., Morsink, C. V., and Algozzine, K. M. (1988). What's happening in self-contained special education classrooms? *Excep. Children* **55,** 259–265.

Allen, D. (1989). Evaluating solutions, monitoring progress, and revising intervention plans. *In* "Curriculum-Based Measurement: Assessing Special Children" (M. Shinn, ed.), pp. 182–201. Guilford Press, New York.

Blankenship, C. S. (1985). Using curriculum-based assessment data to make instructional decisions. *Excep. Children* **52,** 233–238.

Blatt, B. (1958). The physical, personality, and academic status of children who are mentally retarded attending special classes as compared with children who are mentally retarded attending regular classes. *Am. J. Ment. Defic.* **62,** 810–818.

Borg, W. (1980). Time and school learning. *In* "Time to Learn" (C. Denham and A. Lieberman, eds.), pp. 27–43. National Institute of Education, Washington, D.C.

Borsuch, G. D., and Nance, D. D. (1987). Evaluating special education programs: Shifting the professional mandate from process to outcome. *Remed. Special Educ.* **8(3),** 7–16.

Bruininks, R., and Rynders, J. (1971). Alternatives to special class placement for educable mentally retarded children. *Focus Excep. Children* **3,** 1–12.

Budoff, M., and Gottlieb, J. (1976). Special-class EMR children mainstreamed: A study of an aptitude (learning potential) × treatment interaction. *Am. J. Ment. Defic.* **81,** 1–11.

Carlberg, C., and Kavale, K. (1980). The efficacy of special versus regular class placement for exceptional children: A meta-analysis. *J. Special Educ.* **14,** 295–309.

Cegelka, W., and Tyler, J. (1970). The efficacy of special class placement for the mentally retarded in proper perspective. *Train. School Bull.* **65,** 33–65.

Clymer, T., and Bissett, D. J. (1980). Reading 720 Rainbow edition: A lizard to start with. Lexington, Massachusetts: Ginn and Company.

Coulter, W. A. (1985). Implementing curriculum-based assessment: Considerations for pupil appraisal professionals. *Excep. Children* **52,** 277–281.

Deno, S. L. (1985). Curriculum-based measurement: The emerging alternative. *Excep. Children* **52,** 219–232.

Deno, S. L. (1986). Formative evaluation of individual programs: A new role for school psychologists. *School Psychol. Rev.* **15,** 358–374.

Deno, S. L. (1989). Curriculum-based measurement and special education services: A fundamental and direct relationship. *In* "Curriculum-Based Measurement: Assessing Special Children" (M. Shinn, ed.), pp. 1–17. Guilford Press, New York.

Deno, S. L., and Mirkin, P. K. (1977). "Data-Based Program Modification: A Manual." Council for Exceptional Children, Reston, Virginia.

Deno, S. L., Marston, D., Shinn, M. R., and Tindal, G. (1983). Oral reading fluency: A simple datum for scaling reading disability. *Top. Learn. Learn. Disabil.* **2**, 53–59.

Englert, C. S. (1984). Effective direct instruction practices in special education settings. *Remed. Special Educ.* **5(2)**, 38–47.

Epps., S., Ysseldyke, J. E., and Algozzine, B. (1983). Public policy implications of different definitions of learning disabilities. *J. Psychoeduc. Assess.* **1**, 341–352.

Fuchs, L. S. (1989). Evaluating solutions, monitoring progress, and revising intervention plans. *In* "Curriculum-Based Measurement: Assessing Special Children" (M. Shinn, ed.), pp. 153–181. Guilford Press, New York.

Fuchs, L. S., and Shinn, M. R. (1989). Writing IEP objectives. *In* "Curriculum-Based Measurement: Assessing Special Children" (M. Shinn, ed.), pp. 130–152. Guilford Press, New York.

Furlong, M. J., and Yanagida, E. H. (1985). Psychometric factors affecting multidisciplinary team identification of learning disabled children. *Learn. Disabil. Q.* **8**, 37–44.

Gickling, E., and Havertape, J. (1981). "Curriculum-Based Assessment (CBA)." National School Psychology Inservice Training Network, Minneapolis, Minnesota.

Gickling, E. E., and Thompson, V. P. (1985). A personal view of curriculum-based assessment. *Excep. Children* **52**, 205–218.

Glass, G. V. (1993). Effectiveness of special education. *Policy Stud. Rev.* **2**, 65–78.

Goldstein, H. (1964). Mentally retarded children in special programs. *J. Educ.* **147**, 95–100.

Gerber, M., and Semmel, M. (1984). Teachers as imperfect tests: Reconceptualizing the referral process. *Educat. Psychologist* **19**, 137–148.

Good, R. H., and Salvia, J. (1987). Curriculum bias in published, norm-referenced reading tests: Demonstrable effects. *School Psychol. Rev.* **17**, 51–60.

Guskin, S., and Spicker, H. (1968). Educational research in mental retardation. *In* "International Review of Research in Mental Retardation," Vol. 3 (N. Ellis, ed.). pp. 384–417. Academic Press, New York.

Heller, K. A., Holtzman, W. H., and Messick, S. (eds.) (1982). "Placing Children in Special Education: A Strategy for Equity." National Academy Press, Washington, D.C.

Horn, J. L. (1924). "The Education of Exceptional Children: A Consideration of Public School Problems and Policies in the Field of Differentiated Education." Century, New York.

Howell, K. W., and Kaplan, J. S. (1980). "Diagnosing Basic Skills: A Handbook for Deciding What to Teach." Charles E. Merrill, Columbus, Ohio.

Ivarie, J., Hogue, D., and Brulle, A. R. (1984). An investigation of mainstream teacher time spent with students labeled learning disabled. *Excep. Children* **51**, 142–149.

Jenkins, J. R., and Pany, D. (1978). Standardized achievement tests: How useful for special education? *Excep. Children* **44**, 448–453.

Kavale, K. A., and Forness, S. R. (1987). History, politics, and the general education initiative: Sleeter's reinterpretation of learning disabilities as a case study. *Remed. Special Educ.* **8(5)**, 6–12.

Kirk, S. (1964). Research in education. *In* "Mental Retardation: A Review of Research" (H. Stevens and R. Heber, eds.), pp. 217–249. University of Chicago Press, Chicago.

Lerner, J. (1989). "Learning Disabilities," 4th ed. Houghton Mifflin, Boston.

Loeber, R., Dishion, T. J., and Patterson, G. R. (1984). Multiple gating: A multistage assessment procedure for identifying youths at risk for delinquency. *J. Res. Crime Delinq.* **21,** 7–32.

Mager, R. F. (1962). Preparing instructional objectives. Palo Alto, California: Fearon Publishers.

Marston, D. (1987). Does categorical teacher certification benefit the midly handicapped. *Excep. Children* **53,** 423–431.

Marston, D., and Magnusson, D. (1985). Implementing curriculum-based measurement in special and regular education settings. *Excep. Children* **52,** 266–277.

Marston, D. B. (1989). A curriculum-based measurement approach to assessing academic performance: What it is and why do it. *In* "Curriculum-Based Measurement: Assessing Special Children" (M. Shinn, ed.), pp. 18–78. Guilford Press, New York.

Myers, J. K. (1976). The efficacy of the special day school for EMR pupils. *Ment. Retard.* **14,** 3–11.

O'Shea, L. J., and Valcante, G. (1986). A comparison over time of relative discrepancy scores of low achievers. *Excep. Children* **53,** 253–259.

O'Sullivan, P. J., Marston, D., and Magnusson, D. (1987). Categorical special education teacher certification: Does it affect instruction of mildly handicapped pupils. *Remed. Special Educ.* **8(5),** 13–18.

Polloway, E. A., Epstein, M. H., Polloway, C. H., Patton, J. R., and Ball, D. W. (1986). Corrective reading program: An analysis of effectiveness with learning disabled and mentally retarded students. *Remed. Special Educ.* **7(4),** 41–47.

Raspberry, W. (1976). Rascism and victims. *Washington Post* **March 8,** A19.

Rubin, R. A., and Balow, B. (1978). Prevalence of teacher identified behavior patterns: A longitudinal study. *Excep. Children* **44,** 102–111.

Sabatino, D. A. (1971). An evaluation of resource rooms for children with learning disabilities. *J. Learn. Disabil.* **4,** 27–35.

Salvia, J. A., and Ysseldyke, J. E. (1985). "Assessment in Special and Remedial Education," 3rd ed. Houghton Mifflin, Boston.

Samuels, S. J., and Miller, N. L. (1985). Failure to find attention differences between learning disabled and normal children on classroom and laboratory tasks. *Excep. Children* **51,** 358–375.

Sarason, S. B., and Doris, J. (1979). "Educational Handicap, Public Policy, and Social History." Free Press, New York.

Scruggs, T. E., Mastropieri, M. A., and Tolfa-Veit, D. (1986). The effects of coaching on the standardized test performance of learning disabled and behaviorally students. *Remed. Special Educ.* **7(5),** 37–41.

Semmel, M., Gottlieb, J., and Robinson, N. (1979). Mainstreaming: Perspectives on educating handicapped children in the public schools. *In* "Review of Research in

Education" (D. Berliner, ed.), pp. 111–142. American Educational Research Association, Washington, D.C.

Shinn, M. R. (1986). Does anyone care what happens after the refer-test-place sequence: The systematic evaluation of special education effectiveness. *Sch. Psychol Rev.* **15**, 49–58.

Shinn, M. R. (1989). Identifying and defining academic problems: CBM screening and eligibility procedures. *In* "Curriculum-Based Measurement: Assessing Special Children" (M. Shinn, ed.), pp. 90–129. Guilford Press, New York.

Shinn, M. R, and Marston, D. (1985). Differentiating mildly handicapped, low-achieving and regular education students: A curriculum-based approach. *Remed. Special Educ.* **6**, 31–45.

Shinn, M. R., Ysseldyke, J. E., Deno, S. L., and Tindal, G. (1986). A comparison of differences between students labeled learning disabled and low achieving on measures of classroom performance. *J. Learn. Disabil.* **19**, 545–552.

Shinn, M. R., Tindal, G., Spira, D., and Marston, D. (1987). Practice of learning disabilities as social policy. *Learn. Disabil. Q.* **10**, 17–28.

Singer, J. D., and Butler, J. A. (1987). The Education of All Handicapped Children Act: Schools as agents of social reform. *Harv. Educ. Rev.* **57**, 125–152.

Skiba, R. (1989). "Integrating Assessment and Instruction: The Missing Link in Effective Programming." Paper presented at the CEC/CCBD Topical Conference on Behavior Disordered Youth, Charlotte, North Carolina.

Sleeter, C. E. (1986). Learning disabilities: The social construction of a special education category. *Excep. Children* **53**, 46–54.

Summers, E. G. (1986). The information flood in learning disabilities: A bibliometric analysis of the journal literature. *Remed. Special Educ.* **7(1)**, 49–60.

Thompson, R. H., Vitale, P. A., and Jewett, J. P. (1984). Teacher–student interaction patterns in mainstream classrooms. *Remed. Special Educ.* **5(6)**, 51–61.

Thurlow, M. L., and Ysseldyke, J. E. (1979). Current assessment and decision-making practices in model LD programs. *Learn. Disabil. Q.* **2**, 15–24.

Tindal, G. (1985). Investigating the effectiveness of special education: An analysis of methodology. *J. Learn. Disabil.* **18**, 101–112.

Trimble, A. C. (1970). Can remedial reading be eliminated? *Acad. Ther.* **5**, 207–213.

Tucker, J. A. (1985). Curriculum-based assessment: An introduction. *Excep. Children* **52**, 199–204.

United States Department of Education (1988). "Tenth Annual Report to Congress on the Implementation of The Education of the Handicapped Act." Washington, D.C.

Vacc, N. A. (1972). Long term effects of special class intervention for emotionally disturbed children. *Excep. Children* **39**, 15–22.

Walker, D. K., Singer, J. D., Palfrey, J. S., Orza, M., Wenger, M., and Butler, J. A. (1988). Who leaves and who stays in special education: A 2-year follow-up study. *Excep. Children* **54**, 393–402.

Ysseldyke, J. E., and Algozzine, B. (1982). Bias among professionals who erroneously classify students eligible for special education services. *J. Exp. Educ.* **76**, 223–228.

Ysseldyke, J. E., and Algozzine, B. (1983). LD or not LD: That's not the question. *J. Learn. Disabil.* **16**, 29–31.

Ysseldyke, J. E., and Algozzine, B, (1984). "Introduction to Special Education." Houghton Mifflin, Boston.

Ysseldyke, J. E., and Algozzine, B. (1990). "Introduction to Special Education," 2nd ed. Houghton Mifflin, Boston.

Ysseldyke, J. E., and Christenson, S. L. (1987). Evaluating students' instructional environments. *Remed. Special Educ.* **8(3),** 17–24.

Ysseldyke, J. E., Algozzine, B., Regan, R., and Potter, M. (1980). Technical adequacy of tests used by professionals in simulated decision making. *Psychol. Schools* **17,** 202–209.

Ysseldyke, J. E., Algozzine, B., Richey, L., and Graden, J. (1982a). Declaring students eligible for learning disabilities services: Why bother with the data? *Learn. Disabil. Q.* **5,** 37–44.

Ysseldyke, J. E., Algozzine, B., Shinn, M. R., and McGue, M. (1982b). Similarities and differences between low achievers and students labeled learning disabled. *J. Special Educ.* **16,** 73–85.

Ysseldyke, J. E., Thurlow, M. L., Graden, J., Wesson, C., Algozzine, B., and Deno, S. L. (1983). Generalizations from five years of research on assessment and decision making: The University of Minnesota Institute. *Excep. Educ. Q.* **4,** 75–93.

Ysseldyke, J. E., Thurlow, M. L., Mecklenburg, C., and Graden, J. (1984). Opportunity to learn for regular and special students during reading instruction. *Remed. Special Educ.* **5(1),** 29–37.

CHAPTER 3

Attention Disorders

Richard Conte

Editor's Notes

In the first two chapters, we have covered basic topics on the history, conceptual issues, and assessment in learning disabilities (LDs). Starting with this chapter, we begin to examine research in various areas of LDs. We focus first on attentional problems in children with LDs. Conte's chapter informs us about the complexities of the attention-deficits disorder (ADD) construct in terms of definitional and diagnostic problems. It also brings out the richness of the research information, the grounds covered, and the long haul ahead toward unravelling its causal origins and the challenge in devising treatments that allow ready implementation and produce effects that can be sustained and generalized.

Conte's chapter contains multiple themes. These include the relevance of studying ADDs to LDs, definitions and diagnostic measurements of ADD, research on ADD, current research issues on ADD, and practical implications of research on ADD.

Of these, the major theme is Conte's comprehensive summaries of research on ADD. He organizes his report of the research into three broad areas: characteristics and developmental course of ADD, causes of ADD, and treatment of ADD. Within each area of research, Conte meticulously and thoughtfully summarizes substantial bodies of work. He points out the promises and limitations of extant research. He also gives well-considered analyses to the failures of the various treatment approaches to ADD.

I. THE DOMAIN OF ATTENTION

Minimal reflection on human behavior makes it clear that we need a construct to explain the considerable variation both within and among individuals regarding the ability to attend to external events. All of us experience lapses of attention at least some of the time. Every student has been frustrated by an inability to attend, even in situations where consequences for not doing so were extreme. At classical music concerts, we may find ourselves unexpectedly dwelling on the events of the previous day despite the fact that we have paid an exorbitant price for admission. Every parent has wondered why their child can attend to TV cartoons for hours but cannot stand math homework for more than a few minutes.

Attention is a difficult and complicated concept, as evidenced by the variety of terms that have been used to describe it. For example, Moray (1969) identified seven components of attention: mental concentration, vigilance, selective attention, search, activation, set, and analysis by synthesis. Posner (1975) suggested three components to attention: alertness, selection, and effort. In the special education literature, Keogh and Margolis (1976) described coming to attention, decision-making, and sustaining attention. Krupski (1980) viewed attention along two dimensions: voluntary–involuntary and short term–sustained.

Some of the components of attention are readily observable in our everyday experience. Taking Posner's three-component model (alertness, selection, and effort), we know that our alertness or receptivity to external signals varies considerably, even over the course of a single day. Thus, after a hard day at work or study, we may not be as receptive to external stimuli as we are when we are fresh in the morning. If we skip a meal and our blood sugar drops to a critically low level, we may find it difficult to attend to even very simple events. In addition to these internal factors, alertness can vary as a function of external circumstances; i.e., we know that certain types of situations are inherently easier to attend to than others. Thus, children who find it difficult to attend to the teacher's explanation of a math lesson may stay fixated at a computer game for hours. Second, we can heighten our attention by selecting certain elements in the environment for special attention. For instance, our receptivity to external signals can be enhanced if we are given advanced warning of their position in space. Also, if we are given a model (in terms of the physical characteristics or abstract category information) of a stimulus to attend to, our receptivity to such stimuli is greatly enhanced. Third, we know that we have limited resources to deploy when attempting to attend to events. At a noisy party we usually find that we can attend to only one conversation at a time. Experimentally, if we are asked to monitor a message in one ear, we seem to have little conscious awareness of the content of messages delivered to the other ear. Thus, if we deploy attention to a certain place or toward a certain type of content, it seems to decrease our receptivity to nontarget events. Thus, the amount of effort we expend in attending to some events can have consequences for our ability to attend to other events.

II. SCOPE AND SEQUENCE

In this chapter, learning disabilities (LDs) and attention disorders are assumed to be different entities. Whereas LDs are characterized by the specificity of dysfunction (e.g., a deficit in reading or spelling), attention disorders tend to be relatively diffuse and affect functioning in a wide range of contexts. Not everyone agrees with the position that attention disorders and LDs are essentially different (indeed, some have thought that LDs was caused by attention disorder), but this view is consistent with that which was put forward at the most recent National Conference on Learning Disabilities (1987). As will be evident in this chapter, although LDs and attention disorders are different, they often occur together.

In the LDs field, attention has been studied in two different ways, and in each of these the term attention has been defined somewhat differently. One line of research has been concerned with the possibility that LDs is caused by deficiencies in one or more of the components of attention that are described in the preceding section. So, for example, a large number of studies have been conducted in which the performance of learning-disabled (LD) and non-LD children are compared on various measures of selective attention. The second line of research has focused on children with attention-deficit–hyperactivity disorder (ADHD). The primary symptoms of ADHD include short attention span, impulsivity, and overactivity. Research on ADHD is relevant to the study of LDs because many children with LDs also have ADHD. However, in this area of study, attention is not defined in terms of the components of attention; instead, diagnostic criteria have been developed for use by experienced clinicians. These diagnostic criteria (to be described in a subsequent section) consist of descriptions of behaviors that are thought to be characteristic of children with ADHD. In using these criteria, a description of the child's behavior is obtained from direct observation of the child's behavior and from parent and teacher reports, and then this description is compared with the diagnostic criteria.

One other reason that the two approaches to the study of attention are so different is that *some* of the diagnostic criteria for ADHD (e.g., talking excessively, engaging in physically dangerous activities, having difficulty taking turns while playing games) have little similarity to attention as it is described in attention theories.

With respect to attention-deficits disorder (ADD), it is important to note that a variety of labels have been used for this condition: hyperkinesis, hyperactivity, ADD with and without hyperactivity, and ADHD. For the sake of simplicity, we will employ the term in current use: attention-deficit–hyperactivity disorder, or ADHD, as the general term to describe this population. Reference will be made to the different labels when describing some of the changes in the conception of ADHD that have coincided with a name change.

Of the two major approaches to attention that have been described above, the major portion of this chapter is concerned with ADHD. This is justifiable by the fact that far more research has been conducted on issues related to ADHD than on deficiencies in attention components in LDs.

It is important to note that the terms ADHD and LDs stem from different classification systems. ADHD is found in the "Diagnostic and Statistical Manual of Mental Disorders," 3rd ed., revised (DSM-III-R; American Psychiatric Association, 1987), whereas the term LDs may be found (in the United States, at least) in P.L. 94-142. ADHD does not appear in P.L. 94-142; however, LDs is referred to in the DSM-III-R as specific developmental disorders such as developmental arithmatic disorder and developmental reading disorder, among others.

From this chapter readers should understand the following:

1. The role of attention in LDs
2. The characteristics of ADDs
3. Methods of diagnosing ADDs
4. Theories of the causes of ADDs
5. Methods of treating ADDs

III. WHY IS IT IMPORTANT TO STUDY ATTENTION DEFICITS?

In this section, the two approaches to the study of attention that are described above are elaborated upon.

A. Role of Attention Deficits in LDs

The exploration of attention deficits in LDs was motivated by the belief that LDs was caused by deficiencies in attention (Ross, 1976; Dykman *et al.*, 1971). This issue was investigated primarily in terms of performance on two types of attention tasks: selective attention tasks and sustained attention tasks.

1. Selective Attention

Selective attention is usually defined as the ability to maintain attention to target stimuli when distractors are present. Hagen's (1967) incidental learning paradigm will be used to exemplify a selective attention task. In this methodology, a central stimulus (e.g., a picture of an animal) is presented together with an incidental or background stimulus (e.g., a picture of a household object). A subject in such an experiment is told to pay attention to the central stimulus; usually nothing is said about the incidental stimulus. Presumably, a child with good selective attention skills will focus only on the central item, whereas a child with more diffuse attention will attend to both the central and incidental items. These different patterns of behavior are revealed by asking subjects what they remember after exposure to a list of items, each of which contains a central and incidental stimuli. In a large number of studies (for review, see Hallihan and Reeve, 1980), it has been typically found that non-LD children retain more central items than do LD children, but LD children retain more of the incidental items than do non-LD children. On the basis of these findings, it was concluded that LD children were deficient in selective attention.

One of the difficulties in evaluating the role of selective attention in LDs is that the studies described by Hallihan and Reeve (1980) used mixed samples of subjects. Specifically, 30–40% of the LD children also are known to have ADHD, and if such a large proportion of ADHD subjects were included in samples of LD children, then one could argue that the deficit in selective attention may have been due to ADHD rather than the presence of LDs.

To examine this issue, a few studies have segregated subjects into homogeneous groups of LD subjects with and without ADHD. The findings from these studies support the notion that LD subjects are deficient in selective attention. Tarnowski et al. (1986) found that LD children showed deficient selective attention performance relative to normal controls on an incidental learning task, whereas children with ADHD and no LDs did not. Richards et al., (1990) obtained a similar result with a letter-distraction task.

While these studies suggest that LD children are deficient in selective attention, they do not tell us whether or not a selective attention deficit is responsible for the learning problems experienced by LD children. To do this, they would have to establish that a relationship exists between performance on selective attention tests and measures of either the *type of* or *severity of* LDs. Thus far, no such data are available.

2. Sustained Attention

As the name implies, sustained attention means that one must attend for an extended period of time. There does not appear to be a precise definition for what is meant by the term sustained, although most studies involving children seem to use trial durations of at least 10 min. Sustained attention will be exemplified by the continuous performance task. In this task, subjects are instructed to monitor either visually or auditorily presented individual letters or numbers and are required to respond when a certain target stimulus is present. For example, they might be asked to press a button whenever the letter "x" is preceded by the letter "a". This method provides an index of sustained attention because many stimulus presentations are used, but relatively few targets are presented. To do well, a subject must be able to maintain attention for an extended period and withhold responding to nontarget stimuli.

The consistent finding for those studies employing the continuous performance task and that have segregated subjects into LD and ADHD groups (Richards *et al.*, 1990; Chee *et al.*, 1989; Tarnowski *et al.*, 1986) is that LD children do not show a deficit on this task. In contrast, ADHD children tend to make more errors of commission, i.e., make responses to nontarget stimuli (Richards *et al.*, 1990; Chee *et al.*, 1989). This pattern of behavior is usually interpreted as a reflection of impulsive behavior (acting without thinking), which is one of the defining characteristics of ADHD.

Clearly, there are unresolved issues with regard to the role of attention in LDs, and on the basis of the present analysis a number of recommendations can be made regarding future research. First, more research is needed in which a variety of measures of both selective and sustained attention is used with groups of subjects identified as having LDs without ADHD, LDs with ADHD, and ADHD without LDs. Second, these studies should also attempt to demonstrate that the deficit in attention is related to the problems that subjects experience outside the testing situation. For LDs, are deficiencies in selective attention related to the type of LDs? In ADHD, is the deficit in sustained attention related to symptoms that are expressed at school and home?

B. Many Children Have Both LDs and ADHD

Individuals who are responsible for providing service to LD children must be aware of the characteristics of and treatment procedures used for children with ADHD, because they will undoubtedly encounter many of these children in their practice. Recent estimates suggest that at least 30% of LD children also have ADHD (Lambert and Sandoval, 1980; Safer and Allen, 1976). The recent reformulation of the definition of LDs by the National Conference on Learning Disabilities (1987) states that attention disorder *can* be a cause of learning problems but it is not *the* cause of LDs. Presumably, this statement suggests that different characteristics of the learning difficulties are associated with ADHD (e.g., they may be more tractible than learning problems that stemmed from LDs). If some learning problems stem from attention deficits, then it is important for practitioners to be aware of what to look for. Evidence indicates that different cognitive processing difficulties are associated with LDs and ADHD. In addition to the deficits in selective and sustained attention discussed above, Felton and Wood (1989) have shown that rote memory tends to pose problems for ADHD children but not for LD children. In contrast, one segment of the LD population (children with reading disabilities) tends to show deficits on rapid automatized naming (RAN) tasks (Felton and Wood, 1989; Denkla and Rudel, 1976; but for an exception, see Dykman *et al.*, 1985), whereas children with ADHD do as well as controls. In RAN tasks, the speed at which pictures of objects, colors, or symbols can be named is measured. Tant and Douglas (1982) found that on a 20-questions type of task, ADHD children asked less efficient questions and used less efficient strategies than either normal or reading-disabled children. The latter two groups did not differ from each other.

These differences in cognitive processing skills may have important implications for the assessment and treatment of children with LDs and ADHD. The lack of efficient learning strategies in children with ADHD (as indicated by the results of Tant and Douglas, 1982) suggests that learning strategies should be routinely examined during assessment, particularly in children suspected of having ADHD. It seems reasonable that training in the use of more efficient strategies could be of benefit in overcoming the difficulties in rote memory that were described by Felton and Wood (1989). The picture for LD children is more complicated: They appear to have deficiencies in selective attention as well as in RAN tasks. Is it possible that these two areas of difficulty are related? It may be relevant that selective attention tasks and RAN tasks require relatively rapid responses. Perhaps LD children have difficulty with situations that require such quick responses. To confirm this, one would have to examine the performance of LD children in different situations that require speeded responses. Comparisons should be made between tasks that involve selective attention and those that do not, so that relative importance of both processes could be assessed. Regardless of whether LD children are deficient in selective attention or in making rapid responses, how these kinds of problems are related to LDs still is not clear. The ability to attend selectively and the ability to make rapid responses may be thought of as general skills, which apply to many situations. Why would they lead to the specific learning problems that are observed in LDs?

IV. WHAT DO WE MEAN BY AN ATTENTION DISORDER AND HOW CAN IT BE MEASURED?

A. Alternative Conceptions of Attention Disorders

1. DSM-III Criteria

As we have seen in this chapter, the term attention has been used in several different ways. In one sense, attention can signify the various processes (alertness, selection, effort) that are described in attention theories. Thus, a body of literature suggests that selective attention deficits are quite prevalent in the population of LD children. However, as used in describing children with ADHD, the concept of attention is considerably more complicated, and, in fact, attention is only one aspect of the complex symptomatology of ADHD.

Current definitions of ADHD have been heavily influenced by Diagnostic and Statistical Manuals of the American Psychiatric Association. These manuals are based on the results of surveys in which practicing psychiatrists are asked to indicate which symptoms they rely on in formulating diagnoses of various disorders. The results are tabulated and the most frequent responses are used to develop definitions of psychiatric disorders. The DSM-III, (American Psychiatric Association, 1980) defined two types of attention disorder: ADD with hyperactivity and ADD without hyperactivity. The attentional aspect of this disorder consisted of two classes of symptoms: inattention and impulsivity. As should be evident when inspecting the characteristics of attention disorder (see Table 3.1), many of the behaviors have little obvious connection with the concept of attention as it is discussed in attention theories.

Table 3.1

DSM-III Criteria: Attention-Deficit Disorder

A. Inattention (at least three of the following)
   1. Fails to finish things
   2. Often does not seem to listen
   3. Easily distracted
   4. Has difficulty concentrating on schoolwork or other tasks requiring sustained attention
   5. Has difficulty sticking to a play activity
B. Impulsivity (at least three of the following)
   1. Often acts before thinking
   2. Shifts excessively from one activity to another
   3. Has difficulty organizing work (this not being due to cognitive impairment)
   4. Needs a lot of supervision
   5. Frequently calls out in class
   6. Has difficulty awaiting turns in games or group situations
C. Hyperactivity (at least two of the following)
   1. Runs or climbs on things excessively
   2. Has difficulty sitting still or fidgets excessively
   3. Has difficulty staying seated
   4. Moves about excessively during sleep
   5. Is always "on the go" or acts as if "driven by a motor"
D. Age of onset before age 7 yr
E. Duration of at least 6 mo
F. Not due to schizophrenia, affective disorder, or severe or profound mental retardation

2. DSM-III-R Criteria

In the recently revised DSM-III (DSM-III-R; American Psychiatric Association, 1987), the distinction between ADD with and without hyperactivity was abolished because little empirical evidence supports this distinction. Instead, it was decided to treat attention disorder as a unitary construct named attention-deficit–hyperactivity disorder, ADHD, but as one that had a number of different manifestations. Thus, as shown in Table 3.2, 14 symptoms of ADHD are listed. Some of the symptoms are concerned with inattention, some with impulsive behavior, and some with overactivity. To satisfy the criteria for a diagnosis of ADHD, eight of the symptoms must be true of an individual.

3. Unidimensional versus Multidimensional Attention Disorder

There is still disagreement as to the fundamental nature of ADHD. The unidimensional view, as proposed in the DSM-III-R, has come under attack (Lahey *et al.*, 1988) because of data that suggest that the attentional and hyperactivity components are not highly correlated; i.e., some children seem to be primarily hyperactive and others inattentive. In addition, the findings of Lahey *et al.* (1988) indicate that the impulsivity components cannot be clearly

Table 3.2

DSM-III-R Criteria: Attention-Deficit–Hyperactivity Disorder

A. A period of 6 mo or more during which at least eight of the following symptoms are present:
   1. Has difficulty remaining seated
   2. Often fidgets with hands or feet or squirms in seat
   3. Has difficulty playing quietly
   4. Often talks excessively
   5. Often shifts from one uncompleted activity to another
   6. Has difficulty sustaining attention to tasks and play activities
   7. Has difficulty following through on instructions from others (not due to oppositional behavior or failure of comprehension)
   8. Is easily distracted by extraneous stimuli
   9. Often interrupts or intrudes on others (e.g., butts into games)
   10. Often blurts out answers to questions before they have been completed
   11. Has difficulty awaiting turns in games or group situations
   12. Often engages in physically dangerous activities without considering possible consequences (not for the purpose of thrill seeking) (e.g., runs into street without looking)
   13. Often loses things necessary for tasks or activities at school or at home
   14. Often does not seem to listen to what is being said to him or her
B. Onset before the age of 7 yr
C. Does not meet the criteria for pervasive developmental disorder

segregated from those of inattention and hyperactivity. Thus, combining the different classes of symptoms of ADHD may not be legitimate as has been carried out in the DSM-III-R. If the findings of Lahey *et al.* (1988) are replicated, inattention and overactivity would be considered as separate disorders.

4. Situational versus Pervasive ADHD

The diagnostic criteria specified in the DSM-III and DSM-III-R suggest that a diagnosis of ADHD can be made when the symptoms are situational (occur in a limited number of situations; e.g., at home but not at school, or vice-versa) or pervasive (occur in many situations; e.g., at both home and school). According to the DSM-III, information from both school and home should be considered in diagnosing ADHD. In case of disagreement between these two sources, the school report should be given the most weight. In the DSM-III-R, the definition has been broadened with the statement that the symptoms of ADHD may be confined to one situation. Thus, in this system the findings from both school and home are given equal weight.

Relatively few studies have examined the characteristics of children with situational and pervasive ADHD. In the most thorough study, Goodman and Stevenson (1989a) found that only pervasive ADHD subjects could be distinguished from non-ADHD antisocial subjects on the basis of measures of inattention and specific learning problems; in contrast, children with situational ADHD were not distinguishable from non-ADHD antisocial subjects using these measures. Thus, the attentional difficulties of children with situational ADHD may not be sufficiently distinguishable from other populations of atypical children who are not attention-disordered. Goodman and Stevenson (1989a) propose that to be on the safe side investigators should confine the use of the term ADHD to those subjects with pervasive symptoms. Barkley (1981) has made similar recommendations and has developed instruments to measure the pervasiveness of symptoms.

5. ADHD and Conduct Disorder—Same or Different?

Diagnosing ADHD is made even more complex by the fact that other disorders often co-occur with it. The large number of LD children with ADHD has been discussed above. In addition, as detailed in Pelham and Murphy's (1986) review, 30–65% of children diagnosed as ADHD also satisfy the criteria for conduct disorder (CD) (see Table 3.3). Whereas the chief symptoms of ADHD are inattention and impulsivity, CD is characterized by a lack of respect for the basic rights of others. The high degree of overlap between ADHD and CD has prompted the opinion that ADHD and CD are the same thing (Lahey *et al.*, 1980); however, evidence from two recent studies supports the distinction between ADHD and CD. First, Szatmari *et al.* (1989a) found that

Table 3.3

DSM-III-R Criteria: Conduct Disorder

A persistent pattern of conduct in which the basic right of others and major age-appropriate societal norms or rules are violated. The pattern must have continued for at least 6 mo, and at least 3 of the following 13 behaviors must be present:
1. Stolen without confrontation of a victim (more than once)
2. Run away from home overnight (at least twice, or once without returning)
3. Lied
4. Set fires
5. Truant from school
6. Broken into someone else's house, building, or car
7. Deliberate destruction of other's property
8. Physical cruelty to animals
9. Forced someone into sexual activity
10. Used a weapon (in more than one fight)
11. Initiated physical fights
12. Stolen with confrontation of a victim
13. Physical cruelty to people

Subtypes:

The *solitary aggressive type* is characterized by aggressive physical behavior initiated by the child and usually directed toward both adults and peers.

The *group type* is characterized by conduct problems that occur mainly as group activities with peers.

The *undifferentiated type* does not fit neatly into the other two types.

family dysfunction is more likely when ADHD and CD are both present, but not with ADHD alone. Second, Lahey *et al.* (1988) found that a relationship exists between familial psychiatric dysfunction and CD, but not ADHD. Thus, even though ADHD and CD greatly overlap, different etiologic factors seem to be involved in the two disorders.

B. Measures of ADHD

In addition to the procedures specified in the DSM, a number of other instruments are available to measure attention disorder; the Conners Parent–Teacher Questionnaire is perhaps the most commonly used (Fig. 3.1). This questionnaire may be used by parents or teachers who make their ratings on the basis of their interactions with the child over the previous 6-mo period. Generally, if a child obtains a rating that exceeds the average rating obtained by children in the normative sample by 2 or more standard deviations, then this is considered to be consistent with a diagnosis of ADHD. Unlike the DSM-III-R criteria, normative data are available on the Conners Questionnaire. This questionnaire appears to distinguish children with attentional

Child's Name _____

INSTRUCTIONS: Listed below are items concerning children's behavior or the problems they
sometimes have. Read each item carefully and decide how much you think
this child has been bothered by this problem *at this time.*

Information obtained _____ By _____
                            Month   Day   Year

OBSERVATION	Not at All	Just a Little	Pretty Much	Very Much
1. Restless or overactive				
2. Excitable, impulsive				
3. Disturbs other children				
4. Fails to finish things he starts— short attention span				
5. Constantly fidgeting				
6. Inattentive, easily distracted				
7. Demands must be met immediately— easily frustrated				
8. Cries often and easily				
9. Mood changes quickly and drastically				
10. Temper outbursts, explosive and unpredictable behaviour				

	NONE	MINOR	MODERATE	SEVERE
How serious a problem do you think this child has at this time?				

COMMENTS: _____
_____
_____
_____
_____

Figure 3.1   Conners Parent–Teacher Questionnaire

difficulties from those without attention problems. In addition, the Conners scales have been shown to be sensitive to stimulant drug effects. The Conners scales have been criticized for being oversensitive to the overactivity in ADHD and less sensitive to attentional factors. Examples of other ratings scales in common use may be found in Barkley (1981).

V. WHAT HAS BEEN DONE IN THIS RESEARCH AREA?

A. Characteristics and Developmental Course of ADHD

Recent estimates (Szatmari *et al.*, 1989b; Goodman and Stevenson, 1989a) suggest that ADHD affects between 4 and 6% of the school-age population. The prevalence of the disorder is three times more common in males than in females. Developmentally, attention disorders are more common in the age range of 6–8 yrs, perhaps because assessment criteria for ADHD include activity level and, even in normal-functioning children, activity declines as a function of age. Some parents of ADHD children indicate that they identified their child as showing difficult behavior soon after birth; however, the deviant behaviors (noncompliance with parental requests, overactivity) of these children become apparent to most families by the age of 3 or 4 yr.

The difficulties associated with an attention problem tend to stand out even more clearly when a child begins school. The attentional demands placed on a child in school exceed by far those that a child encounters at home or daycare, and very likely these demands exacerbate the symptoms of short attention span. Also the rule structure that is needed to govern the behavior of children at school would also be expected to be problematic for children with ADHD. Because a substantial number of children with ADHD also have learning difficulties, it would be expected that many of these children would require special education services.

As the child with ADHD approaches the teen years, the nature of the problems may undergo change. As is the case in normally developing children, activity level tends to decrease with increasing age. However, other aspects of ADHD assume greater importance. As homework assignments become more and more demanding, difficulties with assignment completion become increasingly apparent. The increasing importance of social relationships is likely to be problematic for children with ADHD. The rules and perceptual cues that govern social interactions are considerably more subtle than those that govern classroom activities, and these messages probably will not be correctly interpreted by the child with ADHD.

In adulthood, as many as 60% continue to show signs of ADHD, while interpersonal problems continue to trouble as many as 75% (Barkley, 1989). Other findings indicate that the long-term prognosis is worsened considerably when CD occurs in combination with ADHD. For instance, Mannuzza *et al.* (1989) found that there is increased risk of criminal behavior only in ADHD children with an associated CD.

B. Causes of ADHD

1. Biological versus Environmental Factors

We approach the study of the causes of ADHD by first considering the relatively broad issue of biological versus environmental causes. More specific factors are considered in subsequent sections.

The investigation of biological factors has included research on the genetics of ADHD and also investigations of physical maladies (delay in developmental milestones, chronic diseases), which appear to be commonly associated with ADHD. Research on environmental factors has considered the importance of psychosocial factors, perinatal influences, and dietary sensitivities.

a. Epidemiological Data   The recent Ontario Child Health Study (OCHS) (Szatmari *et al.*, 1989a) set out to examine the relative contribution of biological versus psychosocial factors in attention disorders by analyzing the characteristics of children with and without ADHD. This study is exemplary because, unlike many previous studies, subjects were randomly sampled from the general population (rather than clinic samples) and because sophisticated statistical procedures were used.

The results of the OCHS indicated that indeed the likelihood of family dysfunction was 2.2 times more likely in a family with a child with ADHD as compared with a child without ADHD. However, when an associated problem was taken into consideration, the relationship between ADHD and family dysfunction did not hold up. This means that family dysfunction was probably more closely related to the associated disorder (e.g., CD) than ADHD. Clearer relationships were obtained when examining biological variables. For instance, it was found that developmental problems (difficulty with speech, clumsiness, slowness to talk, slowness to walk, and low birthweight) were 1.8 times as common in children with ADHD than in those without ADHD. Also, children with ADHD were 1.9 times as likely to have a chronic health problem as children without ADHD. There were few indications of the relevance of psychosocial variables; however, ADHD children apparently were more likely to live in cities than in rural areas. Also, there was an increased likelihood that children with ADHD would come from a family on welfare, but this relationship was restricted to females: A female with ADHD was 3.2 times as likely to be on welfare as females without ADHD; no relationship existed between welfare and ADHD in males. This may mean that ADHD in females is of a quite different character than that observed in males.

In summary, the epidemiological data reviewed here suggest that children with ADHD are distinguished primarily by the presence of a number of developmental abnormalities. These data lend credence to theories of biological causation of ADHD.

b. Twin Studies Information regarding causes of ADHD has also been obtained from twin studies. Goodman and Stevenson (1989b) compared symptoms of ADHD in monozygotic (identical) and dyzygotic (fraternal) same sex twins and found that the ADHD was much more likely to co-occur when the twins were monozygotic. They also investigated the relationship between adverse family factors (marital discord, low parental warmth, high parental criticism) and found that these factors accounted for <10% of the variance when examined in relationship to the measures of ADHD. Thus, consistent with the information obtained by Szatmari *et al.* (1989a), these data also support the biological hypothesis with regard to the causation of ADHD.

c. Adoption Studies Several studies have reported a much higher incidence of adoption in ADHD children than in non-ADHD children. Deutsch *et al.* (1982) reported a 17% rate of nonrelative adoption in children with ADHD. In contrast, the rate of nonrelative adoption for controls (children referred to hospitals for other problems such as kidney transplant or allergies) was <2.5%. The samples of children in this study were drawn from clinic samples in two different cities. In attempting to interpret the significance of these data, Deutsch *et al.* (1982) pointed to the high incidence of psychopathology in unwed mothers, who are the source of most adoptions, and suggested that this may be indicative of genetic factors in the causation of ADHD. However, this line of reasoning is not supported by other data (Lahey *et al.*, 1988) that indicate no association between familial psychopathology and ADHD. Instead, Lahey *et al.* (1988) found that familial psychopathology was only related to cases of CD or where both ADHD and CD were present in the same child.

Dalby *et al.* (1982) obtained a similar rate of adoption (approximately 17%) for children with ADHD obtained from hospital records; however, they suggested that perinatal factors such as poor nutrition, maternal alcohol consumption, or low birthweight may be the relevant factors in determining the high rate of ADHD among adoptees. There does not appear to be any evidence to support this contention. For instance, Goodman and Stevenson (1989b), Nichols and Chen (1981), and Werner and Smith (1977) found no association between pre- and perinatal problems and ADHD. Indeed, the only known relationship that has been verified is that children with fetal alcohol syndrome appear to be at risk for ADHD (Streissguth *et al.*, 1978).

One of the criticisms directed at adoption studies in which samples are drawn from clinics is that the overrepresentation of adoptees in samples of ADHD children may be an artifact of an inordinately high rate of utilization of health care services by adoptive parents. This may be so because adoptive parents tend to be predominantly middle class and also because they may be on the lookout for problems to a greater extent than nonadoptive parents. One way to resolve this issue is to examine the data from studies that have sampled ADHD children from the general population and not from a hospital or clinic. In one study where this procedure was followed (Szatmari *et al.*, 1989a), no connection existed between ADHD and separation from natural parents in the first 4 yr of life. This suggests no relationship exists between adoptive status and ADHD. However, Deutsch (1989) sent out questionnaires to parents in the Ontario Adoption Registry and found an overrepresentation of ADHD children among adoptees as compared with biological children of the same parents. It may be significant that a much lower rate of ADHD was obtained in this study (approximately 10%) as compared with the 17% rate of adoption in the studies that sampled ADHD children from clinics. This lower rate may be due to the fact that a nonclinic sample was studied.

Clearly, there are unresolved issues in the literature on the relationship between adoption and ADHD. One of the factors that may be complicating these data is that most studies of adoption in ADHD (Deutsch *et al.*, 1982; Dalby *et al.*, 1982; Deutsch, in press) have failed to distinguish ADHD children with and without CD. Because a high incidence of psychopathology appears in mothers who give up their children for adoption, and familial psychopathology tends to be related to CD and not ADHD (Lahey *et al.*, 1988), there may be an overrepresentation of adoptees in the population of children with CDs. The relationship between adoption and ADHD that has been found in some studies may be due to the fact that many children with ADHD also have CD.

The implication of these findings is that there is probably substantial biological causation of ADHD, although the exact nature of the cause is not clear. There does not appear to be any uniform abnormality in the nervous system that can be tied to the symptoms. The causes may be nonspecific, and ADHD may be the result of diverse developmental abnormalities. The findings also suggest that faulty parenting or general environmental deprivation are probably not viable candidates as causes of ADHD.

d. Allergies and Dietary Sensitivities   Allergies and dietary sensitivities could be considered as either biological or environmental. There is a clear biological component because, undoubtedly, there must be a biological pre-disposition to develop allergies. At the same time, the allergens that cause allergic symptoms are present in the external environment. Investigation of the role of allergies in ADHD was initially stimulated by the work of Benjamin Feingold (1974). On the basis of his clinical observations, Feingold maintained that about two-thirds of the children in his practice were cured of their attentional difficulties by the modification of their diet. Feingold thought of ADHD as a reaction to a food allergy and pointed to several classes of substances as causal agents including artificial flavors and colors and salicylates.

There has been some empirical support for Feingold's view of the relationship between diet and ADHD. For example, Tryphonas and Trites (1979) found that 47% of the ADHD children referred to their clinic were allergic to at least one food substance. An even higher proportion of food allergies (66%) in children with ADHD was reported by Rapp (1978). These data may be contrasted with the incidence of 6.6–7.5% food allergy in the general population (Marshall, 1989). In addition to these data for food allergies, Kaplan *et al.* (1987) found a high incidence of physical signs and symptoms that are common signs of allergy in children with ADHD as compared with normal children. For the most commonly reported physical signs such as rhinitis, bad breath, skin rash, red cheeks, and dry skin, approximately 70% of children with ADHD were affected as compared with 8–13% of controls.

Even though these studies indicate that allergies are more common in children with ADHD, this should not be taken to mean that food allergies are causally related to ADHD. For instance, food allergies and ADHD may have a common cause. Alternatively, stress reactions to food allergies may exacerbate the symptoms of ADHD in children who have a predisposition to develop them.

2. Neurological Abnormalities

a. Brain Damage   Given the evidence of biological causation of ADHD, one might expect to find specific abnormalities in the nervous system. For many years, there have been suspicions that attention disorders stem from brain damage. This view was reflected in the use of the term *minimal brain dysfunction* in the 1950s and 1960s. Eventually, the term fell into disuse because of a lack of compelling evidence of brain damage. It now appears that <5% of the children with ADHD have documented brain damage (Rutter, 1977). It is also the case that most children with brain damage do not show symptoms of ADHD. More recent studies have pointed to functional deficits, particularly in the frontal lobes of the brain. For instance, Lou *et al.* (1984) found decreased blood flow in the frontal lobes. The findings of Chelune *et al.* (1986) suggested frontal lobe involvement in ADHD because of parallels between the performance of children with ADHD and patients with frontal lobe damage on the Wisconsin Card Sorting Test. On this task, subjects are required to sort multidimensional stimuli according to categories (such as shape, color, and form) that are predefined by the experimenter. Once a criterion level of performance is achieved in one category, the examiner switches categories, and this is made evident by feedback that is received from the examiner. If the examinee inappropriately applies the old categorization rule after the experimenter has switched categories, this is scored as a perseverative error. Chelune *et al.* (1986) found that children with attention disorders performed similarly to patients with damage to the frontal lobes of the brain: They made significantly more perseverative errors than controls. This is at least suggestive evidence of frontal lobe involvement in ADHD.

    b. Neurotransmitter Deficiency   Kornetsky (1970) first stated the hypothesis that implicated catecholamine neurotransmitters (e.g., adreneline, noradreneline, dopamine) in ADHD. This supposition was based on the fact that many of the drugs that seemed to reduce the symptoms of ADHD potentiated the production of catecholamine neurotransmitters. A large body of literature has been devoted to testing this hypothesis, but for the most part the data have been inconclusive. While many studies seem to implicate these neurotransmitters, there are equally as many studies that suggest no relationship between neurotransmitters and ADHD (Zametkin and Rapoport, 1987).

3. Arousal Defect

In terms of the attention components that were discussed previously, *arousal* is a term that carries a meaning similar to *alertness*. Arousal is usually used when discussing physiological measures (heart rate, blood pressure, skin conductance), whereas alertness tends to be applied more often to behavioral indicators. Arousal is often discussed in the context of fight or flight reactions of organisms. When an organism is threatened, resources to cope with the danger are mobilized. Physiologically, such a condition is associated with elevated levels of heart rate, blood pressure, and skin conductance. In terms of more everyday occurrences, arousal varies as a function of time of day. Arousal tends to be lower in early morning and late in the evening. Of perhaps more relevance to the study of ADHD is the fact that arousal varies situationally. In a testing situation, a state of moderate arousal is probably best; excessive arousal may lead to anxiety and disorganization. On the other hand, relaxing at home is associated with a lower state of arousal than the test-taking situation.

There has been some suggestion in the literature that the arousal system does not work properly in children with ADHD. At various times it has been argued that children with ADHD are excessively aroused (Laufer and Denhoff. 1957), they are underaroused (Satterfield and Dawson, 1971), or they cannot adjust their arousal level to suit task demands (Douglas, 1980).

An arousal model that attempted to explain the symptoms of ADHD first appeared in the mid-1950s. Based on their belief that children with ADHD were overaroused, Laufer and Denhoff (1957) showed that they were more sensitive to the effects of the seizure-inducing drug metrazol than were normal children. The theory that attention disorders stemmed from over-arousal implied that stimulant drugs acted paradoxically. In this view it was argued that high arousal was the cause of a high level of activity. Stimulants were hypothesized to act paradoxically because even though they increased arousal, they led to less activity. The overarousal framework also made predictions about an effective treatment for attention disorders. If arousal is increased by stimulus input, then it would seem reasonable to reduce activity level by restricting stimulus input. However, attempts to isolate children have generally not proved successful. In fact, children with ADHD tend to be in-distinguishable from controls in high-stimulation environments, and indeed they show abnormal levels of activity only when the level of stimulation is weak (Kaspar *et al.*, 1971; Zentall and Zentall, 1983).

The lack of empirical support for the overarousal view has prompted many investigators to consider the premise that children with attention disorders are *underaroused*. There are certain advantages to this view. First, it is easier to conceptualize the benefit that ADHD children derive from stimulant medi-cation: Given that stimulants increase arousal, it makes sense that they would benefit children whose arousal levels were low to start with. In support of this view, Conte and Kinsbourne (1988) found that the ADHD children who benefited most on a learning task from stimulants were those with low-resting levels of physiological arousal.

Initially, the low-arousal view of ADHD was bolstered by findings (Satterfield and Dawson, 1971) of lower levels of resting skin conductance levels (i.e., lower arousal level) in ADHD as compared with non-ADHD children. However, subsequent attempts to replicate this finding have not yielded consistent support for the low-arousal view. Other research has indicated that as indexed by physiological measures the construct of arousal may be difficult to work with because there are many measures of arousal, and the various measures rarely seem to agree with one another.

Zentall and Zentall (1983) have argued that arousal may be a more viable construct when examined behaviorally rather than physiologically. They couch their explanation of the behavior of children with ADHD by means of the optimal stimulation theory. According to this theory, organisms requre an optimal level of arousal to function in different situations. Some situations such as a final examination in school require a moderate level of arousal to function optimally. Excessive arousal in this situation would lead to anxiety and disorganization. If arousal is too low, it would lead to fatigue and an inability to think clearly. Other conditions such as a threatening situation require a high level of arousal to function. A lack of arousal here would mean that energy to cope with the threat would be inadequate. Too much arousal such as occurs in states of terror would lead to an inability to function in an organized way. If an organism's state of arousal is not optimal for a given situation, it will attempt to change the environment if it can. Usually this means changing the level of stimulation. Thus, if the level of arousal is too high for an organism, it will lead to stimulus avoidance and a disorganization of behavior. In contrast, a level of stimulation that is too low will result in *stimulus seeking*. Because ADHD children are usually described as stimulus seeking, this suggests that ordinary levels of stimulation are inadequate. The optimal stimulation theory proposed by Zentall and Zentall (1983) would suggest that the stimulus-seeking behavior of ADHD children is a manifestation of a state of low arousal and that these children need to seek stimulation to raise the level of arousal. In these terms the distractibility and stimulus-seeking behaviors of ADHD children may occur because ordinary levels of stimulation are too low. This view of ADHD children would predict that differences between ADHD and normal children would be most evident under conditions of minimal stimulation. As discussed previously, this prediction has been confirmed (Kaspar *et al.*, 1971).

Analysis of the cognitive task performance of ADHD children is also consistent with the optimal stimulation theory. For example, in vigilance tasks subjects are required to monitor infrequently occurring signals. Under such low-stimulation conditions, ADHD children consistently detect fewer signals than controls. Optimal stimulation theory would explain this finding by assuming that the level of stimulation in vigilance tasks is excessively low for ADHD children, prompting them to seek out other sources of stimulation. Presumably, this stimulus-seeking behavior would compete with the type of attentive behavior that is needed to identify targets on a vigilance task. Presumably, a similar mechanism could account for the fact that ADHD children learn less efficiently during associative learning tasks when material is presented at slow rates as compared with more rapid rates of presentation. In contrast, normal control subjects learn equally well at either rate of presentation (Conte *et al.*, 1986).

Is the benefit that ADHD children experience from increasing the level of stimulation sufficiently general that this phenomenon could be used to develop treatment programs? Zentall and her colleagues have attempted a number of experiments in which background stimulation during the presentation of learning tasks has been varied. The findings from these studies have been mixed. Sometimes high levels of stimulation enhance performance and sometimes they don't. Zentall and Zentall (1983) have argued that stimulation tends to impair performance when it overlaps with task-relevant stimulation but benefits performance when it is clearly separable from task-relevant stimulation. These findings suggest that the manipulation of environmental stimulation has to be treated very carefully when attempting to enhance the performance of children with attention disorders.

C. Treatment of ADHD

1. Stimulant Medication

The administration of stimulant medication is the most common treatment for children with ADHD. At the present time, Ritalin (which is the trade name for the generic drug methylphenidate) appears to be the medication of choice, although in the past a number of other amphetamine compounds have been used such as dexedrine and benzedrine. In addition, nonamphetamine stimulants (pemoline) and tricyclic antidepressants have been used with some success.

The mechanism of action of stimulant drugs is at least partially understood. It is well documented that stimulants increase autonomic activity as indexed by changes in heart rate (Porges et al., 1975), blood pressure, and skin conductance (Cohen et al., 1971). Evidence also indicates that stimulants potentiate the production of the neurotransmitters dopamine and norepinephrine in the central nervous system (Levy and Hobbes, 1988).

The research literature on stimulant treatment of children with ADHD is extensive. A number of generalizations can be made about the efficacy of stimulant therapy. First, one-half to two-thirds of the children diagnosed as attention-disordered appear to show at least some benefit from stimulants (Swanson and Kinsbourne, 1976). Furthermore, stimulants appear to exert their effect on a wide range of behaviors. A large number of studies have indicated that stimulants improve students' ability to attend: They increase on-task behavior and reduce fidgeting and motoric activity (Douglas et al., 1988). They also improve performance on a wide range of laboratory tasks such as reaction time (Porges et al., 1975), vigilance (Sykes et al., 1971), and paired associate learning (Swanson and Kinsbourne, 1976).

The evidence is less clear with regard to the effects of stimulants on academic performance. Most studies that have employed achievement tests suggest that there is no benefit from stimulant drugs (Aman, 1980; Gadow, 1983). Many of these studies have been criticized because the achievement tests are not sensitive to short-term changes in behavior. Recent studies that have examined specific aspects of math performance suggest that performance may improve. For example, Douglas *et al.* (1986) have demonstrated that stimulants increase the number of math problems attempted and the number correct, and they also enable students with ADHD to work more quickly. In addition, the number of errors corrected increased. Similar short-term improvements in math skills have also been reported by Pelham (1986) and Tannock *et al.* (1989). While these findings suggest that stimulants enable students with ADHD to operate more efficiently and accurately while working on math problems, it still has not been demonstrated that over the long term stimulants can improve the academic status of ADHD children.

Even when stimulants exert a positive effect on behavior, they rarely normalize behavior. Thus, in his review, Pelham (1986) indicates that after stimulant treatment, measures of deviant behavior of children with ADHD are usually 1 standard deviation or more above the mean for the normative sample. This means that most children with ADHD who are treated with stimulants continue to experience difficulties that require treatment.

Recently, Douglas *et al.* (1988) have questioned the view that only two-thirds of the children show a positive response to stimulants. They argue that this relatively large proportion of nonresponders stems from the fact that most studies use only one measure of performance when evaluating the effects of stimulants. When Douglas *et al.* (1988) based their drug evaluations on a wide range of cognitive and behavioral measures, they found that every child in their study made substantial gains on at least several measures. Thus, the response to stimulants apparently is quite variable across measures, making it very important to sample a range of clinically relevant measures when attempting to evaluate the effects of medication. Obviously, another critical factor in drug evaluations is the method of selecting subjects. The 30% nonresponse rate may be somewhat reflective of the fact that inconsistent subject selection criteria have been used across studies that have investigated the drug response of children with ADHD.

Given that ADHD consists of both cognitive and behavioral components, are these two important functions affected similarly by medication? Sprague and Sleator (1977) presented findings that suggested that cognitive task performance and social behavior were differentially affected by increasing doses of Ritalin. In their research, lower drug doses (0.3 mg/kg) were more effective in enhancing cognitive task performance, whereas relatively high doses (1.0 mg/kg) were more effective in dealing with social behavior. However, recent attempts to replicate these findings using different tasks have not been successful. Tannock *et al.* (1989) found that cognitive and behavioral measures were not differentially affected across doses of 0.3 mg/kg and 1.0 mg/kg. Rather than finding a decrement in cognitive performance at 1.0 mg/kg, they discovered that both cognitive and behavioral measures improved markedly from placebo to 0.3 mg/kg and showed no change from 0.3 to 1.0 mg/kg. One possible drawback of this study is that Tannock *et al.* (1988) sampled their behavioral measures as the students engaged in performing the cognitive tasks, and conceivably this may have inflated the relationship between these measures. Douglas *et al.* (1988) used 0.3 and 0.6 mg/kg and, as in the study of Tannock *et al.* (1989), found a similar pattern of performance across cognitive and behavioral measures. In contrast to Tannock *et al.* (1989), Douglas *et al.* (1988) evaluated the cognitive and behavioral measures in different contexts. Some of the cognitive measures were obtained in a laboratory setting, whereas behavioral measures were obtained from home and school.

Thus, the majority of the existing data seem to suggest that the effects of drug dose on cognitive and behavioral measures may not be different after all. Further research sampling different kinds of behavioral and cognitive measures is needed before any firm conclusions can be made.

While there is general agreement on the short-term benefits of stimulants for the majority of attention-disordered children, the long-term picture is less clear. Virtually every study has failed to find evidence of long-term benefit of stimulant drugs. Before making any firm conclusions regarding the long-term effects of stimulants, it is important to note that long-term drug studies are exceedingly difficult to undertake. Most of these studies have been retrospective and entail the identification of a group of ADHD children that has received stimulants and another group that has not received drug treatment. These two groups are then compared on a mix of academic and behavioral measures. As one might expect, it is extremely unlikely that one can come up with equivalent samples using this approach. Ethically, one cannot systematically withhold treatment from some subjects, so it is not possible to randomly assign subjects to drug and no-drug treatment conditions. Thus, it is possible that the comparison groups in such studies differ in ways that could mask any effects of treatment. The consensus of opinion (e.g., Douglas *et al.*, 1988; Pelham, 1986) is that the existing long-term studies are fraught with so many methodological problems that it is not possible to base any firm conclusions on them.

To summarize, stimulant drugs apparently have extensive cognitive and behavioral effects on ADHD children. They enhance the ability to concentrate and increase on-task behavior, and they apparently improve the acquisition of new material. The mechanism by which stimulants affect behavior is not well understood, but the physiological investigation of the drug is an area of active investigation. Little evidence suggests that stimulants produce long-term improvements in behavior, but methodological problems make it impossible to base firm conclusions on these studies.

2. Dietary Intervention

As noted previously, there has been speculation of a relationship between ADHD and food allergies. While the available evidence indicates a higher incidence of food allergies in ADHD children, this does not mean that the food and ADHD are causally related.

One of the distinguishing features of studies of dietary intervention is the method of selecting subjects. Some studies have selected children indiscriminately from the population of ADHD children. In contrast, other studies have selected ADHD children who showed signs of allergic responses on the assumption that this subgroup would be more likely to respond to dietary intervention. Studies that have examined the response of unselected ADHD children have not produced very consistent results. Two of these studies (Conners et al., 1976; Harley et al., 1978) found that less than one-third of school age subjects responded positively. In contrast, Rapp (1978) using a modified Feingold diet found a response rate of nearly 50%. In those studies that have selected subjects on the basis of allergic symptoms, the results have been quite favorable. Trites et al. (1980) found that 11 of 19 subjects were either rated as better or possibly better when allergic foods were removed from the diet. In contrast, none of the children in a sample of unselected ADHD children showed any response to dietary intervention. Egger et al. (1985) selected subjects on the basis of a history of eczema, asthma, or hay fever and put them on an oligoantigenic diet (a diet in which a limited variety of nonallergenic foods are eaten). In contrast to the findings of Trites et al. (1980), Egger et al. (1985) obtained a similar response rate in selected and unselected subjects. Finally, Kaplan et al. (1989) selected subjects for symptoms of allergy such as skin rashes and rhinitis. Also, relative to other studies that have been conducted, a wider range of substances was eliminated from the experimental diet, including artificial flavors and colors, chocolate, monosodium glutamate, preservatives, caffeine, and any substance that the family reported might affect their child. The diet was low in sugar and was dairy-free if sensitivity to cow's milk was indicated. The findings from this study indicated that 42% of the subjects exhibited a 50% improvement in behavior, and 16% showed a 12% improvement.

Age of subjects has also emerged as a potentially important variable in dietary intervention. As noted above, Harley et al. (1978) found that relatively few of the school-age subjects in their study responded to dietary intervention. In the same study, the same dietary intervention was attempted with a group of preschool subjects, and 10 out of 10 showed a positive response. Interestingly, Kaplan et al. (1989) found a 50% response rate in their study of preschool children.

In summary, review of the dietary intervention studies points to several variables that should be explored further. First, two studies that showed substantial response rates were those that included preschool subjects only. Second, studies that have selected subjects on the basis of signs of allergy (Trites *et al.*, 1980; Egger *et al.*, 1985; Kaplan *et al.*, 1989) have all obtained a substantial rate of positive response to diet. Finally, the positive findings with the oligoantigenic diet of Egger *et al.* (1985) suggest that this diet should be examined further.

As is the case with others forms of treatment for ADHD, even when diet improves the behavior of ADHD children, it rarely normalizes it. For instance, Kaplan *et al.* (1989) noted that even the most positive responders to diet continue to experience behavior problems. Also, Egger *et al.* (1985) reported that even though 82% of the children in their study improved in response to diet, only 27% were cured.

3. Behavior Modification

Behavior modification (BM) is a treatment approach that has been derived from the classical behaviorism of Skinner and other twentieth-century psychologists. In this approach, reward or punishment is made contingent on the performance of certain behaviors. For instance, in using contingent rewards to reduce off-task behaviors, a teacher may give verbal praise to a child who is engaged in an assigned academic task. Alternatively, in a punishment paradigm, a teacher may remove tokens (which are exchangeable for rewards) from a child who is out of his seat at a time when he is supposed to be completing an assignment at his desk. For the most part, a theoretical rationale for using BM for ADHD children has not been well-developed. In most applications, it is viewed as a set of simple procedures to obtain control over the behavior of a child who is out of control much of the time. The one exception to this largely atheoretical approach stems from Barkley's (1989) view of ADHD as a developmental delay in the regulation of behavior by its consequences. From this standpoint, BM is a way of increasing the salience of consequences such that they will exert control over the behavior of the child.

Recent reviews of the BM literature suggest that reducing the levels of inappropriate behavior at home and school is possible with these procedures. However, as detailed in Pelham and Murphy's (1986) review, a number of shortcomings of BM make it less than an ideal treatment. For example, findings from several studies suggest that not all children respond to BM. Even for those who respond, BM does not normalize the behavior of most children, and the effects that are observed usually fail to persist at 1-yr follow-up assessment sessions. Compliance problems are also evident with some studies (Firestone *et al.*, 1981), suggesting that as many as 50% of the parents of ADHD children discontinue the treatment. Bosco and Robin's (1980) findings suggest that only about 10% of ADHD children have been treated with BM.

One of the reactions to the difficulties that have been encountered in implementing BM programs has been to investigate the efficacy of combining BM with stimulant drug therapy. This approach is appealing because it is possible that the cognitive benefits associated with stimulant therapy may make it possible for children to derive greater benefit from BM. While the findings from most studies suggest that BM in combination with stimulant drugs is more effective than either treatment alone, no evidence suggests that the effects of the combined treatment persist after medication has been terminated.

4. Cognitive Behavior Modification

Of all the treatments used with ADHD children, cognitive behavior modification (CBM) appears to be the one that was specifically designed for this population. This is so because CBM attempts to train behaviors such as planning skills, problem-solving skills, and self-regulation, which appear to be deficient in ADHD children.

The theoretical rationale for CBM stems largely from the work of the Russian psychologists Luria and Vygotsky, who stressed the importance of the verbal control of behavior in normal development. According to their theory, one of the most important developmental progressions concerns the increasingly important role played by self-vocalization over the control of behavior.

As applied to ADHD children, it has been argued that the impulsivity that characterizes the behavior of these children is incompatible with the development of self-talk. Consequently, self-talk is less likely to develop spontaneously in ADHD children and, thus, one must provide explicit training in the use of this technique. Thus, a universal element in the implementations of CBM is for students to receive instruction in self-verbalizing the steps they undertake when engaged in task performance.

Another aspect of CBM is specifically directed at the organizational difficulties that are commonly observed in ADHD children. Empirical studies have documented that one manifestation of the lack of organizational skill is an inability to utilize learning strategies, particularly when confronted with problem-solving situations. Thus, in most applications of CBM (Meichenbaum, 1977; Kendall and Braswell, 1984), students are taught skills that are thought to be crucial to effective problem-solving. These include problem definition, solution generation, solution monitoring, and self-reinforcement. In actually carrying out such a program, a child would be taught to ask herself what the nature of the problem is before attempting a solution. Second, once the problem has been defined, a range of possible solutions would be generated. Once a specific solution has been developed, the effectiveness of the solution would be checked. Finally, once all the steps have been followed, the child is instructed to use a self-reinforcing statement.

To take a concrete example in math, if a child were presented with a problem in which two numbers were presented with a plus sign, the child would have to first define the problem as addition. Second, the procedures for solving addition problems would have to be called up from memory. Third, the procedures would have to be adapted to the problem, which would usually require recalling specific factual knowledge. Fourth, once an answer was arrived at, it would have to be checked, say by using a subtraction method. Finally, when the child is satisfied that the answer is correct, she would say "I did a good job." In some applications of CBM, external reinforcers are used to motivate the children to use the CBM strategies appropriately. For example, Kendall and Braswell (1984) start the children out with a number of chips that can be exchanged for concrete rewards. Each time the child fails to follow the CBM steps, one of the chips is taken away.

As is the case with most other treatments for ADHD, most studies have failed to demonstrate generalization of treatment effects over time or across situations. In other words, children tend to use CBM strategies in the situation in which they were trained. When removed from that situation, or when put back in the original training situation a few months after the training has finished, they fail to use the CBM strategies in guiding their problem-solving behavior.

It is not clear why CBM strategies do not generalize. It may be that the skills that are taught in CBM are so antithetical to the temperament of ADHD children that they simply do not perceive the value of using the strategies. Alternatively, the skills taught in CBM may be too difficult to teach to children with severe organizational problems. For instance, one can imagine that when confronted with a novel situation, problem definition may be too formidable a task for a child who is highly distractible. Finally, it is possible that generalization fails to materialize because the strategies that are taught cannot be easily incorporated in the classroom. Thus, unless a child is in a class that has a strong problem-solving orientation to learning, there may be little opportunity to practice the strategies learned in CBM.

At this point in planning future research on cognitive training in ADHD children, it would seem important to attempt to find out what skills do transfer and then attempt to find out the situational factors that seem to promote it. Once such a science of transfer is formulated, we may be in a better position to determine what type of training program is needed for children with ADHD.

5. Parent Training

Difficulties in obtaining transfer of training when using behavioral interventions has led to the view that therapy for ADHD children must be ongoing over a substantial period of time and must be carried out in the environments in which the child's problems are most often expressed. Because it is far too expensive to enlist the services of a therapist for such intensive and long-term intervention, some investigators have begun exploring the efficacy of parent training programs. Parents are usually the only adults who have a continuing daily presence in the child's life, and if they can be taught to deal with the problematic behaviors more effectively, then perhaps it might be possible to obtain long-term control over the child's behavior.

Relatively few studies have investigated parenting intervention programs for children specifically diagnosed with ADHD. However, a much larger body of literature pertains to parenting interventions with heterogeneous groups of aggressive and conduct-disordered children. Because many ADHD children are also aggressive and conduct-disordered, many of the children in these studies would probably meet the diagnostic criteria for ADHD. Parenting programs such as the one developed by Forehand and McMahon (1981) for aggressive and conduct-disordered children are beginning to be adapted for use with ADHD children (see Barkley, 1987).

The program developed by Forehand and McMahon (1981) is perhaps the most extensively investigated, and it has recently been adapted for use with parents of preschool children with ADHD (Pisterman *et al.*, 1989). It is based on the assumption that problem behaviors stem from a number of sources including:

1. A child with developmental disabilities, chronic health problems, or a difficult temperament
2. Other family members with similar characteristics
3. Situational consequences of the behavior
4. Stressful family events

Consistent with evidence (reviewed previously) that ADHD has strong biological causation, points 1 and 2 refer to the fact that some individuals are inherently more difficult to manage than others. Point 3 stems from the view that the outcomes that occur in response to specific behaviors are important determinants of whether or not these behaviors will reoccur. Thus, if a parent placates a whining child with a piece of candy, then it is more likely that whining will reoccur at a later point in time. In other instances, a child may successfully ward off a parental threat of punishment by pleading or yelling at the parent. Success at escaping such undesirable consequences may reinforce the child's coercive behaviors. If this scenario is repeated often enough, coercion will be a permanent fixture in the child's interaction with the parent. Point 4 refers to the fact that stressful family events can exacerbate the frequency of difficult behaviors and can also influence the way in which difficult behaviors are dealt with by caregivers. Thus, financial or emotional stress may heighten the tendency to deal with a child's behavior in a coercive manner.

There are several techniques that are employed in parent training to break the cycle of coercive behaviors between parent and child.

a. Enhancing the Value of Parental Attention   Enhancement of parental attention is included in the program because of evidence suggesting that the value of parental attention is greatly reduced in children with behavior problems relative to nonproblem children (Patterson, 1982). To increase the reinforcing value of parental attention, parents are taught to spend time each day engaging their child in pleasurable activities and not attempt to exert control or consequences over the child's behavior.

b. Attending to Child Compliance   Once the value of parental attention is enhanced, parents are instructed to selectively attend to their child when the child complies with adult commands. This aspect of the program is usually undertaken in conjunction with instruction in how to give more effective commands, such as stating commands clearly, reducing the number of question-commands (e.g., Would you like to ...? or Can you pick up your toys now?). Presumably, parents can increase the child's compliance by consistently giving positive attention (e.g., praise) when the child complies.

c. Establishing a Home Token Economy   A token economy is used because of the assumption that ADHD children require more explicit consequences for their behavior than other children. In implementing a token economy, rules of appropriate conduct are defined and discussed with the child. In addition, the costs and benefits in terms of the number of tokens for compliance and/or noncompliance are discussed. In positive reinforcement systems, a child is given a set number of tokens each time compliance with a rule is demonstrated. In a punishment system, tokens are removed each time the child fails to comply. The tokens, which the child retains (say at the end of the week), can be exchanged for special treats or privileges.

d. Implementing Time Out for Noncompliance   Time out as used in this program means time out from reinforcement. It means that if the techniques discussed above are not effective in obtaining control over the behavior, immediately after the episode of noncompliance, the child is placed in a situation where he or she is denied access to reinforcers. The length of time in time out is left up to the discretion of the parent (not the child). Usually, time out is used for one or two behaviors at any given point in time.

e. Extending the Range of Behaviors   In implementing a behavior management program, one usually begins by selecting a subset of problem behaviors for intervention. As one obtains control over these initial behaviors, the program is extended to other problematic behaviors.

A recent study (Pisterman *et al.*, 1989) that sought to teach parenting skills to parents of preschool children is quite typical of parenting intervention programs for ADHD children. Pisterman *et al.* (1989) conducted a 12-wk intervention program that focused on training parents to cope more effectively with the noncompliant behaviors that occur frequently in ADHD children. Pisterman *et al.* (1989) found that the program was effective in improving compliance with parental commands and in improving the management techniques of the parent. Temporal generalization did occur insofar as the changes in behavior were maintained at a 3-mo follow-up testing session. However, they did not obtain generalization to nontrained behaviors or to the school environment.

The findings from this study suggest that this particular approach to parent training needs to be extended to all problem behaviors if it is to be effective. One cannot expect that the program will spontaneously generalize to behaviors that are not the target of intervention. In addition, the program apparently does not generalize to the school setting. This is a serious limitation, because most ADHD children experience their most serious difficulties in school rather than at home. The lack of transfer to school suggests that the training needs to be extended to school, perhaps by having a professional familiar with the parenting program work with the child's classroom teacher so that the teacher can begin applying similar management strategies as those being used in the home. It should be noted, however, that transfer to the school setting may require more time to happen than is usually allowed for in most studies of parenting intervention.

It should also be noted that the approach outlined above is not the only approach to parent training. Other investigators have developed programs with a different orientation. For instance, Bloomquist and Braswell (1987) have recently developed a parent training program that is based on the principles of cognitive behavior modification. In this program, children are taught to deal with problematic behaviors by making use of planning skills. Parents are taught how to prompt and guide their children in developing and carrying out their plans.

VI. CURRENT RESEARCH ISSUES

A. Cause(s) of ADHD

While many researchers seem to base their work on the assumption that ADHD is a medical condition with specific neurophysiological causes, the evidence reviewed in this chapter suggests that the direct evidence for such biological causation is weak, at best. There is little evidence of brain damage in children with ADHD. Also, the evidence supporting neurotransmitter abnormalities as a cause of ADHD has also been inconsistent. On the other hand, the results of a recent epidemiological study (Szatmari *et al.*, 1989a,b) and a twin study (Goodman and Stevenson, 1989b) provide little evidence indicating that psychosocial factors are causes of ADHD. Thus, family dysfunction, low socioeconomic status, and being on welfare do not appear to be any more common in ADHD than in normal-functioning children. Instead, developmental and chronic health problems (both of which are most likely biological factors) appear to be related to the occurrence of ADHD. The only psychosocial factors that appeared to be relevant to ADHD were living in an urban setting and being on welfare, which was more common in females with ADHD than in females without ADHD. This latter result suggests that ADHD in females may have different causes than it does in males. Because the diagnostic process for ADHD usually involves judgments of children by adults, this finding may be partially attributable to the fact that the public's perception of appropriate behavior is different for males and females.

Thus, while the balance of the evidence seems to favor biological factors as causes of ADHD, little evidence points to specific brain abnormalities. Some behavioral (Chelune *et al.*, 1986) and physiological (Lou *et al.*, 1984) evidence points to abnormal functioning of the frontal lobes, although this does not necessarily mean that there is actual structural damage to this area of the brain. Clearly, more research that explores frontal lobe functioning in ADHD children is needed.

Another promising line of work that is consistent with the biological view of ADHD has focused on the high incidence of allergies. Marshall (1989) has reviewed evidence that allergies apparently are associated with an imbalance in cholinergic and adrenergic neurotransmitter systems. Because these neurotransmitters have been implicated as causes of ADHD in a number of studies, subgrouping of ADHD children with and without allergies may be a useful way of obtaining more homogeneous samples of subjects in future research.

B. What is the Best Way to Characterize ADHD: A Single Disorder or a Multiplicity of Disorders?

The diagnostic criteria that have been established in the DSM-III-R are based on the notion that ADHD is a single disorder with a multiplicity of manifestations. Thus, to satisfy the criteria in the DSM-III-R, any combination of 8 of the 14 symptoms is needed to establish a diagnosis of ADHD. Recent evidence presented by Lahey *et al.* (1988) suggests that this may not be the best way to conceptualize ADHD. In their analysis, the symptoms of inattention and those of overactivity appear to be unrelated. This would mean that many children are primarily inattentive but are not overactive, whereas many others are overactive but not inattentive. If these data are substantiated, it would mean that we could be confusing our understanding of children with ADHD by lumping inattentive children and overactive children into the same category.

Another area of research that has a bearing on whether there is a single attention disorder or a multiplicity of them stems from studies on the relationship between attention and CDs. Even though the surface symptoms of ADHD and CD can be clearly distinguished (compare Tables 3.2 and 3.3), these two disorders often co-occur. This association has prompted some investigators to argue that ADHD and CD are indistinguishable (for review, see Blouin *et al.*, 1989). There are two kinds of evidence to counter this view. First, Blouin *et al.* (1989) point out that much of the evidence that pointed to the overlap of CD and ADHD was probably based on the inappropriate application of a statistical technique. Second, Lahey *et al.* (1988) distinguished ADHD and CD on the basis of etiology: While a relationship exists between familial psychopathology and CD, this relationship does not hold for ADHD.

To summarize, ADHD is a complex disorder with multiple components and associated disorders (e.g., CDs, LDs). The DSM-III-R has attempted to define ADHD in terms of a multiplicity of symptoms including inattention, overactivity, and impulsivity among others. Because evidence suggests that there may be little overlap between inattention and overactivity, it may be more prudent at the present time to avoid attempting to combine these symptoms into a single disorder, at least until additional subtyping studies are completed.

C. How Do ADHD and LDs Interact?

Several studies have shown convincingly that many LD children also have attentional difficulties. One issue that is particularly important for service providers is the manner in which these two disorders interact. Douglas and Peters (1979) argued that both LDs and ADHD can lead to learning problems but they do so for different reasons: Deficits in ADHD children are related to impulsivity and short attention span, whereas those in LD children are due to specific processing deficits. One prediction that could be derived from this view is that ADHD children would show a wider variety of learning problems than LD children.

Beyond the breadth of learning difficulties in ADHD and LD children, a number of issues remain unresolved. For instance, it is not known if the characteristics of learning difficulties associated with ADHD and LDs are different in important respects. If one were to examine performance on a math test, are there substantial differences in the types of errors made by LD children as compared with those with ADHD? Similar analyses could be performed for other content areas. Studies such as these might provide important clues regarding the manner in which these two disorders interact. Does ADHD lead to learning problems that have unique characteristics, or does ADHD tend to exacerbate learning difficulties in LD children? Are the learning problems associated with ADHD easier to remediate that those associated with LD?

D. Treatment Generalization

As outlined in this chapter, behavioral treatments such as BM, CBM, and parent training have been successful in producing relatively short-term changes in behavior. However, there has been relatively little success in generalizing the results among settings or among behaviors. One possible reason for the lack of generalization is that the procedures used in these programs may lack the critical ingredients to encourage the transfer of skills. As Brown *et al.* (in press) point out, experimenters often assume that subjects in training studies will automatically notice the similarities and differences among situations. They suggest that if, indeed, people routinely engaged in these types of comparisons, they would soon be overwhelmed with information. In fact, most transfer tests are conducted without adequately preparing the subject for it. Brown *et al.* (in press) point out that in teaching situations (in contrast to experiments) students are given explicit instruction to apply what they know to a new situation. Furthermore, they are usually informed that what they just learned will help them cope with the new situation, and in fact the transfer situation is generally presented as an illustration of a problem that was recently presented. Brown *et al.* (in press) demonstrated in a number of examples that students do not transfer information across even relatively simple situations if they are not prepared for the transfer situation. However, simply informing them that information that they recently acquired will help them cope with the new situation is often sufficient to promote transfer. It may be the case that in the training studies that have been conducted, subjects have not been adequately prepared to transfer what they have learned to new situations. Perhaps if such training for transfer was emphasized in intervention programs for ADHD children, more evidence of transfer would have been obtained.

There is one additional and perhaps more serious impediment to transfer in behavioral training studies. One of the critical ingredients required to obtain transfer is that the subject has sufficient self-control and is sufficiently motivated to apply the behavioral strategy to a new situation. There is a burgeoning literature (for review, see Deci and Chandler, 1986) that suggests that intrinsic motivation can be enhanced or diminished depending on specific environmental conditions. One of the conditions that appears to diminish subjects' intrinsic interest in a task is excessive external control. Perhaps the heavy reliance on external control (such as token reinforcers, time out, and response cost), which is characteristic of behavioral intervention programs, may lessen the likelihood of obtaining transfer.

Two possibilities present themselves: On the one hand it may be necessary to rely heavily on the use of external incentives to teach appropriate behavior to ADHD children; on the other hand, the use of such strategies may undermine the child's intrinsic motivation to apply the behavioral strategy when the external incentive is not present.

VII. PRACTICAL IMPLICATIONS OF THE RESEARCH ON ADHD

A. Diagnostic Criteria for ADHD

From the analysis provided in this chapter, it should be amply clear that the diagnostic criteria for ADHD have not been firmly established. Diagnostic uncertainty is especially problematic in the treatment of ADHD because of issues associated with the use of stimulant medication. This picture is made even more complicated because the response of ADHD children to stimulants is probably not unique: Rapoport *et al.* (1980) found that normal children showed a favorable behavioral response to stimulant drugs that was quite similar to that of children with ADHD; i.e., they showed improved performance on memory tasks, were less active, and showed increased attention to tasks. Without well-founded diagnostic criteria, there may be a tendency to use (or not use) medication inappropriately. Uncertainty should prompt caution and a conservative approach to the use of medication. Prudence would seem to require that the conditions in which the attentional difficulty is expressed should be thoroughly investigated, and interventions other than medication should be attempted prior to the use of medication. Medication trials should be attempted only when the professionals who are overseeing the child's treatment are convinced that the attention problem is serious and is likely to persist into the future even if available behavioral treatments are implemented. One last cautionary procedure should be to reserve the label of ADHD only to those cases in which symptoms are pervasive.

B. Treatment of ADHD

Evidence reviewed in this chapter indicated that there is no proven treatment for ADHD. Stimulant medication seems to produce the most wide-ranging changes in behavior, yet little evidence indicates that children derive long-term benefit from stimulants. Behavioral treatments seem to be effective in the situations in which they are implemented but do not transfer easily to other situations. The implications of these findings is that treatment programs must actually take place in the situations in which the difficulties are being experienced. From this standpoint, the present popularity of parent training programs appears to be warranted, because, for most children, parents are the only adults who can provide the long-term treatment that is needed to deal effectively with an attention problem. The potential significance of parent training is also implied by previous studies that indicate that parents of ADHD children report higher levels of stress (Befera and Barkley, 1985), lower self-esteem, and increased guilt (Mash and Johnston, 1983). Mothers of ADHD children are less satisfied with their marriages than mothers of normal-functioning children (Befera and Barkley, 1985). Also, Weiss *et al.* (1971) found that poor parental adjustment, poor mother–child relationships, and the excessive use of punishment were related to higher levels of antisocial behavior in adolescent children with ADHD. Clearly, even if there is no direct causal relationship between family functioning and the onset of ADHD, it seems likely that the welfare of ADHD children can be substantially improved if families with ADHD children receive treatment for these problems that beset them. The recent promise shown by parent training programs also suggests that psychosocial approaches to treatment should continue to be explored.

C. What Schools Can Do

1. Providing Continuity in Treatment

Attentional difficulties apparently require long-term intervention, which is often difficult to undertake in school settings. Children in most schools change teachers every year, and thus even if an adequate treatment program is established in one teacher's classroom, there is no assurance that the program will be carried over to the following year. In addition, the distractibility of many ADHD children probably makes it very difficult for them to adapt to new situations. School districts that require students to change teachers with every subject, particularly in the junior high years, also place a special burden on the ADHD child.

To moderate the impact of these structural features of schools, it is important to provide continuity in treatment from one year to the next. At the very least, school-based classroom consultants who are trained in dealing with ADHD children are essential. Such consultants should serve the whole school in such a way that they can monitor the progress of ADHD students over a period of several years. This should be supplemented with in-house professional development programs that focus on dealing with problem behaviors of children.

2. Use of Stimulant Medication in Schools

One of the inherent difficulties in the use of stimulant medication to treat children with attentional difficulties is that the evidence suggests that it offers only symptomatic treatment of attention disorders. None of the long-term studies have indicated any extended benefit from stimulant treatment.

The problem this poses for school personnel is that stimulants may make it appear that a child is making more progress than is actually the case. Also, if there is a perception among school personnel that stimulant medication is "the treatment" for ADHD, and if that treatment is working to some extent, they may feel that there is nothing else to do. Thus, they may feel justified in paying more attention to children who have problems for which no medical intervention is available.

Because no evidence indicates long-term benefit from stimulants, it seems reasonable that practitioners should attempt to provide additional therapy even to those children who respond positively to stimulants. While no data indicate that there is long-term benefit from stimulant medication used in combination with behavioral treatment, there is such evidence from short-term studies.

VII. SUMMARY

The purpose of this chapter has been to provide an overview of the major issues regarding attentional processes in the study of LDs. Early in the chapter, a distinction was made between the meaning of the term attention in (1) attention theories and (2) ADHD. The former refers to processes such as alertness, selection, and effort, which are measured by various attention tasks. In contrast, in ADHD, inferences regarding attention are based largely on the perceptions of a child's overt behavior by parents, teachers, and professionals. Because the two uses of attention have very different operational definitions, they should not be confused with each other.

Two major approaches to the study of attention are presented. In the first, attentional processes such as selective and sustained attention were thought to play a causal role in LDs. The analysis provided in this chapter led to the conclusion that there was evidence of a selective attention deficit associated with LDs and a sustained attention deficit in ADHD. The second point of view presented is that even though LDs and ADHD are often present in the same child, attention disorders and LDs are distinct problems. This is particularly evident in research that has demonstrated that specific processing disorders such as deficits in RAN tasks and phonological awareness underlie some types of LDs, whereas tasks that require the utilization of more general processing strategies such as those that are employed in rote learning are more evident in ADHD. Also, evidence indicates that ADHD children may be deficient in the utilization of efficient learning strategies relative to children with LDs alone.

The major thrust of the chapter is to provide an overview of the various facets of ADHD. This population has received an increasing amount of attention in the research literature because it is the most common cause of referral to child guidance clinics. Generalizations about ADHD must be tempered by the definitional confusion that still besets this area of study. Diagnostic criteria for ADHD are in a state of flux as evidenced by the recent criticisms of the DSM-III and DSM-III-R criteria. However, with this limitation in mind, a number of conclusions regarding ADHD will be offered. First, the findings reviewed in the chapter from epidemiological and twin studies support the view that there is biological causation of attention disorder. This conclusion is derived from studies that indicated that the heritability of ADHD was quite high and also from findings that children with ADHD tended to have an inordinately high frequency of developmental difficulties (slow to talk and walk, chronic health problems, low birthweight). In contrast, little substantive evidence suggests that psychosocial factors (e.g., family dysfunction, low socioeconomic status) play an important causal role in ADHD. Psychosocial factors appear to be more important in conditions such as CD, which often co-occur with ADHD. There is, however, little solid information on the specific biological causes of ADHD. Earlier speculations on the role of brain damage and neurotransmitter deficiencies in ADHD have not been verified in empirical studies. Recent findings primarily from behavioral studies suggest that ADHD stems from a deficiency in the arousal system: chronic low arousal may account for the fact that children with ADHD are often described as stimulus-seeking. It may also provide an explanation for the beneficial effects of stimulants on ADHD. Other evidence suggests that there may be a higher incidence of allergies, particularly food allergies, in children with ADHD. This work requires further explication regarding the prevalence and types of allergies in children with ADHD. Review of the treatment literature suggests that all existing treatments leave much to be desired. Stimulant medication has been the most successful in producing consistent improvements in behavior. However, stimulants reduce symptoms only and are not a cure, and most researchers advocate that stimulants should be combined with other forms of treatment. Several studies indicate that a subset of the ADHD children appear to benefit from dietary intervention. Successful dietary intervention studies have tended to be those that selected ADHD subjects with a history of allergic symptoms. The range of suspected substances that appear to trigger the symptoms of ADHD are quite broad, and further research is needed to elucidate the critical substances and the mechanisms by which diet can influence behavior. It should also be noted that even when children respond positively to dietary intervention (or any other form of intervention for that matter), they continue to experience problems that require treatment.

A large number of studies have indicated that behavioral intervention such as BM and CBM can lead to short-term changes in behavior. Most studies of these treatments have failed to obtain transfer of skills out of the training environment. One response to the lack of transfer has been the development and investigation of parenting programs. The rationale for such programs is that parents are potential therapeutic agents who are usually present throughout a child's life. As such, they can provide the continuity in treatment (and thus overcome the limitations inherent in not obtaining transfer of treatment), which is virtually impossible for professionals to provide. However, this is not to suggest that attempts to obtain transfer of training should be abandoned but, rather, that radically different approaches to treatment must be taken.

References

Aman, M. (1980). Psychotropic drugs and learning problems: A selective review. *J. Learn. Disabil.* **13**, 87–97.

American Psychiatric Association (1980). "Diagnostic and Statistical Manual of Mental Disorders—DSM III." American Psychiatric Association, Washington, D.C.

American Psychiatric Association (1987). "Diagnostic and Statistical Manual of Mental Disorders—DSM-III-R," 3rd ed., revised. American Psychiatric Association, Washington, D.C.

Aylward, E. H., and Whitehouse, D. (1987). Learning disability with and without attention deficit disorder. *In* "Handbook of Cognitive, Social & Neurological Aspects of Learning Disabilities" (S. J. Ceci, ed.), pp. 321–341. Lawrence Erlbaum, Hillsdale, New Jersey.

Barkley, R. A. (1987). "Defiant Children: A Clinician's Manual for Parent Training." Guilford Press, New York.

Barkley, R. A. (1988). Attention deficit disorder with hyperactivity. *In* "Behavioral Assessment of Childhood Disorders," 2nd ed., (E. J. Mash and L. G. Terdal, eds.), pp. 69–104. Guilford Press, New York.

Barkley, R. A. (1989). Attention deficit–hyperactivity disorder. *In* "Treatment of Childhood Disorders," pp. 39–72. (E. J. Mash and R. A. Barkley, eds.). Guilford Press, New York.

Barkley, R. A. (1981). Hyperactive Children: A Manual for Diagnosis and Treatment. Guilford Press, New York.

Befera, M. S., and Barkley, R. (1985). Hyperactive and normal girls and boys: Mother–child interaction, parent psychiatric status and child psychopathology. *J. Child Psychol. Psych.* **26**, 439–452.

Bloomquist, M., and Braswell, L. (1987). "Comprehensive Child and Family Intervention for Attention Deficit–hyperactivity Disorder Children." Unpublished Manuscript, University of Minnesota Hospital, Minneapolis.

Blouin, A., Conners, C. K., Seidel, W., and Blouin, J. (1989). The independence of hyperactivity from conduct disorder: Methodological considerations. *Can. J. Psych.* **34**, 279–282.

Bosco, J., and Robin, S. (1980). Hyperkinesis: Prevalence and treatment. *In* "Hyperactive Children: The Social Ecology of Identification and Treatment" (C. Whalen and B. Henker, eds.). Academic Press, New York.

Brown, A. L., Kane, M., and Long, C. (in press). Analogical transfer in young children: Analogies as tools for communication and exposition. *Appl. Cog. Psychol.*

Carlson, G., and Rapport, M. (1989). Diagnostic classification issues in attention-deficit hyperactivity disorder. *Psych. Ann.* **19**, 576–583.

Chee, P., Logan, G., Schachar, R., Lindsay, P., and Wachsmuth, R. (1989). Effects of event rate and display time on sustained attention in hyperactive, normal, and control children. *J. Abnorm. Child Psychol.* **17**, 371–391.

Chelune, G. J., Ferguson, W., Koon, R., and Dickey, T. (1986). Frontal lobe disinhibition in attention deficit disorder. *Child Psychol. Hum. Dev.* **16**, 221–234.

Cohen, N., Douglas, V. I., and Morgenstern, G. (1971). The effect of methylphenidate on attentive behavior and autonomic activity in hyperactive children. *Psychopharmacologia* **22**, 282–294.

Conners, C. K., Goyette, C. H., Southwick, D. A., *et al.* (1976). Food additives and hyperkinesis: A controlled double-blind experiment. *Pediatrics* **58**, 154–166.

Conte, R., and Kinsbourne, M. (1988). Electrodermal lability predicts presentation rate effects and stimulant drug effects on paired associate learning in hyperactive children. *Psychophysiology* **25**, 64–70.

Conte, R., Kinsbourne, M., Swanson, J., Zirk, H., and Samuels, M. (1986). Presentation rate effects on paired associate learning by attention deficit disordered children. *Child Dev.* **57**, 681–687.

Dalby, J. T., Fox, S. L., and Haslam, R. H. A. (1982). Adoption and foster care rates in pediatic disorders. *J. Dev. Behav. Ped.* **3**, 61–64.

Deci, E., and Chandler, C. (1986). The importance of motivation for the future of the LD field. *J. Learn. Disabil.* **19**, 587–594.

Denkla, M. B., and Rudel, R. G. (1976). Naming of object-drawings by dyslexic and other learning disabled children. *Brain Lang.* **3**, 1–15.

Deutsch, C. K. (1989). Adoption and Attention deficit disorder. *J. Child Psychol. Psych. Supp: Attention–deficit disorder* **IV**, 67–79.

Deutsch, C. K., Swanson, J. M., Bruell, J. H., Cantwell, D. P., Weinberg, F., and Baren, M. (1982). Overrepresentation of adoptees in children with the attention deficit disorder. *Behav. Gen.* **12**, 231–238.

Douglas, V. I. (1980). Higher mental processes in hyperactive children: Implications for training. *In* "Rehabilitation, Treatment, and Management of Learning Disorders" (R. M. Knights and D. J. Bakker, eds.), pp. 65–91. University Park Press, Baltimore.

Douglas, V. I., and Peters, K. B. (1979). Toward a clearer definition of the attentional deficit of hyperactive children. *In* "Attention and the Development of Cognitive Skills" (G. A. Hale and M. Lewis, eds.), pp. 173–247. Plenum Press, New York.

Douglas, V. I., Barr, R., O'Neil, M., and Britton, B. G. (1986). Short term effects of methylphenidate on the cognitive, learning and academic performance of children with attention deficit disorder in the laboratory and the classroom. *J. Child Psychol. Psych.* **27**, 191–211.

Douglas, V. I., Barr, R., Amin, K., O'Neil, M., and Britton, B. (1988). Dosage effects and individual responsivity to methylphenidate in attention deficit disorder. *J. Child Psychol. Psych.* **29**, 453–475.

Dykman, R., Ackerman, P., Clements, S., and Peters, J. (1971). Specific learning disabilities: At attentional deficit syndrome. *In* "Progress in Learning Disabilities," Vol. 2 (H. Myklebust, ed.), pp. 56–93. Grune and Stratton, New York.

Dykman, R., Ackerman, P., and Holcomb, P. (1985). Reading disabled and ADD children: Similarities and differences. *In* "Biobehavioral Measures of Dyslexia" (D. B. Gray and J. F. Kavanaugh, eds.), pp. 47–61. York Press Inc., Parkton, Maryland.

Egger, J., Carter, C. M., Graham, P. J., Gumley, D., and Soothill, J. F. (1985). Controlled trial of oligoantigenic treatment in the hyperkinetic syndrome. *Lancet* **14**, 540–545.

Feingold, B. F. (1974). "Why Your Child is Hyperactive." Random House, New York.

Felton, R. H., and Wood, F. B. (1989). Cognitive deficits in reading disability and attention deficit disorder. *J. Learn. Disabil.* **22**, 3–13.

Firestone, P., Kelly, M. J., Goodman, J. T., and Davey, J. (1981). Differential effects of parent training and stimulant medication with hyperactives. *J. Am. Acad. Child Psych.* **20**, 135–147.

Forehand, R., and McMahon, R. J. (1981). "Helping the Non-compliant Child: A Clinician's Guide to Effective Parent Training." Guilford Press, New York.

Gadow, K. (1983). Effects of stimulant drugs on academic performance in hyperactive and learning disabled children. *J. Learn. Disabil.* **16**, 290–299.

Goodman, R., and Stevenson, J. (1989a). A twin study of hyperactivity—I. An examination of hyperactivity scores and categories derived from Rutter Teacher and Parent Questionnaires. *J. Child Psychol. Psych.* **30**, 671–689.

Goodman, R., and Stevenson, J. (1989b). A twin study of hyperactivity—II. The aetiological role of genes, family relationships and perinatal adversity. *J. Child Psychol. Psych.* **30**, 691–709.

Hagen, J. (1967). The effect of distraction on selective attention. *Child Dev.* **38**, 685–694.

Hallihan, D., and Reeve, R. E. (1980). Selective attention and distractibility. *In* "Advances in Special Education," Vol. 1 (B. Keogh, ed.), pp. 141–181. JAI Press, Greenwich, Connecticut.

Harley, J. P., Ray, R. S., Tomasi, L., *et al.* (1978). Hyperkinesis and food additives: Testing the Feingold hypothesis. *Pediatrics* **61**, 818–828.

Kaplan, B., McNicol, J., Conte, R., and Moghadam, H. K. (1987). Physical signs and symptoms in preschool age hyperactive and normal children. *J. Dev. Behav. Ped.* **8**, 305–310.

Kaplan, B. J., McNicol, J., Conte, R., and Moghadam, H. K. (1989). Dietary replacement in preschool-aged hyperactive boys. *Pediatrics* **83**, 7–17.

Kaspar, J. C., Millichap, J. G., Backus, D. C., Child, D. and Schulman, J. (1971). A study of the relationship between neurological evidence of brain damage in children and activity and distractibility. *J. Consult. Clin. Psychol.* **36**, 329–337.

Kendall, P. C., and Braswell, L. (1984). "Cognitive-Behavioral Therapy for Impulsive Children." Guilford Press, New York.

Keogh, B., and Margolis, J. (1976). Learn to labor and wait: Attentional problems of children with learning disorders. *J. Learn. Disabil.* **9**, 276–286.

Krupski, A. (1980). Attention processes: Research, theory, and implications for special education. *In* "Advances in Special Education," Vol. 1 (B. Keogh, ed.), pp. 101–140. JAI Press, Greenwich, Connecticut.

Lahey, B., Green, K., and Forehand, R. (1980) On the independence of ratings of hyperactivity, conduct problem, and attention deficits in children: A multiple regression analysis. *J. Consult. Clin. Psychol.* **44**, 586–596.

Lahey, B., Pelham, W., Schaughency, E., Atkins, M., Murphy, H., Hynd, G., Russo, M., Hartdagen, S., and Lorys-Vernon, A. (1988). Dimensions and types of attention deficit disorder. *J. Am. Acad. Child Adolesc. Psychiat.* **27**, 330–335.

Lahey, B., Piacentini, J., McBurnett, K., Stone, P., Hartdagen, S., and Hynd, G. (1988). Psychopathology in the parents of children with conduct disorder and hyperactivity. *J. Am. Acad. Child Adol. Psych.* **27**, 163–170.

Lambert, N., and Sandoval, J. (1980). The prevalence of learning disabilities in a sample of children considered hyperactive. *J. Abnorm. Child Psychol.* **8**, 33–50.

Laufer, M. W., and Denhoff, E. (1957). Hyperkinetic behavior syndrome in children. *J. Ped.* **50**, 463–470.

Levy, F., and Hobbes, G. (1988). The action of stimulant medication in attention deficit disorder with hyperactivity: Dopaminergic, noradrenergic, or both? *J. Am. Acad. Child Adol. Psych.* **27**, 802–805.

Lou, H. C., Henriksen, L., and Bruhn, P. (1984). Focal cerebral hypoperfusion in children with dysphasia and/or attention deficit disorder. *Arch. Neurol.* **41**, 825–829.

Mannuzza, S., Gittelman-Klein, R., Konig, P., and Giampino, T. (1989). Hyperactive boys almost grown up: IV. Criminality and its relationship to psychiatric status. *Arch. Gen. Psych.* **46**, 1073–1079.

Marshall, P. (1989). Attention deficit disorder and allergy: A neurochemical model of the relation between the illnesses. *Psycholog. Bull.* **106**, 434–446.

Mash, E. J., and Johnston, C. (1983). Parental perceptions of child behavior problems, parenting self-esteem, and mothers' reported stress in younger and older hyperactive and normal children. *J. Consult. Clin. Psychol.* **51**, 68–99.

Meichenbaum, D. (1977). "Cognitive Behavior Modification." Plenum Press, New York.

Moray, N. (1969). "Attention: Selective Processes in Vision and Hearing." Hutchinson, London.

National Conference on Learning Disabilities (1988). *In* J. F. Kavanagh and Tom J. Truss, eds. "Proceedings of the National Conference on Learning Disabilities." Yorkton Press, Parkton, Maryland.

Nichols, P., and Chen, T. C. (1981). "Minimal Brain Dysfunction: A Prospective Study." Lawrence Erlbaum, Hillsdale, New Jersey.

Patterson, G. R. (1982). "Coercive Family Process." Castalia, Eugene, Oregon.

Pelham, W. E. (1986). The effects of psychostimulant drugs on learning and academic achievement in children with attention-deficit disorders and learning disabilities. *In* "Psychological and Educational Perspectives on Learning Disabilities" (J. Torgesen and B. Wong, eds.), pp. 259–295. Academic Press, New York.

Pelham, W. E., and Murphy, H. A. (1986). Attention deficit and conduct disorders. *In* "Pharmacological and Behavioral Treatment: An Integrative Approach" (M. Hersen, ed.), pp. 108–148. John Wiley & Sons, New York.

Pisterman, S., McGrath, P., Firestone, P., Goodman, J., Webster, I., and Mallory, R. (1989). Outcome of parent-mediated treatment of preschoolers with attention deficit disorder with hyperactivity. *J. Consult. Clin. Psychol.* **57,** 628–635.

Porges, S. W., Walter, G. F., Korb, R. J., and Sprague, R. L. (1975). The influence of methylphenidate on heart rate and behavioral measures of attention in hyperactive children. *Child Dev.* **46,** 727–733.

Posner, M. I. (1975). Psychobiology of attention. *In* "Handbook of Psychobiology" (M. Gazzaniga and C. Blakemore, eds.), pp. 441–479. McGraw-Hill, New York.

Rapport, J. L., Buchsbaum, M., Weingartner, H., Zahn, T., Ludlow, C., and Mikkelson, E. J. (1980). Dextroamphetamnine: Cognitive and behavior effects in normal and hyperactive boys and normal men. *Arch. Gen. Psych.* **37,** 933–934.

Rapp, D. J. (1978). Does diet affect hypersensitivity. *J. Learn. Disabil.* **11,** 56–62.

Richards, G. P., Samuels, S. J., Turnure, J., and Ysseldyke, J. (1990). Sustained and selective attention in children with learning disabilities. *J. Learn. Disabil.* **23,** 129–136.

Ross, A. O. (1976). "Psychological Aspects of Learning Disabilities and Reading Disorders." McGraw-Hill, New York.

Ross, D. M., and Ross, S. A. (1976). "Hyperactivity: Theory, Research and Action." Wiley, New York.

Rutter, M. L. (1977). Brain damage syndromes in childhood: Concepts and findings. *J. Child Psychol. Psych.* **139,** 21–33.

Safer, D., and Allen, R. (1976). "Hyperactive Children: Diagnosis and Management." University Park Press, Baltimore.

Samuels, S., and Edwall, G. (1981). The role of attention in reading with implications for the learning disabled student. *J. Learn. Disabil.* **14,** 353–361.

Satterfield, J. H., and Dawson, M. E. (1971). Electrodermal correlates of hyperactivity in children. *Psychophysiology* **8,** 191–197.

Sprague, R. L., and Sleator, E. (1977). Methylphenidate in hyperkinetic children: Differences in dose effects on learning and social behavior. *Science* **198,** 1274–1276.

Streissguth, A. P., Herman, C. S., and Smith, D. W. (1978). Intelligence, behavior, and dysmorphogenesis in the fetal alcohol syndrome: A report on 20 patients. *J. Ped.* **92,** 363–367.

Swanson, J. M., and Kinsbourne, M. (1976). Stimulant related state dependent learning in hyperactive children. *Science* **192,** 1754–1757.

Sykes, D., Douglas, V., Weiss, G., and Minde, K. (1971). Attention in hyperactive children and the effect of methylphenidate. (Ritalin). *J. Child Psychol. Psych.* **12,** 129–139.

Szatmari, P., Offord, D. R., and Boyle, M. H. (1989a). Correlates, associated impairments and patterns of service utilization of children with attention deficit disorder: Findings from the Ontario Child Health Study. *J. Child Psychol. Psych.* **30,** 205–217.

Szatmari, P., Offord, D. R., and Boyle, M. H. (1989b). Ontario child health study: Prevalence of attention deficit disorder with hyperactivity. *J. Child Psychol. Psych.* **30,** 219–230.

Tannock, R., Schachar, R. J., Carr, R., and Logan, G. (1989). Dose–response effects of methylphenidate on academic performance and overt behavior in hyperactive children. *Pediatrics* **84**, 648–657.

Tant, J. L., and Douglas, V. I. (1982). Problem solving in hyperactive, normal and reading-disabled boys. *J. Abnorm. Child Psychol.* **10**, 285–306.

Tarnowski, K. J., Prinz, R. J., and Nay, S. M. (1986). Comparative analysis of attentional deficits in hyperactive and learning-disabled children. *J. Abnorm. Psychol.* **95**, 341–345.

Tarver, S., and Hallihan, D. (1974). Attention deficits in children with learning disabilities: A review. *J. Learn. Disabil.* **7**, 560–569.

Trites, R. C., Ferguson, H. B., and Tryphonas, H. (1980). Diet treatment for hyperactive children with food allergies. *In* "The Rehabilitation, Treatment, and Management of Learning Disabilities" (R. M. Knights and D. Bakker, eds.), pp. 151–163. University Park Press, Baltimore.

Tryphonas, H., and Trites, R. (1979). Food allergy in children with hyperactivity, learning disabilities, and/or minimal brain dysfunction. *Ann. Allergy* **42**, 22–27.

Weiss, G., Minde, K., Werry, J. S., Douglas, V., and Nemeth, E. (1971). Studies of the hyperactive child: VIII. Five-year follow-up. *Arch. Gen. Psych.* **24**, 409–414.

Werner, P. H., and Smith, R. S. (1977). "Kauai's Children Come of Age." University of Hawaii Press, Honolulu.

Zametkin, A. J., and Rapoport, J. L. (1987). Neurobiology of attention deficit disorder with hyperactivity: Where have we come in 50 years? *J. Am. Acad. Child Adol. Psych.* **26**, 676–686.

Zentall, S. S., and Zentall, T. R. (1983). Optimal stimulation: A model of disordered activity and performance in normal and deviant children. *Psycholog. Bull.* **94**, 446–471.

CHAPTER 4

Learning Disabilities and Memory

H. Lee Swanson and John B. Cooney

Editor's Notes

In the preceding chapter, you learned about attentional problems in children with learning disabilities. In the present chapter, you will learn about their memory skills and problems. Attentional and memory processes are closely related. Hence, from a teacher's point of view, to facilitate your learning, it makes good sense for us to proceed from addressing attentional problems to memory-processing problems in children with learning disabilities.

Here, Swanson and Cooney's chapter is organized around five themes. The first theme concerns the three types of memory research in learning disabilities: (1) descriptive, (2) instructional, and (3) theoretical. The second theme concerns how learning-disabled children's memory functions/skills resemble those in younger, normal-achieving children. They highlight these functional similarities in four specific areas: (1) the distinctions between automatic and effortful processing, (2) the use of cognitive strategies, (3) the development of a knowledge base, and (4) children's awareness of their own memory processes. The third lies in a model of memory and the outlining of processing stages in it. Swanson and Cooney use it to show where memory-processing problems of learning-disabled children occur. The fourth theme lies in a historical review of memory research in learning disabilities, which Swanson and Cooney have divided into early versus contemporary research. The last theme focuses on principles for memory strategy instruction.

I. INTRODUCTION

Simply defined, memory is the ability to encode, process, and retrieve information that one has been exposed to. As a skill, it is inseparable from intellectual functioning and learning. Individuals deficient in memory skills, such as the learning-disabled (LD), would be expected to have difficulty in a number of academic and cognitive domains (Stanovich, 1986; Torgesen *et al.*, 1988). Thus, helping students with learning disabilities (LDs) to better remember information is an important educational goal. The importance of this goal is also bolstered by studies suggesting that the memory skills used by students with LDs do not appear to exhaust, or even to tap, their ability (e.g., Barclay and Hagen, 1982; Brown and Palinscar, 1988; Kolligian and Sternberg, 1987; Scrugg and Mastropieri, 1989; Spear and Sternberg, 1987; Swanson, 1990; Wong, 1982). In the spirit of this broad educational goal, the objective of this chapter is to provide a foundation for our understanding of LD students' memory skills. The chapter attempts to characterize and selectively review current research on LD children's memory skills, describe the components and stages of processing that influence memory performance, and discuss the implication of memory research for the instruction of LD students.

II. INFORMATION PROCESSING

Based mainly on the findings of descriptive and instructional studies, we may characterize LD students' memory skills as similar to those of younger children, particularly in the way they approach memory tasks. For a broader understanding of their immature memory functioning, however, it is necessary to provide a model of memory that outlines some important components that influence performance.

   To date, the study of memory in LD students is conceptualized within an information-processing approach. Greatly simplified, the information-processing approach is defined as the study of how input is transformed, reduced, elaborated, stored, retrieved, and used (Newell, 1980). To understand how each of these processes plays a part in the flow of information, some general components must be identified. Three components that typically underlie information-processing models are (1) a constraint or structural component, akin to the hardware of a computer, which defines the parameters within which information can be processed at a particular stage (e.g., sensory storage, short-term memory, working memory, long-term memory); (2) a control or strategy component, akin to the software of a computer system,

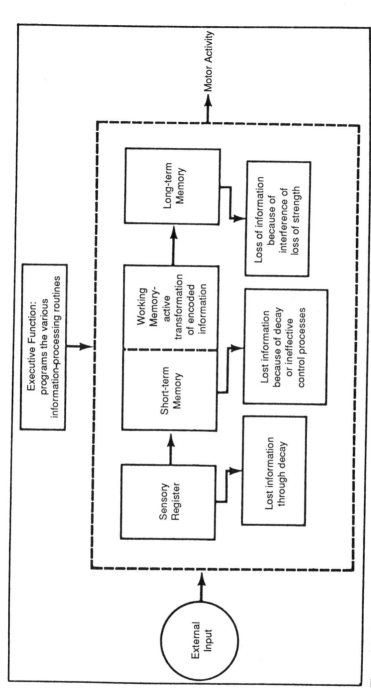

Figure 4.1 Stages and components of information processing. (From H. Lee Swanson, 1987, Information processing and learning disabilities: An overview, *J. Learn. Disabil.* **20**, 3–7.)

which describes the operations of the various stages (to be described); and (3) an executive process, by which learners' activities (e.g., strategies) are overseen and monitored. These components are shown in Figure 4.1.

Briefly, the structural components are sensory, short-term, working, and long-term memory. Sensory memory refers to the initial representation of information that is available for processing for a maximum of 3–5 sec; short-term memory processes information between 3 and 7 sec and is primarily concerned with storage, via rehearsal processes. Working memory also focuses on the storage of information as well as the active interpretation of newly presented information, whereas long-term memory is a permanent storage with unlimited capacity. The executive component monitors and coordinates the functioning of the entire system. Some of this monitoring may be automatic, with little awareness on the individual's part, whereas other types of monitoring require effortful and conscious processing. These components will become clearer when we later discuss current research findings (for a review, also see Jorm, 1983).

Let us now consider research that identifies where in this memory model LD students' memory difficulties may lie. However, it is important to recognize that research findings on memory problems in LD children come primarily from contemporary research. Contemporary research focuses on control and, more recently, executive processes, whereas earlier research focused primarily on the hardware (structural) differences of LD children's memory difficulties.

A majority of the research published prior to 1976 was concerned with perceptual–motor behavior of brain-injured and/or reading-disabled children, and little experimental research dealt directly with memory difficulties (Hallahan and Cruickshank, 1973). Of the studies that were available prior to 1970, most stated merely that LD children perform poorly on certain tasks (e.g., digit span; for a recent review, see Mishra et al., 1985), and the nature of their deficits were isolated to structural (hardware) problems. We now focus on more recent findings of LD children's memory processes/functions.

III. CONTEMPORARY RESEARCH

After 1975, the study of LD children's memory deficits dramatically increased. For example, a survey of LDs journals between 1976 and 1979 revealed that 18% of the reports were concerned with memory processes (Torgesen and Dice, 1980). Let us briefly review important research findings to date. This review is organized according to the basic components outlined in Figure 4.1: sensory register, short-term memory, working memory, long-term memory, and executive function.

A. Sensory Register

As shown in Figure 4.1, basic structural environmental information (e.g., visual, auditory) is assumed first to enter the appropriate sensory register. Information in this initial store is thought to be a relatively complete copy of the physical stimulus that is available for further processing for a maximum of 3–5 sec. An example of sensory registration for the visual modality is an image or icon. In a reading task, if an array of letters is presented tachistoscopically and the child is then asked to write out those letters after a 30-sec delay between instructions, the child can reproduce about six or seven letters. Incoming information from other modalities (auditory, kinesthetic) receives sensory registration, but less is known about their representation. For example, students who are presented a letter of the alphabet may produce a photographic trace that decays quickly, or they may physically scan the letter and transfer the information into an auditory (e.g., echo of sound)–visual–linguistic (meaning) representation. In other words, information presented visually may be recorded into other modalities (e.g., auditory). The transfer of a visual image to the auditory–visual–linguistic store is made at the discretion of the person. In the reading process, each letter or word is scanned against information in long-term memory and the verbal name. Certainly this representation will facilitate transfer of information from the sensory register to a higher level of information processing.

In general, research on the sensory register of LD children suggests it is intact. For example, Elbert (1984) has provided evidence that LD and non-learning-disabled (NLD) students are comparable at the encoding stage of word recognition, but that LD children require more time to conduct a memory search (also see Manis, 1985). Additional evidence that LD and NLD children are comparable at the encoding stage of information processing was provided by Lehman and Brady (1982). Using a release from the proactive inhibition procedure (see Dempster and Cooney, 1982), Lehman and Brady found that reading-disabled and normal readers were comparable in their ability to encode word information (e.g., indicating whether a word was heard or seen and information concerning a word's category). However, reading-disabled children relied on smaller subword components in the decoding process than did normal readers.

Many accounts of poor recognition of quickly presented information by LD students have been attributed to attention deficits—although this conclusion is in question. For example, using a psychological technique free of memory confounds, McIntyre et al. (1978) reported a lower-than-normal span of apprehension in children identified as LD. Subsequently, Mazer et al. (1983) attributed the lower span of apprehension to a slower rate of information pickup from the iconic sensory store. Despite the common assumption of differences between LD and NLD children in attentional to visual and auditory stimuli, Bauer (1977a) has argued that the attentional resources of the LD children are adequate for performance on a variety of memory tasks. In other words, the residual differences are not great enough to account for the differences in memory performance. For example, LD and NLD children are comparable in their ability to recall orally presented sets of three letters or three words within 4 sec after presentation (Bauer, 1979). Similarly, LD and NLD students are comparable in their ability to recognize letters and geometric shapes after a brief visual presentation when recognition is less than 300 msec after stimulus offset (Morrison *et al.*, 1977). In view of these findings, the retrieval of information from sensory storage apparently is an important, although not a major, factor in the memory deficits exhibited in LD children. Taken as a whole, research on attention suggests that the attentional resources of LD children are adequate for performance on most learning and memory tasks (also see Elison and Richman, 1988; Samuels, 1987a,b; Swanson, 1983a).

B. Short-Term Memory

From the sensory register, information is transferred into the limited-capacity short-term memory. Information lost in this memory is assumed to decay or disappear, but actual time of decay is longer than time available in the sensory register. Exact rate of decay of information cannot be estimated, because this component is greatly controlled by the subject. The short-term memory retains information in auditory–verbal–linguistic representations. Using the example of a child recalling letters, the child may subvocally rehearse a letter by voicing the letter as well as the place of articulation in the mouth.

Variation in short-term memory capacity of LD children has been attributed to control processes (such as rehearsal) and the meaningfulness of the material. The crucial factor in capacity is the person's ability to encode units or sequence the items so that they can be recoded into smaller units. Other factors that affect capacity include (1) information load, (2) similarity of items, (3) number of items processed during subsequent activities, and (4) passage of time. The exact nature of problems with the capacity of short-term memory is somewhat obscure in LD students (Cooney and Swanson, 1987). Research has been unclear as to whether the limitation is one of processing capacity, storage capacity, or some interaction between the two.

Control processes in short-term memory include a choice as to which information to scan and a choice of what and how to rehearse. Rehearsal refers to the conscious repetition of information, either subvocally or orally, to recall information at a later date. Learning a telephone number or street address illustrates the primary purpose of rehearsal. Additional control processes also involve organization (ordering, classifying, or tagging information to facilitate retrieval) and mediation (comparing new items with items already in memory). Various organization of strategies may include:

1. Chunking: Grouping items so that each one brings to mind a complete series of items (e.g., grouping words into a sentence).
2. Clustering: Organizing items in categories (e.g., animal, furniture).
3. Mnemonics: Idiosyncratic methods for organizing materials.
4. Coding: Varying the qualitative form of information (e.g., using images rather than verbal labels, substituting pictures for words).

Mediation may be facilitated by

1. Making use of preexisting associations, eliminating the necessity for new ones.
2. Utilizing instructions, either verbal or asking the child to imagine, to aid in retrieval and organization.
3. Cuing at recall by using verbal and imaginary information to facilitate mediation.

Concerning research on short-term memory control processes, Torgesen and Goldman (1977) studied lip movements of children during a memorization task. LD children were found to exhibit fewer lip movements than the NLD students. To the extend that these lip movements reflect the quantity of rehearsal, these data support a rehearsal-deficiency hypothesis. Haines and Torgeson (1979) and others (e.g., Dawson et al., 1980; Koorland and Wolking, 1982) also reported that incentives could be used to increase the amount of rehearsal and, thus, recall by LD students. More recently, Bauer and Emhert (1984) have suggested that the difference between LD and NLD students is in the quality of the rehearsal rather than the quantity of rehearsal, per se.

Another major source of difficulty that LD children experience during their attempts to memorize material has been highlighted by Gelzheiser et al. (1983). These authors recorded a brief statement made by a LD student following an attempt to retain a passage containing four paragraphs about diamonds. The student reported that she could identify major themes of the story but could not categorize the various pieces of information under these major items. She was able to abstract the essence of the story but was unable to use this as a framework to organize the retention of the specific passage.

Swanson (1983c) found that LD children rarely reported the use of an organizational strategy when they were required to rehearse several items. He reasoned that, because these children were capable of rehearsal, the problem was not a deficiency in rehearsal but, instead, was a failure to perform elaborative processing of each word. Elaborative processing was defined as processing that goes beyond the initial level of analysis to include more sophisticated features of the words and ultimately the comparison of these features with others in the list.

Another major source of difficulty related to short-term memory processing has been related to LD children's lack or inefficient use of a phonological code (sound represented). Torgesen (1988) conducted studies on a small group of subjects who performed in the retarded range of verbatim recall on sequences of verbal information. His comprehensive analysis of LD students' performance deficits suggests that they are due to coding errors and represent the phonological features of language. He suggests that LD children's memory problems relate to the acquisition of fluent word identification and word analysis skills.

Additional support for the notion of phonological coding errors comes from studies suggesting that good and poor readers differ in the extent to which they recall similar- and dissimilar-sounding names. An interaction is usually found in which poor readers perform better on "rhyming-word and similar letter-sounding tasks" because they have poor access to a phonological code (e.g., Shankweiler et al., 1979; Siegel and Linder, 1984). That is, good readers recall more information for words or letters that have distinct sounds (e.g., mat vs. book, A vs. F) than words or letters that sound alike (mat vs cat, b vs. d). In contrast, poor readers are more comparable in their recall of similar and dissimilar words or sounds than skilled readers. This finding suggests that good readers are disrupted when words or sounds are alike because they process information in terms of sound (phonological) units. In contrast, poor readers are not efficient in processing information into sound units (phonological codes) and, therefore, are not disrupted in performance if words or letters sound alike. In a recent study by Johnston et al. (1987), 8- and 11-yr-old good and poor readers of average and below-average intelligence were compared on their ability to recall strings of similar and dissimilar sounding letters. When a control was made of differences in memory span between ability groups, high- and low-IQ poor readers were comparable with their chronological age (CA) reading-level matched controls in similarity effects; i.e., the study did not directly support the contention that difficulties in immediate memory are primarily due to difficulty with phonological coding. Some other contrasting studies (e.g., Sipe and Engle, 1986) have suggested that poor readers may be adequate in phonological coding (echoic memory processes) but show a fast decline in their ability to recall as the retention interval (time between item presentation and recall) is increased.

In summary, LD children's poor short-term memory has been related to problems in rehearsal, organization, elaborative processing, and phonological coding; i.e., the previous studies suggest that LD children suffer short-term memory difficulties and these problems manifest themselves in terms of how information is strategically processed (e.g., rehearsal) and how information is mentally represented (e.g., phonological codes).

C. Long-Term Memory

The amount of information as well as the form of information transferred to long-term memory is primarily a function of control processes (e.g., rehearsal). Long-term memory is a permanent storage of information of unlimited capacity. How information is stored is determined by the uses of links, associations, and general organization plans. Information stored in long-term memory is primarily semantic. Forgetting occurs because of item decay (loss of information) or interference.

In comparison to the volume of research on short-term memory processes, research on LD children's long-term memory is meager; however, the availble research provides considerable support for the assertion that storage and retrieval problems are primary sources of individual differences in long-term memory performance (e.g., Bjorklund, 1985; Ceci, 1986; Howe et al., 1985; Vellutino and Scanlon, 1987).

Numerous studies have also shown that LD children are less skilled than NLD peers in the use of rehearsal strategies used to store information in long-term memory (Bauer, 1977a,b, 1979; Tarver et al., 1976; Torgeson and Goldman, 1977). The main source of support for the assertion of rehearsal deficits in LD children is the diminished primary effect (i.e., better recall of items at the beginning of a list over the middle items of the list) of the serial position curve (Bauer, 1979). Primacy performance is a measure of the accessibility of items placed in long-term storage. Thus, the primacy effect is thought to reflect greater rehearsal of those items at the beginning of the list.

Concerning retrieving information from long-term memory, LD children can use organized strategies for selecting retrieval cues (Wong, 1982) and different word attributes (e.g., graphophonic, syntactic, semantic) to guide retrieval (Blumenthal, 1980); however, they appear to select less efficient strategies, conduct a less exhaustive search for retrieval cues, and lack self-checking sklls in the selection of retrieval cues (Wong, 1982). Swanson (1984b, 1987e) also provided evidence suggesting that long-term memory deficits may arise from failure to integrate visual and verbal memory traces of visually presented stimuli at the time of storage or retrieval. His findings suggested that semantic memory limitations underlie LD children's failure to integrate verbal and visual codes. In contrast, Ceci et al. (1980) presented data that suggested separate pathways for auditory and visual inputs to the semantic memory system and that LD children may have an impairment in one or both of these pathways. For children with visual and auditory impairments, the recall deficit arises in both storage and retrieval. When only one modality is impaired, the long-term memory deficit is hypothesized to arise at the time of storage. Furthermore, semantic orienting tasks were found to ameliorate the recall deficits of the children with single modality impairments but not those with impairments in both visual and verbal modalities (Ceci *et al.*, 1980; experiment 2).

Some investigators (for a review, see Worden, 1986) have suggested that LD children's long-term memory is intact, but the strategies necessary to gain access to this information are impaired. This notion has been recently challenged (Baker *et al.*, 1987), and evidence suggests that LD children's long-term memory for tasks that require semantic processing is clearly deficient when compared with that of NLD peers (Swanson, 1986a). Moreover, some experimental evidence suggests that LD children may have problems in the structural component of information processing (e.g., Baker *et al.*, 1987; Cohen, 1981; Swanson, 1987c; Torgesen and Houck, 1980). Specifically, Torgesen and Houck (1980) completed a series of eight experiments in which subgroups of LD and NLD children were compared on a digit span task.

Treatment variations among the eight experimental conditions included manipulations of rehearsal, incentives, and related mnemonic activities. Not all LD subjects benefited from strategy intervention, suggesting that structural or capacity difficulties may exist in some children with LD (also see Swanson, 1986a, 1989).

Taken as a whole, the results reviewed here suggest that the processes involved in entering a memory trace into the long-term store are important sources of ability group differences in children's long-term recall. Additional research to discover methods for remediating these deficits is certainly warranted.

D. Working Memory

Working memory is viewed as a *dynamic* and active system because it simultaneously focuses on both processing and storage demands, whereas short-term memory primarily focuses on the storage of information and is considered a more passive system (Baddeley, 1981). Thus, short-term memory is partly understood as a component of a limited capacity system from accumulating and holding segments of information in order (e.g., speech or orthographic units) as they arrive during a listening or reading task. Material in short-term memory is retained if it is rehearsed. In contrast, working memory is concerned with the interpretation and integrating of information with previously stored information.

How does the formulation of working memory help us understand LD children's memory problems better than the concept of short-term store? First, it suggests that verbal rehearsal plays a smaller role in learning and memory (Baddeley, 1984) an important point because some studies do show that performance deficits of LD children are not related to rehearsal, per se (e.g., see Swanson, 1983b). For example, previous studies of LD children's short-term memory operations such as rehearsal (Bauer, 1979) have not explained how constraints in long-term memory contribute to academic performance; i.e., they have not shown how word knowledge, associations, and attentional capacity contribute to some of the problems we see occurring in short-term memory tasks. Furthermore, measures (e.g., digit span) commonly used in assessing differences between LD and NLD children's memory are weakly correlated with academic ability (Daneman and Carpenter, 1980, 1983), suggesting that such short-term tasks may not capture the essence of academic performance, namely the combination of processing and long-term memory storage functions. Second, the idea of a working memory system is useful because it is viewed as an active memory system directed by a central executive (to be discussed) and the resources stored in long-term memory.

A recent study (Swanson *et al.*, 1989a) sought to determine the *extent* to which less skilled readers suffer from working memory deficiencies. A sentence span task (Daneman and Carpenter, 1980; also see Baddeley *et al.*, 1985) was used to measure the efficiency of storage and processing operations combined. The task requires recalling the last word of several sentences as well as answering a comprehension question about a sentence. Materials for the sentence span task were unrelated declarative sentences, 7–10 words in length. The sentences were randomly arranged into sets of two, three, four, or five. Examples of the sentences for recalling the last word in a series of three sentences for words are

1. We waited in line for a *ticket*.
2. Sally thinks we should give the bird its *food*.
3. My mother said she would write a *letter*.

To ensure that children comprehended the sentences (i.e., processed their meaning) and did not merely treat the task as one of short-term memory, they were required to answer a question after each group of sentences were presented. For the three-sentence set, for example, they were asked "Where did we wait?" The results of this study suggests that LD readers' working memory was inferior to NLD readers. Thus, studies that suggest LD children's memory deficiencies are localized to a short-term store system must be re-evaluated within the context of a model that incorporates the operations of working memory.

E. Executive Function

An executive function is a cognitive activity *that determines the order* in which processes will be performed (Neisser, 1967). In other words, it is the organization directive for various memory strategies. The executive function does not perform the searching task, or organize, and sort out material; instead, it directs the various mental activities to a goal. Computers have the executive built-in; humans can modify and develop overall routines for information retrieval.

Neisser sums up some important points related to executive processing:

1. Retrieval of information consists of many programmed searches simultaneously and independently (parallel search or multiple search).
2. Control of parallel and sequential processes is directed by the executive routine.
3. Executive function and search processes are learned and based on earlier processing, the implication being that:
   a. Individuals learn to organize and retrieve.
   b. There are individual styles of organization.
4. Failure to recall is failure to access, the implication being that there is a misguided search strategy.

Although executive functioning has been researched with respect to its importance and application to mentally retarded children's memory (Campione *et al.*, 1985), its application to LDs is just emerging (Brown and Palinscar, 1988; Pressley *et al.*, 1987b; Swanson, 1987a). A focus on executive processing is an important area of research because planning activities prior to solving a problem, monitoring behavior in action, reorganizing strategies, and evaluating the outcomes of any strategic action have characterized LD students' functioning in a number of academic domains (e.g., Palinscar and Brown, 1984). Strategy deficits in LD learners have been noted in terms of failing to monitor cognitive progress or to notice important task differences in learning tasks (for a review, Pressley *et al.*, 1989). Within this context, the important focus of memory research has been to determine whether or not LD students can review their own cognitive strategies, select and reject them appropriately, and persist in searching for the most suitable task strategies at various stages of performance (Palinscar and Brown, 1984; Pressley *et al.*, 1987). Support for possible problems in LD children's executive functioning can be found in studies where students with LDs have difficulty checking, planning, and monitoring control processes (Palinscar and Brown, 1984). This type of research focuses on how decisions or strategies are prioritized, the kinds of decisions LD children make at a specific point in implementing strategy, and how they make decisions related to an unresolved processing stage (e.g., cannot understand the gist of the passage). In summary, the focus of the executive function is to detail the LD students' coordination, direction, and organization of search strategies. The kinds of decisions that will be made and how decisions will be directed when a sequence of operations may provide unresolved steps is related to the child's metacognitive knowledge (see Chapter 8, later in this volume).

F. Summary

Overall, current research suggests that LD children experience problems with a number of information-processing components. Most of the research has focused on short-term memory, and problems in short-term memory may very likely influence processes related to working memory, long-term memory, and executive processes. As yet, research has not identified the independent effects and contributions of various memory components to LD students' overall memory functioning. Thus, it is best to view their memory difficulties as reflecting interactive problems between and among various memory-processing components.

IV. IMPLICATIONS FROM CONTEMPORARY MEMORY RESEARCH FOR INSTRUCTION

A number of memory researchers have converged on the notion that LD students' ability to access information remains inert, unless they are explicitly prompted to use certain cognitive strategies (e.g., for a review, see Swanson, 1989). For example, LD students may be taught to (1) organize lists of pictures and words in common categories, (2) rehearse the category names during learning, and (3) use the names and retrieval cues at the time of the test (e.g., for a review, see Cooney and Swanson, 1987; Swanson, 1987a). The data suggest that when LD children are explicitly encouraged to use such strategies on some tasks, their performance improves and thus the discrepancy between their general intellectual ability and contextually related memory deficits is lessened.

Based on these findings, the LD learner has been viewed as having poor strategies for approaching the complex requirements of academic tasks and, thus, cannot meet his or her academic potential. Thus, he or her is described as an inefficient learner—one who either lacks certain strategies or chooses inappropriate strategies and/or generally fails to engage in self-monitoring behavior. Critical to the strategy-deficit model is the concept of access. Access refers to the notion that the information necessary for task performance resides within the child. Some children can flexibly access this information; i.e., a particular behavior is not delimited to a constrained set of circumstances (Campione *et al.*, 1985). In addition, some children are "aware" of these processes and can consciously describe and discuss their own cognitive activities that allow them to access information. Based on this extensive literature, some very practical concepts and principles from memory research can serve as guidelines for the instruction of LD students. We will briefly discuss eight in the following

V. PRINCIPLES OF STRATEGY INSTRUCTION

A. Memory Strategies Serve Different Purposes

One analysis of the memory strategy research suggests there is no single best strategy for LD students within or among particular domains (for a review, see Cooney and Swanson, 1987). As can be seen from the studies reviewed in this chapter, research is in pursuit of the best strategy to teach LD students. Some of the memory strategies that have been used to enhance LD children's performance are shown in Table 4.1. A number of studies, for example, have looked at enhancing LD children's performance by using advanced organizers, skimming, asking, questioning, taking notes, summarizing, and so on. But apart from the fact that LD students have been exposed to various types of strategies, the question of which strategies are the most effective is not known. We known in some situations such as remembering facts the key word approach appears to be more effective than direct instruction models (Scruggs *et al.*, 1987), but, of course, the rank ordering of different strategies changes in reference to the different types of learning outcomes expected. For example, certain strategies are better suited to enhancing students' understandingof what they previously read, whereas other strategies are better suited to enhancing students' memory of words or facts. The point is that different strategies can effect different cognitive outcomes in a number of ways.

B. Good Memory Strategies for NLD Students Are Not Necessarily Good Strategies for LD Students and Vice Versa

Strategies that enhance access to information for NLD students will not, in some cases, be well suited for the LD child. For example, Wong and Jones (1982) trained LD and NLD adolescents in a self-questioning strategy to monitor reading comprehension. Results indicated that although the strategy

Table 4.1

Classification of Memory Strategies[a]

1. Rehearsal

   Students are told to rehearse stimuli verbally or to write, look at, go over, study, or repeat the stimuli in some other way. The children may be instructed to rehearse items just once, a finite number of times, or an unlimited number of times.

2. Elaboration

   Students are instructed to use elements of the stimulus material and assign meaning by, for instance, making up a phrase or sentence, making an analogy, or drawing a relationship based on specific characteristics found in the stimulus material.

3. Orienting (attention)

   These strategies direct student's attention to a task. For example, teachers may instruct children to "follow along" or "listen carefully" during lessons.

4. Specific Attentional Aids

   This strategy is similar to the attention strategy, but students are instructed to use objects, language, or a part of their body in a specific way to maintain orientation to a task.

5. Transformation

   Transformation is a strategy suggested by teachers for converting unfamiliar or difficult problems into similar or simpler ones that can then be remembered more easily. Transformations are possible because of logical, rule-governed relationships between stimulus elements.

6. Categorical Information

   Teachers might direct students to use taxomomic information (e.g., pictures accompanying a category) or to analyze the item into smaller units (e.g., looking for interitem associations).

7. Imagery

   This strategy usually consists of nonspecific instructions to remember by taking a mental picture of something or to maintain or manipulate them in the mind.

8. Specific Aids for Problem-Solving and Memorizing

   This strategy involves the use of specific aids in problem-solving or memorizing. For example, teachers may tell children to use blocks or other counters to represent addition or subtraction operations in a concrete way.

9. General Aids

   In contrast to specific aids, teachers recommend the same general aid for a variety of different problems. These aids are designed and used to serve a general reference purpose. Examples include the use of dictionaries or other reference works.

10. Metamemory

    Teachers instructing this strategy tell students that certain procedures will be more helpful for studying and remembering than others. The strategy frequently includes giving hints about the limits of memory, asking students about the task factors that will influence ease of remembering, or helping them understand the reasons for their own performance. Teachers can also tell students that they can devise procedures that will aid their memory or indicate the value of using a specific strategy.

[a] Adapted from Moely *et al.* (1986).

training benefited the adolescents with LDs, it did not positively influence the performance of NLD adolescents.

To illustrate this point further, Swanson, (1989) presented LD, mentally retarded, gifted, and average-achieving students a series of tasks that involved base and elaborative sentences. Their task was to recall words embedded in a sentence. The results of the first study suggested that LD children differ from the other group in their ability to benefit from elaboration. This finding was qualified in the next study (experiment 2) and suggested that the difficulty of the material must be taken into consideration when determining strategy effects, but the results suggest that LD children may require additional strategies to perform comparably to their cohorts. In another study (Swanson *et al.*, 1989b), LD college students were asked to recall words in a sentence under semantic and imagery instructional condition. The results showed LD students were better able to remember words in a sentence during instructional conditions that induced semantic processing. In contrast, NLD readers favored imagery processing over semantic processing conditions. In summary, these results suggest that strategies that are effective for NLD students may, in some situations, be less effective for LD students.

C. Effective Memory Strategies Does Not Necessarily Eliminate Processing Differences

It is commonly assumed that if LD children are presented a strategy that enables efficient processing of information, then improvement in performance is due to the fact that the strategies are affecting the same processes as in NLD students (e.g., Torgesen *et al.*, 1979). This assumption has emanated primarily from studies that have imposed organization on seemingly unorganized material. For example, considerable evidence indicates that LD readers do not initially take advantage of the organizational features of material (e.g., Dallego and Moely, 1980). When instructed to organize information into semantic or related categories (e.g., Torgesen *et al.*, 1979), they improve considerably and perform comparably to NLD students. However, the notion that LD readers process the organizational features of information in the same fashion as NLD students is questionable. For example, Swanson and Rathgeber (1986) found in categorization tasks that LD readers can retrieve information without interrelating superordinate, subordinate, and coordinate classes of information as the NLD children do. Thus, LD children can learn to process information in an organizational sense without implicitly knowing the meaning of the material. Hence, just because LD children are sensitized to internal structure of material via some strategy (e.g., by cognitive strategies that require the sorting of material), it does not follow that they will make use of the organization qualities of the material in a manner consistent with what was intended from the instructional strategy.

D. Comparable Memory Performance Does Not Mean Comparable Strategies

Although the previous principle suggests that different processes may be activated during intervention that are not necessarily the intent of the instructional intervention, it is also likely that LD subjects use different strategies on tasks in which they seem to have little difficulty, and these tasks will probably be overlooked by the teacher for possible intervention. For example, it is commonly assumed that although LD children have isolated processing deficits and require general learning strategies to compensate for these processing deficits, they process information comparable with their normal counterparts on tasks in which they have little trouble. Yet several authors suggest that there are alternative ways for achieving successful performance (Newell, 1980), and some indirect evidence indicates that LD individuals may use qualitatively different mental operations (Shankweiler *et al.*, 1979) and processing routes (e.g., Swanson, 1986a) when compared with their NLD counterparts. A recent study (Swanson, 1988) suggests that LD children use qualitatively different processes on tasks they have little difficulty with; i.e., their performance is comparable to NLD children, but they use different strategies to arrive at the same response as their NLD peers.

E. Memory Strategies in Relation to a Student's Knowledge Base and Capacity

Levin (1986) has suggested that a match must exist between strategy and learner characteristics. For example, Conca (1989) as well as others (Jenkins *et al.*, 1986; Gelzheiser *et al.*, 1987) suggest that LD children are not uniformly inactive strategy users but, rather, tend to be more proficient users when demands on verbal processing are not heavy.

One important variable that has been overlooked in the LD memory literature is the interaction between processing constraints (structures) and memory strategies. Most LD strategy research, either implicitly or explicitly, has considered cognitive to be a confounding variable and has made very little attempt to measure its influence (Swanson, 1987c). Swanson (1984a) has recently conducted three experiments related to LD students' performance on a word-recall task and found that recall is related to cognitive effort (or the mental input) that a limited capacity system expends to produce a response. He found that LD readers were inferior in their recall of materials that made high-effort demands when compared with NLD readers. Furthermore, it was found that skilled readers accessed more usable information form semantic memory for enhancing recall than did LD readers. In a subsequent study (Swanson, 1986b) found that LD children were inferior in the quantity and internal coherence of information stored in semantic memory as well as in the means by which it is accessed.

F. Comparable Memory Strategy May Not Eliminate Performance Differences

It is commonly assumed that without instruction, LD students are less likely to produce strategies than their normal counterparts. However, several studies have indicated that residual differences remain between ability groups even when groups are instructed or prevented from strategy use (Gelzheiser, 1984; Swanson, 1983b, 1989; Wong et al., 1977). For example, in a study by Gelzheiser et al. (1987), LD and NLD children were compared on their ability to use organizational strategies. After relevant instruction, LD and NLD were compared on their ability to recall information on a post-test. The results indicated that LD children were comparable to NLD in strategy use but were deficient in overall performance. In another study, Swanson (1983c) found that the recall performance of the LD group did not improve from baseline level when trained with rehearsal strategies. They recalled less than normal-achieving peers, even though the groups were comparable in the various types of strategy use. The results support the notion that groups of children with different learning histories may continue to learn differently, even when the groups are equated in terms of strategy use.

G. Memory Strategies Taught Do Not Necessarily become Transformed into Expert Strategies

One mechanism that promotes expert performance is related to strategy transformation (e.g., Chi et al., 1988). Children who become experts at certain tasks often have learned simple strategies and, through practice, discover ways to modify them into more efficient and powerful procedures. In particular, the proficient learner uses higher-order rules to eliminate unnecessary or re-dundant steps to hold increasing amounts of information. The LD child, in contrast, may learn most of the skills related to performing an academic task and perform appropriately on that task by carefully and systematically following prescribed rules or strategies. Although LD children can be taught strategies, recent evidence suggests that the difference between LD (experts in this case) and NLD children is that the latter have modified such strategies to become more efficient (Swanson and Cooney, 1985). It is plausible that the LD child remains a novice in learning new information because he or she fails to transform memory strategies into more efficient forms (see Swanson and Rhine, 1985).

G. Strategy Instruction Must Operate on the Law of Parsimony

A "number of multiple-component packages" of strategy instruction have been suggested for improving LD children's functioning. These components have usually encompassed some of the following: skimming, imagining, drawing, elaborating, paraphrasing, using mnemonics, accessing prior knowledge, reviewing, orienting to critical features, and so on. No doubt there are some positive aspects to these strategy packages in that:

1. These programs are an advance over some of the studies that are seen in the LDs literature as rather simple or "quick-fix" strategies (e.g., rehearsal or categorization to improve performances).
2. These programs promote a domain skill and have a certain metacognitive embellishment about them (see Chapter 8, later in this volume).
3. The best of these programs involve (a) teaching a few strategies well rather than superficially, (b) teaching students to monitor their performance, (c) teaching students when and where to use the strategy to enhance generalization, (d) teaching strategies as an integrated part of an existing curriculum, and (e) teaching that includes a great deal of supervised student practice and feedback.

The difficulty of such packages, however, at least in terms of theory, is that little is known about which components best predict student performance, nor do they readily permit one to determine why the strategy worked. The multiple-component approaches that are typically found in a number of LDs strategy intervention studies must be carefully contrasted with a component analysis approach that involves the systematic combination of instructional components known to have an additive effect on performance. As stated by Pressley (1986: 140), good strategies are "composed of the sufficient and necessary processes for accomplishing their intended goal, consuming as few intellectual processes as necessary to do so."

VI. SUMMARY AND CONCLUSION

In summary, we have briefly characterized research on memory and LDs. Our knowledge of LD individuals' memory somewhat parallels our knowledge about the differences between older and younger children's memory. The parallel relies in effortful processing, the focus on cognitive strategies, the development of a knowledge base, and the awareness of one's own memory processes. Memory research may be categorized into three types: (1) descriptive, (2) instructional, and (3) theoretical. Most memory research emanates from an information-processing framework. Earlier research tends to emphasize the structural problems (hardware problems), i.e., brain deficits of memory, whereas more recent studies tend to focus on the representation, control, and executive process (e.g., strategies) of memory. Current research on memory is beginning to examine the interaction of structures and process on performance. A number of principles related to memory strategy instruction have emerged that have direct application to the instruction of children and adults with LDs. These principles are related to (1) the purposes of strategies, (2) parsimony with regard to the number of processes, (3) individual differences in strategy use and performance, (4) learner constraints, and (5) the transfer of strategies into more efficient processes.

References

Baddeley, A. D. (1981). The concept of working memory: A view of its current state and probable future development. *Cognition* **10,** 17–23.

Baddeley, A. (1984). Reading and working memory. *Vis. Language* **18,** 311–322.

Baddeley, A., Logie, R., Nimmo-Smith, T., and Brereton, N. (1985). Components of fluent reading. *J. Mem. Language* **24,** 119–131.

Baker, J. G., Ceci, S. J., and Hermann, N. D. (1987). Semantic structure and processing: Implications for the learning disabled child. *In* "Memory and Learning Disabilities" (H. L. Swanson, ed.), pp. 83–110. JAI Press, Greenwich, Connecticut.

Barclay, C. R., and Hagen, J. W. (1982). The development of mediated behavior in children: An alternative view of learning disabilities. *In* "Theory and Research in Learning Disabilities" (J. P. Das, R. F. Mulcahy, and A. E. Wall, eds.), pp. 61–84. Plenum Press, New York.

Bauer, R. H. (1977a). Memory processes in children with learning disabilities: Evidence for deficient rehearsal. *J. Exp. Child Psychol.* **24,** 415–430.

Bauer, R. H. (1977b). Short-term memory in learning disabled and nondisabled children. *Bull. Psychon. Soc.* **10,** 128–130.

Bauer, R. H. (1979). Memory processes in children with learning disabilities: Evidence for deficient rehearsal. *J. Exp. Child Psychol.* **24,** 415–430.

Bauer, R. H., and Emhert, J. (1984). Information processing in reading-disabled and nondisabled children. *J. Exp. Child Psychol.* **37,** 271–281.

Blumenthal, S. H. (1980). A study of the relationship between speed of retrieval of verbal information and patterns of oral reading errors. *J. Learn. Disabil.* **3,** 568–570.

Brown, A. L., and Palinscar, A. S. (1988). Reciprocal teaching of comprehension strategies: A natural history of one program for enhancing learning. *In* "Intelligence and Cognition in Special Children: Comparative Studies of Giftedness, Mental Retardation, and Learning Disabilities" (J. Borkowski and J. P. Das, eds.), Ablex, New York.

Campione, J. C., Brown, A. L., Ferrara, R. A., Jones, R. S., and Steinberg, E. (1985). Breakdown in flexible use of information: Intelligence related differences in transfer following equivalent learning performances. *Intelligence* **9**, 297–315.

Ceci, S. J. (1986). Developmental study of learning disabilities and memory. *J. Exp. Child Psychol.* **38**, 352–371.

Ceci, S. J., Ringstrom, M. D., and Lea, S. E. G. (1980). Coding characteristics of normal and learning-disabled 10 year olds: Evidence for dual pathways to the cognitive system. *J. Exp. Psychol.: Hum. Learn. Mem.* **6**, 785–797.

Chi, M. T. H., Glaser, R., and Farr, M. (1988). "The Nature of Expertise." Lawrence Erlbaum, Hillsdale, New Jersey.

Cohen, R. L. (1981). Short-term memory deficits in reading disabled children, in the absence of opportunity for rehearsal strategies. *Intelligence* **5**, 69–76.

Conca, L. (1989). Strategy choice by LD children with good and poor naming ability in a naturalistic memory situation. *Learn. Disabil. Q.* **12**, 97–106.

Cooney, J. B., and Swanson, H. L. (1987). Overview of research on learning disabled children's memory development. *In* "Memory and Learning Disabilities" (H. L. Swanson, ed.), pp. 2–40. JAI Press, Greenwich, Connecticut.

Dallego, M. P., and Moely, B. E. (1980). Free recall in boys of normal and poor reading levels as a function of task manipulation. *J. Exp. Child Psychol.* **30**, 62–78.

Daneman, M., and Carpenter, P. A. (1980). Individual differences in working memory and reading. *J. Verbal Learn. Verbal Behav.* **19**, 450–466.

Daneman, M., and Carpenter, P. A. (1983). Individual differences in integrating information between and within sentences. *J. Exp. Psychol.: Learn. Mem. Cognit.* **9**, 561–584.

Dawson, M. H., Hallahan, D. P., Reeve, R. E., and Ball, D. W. (1980). The effect of reinforcement and verbal rehearsal on selective attention in learning-disabled children. *J. Abnorm. Child Psychol.* **8**, 133–144.

Dempster, F. N., and Cooney, J. B. (1987). Individual differences in digit span, susceptibility to proactive interference, and aptitude/achievement test scores. *Intelligence* **6**, 399–416.

Elbert, J. C. (1984). Short-term memory encoding and memory search in the word recognition of learning-disabled children. *J. Learn. Disabil.* **17**, 342–345.

Forrest Pressley, D. D. L., and Gillies, L. A. (1983). Children's flexible use of strategies during reading. *In* "Cognitive Strategy Research: Educational Applications" (M. Pressley and J. R. Levin, eds.). Springer-Verlag, New York.

Gelzheiser, L. (1984). Generalization from categorical memory tasks to prose by learning disabled adolescents. *J. Educ. Psychol.* **76**, 1128–1138.

Gelzheiser, L. M., Solar, R. A., Shephard, M. J., and Wozniak, R. H. (1983). Teaching learning disabled children to memorize: Rationale for plans and practice. *J. Learn. Disabil.* **16**, 421–425.

Gelzheiser, L. M., Cort, R., and Shephard, M. J. (1987). Is minimal strategy instruction sufficient for learning disabled students. *Learn. Disabil. Q.* **10**, 267–275.

Haines, D., and Torgesen, J. K. (1979). The effects of incentives on short-term memory and rehearsal in reading disabled children. *Learn. Disabil. Res. Q.* **2,** 18–55.

Hallahan, D. P., and Cruickshank, W. M. (1973). Psychoeducational foundations of learning disabilities. Prentice-Hall, Englewood Cliffs, New Jersey.

Jenkins, J., Heliotis, J., Haynes, M., and Beck, K. (1986). Does passive learning account for disabled readers' comprehension deficits in ordinary reading situations? *Learn. Disabil. Q.* **9,** 69–76.

Johnson, R. S., Rugg, M., and Scott, T. (1987). Phonological similarity effects, memory span and developmental reading disorders. *Br. J. Psychol.* **78,** 205–211.

Jorm, A. F. (1983). Specific reading retardation and work memory: A review. *Br. J. Psychol.* **74,** 311–342.

Kolligian, J., and Sternberg, R. J. (1987). Intelligence, information processing, and specific learning disabilities: A triarchic synthesis. *J. Learn. Disabil.* **20.** 8–17.

Koorland, M. A., and Wolking, W. D. (1982). Effect of reinforcement on modality of stimulus control in learning. *Learn. Disabil. Q.* **5,** 264–273.

Koppitz, E. M. (1971). "Children with Learning Disabilities: A Five Year Follow-up Study. Grune & Stratton, Orlando, Florida.

Lehman, E. B., and Brady, K. M. (1982). Presentation modality and taxonomic category as encoding dimensions from good and poor readers. *J. Learn. Disabil.* **15,** 103–105.

Levin, J. R. (1986). Four cognitive principles of learning strategy instruction. *Educ. Psycholog.* **21,** 3–17.

Manis, F. R. (1985). Acquisition of word identification skills in normal and disabled readers. *J. Educ. Psychol.* **27,** 28–90.

Mazer, S. R., McIntyre, C. W., Murray, M. E., Till, R. E., and Blackwell, S. L. (1983). Visual persistence and information pick-up in learning disabled children. *J. Learn. Disabil.* **16,** 221–225.

McIntyre, C. W., Murray, M. E., Coronin, C. M., and Blackwell, S. L. (1978). Span of apprehension in learning disabled boys. *J. Learn. Disabil.* **11,** 13–20.

Mishra, S. P., Shitala, P., Ferguson, B. A., and King, P. V. (1985). Research with the Wechsler digit span subtest: Implications for assessment. *School Psychol. Rev.* **14,** 37–47.

Moely, B. E., Hart, S. S., Santulli, K., Leal, L., Johnson, T., and Rao, N. (1986). How do teachers teach memory skills? *Educ. Psycholog.* **21,** 55–57.

Morrison, F. J., Giordani, B., and Nagy, J. (1977). Reading disability: An information processing analysis. *Science* **196,** 77–79.

Neisser, U. (1967). "Cognitive Psychology." Appleton-Century-Crofts, New York.

Newell, A. (1980). Reasoning, problem solving and decision processes: The problem space as a fundamental category. *In* "Attention and Performance VIII". (R. Nickerson, ed.). Lawrence Erlbaum, Hillsdale, New Jersey.

Palinscar, A. S., and Brown, A. L. (1984). Reciprocal teaching of comprehension-fostering and monitoring activities. *Cognit. Instruct.* **1,** 117–175.

Pressley, M. (1986). The relevance of the good strategy user model to the teaching of mathematics. *Educ. Psycholog.* **21,** 139–161.

Pressley, M., Borkowski, J. G., and O'Sullivan, J. T. (1984). Memory strategy instructions is made of this: Metamemory and durable strategy use. *Educ. Psycholog.* **10,** 94–107.

Pressley, M., Johnson, C. J., and Symons, S. (1987). Elaborating to learn and learning to elaborate. *J. Learn. Disabil.* **20,** 76–91.

Pressley, M., Symons, S., Snyder, B. L., and Cariglia-Bull, T. (1989). Strategy instruction research is coming of age. *Learn. Disabil. Q.*

Samuels, S. J. (1987a). Information processing and reading. *J. Learn. Disabil.* **20,** 18–22.

Samuels, S. J. (1987b). Why is it difficult to characterize the underlying cognitive deficits in special education populations. *Excep. Children* **54,** 60–62.

Schneider, W., and Pressley, M. (1989). "Memory Development between 2 and 20." Springer-Verlag, New York.

Schneider, W., and Sodian, B. (1988). Metamemory–memory relationships in pre-school children: Evidence from a memory-for-location task. *J. Exp. Child Psychol.* **45,** 209–233.

Scruggs, T. E., and Mastropieri, M. A. (1989). Mnemonic instruction of LD students: A field-based evaluation. *Learn. Disabil. Q.* **12,** 119–125.

Scruggs, T. F., Mastropieri, M. A., Levin, J. R., and Gaffney, J. S. (1987a). Facilitating the acquisition of science facts in learning disabled students. *Am. Educ. Res. J.* **22,** 575–586.

Scruggs, T. E., Mastropieri, M. A., and Levin, J. R. (1987b). Transformational mnemonic strategies for learning disabled students. *In* "Memory and Learning Disabilities" (H. L. Swanson, ed.), pp. 225–244. JAI Press, Greenwich, Connecticut.

Shankweiler, D., Liberman, I. Y., Mark, S. L., Fowler, L. A., and Fischer, F. W. (1979). The speech code and learning to read. *J. Exp. Psychol.: Hum. Learn Mem.* **5,** 531–545.

Siegel, L., and Linder, B. A. (1984). Short-term memory processing in children with reading and arithmetic learning disabilities. *Dev. Psychol.* **20,** 200–207.

Sipe, S., and Engle, R. (1986). Echoic memory processes in good and poor readers. *J. Exp. Psychol.: Learn. Mem. Cognit.* **12,** 402–412.

Snow, J. H., Barnett, L., Cunningham, K., and Ernst, M. (1988). Cross-model development with normal and learning disabled children. *Int. J. Clin. Neuropsychol.* **10,** 74–80.

Spear, L. C., and Sternberg, R. J. (1987). An information-processing framework for understanding reading disability. *In* "Handbook of Cognitive, Social and Neuropsychological Aspects of Learning Disabilities" (S. Ceci, ed.), pp. 3–32. Lawrence Erlbaum, Hillsdale, New Jersey.

Stanovich, K. (1986). Matthew effects in reading: Some consequences of individual differences in the acquisition of literacy. *Read. Res. Q.* **21,** 360–387.

Sternberg, R. J. (1987). A unified theory of intellectual exceptionality. *In* "Intelligence and Exceptionality: New Directions for Theory, Assessment, and Instructional Practices." (J. D., Day and J. G. Borkowski, eds.), pp. 135–172. Ablex, Norwood, New Jersey.

Swanson, H. L. (1983a). A developmental study of vigilance in learning disabled and non-disabled children. *J. Abnorm. Child Psychol.* **11,** 415–429.

Swanson, H. L. (1983b). A study of nonstrategic linguistic coding on visual recall of learning disabled and normal readers. *J. Learn. Disabil.* **16,** 209–216.

Swanson, H. L. (1983c). Relations among metamemory, rehearsal activity and word recall in learning disabled and nondisabled readers. *Br. J. Educ. Psychol.* **53,** 186–194.

Swanson, H. L. (1984a). Effects of cognitive effort and word distinctiveness on learning disabled and nondisabled readers' recall. *J. Educ. Psychol.* **76**, 894–908.

Swanson, H. L. (1984b). Semantic and visual memory codes in learning disabled readers. *J. Exp. Child Psychol.* **37**, 124–140.

Swanson, H. L. (1986a). Do semantic memory deficiencies underlie disabled readers encoding processes? *J. Exp. Child Psychol.* **41**, 461–488.

Swanson, H. L. (1986b). Learning disabled readers' verbal coding difficulties: A problem of storage or retrieval? *Learn. Disabil. Res.* **1**, 73–82.

Swanson, H. L. (1987a). Information processing theory and learning disabilities: An overview *J. Learn. Disabil.* **20**, 3–7.

Swanson, H. L. (1987b). The combining of multiple hemispheric resources in learning disabled and skilled readers' recall of words: A test of three information processing models. *Brain Cognit.* **6**, 41–54.

Swanson, H. L. (1987c). Verbal coding deficits in the recall of pictorial information in learning disabled readers: The influence of a lexical system. *Am. Educ. Res. J.* **24**, 143–170.

Swanson, H. L. (1988). Learning disabled children's problem solving: Identifying mental processes underlying intelligent performances. *Intelligence* **12**, 261–278.

Swanson H. L. (1989). Central processing strategy differences in gifted, average, learning disabled and mentally retarded children. *J. Exp. Child Psychol.* **47**, 370–397.

Swanson, H. L. (1990). Intelligence and learning disabilities. *In* "Learning Disabilities and Research Issues" (H. L. Swanson and B. K. Keogh, eds.), pp. 97–113. (Lawrence Erlbaum, Hillsdale, New Jersey.

Swanson, H. L., and Cooney, J. (1985). Strategy transformations in learning disabled children. *Learn. Disabil. Q.* **8**, 221–231.

Swanson, H. L., and Rathgeber, A. (1986). The effects of organizational dimensions on learning disabled readers' recall. *J. Educ. Res.* **79**, 155–162.

Swanson, H. L., and Rhine, B. (1985). Strategy transformation in learning disabled children's math performance: Clues to the development of expertise. *J. Learn. Disabil.* **18**, 596–603.

Swanson, H. L., Cochran, K., and Ewers, C. (1989a). Working memory and reading disabilities. *J. Abnorm. Child Psychol.* **17**, 745–756.

Swanson, H. L., Cooney, J. D., and Overholser, J. D. (1989b). The effects of self-generated visual mnomics on adult learning disabled readers' word recall. *Learn. Disabil. Res.* **4**, 26–35.

Tarver, S. G., Hallahan, D. P., Kauffman, J. M., and Ball, D. W. (1976). Verbal rehearsal and selective attention in children with learning disabilities: A developmental lag. *J. Exp. Child Psychol.* **22**, 375–385.

Torgesen, J. K. (1978). Memorization process in reading-disabled children. *J. Educ. Psychol.* **69**, 571–578.

Torgesen, J. K. (1988). Studies of children with learning disabilities who perform poorly on memory span tasks. *J. Learn. Disabil.* **21**, 605–612.

Torgesen, J. K., and Dice, C. (1980). Characteristics of research on learning disabilities. *J. Learn Disabil.* **13**, 531–535.

Torgesen, J. K., and Goldman, T. (1977). Rehearsal and short-term memory in second grade reading disabled children. *Child Dev.* **48,** 56–61.

Torgesen, J. K., and Houck, D. G. (1980). Processing deficiencies of learning disabled children who perform poorly on the digit span task. *J. Educ. Psychol.* **72,** 141–160.

Torgesen, J. K., Bowen, C., and Ivey, C. (1978). Task structure vs. modality of the visual–oral digit span test. *J. Educ. Psychol.* **70,** 451–456.

Torgesen, J. K., Murphy, H. A., and Ivey, C. (1979). The effects of an orienting task on the memory performance of reading disabled children. *J. Learn. Disabil.* **12,** 396–402.

Torgesen, J. K., Rashotte, C. A., and Greenstein, J. (1988). Language comprehension in learning disabled children who perform poorly on memory span tests. *J. Educ. Psychol.* **80,** 480–487.

Vellutino, F. R., and Scanlon, D. M. (1987). Linguistic coding and reading ability. *In* "Advances in Applied Psycholinguistics," Vol. (S. Rosensberg, ed.), pp. 71–69. Cambridge University Press, New York.

Wong, B. Y. L. (1982). Strategic behaviors in selecting retrieval cues in gifted, normal achieving and learning disabled children. *J. Learn. Disabil.* **15,** 33–37.

Wong, B. Y. L., and Jones, W. (1982). Increasing metacomprehension in learning-disabled and normally-achieving students through self-questioning training. *Learn. Disabil. Q.* **5,** 228–240.

Wong, B. Y. L., Wong, R., and Foth, D. (1977). Recall and clustering of verbal materials among normal and poor readers. *Bull. Psychon. Soc.* **10,** 375–378.

Worden, P. E. (1986). Comprehension and memory for prose in the learning disabled. *In* "Handbook of Cognitive, Social and Neuropsychological Aspects of Learning Disabilities," Vol. 1 (S. J. Ceci, ed.), pp. 241–262. Lawrence Erlbaum, Hillsdale, New Jersey.

Worden, P. E., Malmgren, P., and Gabourie, P. (1982). Memory for stories in learning disabled adults. *J. Learn. Disabil.* **15,** 145–152.

Worden, P. E., and Nakamura, G. V. (1983). Story comprehension and recall in learning-disabled vs. normal college students. *J. Educ. Psychol.* **74,** 633–641.

CHAPTER 5

Language Problems: A Key to Early Reading Problems

Virginia Mann

Editor's Notes

You have read about memory-processing problems in children with learning disabilities in the previous chapter. You will discover that their phonetic short-term memory problems contribute to their difficulties in learning to read as you read the present chapter. Clearly, memory-processing problems are more than a characteristic of children with learning disabilities.

In this chapter, Mann's major theme concerns her exposition that extant research findings support a language-oriented view of reading disability. She approaches her task by first considering the question of what cognitive processes are involved in reading. This is an important question for a twofold reason: (1) it uncovers the commonalities between some of the processes in spoken and written language; and (2) the cognitive processes involved in reading differentiate importantly between good and poor readers.

Reading subsumes two component processes: language-processing skills and phonemic awareness. Language-processing skills comprise speech perception, vocabulary skills as in naming, linguistic short-term memory, syntax, and semantics. Phoneme awareness is the sensitivity to the constituent phonemes in words. It is intricately associated with the English language system of alphabets. Mann examined the research in these two areas of component processes in reading. The research findings indicated that poor readers were deficient in all aspects of language-processing skills, excepting syntax and semantics, and consistently pointed to the power of phonemic awareness in predicting future reading ability and achievements among beginning readers.

Although we subscribe to a language-oriented view of reading disability, we must not forget that for a minority of poor readers and students with learning disabilities visual factors apparently compound their reading difficulties. In the next chapter, Dale Willows examines the role of visual factors in reading disability.

I. INTRODUCTION: THE LINK BETWEEN READING PROBLEMS AND LANGUAGE PROBLEMS

What makes a poor reader a *poor reader*? Why do some children fail to learn to read in the very same classrooms where other children succeed and even excel? Although reading is a task that most children accomplish quite readily, it poses a specific difficulty for some 4–10% of children who may be labeled as dyslexic or reading-disabled. It is often noted that such children cannot be distinguished from their more successful peers by general intelligence, motivation, or prior classroom experience; in fact, this "unexpected" aspect of the problem is at the core of the definition of dyslexia.

Are early reading problems really so unexpected? Can we not identify some factor or factors that have limited certain children's success in learning to read? The objective of the following pages is to introduce the very fruitful approach to the problem of early reading disability that is being guided by the assumption that reading is first, and foremost, a language skill. In Section II, we begin with the rationale behind this approach before turning to the many interesting results that it has produced. Psychologists, educators, and medical doctors have all, in one way or another, tried to identify the basis of early reading difficulty, and their efforts have always been guided by a rationale of some sort or another that reflects some basic assumptions as to what skilled reading is "all about." For this reason, a basic understanding of the assumptions behind the studies and experiments that seek to explain early reading problems is an obvious place to begin. To introduce these assumptions, Section II first describes how the English alphabet functions as "written language" by mapping onto the structure of spoken English. This theoretical point will then be complemented by a brief review of experimental evidence that shows that adult readers use certain spoken language skills to read well. Section III turns to the real substance of the chapter; it outlines two categories of spoken language skills—language processing and phoneme awareness—that are essential to beginning readers and then proceeds to a survey of research that links early reading difficulty to problems within each of these areas. This section also offers a few comments on some less successful accounts of early reading problems. Section IV presents some plausible explanations of the language deficiencies that have been found among poor beginning readers, considering constitutional factors and environmental factors in turn. Section V concludes the chapter with a brief summary and some concluding remarks about directions for future research and practical applications.

II. WHY SPOKEN LANGUAGE IS SO CRITICAL TO READERS

A necessary first step toward understanding the role of language problems in poor reading is to understand something about how writing systems function as written language and the language skills that allow skilled readers to read. Those researchers who have approached the question "What makes a poor reader a *poor reader*?" by first identifying the skills that are involved in reading have made some of the greatest contributions to the field. The success of their approach will become obvious in Section III, when we turn to surveying the abilities and disabilities of poor readers.

What skills are involved in reading? Obviously, reading involves the processes of perceiving, recognizing, remembering, and interpreting the various letters and the words, sentences, etc. that they form. Certain aspects of these processes are visual, but others are linguistic in that they use some of the spoken language skills that allow us to be speakers and hearers of our language. Two insights about the linguistic aspects of reading have been particularly helpful in pointing out potential causes of reading problems: (1) that writing systems are designed to make use of language skills as well as visual skills and (2) that skilled readers make active use of some of the same skills that allow them to be fluent speakers and hearers of their language. The following sections will review the basis for each of these two insights.

A. How Writing Systems Represent Language

Writing systems, or orthographies, are systems of symbols that represent, or transcribe, spoken language, which is to say that a writing system writes language. The focus of this section will be on how alphabets work, because most readers of this chapter will be interested in children who are having problems with the English alphabet. Like all writing systems, alphabets represent units of the spoken language. Various systems have come to exist because of the variety of different types of linguistic units that can be represented. Ideographies, like American Indian petroglyphs, represent language at the level of ideas: logographies, like the Chinese writing system (and Japanese Kanji), represent units called morphemes; syllabaries, like Hebrew and Japanese Kana, represent syllables; and alphabets, like those used for English, French, and most of the European languages, represent units called phonemes. Each of these systems makes slightly different demands on the beginning reader because each transcribes a different type of unit. Their history and diversity is quite fascinating to consider, and, for interesting discussions, the reader might want to read Hung and Tzeng (1981) and Watt (1989).

Because a writing system represents certain units of spoken language, the language user's realization that these units are a part of his or her speech will be an important key to understanding how written words relate to their spoken language counterparts (for discussion, see Hung and Tzeng, 1981; Liberman *et al.*, 1980a). Alphabets represent phonemes, so someone who wishes to learn how an alphabet functions should be sensitive to the fact that spoken language can be broken down into phonemes. As we shall see in Section III.D, much evidence indicates that this "sensitivity," which is referred to as phoneme awareness, is a problem for many young children and, in particular, for poor readers.

1. The English Alphabet: A Morphophonological Transcription

Alphabets represent phonemes, the consonants and vowels of language. To be a bit more precise, the English alphabet does not provide the one-to-one mapping of letter to phonemes that one finds, for example, in Spanish. Rather, it provides a "deeper," more abstract level of representation, which has been referred to as a morphophonological transcription (morphological and phonological transcription). Morphophonological transcription corresponds not so much to the consonants and vowels that speakers and hearers think they pronounce and perceive, as to the way theoretical linguists assume that words are abstractly represented in the ideal speaker/hearer's mental dictionary, or lexicon (Chomsky, 1964). According to these linguists, words are represented as sequences of systematic phonemes in such a way as to preserve (on the whole) the basic units of meaning that we refer to as morphemes. To convert the morphophonological representations of words in the lexicon to the less abstract, phonetic representations that are used in pronunciation and perception, language users are thought to employ ordered series of phonological rules that alter, insert, or delete segments.

As discussed in Liberman *et al.* (1980a), an example of the morphophonological nature of transcription by the English alphabet can be found in the way we use "ea" to transcribe the vowels in "heal" and "health," preserving their abstract morphological and phonological similarity, while blurring certain phonetic distinctions. Insofar as the letter sequences in "heal" and "health" stand for the morphophonological (morphological and phonological) representations of these words, they can provide a means of access to lexical information, including each word's meaning and grammatical properties. To pronounce a written word, the reader who has recovered the appropriate morphophonological representation need only apply the phonological rules of his language—the same rules that otherwise exist for the perception and pronunciation of "heal" and "health" in normal speech.

This account of the English orthography is, of course, somewhat idealized. Sometimes words are transcribed at a shallower, more phonetic level than the morphophonological ideal, hence the different spelling of the vowels in "well" and "wealth." Sometimes, too, the spelling of a word seems neither phonetically nor phonologically principled, as in the spelling of "sword." Some of these exceptions have the advantage of disambiguating homophones; others are historically based, but their existence does not seriously undermine Chomsky's claim about the basic operating principle of the English orthography (Liberman *et al.*, 1980a).

2. Virtues of Alphabetic Systems

Why should English be transcribed with an alphabetic system? Are there any advantages to using an alphabetic orthography and to the English morphophonological system, in particular? One general benefit of alphabets stems from the fact that they transcribe phonemes as opposed to some other unit of language—syllables, for example, or words. This greatly reduces the number of characters that the would-be reader must learn to recognize and reproduce. There are only 26 letters in the English alphabet, whereas between 2,000 and 3,000 characters are needed to read a newspaper written in the Chinese logography.

A benefit of the English morphophonological system, in particular, stems from the fact that, by transcribing a deep, relatively abstract level of phonological structure, it preserves the relation between words such as "heal" and "health" and thereby can facilitate our appreciation of word meaning. The transcription of a morphophonological level of representation also avoids the need to create different spelling patterns for people who speak with different accents. Were English a more "shallow" alphabet, speakers from Boston would spell "cot" and "cart" the same way, and speakers from the South would spell "pen" and "pin" the same—imagine the inconveniences this could cause.

Another virtue to alphabets, aside from being economical, is that they are highly productive. In alphabets and morphophonological transcription, the relation between written words and spoken words is highly rule-governed. Knowledge of the rules that relate between written words and spoken words—the rules that relate letter sequences, morphophonological representations, and their pronunciation—allows the reader to read not only highly familiar words but also less familiar ones such as "skiff" and even nonsense words such as those that Dr. Seuss so cleverly employs. Consider that a skilled reader of the Chinese logography must have memorized thousands of distinct characters—and even then may encounter difficulty in reading a new word. In contrast skilled readers of English need to know only a limited set of phoneme–grapheme correspondences and the phonological rules of their spoken language to "decode" most words on the page (and any phonologically plausible nonword such as "bliggle").

This is not to imply that there is anything inherently undesirable about reading a syllabary or logography. Ultimately, the utility of a given orthography rests on the nature of the spoken language it transcribes. For example, a logography is appropriate for Chinese because it allows people to read the same text even though they cannot understand each other's speech. Likewise, for Japanese, the Kana syllabaries are quite well suited to the hundred or so syllables in the Japanese language. English, however, has less profound dialectical variation than Chinese, and English employs more than 1,000 syllables. Hence, an alphabet is appropriate, and it would be a disservice to present the English writing system otherwise. However, to present it in its true light requires that the would-be reader possess both language-processing skills and phonological sophistication.

3. Phoneme Awareness: A Special Requirement of Alphabetic Systems

Alphabets may have clear advantages, but they nonetheless pose an obstacle for poor readers. There are a variety of reasons why children might become poor readers. They might have problems distinguishing between the various letter shapes. They might have problems with the linguistic units that the written words represent. But children must "know" these units when they "know" spoken English, so why isn't every child who speaks English able to become a successful beginning reader? The answer to this question is that "knowing" spoken English is not enough: Would-be readers must go one step further than merely being a speaker/hearer of their language; they must be "aware" of certain aspects of their language and aware of phonemes in particular (Mattingly, 1972).

The awareness of phonemes is critical because alphabets work best for readers who are aware that letters represent phonemes; however, readers cannot be aware of this relationship unless they are aware of phonemes in the first place. Unless they are sensitive to the fact that words can be broken down into phonemes (i.e., units the size of consonants and vowels), the letter–phoneme correspondences will be useless. This sensitivity is not something that we use in the normal activities of speaking and hearing, although we use it in certain "secondary language activities" such as appreciating verse (i.e., alliteration), making jokes (i.e., Where do you leave your dog? In a barking lot.), and talking in secret languages (i.e., Pig Latin). We refer to this sensitivity as phoneme awareness.

One slight problem with the term phoneme awareness is that it is often used interchangeably with several other terms: phonological awareness, metalinguistic awareness, and linguistic awareness, to name a few. By using the term phoneme awareness, we confine the issue to sensitivity about phonemes. Phonological awareness would also include sensitivity to syllables, morphemes, and the phonological rules that operate upon them; linguistic awareness and metalinguistic awareness would further include sensitivity to syntax (i.e., grammar), semantics (i.e., meaning), and their rules. These broader levels of awareness are of interest in their own right and could be an interesting topic for research. To date, awareness of phonemes has been most often studied and appears to be directly related to the beginning reader's progress.

B. Language Skills that Skilled Readers Use

Considerations about the way in which the English alphabet transcribes language offer one form of evidence about the importance of spoken language skills to reading. A second source of evidence comes from studies of skilled readers. These show a clear involvement of certain spoken language skills in the skilled reading of words, sentences, and paragraphs. Such studies are important to consider, not only because they show that reading is really quite "parasitic" upon spoken language processes, but because they have inspired certain studies of the differences between good and poor beginning readers.

1. Language Skills and Word Recognition

The question of whether or not written words must be recoded into some type of "silent speech" has been a topic in much of the research on the psychology of skilled reading. It has especially preoccupied those who study the processes that make it possible to recognize the words of our vocabulary, a process often referred to as lexical access, or word perception (for recent reviews, see Crowder, 1982; Perfetti and McCutchen, 1982; Taylor and Taylor, 1983). Under some circumstances, silent speech can appear unnecessary for word recognition; some words may be directly perceived as visual units, instead of being decoded into a string of phonemes. But clear evidence also implicates at least some speech code involvement in word perception, making many psychologists favor a "dual access" or "parallel racehorse" model in which both phonetic and visual access occur in parallel. The speech code, or phonetic, route is most heavily used in the case of less frequent or unfamiliar words, the visual, or whole word, route is most important for very familiar words and words with irregular spelling patterns.

Regardless of how a word is recognized, it will be remembered from Section I that the mental lexicon of words contains the morphophonological representation of each word in the reader's vocabulary, and that representation is the key to realizing the word's semantic extensions (its meaning) and its syntactic properties (its part of speech: noun, action verb, etc.) as well as its pronunciation. Hence, it is appropriate that English transcribes spoken words in terms of their morphophonological representations. It may not be necessary to recode print into a speech code in the process of gaining access to this dictionary (referred to as the mental lexicon), and it may not even be feasible if we accept Chomsky's (1964) contention, but morphophonological recoding clearly must occur, or else the reading of phrases, sentences, etc. would not be possible.

2. Language Skills and the Reading of Sentences and Paragraphs

From the point of word perception onward, the involvement of speech processes in reading is quite clear (Perfetti and McCutchen, 1982). First of all, considerable evidence indicates that temporary or short-term memory for written material involves recoding the material into some kind of silent speech, or phonetic representation. This type of representation is used whether the task requires temporary memory for isolated letters, printed nonsense syllables, or printed words. In all of these cases, both the nature of the errors that subjects make in recalling such material and the experimental manipulations that help or hurt their memory performance have shown us that a phonetic representation is being used; i.e., subjects are remembering the items in terms of the consonants and vowels that form the name of each item, rather than the visual shape of the letters, the shape of the words, etc. (cf., e.g., Baddeley, 1978; Conrad, 1964, 1972; Levy, 1977). Furthermore, subjects apparently rely on phonetic representation when they are required to comprehend sentences written in either alphabetic (Kleiman, 1975; Levy, 1977; Slowiaczek and Clifton, 1980) or logographic orthographies (Tzeng et al., 1977). This is one reason why we may observe such significantly high correlations between reading and listening comprehension among a variety of languages and orthographies, including English (cf. Curtis, 1980; Daneman and Carpenter, 1980; Jackson and McClelland, 1979), Japanese, and Chinese (Stevenson et al., 1982).

Thus, regardless of the way in which the reader recognizes each word, the processes involved in reading sentences and paragraphs apparently place certain obvious demands on temporary memory, and temporary memory for language apparently makes use of phonetic representation in short-term memory. The fact that readers make active use of a phonetic representation is an important thing to keep in mind. In Section III.C, we will see that problems with phonetic representation are often found among poor beginning readers in the form of short-term memory problems.

III. LANGUAGE PROBLEMS AS CAUSES OF EARLY READING PROBLEMS

Without spoken English, there would be nothing for the English orthography to transcribe; the well-known difficulties of deaf readers attest to the importance of spoken language skills for successful reading. But deaf children are not the only ones for whom deficient language abilities are a cause of reading problems. As we will see, many hearing children who are poor readers also suffer from spoken language problems, and, although their problems are considerably more subtle than those of the deaf, they are no less critical. However, before discussing this fact, let us first summarize the language skills needed by beginning readers and then mention some of the previously held theories about the causes of reading problems and some of the general evidence that points to a link between reading and language problems. Then we may more appropriately turn to a more detailed survey of various forms of evidence about the types of language skills that are lacking in poor readers and are typical of kindergarten children who will become poor readers in the early elementary grades.

A. Two Types of Language Skills that Are Essential to Beginning Readers

What skills does a child need to learn to read well? Obviously, would-be readers need to possess the visual skills that allow them to differentiate and remember various letter shapes. They also need language-processing skills to perceive and recognize the teacher's words and to combine them into phrases, sentences, and paragraphs as well as to meet the requirements of skilled reading discussed in Section II.B. Finally, they will need to possess phoneme awareness if they are to make any real sense of the way in which the alphabet works.

1. Language-Processing Skills

Beginning readers should possess language-processing skills at four different levels. First, they need the speech perception skills that make it possible to distinguish the words of their vocabulary (e.g., the difference between "cat" and "hat"). They also need vocabulary skills, although they need not necessarily possess mature morphophonological representations in their lexicons, given some evidence that the experience of reading, in and of itself, serves to stimulate and further phonological development (Moskowitz, 1973; Read, 1986). Beginning readers should also have an adequate linguistic short-term memory, because this is not only critical to skilled readers but also supports retention of sufficient words to understand sentences and paragraphs. Finally, they should further be able to recover the syntactic and semantic structure of phrases and sentences (although their mastery of these aspects of language, like their mastery of phonology, may be facilitated by the experience of reading [Goldman, 1976]).

2. Phoneme Awareness

Language-processing skills, however, are only one aspect of the language skills needed by would-be readers of English. As noted in Section II.A, the English orthography requires that successful readers not only be able to process spoken language but also be conscious of certain abstract units of that language—in particular, phonemes. Otherwise, the alphabet will make no sense as a transcription of spoken English. Whereas sophistication about words is sufficient for learning a logography, and sophistication about words and syllables is sufficient for syllabaries, children must know about these units and also about phonemes if the alphabet is to make sense and if they are to use it to its fullest advantage.

Section II.A hinted that phoneme awareness might pose a problem, but why should this be the case? One reason is that phonemes are quite abstract units of language, considerably more abstract than either words or syllables. We reflexively and unconsciously perceive them when we listen to the speech stream, because we have a neurophysiology uniquely and elegantly adapted to that purpose (cf. A. M. Liberman, 1982). However, phonemes cannot be mechanically isolated from each other nor produced in isolation (Liberman et al., 1967) as can syllables and words. There are some very interesting indications that infants may distinguish phonemes (for a recent review of the speech perception capabilities of infant listeners, see Miller and Elmas, 1983), and preschool-aged children most certainly employ phonetic representation when holding linguistic material in short-term memory (Alegria and Pignot, 1979; Elmas, 1975). Yet these are automatic, tacit aspects of language-processing ability, and the child who "knows" his or her language well enough to perceive and remember phonemes can still be blissfully unaware of the fact that these units exist—much the same way that you and I are blissfully unaware of the rods and cones that allow us to see.

The problems with using written language is that the tacit must also become explicit. Successful beginning readers must not only know the difference between words such as "cat" and "hat," and how to hold these words in memory. They must further possess the awareness of phonemes, which allows them to appreciate the fact that, among other things, "cat" and "hat" differ in one phoneme, namely the first, and share a final phoneme, which is the initial one in "top"; otherwise the alphabet will remain a mystery to them, and its virtues are unrealized.

B. The Problem of Specific Reading Difficulty

One way to discover the problems that limit success in learning to read is to examine the differences between children who become poor readers and those who become skilled readers. We have now developed some ideas about where to look for those differences, for it is clear that language-processing and phoneme awareness problems might lead to reading problems. But before we turn to a survey of research that concerns each of these two areas, a bit more background is in order. It is appropriate to consider some of the ways in which psychologists and educators have tried to explain reading disability in the past. We might also ask if there are any indications that a linguistic account of poor reading will be more successful than some of the previously popular theories have been.

1. Some Less Successful Accounts of Poor Reading

As Rutter (1978) has noted, learning to read is a specific example of a complex learning task, which correlates about 0.6 with IQ. Yet a low IQ cannot be the sole basis of reading problems, because some children are backwards in reading ability but average in intelligence (Rutter and Yule, 1973). Children who possess a seemingly adequate IQ (typically 90 or higher) but nonetheless encounter reading problems are said to have a specific reading difficulty, as their actual reading ability lags between 1 and 2 yr behind that which is predicted on the basis of their age, IQ, and social standing. For these children, something other than general intelligence must be the primary cause of many instances of poor reading.

In attempting to discover the cause of early problems, many early theories were biased by an assumption that influenced psychologists and educators alike. That assumption stemmed from the view that reading is first and foremost a complex visual skill that demands differentiation and recognition of visual stimuli. Owing to it, models of skilled reading have often been biased toward clarification of how readers see and recognize the various letter and word shapes, and many studies of the cause of poor reading tried to blame early reading difficulty on some problem in the visual domain. Recently, however, visual theories of reading disability have become less and less popular, for it seems that, at best, only a few of the children who are poor readers actually suffer from perceptual malfunctions that somehow prevent recognition, differentiation, or memory of visual forms. In short, visual skills do not reliably distinguish among children who differ in reading ability (for recent reviews of these findings, see Rutter, 1978; Stanovich, 1982a; Vellutino, 1979), so visual problems would not seem to be the primary cause of many instances of reading problems.

Let me follow Mann and Brady (1988) in mentioning two pieces of supporting evidence that show just how unfair it is to blame the majority of early reading problems on visual problems. First, 5- to 6-yr-old children who were identified as having deficient visual perception and/or visuomotor coordination skills show no more instances of reading difficulty at age 8–9 yr than do matched controls who possess no such deficits (Robinson and Schwartz, 1973). Second, while it is true that all young children tend to confuse spatially reversible letters such as "b" and "d" and "p" and "q" until they are 7 or 8 yr old (Gibson *et al.*, 1962), letter and sequence reversals actually account for only a small proportion of the reading errors that are made by children in this age range. Even children who have been formally diagnosed as dyslexic make relatively few letter and sequence reversal errors (Fisher *et al.*, 1977).

Theories that placed primary emphasis on cross-modal integration have also been popular at one time or another (Birch and Belmont, 1964; see reviews by Benton, 1975; Rutter and Yule, 1973). Their misconception was that reading involved translating visual information into auditory information and that this cross-modal match was the source of the problem. Such theories have met much of the same fate as theories that emphasized visual deficiencies as the cause of reading problems. When investigators carefully examined the behavior of skilled readers, they realized that the translation was not directly from visual to auditory information, visual information was first translated into an abstract linguistic code. When they considered children's ability to map between information presented to the visual and auditory modalities, they also began to realize that an abstract linguistic code was often the basis for the cross-modal integration. Finally, researchers began to realize that when visual–auditory integration problems were present, then so were auditory–auditory problems and even visual–visual ones. Thus, the poor reader's problems with visual–auditory integration have come to be viewed as one of the many consequences of a more general linguistic coding problem, which hurts integration within modalities as well as between them (for a review, see Vellutino, 1979).

Other theories have suffered from similar attempts to explain an observation about poor readers in terms that are somehow too general. For example, certain theories were preoccupied by the fact that reading involves remembering an ordered sequence of letters in a word and of words in a sentence, etc. Hence, it was suggested that poor sequential order memory (Corkin, 1974) or poor short-term memory (Morrison *et al.*, 1977) might be a cause of poor reading. A focus on memory problems was not a bad direction for theories to take, but some other observations about the specific pattern of poor readers disabilities and abilities indicate that some refinements are in order. Good and poor readers do not differ on all tasks that require temporary memory of items or their order. Good and poor beginning readers are equivalent, for example, in ability to remember faces (Liberman *et al.*, 1982) or visual stimuli that cannot readily be assigned verbal labels (Katz *et al.*, 1981; Liberman *et al.*, 1982; Swanson, 1978). Only when the to-be-remembered stimuli can be linguistically coded do children who are poor readers consistently fail to do as well as good readers (Liberman *et al.*, 1982; Katz *et al.*, 1981; Swanson, 1978).

Various other general or visual accounts of reading disability have been offered in the literature (for a review, see, Carr (1981). These tend to be inadequate because they fail to explain why poor readers often do as well as good readers on nonlinguistic tasks, yet lag behind good readers in performance on many linguistic tasks (for recent reviews, see Mann and Brady, 1988; Stanovich, 1982a,b; Vellutino, 1979). For the sake of brevity, such general accounts will not be discussed here; instead, let us turn to the more positive task of reviewing that evidence which links language and reading problems.

2. A Language-Based Perspective May Offer a Better Account

The previous paragraphs mentioned several studies that demonstrate that good and poor readers are distinguished by their performance on certain linguistic tasks but not by their performance on comparably demanding nonlinguistic ones (e.g., as shown by Brady *et al.*, 1983; Katz *et al.*, 1981; Liberman *et al.*, 1982; Mann and Liberman, 1984; Swanson, 1978). That evidence receives further support from a consideration of the frequency of reading difficulties in children with various sorts of handicaps. As Rutter (1978) observes, whereas children deficient in visual–perceptual and/or visual–motor skills do not encounter reading difficulty any more frequently than matched controls (Money, 1973; Robinson and Schwartz, 1973), speech- and language-retarded children encounter reading problems at least six times often than controls do (Ingram *et al.*, 1970; Mason, 1976). But we can ask whether there is a more fine-grained analysis of the language problems found among poor readers. Are some areas of language skill more problematic than others? Considered broadly, the language disabilities that tend to be found among poor beginning readers fall within the two categories of language processing and phoneme awareness. Let us now proceed to examine the evidence within each area.

C. Language-Processing Problems Associated with Poor Reading

Since the mid-1970s, activity in the psychology of early reading problems has been considerable, and study after study has uncovered some link between difficulties in learning to read and difficulties with some aspect of spoken language processing. Such a link is clearly established beyond question, not only in English (for a review, cf. Mann, 1986) but in Swedish (Lundberg *et al.*, 1980), Japanese, and Chinese (Stevenson *et al.*, 1982) as well. In the case of English, there have also been considerable attempts to more precisely specify the nature of the language problems that typify poor beginning readers. These attempts can be organized in terms of the four levels of language processing that were identified in Section III.A.1 as being important to beginning reading: speech perception, vocabulary skills, linguistic short-term memory, and syntax and semantics.

1. Speech Perception

The possibility that some aspect of speech perception might be a special problem for poor readers receives support from a study by Brady *et al.* (1983). Their research considered a group of beginning readers who did not differ from each other in age, IQ, or audiometry scores but strongly differed in reading ability. The children were asked to identify spoken words or environmental sounds under a normal listening condition and under a noisy condition, and the performance of the good and poor readers was compared. The results indicated that the good and poor readers could equally identify the environmental sounds, whatever the listening condition. As long as the words were not masked by noise, the good and poor readers performed equivalently on these items as well, but the poor readers made almost 33% more errors than the good readers when they were asked to identify the spoken words in the noisy condition. This result implies, as other research has suggested (Goetzinger *et al.*, 1960), that poor readers have difficulties with speech perception when the listening conditions are less than optimal.

Another suggestion to this effect comes from studies that compare the categorical perception of synthetic speech stimuli by good and poor beginning readers. In such studies, categorical perception was evident in both groups of subjects; yet the poor readers differed from the good readers either in failing to meet the level of intercategory discrimination predicted on the basis of their identification responses (Brandt and Rosen, 1980) or in failing to give as consistent identification responses (Godfrey *et al.*, 1981). These findings have been interpreted as the reflection of deficient speech perception processes on the part of poor readers (but they may also relate to a problem with remembering speech sounds, because memory plays an obvious role in discrimination tasks as well as in many identification tasks).

2. Vocabulary Skills

There are quite a few indications that reading ability is related to certain vocabulary skills, depending on how reading ability is measured and on what type of vocabulary skill is at issue. Reading ability can be measured in terms of the ability to read individual words (decoding) or to understand the meaning of sentences and paragraphs (comprehension). In the case of beginning readers, decoding and comprehension tests are correlated quite highly, implying that children who differ on one type of test will usually differ on the other as well. Still, in some cases the two types of tests identify different groups of good and poor readers that may lead researchers to different conclusions about the cause of poor reading (for discussion, see Stanovich, 1988). Vocabulary skills is a case in point; future research may uncover other cases as well.

Vocabulary skills are also tested with two different types of test. One type is recognition vocabulary tests such as the Peabody Picture Vocabulary Test, which requires the child to point to a picture that illustrates a word. Recognition vocabulary has sometimes been related to early reading ability (see Stanovich et al., 1984b), although it is not always a very significant predictor (see Wolf and Goodglass, 1986). The utility of this test may depend on how reading ability is measured, as the relationship seems stronger for tests of reading comprehension like the Reading Survey of the Metropolitan (see Stanovich et al., 1988) than for tests of word recognition such as the Word Identification and Word Attack tests of the Woodcock (see Mann and Liberman, 1984).

The other type of vocabulary test is naming or productive vocabulary tests such as the Boston Naming Test, which requires the child to produce the word that a picture illustrates. Productive vocabulary gives clearer indications of a link between reading ability and vocabulary skill, and evidence indicates that this link exists whether reading skills are measured in terms of decoding or comprehension. Performance on the Boston Naming Test predicted both the word recognition and the reading comprehension ability of kindergarten children far more accurately than did performance on the Peabody Picture Vocabulary Test (Wolf, 1984; Wolf and Goodglass, 1986). Tests of continuous naming (sometimes called rapid automatized naming), which require children to name a series of repeating objects, letters, or colors, also show that children who are poor readers require more time to name the series than good readers do (see, e.g., Denckia and Rudel, 1976; Blachman, 1984; Wolf, 1984).

A causal link between naming problems and reading problems is indicated by the discovery that performance on naming tests can predict future reading ability. Wolf (1984) noted that, whereas continuous naming tests using objects and colors are predictive of early problems with word recognition, problems with rapid letter recognition and retrieval play a more prolonged role in the reading of severely impaired readers, even in reading comprehension. In the author's laboratory, students and the author have been using a test of letter-naming ability in longitudinal studies of kindergarten children (Mann, 1984; Mann and Ditunno, 1990) and have consistently found that kindergarteners who take more time to name a randomized array of the capital letters are significantly more likely to perform poorly on word decoding tests and comprehension tests that are administered in first grade. Furthermore, present letter naming apparently predicts future reading ability more consistently than present reading ability predicts future letter naming ability (for relevent evidence, see Mann and Ditunno, in press; also see Stanovich *et al.*, 1988). Thus, something other than a lack of educational experience probably is preventing these children from naming the letter names as fast as other children can, and that something could be a problem with productive vocabulary skills.

A final piece of evidence about the vocabulary problems of poor readers comes from a study by Katz (1986), who found that children who perform poorly on a decoding test are particularly prone to difficulties in producing low-frequency and polysyllabic names and suggested that, for such words, these children may possess less phonologically complete lexical representations than good readers do. On the basis of his research, he further suggests that, because poor readers often have access to aspects of the correct phonological representation of a word, even though they are unable to produce that word correctly, their problem may be attributable to phonological deficiencies in the structure of the lexicon rather than to the process of lexical access, per se.

3. Phonetic Short-Term Memory

The observation that poor readers perform less well than good readers on a variety of short-term memory tests has given rise to one of the more fruitful lines of research in the field (see Mann and Brady, 1988). It has often been noted that poor readers tend to perform less well on the digit span test and are deficient in the ability to recall strings of letters, nonsense syllables, or words in order, whether the stimuli are presented by ear or by eye. Poor readers even fail to recall the words of spoken sentences as accurately as good readers do (for references to these effects, see Jorm, 1979; Mann *et al.*, 1980). Evidence that these differences are not merely consequences of differences in reading ability has come from a longitudinal study that showed that problems with recalling a sequence of words can precede the attainment of reading ability and may actually serve to presage future reading problems (Mann and Liberman, 1984).

In searching for an explanation of this pattern of results, researchers turned to the research that was discussed in Section II.B, namely that research that indicated that linguistic materials such as letters, words, etc. are held in short-term memory through use of phonetic representation. Liberman, Shankweiler, and their colleagues (Shankweiler *et al.*, 1979) were the first to suggest that the linguistic short-term memory difficulties of poor readers might reflect a problem with using this type of representation. Several experiments have supported this hypothesis. These show that when recalling letter strings (Shankweiler *et al.*, 1979), word strings (Mann *et al.*, 1980; Mann and Liberman, 1984), and sentences (Mann *et al.*, 1980) poor readers are much less sensitive than good readers to a manipulation of the phonetic structure of the materials (i.e., the density of words that rhyme). Indeed, good readers can be made to appear like poor readers when they are asked to recall a string of words in which all of the words rhyme (such as "bat," "cat," "rat," "hat," and "mat"), whereas poor readers perform at the same level whether the words rhyme or not. This observation had led to the postulation that poor readers— and children who are likely to become poor readers—are for some reason less able to use phonetic structure as a means of holding material in short-term memory (Mann *et al.*, 1980; Mann and Liberman, 1984; Shankweiler *et al.*, 1979).

One might ask, at this point, whether poor readers are avoiding phonetic representation altogether or merely using it less well. We have obtained little evidence that poor readers employ a visual form of memory instead of a phonetic one (Mann, 1984), although there have been indications that they may place greater reliance on word meaning (Byrne and Shea, 1979). Evidence that poor readers are attempting to use phonetic representation has been found in the types of errors that they make as they attempt to recall or recognize spoken words in a short-term memory task (Brady *et al.*, 1983, 1989). These errors reveal that poor readers make use of many of the same features of phonetic structure as good readers do. They make the same sort of phonetically principled errors—they merely make more of them.

4. Syntax and Semantics

Do poor readers have a problem with the syntax (grammar) and the semantics (meaning) of language in addition to their problem with speech perception, vocabulary, and using phonetic structure in short-term memory? The observation that poor readers cannot repeat sentences as well as good readers has led to some obvious questions about these higher-level language skills and their involvement in reading problems.

Quite a few studies have examined the syntactic abilities of poor readers. An accumulating body of evidence indicates that poor readers do not comprehend sentences as well as good readers do (for a review, see Mann *et al.*, 1989). It has been shown that good and poor readers differ in the ability both to repeat and to comprehend spoken sentences that contain relative clauses such as "the dog jumped over the cat that chased the monkey" (Mann *et al.*, 1985). They also perform less well on instructions from the Token Test such as "touch the small red square and the large blue triangle" (Smith *et al.*, 1987). They also are less able to distinguish the meaning of spoken sentences such as "he showed her bird the seed" from "he showed her the birdseed," which use the stress pattern of the sentence (its prosody) and the position of the article "the" to mark the boundary between the indirect object and the direct object.

To explain these and other sentence comprehension problems that have been observed among poor readers, the author and her colleagues have been struck by the fact that a short-term memory problem could lead to problems with comprehending sentences whose processing somehow stresses short-term memory. When they examined the results of the studies mentioned above, they found little evidence that the poor readers were having trouble with the grammatical structures being used in the sentences that caused them problems. In fact, the structures were often ones that young children master within the first few years of life and ones that the poor readers could understand if the sentence was short enough (for a discussion, see Mann *et al.*, 1989). Instead, they found much evidence that the comprehension problem was predominantly due to the memory problem discussed in the previous section. It seems as if poor readers are just as sensitive to syntactic structure as good readers; they fail to understand sentences because they cannot hold an adequate representation of the sentence in short-term memory (for discussion, see Mann *et al.*, 1985, 1989; Smith *et al.*, in press).

At present, then, while it is clear that poor readers do have sentence comprehension problems, there is little reason to think that their difficulties reflect a problem with the syntax of language. But the issue of whether or not poor readers are deficient in syntactic skills is far from resolved and will have to await further research. Goldman (1976) is correct in noting that such syntactic differences as have been reported among good and poor readers could be either the cause of reading difficulty or a consequence of different amounts of reading experience. It is also worth noting that such deficits as do exist are relatively subtle, with poor readers merely performing as somewhat younger children rather than as good readers.

As for the question of semantic impairments among poor readers, here, there is no reason to presume any real deviance exists. If anything, poor readers place greater reliance on semantic context and semantic representation than good readers do, perhaps in compensation for their other language difficulties (for a review, see Stanovitch, 1982b; also see Byrne and Shea, 1979; Simpson *et al.*, 1983.)

D. Problems with Phoneme Awareness Associated with Poor Reading

Possessing adequate phonetic perception and short-term memory skills, an adequate mental lexicon, and the ability to recover the syntactic and semantic structure of utterances is only part of the requirement of reading success. As noted in Section II.B, successful readers of the alphabet must go beyond these tacit language-processing abilities to achieve an explicit awareness of phonemes. Let us now turn to studies concerned with the pertinence of phonological sophistication to success in learning to read an alphabetic orthography.

1. Evidence from the Analysis of Reading Errors

The errors that a person makes can be informative about the difficulties that produce those errors, and oral reading errors can offer an important source of evidence about the cause of reading problems. A consideration of these errors has shown that a lack of phoneme awareness is responsible for making beginning reading difficult for all young children (Shankweiler and Liberman, 1972), including dyslexic ones (Fisher *et al.*, 1977). As noted earlier, such errors do not tend to involve visual confusions or letter or sequence reversals to any appreciable degree. What they did apparently reflect is a problem with integrating the phonological information that letter sequences convey. Hence, children often tend to be correct as to the pronunciation of the first letter in a word but have more and more difficulty with subsequent letters, with a particular problem with vowels as opposed to consonants. For more detailed presentation of these findings and their implications, the reader is referred to papers by Shankweiler and Liberman (1972) and Fisher *et al.* (1977) and also to a paper by Russell (1982b), which suggests that deficient phoneme awareness may account for the reading difficulties of adult dyslexics.

2. Evidence from Tasks that Measure Awareness Directly

Most of the studies of phoneme awareness have concerned tasks that directly measure awareness. These tasks require children to play language "games" that manipulate the phonemes within a word in one way or another: counting them, deleting them, choosing words that contain the same phoneme, etc. The use of these tasks has revealed that phoneme awareness develops later than phonetic perception and the use of phonetic representation and remains a chronic problem for those individuals who are poor readers.

Research involving such tasks began with a study by Liberman and her colleagues who asked whether or not a sample of 4–6-yr-olds could learn to play syllable counting games and phoneme counting games in which the idea was to tap the number of syllables–phonemes in a spoken word (Liberman *et al.*, 1974). It was discovered that none of the nursery school children could tap the number of phonemes in a spoken word, while half of them managed to tap the number of syllables. Only 17% of the kindergarteners could tap phonemes, while, again, about half of them could tap syllables. At 6 yr old, 90% of the children could tap syllables, and 70% could tap phonemes. From such findings about children's sensitivity to the number of phonemes and syllables in spoken words, the awareness of phonemes and syllables clearly develops considerably between the ages of 4 and 6 yr. It is also clear that awareness of phonemes is slower to develop than awareness of syllables. Finally, both types of awareness markedly improve at just the age when children are learning to read (Liberman *et al.*, 1974).

Numerous experiments involving widely diverse subjects, school systems, and measurement devices have shown a strong positive correlation between a lack of awareness about phonemes and current problems in learning to read (see, e.g., Alegria *et al.*, 1982; Fox and Routh, 1976; Lundberg *et al.*, 1980; Liberman *et al.*, 1980b; Perfetti, 1985; Yopp, 1988). Also, evidence indicates that lack of awareness about syllables is associated with reading disability (Katz, 1986). Finally, studies of kindergarten children provide evidence that problems with phoneme segmentation (Blachman, 1984; Helfgott, 1976) and problems with syllable segmentation (Mann and Liberman, 1984; Wagner *et al.*, in press) can presage future reading difficulty. For example, we have found that 85% of a population of kindergarten children who went on to become good readers in the first grade correctly counted the number of syllables in spoken words, whereas only 17% of the future poor readers could do so (Mann and Liberman, 1984). In another study, a kindergarten battery of tests that assessed phoneme awareness accounted for 66% of the variance in children's first-grade reading ability (Stanovich *et al.*, 1984a).

IV. SOME PLAUSIBLE ORIGINS OF THE LANGUAGE PROBLEMS THAT LEAD TO READING PROBLEMS

Having surveyed some, though certainly not all, of the many findings that link reading difficulty to problems with language skills, we can now appropriately consider a related line of research that concerns the causes of the language problems that lead to reading problems. Both theoretical and practical matters are at stake in such research, because if we knew why poor readers are lacking in certain language skills, then we might be able to develop more effective means of early diagnosis and more remedies for reading difficulty.

Much of the available literature on the causes of language-processing problems is centered on what will be referred to here to as constitutional causes. These involve those factors that are somehow intrinsic to the child, such as his or her brain structure, genetic makeup, and rate of physical development. Problems with phoneme awareness have also been explained in these terms, but it has been more common to attribute problems in this area to a lack of sufficient experience, such as insufficient exposure to instruction in the use of an alphabetic writing system. We shall consider constitutional explanations and experiential explanations in turn.

A. Constitutional Factors

As representative examples of theories that place the cause of a child's language problems within the child's constitution, genetic theories, neuropsychological theories, and the theories that postulate some type of developmental lag have been chosen. Each of the following sections contains a representative, but by no means exhaustive, summary of each type of account, and the different accounts should not be taken as mutually exclusive. For example, a genetic account might help a neuropsychological account to explain why the brains of poor readers are subtly different from those of good readers, and both of these accounts may help to explain why the language development of many poor readers seem delayed.

1. Genetic Theories

That reading problems and language problems do tend to run in certain families was first noted by Thomas (1905), and has received considerable attention in recent literature as well (see, e.g., Owen, 1978; Owen et al., 1971; Rutter, 1978). In fact, whether or not a child comes from a family that contains other dyslexic individuals is one of the most important factors to consider when attempting to predict that child's likelihood of becoming a poor reader (see Scarborough, 1988).

Further evidence about the genetic basis of dyslexia has become available through the use of more sophisticated forms of analysis. Ample evidence now indicates that the concordance rate of dyslexia in monozygotic (i.e., identical) twins is consistently higher than in dizygotic (fraternal) ones, and the Colorado Twin Study is addressing this point (see DeFries et al., 1987). There is also interesting information about the type of genetic transmission. Some instances of dyslexia have been linked to an aberration on chromosome 15 (Smith et al., 1983). There are also some indications of considerable genetic heterogeneity (Smith et al., 1986). Research on the genetic basis of dyslexia will surely be an exciting area for years to come.

2. Neuropsychological Accounts

Neuropsychological accounts seek to place the cause of the language problem within the brain structure of the affected child. One of the first accounts of this sort was offered by Orton (1937) in his now famous theory of strephosymbolia. In that theory, mirror reversals (which Orton erroneously thought to be the predominant symptom of reading disability) were attributed to insufficiently developed cerebral dominance. This insufficiency further manifested itself, according to Orton, in such abnormalities of lateral preference as mixed dominance.

Orton's theory has given rise to considerable research. On the one hand, it has been falsified by findings that reading difficulty is not associated with any particular pattern of handedness, eyedness, or footedness (for a review, see Rutter, 1978). It has also motivated quite a number of studies of cerebral lateralization for language processing among good and poor readers, with mixed results. Some such studies have provided evidence that poor readers show a reversal of the normal anatomical assymmetries between the left and right hemispheres, in conjunction with a lower verbal IQ (Hier *et al.*, 1978). Others have reported that poor readers may show a lack of cerebral dominance for language processing (see, e.g., Keefe and Swinney, 1979; Zurif and Carson, 1970). But, at best, only a weak association can exist between abnormal lateralization and poor reading, because not all of the individuals who display abnormal cerebral lateralization are poor readers (Hier *et al.*, 1978). It must also be recognized that several other studies have failed to find that good and poor readers differ in the extent or direction of the lateralization for language processing (Fennel *et al.*, 1983; McKeever and van Deventer, 1975).

Overall, the data are not particularly supportive of Orton's thesis about incomplete cerebral dominance as the explanation of reading difficulty; however, Orton may still have been correct in the spirit, if not the letter, of his explanation. If we accept the left hemisphere to be the mediator of language processing (in the majority of individuals), and if we accept that language processes are deficient among poor readers, then certainly we may suppose that some anatomical or neurochemical abnormality of the left hemisphere is involved in early reading difficulty. This is the position taken in a new neuropsychological theory by Geschwind and Galaburda (1987), which views developmental dyslexia as a consequence of slowed development of the left hemisphere. The slowed development is postulated to be a consequence of early exposure to the hormone testosterone, which explains the greater instance of reading problems among young boys. Thus far, the Geschwind and Galaburda theory is supported by autopsies of the brains of several adult dyslexics and by a certain profile of disabilities (language problems), abilities (spatial skills), and other traits (left handedness, allergies) that distinguish the population of dyslexics from the general population. Further tests of this theory are a topic for future research.

3. Maturational Lag Accounts

The third class of constitutional explanations seeks to explain poor readers' language difficulties as the consequence of a maturational lag in development (see, e.g., Fletcher *et al.*, 1981), which may be specific to language development (Mann and Liberman, 1984), especially in the case of dyslexic children (Stanovich, 1988). Maturational lag has been offered to explain the problems of young children who are poor readers, their word decoding problems (Stanovich, 1988), their speech perception difficulties (Brandt and Rosen, 1980), their problems with phonetic representation in temporary memory and their problems with phoneme awareness (Mann and Liberman, 1984; Watson and Engle, 1982), and their sentence comprehension problems (Mann et al., 1989). Such theories also provide an interesting account of adolescent learning disability, (Wong et al., 1989).

Maturational lag theories have the virtue of providing a ready explanation of one of the more common findings in the field, namely that the performance of poor readers never really deviates from that of good readers but, rather, merely involves more of the kinds of errors typical of slightly younger children (Mann et al., 1989). They are also consistent with some other observations about the population of poor readers. First, there is the observation that boys encounter reading problems more often than girls (Mann and Liberman, 1980; Rutter and Yule, 1973). It is well known that boys mature less rapidly than girls do. It has also been shown that a slower rate of physical maturation tends to be associated with a pattern of mental abilities in which spatial processing skills are superior to language (Waber, 1977). Given these observations, one should expect to find disproportionately many boys with lesser language skills and, hence, disproportionately many boys who encounter reading difficulty among children at a given age. It is also the case that children with low birthweight are at risk for reading problems (Rutter and Yule, 1973). Low birthweight often reflects a premature birth, and prematurely born infants may reach the first milestones of language development relatively later in postgestational life than do those infants born at full term (Gleitman, 1981). Hence, they show a lag in language development and would be expected to encounter reading problems.

The primary difficulty with the concept of maturational lag is that it cannot, as yet, explain why only certain language difficulties tend to be found among poor readers. Perhaps we might want to conceive of a maturational lag that is confined to one area of language skill, given the findings summarized earlier. We will have more to say about the identity of this area in the final section of this chapter. Another problem with maturational lag theories is that the language-processing difficulties of poor readers can persist after early childhood to adolescence (McKeever and van Deventer, 1975) and beyond (Scarborough, 1984; Jackson and McClelland, 1979); i.e., the language-processing skills of poor readers may never really catch up to those of good readers. Perhaps the concept of a lag in development will need to be refined to allow for the possibility that language development in poor readers is not only delayed but also reaches a premature plateau. In any event, such problems are not insurmountable, and the possibility that reading difficulty involves a specific maturational lag in the development of language-processing skills is a most intriguing one, which should spark considerable research in the years to come.

B. Experiential Factors

Rutter and Madge (1976) noted that poor reading and low verbal intelligence tend to associate with low socioeconomic status and large family size. In discussing their findings about "cycles of disadvantage," these investigators note that both genetic and environmental influences are to be held responsible. We have already discussed the possibility of a genetic basis for reading problems, so let us now turn to the evidence that the environment can play an important role in the language skills that are important to reading. Experience is no doubt important to the child's development of the language-processing skills involved in speech perception, vocabulary, etc.; however, the role of the environment in poor readers' problems in these areas has not been very well explored and remains a topic for future research. However a wealth of evidence exists on the role of the environment—the educational environment—in the development of phoneme awareness.

In considering the role of the environment in the development of phoneme awareness, let us return to the spurt in phoneme awareness that occurs at the age of 6 yr (Liberman *et al.*, 1974). Why should such a spurt occur? Phoneme awareness is a cognitive skill of sorts, and, as such, must surely demand the attainment of a certain degree of intellectual maturity. Yet, 6 yr is the age at which most children in America begin to receive instruction in reading and writing, and there is reason to suspect that not only may phoneme awareness be important for the acquisition of reading, being taught to read may at the same time help to develop phoneme awareness (see, e.g., Alegria, *et al.*, 1982; Liberman *et al.*, 1980b; Morais, *et al.*, 1979).

It has been reported that illiterate adults are unable to manipulate the phonetic structure of spoken words (Morais *et al.*, 1979). Another study, conducted in Belgium, reveals that first graders taught largely by a phonics method did spectacularly better on a task requiring phoneme segmentation than did other children taught by a largely whole-word method (Alegria *et al.*, 1982). It would seem that awareness of phonemes is enhanced by methods of reading instruction that direct the child's attention to the phonetic structure of words, and it may even depend on such instruction.

However, experience alone cannot be the only factor behind some children's failure to achieve phoneme awareness. This is aptly shown by a finding that among a group of 6-yr-old skilled readers and 10-yr-old disabled readers who were matched for reading ability, the disabled readers performed significantly worse on a phoneme awareness task, even though they would be expected to have had more reading instruction than the younger children (Bradley and Bryant, 1978). Here it could be argued that some constitutional factor limited the disabled readers' ability to profit from instruction and, thus, limited their attainment of phonological sophistication. Indeed, Pennington *et al.* (in press) have offered some new and interesting evidence that deficient phoneme awareness is the primary trait of individuals who are familiar dyslexics.

V. SUMMARY AND CONCLUDING REMARKS

This chapter has proceeded from a consideration of the importance of certain language skills to reading, to a survey of evidence that links problems with these language skills to early reading disability, to a consideration of some plausible origins of these problems. By way of a conclusion, a generalization about the type of language problems that cause reading problems and about how we might improve upon our characterization of the relation between reading and language problems is now offered. Also, a few words speculate about the prospects for future research in the prediction and prevention of reading problems.

A. The Phonological Core Deficit: A Language-Oriented Perspective on Reading Problems

The survey of the literature on the relation between language-processing skills and reading problems indicates that poor readers—and children who are likely to become poor readers—tend to have problems with phoneme awareness and also with three aspects of language-processing skill: (1) speech perception under difficult listening conditions; (2) vocabulary, especially when vocabulary is measured in terms of naming ability; and (3) using a phonetic representation in linguistic short-term memory. A logical interrelation exists among these difficulties, for they all involve phonological processes that concern the sound pattern of language. Hence, we may speculate that the cause of many instances of reading disability is some problem within the phonological system, something that could be referred to as a phonological core deficit (see Mann, 1986; Stanovich, 1988).

In this chapter, the emphasis has been on the language problems of reading-disabled children, in general, and no attempt has been made to differentiate between dyslexic children and so-called "garden-variety" poor readers. From the perspective of present research, both groups of children seem to form a continuous distribution (see Stanovich, 1988). Both have problems with the phonological skills of primary interest in this paper, and the phonological core deficit seems just as characteristic of dyslexic children as of garden-variety poor readers. To date, the only language measure that distinguishes the two groups of children is receptive vocabulary, which may account for the lack of consensus about the role of receptive vocabulary problems in reading, as discussed in Section III.C.2. All other differences among the groups seem to involve real world knowledge and strategic abilities: The dyslexic children possess superior skills in these nonlinguistic areas, hence the discrepancy between their IQ and their reading ability, whereas the garden-variety poor readers may show a developmental delay in these skills as well as in their phonological ones (for a discussion, see Stanovich, 1988).

Future research can help us approach a more accurate description of the phonological core deficit and its role in the reading problems of different groups of children. For example, it may also help us discern the extent of differences among children within each group, informing us as to whether there are different problems or different clusters of problems for different children. In this regard, it is interesting to note Pennington and his colleagues' observation that the language problems of adults from dyslexic families tend to be restricted to phenome awareness, whereas those of individuals from nondyslexic families demonstrate problems with linguistic short-term memory as well as problems with phoneme awareness (Pennington et al., in press). In the future, researchers will surely try to determine whether or not this distinction applies to the population of young children who have reading problems as well as it applies to that of adult disabled readers.

B. Practical Applications and Implications for Future Research

One of the practical benefits of the research described in this chapter is its potential for suggesting ways of predicting and remediating early reading difficulty. One obvious benefit concerns screening devices for identifying children at risk for early reading problems. Phonological processing skills such as the ability to rapidly access the names of objects and the ability to make effective use of phonetic representation in short-term memory have already been shown to be effective kindergarten predictors of first-grade reading success (see, e.g., Blachman, 1984; Mann and Liberman, 1984; Mann, 1984; Mann and Ditunno, 1990). It is a task for future research to consider other tests such as tests of speech perception and tests of the ability to comprehend sentences that place special demands on short-term memory. It will also be important for future studies to address the very practical matter of how to administer such tests to groups of children; thus far, the studies that have successfully predicted future reading problems have involved two or more sessions of individual testing and would not be practical for large-scale use in public school systems.

Some evidence indicates that tests of phoneme and syllable awareness may be even better predictors of reading ability than tests of language processing (Mann and Ditunno, 1990; Yopp, 1988). Thus, it is even more important that such tests be refined for practical administration to groups of children. In this regard, the author and her students have had some success in developing an "invented spelling test," in which preliterate children are asked to try to write some familiar words. Their responses are quite unconventional but show considerable creativity and considerable awareness of the fact that words can be broken down into smaller phonological units. When those responses are scored in terms of their ability to capture the sound of the word the child is trying to spell, we find this score to be a very successful kindergarten predictor of first-grade reading ability (for discussion of the test, see Mann *et al.*, 1987; Mann and Ditunno, 1990).

The research surveyed by this chapter may also be of interest to those who are concerned with the remediation of reading problems. As we come closer to identifying the linguistic problems associated with specific reading difficulty—and their causes—we should also come closer to pointing the way toward more effective procedures for remediation of those problems. For example, if a maturational lag in language development is the cause of reading difficulty, then perhaps we should attempt to identify children at risk for such a lag and consider delaying beginning reading instruction until a point in time when those children have language skills that are more optimal. However, we would not want to delay all education—math, geography, etc.—for it is far from clear that poor readers, especially dyslexic ones, are lagging in those areas of development that support the ability to learn other types of curriculum (see Mann *et al.*, 1989; Stanovich, 1988). We might also want to continue researching the possibility that environmental enrichment can decrease the extent of these children's language-processing problems and pursue research to that effect.

Certainly the brightest prospects for remediation are offered by research that has shown that various types of training can facilitate phoneme awareness. Elsewhere, the author and her colleagues have suggested that the best favor we can do for all children is to promote their phoneme awareness so that we may let them in on the secrets of the alphabetic principle as early as possible. (I. Y. Liberman, 1982; Liberman and Mann, 1980; Mann, 1986). Some very interesting and very practical advice on how to facilitate phoneme awareness is currently available from the work of such researchers as Liberman, Blachman, Bradley, and their colleagues (Blachman, 1984, 1989; Bradley and Bryant, 1985; I. Y. Liberman, 1982; Mann and Liberman, 1984; Liberman *et al.*, 1980b). They offer a variety of word games, nursery rhymes, and other prereading activities that will encourage the child's awareness of the way in which words break down into phonemes. Such activities will undoubtedly pave the way for phonics-oriented methods of instruction so obviously favored by current research (see Chall, 1979; Morais, in press) and so obviously in keeping with this chapter's focus on the importance of phoneme awareness in early reading.

Acknowledgments

Much of the research herein described was funded by NICHD Grant HD-01994 and BRS Grant 05596 to Haskins Laboratories, Inc. Many of the same points were made in two other technical papers (Mann, 1986; Mann and Brady, 1988).

References

Alegria, J., and Pignot, E. (1979). Genetic aspects of verbal mediation in memory. *Child Dev.* **50,** 235–238.

Alegria, J., Pignot, E., and Morais, J. (1982). Phonetic analysis of speech and memory codes in beginning readers. *Mem. Cognit.* **10,** 451–456.

Baddeley, A. D. (1978). The trouble with levels: A reexamination of Craik and Lockhardt's framework for memory research. *Psycholog. Rev.* **85,** 139–152.

Benton, A. (1975). Developmental dyslexia: Neurological aspects. *In* "Advances in Neurology," Vol. 7 (W. J. Freelander, ed.). Raven Press, pp. 1–47. New York.

Birch, H. G., and Belmont, L. (1964). Auditory–visual integration in normal and retarded readers. *Am. J. Orthopsych.* **34,** 852–861.

Blachman, B. (1984). Relationship of rapid naming and language analysis skills to kindergarten and first-grade reading achievement. *J. Educ. Psychol.* **76,** 610–622.

Blachman, B. (1989). Phonological awareness and word recognition: Assessment and intervention. *In* (A. G. Kamhi and H. W. Watts, eds.), "Reading Disabilities: A Developmental Language Perspective" pp. 133–158. College Hill, Boston.

Bradley, L., and Bryant, P. E. (1978). Difficulties in auditory organization as a possible cause of reading backwards. *Nature* **271,** 746–747.

Bradley, L., and Bryant, P. (1985). "Rhyme and Reason in Reading and Spelling." University of Michigan Press, Ann Arbor.

Brady, S., Shankweiler, D., and Mann. V. (1983). Speech perception and memory coding in relation to reading ability. *J. Exp. Child Psychol.* **35,** 345–367.

Brandt, J., and Rosen, J. J. (1980). Auditory phonemic perception in dyslexia: Categorical identification and discrimination of stop consonants. *Brain Lang.* **9,** 324–337.

Bryden, M. P. (1972). Auditory–visual and sequential–spatial imaging in relation to reading ability. *Child Dev.* **43,** 824–832.

Byrne, B., and Shea, P. (1979). Semantic and phonetic memory in beginning readers. *Mem. Cognit.* **7,** 333–338.

Carr, T. H. (1981). Building theories of reading ability: On the relation between individual differences in cognitive skills and reading comprehension. *Cognition* **9**, 73–114.

Chall, J. (1979). The great debate: Ten years later with a modest proposal for reading stages. *In* "Theory and Practice of Early Reading," Vol. 1 (L. Resnick and P. Weaver, eds.), pp. 29–55. Lawrence Erlbaum, Hillsdale, New Jersey.

Chomsky, N. (1964). Comments for project literacy meeting. Project Literacy Report No. 2, pp. 1–8. (M. Lester, ed.). "Reading in Applied Transformational Grammar" Reprinted *in* Holt Rienhardt and Winston, New York.

Conrad, R. (1964). Acoustic confusions in immediate memory. *Br. J. Psychol.* **55**, 75–84.

Conrad, R. (1972). Speech and reading. *In* "Language by Ear and by Eye: The Relationships between Speech and Reading" (J. F. Kavanaugh and I. G. Mattingly, eds.). pp. 205–240. MIT Press, Cambridge.

Corkin, S. (1974). Serial-order deficits in inferior readers. *Neuropsychologia* **12**, 347–354.

Crowder, R. (1982). "The Psychology of Reading." Academic Press, New York.

Curtis, M. E. (1980). Development of components of reading skill. *J. Educ. Psychol.* **72**, 656–669.

Daneman, M., and Carpenter, P. A. (1980). Individual differences in working memory and reading. *J. Verbal Learn. Verbal Behav.* **19**, 450–466.

Daneman, M., and Case, R. (1981). Syntactic form, semantic complexity and short-term memory: Influences on children's acquisition of new linguistic structures. *Dev. Psychol.* **17**, 367–378.

DeFries, J. C., Fulker, D. W., and LaBuda, M. C. (1987). Evidence for a genetic etiology in reading disability of twins. *Nature* **329**, 537–539.

Denckla, M. B., and Rudel, R. G. (1976). Naming of object drawings by dyslexic and other learning-disabled children. *Brain Lang.* **3**, 1–15.

Eimas, P. D. (1975). Distinctive feature codes in the short-term memory of children. *J. Exp. Child Psychol.* **19**, 241–251.

Fennell, E. B., Satz, P., and Morris, R. (1983). The development of handedness and dichotic ear assymetries in relation to school achievement: A longitudinal study. *J. Exp. Child Psychol.* **35**, 248–262.

Fisher, F. W. Liberman, I. Y., and Shankweiler, D. (1977). Reading reversals and developmental dyslexia: A further study. *Cortex* **14**, 496–510.

Fletcher, J. M., Satz, P., and Scholes, R. (1981). Developmental changes in the linguistic performance correlates of reading achievements. *Brain Lang.* **13**, 78–90.

Fox, B., and Routh, D. K. (1976). Phonemic analysis and synthesis as word-attack skills. *J. Educ. Psychol.* **69**, 70–74.

Geschwind, N., and Galaburda, A. M. (1987). "Cerebral Lateralization." Bradford Books, Cambridge.

Gibson, E. J. Gibson, J. J. Pick, A. D., and Osser, R. (1962). A developmental study of the discrimination of letter-like forms. *J. Comp. Physiolog. Psychol.* **55**, 897–906.

Gleitman, L. R. (1981). Maturational determinants of language growth. *Cognition* **10**, 103–114.

Godfrey, J. L., Syrdal-Lasky, A. K., Millay, K. K., and Knox, C. M. (1981). Performance of dyslexic children on speech perception tasks. *J. Exp. Child Psychol.* **32,** 401–424.

Goetzinger, C., Dirks, D., and Baer, C. J. (1960). Auditory discrimination and visual perception in good and poor readers. *Ann. Otol. Rhinol. Laryngol.* **69,** 121–136.

Goldman, S. R. (1976). Reading skill and the minimum distance principle: A comparison of listening and reading comprehension. *J. Exp. Child Psychol.* **22,** 123–142.

Hicks, C. (1980). The ITPA Visual Sequential Memory Test: An alternative interpretation of the implications for good and poor readers. *Br. J. Educ. Psychol.* **50,** 16–25.

Hier, D., LeMay, M., Rosenberger, P., and Perlo, V. (1978). Developmental dyslexia. *Arch. Neurol.* **35,** 90–92.

Hung, D. L., and Tzeng, O. J. L. (1981). Orthographic variations and visual information processing. *Psycholog.* **90,** 377–414.

Ingram, T. T. S., Mason, A. W., and Blackburn, I. (1970). A retrospective study of 82 children with reading disability. *Dev. Med. Child Neurol.* **12,** 271–281.

Jackson, M., and McClelland, J. L. (1979). Processing determinants of reading speed. *J. Exp. Psychol.: Gen.* **108,** 151–181.

Jorm, A. F. (1979). The cognitive and neurological basis of developmental dyslexia: A theoretical framework and review. *Cognition* **7,** 19–33.

Katz, R. B. (1986). Phonological deficiencies in children with reading disability: Evidence from an object naming task. *Cognition* **22,** 225–257.

Katz, R. B., Shankweiler, D., and Liberman, I. Y. (1981). Memory for item order and phonetic recoding in the beginning reader. *J. Exp. Child Psychol.* **32,** 474–484.

Keefe, B., and Swinney, D. (1979). On the role of hemispheric specialization in developmental dyslexia. *Cortex* **15,** 471–481.

Kleiman, G. (1975). Speech recoding in reading. *J. Verbal Learn. Verbal Behav.* **14,** 323–339.

Levy, B. A. (1977). Reading: Speech and meaning processes. *J. Verbal Learn. Verbal Behav.* **16,** 623–638.

Liberman, A. M. (1982). On finding that speech is special. *Am. Psycholog.* **37,** 148–167.

Liberman, A. M., Cooper, F. S., Shankweiler, D., and Studdert-Kennedy, M. (1967). Perception of the speech code. *Psycholog. Rev.* **74,** 431–461.

Liberman, I. Y. (1982). A language-oriented view of reading and its disabilities. *In* "Progress in Learning Disabilities," Vol. 5 (H. Mykelburst, ed.). pp. 81–101. Grune and Stratton, New York.

Liberman, I. Y., and Mann, V. A. (1980). Should reading remediation vary with the sex of the child? *In* "Sex Differences in Dyslexia" (A. Ansara, N. Geschwind, A. Galaburda, N. Albert, and N. Gartrell, eds.). pp. 151–168. The Orton Society, Towson, Maryland.

Liberman, I. Y., Shankweiler, D., Fisher, F. W., and Carter, B. (1974). Explicit syllable and phoneme segmentation in the young child. *J. Exp. Child Psychol.* **18,** 201–212.

Liberman, I. Y., Shankweiler, D., Liberman, A. M., Fowler, C., and Fischer, F. W. (1977). Phonetic segmentation and recoding in the beginning reader. *In* "Towards a Psychology of Reading: The Proceedings of the CUNY Conference" (A. S. Reber and D. Scarborough, eds.). Lawrence Earlbaum, Hillsdale, New Jersey.

Liberman, I. Y., Liberman, A. M., Mattingly, I. G., and Shankweiler, D. (1980a).

Orthography and the beginning reader. *In* "Orthography, Reading and Dyslexia" (J. Kavanaugh and R. Venezky, eds.). University Park Press, Baltimore.

Liberman, I. Y., Shankweiler, D., Blachman, B., Camp, L., and Werfelman, M. (1980b). Steps towards literacy. Report prepared for Working Group on Learning Failure and Unused Learning Potential, President's Commission on Mental Health, November 1, 1977. *In* "Auditory Processing and Language: Clinical and Research Perspectives" (P. Levinson and C. H. Sloan, eds.). pp. 189–215. Grune & Stratton, New York.

Liberman, I. Y., Mann, V. A., Shankweiler, D., and Werfelman, M. (1982). Children's memory for recurring linguistic and non-linguistic material in relation to reading ability. *Cortex* **18**, 367–375.

Lundberg, I., Oloffson, A., and Wall, S. (1980). Reading and spelling skills in the first school years predicated from phoneme awareness skills in kindergarten. *Scand. J. Psychol.* **21**, 159–173.

Mann, V. A. (1984). Longitudinal prediction and prevention of early reading difficulty. *Ann. Dyslex* **34**, 117–136.

Mann, V. A. (1986). Why some children encounter reading problems: The contribution of difficulties with language processing and linguistic sophistication to early reading disability. *In* "Psychological and Educational Perspectives on Learning Disabilities" (J. K. Torgesen and B. Y. Wong, eds.), pp. 133–159. Academic Press, New York.

Mann, V. A., and Brady, S. (1988). Reading disability: The role of language deficiencies. *J. Consult. Clin. Psychol.* **56**, 811–816.

Mann, V. A., and Liberman, I. Y. (1984). Phonological awareness and verbal short-term memory: Can they presage early reading success? *J. Learn. Disabil.* **17**, 592–598.

Mann, V. A., Liberman, I. Y., and Shankweiler, D. (1980). Children's memory for sentences and word strings in relation to reading ability. *Mem. Cognit.* **8**, 329–335.

Mann, V. A., Shankweiler, D., and Smith, S. T. (1985). The association between comprehension of spoken sentences and early reading ability: The role of phonetic representation. *J. Child Lang.* **11**, 627–643.

Mann, V. A., Cowin, E., and Schoenheimer, J. (1989). Phonological processing, language comprehension and reading ability. *J. Learn. Disabil.* **22**, 76–89.

Mann, V. A., and Ditunno, P. (1990). Phonological deficiencies: Effective predictors of reading problems. *In* "Dyslexia: Neurophysiological and learning perspectives." (6, Pavlides, ed.) Wiley and Sons: New York.

Mann, V. A., Tobin, P., and Wilson R. (1987). Measuring phonological awareness through the invented spellings of kindergarten children. *Merill-Pelmer Quart.* **33**, 365–391.

Mason, W. (1976). Specific (developmental) dyslexia. *Dev. Med. Child Neurol.* **9**, 183–190.

Mattingly, I. G. (1972). Reading, the linguistic process, and linguistic awareness. *In* "Language by Ear and by Eye: The Relationship between Speech and Reading" pp. 133–148. MIT Press, Cambridge.

McKeever, W. F., and van Deventer, A. D. (1975). Dyslexic adolescents: Evidence of impaired visual and auditory language processing associated with normal lateralization and visual responsivity. *Cortex* **11**, 361–378.

Miller, J. L., and Eimas, P. D. (1983). Studies on the categorization of speech by infants. *Cognition* **13**, 135–166.

Money, J. (1973). Turner's syndrome and parietal lobe functions. *Cortex* **9**, 387–393.

Morais, J. (in press). Constraints on the development of phonological awareness. *In* "Phonological Processes in Literacy" (S. Brady and D. Shankweiler, eds.). Lawrence Erlbaum, Hillsdale, New Jersey.

Morais, J., Cary, L., Alegria, J., and Bertelson, P. (1979). Does awareness of speech as a sequence of phonemes arise spontaneously? *Cognition* **7**, 323–331.

Morrison, F. J., Giordani, B., and Nagy, J. (1977). Reading disability: An information processing analysis. *Science* **196**, 77–79.

Moskowitz, B. A. (1973). On the status of vowel shift in English. *In* "Cognitive Development and Acquisition of Language" (T. Moore, ed.), pp. 223–260. Academic Press, New York.

Orton, S. T. (1937). "Reading, Writing and Speech Problems in Children." Norton, New York.

Owen, F. W. (1978). Dyslexia—Genetic aspects. *In* "Dyslexia: An Appraisal of Current Knowledge" (A. L. Benton and D. Pearl, eds.), pp. 265–284. Oxford University Press, New York.

Owen, F. W., Adams, P. A., Forrest, T., Stolz, L. M., and Fischer, S. (1971). Learning disorders in children: Sibling studies. *In* "Monographs of the Society for Research in Child Development," **36**. University of Illinois Press, Chicago.

Pennington, B. F., Van Orden, G., Kirson, D., and Haith, M. (in press). Phonological processing skills in adult dyslexics. *In* "Phonological Processes in Literacy." Lawrence Erlbaum, Hillsdale, New Jersey.

Perfetti, C. A. (1985) "Reading Skill." Lawrence Erlbaum, Hillsdale, New Jersey.

Perfetti, C. A., and McCutchen, D. (1982). Speech processes in reading. *Speech Lang.: Adv. Basic Res. Practice* **7**, 237–269.

Read, C. (1986). "Children's Creative Spelling." Routledge & Kegan Paul, London.

Robinson, M. E., and Schwartz, L. B. (1973). Visuo-motor skills and reading ability: A longitudinal study. *Dev. Med. Child Neurol.* **15**, 280–286.

Russell, G. (1982). Impairment of phonetic reading in dyslexia and its persistence beyond childhood—Research note. *J. Child Psychol. Child Psych.* **23**, 459–475 (b).

Rutter, N. (1978). Prevalence and types of dyslexia. *In* "Dyslexia: An Appraisal of Current Knowledge" (A. L. Benton and D. Pearl, eds.), pp. 3–28. Oxford Press, New York.

Rutter, M., and Madge, N. (1976). "Cycles of Disadvantage: A Review of Research." Heinemann Educational, London.

Rutter, M., and Yule, W. (1973). The concept of specific reading retardation. *J. Child Psych.* **16**, 181–198.

Scarborough, H. S. (1984). Continuity between childhood dyslexia and adult reading. *Br. J. Psychol.* **75**, 329–348.

Scarborough, H. S. (1988). Early language development of children who became dyslexic. Paper presented to the New York Child Language group.

Shankweiler, D., and Liberman, I. Y. (1972). Misreading: A search for the causes. *In* "Language by Ear and by Eye: The Relationships between Speech and

Reading" (J. F. Kavanaugh and I. G. Mattingly, eds.), pp. 293–318. MIT Press, Cambridge.

Shankweiler, D., Liberman, I. Y., Mark, L. S., Fowler, C. A., and Fischer, F. W. (1979). The speech code and learning to read. *J. Exp. Psychol.: Hum. Percep. Perform.* **5,** 531–545.

Simpson, G. B., Lorsbach, T. C., and Whitehouse, D. (1983). Encoding and contextual components of word recognition in good and poor readers. *J. Exp. Child Psychol.* **35,** 161–171.

Slowiaczek, M. L., and Clifton, C. (1980). Subvocalization and reading for meaning. *J. Verbal Learn. Verbal Behav.* **19,** 573–582.

Smith, S. D., Kimberling, W. J., Pennington, B. F., and Lubs, H. A. (1983). Specific reading disability: Identification of an inherited form through linkage analysis. *Science* **219,** 1345–1347.

Smith, S. D., Pennington, B. F., Fain, P. E., Kimberling, W. J., and Lubs, H. A. (1986). Genetic heterogeneity in specific reading disability. *Am. J. Hum. Gen.* **39,** A169.

Smith, S. T., Macaruso, P., Shankweiler, D., and Crain, S. (in press). Syntactic comprehension in young poor readers. *Appl. Psycholing.*

Smith, S. T., Mann, V. A., and Shankweiler, D. C. (1986). Spoken sentence comprehension by good and poor readers: A Study with the Token Test. *Cortex* **22,** 627–632.

Spring, C. (1976). Encoding speech and memory span in dyslexia children. *J. Special Educ.* **10,** 35–40.

Stanovich, K. (1982a). Individual differences in the cognitive processes of reading: I. Word decoding. *J. Learn. Disabil.* **15,** 485–493.

Stanovich, K. (1982b). Individual differences in the cognitive processes of reading: II. Text-level processes. *J. Learn. Disabil.* **15,** 549–554.

Stanovich, K. (1988). Explaining the differences between the dyslexic and the garden-variety poor reader: The phonological-core variable difference model. *J. Learn. Disabil.* **21,** 590–604.

Stanovich, K. E., Cunningham, A. E., and Cramer, B. B. (1984a). Assessing phonological awareness in kindergarten children: Issues of task comparability. *J. Exp. Child Psychol.* **38,** 175–190.

Stanovich, K. E., Cunningham, A. E., and Feeman, D. J. (1984b). Intelligence, cognitive skills and early reading progress. *Read. Res. Q.* **19,** 278–303.

Stanovich, K. E., Nathan, R. G., and Zolman, J. E. (1988). The developmental lag hypothesis in reading: Longitudinal and matched reading-level comparisons. *Child Dev.* **59,** 71–86.

Stevenson, H. W., Stiegler, J. W., Lucker, G. W., Hsu, C.-C., and Kitamura, S. (1982). Reading disabilities: The case of Chinese, Japanese and English. *Child Dev.* **53,** 1164–1181.

Swanson, L. (1978). Verbal encoding effects on the visual short-term memory of learning-disabled and normal children. *J. Educ. Psychol.* **70,** 539–544.

Taylor, I., and Taylor, M. M. (1983). "The Psychology of Reading." Academic Press, New York.

Thomas, C. C. (1905). Congenital 'word blindness' and its treatment. *Opthalmoscope* **3,** 380–385.

Torgesen, J. K. (1977). Memorization processes in reading-disabled children. *J. Educ. Psychol.* **69,** 551–578.

Torgesen, J. K., and Hoack, D. J. (1980). Processing deficiencies of learning-disabled children who perform poorly on the digit spaan test. *J. Educ. Psychol.* **72,** 141–160.

Tzeng, O. J. L., Hung, D. L., and Wang, W. S.-Y. (1977). Speech recoding in reading Chinese characters. *J. Exp. Psychol.: Hum. Learn. Mem.* **3,** 621–630.

Vellutino, F. R. (1979). "Dyslexia: Theory and Research." MIT Press, Cambridge.

Waber, D. P. (1977). Sex differences in mental abilities, hemispheric lateralization, and rate of physical growth at adolescence. *Dev. Psychol.* **13,** 29–38.

Wagner, R., Balthazor, M., Hurley, S., Morgan, S., Rashotte, C., Shaner, R., Simmons, K., and Stage, S. (1987). The nature of prereaders' phonological processing abilities. *Cog. Dev.* **2,** 355–373.

Watt, W. C. (1989). Getting writing right. *Semiotica* **75,** 279–315.

Wolf, M. (1984). Naming, reading and the dyslexias: A longitudinal overview. *Ann. Dyslexia* **34,** 87–115.

Wolf, M., and Goodglass, H. (1986). Dyslexia, dysnomia and lexical retrieval: A longitudinal investigation. *Brain Lang.* **28,** 159–168.

Wong, B. Y. L., Wong, R., and Blenkinsop, J. (1989). Cognitive and metacognitive aspects of learning-disabled adolescents' composing problems. *Learn. Disabil. Q.* **12,** 300–322.

Yopp, H. K. (1988). The validity and reliability of phonemic awareness tests. *Read. Res. Q.* **23,** 159–177.

Zurif, E. B., and Carson, G. (1970). Dyslexia in relation to cerebral: Dominance and temporal analysis. *Neuropsychologia* **8,** 351–361.

CHAPTER 6

Visual Processes in Learning Disabilities

Dale M. Willows

Editor's Notes

In this chapter, Willows' theme is that it is premature to dismiss the potential role of visual processing problems in reading disabilities. In support of her theme, she presents impressive data on early visual information processing where younger nondisabled and disabled readers clearly differ. Additionally, she examines data from visual memory research and concludes that the data suggest the possibility of a developmental lag in visual memory in younger disabled readers. She also points out the consistent discovery in subtype research studies in reading disabilities of a cluster of disabled readers sharing visual deficits.

However, it is pertinent to note that Willows does not dispute the research findings on the role of linguistic factors in reading disability, which are elucidated in Mann's previous chapter. Nor is she championing a visual deficits viewpoint about reading disabilities. In fact, she does not support research that attempts to link reading disabilities to one source of causal factors, be they linguistic or otherwise. Rather, she simply wants us to be researchers unfettered by self-imposed blinkers, to explore all possible factors or combinations of factors regarding the causes of reading disabilities.

Learning about Learning Disabilities

I. INTRODUCTION

This chapter describes the visual perception and visual memory abilities of individuals who have difficulties in processing written language. A very high proportion of those designated as learning-disabled might more accurately be termed written-language-disabled, because their most salient difficulties are manifested in the areas of reading, spelling, handwriting, and written composition. Many learning-disabled individuals may also be language-disabled in a more general sense, showing problems in their receptive and expressive aural/oral language processes as well as in the written domain. Many others, however, seem to function very well in the aural/oral domain, but they have great difficulty when they have to deal with print. Despite the fact that spelling, handwriting, and written composition difficulties are almost invariably involved, the term reading-disabled is commonly used to refer to those individuals who have written-language disabilities. The many variants on this term include specific reading disability, developmental reading disability, congenital reading disability, dyslexia, specific dyslexia, developmental dyslexia, etc., but because there are no satisfactory distinctions in the definitions of these terms, the term reading disability will be used here to encompass them all.

Although listening, speaking, reading, and writing are all language processes, the latter two are distinct from the former by virtue of the fact that they involve a visual symbol system. For skilled readers/writers, the visual symbols in the writing system are so familiar that it is very difficult for them to recall a time when printed words were just meaningless marks on the page; however, for beginning readers/writers, young or old, this is exactly the case. The person who is just starting to learn to read and write must differentiate and remember the symbols in their writing system, be they alphabetic like the Arabic system, logographic like the Chinese, or syllabic like the Cree.

If people differ from each other in their abilities to perceive, discriminate, identify, and remember visual symbols (as they differ from each other in virtually every other area of cognitive–linguistic functioning), then it might be expected that those who have weaknesses in these visual abilities would have trouble learning the symbol system of their written language and, as a consequence, might become disabled in their learning to read and write. Despite this obvious possibility, the topic of visual processes in reading–writing disabilities is a very controversial one. This chapter is about why clinicians and educators have long considered visual processing deficits to be potential contributing factors in written-language disabilities, and about what current research tells us about the relation between visual processing deficits and reading disabilities. It is also about why some theorists and researchers dismiss the importance of visual factors in written-language disabilities, and why others believe that progress toward an understanding of reading disabilities is being hampered by a failure to consider the possibility of a contribution by visual processing factors.

The chapter begins by considering the visual demands of learning to read, write, and spell. It then goes on to present clinical case studies and correlational evidence that seem to support the long-standing belief that visual processing weaknesses play some role in written-language disabilities. The next section presents a review of the key basic research in the area, beginning with a discussion of a central point of controversy—whether reading disabilities are caused by one or more types of processing deficit. The research review covers a large number of studies that compare the visual processing abilities of disabled readers with those of normal readers. One major group of studies examines the initial stages of visual processing (visual perception), and another group of studies deals with later processing stages (visual memory). The chapter concludes with a discussion of the implications of the findings concerning visual processing deficits and reading disabilities for future research directions and practical applications.

II. VISUAL COMPONENTS IN READING AND WRITING

Before considering potential areas of visual processing difficulty among the reading-disabled, the visual processing demands of learning to read, spell, and write are examined. To understand what the child, or anyone just beginning to learn the written form of a language, is faced with, consider the messages printed in Figure 6.1. Unless you are familiar with the written languages of Chinese (1), Korean (2), Japanese (3), Hindi (4), Arabic (5), or Urdu (6), all of the characters and words in Figure 6.1 are just meaningless marks on the page. In fact, all six writing samples represent highly meaningful expressions—the first three languages all ask the question "How are you?" and the latter three ask the question "What is your name?" Despite the fact that the content of the messages is familiar, novice readers of the language (whether or not fluent in the oral language) must learn to pay close attention to the visual information on the page to extract the underlying meaning. For more experienced readers of these languages, the visual component is processed unconsciously and effortlessly and may seem to be of little or no importance. For the beginner, the visual task of dealing with written language involves several types of demands,

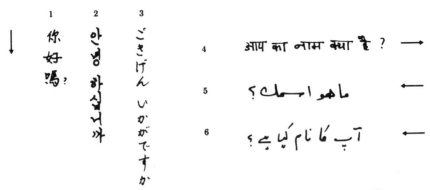

Figure 6.1 Samples of the written languages of Chinese (1), Korean (2), Japanese (3), Hindi (4), Arabic (5), and Urdu (6).

including the following:

1. Accurate visual perception of letters and words
2. Visual analysis of letter forms and the extraction of invariant features (so that variations of handwriting and type style will not interfere with reading)
3. Visual discrimination between similar forms in the writing system (in the English lowercase alphabet, letter-pairs such as "h" and "n," "f" and "t," "b" and "d," and "c" and "e" have a high degree of visual similarity)
4. Visual memory for the patterns of individual letters, of letter-strings (e.g., "ph," "ght," "oi," "th," "ing") that make up orthographic (i.e., spelling) patterns of the language, and of whole words—both to recognize them for reading and to recall or "revisualize" them for writing
5. Visual–spatial and scanning ability to track print from left to right and top to bottom on the page (or whatever direction is appropriate for the writing system involved)
6. Visual–motor ability to reproduce letters and words in writing
7. Visual–linguistic integration to associate letters and words with sounds and word meanings (Dunn-Rankin, 1978; Gibson and Levin, 1975; Rayner and Pollatsek, 1989; Vernon, 1971)

The above demands are present for all novice readers, but, over time, with maturation and reading experience, most individuals master them. The extent to which the visual demands of reading and writing serve as a barrier to progress may vary considerably from one individual to another.

III. CLINICAL CASE STUDIES

A. Historical Perspectives

The earliest evidence suggesting that individual differences in visual process-ing abilities might be a basis for some reading disabilities comes from clinical reports before the turn of the century. In 1895, James Hinshelwood, a Scot-tish opthalmologist with a special interest in neurology, began to present his observations of individuals who exhibited a mysterious phenomenon, the sudden loss of reading ability. This acquired word-blindness, as Hinshelwood described it, is a condition in which an individual with normal vision can no longer interpret written or printed language because of some brain injury. A series of fascinating clinical cases in which the ability to recognize faces and objects was retained but the ability to read words was lost led Hinshelwood to conclude that the "inability to read was... not due to any failure of visual power, but to a loss of the visual memory for words and letters" (Hinshelwood, 1917: 3).

On the basis of Hinshelwood's descriptions of acquired word-blindness, the medical community raised the possibility that there might be cases of congenital word-blindness in which an individual was impaired in her or his ability to process letters and words from birth. Pringle Morgan published a brief note in the *British Medical Journal* in 1896 describing a 14-yr-old boy who might represent such a case. Hinshelwood's book "Congenital Word-Blindness" (1917), however, clearly described what seemed to be convincing evidence of congenital word-blindness. With its thorough and perceptive case histories, it outlines what has now come to be known as "specific dyslexia," "specific reading disability," or, simply, "reading disability." The case de-scriptions in Hinshelwood's book match very well those currently reported by educators and clinicians.

A few years later, in 1925, Dr. Samuel Orton, a medical doctor with a special interest in neurology (who is now considered by many to be the father of the field of reading disabilities), published the article "Word-blindness in school children." In it he described a range of phenomena associated with congenital word-blindness, with a particular emphasis on the confusions of letter and word orientation ("b" and "d," "was" and "saw"), the so-called reversal errors that clinicians often observe in the reading and writing of children with reading disabilities (e.g., see Fig. 6.2). Based on his observations of word-blindness, which he preferred to call strephosymbolia (twisted symbols), Orton developed a theory of reading disability that also focused on visual processes.

To understand why these early clinicians formulated visual processing interpretations of reading disabilities, it is instructive to read Hinshelwood's

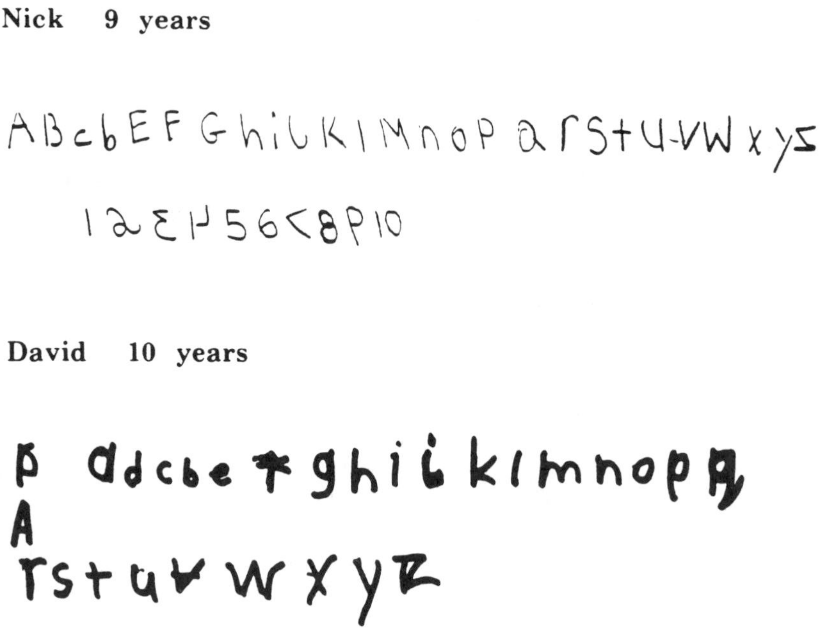

Nick   9 years

ABcbEF GhiLKIMnoP a rSt4-vW x y≤

I 2 Ɛ Ʊ 56 ⟨8 Ƥ 10

David   10 years

Figure 6.2   Examples of the "reversal errors" that clinicians often observe in the writing of reading-disabled children.

original descriptions of cases of congenital word-blindness. The discrepancy between the children's oral/aural language facility and their specific weaknesses in processing visual symbols is consistent with present-day observations. One such case is presented below.

Case I.—In March 1900 a boy, aged 11 years, was brought to me at the Glasgow Eye Infirmary by his father, who gave the following history: This boy had been at school for four and a half years, but was finally sent away, because he could not be taught to read. His father informed me that he was at school a considerable time before his defect was noticed, as he had such an excellent memory that he learned his lessons by heart; in fact, his first little reading book he knew so well that whenever it came to his turn he could from memory repeat his lesson, although he could not read the words. His father also informed me that in every respect, unless in inability to read, the boy seemed quite as intelligent as any of his brothers or sisters. His auditory memory was excellent, and better than that of any of the other members of the family. When a passage was repeated to him aloud, he could commit it to memory very rapidly. When I first saw the boy and his father at the Eye Infirmary, I asked them to call at my house and I wrote down the address on an envelope. A few days thereafter the father could not find the envelope, but the boy at once told him my address correctly, having remembered it from hearing me state it once. When I examined the boy, he seemed a smart and intelligent lad for his years. He knew the alphabet by heart, repeating it rapidly and correctly. He could recognize by sight, however, only a very few letters, and these not with any degree of certainty, after being four and a half years at school. He could spell [aloud] correctly most simple words of one syllable, such as "cat," "dog," "man," "boy," etc., but he could not recognize by sight even the simplest and commonest words such as "the," "of," "in," etc. He had no difficulty in recognizing all other visual objects such as faces, places and pictures. On each page of the little primer in which I tested him, there was a picture of some object, which was followed by some simple letterpress about it. He at once recognized and named the pictures, e.g. "a cat," "a dog." I would then ask him to spell [aloud] the word, which he nearly always did correctly. On asking him to pick out the word "cat" on the page, he was unable to do it. I repeated this experiment with the same result on page after page of the little primer. On testing him with figures [numbers] I found that he could repeat from memory fluently and correctly numbers up to a hundred. He could also perform mentally simple sums of addition. He could not, however, recognize all the figures by sight, but he knew them better than the letters, and recognized a greater number of them. (Hinshelwood, 1917: 45–46)

In the next section, a summary of common clinical characteristics of reading-disabled children based on more recent reports is presented. From a comparison of the case above with this more recent clinical profile, it should be evident that Hinshelwood's term congenital word-blindness was undoubtedly describing present-day specific dyslexia or reading disability.

B. A Clinical Profile

Consistent with the thoughtful observations of Hinshelwood and Orton, the case reports of clinicians observing the patterns of difficulties in the reading, writing, and spelling of reading-disabled children have confirmed over the last 60–70 years that a substantial proportion of these individuals seem to have difficulties with the visual demands of the tasks. Although there are good reasons to exercise great caution in interpreting subjective clinical reports that have not been confirmed through properly controlled experimental testing

(Nisbett and Ross, 1980), a type of information is available in clinical case studies that is extremely difficult to test directly with controlled research. Clinicians and educators who often work with the same individuals over weeks, months, and even years have an opportunity to observe patterns in the abilities and learning of reading-disabled individuals that short-term laboratory studies cannot assess. Only well-conceived longitudinal studies that follow the same children for an extended period can begin to capture the complex patterns of development over time. Few such studies exist.

A review of clinical reports suggests a common profile or pattern of difficulties in the reading and writing of many learning-disabled individuals over time, a pattern that seems to support the importance of some type of visual component processes. Students who experience great difficulty in their written-language acquisition, irrespective of whether or not they manifest any sign of processing difficulties in their aural/oral language (indeed, some may have superior oral-language abilities), often show the following characteristic set of problems as they are learning to read and write:

In reading:
- difficulty learning to recognize letters and numbers
- confusion between similar-looking letters and words
- great difficulty recognizing words "by sight"
- over-reliance on context for word recognition
- failure to analyze the internal structure of words
- slow word-by-word reading

In writing:
- difficulty learning how to form letters
- confusion between similar-looking letters
- mirror-image printing of letters and numbers
- difficulty in remembering "how words look" to spell them
- phonetic spelling, based on the sounds in words

Aspects of this profile have been confirmed in a large number of clinical case reports (e.g., Boder, 1973; Farnham-Diggory, 1978; Golick, 1978; Kaufman, 1980; Money, 1966; Rawson, 1982; Saunders, 1962; Simpson, 1979; Spache et al., 1981; Willows et al., 1986). A comparison of the above pattern of difficulties manifested by many disabled readers with the earlier section on the "visual demands" of learning to read suggests that overlap between the two lists is considerable; i.e., the difficulties of disabled readers seem to involve visual perception and visual memory of printed symbols. It's no wonder, then, that early workers in the field, such as Hinshelwood and Orton, focused on visual factors.

IV. CLINICAL AND NEUROPSYCHOLOGICAL RESEARCH

A. Standardized Psychometric Tests

During the 1960s, a considerable number of studies related children's development of visual–perceptual and visual–motor abilities to their development of reading skill. Much of this research relied on standardized paper-and-pencil psychometric measures such as the Bender Visual–Motor Gestalt Test, the Frostig Developmental Test of Visual Perception, and the Memory-for-Designs test. For example, several studies examined the relation between performance on the Bender Test and scores on tests of reading achievement. Based on such evidence, researchers reported a significant correlation between poor analysis of complex visual patterns and reading difficulties (e.g., Crosby, 1968; Lachmann, 1960). Moreover, two studies were predictive. The perceptual ability tests were administered before the children began learning to read, so inadequacy in reading could not have caused their poor visual analysis abilities (de Hirsch et al., 1966; Smith and Keogh, 1962).

This type of correlational evidence resulted in the development of visual discrimination exercises for the express purpose of improving reading skills (Frostig, 1968). Such training programs, often involving discriminating between geometric shapes, were notoriously unsuccessful because their effects were specific to the training stimuli and did not generalize to letters and words (Cohen, 1967; Rosen, 1966). One important conclusion that these training studies provide is that the type of training required to improve reading achievement is not a generic training of perceptual abilities but, rather, must be a more specific training of reading skills (e.g., letter and word recognition). An additional conclusion is that researchers must be careful in their interpretation of correlational findings. This caution is as important in the interpretation of present-day findings as it was 25–30 years ago. Evidence of a significant correlation between levels of performance on tests of perceptual skills, or any other type of processing, and reading achievement should not be assumed to reflect a causal link.

Performance on standardized psychometric tests is often open to a variety of interpretations because, although the test may be called a "visual" test and may seem to assess some sort of visual ability, other types of factors such as verbal abilities and attentional processes may also be involved over and above what the test purports to measure. Although current research continues to employ standardized psychometric measures to examine the possible role of visual processes in reading disability, such tests are usually used in conjunction with more controlled experimental tasks designed to assess "purer" visual processes.

B. Visual Deficit Subtypes

More recently, some researchers, primarily clinicians and neuropsychologists, have investigated the possibility that groups of reading-disabled children might be subdividable into relatively homogeneous subgroups or subtypes; i.e., different types of processing deficits might play a role in the reading disabilities of different groups of reading-disabled individuals. Subtyping research usually involves administering a battery of tests (standardized and/or experimental) to groups of learning-disabled individuals. Based on a variety of methodological and statistical approaches, researchers have come up with two, three, or more classifications of reading disabilities, often including a visual deficit subtype, variously labeled visual dyslexic (Johnson and Myklebust, 1967), dyseidetic (Boder, 1973), visual–perceptual (Denkla, 1977; Lyon and Watson, 1981), visual–spatial (Bakker, 1979; DeFries and Decker, 1982; Petrauskas and Rourke, 1979; Pirozzolo, 1979), and visual perceptual–motor (Satz and Morris, 1981). Although the subtyping procedures vary widely from one study to another, the frequent finding of a subgroup of reading-disabled children who seem to have difficulties with visual aspects of reading and writing has convinced some that "resolution of problems regarding dyslexia in all likelihood depends on our identifying specific subgroups of dyslexia and treating them separately rather than continuing to view all dyslexia as a unitary syndrome" (Malatesha and Dougan, 1982: 89). This conclusion is not universally accepted, however. Other researchers strongly contend, on the basis of the type of basic research evidence discussed in the next section, that there is essentially only one type of reading disability. Vellutino, for example, has argued that "far from being a visual problem, dyslexia appears to be the consequence of limited facility in using language to code other types of information" (Vellutino, 1987: 34).

V. BASIC EXPERIMENTAL RESEARCH

A. Unitary or Multiple Factors

A major source of contention among present-day theorists concerns the above issue of whether reading disabilities are the result of one or more than one type of processing problem. Theorists such as Vellutino argue that all reading disabilities are a result of subtle and not-so-subtle linguistic processing deficits (e.g., Mann, 1984; Swanson, 1984). Others, however, believe that a variety of factors may contribute to reading disabilities (e.g., Malatesha and Dougan, 1982; Rayner and Pollatsek, 1989), with different reading-disabled individuals being more or less affected by linguistic, visual, and other types of processing deficits.

Those who claim that the unitary cause of reading disabilities is some type of underlying linguistic deficit use as the basis for their argument (1) that an enormous amount of evidence relates language problems in phonology, syntax, and semantics to reading disabilities and (2) that a large body of evidence indicates that no visual processing differences exist between disabled and normal readers (Vellutino, 1979, 1987; Stanovich, 1982, 1985). Those who question the unitary causation position argue instead for a multiple causation position, suggesting either that there are different subtypes of reading disabilities or that two or more areas of processing weakness in combination may underlie reading disabilities. Those who hold a multiple-causation view agree with the unitary-causation theorists that research evidence suggests that linguistic processing factors are involved in some, if not all, cases of reading disabilities, but they question the validity of the second conclusion: that a large body of evidence indicates that no visual processing differences exist between disabled and normal readers (Di Lollo et al., 1983; Doehring, 1978; Fletcher and Satz, 1979a,b; Gross and Rothenberg, 1979; Lovegrove et al., 1986). Rather, on the basis of evidence demonstrating the existence of basic visual processing differences between disabled and normal readers, they argue that, in addition to linguistic factors, visual perceptual and/or visual memory factors may also be involved in causing reading disabilities.

The basic research reviewed in this section reflects directly on this main point of dispute between the unitary- and multiple-factor theorists. It deals with the question of whether or not disabled and normal readers demonstrate differences in their basic visual perceptual and visual memory processes.

B. Methodological Considerations

1. Operational Definitions

Throughout this section on basic research, the term reading disabilities will be defined by the conventional discrepancy definition that includes the following elements:

1. reading performance of 2 or more years below what is expected for an individual's age and general level of cognitive ability,[a]
2. evidence of at least normal cognitive ability as reflected by scores on standardized IQ tests and/or areas of school achievement that do not involve written language,

[a] Note: For children who are below the age of 8 yr, and therefore cannot be more than 2 yr below grade level, it is commonly accepted in research to designate an individual who is at least 1 yr below age/grade at age 7 yr or at least 6 mo below age/grade expectation at age 6 yr as being reading-disabled.

3. normal educational opportunity to learn to read,
4. no organic deficiencies of vision or hearing, and
5. no behavioral or emotional disorders.

Virtually all of the studies examining the role of visual processes in reading disabilities have compared the performance of a group of disabled readers with that of normal-achieving readers. Although most researchers have adopted an acceptable definition of reading disabilities, some have not. Because the operational definition of the groups of readers (i.e., how they are selected) is key to the interpretation of the data produced by research, this review focuses on studies that provide evidence of having met the conventional discrepancy definition for selecting the reading-disabled group and also of having employed an appropriate comparison group of nondisabled "normal" readers that differs from the disabled readers on measures of written language (e.g., reading, spelling) but that is similar to them on factors such as age and general cognitive ability.

2. Language–Labeling Confounds

Although intuitively the most direct way of assessing for visual processing differences between disabled and normal readers might be to test them with letters and words, this approach has serious problems. In view of the fact that linguistic processing deficits undoubtedly play a very significant role in reading disabilities (as Chapter 5 has clearly shown), an important factor to consider in defining experimental tasks thought to be assessing visual processes is whether or not performance on the task may involve the use of linguistic processes that are confounded with the visual processes of interest. Some studies attempting to assess visual processes in reading disabilities may inadvertently have been assessing verbal as well as visual factors. Most studies in which the goal bas been to assess visual factors free of linguistic–verbal confounds have avoided this pitfall by employing stimuli that are very difficult to label verbally, by using procedures in which performance could not be affected by verbal labeling, or by taking precautions of both types. This review reports only studies that have attempted to exclude the possibility that the "visual" task could have been performed by labeling the stimuli. Thus, studies that report the performance of subjects who apparently have visual processing strengths or weaknesses on a task but who, in fact, might have relied on linguistic–verbal rather than visual processes to complete it are not included in this review.

3. "Levels" of Visual Processing

Probably because of the longstanding views of clinicians and educators that reading disabilities have some underlying basis in visual processes, a great deal of basic research has attempted to examine the possibility that visual processing deficits play some role in reading disabilities. This research, which generally fits within an information-processing framework, has involved a wide range of methodologies. To understand the current status of our knowledge about visual processing, it is essential to review the research within the context of the types of methodologies involved.

The type of visual process investigated varies from one study to another. To understand the need to examine different aspects or levels of visual processing, it is helpful to consider that from the instant a visual stimulus reaches the eye, the visual information begins to undergo "processing," proceeding from the retina to the visual cortex, to various association areas of the brain. Deficits in any or all of the levels of visual processing might play some role in reading, spelling, and writing disabilities. Some researchers have focused their efforts on understanding the earlier levels of visual processing, immediately after the information has entered the visual system, whereas others have been more interested in later levels of processing in which higher cognitive processing may play a greater role. Some studies simply require that subjects indicate when they see a stimulus on a screen, whereas others may require that subjects correctly recognize what they saw at some later point or even that they be able to reproduce accurately what they saw. Because the interpretation of any particular study depends on the level of processing demanded in the experimental task, the studies reviewed in the following sections are roughly organized from earlier to later levels of visual processing.

C. Visual–Perceptual Processes

Clinical observations indicating that disabled readers seem to confuse similar-looking letters and words in their reading and writing suggest that, in comparison with normal readers, they may have some underlying difficulty in basic visual perception. A large number of studies have been undertaken to investigate this possibility. These studies have attempted to determine whether or not disabled and normal readers differ in their perception of visual stimuli in the early stages of processing before higher-level cognitive processes have had time to come into play.

Much of the research comparing the early stages of visual information processing of disabled and normal readers has involved two main techniques: temporal integration tasks and backward masking tasks. These tasks are used to determine whether or not disabled and normal readers differ in how quickly they can perceive and extract information from a visual stimulus. Because visual information processing occurs at very rapid rates, highly sophisticated procedures are required in this type of research. Tachistoscopes (or T-scopes), oscilloscopes, and computer presentation technologies are used to control the time intervals, which are measured in thousandths of a second (msec).

1. Temporal Integration

The visible trace of a stimulus persists for a fraction of a second after the stimulus has been removed from view. The duration of this visible persistence can be measured by presenting two stimuli in very close temporal sequence and assessing whether the stimuli have been perceived as two separate stimuli or as a single stimulus. Two main types of temporal integration task have been used to compare the initial stages of visual information processing in disabled and normal readers. One type involves the presentation of two different stimuli with a variable time interval, the interstimulus interval (ISI), between them. The minimum length of the ISI required for a person to perceive the two stimuli as separate is considered to reflect the duration of the visible persistence of the first stimulus. This is often referred to as the separation threshold. An example may make this procedure clearer. In a well-known study by Stanley and Hall (1973), groups of disabled readers and normal readers were shown the pairs of stimuli in Figure 6.3. To begin with, each pair of stimuli was presented simultaneously so that they would be perceived as a single image. It can be seen from the examples in Figure 6.3 that if each pair of stimuli were displayed simultaneously in the same location they would combine to make the word NO, a cross, and a cross within a square, respec-

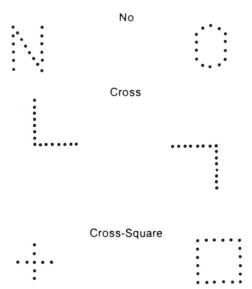

Figure 6.3   The three sets of two-part stimuli used by Stanley and Hall (1973) to investigate temporal integration of visual information.

tively. Next, the procedure involved increasing, by very small steps (20 msec), the time interval between each pair of stimuli until the child reported that she or he saw two shapes instead of one. The results of Stanley and Hall's research indicated that the disabled readers' separation threshold before they reported seeing two separate images was significantly longer than that of the normal readers. This pattern of results showing longer visual persistence among the reading-disabled has been found in other studies using similar procedures (Lovegrove and Brown, 1978; Stanley, 1975).

A second type of temporal integration task involves the presentation of two identical stimuli (such as two identical straight lines or sets of parallel lines called gratings) in close temporal sequence, also to assess the visible persistence of the first stimulus. The task begins by presenting the two stimuli simultaneously, and then the ISI is increased by very small steps until the subject reports that the stimulus is flashing rather than constant. Using this type of temporal integration task, researchers have amassed considerable evidence also indicating that disabled readers have longer visible persistence than normal readers (Di Lollo *et al.*, 1983; Lovegrove *et al.*, 1978; O'Neill and Stanley, 1976). The evidence suggests that the processing deficit is not at the level of the retina but occurs later in processing, at the level of the visual cortex (Slaghuis and Lovegrove, 1985, 1986). Moreover, 75% of disabled readers in a series of studies of early visual processing exhibited evidence of such deficits (Lovegrove *et al.*, 1986). An impressive program of research is still ongoing to clarify the nature of the processing mechanisms involved in these early visual processing deficits among disabled readers (Badcock and Lovegrove, 1981; Lovegrove, 1988; Lovegrove *et al.*, 1980a,b, 1982; Martin and Lovegrove, 1984).

2. Backward Masking

When the onset of one visual stimulus, called the target, is followed almost immediately by the onset of another visual stimulus (known as a masking stimulus or, simply, a mask), the second stimulus interferes with the processing of the first. This effect is known as backward masking. Whereas the temporal integration tasks described earlier are thought to provide an index of the visible persistence of a stimulus after its termination, backward masking tasks are thought to provide a measure of the rate of information pick up in the initial stages of visual information processing. In a typical backward masking experiment, a target stimulus (a figure or letter) is briefly presented, then a mask is presented, and then a test stimulus is presented. The task involves a same–different paradigm (i.e., test format) such that one key is pressed to indicate that the test stimulus is the same as the target or another key is pressed to indicate that it is different. On every trial, there is a 50/50 chance of a "same" or "different" response being correct. The time interval between the target and the mask is varied until a performance level of 75% accuracy is achieved. The ISI at which a reader can perform at 75% accuracy is referred to as the critical ISI. The results of several experiments comparing performance on backward masking tasks have shown that disabled readers process visual information more slowly (their critical ISI is longer) than normal readers (Di Lollo et al., 1983; Lovegrove and Brown, 1978; Mazer et al., 1983; O'Neill and Stanley, 1976; Stanley and Hall, 1973).

Overall, then, the pattern of results from both types of temporal integration task and from studies involving backward masking indicates that disabled readers do not process visual information as quickly as normal readers of similar age and IQ. Some suggestive evidence also indicates that this visual processing deficit may diminish with increasing age (Badcock and Lovegrove, 1981; Di Lollo et al., 1983; Lovegrove and Brown, 1978).

3. Consistency of Findings

Not all studies using temporal integration and backward masking tasks have produced the same patterns of early visual processing differences between disabled and normal readers reported here. A few studies have been repeatedly cited in the literature as sources of contrary evidence (e.g., Arnett and Di Lollo, 1979; Fisher and Frankfurter, 1977; Morrison et al., 1977). Although the existence of studies reporting conflicting evidence suggests that caution is certainly warranted in drawing conclusions, the evidence in support of early visual processing differences between disabled and normal readers is almost overwhelming. Moreover, careful review of the research articles reporting conflicting findings has usually uncovered possible explanatory factors, often involving inadequacy of the operational definition of reading disabilities employed in the studies. For example, Di Lollo et al. (1983) point out that in the earlier study by Arnett and Di Lollo (1979), the fact that only a 1-yr discrepancy existed between the "disabled" and normal reader groups may account for the lack of significant difference between those two groups. Also, the very unusual finding by Fisher and Frankfurter (1977) of a disabled reader superiority in early visual processes may be the result of these authors having failed to control for general cognitive ability of their disabled and normal groups. The disabled readers in their sample may, in fact, have been superior in IQ to the age- and reading-level-matched normal groups with which they were compared. Perhaps brighter children process visual information faster. Another often-cited source of contrary evidence is an article by Morrison et al. (1977) in which no early visual processing differences were found between disabled and normal readers. Like Fisher and Frankfurter (1977), however, these authors failed to match their disabled and normal groups on measures of general intelligence. In addition, the Morrison et al. (1977) study had a small sample size, with only nine disabled and nine normal readers. Their failure to find reading group differences in early visual processes may have resulted from their having tested too small a sample of children.

Virtually all of the studies cited here that have found early visual processing deficits among disabled readers have employed the conventional operational definition of reading disabilities and an age- and IQ-matched normal reader group. Also, the sample sizes in the studies reporting differences have been quite large, with most of the studies having a minimum of 15 subjects per reading-ability group, and many having sample sizes substantially greater. Thus, although this type of *post hoc* explanation of conflicting findings cannot be considered definitive, it does cast doubt on the reliability of the results of the studies. If the conflicting findings prove in the future to be replicable, then they should be considered more seriously. At this point, however, the evidence of early visual processing deficits among disabled readers is very persuasive.

4. Relation to Reading Processes

Some researchers argue that the types of methodologies used to assess early visual processing differences between disabled and normal readers "are remote from the perceptual conditions facing a child learning to read" (Hulme, 1988: 373), but others argue just as persuasively that the types of measures of visual perception described here are more sensitive and powerful approaches to comparing the visual–perceptual functioning of disabled and normal readers (Di Lollo et al., 1983; Gross and Rothenberg, 1979; Lovegrove et al., 1986). Other types of procedures may be confounded with higher cognitive processes (e.g., verbal labeling, rehearsal, cognitive strategies). Moreover, evidence from studies of letter, number, and word perception, stimuli that are more closely related to reading, seems to confirm that disabled readers require stimuli to be exposed for a longer duration than normal readers to produce a given level of correct response (e.g., Allegretti and Puglisi, 1986; Gross et al., 1978; Stanley, 1976). These findings appear to confirm that when brief visual presentations are used to measure adequacy of visual–perceptual functioning disabled readers show deficits relative to normal readers.

5. Conclusions Concerning Early Visual Processes

Returning to the question of whether or not disabled readers differ from normal readers in their visual–perceptual processes, the answer seems to be in the affirmative. Many well-controlled studies have employed temporal integration and backward masking tasks to compare the early visual information processing abilities of disabled and normal readers, and most of them have resulted in similar patterns of results. In general, it seems quite clear that the early visual information processes of disabled readers are different from those of nondisabled normal readers (Di Lollo et al., 1983; Hulme, 1988; Lovegrove et al., 1986).

To answer the more fundamental question of whether or not perceptual deficits are among the causes of reading disabilities, more research is necessary. The role of these early visual processing differences in reading disabilities is not yet well understood. They may have some direct causal role in the perception, discrimination, and analysis of the visual features of letters and words. On the other hand, they may be reflecting some more basic underlying processing differences between disabled and normal readers, such as speed of information processing, which in turn may have some causal role in reading disabilities (Di Lollo *et al.*, 1983). It has even been suggested that disabled–normal reader differences could be a result of reading experience, although evidence argues against this interpretation (Di Lollo *et al.*, 1983; Lovegrove *et al.*, 1986). Whatever the case, the visual–perceptual differences between disabled and normal readers appear to be very real, and, whatever their explanation, theories and models of reading disabilities must take them into account.

D. Visual Memory Processes

To remember the letters and groups of letters that characterize the spelling patterns and words of the language—to recognize them for reading and to recall them for writing and spelling—an individual must retain a record of them in memory and have easy access to that stored information.

After visual information has passed from the very brief visual persistence level to a short-term memory storage level, the information must be processed further in long-term memory if it is to be retained for later recognition and recall (Craik and Lockhart, 1972; Rayner and Pollatsek, 1989). A variety of experimental procedures have been used to determine whether or not differences exist between disabled and normal readers at these later processing stages. Most of the studies designed to investigate visual memory differences between disabled and normal readers have employed one of four main types of task, involving visual recognition memory, reproduction from visual memory, visual–visual paired-associate learning, and serial learning of visual designs. All of these types of tasks are designed to investigate how well individuals remember visual information that they have perceived, to recognize or reproduce it from memory later.

1. Visual Recognition Memory

To recognize words with speed and accuracy, a reader must make use of information such as the overall shape of words. A series of investigations by Lyle and Goyen was designed to examine how accurately disabled readers and normal readers recognize unfamiliar visual stimuli that resemble "word contours" or "word shapes." Sample stimuli from their research are shown in

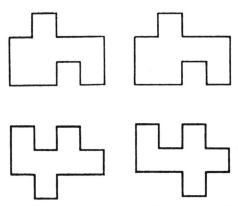

Figure 6.4 Samples of "word contours" used as stimuli in the research by Lyle and Goyen. The top pair are identical (same), the bottom pair nonidentical (different).

Figure 6.4. In five experiments, Lyle and Goyen, using tachistoscopic procedures, presented a series of different word shapes to disabled and normal readers (Goyen and Lyle, 1971a,b, 1973; Lyle and Goyen, 1968, 1975). Shortly after the presentation of each word-shape target, one of two test formats was used. In one test situation, a set of several test word shapes was presented, and the child's task was to select the target stimulus she or he had just seen. In the other test format, involving a same–different paradigm, the child had to press one key to indicate that the test shape was the same as the target or another key if it was different. Lyle and Goyen were interested not only in determining whether or not disabled readers differed from normal readers in their visual recognition of the word shapes, but also whether or not younger children (age 6–8 yr) in the two reading groups differed from older (age 8–10 yr). In addition, they wanted to know whether or not the exposure duration of a word shape (ranging from 0.10 to 5.0 sec) and the degree of similarity among the set of test alternatives affected accuracy of responding.

The results of Lyle and Goyen's research showed clearly that, at the younger age level, disabled readers were less accurate in recognizing word shapes than were normal readers. Such differences were not found at the older age level. These differences between disabled and normal readers were found at the shorter stimulus duration rates (0.10 and 1.0 sec) but not at longer ones (5.0 sec). Consistent with the findings of the studies described in the previous sections, Lyle and Goyen concluded from their research that "the perceptual deficit manifested by young [disabled] readers on tachistoscopic tasks involves the input or processing of visual information at rapid exposures. The relative deficit of young [disabled] readers appears to arise not through short-term memory deficits or difficulty in discriminating between alternatives on response cards but through incomplete analysis of the tachistoscopically presented stimulus, so that certain distinctive features or their interrelationships are not taken into account" (Lyle and Goyen, 1975: 675–676).

More recently, Willows *et al.* (1988) conducted a study of children's visual recognition memory for unfamiliar visual symbols (letters from the Hebrew alphabet) using a same–different paradigm in a "computer game" format. Disabled and normal readers at three age levels (6, 7, and 8 yr) were tested. On each trial in the computer game, the child was shown a target stimulus selected randomly from a pool of 18 Hebrew letters (shown in Fig. 6.5, in six sets of three). After a brief interval, they were shown the test stimulus,

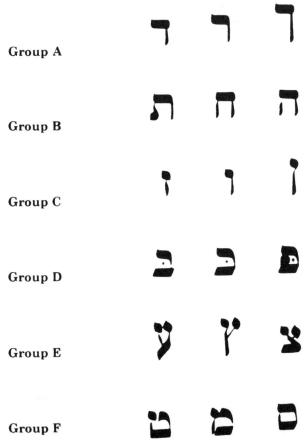

Figure 6.5   The stimulus pool of 18 Hebrew letters, grouped in six visually distinct sets of three visually similar items, used in the visual recognition studies by Willows *et al.* (1988).

either the same letter again or a different, but similar-looking, letter from the same set. The child had to press one key to indicate that the test item was the same as the target and another if it was different. The delay between the target and test stimuli was varied to determine whether disabled readers' visual processing difficulty was at the level of initial input or it was a result of some memory difficulty. The results of this research were consistent with Lyle and Goyen's findings: Reading-disabled children were less accurate and slower in their visual recognition performance. Moreover, there was a developmental pattern (i.e., the effect was greater among younger than older disabled readers) and the deficit appeared to be at the level of initial visual perception rather than visual memory.

Taken together then, the pattern of results from studies of visual recognition that involve rapid stimulus presentation is clear and consistent. Younger disabled readers make more errors and are slower at responding than normal readers of similar age and IQ. The disabled readers' difficulty seems to occur at the initial input stage rather than at a later storage stage. In other words, the findings of these studies that assessed both early and later stages of processing add to the evidence of early visual information processing differences between disabled and normal readers.

2. Reproduction from Visual Memory

In learning to read and write, the child must attend to and remember the visual information in the symbols to recognize them for reading and reproduce them for writing. A widely cited series of studies was undertaken by Vellutino and his colleagues to investigate the possibility of visual memory differences between disabled and normal readers. These studies all involved having children view difficult-to-label visual shapes or strings of letters from the Hebrew alphabet and then, after the stimuli had been removed, "copy" them from memory. The performance of younger and older disabled and normal readers was compared. Based on the findings of the three key studies (Vellutino et al., 1973a, 1975b,d) involving the ability to reproduce unfamiliar visual shapes from memory, Vellutino and his colleagues concluded that: "In all these investigations, poor readers performed as well as normals in short- and long-term memory of Hebrew letters and words—symbols unfamiliar to both groups." (Vellutino et al., 1977: 57).

Other evidence, however, suggests that disabled and normal readers may differ in a draw-from-memory task (Lyle, 1968). In that research, Lyle compared the abilities of large samples of disabled and normal readers to draw unfamiliar visual patterns from memory using the Memory-for-Designs test. The results showed that the disabled were significantly inferior to the normal readers in their reproductions of the designs. Moreover, the previously mentioned findings by Willows et al. (1988), showing disabled–normal reader differences in visual recognition (a less demanding task than reproduction from visual memory) of Hebrew letters, the type of stimuli used in the Vellutino and his colleagues' studies, suggest that caution is warranted in drawing definitive conclusions at this point.

The evidence reported by Vellutino and his colleagues on reproduction from visual memory does not contradict that from research on early stages of processing, because all of the studies by Vellutino and his colleagues involved "long" stimulus exposures. In the studies using Hebrew letters as stimuli, for example, the children examined the string of letters for 3–5 sec. These are exposure durations that are longer than those at which the research on visual perception found disabled–normal reader differences in performance.

3. Visual–Visual Paired-Associate Learning

In the context of attempting to compare disabled and normal readers' abilities to associate unfamiliar visual shapes with sounds and words, as the child must do in learning to read, Vellutino and his colleagues undertook research in which they had disabled and normal readers learn to associate pairs of unfamiliar visual designs with each other. These studies also involved having the children associate visual designs with verbal responses, but this visual–verbal association aspect of the research is concerned with the children's ability to use verbal labels and is essentially irrelevant to questions about visual perception and memory processes. Thus, only the visual–visual paired-associate tasks are discussed here. In these tasks, the child was shown pairs of difficult-to-label shapes (such as those in Fig. 6.6) and told "to try to remember what two designs go together" (Vellutino *et al.*, 1973b: 117). On test trials, the children were shown one of each stimulus pair and required to select its mate from a set of five choices. In both experiments, Vellutino and his colleagues found no differences between disabled and normal readers' abilities to associate visual designs with each other (Vellutino *et al.*, 1973b, 1975a). These results have been interpreted as additional evidence that no visual processing differences exist between disabled and normal readers.

TRAINING SERIES

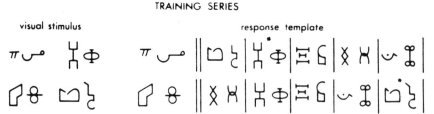

Figure 6.6 Samples of the pairs of difficult-to-label shapes used in the visual–visual paired-associate learning research by Vellutino and his colleagues.

The consistency of these results, using a visual–visual paired-associate task, with the earlier findings, using a reproduction from visual memory task, appears to add weight to Vellutino *et al.*'s (1977) conclusion that no disabled–normal reader differences exist on tasks designed to measure visual memory; however, the results do not contradict the evidence on visual perception. The disabled and normal readers in these studies were in an older age range, between about 9.5 and 12.5 yr of age, and the stimulus presentation rates were relatively slow.

4. Serial Learning of Visual Designs

Based on the work of Vellutino and his colleagues, Swanson also undertook a series of studies designed to compare disabled and normal readers' abilities to remember difficult-to-label visual shapes under conditions in which verbal labels were either excluded or included. Swanson used a probe-type serial memory task in which he presented six nonsense shapes (such as those shown in Fig. 6.7). Again, the task involving the use of verbal labels, although interesting, is not relevant to the present discussion about visual memory processes. Only the unnamed condition is discussed here. In the unnamed condition, a set of six cards, each with a different shape printed on it, was placed face down in front of the child. From left to right, each of the cards was then turned up for a few seconds and then turned down again. A probe (one of the six shapes) was then shown, and the child had to point to the card

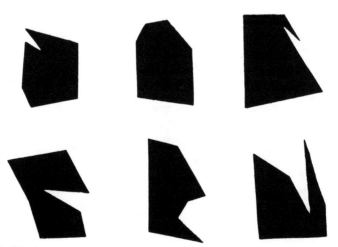

Figure 6.7 The six nonsense shapes (unnamed condition) used by Swanson in his studies involving a visual serial learning task.

in the row in front of her or him that matched the probe. Their task was essentially a visual–spatial task, because they were shown a probe and had to remember where they had seen it. In three experiments involving children from 7 to 12 yr of age, Swanson consistently found no differences between disabled and normal readers in serial memory for unnamed stimuli (Swanson, 1978, 1982, 1983).

Other research examining visual–spatial memory has produced a different pattern of results, however. Willows *et al.* (1988) presented strings of Hebrew letters to 6–8 yr-old disabled and normal readers in a computer game. After each string of three visually distinct letters (each of the three was taken from a different set in Fig. 6.5), one of the same three letters was shown in one of the three spatial positions that the original string had occupied. The child's task was simply to press one of two keys to indicate whether the letter was in the same or a different position from the one she or he had just seen it in. The results on both accuracy and response speed measures indicated that disabled readers were less able than normal readers to remember visual–spatial information. The disabled–normal reader differences were greater at the younger age levels.

5. Statistical Limitations

Although the failure to find disabled–normal reader differences on tasks tapping visual memory is a consistent pattern in the studies by both Vellutino and Swanson, several other researchers have been critical of the "no-difference" conclusions from their findings. They argue that some of the studies have statistical ceilings and floors that prevent finding disabled–normal differences, especially among the younger readers, even if such differences actually exist (Doehring, 1978; Fletcher and Satz, 1979a; Gross and Rothenberg, 1979; Satz and Fletcher, 1980; Singer, 1979; Willows *et al.*, 1986). These statistical problems are very serious because they result in no-difference conclusions when real differences may exist. If, for example, 10-yr-old disabled and normal readers were compared on their ability to read first-grade-level words, all children might read the words almost perfectly; i.e., their performance might be at a statistical ceiling. Conversely, if 6-yr-old disabled and normal readers were compared on their ability to read fifth-grade-level words, all of the children might do very poorly, their performance being at the statistical floor. A failure to find disabled–normal reader differences with such tasks might simply indicate that the tasks were too easy (ceiling effect) or too difficult (floor effect) to detect differences.

6. Conclusions Concerning Later Visual Processes

The answer to the question of whether or not visual memory differences exist between disabled and normal readers is still uncertain. The evidence with respect to older children is fairly consistent. It seems quite unlikely that visual memory differences exist between older (over age 8 yr) disabled and normal readers on the types of tasks reviewed here. At the younger age level, however, the possibility of some sort of developmental lag in visual memory still exists. Evidence suggests that younger disabled readers have difficulty in remembering visual information in a variety of task types. These difficulties may be due to differences in early perceptual processes, because most of the studies that have found differences in visual memory tasks have involved brief stimulus presentation rates, whereas studies that have failed to find such differences have usually presented stimuli at slower rates. Further carefully done research is required to clarify the relation between "later" visual process and reading disabilities, particularly in the younger age range (up to age 8 yr).

VI. CONCLUSIONS AND FUTURE DIRECTIONS

A. Research Directions

Combining the high degree of consistency of the early visual processing evidence with the inconclusiveness of the later visual processing evidence, it appears that visual–perceptual and visual memory deficits may be implicated in reading disabilities. The conclusion of the unitary-deficit theorists that disabled readers have no visual processing difficulties appears to have been premature. There may be more to reading disabilities than the verbal labeling and verbal memory problems that have been widely identified. It is incumbent on researchers to explore all factors that may contribute to reading disabilities and not to limit themselves to those that may seem to fit currently popular models.

Ultimately, the goal of research examining the visual processing of readers of different ability levels is to determine the role that visual processes play in learning to read and in reading failure. However, establishing whether a weakness in any particular processing ability is causal in reading acqustion or reading failure is a difficult problem. Nearly all of the research examining the strengths and weaknesses of children who differ in reading abilities is correlational in nature. It can tell us which factors are related to levels of reading ability, but it cannot tell us why. Very little research on reading disabilities can validly be interpreted as demonstrating a causal link between a particular processing deficit and reading failure. Deficits in some well-documented correlates of reading ability, such as phonemic awareness, have been suggested as causes of reading disabilities, but even these have not passed crucial experimental tests (Hulme, 1987; Bryant and Goswami, 1987) demonstrating a causal link.

Future research examining the relation between visual processing deficits and reading disabilities should focus particular attention on the possibility of visual memory deficits among reading-disabled children in the age range from 6 to 8 yr. In addition, future research should attempt to explore the underlying causal factors that are responsible for the relation between visual deficits and reading disabilities. Perhaps, for example, both visual and linguistic deficits reflect a more basic weakness in the processing of the left hemisphere of the brain. The challenge for future researchers is not to demonstrate whether reading disabilities are related to visual, linguistic, or other types of processing factors but, rather, to explain how basic processing weaknesses of various types may be related to each other or may interact in causing reading disabilities.

B. Practical Implications

If some disabled readers have delays or deficits in their visual processing abilities, such weaknesses could be a factor in their apparent difficulties in differentiating between similar-looking letters and words, especially in analyzing and remembering the orthographic (i.e., spelling) patterns in words and in processing letters and words at rapid rates in text. Clinical observations and case reports, correlational evidence from studies using standardized psychometric instruments, and visual deficit subtypes from clinical and neuropsychological studies all point to some role of visual processing deficits in reading disabilities. Evidence from information-processing research involving basic visual perception and visual memory also suggests that some relation exists between visual processing deficits and reading disabilities. At this point, however, the potential role of visual processing weaknesses in written-language problems is not well enough understood to draw confident conclusions about practice.

Clinicians and educators in the field of learning disabilities should certainly keep an open mind about the possibility that visual processing deficits contribute in some way to reading disabilities. Prudence would dictate that both assessment approaches and teaching techniques should be devised on the assumption that the reading-disabled child may have some difficulty in coping with the visual demands of the task. The findings indicating that younger disabled readers (6–8 yr of age) may be more likely to have some sort of visual perceptual and/or visual memory deficits are worthy of special note. The visual demands of the beginning stages of reading acquisition are probably more significant than those at later stages of reading acqustion when linguistic processes may play a greater role (Chall, 1983; Vernon, 1977).

References

Allegretti, C. L., and Puglisi, J. T. (1986). Disabled vs nondisabled readers: Perceptual vs higher-order processing of one vs three letters. *Percep. Motor Skills* **63**, 463–469.

Arnett, J. L., and Di Lollo, V. (1979). Visual information processing in relation to age and to reading ability. *J. Exp. Child Psychol.* **27**, 143–152.

Badcock, D., and Lovegrove, W. (1981). The effects of contrast, stimulus duration, and spatial frequency on visible persistence in normal and specifically disabled readers. *J. Exp. Psychol.: Hum. Percep. Perform.* **7**, 495–505.

Bakker, D. J. (1979). Hemispheric differences and reading strategies: Two dyslexias? *Bull. Orton Soc.* **29**, 84–100.

Boder, E. (1973). Developmental dyslexia: A diagnostic approach based on three atypical reading–spelling patterns. *Dev. Med. Child Neurol.* **15**, 663–687.

Bryant, P. E., and Goswami, U. (1987). Development of phonemic awareness. *In* "Cognitive Approaches to Reading" (J. Beech and A. Colley, eds.). (pp. 213–244). Wiley, Chichester, England.

Chall, J. S. (1983). "Stages of Reading Development." McGraw-Hill, New York.

Cohen, R. (1967). Remedial training of first grade children with visual perceptual retardation. *Read. Horizons* **45**, 60–63.

Craik, F. I. M., and Lockhart, R. S. (1972). Levels of processing: A framework for memory research. *J. Verbal Learn. Verbal Behav.* **11**, 671–684.

Crosby, R. M. N. (1968). "Reading and the Dyslexic Child." Souvenir Press, London.

de Hirsch, K., Jansky, J. J., and Langford, W. S. (1966). "Predicting Reading Failure." Harper & Row, New York.

DeFries, J. C., and Decker, S. N. (1982). Genetic aspects of reading disability: A family study. *In* "Reading Disorders: Varieties and Treatments" (R. N. Malatesha and P. G. Aaron, eds.). (pp. 255–280). Academic Press, Toronto.

Denkla, M. B. (1977). Minimal brain dysfunction and dyslexia: Beyond diagnosis by exclusion. *In* "Topics in Child Neurology" (M. Blaw, I. Rapin, and M. Kinsbourne, eds.). (pp. 223–268). Spectrum, New York.

Di Lollo, V., Hanson, D., and McIntyre, J. S. (1983). Initial stages of visual information processing in dyslexia. *J. Exp. Psychol.: Hum. Percep. Perform.* **9**, 923–935.

Doehring, D. G. (1978). The tangled web of behavioral research on development dyslexia. *In* "Dyslexia: An Appraisal of Current Knowledge" (A. L. Benton and D. Pearl, eds.). Oxford University Press, New York.

Dunn-Rankin, P. (1978). Visual characteristics of words. *Sci. Am.* **238(1)**, 122–130.

Farnham-Diggory, S. (1978). "Learning Disabilities: A Psychological Perspective." Harvard University Press, Cambridge.

Fisher, D. F., and Frankfurter, A. (1977). Normal and disabled readers can locate and identify letters: Where's the perceptual deficit? *J. Read. Behav.* **9**, 31–43.

Fletcher, J. M., and Satz, P. (1979a). Unitary deficit hypotheses of reading disabilities: Has Vellutino led us astray? *J. Learn Disabil.* **12(3)**, 155–159.

Fletcher, J. M., and Satz, P. (1979b). Has Vellutino led us astray? A rejoinder to a reply. *J. Learn. Disabil.* **12(3)**, 168–171.

Frostig, M. (1968). Education of children with learning disabilities. *In* "Progress in Learning Disabilities" (H. R. Myklebust, ed.). (pp. 234–266). Grune & Stratton, New York.

Gibson, E. J., and Levin, H. (1975). "The Psychology of Reading." MIT Press, Cambridge.

Golick, M. (1978). Learning disabilities and the school age child. *Learning Disabilities: Information Please*, 1–8.

Goyen, J. D., and Lyle, J. G. (1971a). Effect of incentives and age on the visual recognition of retarded readers. *J. Exp. Child Psychol.* **11**, 266–273.

Goyen, J. D., and Lyle, J. G. (1971b). Effect of incentives upon retarded and normal readers on a visual-associate learning task. *J. Exp. Child Psychol.* **11**, 274–280.

Goyen, J. D., and Lyle, J. G. (1973). Short-term memory and visual discrimination in retarded readers. *Percep. Motor Skills* **36**, 403–408.

Gross, K., and Rothenberg, S. (1979). An examination of methods used to test the visual perceptual deficit hypothesis of dyslexia. *J. Learn. Disabil.* **12**, 670–677.

Gross, K., Rothenberg, S., Schottenfeld, S., and Drake, C. (1978). Duration threshold for letter identification in left and right visual fields for normal and reading-disabled children. *Neuropsychologia* **16**, 709–715.

Hinshelwood, J. (1895). Word-blindness and visual memory. *Lancet* **2**, 1564–1570.

Hinshelwood, J. (1917) "Congenital Word-Blindness." H. K. Lewis & Co., London.

Hulme, C. (1987). Reading retardation. *In* "Cognitive Approaches to Reading" (J. Beech and A. Colley, eds.). (pp. 245–270). Wiley, Chichester, England.

Hulme, C. (1988). The implausibility of low-level visual deficits as a cause of children's reading difficulties. *Cog. Neuropsychol.* **5**, 369–374.

Johnson, D. J., and Myklebust, H. R. (1967). "Learning Disabilities: Educational Principles and Practices." Grune & Stratton, New York.

Kaufman, N. L. (1980). Review of research on reversal errors. *Percep. Motor Skills* **51**, 55–79.

Lachmann, F. M. (1960). Perceptual-motor development in children retarded in reading ability. *J. Consult. Psychol.* **24**, 427–431.

Lovegrove, W. (1988). The relationship of visual deficits to short-term memory processes and phonological recoding in normal and specifically disabled readers. Paper presented in August 1988 as part of the symposium "Visual Factors in Learning Disabilities," at the XXIV International Congress of Psychology, Sydney, Australia.

Lovegrove, W., and Brown, C. (1978). Development of information processing in normal and disabled readers. *Percep. Motor Skills* **46**, 1047–1054.

Lovegrove, W., Billing, G., and Slaghuis, W. (1978). Processing of visual contour orientation information in normal and disabled reading children. *Cortex* **14**, 268–278.

Lovegrove, W., Bowling, A., Badcock, D., and Blackwood, M. (1980a). Specific reading disability: Differences in contrast sensitivity as a function of spatial frequency. *Science* **210**, 439–440.

Lovegrove, W., Heddle, M., and Slaghuis, W. (1980b). Reading disability: Spatial frequency specific deficits in visual information store. *Neuropsychologia* **18**, 111–115.

Lovegrove, W., Martin, F., Bowling, A., Blackwood, M., Badcock, D., and Paxton, S. (1982). Contrast sensitivity functions and specific reading disability. *Neuropsychologia* **20**, 309–315.

Lovegrove, W., Martin, F., and Slaghuis, W. (1986). A theoretical and experimental case for a visual deficit in specific reading disability. *Cog. Neuropsychol.* **3**, 225–267.

Lyle, J. G. (1968). Performance of retarded readers on the Memory-for-Designs test. *Percep. Motor Skills* **26**, 851–854.

Lyle, J. G., and Goyen, J. D. (1968). Visual recognition, developmental lag, and strephosymbolia in reading retardation. *J. Abnorm. Psychol.* **73**, 25–29.

Lyle, J. G., and Goyen, J. D. (1975). Effect of speed of exposure and difficulty of discrimination on visual recognition of retarded readers. *J. Abnorm. Psychol.* **84**, 673–676.

Lyon, R., and Watson, B. (1981). Empirically derived subgroups of learning disabled readers: Diagnostic characteristics. *J. Learn. Disabil.* **14**, 256–261.

Malatesha, R. N., and Dougan, D. R. (1982). Clinical subtypes of developmental dyslexia: Resolution of an irresolute problem. *In* "Reading Disorders: Varieties and Treatments" (R. N. Malatesha and P. G. Aaron, eds.). (pp. 69–92). Academic Press, Toronto.

Mann, V. (1984). Reading skill and language skill. *Dev. Rev.* **4**, 1–15.

Martin, F., and Lovegrove, W. (1984). The effects of field size and luminance on contrast sensitivity differences between specifically reading disabled and normal children. *Neuropsychologia* **22**, 73–77.

Mazer, S. R., McIntyre, C. W., Murray, M. E., Till, R. E., and Blackwell, S. L. (1983). Visual persistence and information pick up in learning disabled children. *J. Learn. Disabil.* **16(4)**, 221–225.

Money, J. (1966). Case 1: Space-form deficit. *In* "The Disabled Reader: Education of the Dyslexic Child" (J. Money, ed.). (pp. 263–276). Johns Hopkins Press, Baltimore.

Morgan, W. P. (1896). A case of congenital word-blindness. *Br. Med. J.* **2**, 1378.

Morrison, F. J., Giordani, B., and Nagy, J. (1977). Reading disability: An information-processing analysis. *Science* **19**, 77–79.

Nisbett, R., and Ross, L. (1980). "Human Inference: Strategies and Shortcomings of Social Judgement. Prentice-Hall, Englewood Cliffs, New Jersey.

O'Neill, G., and Stanley, G. (1976). Visual processing of straight lines in dyslexic and normal children. *Br. J. Educ. Psychol.* **46**, 323–327.

Orton, S. T. (1925). "Word-blindness" in school children. *Arch. Neurol. Psych.* **14**, 581–615.

Petrauskas, R. J., and Rourke, B. P. (1979). Identification of subtypes of retarded readers: A neuropsychological, multivariate approach. *J. Clin. Neuropsychol.* **1**, 17–37.

Pirozzolo, F. J. (1979). "The Neuropsychology of Developmental Reading Disorders." Praeger, New York.

Rawson, M. B. (1982). Louise Baker and the Leonardo syndrome. *Ann. Dyslexia* **32**, 289–304.

Rayner, K., and Pollatsek, A. (1989). "The Psychology of Reading." Prentice Hall, Englewood Cliffs, New Jersey.

Rosen, C. (1966). An experimental study of visual perceptual training and reading achievement in first grade children. *Percep. Motor Skills* **22**, 979–986.

Satz, P., and Fletcher, J. M. (1980). Minimal brain dysfunctions: An appraisal of research concepts and methods. *In* "Handbook of Minimal Brain Dysfunctions: A Critical View" (H. E. Rie and E. D. Rie, eds.). (pp. 669–715). Wiley, New York.

Satz, P., and Morris, R. (1981). Learning disability subtypes: A review. *In* "Neuropsychological and Cognitive Processes in Reading" (F. J. Pirozzolo and M. C. Wittrock, eds.). (pp. 109–144). Academic Press, New York.

Saunders, R. E. (1962). Dyslexia: Its phenomenology. *In* "Reading Disability" (J. Money, ed.). Johns Hopkins Press, Baltimore.

Simpson, E. (1979). "Reversals: A Personal Account of Victory Over Dyslexia." Houghton Mifflin, Boston.

Singer, H. (1979). On reading, language and learning. *Harv. Educ. Rev.* **49**, 125–128.

Slaghuis, W. L., and Lovegrove, W. J. (1985). Spatial-frequency-dependent persistence and specific reading disability. *Brain Cognit.* **4**, 219–240.

Slaghuis, W. L., and Lovegrove, W. J. (1986). The effect of physical flicker on visible persistence in normal and specifically disabled readers. *Aust. J. Psychol.* **38**, 1–11.

Smith, C. E., and Keogh, B. K. (1962). The group Bender-Gestalt as a reading readiness screening test. *Percep. Motor Skills* **15**, 639–645.

Spache, G. D., McIroy, K., and Berg, P. C. (1981). "Case Studies in Reading Disability." Allyn and Bacon, Inc., Boston.

Stanley, G. (1975). Two-part stimulus integration and specific reading disability. *Percep. Motor Skills* **41**, 873–874.

Stanley, G. (1976). The processing of digits by children with specific reading disability (dyslexia). *Br. J. Educ. Psychol.* **46**, 81–84.

Stanley, G., and Hall, R. (1973). Short-term visual information processing in dyslexics. *Child Dev.* **44**, 841–844.

Stanovich, K. E. (1982). Individual differences in the cognitive processes of reading: 1. Word decoding. *J. Learn Disabil.* **15**, 485–493.

Stanovich, K. E. (1985). Explaining the variance in terms of psychological processes: What have we learned? *Ann. Dyslexia* **35**, 67–96.

Swanson, L. (1978). Verbal encoding effects on the visual short-term memory of learning disabled and normal readers. *J. Educ. Psychol.* **70(4)**, 539–544.

Swanson, L. (1982). Verbal short-term memory encoding of learning disabled, deaf, and normal children. *Learn. Disabil. Q.* **5**, 21–28.

Swanson, L. (1983). A study of nonstrategic linguistic coding on visual recall of learning disabled readers. *J. Learn. Disabil.* **16(4)**, 209–216.

Swanson, L. (1984). Semantic and visual memory codes in learning disabled readers. *J. Exp. Child Psychol.* **37**, 124–140.

Vellutino, F. R. (1979). "Dyslexia: Theory and Research." MIT Press, Cambridge.

Vellutino, F. R. (1987). Dyslexia. *Sci. Am.* **256(3)**, 34–41.

Vellutino, F. R., Steger, J. A., and Kandel, G. (1972). Reading disability: An investigation of the perceptual deficit hypothesis. *Cortex* **8**, 106–118.

Vellutino, F. R., Pruzek, R., Steger, J. A., and Meshoulam, U. (1973a). Immediate visual recall in poor and normal readers as a function of orthographic-linguistic familiarity. *Cortex* **9**, 368–384.

Vellutino, F. R., Steger, J. A., and Pruzek, R. (1973b). Inter- versus intra-sensory deficiency in paired-associate learning in poor and normal readers. *Can. J. Behav. Sci.* **5**, 111–123.

Vellutino, F. R., Harding, C. J., Phillips, F., and Steger, J. A. (1975a). Differential transfer in poor and normal readers. *J. Gen. Psychol.* **126**, 3–18.

Vellutino, F. R., Smith, H., Steger, J. A., and Kaman, M. (1975b). Reading disability: Age differences and the perceptual deficit hypothesis. *Child Dev.* **46**, 487–493.

Vellutino, F. R., Steger, J. A., DeSetto, L., and Phillips, F. (1975c). Immediate and delayed recognition of visual stimuli in poor and normal readers. *J. Exp. Child Psychol.* **19**, 223–232.

Vellutino, F. R., Steger, J. A., Kaman, M., and DeSetto, L. (1975d). Visual form perception in deficient and normal readers as function of age and orthographic linguistic familiarity. *Cortex* **11**, 22–30.

Vellutino, F. R., Steger, J. A., Moyer, B. M., Harding, S. C., and Niles, C. J. (1977). Has the perceptual deficit hypothesis led us astray? *J. Learn. Disabil.* **10**, 54–64.

Vernon, M. D. (1971). "Reading and Its Difficulties: A Psychological Study." The University Press, Cambridge, England.

Vernon, M. D. (1977). Varieties of deficiency in reading processes. *Harv. Educ. Rev.* **47**, 396–410.

Willows, D. M., Kershner, J. R. and Corcos, E. (1986). Visual processing and visual memory in reading and writing disabilities: A rationale for reopening a "closed case". Paper presented in April 1986 as part of the symposium "The Role of Visual Processing and Visual Memory in Reading and Writing" at the Annual Meeting of the American Educational Research Association, San Francisco, California.

Willows, D. M., Corcos, E., and Kershner, J. R. (1988). Disabled and normal readers' visual processing and visual memory of item and spatial-order information in unfamiliar symbol strings. Paper presented in August 1988 as part of the symposium "Visual Factors in Learning Disabilities," at the XXIV International Congress of Psychology, Sydney, Australia.

CHAPTER 7

Social Problems and Learning Disabilities

Tanis Bryan

Editor's Notes

In the remaining chapters in Section I, we examine research areas that began to attract interest among learning disabilities researchers within the last two decades. To be more precise, on the topic of social problems in learning-disabled children, programmatic research studies began to appear in journals in the 1970s, and on the topic of metacognition and learning disabilities, publications first appeared in the early 1980s. We turn now to the topic of social problems and learning disabilities. In this chapter, Bryan focuses on research in four areas of social problems in children and adolescents with learning disabilities: learning-disabled students' attitudes toward themselves, social competence, communicative competence, and teachers' judgments and classroom behavior. Bryan consistently organizes the contents in each area of research along three themes: a summary of the research, a specification of problems in the research as well as insightful perception of issues that should receive empirical attention, and suggestions for teachers.

I. RATIONALE

Two decades have passed since the term learning disabilities (LDs) was invented. During this time, the field has made amazing progress in establishing services for children, training teachers to provide these services, and developing a research base to help us understand LDs. Very recently, however, formal recognition has been given to the notion that individuals with LDs are at risk for problems in the social domain. Such formal recognition refers to efforts to include social problems as characteristics in the definition of LDs. The two most recent efforts to revise and refine the definition include problems in the social domain as characteristics of LDs (Association for Children and Adults with Learning Disabilities, 1985; Kavanagh and Truss, 1987).

Although alterations in the federal definition of LDs, i.e., the definition included in P.L. 94-142, are unlikely in the near future, attempts to include social problems as part of the concept of LDs represent widespread acknowledgment from professionals and parents of the growing body of clinical and research data that attest to their social risk status.

Several reasons dictate professional and parental concern for social problems. Across cultures, peer relationships are second only to parent relationships in their importance for child development. Abundant evidence attests to the importance of peer interaction in children's development of reasoning in personal, societal, and moral domains of knowledge (Turiel, 1983). Abundant evidence also links problems in peer relationships to problems in school achievement (Parker and Asher, 1987). In addition, early problems in peer relationships are predictive of problems in mental health and adjustment and, in combination with aggression, of adult criminality (Parker and Asher, 1987; Cowen et al., 1973). Thus, there are many good reasons to be concerned about children's peer relationships.

Second, teaching and learning are essentially social events. This is acknowledged, for example, in taxonomies of learning that include affective factors as a primary category (Bloom, 1976; Kolligian and Sternberg, 1986). We suspect social problems play a role in the referral and identification of children as learning-disabled (LD). This suspicion is based on studies showing a significant overlap between scores on psychometric and achievement tests among LD and other low-achieving—but not referred—students. Poor academic achievement in and of itself apparently does not move teachers to initiate the referral process (Ysseldyke et al., 1982). Teachers' referrals apparently relate to a child's lack of academic achievement and to teachers' judgments of children's "teachability" (Keogh, 1983), of teachers finding these children unresponsive to the teaching–learning process (Bay and Bryan, 1989; Bryan et al., 1990). Thus, although social problems are not among the characteristics included in the federal definition, and children are not referred for problems in the social domain, teacher–child interactions may be a decisive factor in this process.

Third, parents of students with LDs have long campaigned for recognition of problems in the social domain (Bader, 1975). Parent recognition of social problems was recently demonstrated by the Association for Children and Adults with Learning Disabilities (ACLD). The ACLD adopted a definition of LDs that includes the statement that "throughout life the condition can affect self-esteem, education, vocation, socialization, and/or daily living activities" (Association for Children and Adults with Learning Disabilities, 1985). Parent concerns have been legitimized by evidence that social difficulties may persist beyond the elementary and secondary school years. LD high-school students and postsecondary adults have indicated that they experience significant social problems (Gregory *et al.*, 1986; White, 1985), and these problems extend to the work place (Minskoff *et al.*, 1987). For professionals in the field to ignore the observations, concerns, and complaints of parents and of persons with LDs, as they seek help for such problems, would be irresponsible, to say the least. This is important because teachers in the United States do not consider problems in children's social relationships to be very important, nor do they consider such problems to be part of their responsibilities (Walker and Lamon, 1987).

Fourth, LDs have been conceptualized as problems in information processing that affect children's thinking, speaking, listening, and so forth. Speaking, thinking, and listening are generic human behaviors that are involved in almost everything we do. To limit our concern in LDs to the acquisition of reading and math skills and to ignore thinking, listening, and speaking in interpersonal relations limits the likelihood that we can help children, or grow in our understanding of the nature of LDs. It is of heuristic and therapeutic importance to consider how problems in attention, memory, visual perception, and the like affect (or fail to affect) children's social cognitive development.

In summary, social development is an important part of child development, and problems in peer interactions are predictive of future adjustment difficulties. Social factors influence events in the classroom and at home and may influence the referral and identification of LDs. The importance of social problems is underscored by parents' strong support of professional attention to problems in the social domain and by evidence that such problems may persist beyond secondary school. Finally, attention to social problems as deficits in information processing should contribute to our understanding of the nature of LDs.

II. SCOPE AND OBJECTIVES

This chapter provides an overview of the research on social factors in LDs. The material included reflects the belief that social problems reflect (1) intra- and interpsychic difficulties that result from the experience of school failure and (2) deficits in information processing that influence the person's understanding of social situations and/or their behavior. A summary of research on those aspect of the social domain that have been studied using populations of students with LDs will be presented. This includes studies of LD students' attitudes toward themselves (self concept and attributions), teachers' attitudes toward the LD, and classroom behavior, social cognitive, and linguistic skills. At the end, readers should have an understanding of LD students' problems with

1. acquiring positive notions about themselves and beliefs in their self-efficacy,
2. generating negative attitudes and judgments of others, and
3. understanding and responding to complex, ambiguous social situations.

Readers should get a sense of how such problems start at a very early age and continue through young adulthood (the latest age tested). In reviewing the social status of persons with LDs, the plan is to define the construct, describe how it is measured, and then present highlights of research that captures our general understanding of LD status.

III. LD STUDENTS' ATTITUDES TOWARD THEMSELVES

A. Self-Efficacy

The review of social status begins with a consideration of LD students' attitudes, perceptions, and judgments about themselves. The reason for this stems from the important influence that attitudes about ourselves have on our responsiveness to others. Our effectiveness in social relationships depends in part on how we feel about ourselves. People's perceptions and opinions of themselves are complex and multidimensional and have multiple sources. Distinctions are made between self-concept, self-esteem, self-efficacy, and attributions, all being components that together comprise self-judgments.

Self-concept refers to a person's awareness of his or her own characteristics and the ways in which he or she is like and unlike others (McCandless and Evans, 1973). Self-esteem refers to the value a person puts on oneself and one's behavior (e.g., one's judgments about one's goodness or badness). Perceived self-efficacy refers to a person's judgments of competence to execute courses of action required to deal with prospective situations. Attributions refer to a person's explanations for successful and failure outcomes. People who assume that their outcomes result from their personal attributes (e.g., their ability, their effort) have an internal locus of control; people who assume that their outcomes result from forces external to themselves (e.g., task difficulty, luck) have an external locus of control. The distinctions between internal and external locus of control are further refined by the temporalness of the attribution. Some attributions are seen as stable (e.g., attributions about ability); others are seen as temporal, (e.g., attributions about effort). The stability of attributions is important because of its implications for personal control of outcomes. Stable attributions are perceived as less alterable than are temporal attributions.

What is important is that our views of ourselves, although complex, influence the way we respond in social situations (Bandura, 1982). Irrespective of whether or not our self-judgments are accurate, they influence our choices of activities and settings. "People avoid activities they believe exceed their coping capabilities, but they undertake and perform assuredly those that they judge themselves capable" (Bandura, 1982: 123). A large body of data show how self-judgments influence children's achievement and behavior (Wittrock, 1986; Dweck and Reppucci, 1973), so it is not surprising that concern for how such beliefs might influence the LD has arisen. A summary of this research follows.

B. Self-Concept

Students with LDs have been described in the clinical literature as having poor self-concepts. A review of the research suggests that although the LD never demonstrate more positive self-concepts than their peers, their negative judgments may be limited to their performance on academic tasks.

Several studies have used the Piers–Harris Self Concept Scale (Piers and Harris, 1969) to compare the self-concepts of the LD with those of normal-achieving students. The Piers–Harris scale consists of 80 declarative statements written at a third-grade level requiring children to respond "yes" or "no" to statements describing themselves. A number of studies have found that LD children rate themselves more negatively on this scale than non-learning-disabled (NLD) classmates (Rogers and Saklofske, 1985; Margalit and Zak, 1984; Jones, 1985), but a number of studies have found no differences between LD and normal-achieving classmates on this measure (Boersma, *et al.*, 1979; Strang *et al.*, 1978; Silverman and Zigmond, 1983). Whether the inconsistent findings relate to properties of the Piers–Harris scale, differences in the samples of children, or the methodology used is not clear.

In an attempt to sort out which components in the scale may contribute to differences in self-concept, Margalit and Zak (1984) and Jones (1985) used factor analysis. Margalit and Zak (1984) found LD children scored worse than NLD children on only one of three factors—self-dissatisfaction. Jones (1985) found LD subjects differed on their estimations of intellectual abilities, social status, physical appearance, and attributes but not on social popularity, anxiety, and happiness and satisfaction.

The Coopersmith Self-Esteem Inventory is a second instrument used to study self-concept (Coopersmith, 1967). The Coopersmith Inventory consists of 50 items related to general self-esteem, self-peers, home-parents, and school academic self-esteem. Students indicate whether the item does or does not describe them. One study found that LD children differ from normal-achieving classmates on the social self-peer scale by rating themselves as less easy to like, less fun to be with, and less popular with peers (Rosenberg and Gaier, 1977), whereas another study found they differed only on the School/Academic subscale (Winnie et al., 1982).

A scale used with older students is the Rosenberg Self-Esteem Scale (Rosenberg, 1965). This scale differs from the Piers–Harris and the Coopersmith scales because it contains no items on academic performance or peer relationships. The items are restricted to ratings of one's personal characteristics (e.g., "I'm a nice person"). This is important, because low self-concept scores on scales that include ratings of academic achievement may simply reflect children's honest reporting of academic difficulties. Only two studies used this scale. The results of one suggest that females with LDs may have lower self-esteem than males with LDs (Pearl and Bryan, 1982), and the second found no differences (Tollefson et al., 1982).

Clear-cut differences between LD and normal-achieving students are found when the items on the scale are restricted to students' concepts about their academic selves. The Students' Perception of Ability Scale (Chapman, 1985; Boersma et al., 1979) measures students' perceptions of their general ability, arithmetic ability, reading and spelling ability, penmanship and neatness, confidence in academic ability, and general school satisfaction. Studies using this scale find that LD students score lower than their NLD classmates, except for their ratings of penmanship and neatness (Hiebert et al., 1982; Chapman, 1985).

Another scale that has found differences between LD and normal-achieving students is Harter's Perceived Competence Scale for Children (Harter, 1985). The Harter scale asks children to rate themselves on scholastic competence, social acceptance, athletic competence, physical appearance, behavioral conduct, and global self-worth. LD students rate themselves lower on all of these scales than NLD students; they perceive themselves as having less ability in both academic and nonacademic areas and report having lower self-esteem than normal-achieving classmates (Kistner and Osborne, 1987).

C. Summary

By and large, it is safe to conclude that students with LDs have lower self-concepts on scales that measure academic self-concept. This is hardly surprising given their experiences of school failure. Of concern is evidence suggesting that they generalize their negative views to content areas on which they have had little or no experience (Chapman and Boersma, 1978; Hiebert *et al.*, 1982) and that lower academic self-concepts persist across time (Kistner and Osborne, 1987). This is discouraging because it suggests that special education services do not eliminate the likelihood that children who experience school failure will adopt poor self-concepts.

Therefore, it is important to note evidence that self-concept scores are susceptible to situational and instructional influences. Strang *et al.* (1978) found that LD students' self-concept scores on the behavior and popularity subscales of the Piers–Harris scale increased when they were partially mainstreamed. LD students who spend at least some time in a special education setting with other mildly handicapped students have higher self-concepts than LD students who spend all of their time in mainstream classrooms (Morrison *et al.*, 1983; Schurr *et al.*, 1972; Strang *et al.*, 1978). LD students in resource room programs tend to perceive themselves as increasingly less competent than classmates across grades three through eight in the regular classroom but maintain high perceptions of academic competence when making self-evaluations in their resource rooms (Renick, 1985).

These results suggest the importance of social comparisons. Our self-perceptions are based on how we think others view us and on comparisons of our performances with those of others (Festinger, 1954). Children who are the lowest achievers in the regular classroom may feel better about themselves when they can compare themselves with other students who are also experiencing difficulty in the special education resource or self-contained setting.

Because mainstreaming handicapped children into regular classrooms is a policy that is strongly endorsed nationwide, children with LDs are at risk for negative self-concepts, if only because they compare themselves with classmates who learn with greater facility. Yet it may be possible to structure the classroom so that individual differences in achievement are not a focal point for comparison and consequent ill will. One way to structure the classroom is through the control of evaluative feedback that teachers give to children. Teachers' feedback to children about their performance is an important source of information to children, one that contributes to their development of ideas about their self-worth. Fortunately, teachers' evaluative feedback is a dimension of instruction over which we have control. Let us consider a study in which children were in classrooms that differed on the dimension of evaluative feedback. In this study (Stipek and Daniels, 1988), comparisons were made between kindergarten and fourth-grade children's perceived competence in classrooms that differed in evaluative feedback. In one group of classrooms, feedback was based on normative criteria and was made very salient and public. In the second type of classroom, normative evaluation was de-emphasized and infrequent. For instance, in the classes in which normative evaluation was salient, assignments were graded with checks, stars, and happy and sad faces or letter grades; "A" papers were placed on bulletin boards; and students were given positive or negative feedback after tests, sometimes verbally. In the classrooms in which normative evaluation was de-emphasized, instructional groups were flexible; comments, but not grades, were given on assignments and report cards; the curriculum was individualized; comparisons with others were discouraged; children were encouraged to seek help from classmates; and projects were frequently completed in groups.

The hypothesis was that children would have higher self-perceptions in the classrooms where evaluation was de-emphasized compared with classrooms in which it was emphasized because children (and adults) tend to have positive expectations in the absence of evidence to the contrary (Crandall et al., 1955). The results found that kindergartners in classes in which normative feedback was salient rated their competence lower than did kindergartners in classes in which normative evaluation was de-emphasized. However, the kindergartners were more optimistic in their predictions for future academic achievement than the fourth-graders. Evaluative feedback differences did not affect the fourth-graders, but the kindergartners' self-ratings were like the fourth-graders in the classrooms that emphasized feedback evaluation. Thus, the decline associated with age in children's perceptions of competence (Benenson and Dweck, 1986; Stipek and Tannatt, 1984) already may have occurred. This study is important because it demonstrates how children's self-concepts for academic achievement can be significantly influenced at an early age by teachers' evaluative feedback. Teachers probably use evaluative feedback with good intentions but, unwittingly, may make it difficult for some children to feel good about their school performance. Because feedback is an aspect of instruction that is under teachers' control, we can hope that informed teachers will moderate instruction to take this information into account. Children with LDs are more likely to prosper in a classroom in which evaluative feedback is de-emphasized and not so public.

D. Self-Esteem

Studies of self-esteem focus on perception of self-worth (e.g., "I am able to do things as well as most other people," "I take a positive attitude toward myself," "At times I think I am no good at all"). Studies of self-esteem have not found differences between elementary and junior high-school students with LDs and normal-achieving students (Lincoln and Chazan, 1979; Tollefson et al., 1982; Winne et al., 1982). However, in a large national survey of high-school seniors in which 439 of 26,147 identified themselves as LD, the LD reported lower estimates of adjustment (e.g., "I'm satisfied with myself") than classmates

(Gregory *et al.*, 1986). A study of LD adults, 18–36 yr old, indicated that problems in self-esteem and confidence ranked high in their concerns (White, 1985). Similarly, interviews with LD adults found that three of the five problems most frequently mentioned are self-image, affect, and motivation (along with hyperactivity and organization; Buchanan and Wolf, 1986).

In summary, problems in self-esteem apparently surface when persons with LDs reach high-school age and beyond. The results are particularly compelling when gathered in anonymous surveys, as opposed to when people are seeking help for problems.

E. Attributions/Locus of Control

There have been several studies of LD students' attributions for outcomes in achievement situations. One of the most frequently used measures is the Intellectual Achievement Responsibility Scale (IAR; Crandall *et al.*, 1965). On this scale, children select either an internal (e.g., ability, effort) or external (e.g., luck) explanation in response to descriptions of hypothetical success and failure outcomes. Children are scored for their responses to the success and failure outcomes. The IAR does not provide information about specific academic versus other domains (e.g., social status), so a second instrument used is one in which children are asked to rate the importance of effort, ability, task difficulty, and luck for each selected domain (e.g., doing well–poorly in reading, doing well–poorly in math, getting along–not getting along with others).

The results of several studies are consistent in finding that students with LDs express different explanations for their successes and failures than normal-achieving classmates. Developmentally, children generally become more internal in their attributions for success and failure outcomes. Students with LDs, however, are likely to become internal in their attributions for failure but are less likely than normal-achieving classmates to become internal for their attributions for success. The LD are more likely to believe that their failures indicate that they lack ability, while normal-achieving youngsters attribute failure to lack of effort. Some studies also find that the LD are more likely to attribute their successes to luck, whereas normal-achieving youngsters attribute success to ability and effort. Not all LD students differ in their patterns of beliefs about outcomes. We are concerned about those students who do because of numerous studies that show that believing sucess and failure are beyond personal control is related to a lack of persistence in the classroom and to poor achievement. Because children may be debilitated by such beliefs, educational researchers are pursuing this topic in a variety of ways.

One of the directions being pursued is to look more closely at attributions in terms of the dimension of stability. As mentioned earlier, both attributions of ability and effort have an internal locus; however, ability is seen as a stable characteristic and beyond our control, whereas effort is something we can control. Thus, it is more adaptive to interpret failure as the result of insufficient effort because we can expend more effort the next time. Researchers are concerned with how such attributions affect children's achievement across time. Kistner *et al.* (1988) conducted a longitudinal study across a 2-yr span employing children in grades three through eight. Using the two scales described above, they studied the relationship among children's attributions, academic achievement, and teacher ratings. They found that attributions of failure to insufficient effort was positively related to achievement gains on the Peabody Individual Achievement Test, whereas attributions of failure to insufficient ability was negatively related to academic progress. Children's IQ scores were not related to children's attributions, but teacher ratings of children's classroom behavior were related. Children who tended to attribute their difficulties to insufficient effort were rated as more successful students, as more capable of independent classwork, and as demanding less time from the teacher. Children's attributions of failure to insufficient ability was related to teacher judgments of less success, less independence, and more demands for help from the teacher.

On the follow-up study, the LD children were less likely than normal-achieving classmates to attribute failure to insufficient effort and more likely to attribute failure to insufficient ability on one of the two scales. On the second scale (the IAR), the results were that LD and normal-achieving children's attributions for success and failure became significantly more internal across the 2-yr period. This study is important because it shows how students' attributions about achievement are related to both their academic progress across time and teacher ratings of their classroom behavior.

A second direction being followed by researchers is to assess how children's attributions interact with teachers' instructional strategies. Here we are concerned with how to take into account children's beliefs as we design instructional programs. Two studies showed how teachers' instructional strategy interacts with students' beliefs to influence achievement outcomes. Pascarella and Pflaum (1981) exposed LD and normal-achieving classmates to one of two types of reading instruction. In the high-structure program, teachers corrected reading errors and confirmed correct responses during specially designed reading lessons. In the low-structure program, teachers encouraged children to determine the adequacy of their responses. Using pre- and posttreatment measures of reading, they found that LD children and poor readers with high scores on internality benefited more from the low-structure teaching strategy, whereas LD children and poor readers with low scores on internality benefited more from the high-structure teaching strategy. In the same vein, Bendell *et al.* (1980) had LD junior-high males do their spelling assignment in either a high- or a low-structured condition. In the high-structured situation, students were directed to trace words they felt they had missed, write them three times, and say the word and the letter to themselves each time they wrote it. In the low-structured situation, students were given no specific study procedure but were reinforced with a nickel for each correctly spelled word. The results were that students high on internal locus of control did better in the low-structure situation, whereas students low on internal locus of control did better in the high-structure situation. These studies are important because they show how the outcome of instruction is affected by students' beliefs. Students who believed in their control over outcomes (i.e., high internal students) did better in a teaching structure that maximized their control; students who did not believe in their control over outcomes (i.e., high external students) did better when they had minimum control over their learning. This suggests that when a student fails to respond to instruction it may be due to a mismatch between the teaching strategy and the student's beliefs about outcomes.

A third direction being pursued by researchers is attribution retraining. Here the goal is to change students' attributions so that they attribute successful outcomes to their effort and ability and their failures to a lack of effort (but not to a lack of ability). Let us consider a study by Borkowski *et al.* (1988) in which LD students' reading comprehension was improved through instructions about summarization strategies and task-specific attribution retraining. The notion is that even though children come to a task with long-standing maladaptive attributions, these attributions can be changed if they acquire new skills and the acquisition of these new skills is accompanied by adaptive interpretations of this learning. To test this hypothesis, LD children and adolescents, ages 10–14 yr, were assigned to one of four training conditions. In one condition, Reading Strategies Plus Complex Attribution, there were two phases. In the first phase, students were taught strategies that improve sort-recall and paired-associate learning. For example, students were asked to try and remember pairs of pictures and then were trained to use an associational strategy so they could remember them better. Attribution training was integrated into the instruction. The instructor made errors on purpose that were followed by an attributional dialog. In the dialog, the instructor noted the error, engaged the student in a discussion about the reasons for failure on school tasks, and emphasized the importance of not attributing failure to uncontrollable factors. In addition, the instructor modeled the positive self-attribution, "I need to try and use the strategy" while using the strategy to successfully perform the previously failed item. Then the instructor tested himself or herself and repeated the need to use the strategy for good recall. Next, the instructor discussed the relation between effortful strategy use and successful performance. A cartoon character, used to guide the discussion, showed "I tried hard, used the strategy, and did well." Then the students' errors were used to stress the importance of controllable factors in outcomes. The child was asked to explain the reason for each error by using the cartoon characters, to perform the previously failed item, and to discuss the reasons for successful performance. Self-attributions about uncontrollable outcomes were rephrased with positive belief statements about the role of effort. In the second phase of this condition, students were taught summarization strategies and given attribution retraining related to strategy-based reading. The summarization strategies included main ideas and details, topic sentence, and summarization. The same procedure of having the instructor make an error by not using the strategy, model the strategy, and discuss the reasons for the mistake as being controllable was followed.

The other three conditions of the study were designed to control for each of the types of training combined in the first condition. Thus, in the second condition, Reading Strategies Plus Attribution, students did the same tasks as in Phase I above but did not get any of the training. In Phase 2, they received training on the reading strategy and attributions. In the third condition, attribution control, they were taught the reading strategies in phases 1 and 2, but did not get any of the attribution training. In the fourth condition, Reading Strategies Control, students practiced all of the tasks without either reading or attribution training.

The results of the study found that only the attributional strategy-trained groups improved from pre- to post-test in their summarization skills. What is striking is that students in the combined attribution plus strategy training group showed about a 50% improvement in summarizing paragraphs compared with a 15% improvement in subjects who received only the reading strategy. In addition, there was a 6-month improvement in inferencing ability for main ideas in short paragraphs in the combined attribution strategy training group. This study is important because it shows how taking into account children's attributions while teaching them specific skills has much greater impact on children's reading comprehension than just teaching them the reading strategies. It should be noted that changes in attributions were restricted to performance on the reading strategies tests and did not generalize to other areas such as math. This suggests that teaching specific skills in reading, math, social studies, and so forth should integrate adaptive attributions into the instructional process. At the least, this is likely to enhance LD students' acquisition of specific subject matter and adaptive attributions about that subject. Hopefully, with enough experiences of this sort, the adaptive attributions will offset the general attributional beliefs about their responsibility for failure that are held by many students with LDs.

F. Research Issues

The research on self-efficacy has demonstrated the powerful influence played by student's self-perceptions on their responsiveness to instruction. Furthermore, it has shown that attribution retraining, in combination with specific skill instruction, can have a positive impact on performance and attributions to controllable factors. Many questions remain unanswered. First, we do not know the origins of the general maladaptive attributions; the relative impact of experience versus feedback from teachers and parents. Should early intervention target parents and teachers evaluative feedback to children? Another question has to do with the emphasis on effort explanations in attribution retraining. If children are already trying hard, do effort attributions exacerbate rather than alleviate their poor attitudes? Because children with LDs attribute failure to a lack of ability, we might try to emphasize increases in ability as a function of the acquisition of new skills. This requires recasting ability from a stable to a more temporal characteristic, so that ability is a characteristic we acquire as we work hard. Third, several of the attribution retraining studies find an increase in student persistence as a result of training but no changes in attributions. Clearly, we need more research on interventions to sort out what influences students' beliefs and performance. In addition, none of the studies have examined the long-term durability of effects. Finally, because some evidence indicates that teachers do not make attributional statements in the regular course of instruction, we need research to explore how to best integrate this knowledge base into practice.

G. Implications for Teaching

The importance of self-concept in student achievement has been recognized for many years. But early attempts to change children's self-concepts were largely ineffectual. These efforts depended pretty much on parents' and teachers' exhortations to students. The results of the more recent attribution training, or retraining, is promising. This type of intervention is cost-effective, easy to integrate into the regular curriculum, and requires no special equipment, materials, or training. Overwhelming evidence seems to indicate that children's beliefs mediate their responsiveness to instruction. The research suggests that classroom teachers, special educators, and parents use techniques that direct children to make attributions to controllable forces for success and failure outcomes. Teachers and parents should model effort self-statements and statements that attribute success to getting smarter. Children should be directed and reinforced for making such statements themselves in response to success and to failure outcomes. If criticism is given, it should be specific to the task and used only when the teacher is reasonably certain that the child has not put forth his or her best effort. If the child is trying hard, and the teacher misperceives the child's effort, the child will probably experience feelings of frustration and helplessness. It is important that the teacher give the child credit where credit is due and not take personal credit for the child's success. Social comparisons with other children should be de-emphasized and children's progress put in the context of learning new strategies, trying hard, and getting smarter.

IV. SOCIAL COMPETENCE

A. Problems in Defining Social Competence

Much of the rationale for concern for the social status of students with LDs was generated by sociometric studies. Two sociometric scales have been used in most of these studies. One requires children to rate every other child in the classroom on a 4- to 7-point scale (like a lot–don't like much). On the second scale, children nominate up to five classmates for various prosocial and anti-social roles (e.g., who is dirty and messy–who does everyone like to have around). Children's scores on these measures can be used to rank children as popular (a lot of positive nominations or high rankings–few or no negative votes), rejected (a lot of negative nominations or low rankings–few or no positive votes), isolated (few nominations on either popular or rejection items), or tolerated (medium rankings). About 25 research studies have compared the popularity and rejection nominations and rankings of students with LDs and their normal-achieving classmates. The majority of these studies have found LD students to differ from their classmates on sociometric scales. Some studies find the LD to be more rejected, others find them to be less popular but not more rejected, and a few find no differences. The problem with sociometric studies is that they provide no clues as to why a child is popular, rejected, or tolerated. To understand the social problems of a child, we need behavioral measures of social competence. Sociometric studies do not tell us how many children with LDs have problems in peer relationships, nor do we have any idea as to how problems in the social domain relate to problems in the cognitive and academic domains.

In addition, social competence involves many behaviors, and not all of the behaviors that shape our judgments of others are social. For instance, social competence in the classroom includes appropriate peer-interaction skills but also behaviors to cope with the demands of the classroom setting (e.g., being on-task, completing work, gaining attention appropriately; Reschly *et al.*, 1984). Second, our judgments of others is somewhat idiosyncratic. For instance, teachers differ in their tolerance of long hair, swearing, and messiness. This means that judgments of social competence are affected by characteristics of the person making the judgments as well as the person being judged. Third, the appropriateness of social behaviors is influenced by the social context in which they occur. Social status is a function of both individual and group characteristics. For instance, Wright *et al.* (1986) showed how aggressive children are more likely to be popular in groups that have many aggressive children but unpopular in groups that have few aggressive children. In contrast, withdrawn children are likely to be popular in groups that have few aggressive children but not popular in groups that have many aggressive children. Popularity is thus related to "distinctiveness," the degree to which one is similar to or different from one's social group. Finally, changing one's behavior to be more appropriate does not guarantee that others' judgments will change in response (Bierman and Furman, 1984).

Models of social competence that try to take into account the complex relationships between children's characteristics and behaviors have been developed. These models have been based on the results of research comparing socially competent with incompetent (e.g., behavior disordered) children. One model developed and tested by Dodge and his colleagues (cf. Dodge, 1986; Dodge and Murphy, 1984; Dodge and Newman, 1981) divides social competence into three components. In the first, the individual must perceive, decode, and interpret social cues. The second component is the selection of an optimal social response, and the third component is the adequate enactment of a behavioral response. Thus, social competence requires the child to read social situations, generate the appropriate strategies, and engage in a strategic response. In the following sections, the research on the social competence of students with LDs is summarized. Readers should note that the research is fragmented as no systematic studies have examined any one group of LD students' skills on all three components of social competence.

B. Social Cognition

The area of social cognition attempts to understand the linkages between social development and cognitive development and between social behavior and social cognition (Schantz, 1983). The importance of social cognition stems from recognition that behavior is a function of knowledge about the situations in which various behaviors are to be used (Chi *et al.*, 1981). The research on LD students' social cognitive development has assessed their perspective-taking, comprehension of nonverbal communication, moral development, social problem-solving skills, and communicative competence (i.e., expressive language skills in social interactions).

Assessments of children's *perspective-taking* focus on children's ability to understand how others would see or interpret social events. Measures of perspective-taking typically provide the child with information about a social situation and then ask the child to report how someone else who has less or different information would interpret the situation. To date, nine studies using five different measures have compared samples of LD and normal-achieving students on perspective taking. Let us consider two studies that used the same measure.

Dickstein and Warren (1980) and Bruck and Hebert (1982) measured cognitive, affective, and perceptual perspective-taking. Each measure had 10 questions. Five questions were egocentric: They required children to respond from their own perspective and were intended to verify that children understood the task requirements. Five questions were nonegocentric: They required children to take into account a point of view that differed from their own. The children responded to each question nonverbally by pointing to one of three objects.

The cognitive task measured the child's ability to predict the thoughts of others. In the egocentric questions, the child is told a short story in which no conflict exists between the information possessed by the child and the person in the story. For the nonegocentric questions, a conflict exists between the information possessed by the child and the person in the story (e.g., "Andy told his Dad he was going to draw a lion in art class. When Andy got to school, his teacher told him he could draw a zebra, a giraffe, or a lion. Andy decided to draw a giraffe instead and brought the picture home in his school bag. Point to the one Daddy will think Andy drew in art class.")

The affective task measured the child's ability to predict another's feelings. The children pointed to one of three plastic "eggheads" looking happy or sad or showing no emotion in response to story questions. The story was worded so that there was conflict or no conflict between the affect of the story character and the child. For example, if the child indicated she liked to take baths, the egocentric story would relate: "Sally likes to take baths. Sally's Mom tells Sally it is time to take a bath. Point to the fact that shows how Sally feels." The nonegocentric question would start: "Sally doesn't like to take baths ...."

The perceptual task measured the child's ability to take the visual perspective of others. Children were presented with groups of toys mounted on two turntables, and a third group with toys mounted on a rectangular platform, and two dolls. Children had to indicate the animal a doll would see when the turntable would allow both dolls to see the same animals (egocentric questions) or different animals (nonegocentric questions).

Dickstein and Warren (1980) tested LD children ages 5–11 yr and NLD children ages 5–9 yr. They found no group differences on the egocentric questions. On the nonegocentric questions, the LD performed more poorly than the NLD children. The NLD children showed a ceiling effect by age

8 yr; i.e., they were able to get all the questions correct. But the LD children did not show this ceiling effect. Although they improved with age, the LD children showed no better performance at age 10 yr than they had at age 8 yr.

Bruck and Hebert (1982) found that LD children did more poorly than the NLD on the nonegocentric questions, thus replicating Dickstein and Warren's (1980) results. In this study, they also looked at the relationship of hyper-activity and perspective-taking. They found that LD students' performance on the perspective-taking measures could not be attributed to hyperactivity.

Although we have no data about the reliability or validity of the perspective-taking measures used in these studies, they are reported here for a number of reasons. First, it is important that the results of the studies replicated. It is notable when two researchers using different samples of children get the same results. Second, by distinguishing between egocentric and nonegocentric questions, it was ensured that group differences could not be attributed to LD children's failure to understand the task or to receptive language differences. Third, because students had only to point as a response, group differences cannot be dismissed as a function of expressive language problems. Fourth, although older LD subjects performed much like younger LD subjects, the outcomes cannot be attributed to a developmental delay. Their performance was stable across ages 5–11 yr.

In summary, although factors such as attention, listening skills, memory, and expressive language are likely to play a role in understanding others' perspectives, these studies found LD students to differ from NLD students under conditions that controlled for at least some of these other factors. Because in reality perspective-taking occurs in response to events that are fleeting in time and space, and demonstrations of understanding are likely to require verbal and nonverbal responses, these studies may provide con-servative estimates of group differences. On the other hand, one could argue that in reality perspective-taking might be easier as more information (sight, sound, and past history) is available and clues for how to respond may be provided by others.

C. Comprehension of Nonverbal Communication

Nonverbal behaviors such as smiling, eye contact, and body leaning play an important role in social interactions. These behaviors communicate our feelings about the other person, the situation, the message, our desire to continue or to terminate the communication, and whether the conversation is going well or badly. Measures of children's ability to accurately interpret others' nonverbal communication thus provide an important way to measure their social perception and cognition.

A number of studies have used the Profile of Nonverbal Sensitivity (PONS; Rosenthal, *et al.*, 1979) to assess LD students' comprehension of nonverbal communication. On this test, subjects are shown a 45-min black-and-white videotape containing 220 items, each a 2-sec clip of a young woman portraying an emotional response. Three visual presentations (face, body, figure) and two auditory presentations (scrambled speech and electronically filtered speech) are shown, both alone and in combination. The subject views or listens to each clip and chooses one of two descriptions as the correct description of the scenario.

The studies that have used the PONS to compare LD with NLD children have found that the LD perform less accurately than their NLD classmates (Axelrod, 1982; Bryan, 1977; Jackson *et al.*, 1987). One study, however, did not find differences between LD and NLD students on the PONS. Stone and LaGreca (1984) hypothesized that differences in accuracy on the PONS were related to LD students' attentional deficits and not to differences in their comprehension of nonverbal communication. To test this hypothesis, Stone and LaGreca (1984) reminded students to pay careful attention prior to showing each clip on the test. The results of this study showed no differences between the LD and NLD subjects on the PONS. This is of theoretical importance as we try to advance our understanding of LD students' performance on measures of social cognition. We need to know if differences in performance between the LD and NLD students are nested in attentional deficits, deficits in perception, or deficits in cognition.

D. Moral Development

Another way of looking at children's social cognition is to assess their understanding of the culture's moral principles. There is a body of research on children's development of morality showing an age–stage progression in their acquisition of these concepts. The most well-known model of moral development was developed by Lawrence Kohlberg (Kohlberg *et al.*, 1978). This model is an age–stage model with six levels of moral reasoning: (1) punishment–obedience (what is right to avoid punishment), (2) individual instrumental purpose and exchange (right is doing what's best for one's own or another person's needs), (3) mutual interpersonal expectations, relationships, and conformity (what is right is performing the way that others in your group expect), (4) social system and conscience maintenance (right is doing one's duty in maintaining the system), (5) prior rights and social contracts (judgments based on the basic rights, values, and legal contract of society, even when they conflict with the rules and laws of a group), and (6) universal ethical principles (right is guided by universal ethical principles that all humanity should follow).

The moral judgment interview (Kohlberg et al., 1978) is used to assess children's developmental levels of moral maturity. The interview presents three hypothetical dilemmas involving conflicting moral issues in which the protagonist must choose to do one of two actions. The conflicting issues are (1) life versus law (e.g., should Heinz break the law to save his wife's life?), (2) punishment versus conscience (should Heinz be punished if he was acting according to his conscience?), and (3) contract versus authority (should Joe obey his father or maintain a contractual agreement?).

Studies that have used the moral judgment interview with LD samples have mixed results. Fincham (1977) found no differences between LD and NLD (8- and 9-year-old males, but Derr (1986) found differences between 14.3- and 18.5-yr-old LD and NLD males. In the Derr study, the LD males responses resembled those of NLD children ages 10–14 yr. Fincham's failure to find group diferences may be related to the efforts he made to eliminate the language complexity in the stimulus materials, to the restricted range of responses he found across both groups (they all scored in the lower three levels on the scale), and to possible school effects. Apparently, the LD attended a school that used an "induction" type of discipline, in which explanations pointing to the consequences for others rather than punishment were emphasized. These studies differed on so many dimensions that it is difficult to interpret their results.

E. Comprehension of Other Social Mores

Other researchers have examined LD children's social cognition by assessing their attitudes and views on such diverse topics as altruism and ingratiation. In the case of understanding altruism, children were administered a questionnaire about giving money to charity, doing good deeds for others, and the like. LD children did not differ in their understanding of the "shoulds." However, on a questionnaire that asked students the likelihood that they would conform to peer pressure to engage in prosocial and antisocial actions, the LD indicated greater willingness than NLD students to conform to pressure on the antisocial scenarios (Bryan et al., 1982). Although their understanding of "shoulds" was comparable, their expressed intentions of how they might act differed.

Similar results were found in a series conducted by James Bryan (Bryan et al., 1981; Bryan and Sonnefeld, 1981). In these studies, children's attitudes toward how best to ingratiate peers, parents, teachers, and adults were tested. The results found that LD students showed no deficit in their knowledge concerning the social desirability of various ingratiation tactics addressed to different audiences; however, evidence indicated that they might select less socially desirable strategies than NLD children.

In summary, studies examining LD students' knowledge about society's modes and morals find that LD students understand these principles as well as their peers. Group differences emerge when asked how they might respond in social situations involving these principles. The LD indicate greater willingness to violate social norms. Whether they actually do so, however, remains to be tested.

F. Social Problem Solving

Still another way to assess children's social cognition is to involve them in social problem solving. In these studies, students are typically presented with some type of social conflict and then asked to role play how they might respond. The assessment of social cognition in these studies is, thus, intertwined with assessment of children's receptive and expressive language skills. LD students' performance might differ from higher-achieving students, but such differences may be due to deficits in social cognition, receptive language, and/or expressive language.

In two studies, researchers used several measures of social cognition–role playing to compare LD with NLD students. Silver and Young (1985) compared LD, low-achieving, and NLD eighth-grade boys, and Schneider and Yoshida (1988) compared LD with NLD junior high-school students. The studies used such measures as the Means–Ends Problem Solving (Platt and Spivack, 1975), the Social Interaction Role Play Assessment (Waddell, 1984), and the Awareness of Consequences Test (Platt and Spivack, 1975). In both studies, the LD males scored lower than normal-achieving males. It should be noted that the differences between groups of subjects cannot be dismissed on the basis of IQ. In the Silver and Young (1985) study, the LD did more poorly than a group of normal-achieving classmates, but they did not perform differently than a group of low achievers, although the low achievers had lower IQs than the LD. If IQ were the reason for performance on these measures, the LD should have performed better because they had higher IQs than the low achievers. In the Schneider and Yoshida (1988) study, LD and normal-achieving subjects had comparable IQs.

A third study that used role plays to assess LD adolescents' social cognition was conducted by Pearl et al. (1990). In this study, the focus was on adolescents' expectations for situations in which one adolescent invites another to engage in antisocial or illegal activities. Students were asked to role-play how a teenager might respond in situations in which one teenager asked another to participate in an act of misconduct such as stealing a car, shoplifting, or taking marijuana or in prosocial acts such as shoveling snow for a neighbor or collecting money for charity. The study found that the LD students expected others to make their pitch using simple requests, whereas

NLD students expected requests that stressed the payoff to the listener, minimized the negative consequences, and maximized the positive consequences of the act. The LD adolescents also showed less insight about suggestions to engage in illegal activities as they suggested fewer reasons why someone should accept or refuse the request and suggested fewer scenarios for what might happen if such a response were made.

These studies are limited in a number of ways. As mentioned, it is hard to differentiate between social cognition and expressive language skills in these studies. Second, what adolescents might really do in such situations is not clear. How much knowledge and what kind of knowledge do people need to be socially competent? And, in the Pearl et al. (in press) study, how many strategies do adolescents need to protect themselves from being led down the garden path? It is notable that these studies focused primarily on preteens and teenagers, that differences in IQ do not explain the poorer performance of the LD and that researchers are struggling to find realistic measures of children's social skills.

G. Social Cognition: Videotape Measures

One of the criticisms made of measures of social cognition is that they are not realistic. Asking children to respond to short scenarios, to questionnaires, or to role plays fails to present them with realistic social scenarios. Hence, a number of researchers have used videotapes or television to present real lifelike sequences of behavior to children. The notion is that better estimates of social cognition can be obtained when children are exposed to realistic scenarios that include sight and sound portrayals of real-life events. On the surface, the argument that video presentations are more realistic than paper and pencil tests or role-play tests is very appealing. In reality, social events offer complete (visual and auditory inputs) and often redundant information, historical and contextual cues, and feedback. In reality, however, the social scene is often complex, and events occur rapidly so there is not much time to think about how to respond. Events seldom occur twice, and information about the proper mode of behavior is seldom made explicit beforehand, at least outside of the classroom. So, the more realistic the presentation, the more difficult it may be to comprehend.

To date, three studies used some type of video presentation to assess the social cognition of LD and NLD children. In one study (Maheady et al., 1984), children were presented with a 30-min scenario showing 20 natural sequences of social interaction. Viewers answered an interpretive question about the people in the scene; for example, viewers were asked to identify which of two women playing with a baby is the mother. Used with 7–11- and 13–17-yr-old LD, emotionally disturbed, educable mentally retarded, and NLD males, the results found that the educable mentally retarded children made fewer correct responses than the other groups. No differences were found between the LD and other groups.

Weiss (1984) used videotapes of 4–16-sec scenes that depicted different social interactions between 2 or 3 boys: neutral, friendly, cooperative, teasing, horseplay, fighting, or angry. After viewing the scene, subjects described it and rated it on a scale (very, very friendly–very, very unfriendly). The study involved LD and NLD, aggressive and nonaggressive 11–15-yr-old males. The results were that the LD groups (aggressive and nonaggressive) viewed the scenarios as more unfriendly.

In the third study, Pearl and Cosden (1982) used segments from televised soap operas to assess junior-high LD and normal-achieving students' inferences about the televised characters' feelings and intentions and the social amenities that they used. The LD performed more poorly than their classmates, as they had a lower proportion of correct responses.

It seems that the differences between the results of the Maheady *et al.* (1984) study and the Weiss (1984) and Pearl and Cosden (1982) studies rest in the complexity of the social scenarios and the level of comprehension demanded by the task. In the Maheady *et al.* (1984) study, the stimuli seem to be concrete and familiar. In the other two studies, students were required to make inferences on the basis of subtle verbal and behavioral cues. This suggests that LD students will not differ from normal-achieving classmates when the social situation is familiar, the stimuli concrete, and/or the response well known. They are more likely to show social cognitive deficits when the situation is complex, the intentions of persons are related through nonverbal, subtle communications, and/or inferences about antecedents, intentions, and consequences must be made. The results of the Weiss (1984) study, showing LD adolescents to misinterpret social interactions as more unfriendly, needs to be replicated with a sample of LD students who are getting along in mainstream settings. If the results replicate with a school-selected sample, we might have a much better understanding of why students with LDs so often do poorly on sociometric measures.

In summary, studies of social cognition have found LD students to differ from normal achieving classmates. Irrespective of the type of measure, paper and pencil, role play, or video presentations and across a wide age span, they perform more poorly than their classmates. Differences were not found, however, when adjustments were made in the complexity of the stimulus materials (Fincham, 1977; Maheady *et al.*, 1984) or when extra special care was taken to control for students attention (Stone and LaGreca, 1984). Hence, we cannot be sure as to the origin of performance differences. The differences cannot be explained on the basis of IQ, but more work is needed to ferret out the relative importance of perception, cognition, memory, and language in determining differences between LD and NLD students' social cognitive skills and development.

H. Implications for Research

There is much to learn about children's social cognitive development. For starters, we have limited understanding of the developmental age–stage sequences in children's acquisition of such skills. Second, we have very limited understanding of how perception, cognition, memory, and language interact to influence children's acquisition of such skills. Third, the measures of social cognition have not been developed within the constraints of psychometry; hence, most assessment devices that serve as the basis of this body of research are lacking indices of reliability, validity, and normative data. Studies delineating the interaction of child cognition and environment are also lacking. Children do not acquire these skills in a vacuum; what they learn and how they behave is influenced by characteristics of the school and home.

In this chapter, little space was given to descriptions of the LD and NLD students; this was intentional. When the results of research studies based on the performances of presumably heterogeneous groups of children and adolescents consistently find differences between the LD and NLD students, a common thread has been identified. Given the diversity of samples in these studies, LD youngsters clearly are at risk for poorer understanding of social situations. That their problems may be minimized by controlling for the complexity of language or calling their attention to the upcoming stimuli does not diminish their problems. At the same time, we have much to learn about the social cognitive development of students with LDs. At what age and in what way do such problems manifest themselves? Which children with LDs are at risk for problems in this domain? How do such problems relate to their LDs in the academic domains?

I. Implications for Teaching

Clues for how teachers might use this information is nested in the results of the studies. If we can improve children's performance in the social domain by attending to children's attention spans, the linguistic complexity of our communications to children, and to the linguistic complexity of the responses demanded from children, we have begun to embed our knowledge of social cognitive development into instruction. It is important that teachers recognize that aberrant behavior may reflect a child's failure to "tune in" to the social situation or the child's misreading of the situation. Thus, the LD child may behave appropriately in some situations but fail to recognize when changes in situations demand alterations in behavior. Teachers should be alert to naturally occurring situations that they can use to instruct children about others' feelings, intentions, antecedents and consequences, and the like. Although there are gaps in our knowledge of children's cognitive development, there is no end to the naturally occurring events in classrooms, lunchrooms, and playgrounds that teachers could use as material for social cognitive assessment and intervention.

V. COMMUNICATIVE COMPETENCE

Communicative competence refers to children's knowledge of the rules that govern communication exchanges in social situations, the use of language in social contexts. Up to this point, we have reviewed research on children's attitudes and cognitions and on estimates of how they decode, interpret, and comprehend social events. Now we turn to their performance. Given their understanding of a social situation, how do children choose to respond? In light of the importance of expressive language in social interactions, researchers should consider the communicative competence of students with LDs.

There is good reason to hypothesize that problems in communicative competence affect the social status of the LD. First, language deficits are part of the definition of LDs. Second, abundant evidence links deficits in syntax and semantics to deficits in the acquisition of reading skills. Thus, it seems likely that the use of language in social contexts would be similarly affected. Third, despite the prevalence of language disorders among LD students, few students with LDs actually receive special services from speech–language pathologists. For instance, a recent study of the prevalence of language disorders among 8.6–12.6-yr-old LD students found that 90.5% of the sample evidenced language impairments, but only 6% were receiving services from speech–language pathologists (Gibbs and Cooper, 1989).

Communicative competence involves a variety of skills. We learn how to engage in conversational turn-taking, how to construct a message so it is meaningful to the listener, and how to take into account characteristics of the listener in relation to us. For instance, we learn how to signal to a speaker that he or she should continue to speak or stop, and we interpret others' behaviors regarding our own output. Our messages must contain enough information so that others can interpret their meaning, and we use direct or indirect terms depending on our assessment of how familiar the information is to our listener. We speak differently to people we know well than we do to strangers, to young versus old people, to men versus women. Children start to acquire these skills very early, with considerable automaticity as they become speakers of their native tongues.

A number of studies have compared the communicative competence of students with LDs and their achieving peers. Let us consider two of these studies. In one study, LD children's persuasion skills were assessed (Bryan *et al.*, 1981a). Triads of LD and normal achieving third- through sixth-graders independently rank-ordered 15 possible gift choices for their class (e.g., candy, two tickets to a movie, perfume for the teacher). The children were then assembled in triads (one LD and two normal-achieving children or three normal-achieving children) to do the ranking of gift choices together. The children were videotaped during their discussions. The analysis looked at the correspondence between the children's top choices when they worked independently and the group's top choices. In addition, children's verbal exchanges during the discussion were analyzed. The results found that LD children were less persuasive because their top choices were less likely to be among their group's first choices than were those of their classmates. The reasons for their failure to be as persuasive are seen in the analysis of the triads' discussions. In comparison to their classmates, the LD were more likely to agree, less likely to disagree, and less likely to argue their case than the normal-achieving children. They were less likely to monitor the group's progress (i.e., keep the group on task by making statements such as "let's get this settled now"). The LD also were less likely to attempt to "hold the floor" (i.e., make statements like "wait" and "ummm"). Such statements serve the function of allowing a person to think while not letting someone else take over the conversation. It is important to note that the LD talked as much as the other children, they were as likely to initiate topics, and they were more likely to respond to requests for opinions addressed to the whole group. The LD children's lack of persuasiveness apparently is linked to the conversational strategies they used in the situation. They produced messages that were acquiescent and unassertive. They selected conversational strategies that allowed them to participate, yet in a rather passive way.

In the second study, Bryan *et al.*, (1981b) tested LD children's verbal passivity by placing them in a social situation that demanded they be verbally dominant. In this study, LD and NLD second- and fourth-graders were cast in the role of television talk show hosts. Randomly selected classmates played the role of television talk show guests. After the children were given instructions on how to play the roles of host and guest, they were videotaped for 3 min while they pretended to put on a television talk show.

The analysis of the videotaped discussions found that the LD talked as much as the NLD talk show hosts. As in the "persuasion" study, the LD students were full participants in the social exchanges. What differed, however, were the verbal strategies used by the LD. In contrast to their peers, the LD asked fewer questions of their guests, and their questions were less likely to be open-ended (a good strategy for eliciting longer responses from one's partner than questions that elicit "yes" or "no" answers). In addition, the guests of the LD provided fewer elaborated responses to the questions, and they asked the LD more questions. This suggests that some role switching was taking place.

Two studies thus found that elementary-aged LD students differed not in their amount of verbal participation but in the communication strategies they employed in their peer interactions. Cursory observations of their peer exchanges would not likely arouse concern for their verbal skills. Indeed, being agreeable and letting others talk is certainly adaptive behavior—under certain conditions. The issue is whether or not the LD use these strategies because of communication limitations. It is cognitively and linguistically easier to say yes than to argue one's position. Perhaps it is easier to formulate a direct question ("Do you like Star Wars?") than an open-ended query ("How do you feel about crime on television?"). LD students' performance may be related to their social status. Perhaps children who have low social status play a more passive social role because the more popular children play the more active roles in their social groups.

A. Research Issues

There are many research questions here. First, the research has not been comprehensive in testing all the components of communicative competence. We do not know how performance in one category relates to performance in another. Second, we need research to link communicative competence to other linguistic skills (syntax and semantics) and to reading skills (decoding and comprehension). Third, we need to link communicative competence to children's sociometric status.

B. Teaching Issues

Because LD children apparently participate as much as other children in social exchanges with peers, classroom teachers will probably not notice that they selectively use certain strategies. We all know that it is important to learn how to be persuasive, how to be tactful, and how to present our own position on issues. It is very important that children learn how to defend themselves verbally, how to verbally carry on a disagreement, how to respond to negative feedback and evaluations, and how to express negative feelings and judgments in socially appropriate ways. Teachers need to tune into such needs in developmentally appropriate ways and provide the structure whereby children can observe, model, and practice such skills.

VI. TEACHERS' JUDGMENTS AND CLASSROOM BEHAVIOR

Now we turn to the research on LD students' social behavioral competence, i.e., how they actually act in social situations. This research is based on teacher ratings of children's behavior, laboratory studies of communicative competence, and classroom observations of social interactions and work-related activities.

A. Teachers' Ratings

Several studies have used teacher rating scales to assess the social competence and behavior of students with LDs. Several investigators used the Behavior Problem Checklist (BPC; Epstein *et al.*, 1984, 1985, 1986; Bursuck, 1989). This measure consists of 55 items, each a statement of some child adjustment problem. The BPC, developed by Quay and Peterson (unpublished), yields scores that have been subgrouped to describe three dimensions of child maladjustment: conduct disorder, personality problem, and inadequacy–immaturity. Conduct disorder items relate to disruptiveness, aggression, and acting-out behaviors. Personality problem items relate to nervousness, fearfulness, and lack of interpersonal competencies. Inadequacy–immaturity items refer to functioning like younger children.

To summarize the results of these studies, each one finds that teacher ratings of LD students on the BPC is indicative of problems in the personality or conduct domains. Among younger LD males and females, the problems seem to relate to attentional deficits. Older LD students were more likely to show predelinquent behavior problems (e.g., "stays out at night") than younger children. LD males tended to externalize their problems (e.g., "disruptive," "disobedient"), and LD females tended to internalize their problems (e.g., "self-conscious").

Studies that used other measures find essentially the same results; teachers rate LD students as less socially competent than their higher-achieving peers (Bender, 1985; Gresham and Reschly, 1986). For instance, Bender (1985) used the Teacher Temperament Questionnaire (Thomas and Chess, 1977), a scale in which teachers rate the child on persistence, distractibility, activity level, adaptability, approach–withdrawal, positive mood, intensity of response, and threshold of response. The Walker Problem Behavior Identification Checklist (Walker, 1976), a measure of acting out, withdrawal, distractibility, disturbed peer relations, and immaturity, was also used. The results found that teachers rated LD students lower on task orientation on the Temperament Questionnaire and higher on acting-out behavior, distractibility, and disturbed peer relations on the Walker Checklist. It should be noted that essentially the same results are found when rating scales are completed by parents of LD and NLD students, and these results hold for black and white and rural and urban samples (Gresham and Reschly, 1986).

B. Classroom Behavior

Studies of LD children's social competence have extended to observational studies of their behavior in the classroom and on the playground. What is amazing is that with the exception of teacher ratings on attention, there appears to be no correspondence between the results of observation studies and teacher ratings of social behavior. Virtually no evidence generated by classroom observation studies or playground studies indicate that children with LDs exhibit conduct and personality problems.

By and large, the results of classroom observation studies indicate that compared with normal-achieving classmates, LD children are more likely to be off-task and to interact with teachers (Feagans and McKinney, 1981; McKinney and Speece, 1983). McKinney and Feagans (1984) carried this work further by classifying students into subtypes on the basis of teacher ratings, measures of intelligence, and achievement. Using teacher ratings of first- and second-graders, they identified four categories: (1) behavior deficits in independent and task orientation, but strong in social adjustment, with average verbal skills, and mildly deficient in achievement; (2) deficits in all behavioral areas, uneven cognitive abilities, and severely deficient in achievement; (3) deficits on task orientation, high on extroversion and hostility, and average cognitive ability but mildly deficient in achievement; and (4) no behavioral problems and deficient only in academic achievement.

Work on subtyping students with LDs will no doubt help us sort out why teacher ratings indicate rather serious problems in conduct and personality; however, observation studies reveal primarily attentional deficits. Several facts should be noted. Most of the observation studies have been done with young children. As pointed out by Epstein and his colleagues (1985, 1986) attention deficits in young children may evolve into conduct problems later. Also, problems noted by teachers perhaps do not show up on classroom observations because these behaviors are likely to be low frequency, thus they may not manifest themselves when observers are present or may not show up in data analyses based on frequencies of behavior. Low-frequency behaviors may be insignificant in statistics but very significant in human relations. It also should be noted that the categories used in observation studies focus primarily on on- and off-task behavior. The interactions that take place among children, especially as they grow older, are not accessible to adults. Children's social interactions become increasingly private. In the classroom, where children's opportunities to interact are limited, social communications are whispered or conducted out of adult view. Still, these explanations fail to account for teacher characterizations of LD children as having problems in the conduct and personality domains.

C. Research Questions

Teacher ratings of LD children's behavior finds them characterized as having problems in conduct and personality. But classroom observation studies find that LD students are differentiated from normal-achieving students on the dimension of on- and off-task behavior. Although McKinney and Feagans (1984) research on subtypes of LDs helps us to sort out teacher ratings of behavior, cognitive ability, and achievement, we have yet to understand how teacher ratings on the BPC correspond to students' classroom behavior. Thus, we have a major gap in our knowledge of LD students social competence. There is extraordinary consistence in peer sociometric studies, teacher and peer ratings finding that the LD rated more negatively on various dimensions than their higher-achieving classmates. But we have yet to isolate the behaviors, social or otherwise, that account for these negative ratings. Our clearest source of differences between the LD and their normal-achieving classmates is generated by research on social cognition. Therefore, it seems that a next step for researchers would be to expand our understanding of how social cognitive development and deficits might interact with social behavior in situations that vary in their linguistic and social complexity.

D. Implications for Teaching

First, teachers must not underestimate the importance of children's classroom competence in behavior and social relationships. Children who are experiencing problems in establishing satisfactory social relationships may be preoccupied with their social problems. Teacher priorities may rest with academics, but it is not at all clear that children share teacher, priorities. Therefore, it is incumbent upon teachers to explore ways to organize the class for instruction to facilitate children's acquisition of social skills and adequate social relationships. It is beyond the scope of this chapter to discuss social skills programs, but most promising is cooperative goal structures. In cooperative goal structures, children are rewarded for group products and work together in small groups. A large body of data show that children in cooperative goal structures feel better about themselves and their classmates, and their learning does not suffer, in comparison to other goal structures (i.e., individualized, competitive).

VII. THE LAST WORD

This chapter summarized a great deal of research, most of it conducted within the last 10 years. The chapter searched for the origins of the LD person's social problems. Studies that compared LD and NLD students' attitudes and judgments about themselves, their knowledge of social norms, social cognition, communication skills, and behavior in classrooms were covered. With the exception of knowledge of social norms, evidence indicated that the LD are not as socially competent as their normal-achieving classmates. The results of the studies suggest that even though the LD have adequate knowledge of social norms, they indicate greater willingness to violate these norms. Studies of social cognition and communicative competence suggest that the LD may have some difficulty in understanding others' affective states or in assuming a socially dominant role, at least in socially complex or ambiguous situations.

The research also shows that the reasons, or origins, of the LD person's social problems have not been identified. Each section of the chapter outlined areas of research and gaps in our knowledge. Ultimately, we must integrate the research so that we know which LD children are vulnerable for which types of social problems and under what conditions. In the meantime, special educators and regular classroom teachers can do much to facilitate the development of social cognition and communicative competence. Although LD youngsters who experience severe problems in the acquisition of social cognitive and communication skills may need individual therapy or social skills training, this chapter has tried to include suggestions that teachers could follow in the normal course of instruction. It is important that research continue to identify the dynamics and origins of the social problems of LD persons. It is equally important that practitioners attend to these problems in the classroom.

References

Asher, S. R., and Renshaw, P. D. (1981). Children without friends: Social knowledge and social skill training. *In* "The Development of Children's Friendships" (S. R. Asher and J. M. Gottman, eds.). (pp. 273–296). Cambridge University Press, New York.

Association for Children and Adults with Learning Disabilities (1985). "Special Education Today," Vol. 2, No. 5. Set Press, LTD.

Axelrod, L. (1982). Social perception in learning disabled adolescents. *J. Learn. Disabil.* **15**, 610–613.

Bader, B. W. (1975). "Social Perception and Learning Disabilities." Moon Lithographing & Engraving, Des Moines, Iowa.

Bandura, A. (1982). Self-efficacy mechanism in human agency. *Am. Psycholog.* **37**, 122–147.

Bay, M., and Bryan, T. (1989). "A Case Study Using Videotape to Increase On-Task Behavior in a Head Start Classroom." Unpublished manuscript, University of Illinois at Chicago.

Bendell, D., Tollefson, N., and Fine, M. (1980). Interaction of locus-of-control orientation and the performance of learning disabled adolescents. *J. Learn. Disabil.* **13**, 32–35.

Bender, W. N. (1985). Differences between learning disabled and non-disabled children in temperament and behavior. *Learn. Disabil. Q.* **8**, 11–18.

Benenson, J., and Dweck, C. (1986). The development of trait explanations and self-evaluations in the academic and social domains. *Child Dev.* **57**, 1179–1187.

Bierman, K. L., and Furman, W. F. (1984). The effects of social skills training and peer involvement on the social adjustment of preadolescents. *Child Dev.* **55**, 151–162.

Bloom, B. S. (1976). "Human Characteristics and School Learning." McGraw-Hill, New York.

Boersma, F. J., Chapman, J. W., and Maguire, T. O. (1979). The Student's Perception of Ability Scale: An instrument for measuring academic self-concept in elementary school children. *Educ. Psycholog. Measure.* **39**, 1035–1041.

Borkowski, J. G., Weyhing, R. S., and Carr, M. (1988). Effects of attributional retraining on strategy-based reading comprehension in learning-disabled students. *J. Educ. Psychol.* **80**, 46–53.

Bruck, H., and Hebert, M. (1982). Correlates of learning disabled students' peer-interaction patterns. *Learn. Disabil. Q.* **5**, 353–362.

Bryan, J. H., and Sonnefeld, J. (1981). Children's social ratings of ingratiation tactics. *J. Learn. Disabil.* **5**, 605–609.

Bryan, T. (1977). Children's comprehension of nonverbal communication. *J. Learn. Disabil.* **10**, 501–506.

Bryan, T., Donahue, J., and Pearl, R. (1981a). Learning disabled children's peer interactions during a small-group problem-solving task. *Learn. Disabil. Q.* **4**, 13–22.

Bryan, T., Donahue, M., Pearl, R., and Sturm, C. (1981b). Learning disabled children's conversational skills: The "TV talk show." *Learn. Disabil. Q.* **4**, 250–259.

Bryan, T., Werner, M. A., and Pearl, R. (1982). Learning disabled students' conformity responses to prosocial and antisocial situations. *Learn. Disabil. Q.* **5**, 344–352.

Bryan, T., Bay, M., Shelden, C., and Simon, J. (1990). Teachers and at-risk students simulated recall of instruction. *Exceptionality*, **1**, 167–179.

Buchanan, M., and Wolf, J. S. (1986). A comprehensive study of learning disabled adults. *J. Learn. Disabil.* **19**, 34–38.

Bursuck, W. (1989). A comparison of students with learning disabilities to low achieving and higher achieving students on three dimensions of social competence. *J. Learn. Disabil.* **22**, 188–194.

Chapman, J. W. (1985). "Self-Perceptions of Ability, Learned Helplessness and Academic Achievement Expectations of Children with Learning Disabilities." Education Department, Massey University, Massey, New Zealand.

Chapman, J. W., and Boersma, F. J. (1978). "The Projected Academic Performance Scale." Unpublished instrument, University of Alberta. Edmonton, Canada.

Chi, M. T. H., Feltovich, P., and Glaser, R. (1981). Categorization and representation of physics problems by experts and novices. *Cog. Sci.* **5**, 121–152.

Coopersmith, S. (1967). "The Antecedents of Self-Esteem. "University of California–Davis; W. H. Freeman and Company, San Francisco.

Cowen, El., Pederson, A., Babigion, M., Izzo, L. D., and Trost, M. A. (1973). Long-term follow-up of early detected vulnerable children. *J. Consult. Clin. Psychol.* **41**, 438–446.

Crandall, V., Solomon, D., and Kelleway, R. (1955). Expectancy statements and decision times as a function of objective probabilities and reinforcement values. *J. Person.* **24**, 192–203.

Crandall, V. C., Katkovsky, W., and Crandall, F. J. (1965). Children's beliefs in their own control of reinforcements in intellectual–academic situations. *Child Dev.* **36**, 91–109.

Derr, A. M. (1986). How learning disabled adolescent boys make moral judgements. *J. Learn. Disabil.* **19**, 160–164.

Dickstein, E., and Warren, D. (1980). Role-taking deficits in learning disabled children. *J. Learn. Disabil.* **13**, 378–382.

Dodge, K. A. (1986). "A Social Information Processing Model of Social Competence in Children." In M. Perlmutter (ed.), Minnesota Symposium on Child Psychology, **18**, 77–125. Hillsdale, New Jersey: Erlbaum.

Dodge, K. A., and Murphy, R. R. (1984). The assessment of social competence in adolescents. *In* "Adolescent Behavior Disorders," Vol. 4, "Advances in Child Behavioral Analysis and Therapy" (P. Karoly and J. J. Steffen, eds.). Lexington Books, Lexington, Massachusetts.

Dodge, K. A., and Newman, J. P. (1981). Biased decision making processes in aggressive boys. *J. Abnorm. Psychol.* **90**, 375–379.

Dweck, C. S., and Reppucci, N. D. (1973). Learned helplessness and reinforcement responsibility in children. *J. Person. Social Psychol.* **25**, 109–116.

Epstein, M. H., Cullinan, D., and Nieminen, G. (1984). Social behavior problems of learning disabled and normal girls. *J. Learn. Disabil.* **17**, 609–611.

Epstein, M. H., Bursuck, W., and Cullinan, D. (1985). Patterns of behavior problems among the learning disabled: Boys aged 12–18, girls aged 6–11, and girls aged 12–18. *Learn. Disabil. Q.* **8**, 123–129.

Epstein, M. H., Cullinan, D., and Lloyd, J. W. (1986). Behavior-problem patterns among the learning disabled: Ill-replication across age and sex. *Learn. Disabil. Q.* **9**, 43–54.

Feagans, L., and McKinney, J. D. (1981). The pattern of exceptionality across domains in learning disabled children. *J. Appl. Dev. Psychol.* **1**, 313–328.

Festinger, L. (1954). A theory of social comparison processes. *Hum. Relations* **7**, 117–140.

Fincham, F. A. (1977). Comparison of moral judgment in learning disabled and normal achieving boys. *J. Psychol.* **96**, 153–160.

Gibbs, D. P., and Cooper, E. G. (1989). Prevalence of communication disorders in students with learning disabilities. *J. Learn. Disabil.* **22**, 60–68.

Gregory, J. F., Shanahan, T., and Walberg, H. J. (1986). A profile of learning disabled twelfth-graders in regular classes. *Learn. Disabil. Q.* **9**, 33–42.

Gresham, F. M., and Reschly, D. J. (1986). Social skills deficits and low peer acceptance of mainstreamed learning disabled children. *Learn. Disabil. Q.* **9**, 23–32.

Harter, S. (1985). Processes underlying the construction maintenance, and enhancement of the self-concept in children. *In* "Psychological Perspectives on the Self, Vol. 3 (J. Suls and A. Greenwald, eds.). Lawrence Erlbaum, Hillsdale, New Jersey.

Hiebert, B., Wong, B., and Hunter, M. (1982). Affective influences on learning disabled adolescents. *Learn. Disabil. Q.* **5,** 334–343.

Jackson, S. C., Enright, R. D., and Murdock, J. Y. (1987). Social perception problems in learning disabled youth: Developmental lag versus perceptual deficit. *J. Learn. Disabil.* **20,** 361–364.

Jones, C. J. (1985). Analysis of the self-concepts of handicapped students. *Remedial and Special Education,* **6,** 32–36.

Kavanagh, J. F. and Truss, T. J. (1987). "Learning Disabilities: Proceedings of the National Congress, Parkton, Maryland York.

Keogh, B. K. (1983). Individual differences in temperament: A contributor to the personal–social and educational competence of learning disabled children. *In* "Current Topics in Learning Disabilities," (pp. 33–56). Vol. 1 (J. D. McKinney and L. Feagans, eds.). Ablex, Norwood, New Jersey.

Kistner, J. A., and Osborne, M. (1987). A longitudinal study of LD children's self evaluations. *Learn. Disabil. Q.* **10,** 258–266.

Kistner, J. A., Osborne, M., and LeVerrier, L. (1988). Causal attributions of learning-disabled children: Developmental patterns and relation to academic progress. *J. Educ. Psychol.* **80,** 82–89.

Kohlberg, L., Colby, A., Gibbs, J., Spicher-Dubin, B., and Power, C. (1978). "Assessing Moral Stages: A Manual, Preliminary Edition," July. Center for Moral Education, Harvard University, Cambridge.

Kolligian, J., and Sternberg, R. J. (1986). Intelligence, information processing, and specific learning disabilities: A triarchic synthesis. *J. Learn. Disabil.* **20,** 8–17.

Lincoln, A., and Chazan, S. (1979). Perceived competence and intrinsic motivation in learning disability children. *J. Clin. Child Psychol.* **8,** 213–216.

Maheady, L., Maitland, G., and Sainato, D. (1984). The interpretation of social interactions by mildly handicapped and nondisabled children. *J. Special Educ.* **18,** 151–159.

Margalit, M., and Zak, I. (1984). Anxiety and self-concept of learning disabled children. *J. Learn. Disabil.* **17,** 537–539.

McCandless, B. R., and Evans, E. D. (1973). "Children and Youth: Psychological Development." Hinsdale, Illinois. Dryden.

McKinney, J. D., and Feagans, L. (1984). Adaptive classroom behavior of learning disabled students. *J. Learn. Disabil.* **16,** 360–367.

McKinney, J. D., and Speece, D. L. (1983). Classroom behavior and academic progress of LD students. *J. Appl. Dev. Psychol.* **4,** 149–161.

Minskoff, E. H., Sautter, S. W., Hoffmann, F. J., and Hawks R. (1987). Employer attitudes toward hiring the learning disabled. *J. Learn. Disabil.* **20(1),** 53–57.

Morrison, G. M., Forness, S. R., and MacMillan, D. L. (1983). Influences on the sociometric ratings of mildly handicapped children: A path analysis. *J. Educ. Psychol.* **75,** 63–74.

Parker, J. G., and Asher, S. R. (1987). Peer relations and later personal adjustment: Are low-accepted children at risk? *Psycholog. Bull.* **102(3),** 357–389.

Pascarella, E. T., and Pflaum, S. W. (1981). The interaction of children's attribution and level of control over error correction in reading instruction. *J. Educ. Psychol.* **73**, 533–540.

Pearl, R., and Bryan, T. (1982). Mothers' attributions for their learning disabled child's successes and failures. *Learn. Disabil. Q.* **5**, 53–57.

Pearl, R., and Cosden, M. (1982). Sizing up a situation: LD children's understanding of social interactions. *Learn. Disabil. Q.* **5**, 371–373.

Pearl, R., Bryan, T., and Herzog, A. (1990). Resisting or acquiescing to peer pressure to engage in misconduct: Adolescents' expectations of probable consequence. *J. Youth Adolesc.* **19**, 43–55.

Piers, E., and Harris, D. (1969). "The Piers–Harris Children's Self-Concept Scale." Counselor Recordings and Tests, Nashville.

Platt, J. J., and Spivack, G. (1975). "Manual for the Means-Ends Problem Solving Procedure (MEPS): A Measure of Interpersonal Cognitive Problem-Solving Skill.

Quay, H. C., and Peterson, D. P. (1975). "Manual for the Behavior Problem Checklist." Unpublished manuscript.

Renick, M. J. (1985). "The Development of Learning Disabled Children's Self-Perceptions. National Institute of Child Health and Human Development, Bethesda.

Reschly, D. J., Gresham, F. M., and Graham-Clay, S. (1984). "Multifactored nonbiased Assessment: Convergent and Discriminant Validity of Social and Cognitive Measures with Black and White Regular and Special Education Students." Office of Special Education, Grant Number G0081101156, Assistance Catalog Number CFDA: 84.023E, Washington, D.C.

Rogers, H., and Saklofske, D. H. (1985). Self-concept, locus of control and performance expectations of learning disabled children. *J. Learn. Disabil.* **18**, 273–278.

Rosenberg, B. S., and Gaier, E. L. (1977). The self-concept of the adolescent with learning disabilities. *Adolescence* **12**, 490–497.

Rosenberg, M. (1965). "Society and Adolescent Self-Image." Princeton University Press, Princeton, New Jersey.

Rosenthal, R. Hall, J. A., Mateo, J. R., Rogers, P. L., and Archer, D. (1979). "Sensitivity to Nonverbal Communication: The PONS Test." Johns Hopkins University Press, Baltimore.

Schantz, C. U. (1983). Social cognition. *In* "Handbook of Child Psychology," 4th ed. (P. H. Mussen, ed.), pp. 495–555. John Wiley, New York.

Schneider, M., and Yoshida, R. K. (1988). Interpersonal problem-solving skills and classroom behavioral adjustment in learning-disabled adolescents and comparison peers. *J. School Psychol.* **26**, 25–34.

Schurr, K. T., Towne, R. C., and Joiner, L. M. (1972). Trends in self-concept of ability over 2 years of special-class placement. *J. Special Educ.* **6**, 161–166.

Silver, D. S., and Young, R. D. (1985). Interpersonal problem-solving abilities, peer status and behavioral adjustment in learning disabled and non-learning disabled adolescents. *Adv. Learn. Behav. Disabil.* **4**, 201–223.

Silverman, R., and Zigmond, N. (1983). Self-concept in learning disabled adolescents. *J. Learn. Disabil.* **16**, 478–482.

Stipek, D. J., and Daniels, D. H. (1988). Declining perceptions of competence: A consequence of changes in the child or in the educational environment? *J. Educ. Psychol.* **80,** 352–356.

Stipek, D. J., and Tannatt, L. (1984). Children's judgments of their own and their peers' academic competence. *J. Educ. Psychol.* **76,** 75–84.

Stone, W. L., and LaGreca, A. M. (1984). Comprehension of nonverbal communication: A reexamination of the social competencies of learning-disabled children. *J. Abnorm. Child Psychol.* **12,** 505–518.

Strang, L., Smith, M. D., and Rogers, C. M. (1978). Social comparison, multiple reference groups, and the self-concepts of academically handicapped children before and after mainstreaming. *J. Educ. Psychol.* **70,** 487–497.

Thomas, A., and Chess, S. (1977). "Temperament and Development." Brunner, New York.

Tollefson, H., Tracy, D. B., Johnsen, E. P., Buenning, M., Farmer, A., and Barke, C. R. (1982). Attribution patterns of learning disabled adolescents. *Learn. Disabil. Q.* **5,** 14–20.

Turiel, E. (1983). "The Development of Social Knowledge." Cambridge University Press, Cambridge.

Waddell, J. (1984). The self-concept and social adaptation of hyperactive children in adolescence. J. Clin. Child Psychol. **13,** 50–55.

Walker, H. M. (1976). "Walker Problem Behavior Identification Checklist." Western Psychological Services, Los Angeles.

Walker, H. M., and Lamon, W. E. (1987). Social behavior standards and expectations of Australian and U.S. teacher groups. *J. Special Educ.* **21,** 56–82.

Weiss, E. (1984). Learning disabled children's understanding of social interactions of peers. *J. Clin. Child Psychol.* **13,** 50–55.

White, W. J. (1985). Perspectives on the education and training of learning disabled adults. *Learn. Disabil. Q.* **86,** 231–236.

Winne, P. H., Woodlands, M. H., and Wong, B. Y. L. (1982). Comparability of self-concept among learning disabled, normal and gifted students. *J. Learn. Disabil.* **15,** 470–475.

Wittrock, M. C. (ed.) (1986). "Handbook on Research on Teaching," 3rd ed. Macmillan, New York.

Wright, J. C., Giammarino, M., and Parad, H. W. (1986). Social status in small groups: Individual-group similarity and the social "misfit". *J. Pers. Soc. & Psych.,* **50,** 523–536.

Ysseldyke, J. E., Algozzine, B., Shinn, M., and McGue, M. (1982). Similarities and differences among low achievers and students labeled learning disabled. *J. Special Educ.* **16,** 73–85.

CHAPTER 8

The Relevance of Metacognition to Learning Disabilities

Bernice Y. L. Wong

Editor's Notes

Metacognition is an important construct in reading research, and metacognitive strategies have been shown to differentiate between skilled and unskilled readers. More important, reading researchers have shown that teaching students metacognitive strategies in reading enhanced their reading comprehension.

What does all that have to do with us in learning disabilities? My chapter answers this question by explaining to you the relevance of metacognition to learning disabilities. This relevance concerns the invalidity in interpreting all learning and performance problems in individuals with learning disabilities as deep-seated cognitive deficiencies, as well as the necessity to include metacognitive strategies in reading and writing in instructional remediations of those individuals. The relevance of metacognition to learning disabilities is realized through an appreciation of A. L. Brown's conceptualization of the crucial role of metacognition in successful reading and learning and of the empirical research on metacognitive skills in reading that discriminated among younger readers, poor readers, and skilled readers.

I. RATIONALE

Every young science begins its development by adopting theories and experimental methods and approaches from other more established sciences. Psychology is a prime example. The psychologist Murray (1984) shows how the development of psychology as an experimental science has been shaped by various theories from other disciplines.

Learning disabilities (LDs) is a very young scientific discipline. Its development began in the late 1960s and is influenced by advances in the theories and research in related fields such as cognitive psychology, reading, and instructional psychology. In this chapter, we will see the influence of a theoretical construct from cognitive psychology, metacognition and its research, on the LDs field.

Metacognition is one of the important theoretical constructs in cognitive psychology. It was originated by Flavell (1976) and arose from the context of research in memory processes. It has generated much theoretical and empirical interest. The construct was then applied to academic areas by A. L. Brown (1980), who conceptualized the important role of metacognition in effective learning and reading. Subsequently, research findings were obtained that clearly separated good and poor/learning-disabled (LD) readers in metacognitive skills in reading. Against the backdrop of Brown's conceptualizations and the metacognitive research findings differentiating between good and poor/LD readers, the question of the relevance of metacognition assumes research and practical significance for LD professionals.

II. SCOPE AND SEQUENCE

The topic of metacognition and LDs revolves around the relevance of this theoretical construct and its accompanying research to LDs. This chapter focuses on explicating that relevance. First, the theoretical construct of metacognition is defined. Then, its crucial role in effective learning and efficient reading is explained. A summary of research differentiating between the metacognitive skills of good and poor/LD readers follows. The preceding conceptual and empirical expositions provide the necessary framework for explaining the relevance of metacognition to LDs. Both the advantages and limitations of applying metacognition to LDs are then considered. The limitations appear to be redressed by the most recently developed model of metacognition by Borkowski et al. (1989).

From this chapter, readers should understand the following:

1. why metacognition is crucial to effective learning and efficient reading,

2. why metacognition is relevant to LDs and the implications of this relevance for LDs professionals, and
3. the heuristic value of the model of metacognition developed by Borkowski *et al.* (1989) for instructional research with individuals with LDs.

Although both males and females have LDs and problems in metacognition, in the interest of clarity and a smoother flow of writing, reference will be made to the masculine gender throughout this chapter.

III. METACOGNITION: DEFINITION, ASPECTS, AND CHARACTERISTICS

Flavell (1976: 232) stated that "metacognition refers to one's knowledge concerning one's own cognitive processes and products of anything related to them, e.g., the learning-relevant properties of information or data." Included in that statement are two kinds of activities: knowledge about cognition and regulation of cognition (Baker and Brown, 1984b).

Knowledge about cognition concerns an individual's knowledge about his own cognitive resources and the compatibility between himself as a learner and the learning situation. Specifically, Flavell (1987) proposes three categories of knowledge about cognition: person variables, task variables, and strategy variables. Person variables refer to an individual's knowledge and beliefs that he has learned through his experiences about human beings as cognitive organisms. Thus, an individual may believe that he is good at processing abstract, conceptual materials but poor at processing information about machines. He may consider himself to be more musically talented than his classmates but realizes that in other schools, some peers surpass himself in musical talent. Then there is some universal or general knowledge that we gain in the course of growing up. For example, we all realize that we think and operate less efficiently when we are hungry or tired. The above examples correspond to the three subcategories of person variables proposed by Flavell (1987): intraindividual (within the individual, i.e., within onself), interindividual (between individuals), and universal (applies to everyone).

Knowledge about task variables refers to the individual's learning from experience that different kinds of tasks exert different kinds of information-processing demands on him. For example, memorizing an entire poem word for word involves much more work (information processing) than remembering its theme. Realizing the need for different information processing for different tasks helps us plan appropriate allocation of our cognitive resources in completing them successfully.

Strategy variables refer to two kinds of strategies: cognitive and metacognitive. Cognitive strategy is a procedure that enables an individual to reach a goal. For example, one can learn a summarization strategy to record efficient notes from one's reading. A metacognitive strategy is a procedure that involves self-monitoring, self-testing, or self-evaluation. For example, one can learn a strategy that helps one to self-check whether or not one has properly carried out the summarization strategy. This self-monitoring strategy may consist of self-questions such as: "Have I included all the important points from this passage in my summary?" A self-evaluative strategy may have these self-questions: "How good is my summary? Is it sufficiently concise? Have I paraphrased all the important points?" Clearly both kinds of strategies, cognitive and metacognitive, are important in our successful learning and performance.

The studies of Flavell and Wellman (1977) and Flavell (1987) emphasize the interactions among person, task, and strategy variables. We develop intuitions about interactions among these variables. For example, we become aware of the superiority–inferiority of certain strategies, as we consider our own particular cognitive resources and the specific task (Flavell, 1987).

The regulation of cognition concerns the self-regulatory mechanisms used by an active learner during an ongoing attempt to solve problems (Brown, 1980; Baker and Brown, 1984a). The metacognitive activities here include planning, monitoring, testing, revising, and evaluating.

The two aspects of metacognition—knowledge about cognition and regulation of cognition—direct, guide, and govern successful learning, efficient reading, and effective studying (Brown, 1980; Baker and Brown, 1984a,b). Although they are very closely related, the two aspects of metacognition have different characteristics. Knowledge about cognition is "stable, statable but fallible, and late-developing"; i.e., we can verbalize our own awareness of our cognitive strengths and weaknesses. These cognitive strengths and weaknesses are, by and large, consistent. However, our knowledge about cognition is fallible in the sense that a child or an adult may "know" some facts about something (e.g., mathematics) that are untrue. Regulation of cognition, on the other hand, is "relatively unstable, rarely statable and relatively age independent" (Brown, 1987). The regulating activities as stated earlier (planning, monitoring, testing, revising, and evaluating) are unstable and age-independent in that their consistent use in individuals may not be assumed. For example, although older children and adults use self-regulating activities more often than younger children, they do *not* always use them. Even young children monitor their activities on a simplified task (Patterson *et al.*, 1980). Moreover, adults–fluent readers may only be aware of their regulating activities such as comprehension monitoring when they have a reading comprehension failure (Anderson, 1980). Thus, active comprehension monitoring is often an unconscious process and, therefore, an unstatable experience (Baker and Brown, 1984a,b).

IV. ORIGIN OF THE CONSTRUCT OF METACOGNITION AND ITS SUBSEQUENT APPLICATION TO READING

The construct of metacognition originated in Flavell's research on young children's memory processes. He proposed this construct in an attempt to explain young children's failure to maintain and generalize learned mnemonic strategies. Metamemory, awareness of parameters that govern effective recall, was assumed to be deficient among young children, and this deficiency explained their problems in strategy maintenance and generalization (Flavell, 1976). Subsequently in a seminal paper, Ann Brown (1980) related the theoretical construct of metacognition to reading. Brown (1980: 456) stated: "Any description of effective reading includes active strategies of monitoring, checking and self-testing, whether the task under consideration is reading for remembering (studying) or reading for doing (following instructions)."

V. METACOGNITION AND EFFECTIVE LEARNING

Jenkins' (1979) model of memory outlines four basic sources of influence on a learner's remembering in a learning situation. These include characteristics of the learner, criterial task, nature of the materials to be learned, and learning activities engaged in by the learner. Jenkins' model was borrowed and modified for use by Bransford (1979). It was subsequently borrowed from Bransford by Brown (1982) to apply to the educational scene. Brown's (1980) model contained the same factors as Jenkins' original model.

The *characteristics of the learner* refer to the cognitive and strategic repertoires that the individual brings to the learning situation. Individual differences in knowledge and procedural repertoires affect how the individuals learn (Brown, 1982). For example, students with a psychology background would find it easier to understand the research summaries in this and other chapters of this book than someone without such a background. The *nature of the materials to be learned* refers to the organizational nature of the materials, materials that match the readers' prior knowledge, etc. The nature of the materials to be learned affects the individuals' learning outcome. For example, materials that match subjects' prior knowledge are more easily understood by subjects (Anderson, 1982; Brown, 1978). Organized lectures facilitate student understanding and notetaking. The *criterial task* is the end product in any learning. For example, the criterial task in this course in LDs comprises a midterm and a final examination. The efficient learner is aware of the criterial task and tailors his learning activities accordingly (Baker and Brown, 1984b). For example, knowing that the final examination in a course involves short essay questions would lead a student to rely less on memorization of materials. Instead, he would focus on understanding the course material, and thinking hard about implications of what is read. Thus, the criterial task sets the learner's purpose in learning, as well as providing him with standards for evaluating his learning (Brown, 1980; Anderson, 1980). *Learning activities* refer to the activities the student engages in while learning. He could spontaneously deploy suitable learning activities or be taught to do so. As children grow older, they gradually learn a repertoire of learning activities. With extensive use, these learning activities–strategies become automatic and their deployment unconscious (Brown, 1982). Engaging in appropriate learning activities greatly influences students' learning outcome. For example, failure to categorize items into discrete categories such as food, clothing, furniture, or vehicles impairs recall in children with LDs. Unobtrusively prompting them to put related items into suitable categories remarkably improved their recall (Wong, 1978).

The literature in cognitive psychology and developmental psychology has shown us clearly how each of the above factors governs the likelihood of a student's successful learning. To demonstrate the point that these four factors and their interactions are important determinants of learning, two illustrative studies are described.

The influence of knowledge of criterial task on students' performances and perception of the ease/difficulty in task learning was shown by Wong *et al.* (1982). In two experiments involving normal-achieving and LD children, Wong *et al.* (1982) investigated the hypothesis that poor comprehension and recall in LD children might stem from a vague perception of criterion tasks (task demands) and that provision of clear knowledge of criterion tasks would enhance their performance. This performance enhancement comes about when students focus their study efforts on relevant parts of the exercise, in light of knowledge of criterion task.

In the comprehension task, children given knowledge of criterion task were explicitly told to attend to pre-paragraph questions in two expository pas-sages, because they modeled test questions the children would receive later. In the recall task, the children in the treatment condition were told to study the two expository passages for subsequent recall.

The results in the comprehension task substantiated the hypothesis under investigation. Wong *et al.* (1982) found that both normal-achieving and LD children, given knowledge of criterion task, correctly answered more questions than their respective counterparts in the control condition. However, the results in the recall task did not indicate reliable differences between treatment and control groups. The investigators attributed this outcome to the imprecision in the instructions given to the treatment groups. It is recalled that these children were simply told to expect a recall test. Unlike the comprehension task, they were not guided on which parts of the text to focus on in studying.

In a follow-up experiment, Wong *et al.* (1982) improved the methodology in the recall task. They instructed the children in the treatment condition to study the passages for subsequent recall and to attend specifically to certain important parts of the passages in their study. The children in the control condition were simply told to study the passages for subsequent recall. The results clearly indicated that given explicit knowledge of criterion task, both normal-achieving and LD children recalled substantially more of the passages than their respective control groups. In summary, Wong *et al.* (1982) showed that explicit knowledge of criterion task induced appropriate studying activities in children. The children could focus their attention on relevant contents in the passages, because of knowledge of criterion task.

Equally important influences on a student's successful learning are exerted by the interactions between the four factors of characteristics of learner, nature of materials to be learned, criterial task, and learner activities. Miyake and Norman's (1979) study illustrates the interactive influences between the nature of the materials to be learned (in this case, conceptual difficulty) and learning activities employed by students. Miyake and Norman (1979) investigated the effects of prior knowledge on student's questioning behavior. They used two groups of college students. One group knew little about computers and text-editors. The other group was given sufficient training in the use of a text-editor. The criterion in training was the students' editing one text unaided. Subsequently both groups were instructed to learn to operate a different text-editor by following either an easy nontechnical manual or a difficult technical manual. The students were further instructed to verbalize their thoughts and questions as they learned the new text-editor. Miyake and Norman (1979) found an interesting interaction in their study: Novice students in computer science asked more questions on the easy manual but very few on the hard manual. The reverse pattern of questioning was obtained for the trained students. Miyake and Norman interpreted the findings to suggest that to ask a question, you have to have an *optimal* amount of prior knowledge for the *particular* subject matter at hand. Because educators have long stressed the importance of cultivating questioning behaviors to facilitate learning in students, Miyake and Norman's findings imply that teachers should attend to students' existing prior knowledge as a concomitant condition in teaching students to generate questions. The preceding study of Miyake and Norman (1979) presents a mere glimpse into the web of interactions of various parameters underlying successful learning.

VI. METACOGNITION AND BROWN'S MODEL

One impetus responsible for the development of metacognitive theory and research is that an individual's successful learning requires more than background knowledge or learning strategies. Equally, if not more important, the individual must be able to use his background and strategic knowledge effectively during learning (Brown, 1980). If an individual is unaware of his own repertoire of strategies, he would be unlikely to deploy suitable strategies flexibly and precisely in tune with task demands. Occasionally, children and adults fail to use appropriate strategies for learning despite having them in their repertoire of strategies (Brown, 1980). The term production deficiencies has been applied to these occasions by Flavell (1976) and called inert knowledge by Scardamalia and Bereiter (1987). For the learner to be able to use and control appropriately his background knowledge and knowledge of strategies, he needs to develop metacognitive skills (Brown, 1980; Baker and Brown, 1984b).

It is recalled that metacognition refers to the awareness of knowledge and control and regulation of that knowledge (Baker and Brown, 1984a,b). The distinction between cognition and metacognition is the "distinction between knowledge and the understanding of knowledge in terms of *awareness and appropriate use*" (Brown, 1980: 453, italics added). Metacognitive skills are those that have been attributed to the "executive" in numerous theories of human memory and artificial intelligence. They are the essential characteristics of efficient thinking in a broad range of learning situations, including efficient reading and effective studying (Anderson, 1980; Brown, 1980; Baker and Brown, 1984b). The following example gives some flavor of how good students deploy metacognitive strategies in their studying. After being informed that there will be a midterm examination involving short essay answers, the good students begin to plan their study schedule. With 3 weeks left before the midterm, they start reading their lecture notes and corresponding chapters from their textbooks. They underline important parts of these materials and denote parts that they understand well. In addition, they identify those sections not understood thoroughly. They seek out the teaching assistant and the professor for help over parts of their notes and texts on which they lack thorough understanding. Having received the necessary help, they concentrate their efforts at studying the important parts of their notes and texts. Remembering that short essay answers rather than multiple choice questions will be on the midterm, good students spend time thinking about what they are studying, in particular, the implications of what they have studied.

In the above example, the good students ascertain what they already know or understand and what they need to clarify in their lecture notes and texts (assessing own knowledge repertoire). Their awareness of the need to get clarification for certain parts of their notes and chapters leads them to seek help from the appropriate sources: the teaching assistant and the professor (awareness leads to proper action). Having clarified their notes and texts, they settle down to diligent studying (self-regulation). However, they are mindful of the criterial task (short essay answers in the midterm), which leads them to engage in appropriate studying behaviors (concentrating on thinking about rather than rote memorization of notes and text). Metacognition enables good students to coordinate their awareness of their state of knowledge with appropriate problem-solving behaviors and guides them to link up appropriate studying behaviors with the task demands of the midterm. Surely the consequence of such well-coordinated, planful, and intelligent studying behaviors is a first class performance on the midterm.

The above description indicates how good students consciously and deliberately coordinate their efforts in studying. The skills they have mobilized in coordinating and regulating their efforts in studying are metacognitive skills. What they have coordinated and regulated are their own knowledge, their notes and texts, their own learning activities, and the criterial task. These are factors depicted in Brown's model. Thus, it can be seen that metacognitive skills are essential in effective coordination of the four factors in that model, and this coordination greatly affects the student's success in learning. Put differently, executive processes are needed to direct, coordinate, and regulate the interactions among those four factors. It is effective coordination, or "orchestration" (to borrow the word from Brown, 1980) of these interactions that is responsible for the success of any learning outcome. These executive processes are the individual's metacognitive skills.

VII. METACOGNITIVE SKILLS AND EFFICIENT READING

Good readers who possess metacognitive skills in reading are aware of the purpose of reading and differentiate between task demands, for example, in reading a text for class assignment versus reading a magazine for pleasure. They actively seek to clarify the purposes or task demands through self-questioning prior to reading the given materials (Anderson, 1980). Their awareness of reading purpose leads to the use of suitable reading strategies. For example, a good reader varies his reading rate and concentration level as a function of materials being read—text or magazine. He reads his text slower and with more intense concentration than his magazine. The awareness of the purpose in reading also leads a good reader to monitor his state of reading comprehension. For example, when he encounters difficulty in comprehending material, he uses debugging problem-solving strategies. These problem-solving attempts indicate self-regulation (Anderson, 1980; Brown, 1980). Moreover, good readers evaluate their own comprehension of materials read. Evaluating one's own comprehension of given instructions or of materials read has important consequences (Markman, 1977, 1979). This last reading strategy involves a very basic form of self-awareness (Brown, 1980). If a reader does not realize that he has not understood a particular part of the given materials, he will not employ suitable "debugging devices" (problem-solving strategies) such as backtracking or scanning ahead for possible clues to shed light on the part that currently presents difficulties in comprehension (Anderson, 1980; Baker, 1979). In contrast, LD readers show little indication of such coordination between task demands and suitable reading strategies. They lack the requisite metacognitive skills in reading (Wong, 1985).

The fluent or mature reader is rarely conscious of his own comprehension monitoring. Only when a comprehension failure arises in reading does the fluent reader realize that comprehension monitoring has occurred (Anderson, 1980). The individual immediately slows down his rate of reading and either reviews the difficult section or reads on, seeking enlightenment in subsequent text.

It remains to be shown if younger or immature readers, poor readers, and children and adolescents with LDs have deficient metacognitive skills in the reading process. Two excellent summaries of metacognitive research in reading (Baker and Brown, 1984a,b) document deficiencies in metacognitive skills of reading in poor readers and young children. Readers should study those papers.

How does the importance of metacognitive skills in reading affect our understanding of reading problems in students with LDs? Put differently, what is the relevance of metacognitive skills in reading to LDs?

VIII. METACOGNITION AND LEARNING DISABILITIES

Wong realized the relevance of the theoretical construct of metacognition and metacognitive research to special education, in particular, to the education of the LD. She sought to relate metacognition to LDs because basically she felt there has been an indiscriminate tendency among LDs professional to interpret performance failures in children and adolescents with LDs as cognitive deficits. She felt there is a need to discern between performance failures that genuinely reflect more deep-seated processing problems versus problems that are of a strategic nature. Because metacognitive research unequivocally demonstrates that skilled reading involves decoding, reading comprehension, *and* metacognitive skills, Wong felt that LDs professionals need to look afresh at how they interpret reading problems manifested by LD students. Specifically, they would not be justified in indiscriminately inferring deep-seated processing deficits in any child or adolescent with LDs who has a reading disability. Likewise, they would not be justified in focusing exclusively on decoding and comprehension skills in remediating reading problems in students with LDs (Wong, 1985, 1986, 1987, 1990).

Essentially, metacognition is relevant to LDs because it broadens our perception and understanding of reading problems in LD students and highlights the need to teach them metacognitive skills in reading *in addition* to decoding and comprehension skills. However, we must not lose sight of the limitations of a metacognitive perspective in LDs (Wong, 1986). Specifically, we must not embrace a wholesale interpretation of academic failures in LD students in terms of strategic deficits because there will be occasions when failures are caused by insufficient knowledge and/or ability. Moreover, metacognition alone does not suffice in students' maintenance and generalization of what has been learned. Students' motivation is pivotal in such maintenance and generalization (Wong, 1986: 22–24).

Of more serious concern is Stanovich's point that linking metacognition to LDs may in fact attenuate the assumption of specificity, which underlies the concept of LDs (Stanovich, 1986a,b, 1988). The assumption of specificity holds that dyslexics have a severe disability in one particular cognitive domain, typically reading, but in other cognitive domains, they are relatively adequate. It is essential that the cognitive disability be restricted to one specific area, otherwise the individual would be labeled slow learner or mentally retarded. The latter type of learners characteristically have widespread cognitive deficits (Stanovich, 1986a).

Stanovich (1986a,b, 1988) pointed out that recent theoretical formulations in intelligence tend to include metacognition as an integral component, as shown, for example, in Sternberg's work. Thus, if metacognition is treated or seen as a characteristic of individuals with LD, it would logically lead to the conclusion or statement that they have lower intelligence. Clearly this conclusion would undermine the discrepancy notion, and cause the disintegration of the assumption of specificity in LDs.

How can we resolve this problem? One way to resolve it is to invoke Stanovich's hypothesis of Matthews Effects (Stanovich, 1986b). In his phonological core-variable model (Stanovich, 1988), Stanovich posits that dyslexic children begin with a very specific, circumscribed cognitive problem in phonological processing. This phonological processing problem impedes the child's learning to read because he would experience enormous difficulties in learning letter–sound associations. Early and persistent failures to learn to read inevitably create motivational problems in the young child (Torgesen, 1977). The child becomes anxious with the reading task, comes to loathe reading, and develops problems with self-esteem.

These motivational problems eventually generalize to academic areas outside of reading (Butkowsky and Willows, 1980) and adversely affect the child's motivation to learn in school. Because the child cannot read and dislikes reading, because reading reminds him of his disability and presents continual frustrations, he ends up having substantially less reading experience outside of school. Similarly, in remedial reading sessions, the child typically receives phonics drills or drills in word recognition rather than passage reading; therefore, he is exposed to much less reading for meaning than his peers in school (Allington, 1980). These motivational and experiential deficiencies bode ill for the dyslexic child because many school subjects involve reading. Hence, the child's reading disability and the resultant motivational problems impede his learning of other academic subjects in school. Consequently, his academic problem is not confined to reading. In time, as he ages, the dyslexic child presents a picture of more generalized cognitive and cumulative deficits.

Stanovich uses the Biblical analogy of Matthews Effects to describe the generalized deficits that dyslexic individuals manifest. It's the case of the poor getting poorer as contrasted with the rich getting richer version of learning to read in the normal-achieving child. Normal-achieving children literally take off after mastering letter–sound associations or cracking the spelling-to-sound code. They begin to read much more, enjoy reading more, and comprehend more. Independent reading for pleasure and in-class reading provide normal-achieving children with reading experiences that are essential for their growth in various kinds of knowledge: vocabulary, syntax, and knowledge about the world and specific topics (e.g., dinosaurs). In turn, such growth in knowledge promotes knowledge acquisition in other related areas. Current schema theories and research in reading comprehension indicate the importance of prior knowledge in the acquisition of knowledge (Schallert, 1982). Thus, children who learned to read well can add much to this cognitive foundation. Cognitively speaking, they get richer and richer. The analogy is most apt *vis-à-vis* skilled readers.

The Matthews Effects hypothesis provides us with a potential solution for the problem of linking metacognition with LDs. We can treat metacognitive problems in the LD as a joint by-product of their lack of reading exposure or experience and motivational problems. Metacognition about reading develops in the context and experiences of reading. An individual cannot develop metacognition about reading in a vacuum. Similarly, the self-regulatory component of metacognition depends on motivation for its deployment. As children with LDs get poorer and poorer in learning, they develop metacognitive problems, which are essentially a second-order problem. In the picture of more widespread and generalized cognitive problems, metacognitive deficiencies are also present.

It is important to remember that we can avoid the problem highlighted by Stanovich only by treating metacognitive problems as a second-order problem—a joint by-product of deficient reading experiences and motivation. It is not a first-order problem such as a phonological processing problem. Seen from the perspective of the negative effects of Matthews Effects, metacognitive deficits may be legitimately used to describe the LD.

Having addressed the issue of the relevance of metacognition to LDs and the caveats in embracing a metacognitive perspective, it is opportune to consider the question of metacognitive deficiencies in reading in students with learning disabilities.

IX. METACOGNITION IN STUDENTS WITH
LEARNING DISABILITIES

The assumption that LD students generally lack metacognitive skills in reading is invalid. Rather, they appear to have less sophisticated metacognitive skills than non-learning-disabled peers in reading (Wong and Wong, 1986).

Wong and Wong (1986) investigated how metacognitive knowledge of vocabulary difficulty and passage organization of given passages affected study time of the same passages in above-average, average, and LD students from grades five through seven. The investigators first interviewed each subject individually on his knowledge/awareness of how easy/difficult vocabulary and the organized/disorganized nature of a passage affected the ease in studying a particular passage. Altogether, four passages were used. In two of these, level of vocabulary difficulty was manipulated. The "Oyster" passage contained difficult words such as "mollusks, plankton, immediate, environment, unexpectedly, especially, maturity." In comparison, the "Whooping Crane" passage contained relatively easy words. Passage organization was manipulated through two alternate versions of a passage either about a fox or polar bears. Each passage contained 12 short sentences, which clustered in fours around a specific subtopic about the respective animal: physical features, food, and habitat. One version of the "Fox" and the "Polar Bear" passages was organized so that the four sentences clustering each of the three subtopics were related to the particular subtopic and logically sequenced. In the disorganized version of the passages, thematic cohesion within each cluster of sentences was clearly lacking.

Each child was seen individually and, depending on order of passage presentation, was given either the organized/disorganized pair or the pair with hard/easy vocabulary first. With respect to the pair of passages with hard/easy vocabulary, the child was told that two students (A and B) studied the Oyster (hard vocabulary) and Whooping Crane (easy vocabulary) passages. Student A spent 15 min studying each passage. Student B spent 30 min on the Oyster passage and 15 min on the Whooping Crane passage. The child was asked which student would remember more of the passages, especially the Oyster passage, and why. To facilitate the child's responding, a schematic depiction of the hypothetical students' study behaviors and the Oyster and Whooping Crane passages were placed before the child. With respect to the organized/disorganized pair of passages, the child was told that again two students (C and D) studied them. Student C spent 15 min on the organized passage and 30 min on the disorganized passage. Student D, however, studied them for 15 min each. The child again was asked which student would remember more of the passages, especially the disorganized one, and why. Again, to facilitate the child's responding, a schematic depiction of the hypothetical students' study behaviors and the organized and disorganized passages were placed before the child.

About 3 weeks after the interview, the children were again seen individually. Half the children were randomly assigned to receive the passage-pair with hard/easy vocabulary first, followed by the organized/disorganized passage-pair. The remaining children had the passage-pairs in the reverse order. When given the previously seen organized/disorganized passage-pair, the child was told to study for subsequent recall of both passages. When given the passage-pair with hard/easy vocabulary, the child was told to study for a subsequent reading comprehension test on each passage. Within each pair of passages, the order of passage presentation was randomized. Moreover, there was a 3-min break between passages within a pair of passages and a 5-min break between the two sets of passages. The child was self-paced and given unlimited time to study the passages. Also, an aide pronounced and carefully explained the meanings of key vocabulary words in the Oyster and Whooping Crane passages. For the benefit of the LD readers, words that might pose decoding or vocabulary difficulties were pronounced clearly and explained thoroughly. Additionally, the child was encouraged to seek help with any other decoding or vocabulary difficulties. When ready for the recall or comprehension test, the child signaled to the experimenter. The child was told not to worry about spelling errors in written answers to the short comprehension questions. Study times in minutes and seconds were recorded with a stopwatch. The children's recall was tape-recorded and later transcribed.

The results indicated that above-average readers were substantially more aware that the level of vocabulary difficulty and passage organization affect the ease of studying a given passage. Examination of the children's individual protocols indicated that few fifth-grade children scored more than one point in the justification responses, which had a scoring range of 0–4. Those who obtained two points were above average. Among the sixth-grade children, above-average readers did very well because none had scores less than two points. Apart from one fifth-grade child, the average readers' performance was generally lacklustre. Among LD readers, two seventh-grade subjects had four points each in justifying why the hypothetical student studying the disorganized passage a longer time would do better. Their respective responses were "30 min for disorganized passage—disorganized passage would be harder to learn so would need more time," and "Studied longer on the disorganized passage ... it's harder to remember ... need to study longer." Thus, examination of individual protocols indicated that although above-average readers were substantially more advanced in metacognitive knowledge about vocabulary difficulty and passage organization, the same awareness appeared to be present in LD readers. Such awareness, however, appeared only in two out of four of the *oldest* (grade seven) readers.

More importantly, Wong and Wong (1986) found a significant interaction between reader and passage. This finding indicated that whereas LD readers were most sensitive to level of vocabulary difficulty in a passage, above-average readers were most sensitive to the organization of a passage. Within the pair of passages with easy and difficult vocabulary, only LD readers showed reliable differences in study times, studying significantly longer the passage with difficult vocabulary. Within the pair of passages with organized/disorganized sentences, only above-average readers showed reliable differences in study times, studying significantly longer the disorganized passage.

This pattern of differential study times among above-average readers and LD readers is important. The data for LD readers challenge the ubiquitous assumption of metacognitive deficiency in reading among LD readers. LD readers apparently do possess metacognitive knowledge about one particular aspect of reading investigated, namely level of vocabulary difficulty. Moreover, LD readers' sensitivity to differential vocabulary difficulty in the two passages led them to deploy suitable reading strategies. They studied the passage with difficult vocabulary much longer. One possible reason for LD readers' possession of such metacognitive awareness may be due to their decoding problems, from which ensues an acute awareness of vocabulary difficulty in the reading materials and the development of a strategy to overcome the problems, namely reading slowly.

X. MODEL OF METACOGNITION

A very recently developed model of metacognition by Borkowski and his associates clearly establishes the relevance of metacognition to the instruction of individuals with LDs. The following is a condensed description of their model. However, before proceeding to that description, some explanatory notes are necessary. Specifically, the original term metamemory acquisition procedures (MAPs), used in Pressley et al. (1985), is equivalent to executive processes in later papers by Borkowski and his associates (see Borkowski et al., 1989, Groteluschen et al., in press). Whereas Borkowski, Pressley, and their associates refer to a person's entire stock of knowledge of a particular strategy as specific strategy knowledge, others have used the term meta-memorial knowledge. Lastly, in earlier versions of the models (e.g., Borkowski et al., 1987), attributions were subsumed under General Strategy Knowledge. In the most recent paper, however, attributions are conceptualized as correlates of General Strategy Knowledge (Groteluschen et al., in press).

A. Model of Metacognition Developed by Borkowski et al. (1989)

1. Components of the Model

The components within this model of metacognition are specific strategy knowledge, relational strategy knowledge, general strategy knowledge, and MAPs.

Specific strategy knowledge refers to the individual's repertoire of cognitive–learning strategies, which enhance learning and performance, and his knowledge of their uses. For example, a child or an adolescent may know and use an elaboration strategy as an aid to learning French vocabulary. Children develop specific strategy knowledge slowly as they grow up. Such knowledge means they understand (1) what a particular strategy would achieve for them; (2) what tasks match its use in appropriateness; (3) the range of its usefulness, i.e., what tasks it should or should not be used for; (4) the benefits from regular use of the strategy; (5) how much effort is involved in using the strategy; and (6) how enjoyable or laborious is the strategy use.

With specific strategy knowledge about various strategies and their uses, the child can make enlightened decisions about which to use to aid the learning of new tasks. Thus, specific strategy knowledge is requisite in intelligent deployment of strategies. Moreover, a reciprocal beneficial relationship exists between strategy use and specific strategy knowledge. While the individual's specific strategy knowledge guides his use of particular strategies, consistent use of them broadens and refines his specific strategy knowledge about those particular strategies. These elaborations and refinements result in detailed representations of them in specific strategy knowledge. In turn, the expanded and refined specific strategy knowledge improves future use of those strategies.

As specific strategy knowledge cumulates, two other components develop: relational strategy knowledge and general strategy knowledge. Relational strategy knowledge refers to the child's knowledge of the comparative characteristics of various strategies in his repertoire. This knowledge enables the child to choose the appropriate strategy to match task demands and to switch strategies when necessary.

General strategy knowledge refers to the child's awareness that strategy use involves effort expenditure, that a planned and strategic approach to learning is much more likely to result in successful learning. The conceptual uniqueness of general strategy knowledge is its motivational aspect. Borkowski and his associates highlight attributions as the motivational correlate of general strategy knowledge. Effort-related attributions enhance the individual's self-efficacy and self-esteem and induce him to value strategy use in learning. The individual's enhanced self-efficacy motivates/energizes him to tackle difficult tasks and to maintain and generalize learned strategies.

2. MAPs

As conceptualized by Pressley *et al.* (1985), MAPs have a twofold function. First, these procedures refer to the child's problem-solving attempts to fill in gaps that occur in the teacher's incomplete instructions. Second, they refer to the child's self-regulation, i.e., his self-monitoring of proper use of strategy, the effects of it on his performance (evaluation of strategy use), and deciding on change or modification of strategy in use. MAPs are very important because they constitute the executive processes (self-control or self-regulation). Without knowledge of MAPs, the child would not be able to engage in self-monitoring or self-evaluation of strategy use. It is these executive processes that are energized by enhanced self-efficacy and self-esteem. Such enhanced self-efficacy and self-esteem are brought about by effort-related attributions and a new-found belief in the value of a strategy approach to learning. MAPs are manifested by the following behaviors: self-directed, self-initiated learning or behaviors, self-reliance (independence) in problem solving, and persistence at difficult tasks. Figure 8.1 presents schematically the model of metacognition developed by Borkowski *et al.* (1989).

B. Relevance of the Model of Metacognition to LD

Although intervention research with LD students focuses on inculcation of cognitive strategies, it would be erroneous to assume that they have entirely

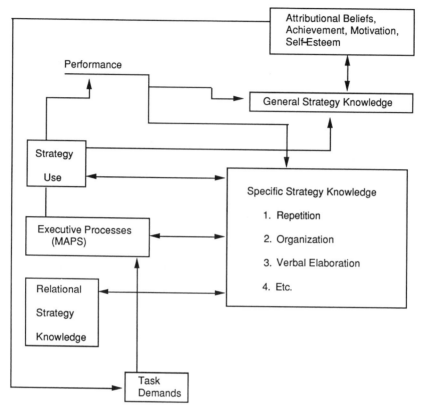

Figure 8.1   A model of metacognition (Borkowski *et al.*, 1989).

no specific strategy knowledge; rather, it would be more valid to consider that these students possess faulty or ineffectual strategies. In support of this consideration, Garner (1981) found that poor readers read in a word-by-word fashion greatly straining short-term memory and that they showed "piece-meal processing" in that they did not integrate textual information across sentences, which may well impede inferential comprehension. Moreover, when LD students possess knowledge of appropriate strategies, their knowledge appears to be "inert" in that they do not spontaneously activate their use. External prompting for strategy mobilization is required (Wong, 1978; Torgesen, 1979; Torgesen and Goldman, 1977).

How do we explain such "inert" strategy knowledge in LD children and their failure to maintain and generalize learned strategies? One plausible answer to this question is their lack of executive control or self-regulation.

Insufficient self-regulation in learning explains LD students' lack of initiation and selection of appropriate strategies, subsequent monitoring, evaluation, and modification of the strategy in use.

C. Empirical Support for the Suggestion that LD Students Lack Executive Control, or Self-Regulation

LD students lack executive control (self-regulation). Observations of deficient executive control in LD students span a number of areas. Specifically, LD students frequently need external prompting to mobilize strategy use (Wong, 1978). They tend not to spontaneously deploy strategies (Torgesen and Kail, 1980). They also have difficulty in choosing suitable problem-solving devices for tasks ranging from reading comprehension (Kavale, 1980), to analytical reasoning (Barton, 1988), to arithmetic problems (Fleischner and Garnett, 1987). Additionally, they show problems in comprehension monitoring, which is an important constituent of mature executive processing (Bos and Filip, 1982; Kotsonis and Patterson, 1980; Wong and Jones, 1982).

In turn, why do LD students show lack of executive control or self-regulation in learning? Put differently, why do LD students fail to develop self-regulation? How have they become passive learners?

The answer mainly resides in the self-systems in LD students. Self-system comprises self-efficacy, self-esteem, and attributions. LD students have a history of academic failure (Torgesen, 1977). Consistent academic failures have at least three negative consequences: (1) erode their motivation to learn, (2) result in nonbeliefs of the value of effortful strategic learning because applications of their own faulty strategies inevitably result in poor learning outcomes, and (3) produce low self-concept ("I am dumb"). At the same time, LD students develop maladaptive attributional patterns. They attribute success in learning to external factors such as luck or "teacher likes me," whereas they attribute failure to internal factors such as ability (Pearl *et al.*, 1980, 1986; Pearl, 1982). These faulty attributions reinforce their incredulous attitudes toward expending effort at strategy-based learning as well as lower their self-esteem. Clearly, compared with normal-achieving students, the self-systems in LD students are warped in development.

The unwholesome self-systems of LD students lead them to avoid challenging tasks, to give up readily at difficult tasks after initial setbacks. Hence, they rob themselves of opportunities in generating problem-solving strategies and fail to apply and modify learned strategies flexibly to suit the task demands. The net result of such poorly developed self-systems is to restrict LD students' development in self-efficacy and self-regulation and make them into passive learners.

To turn LD students into active learners involves a direct assault on their maldeveloped self-systems. How can we achieve this turn-around in their self-systems? One feasible way has been suggested by Borkowski and his associates (Borkowski *et al.*, 1988, 1989; Groteluschen *et al.*, in press). They advocate reattribution training. They reason that LD students have faulty attributions, and need to learn to make effort-related attributions once they have mastered a cognitive strategy. When they succeed at the task, they should be shown clearly that their effortful use of an appropriate learning strategy is responsible for the positive learning outcome. When they fail, they should be taught to analyze the cause(s) of failure—is it due to insufficient effort or insufficient domain knowledge, or should the strategy be changed, etc.? Failure should be *depersonalized*. It should in no way be taken to reflect low ability.

The goal of reattribution training is to change LD students into active learners by restoring responsibility of learning to them. They must be the agents of their own learning and learning outcomes. The end product of reattribution training is that LD students develop a sense of self-efficacy because, through such training, they come to realize that they are indeed in control of their own learning: They alone are responsible for their learning outcomes. This sense of self-efficacy (1) provides the confidence to select or activate the use of a learned strategy, (2) mobilizes self-regulation (executive control processes) to monitor and evaluate the impact of strategy use on learning and performance, and (3) motivates and energizes maintenance and generalization of strategy. Put differently, for the LD student, a sense of self-efficacy translates into self-statements such as "I can do it." It empowers LD students to select a task-appropriate strategy, take the responsibility of monitoring and evaluating it, and maintain and generalize its use. Concomitant to the development of self-efficacy, their self-esteem would soar as they experience increasing success in learning.

However, Borkowski and his associates are quick to point out the need to accompany reattribution training with training in executive processes or self-regulation procedures. LD students need to learn how to monitor and evaluate the impact or effect of strategy use on their learning and performance so that they can use and modify learned strategies adaptively. Earlier in this chapter, we summarized the research literature on their lack of self-regulation (executive control). Hence, we must not neglect to teach them requisite self-regulation procedures such as self-monitoring. In short, we need to teach them MAPs.

In light of the above account of how to turn LD students into active learners, we can see the relevance of the metacognition model put forth by Borkowski and his associates to LDs. Their model provides the most comprehensive framework in understanding the cognitive, metacognitive, and affective motivational needs of LD individuals. More importantly, it gives the most plausible conceptualization of their failure to maintain and transfer learned strategies. The model highlights the necessity of the interactive roles of specific strategy knowledge, executive processes (self-regulation), and general beliefs about self-efficacy (effort-related attributions) in inducing successful strategy maintenance and transfer in LD individuals. Borkowski and his associate's repeated emphasis on a twin foci in intervention research with the LD, i.e., an equal focus on executive process and reattribution training, is supported by Reid and Borkowski's (1987) study.

Reid and Borkowski (1987) investigated the effects of three instructional conditions on strategy maintenance and generalization in hyperactive children with LDs. Children in the control condition received specific strategy training, which involved learning the use of an interrogative associative strategy for a paired-associate task and a cluster-rehearsal strategy for a sort-recall readiness task. Children in the self-control (or executive process) condition learned the same strategies as those in the control condition. In addition, they learned self-regulatory procedures in the form of self-statements such as "look to see how the problem might be solved" and "stop and think before responding." These self-regulatory procedures were modeled for them by the instructor in the context of using those strategies. Children in the self-control plus attribution retraining group received specific strategies training and self-control (executive process) training as well as attribution retraining. Specifically, they received two forms of attribution retraining: (1) Antecedent attributional training involved a discussion between instructor and student on prevalent beliefs about the causes of success and failure; and (2) program-specific attributions comprised feedback from the instructor about the link between the child's strategic behavior or his lack of it and his performance during learning. The child was shown individual items in which right or wrong answers depended on whether or not he had used the learned strategy.

The results indicated substantially superior performance of those children in the self-control plus attribution retraining condition across a wide range of performance measures. Not only did they demonstrate better strategy maintenance and generalization, they also attained higher personal causality scores that endorsed effort. Moreover, these hyperactive children with LDs showed less impulsivity than the others in the remaining two conditions of self-control training and the control comparison condition.

Most significant was the finding that after 10 months, children in the combined self-control plus attribution retraining condition were found to use more strategies, maintained effort-related attributions, and showed more advanced metamemories. In short, the combined training appeared to have established some rather permanent improvements in the hyperactive children with LD.

The impressive results of Reid and Borkowski's (1987) intervention study speak to the importance of training both executive processes (self-control/self-regulation) and reattribution in children and adolescents with LDs. Training-specific strategies are clearly insufficient, as is training solely in executive processes (self-control).

XI. RESEARCH ISSUES

Concerning metacognition and LDs several areas appear to call for research. These are briefly discussed below.

A. Development of Metacognition

How normal-achieving children and children and adolescents with LDs develop the various kinds and levels (higher order versus lower order) of metacognitive skills in academic domains, such as reading and writing, remains an empirical question. At present, we only know that, compared with LD children, normal-achieving children possess more sophisticated metacognitive skills in reading (Wong and Wong, 1986). Understanding the developmental processes here would greatly facilitate the design of instructions to inculcate metacognitive skills in reading.

B. Cumulative Strategy Instruction

The effects of long-term cumulative strategy instruction on normal-achieving children and LD children have not been researched. Conducting this kind of research appears to be very profitable because we would be informed about the nature of strategic learners that results from such training; how the learners modify the learned strategies for their own purposes: whether or not savings in learning occur across cumulative strategies inculcation; and how the learners transfer all the learned strategies.

C. Instructional Modes

Hitherto in research and in classroom practice, strategy instruction has been conducted by an adult. We have not researched the efficacy of peer instruction in strategy training. Having an older LD student teach a younger LD student a metacognitive strategy, such as comprehension monitoring ("Is there anything I don't understand in this story?") may be a worthwhile study. We would hypothesize that self-efficacy and self-esteem in the older LD student should increase as the younger one improves his reading comprehension by using comprehension monitoring in his reading.

D. Metacognitive Skills in Writing

Research in metacognitive skills in writing is nascent (Englert, 1990). We need to expand this area of research to better understand the role of metacognition in effective writing.

E. Metacognitive Model

The model of metacognitive proposed by Borkowski and his colleagues invites research. It has much heuristic value for instructional research with LD individuals.

XII. TEACHING IMPLICATIONS: METACOGNITIVE ASSESSMENT AND CURRICULA

To date, Scott Paris and his associates (Jacobs and Paris, 1987) have developed the only metacognitive strategies assessment device in reading. In the Index of Reading Awareness (IRA), Jacobs and Paris (1987) have produced a very useful questionnaire to measure students' strategies in reading. The questionnaire is divided into four sections: evaluation, planning, regulation, and conditional knowledge with five questions per section. It also contains multiple-choice answers. One example from each of the four sections is shown below:

Evaluation (Jacob and Paris, 1987; 269)
1. What is the hardest part about reading for you?
   a. Sounding out the hard words.
   b. When you don't understand the story.
   c. Nothing is hard about reading for you.
Planning (Jacob and Paris, 1987; 269)
4. Before you start to read, what kind of plans do you make to help you read better?
   a. You don't make any plans. You just start reading.
   b. You choose a comfortable place.
   c. You think about why you are reading.
Regulation (Jacob and Paris, 1987; 270)
2. Why do you go back to read things over again?
   a. Because it is good practice.
   b. Because you didn't understand it.
   c. Because you forgot some words.

Conditional Knowledge (Jacob and Paris, 1987; 270)
   3. If you are reading for a test, which would help the most?
      a. Read the story as many times as possible.
      b. Talk about it with somebody to make sure you under-
         stand it.
      c. Say the sentences over and over.

Clearly, the IRA assessment is applicable to LD students. It can be used for both research and practical purposes. Currently, there is only information on its use in research. However, it can be profitably used by teachers of LD students as both a pretraining assessment and post-training measure.

Similarly, Paris has produced the only metacognitive curricula, the Reading and Thinking Strategies curricula. He has produced three sets/modules of reading and thinking strategies, one for each of the following grades: third–fourth, fifth–sixth, seventh, and eighth. There are clear merits to these metacognitive curricula, not the least of which is the theoretical framework and empirical base on which they were built.

The instructional principles underlying the Reading and Thinking Strategies curricula are direct explanation, metaphors for strategies, group dialogues, guided practice, and integration with content area reading (Paris et al., 1986). Elsewhere I have detailed the uniqueness of Paris' Reading and Thinking Strategies curricula, its theoretical and empirical underpinnings (Wong, 1990).

XIII. SUMMARY

As assessment of metacognitive practice in LDs suggests that practical applications may still only be at the stage of a promising start. This is due largely to the lack of development of metacognitive assessment tools and curricula. However, this state of affairs may not last. To date, Scott Paris and his associates have blazed the trail in developing a strategy assessment questionnaire that is immensely applicable in LDs research and practice. More importantly, he has developed a systematic set of metacognitive curricula for instructional purposes—the Reading and Thinking Strategies curricula. Close scrutiny of them suggests immediate possibilities for use with LD students in instructional research and actual remedial practices. Paris' strategy assessment device and curricula should serve as models for similar developments by LDs professionals in the future.

Acknowledgments

I greatly appreciate Jenny Alexander's helpful comments and editing of the first draft of this chapter. I thank Rod Wong for reading the final draft and Eileen Mallory for cheerfully word-processing the various drafts of this chapter.

References

Allington, R. L. (1980). Poor readers don't get to read much in reading groups. *Lang. Arts* **57**, 872–876.

Anderson, R. C. (1982). Role of the reader's schema in comprehension, learning and memory. *In* "Learning to Read in American Schools: Basal Readers and Content Texts" (R. C. Anderson, J. Osborn, and R. J. Tierney, eds.), pp. 243–257. Lawrence Erlbaum, Hillsdale, New Jersey.

Anderson, T. H. (1980). Study strategies and adjunct aids. *In* "Theoretical Issues in Reading Comprehension" pp. 484–502. Lawrence Erlbaum, Hillsdale, New Jersey.

Baker, L. (1979). "Do I Understand or Do I Not Understand: That is the Question." Reading Education Report No. 10, July 1979. Center for the Study of Reading, University of Illinois, Urbana.

Baker, L., and Brown, A. L. (1984a). Cognitive monitoring in reading. *In* "Understanding Reading Comprehension" (J. Flood, ed.), pp. 21–44. International Reading Association, Newark, Delaware.

Baker, L., and Brown, A. L. (1984b). Metacognition skills of reading. *In* "Handbook on Research in Reading" (D. P. Pearson, ed.), pp. 353–394. Longman, New York.

Barton, J. A. (1988). Problem-solving strategies in learning disabled and normal boys: Developmental and instructional effects. *J. Educ. Psychol.* **80**, 184–191.

Borkowski, J. G., Johnston, M. B., and Reid, M. K. (1987). Metacognition, motivation and controlled performance. *In* "Handbook of Cognitive, Social and Neurological Aspects of Learning Disabilities," Vol. 2. (S. Ceci, ed), pp. 147–174. Lawrence Erlbaum, Hillsdale, New Jersey.

Borkowski, J. G., Milstead, M., and Hale, C. (1988). Components of children's metamemory: Implications for strategy generalization. *In* "Memory Development: Universal Changes and Individual Differences" (F. E. Weinert and M. Perlmutter, eds.), pp. 73–100. Lawrence Erlbaum, New Jersey.

Borkowski, J. G., Estrada, M. T., Milstead, M., and Hale, C. A. (1989). General problem-solving skills: Relations between metacognition and strategic processing. *Learn. Disabil. Q.* **12(1)**, 57–70.

Bos, C., and Filip, D. (1982). Comprehension monitoring skills in learning disabled and average students. *Top. Learn. Learn. Disabil.* **2**, 79–85.

Bransford, J. D. (1979). "Human Cognition: Learning, Understanding and Remembering. Wadsworth, Belmont, Califonia.

Brown, A. L. (1978). Knowing when, where, and how to remember: A problem of metacognition. *In* "Advances in Instructional Psychology" (R. Glaser, ed.). Lawrence Erlbaum, Hillsdale, New Jersey.

Brown, A. L. (1980). Metacognitive development and reading. *In* "Theoretical Issues in Reading Comprehension" (R. J. Spiro, B. B. Bruce, and W. F. Brewer, eds.), pp. 453–481. pp. 77–165. Lawrence Erlbaum, Hillsdale, New Jersey.

Brown, A. L. (1982). Learning and development: The problems of compatibility, access and induction. *Hum. Dev.* **25,** 89–115.

Brown, A. L. (1987). Metacognition, executive control, self-regulation and other even more mysterious mechanisms. *In* "Metacognition, Motivation & Learning" (R. H. Kluwe and F. E. Weinert, eds.), pp. 65–116. Lawrence Erlbaum, Hillsdale, New Jersey.

Brown, A. L., and Palincsar, A. S. (1982). Inducing strategic learning from texts by means of informed, self-control training. *Top. Learn. Learn. Disabil.* **2,** 1–17.

Butkowsky, J. S., and Willows, D. M. (1980). Cognitive-motivational characteristics of children varying in reading ability: Evidence for learned helplessness in poor readers. *J. Educ. Psychol.* **72,** 408–422.

Englert, C. S. (1990). Unravelling the mysteries of writing through strategy instruction. *In* "Intervention Research in Learning Disabilities" (T. E. Scruggs and B. Y. L. Wong, eds.). pp. 186–223. Springer-Verlag, New York, in press.

Flavell, J. H. (1976). Metacognitive aspects of problem solving. *In* "The Nature of Intelligence" (L. B. Resnick, ed.), pp. 231–235. Lawrence Erlbaum, Hillsdale, New Jersey.

Flavell, J. H. (1987). Speculations about the nature and development of metacognition. *In* "Metacognition, Motivation and Learning" (R. H. Kluwe and F. E. Weinert, eds.), pp. 21–39. Lawrence Erlbaum, Hillsdale, New Jersey.

Flavell, J. H., and Wellman, H. M. (1977). Metamemory. *In* "Perspectives on the Development of Memory and Cognition" (R. V. Kail and J. W. Hagen, eds.), Lawrence Erlbaum, Hillsdale, New Jersey.

Fleischner, J. E., and Garnett, K. (1987). Arithmetic difficulties. *In* "Handbook of Learning Disabilities," Vol. 1, "Dimensions and Diagnosis" (K. Kavale, S. Forness, and M. Bender, eds.), pp. 189–209. Little, Brown & Co., Boston.

Garner, R. (1981). Monitoring of passage inconsistency among poor comprehenders: A preliminary test of the "Piecemeal Processing" explanation. *J. Educ. Res.* **74,** 159–162.

Garner, R. (1987). "Metacognition and Reading Comprehension." Ablex, Norwood, New Jersey.

Groteluschen, A. K., Borkowski, J. G., and Hale, C. (in press). Strategy instruction is often insufficient: Addressing the interdependency of executive and attributional processes. *In* "Intervention Research in Learning Disabilities." T. E. Scruggs and B. Y. L. Wong (eds.), pp. 81–102. Springer-Verlag, New York.

Hagen, J. W., and Barclay, C. R. (1981). The development of memory skills in children: Portraying learning disabilities in terms of strategy and knowledge deficiencies. *The Best of ACLD.*

Jacobs, J. E., and Paris, S. G. (1987). Children's metacognition about reading: Issues in definition, measurement and instruction. *Educ. Psycholog.* **22(3/4),** 255–278.

Jenkins, J. J. (1979). Four points to remember: A tetrahedral model and memory experiments. *In* "Levels and Processing in Human Memory" (L. S. Cermak and F. I. M. Craik, eds.), pp. 429–446. Lawrence Erlbaum, Hillsdale, New Jersey.

Kavale, K. A. (1980). The reasoning abilities of normal and learning-disabled readers on measures of reading comprehension. *Learn. Disabil. Q.* **3**, 34–45.

Kotsonis, M. E., and Patterson, C. J. (1980). Comprehension monitoring skills in learning disabled children. *Dev. Psychol.* **16**, 541–542.

Markman, E. M. (1979). Realizing that you don't understand: Elementary school children's awareness of inconsistencies. *Child Development* **50**, 643–655.

Markman, E. M. (1977). Realizing that you don't understand: A preliminary investigation. *Child Development* **43**, 986–992.

Miyake, N., and Norman, D. A. (1979). To ask a question, one must know enough to know what is not known. *J. Verbal Learn. Verbal Behav.* **18**, 357–864.

Murray, F. B. (1984). The application of theories of cognitive development. *In* "Applications of Cognitive-Developmental Theory" (B. Gholson and T. L. Rosenthal, eds.), pp. 3–18. Academic Press, New York.

Paris, S. G., Wixson, K. K., and Palincsar, A. S. (1986). Instructional approaches to reading comprehension. *In* (E. Z. Rothkopf, ed.), *Rev. Res. Educ.* **13**, 91–128.

Patterson, C. J., Cosgrove, J. M., and O'Brien, R. G. (1980). Nonverbal indicants of comprehension and noncomprehension in children. *Dev. Psychol.* **16**, 38–48.

Pearl, R. (1982). Learning-disabled children's attributions for success and failure: A replication with a labeled learning-disabled sample. *Learning Disability Quarterly* **5**, 183–186.

Pearl, R., Bryan, T. H., and Donahue, M. (1980). Learning-disabled children's attributions for success and failure. *Learn Disabil. Q.* **3**, 3–9.

Pearl, R., Donahue, M., and Bryan, T. (1986). Social relationships of learning-disabled children. *In* "Psychological and Educational Perspectives on Learning Disabilities" (J. K. Torgesen and B. Y. L. Wong, eds.), pp. 194–224. Academic Press, New York.

Pressley, M., Borkowski, J. G., and O'Sullivan, J. (1985). Children's metamemory and the teaching of memory strategies. *In* "Metacognition, Cognition and Human Performance" (D. L. Forrest-Pressley, D. MacKinnon, and T. G. Waller, eds.), pp. 111–153. Academic Press, San Diego.

Reid, M. K., and Borkowski, J. G. (1987). Causal attributions of hyperactive children: Implications for training strategies and self-control. *J. Educ. Psychol.* **76**, 225–235.

Scardamalia, M., and Bereiter, C. (1987). Knowledge telling and knowledge transforming in written composition. *In* "Advances in Applied Psycholinguistics," Vol. 2, "Reading, Writing and Language Learning" (S. Rosenberg, ed.), pp. 142–175. Cambridge University Press, Cambridge.

Schallert, D. L. (1982). The significance of knowledge: A synthesis of research related to schema theory. *In* "Reading Expository Material" (W. Otto and S. White, eds.), pp. 13–49. Academic Press, New York.

Stanovich, K. E. (1986a). Cognitive processes and the reading problems of learning-disabled children: Evaluating the assumption of specificity. *In* "Psychological and Educational Perspectives in Learning Disabilities" (J. K. Torgesen and B. Y. L. Wong, eds.), pp. 110–131. Academic Press, New York.

Stanovich, K. E. (1986b). Matthew effects in reading: Some consequences of individual differences in the acquisition of literacy. *Read. Res. Q.* **XXI(4)**, 360–407.

Stanovich, K. E. (1988). Explaining the differences between the dyslexic and the garden-variety poor reader: The phonological-core variable-difference model. *J. Learn. Disabil.* **21(10)**, 590–612.

Torgesen, J. K. (1977). The role of nonspecific factors in the task performance of learning-disabled children: A theoretical assessment. *J. Learn. Disabil.* **10**, 27–34.

Torgesen, J. K. (1979). Factors related to poor performance on rote memory tasks in reading-disabled children. *Learn. Disabil. Q.* **2**, 17–23.

Torgesen, J. K., and Goldman, T. (1977). Rehearsal and short-term memory in reading disabled children. *Child Dev.* **48**, 56–60.

Torgesen, J. K., and Kail, R. V. (1980). Memory processes in exceptional children. *Adv. Special Educ.* Vol. 1, JAI.

Wong, B. Y. L. (1978). The effects of directive cues on the organization of memory and recall in good and poor readers. *J. Educ. Res.* **72**, 32–38.

Wong, B. Y. L. (1985). Metacognition and learning disabilities. *In* "Metacognition, Cognition and Human Performance" (T. G. Waller, D. Forrest-Pressley, and E. MacKinnon, eds.), pp. 137–180. Academic Press, New York.

Wong, B. Y. L. (1986). Metacognition and special education: A review of a view. *J. Special Educ.* **20(1)**, 9–29.

Wong, B. Y. L. (1987). Metacognition and learning disabilities. *Learn. Disabil. Q.* **10(3)**, 189–195.

Wong, B. Y. L. (1991). Assessment of metacognitive research in learning disabilities: Theory, research and practice. *In* "Handbook on the Assessment of Learning Disabilities: Theory, Research and Practice" (L. Swanson and B. Keogh, ed.), (pp. 265–283). College Hill Press.

Wong, B. Y. L., and Jones, W. (1982). Increasing metacomprehension in learning-disabled and normally-achieving students through self-questioning training. *Learn. Disabil. Q.* **5**, 228–240.

Wong, B. Y. L., and Wong, R. (1986). Study behavior as a function of metacognitive knowledge about critical task variables: An investigation of above average, average and learning-disabled readers. *Learn. Disabil. Res.* **1**, 101–111.

Wong, B. Y. L., Wong, R., and LeMare, L. J. (1982). The effects of knowledge of criterion tasks on the comprehension and recall of normally-achieving and learning-disabled children. *J. Educ. Res.* **76**, 119–126.

Wong, B. Y. L., Wong, R., and Blenkisop, J. (1989). Cognitive and metacognitive aspects of composing problems in learning-disabled adolescents. *Learn. Disabil. Q.* **12(4)**, 300–322.

Assessment and Instructional Aspects of Learning Disabilities

Early Reading and Instruction

Lynn M. Gelzheiser and Diana Brewster Clark

Editor's Notes

With this chapter, we begin Section II, which focuses on the practical aspects of learning disabilities. Gelzheiser and Clark's chapter has three themes. The first centers on what reading involves and provides a necessary context for identifying sources of reading difficulty for beginning readers and older disabled readers. Readers should note how the materials here relate to Virginia Mann's chapter (Chapter 5, earlier in this volume) on language problems in children's failures to learn to read. The second theme focuses on stages in children's development of reading proficiency, which in turn provides the framework for the third theme of instruction. The latter focuses on general and more specific instructional suggestions on developing the component skills necessary in learning to read as well as considering factors that affect effective implementation of special reading instruction.

Many children classified as learning-disabled have not learned to read through traditional basal reading instruction. Of these reading-disabled students, this chapter focuses on those who have failed to master basic decoding skills. It outlines several direct approaches for teaching decoding that could be used in a remedial program. Some of these approaches are also appropriate for classroom reading instruction for the at-risk reader, a term used to refer to the beginning reader who may develop reading disabilities. Typically, at-risk readers show extraordinarily slow progress in reading despite traditional instruction. Instructional methods have been selected to represent a variety of approaches. Their efficacy has been examined with at-risk or learning disabled populations.

This chapter begins with a brief overview of early reading. It then focuses on the specific reading competencies learning disabled pupils most often lack. Instruction designed to address these areas of special need is then described in some detail. Finally, issues related to implementation of reading instruction with learning disabled pupils are discussed.

I. WHAT IS READING?

Learning to read is not a natural act (Gough and Hillinger, 1980). In English, the alphabetic code (i.e., the relationship between letters and sounds) is both abstract and complex. Text provides several different levels of cues including letters, context, and structural cues. The mature reader attends to and interprets all of these simultaneously. One goal of reading instruction is to make the reader aware of each of these cue systems and to provide him or her with the knowledge needed to interpret the available cues. The information about the text provided in these cues is, in turn, one source utilized by the reader as he or she derives meaning while reading.

Letters on the page are a first set of cues. Single letters, letter patterns (e.g., -tion), and even written whole words may cue the reader to the sounds of words, provided the reader has knowledge of the correspondences needed to interpret these cues. Instruction for beginning readers includes teaching them to attend carefully to letter cues as well as the knowledge of correspondences that is needed to interpret letter cues. While it might appear to be a visual task, decoding places great demands on the phonological system as it requires mapping sounds to letters.

In text, every word is surrounded by a context of other words. If a word is not recognized, the context provides clues as to the part of speech of the word. If the reader guesses at an unknown word, the context is used to determine whether or not the guess is syntactically acceptable and whether or not the idea makes sense. Thus, experienced readers take advantage of a system of context cues.

Just as with the letter cues, the student learning to read must become aware of context cues. However, in contrast to the letter cues, most readers bring to school much of the knowledge needed to interpret context cues; i.e., they have knowledge of acceptable sentence structure and knowledge about the world.

A final cue system consists of structural cues. Print is structured according to conventions: In English, it is written from left to right, top of page to bottom. Pictures and words convey interconnected ideas. Most often, each paragraph has a central idea. Stories and content area text each follow a predictable structure. Reading instruction ensures that students attend to these cues and have the knowledge needed for their interpretation.

II. WHERE DO DISABLED READERS FAIL?

In comparison with normally developing readers, many poor readers have difficulty in learning to use letter cues to decode words. Vellutino and Scanlon (in press) report that 83% of second-grade poor readers were deficient in their knowledge and/or use of letter–sound correspondences. More strikingly, by sixth grade, 70% of poor readers still lacked phonetic word-attack skills.

Research indicates that reading-disabled students have difficulty with certain phonological skills prerequisite to remembering how sounds match symbols. Specifically, these poor readers have difficulty in focusing attention on individual sounds in words, a task referred to as phonemic awareness, or phonemic segmentation. Young children tend to direct their attention toward the meaning of words. Because the isolated sounds that make up words are not useful in communication, it is not surprising that children must be directed to attend to them.

Furthermore, many phonemes cannot be presented in isolation but must be abstracted from words. For example, none of the stop consonants (e.g., "b," "c," "d") can be produced without the addition of a vowel sound (*schwa*); the only way to gain a precise understanding of the \b\ sound is to hear it as the beginning sound in "ball" or the ending sound in "tub." The task of attending to phonemes is further complicated because many are influenced by surrounding sounds; many reading programs treat the \a\ in "fan" as equivalent to the \a\ in "fat," although the sound is not identical in the two contexts.

Because decoding requires students to map letters to phonemes, it is not surprising that phonemic awareness is related to success in learning to read. For example, Liberman *et al.* (1974) found that those first-graders who had the greatest difficulty in identifying the number of phonemes in a word were the poorest readers at the end of second grade. Vellutino and Scanlon (1986) found that second- and sixth-grade poor readers did poorly on a phonemic awareness task; those poor readers who were subsequently instructed to attend to phonemes were more facile in decoding unfamiliar words than were uninstructed peers. These findings support recommendations for phonemic awareness instruction for disabled readers.

It has been argued that poor readers' difficulty with phonemic awareness and decoding tasks is a consequence of a more basic disorder, a deficit in phonological coding (Vellutino and Denkla, 1990). A spoken word stored in memory has sound (phonological), meaning, and grammatical attributes.

Various measures suggest that poor readers are inefficient in storing and/or retrieving sound information and rely more on meaning. This phonological coding deficit makes it especially difficult for the student to learn non-meaningful information such as the sounds the letters make.

III. DEVELOPMENT OF READING PROFICIENCY

The beginning reader does not simultaneously master use of the three cue systems. Instead, the process of learning to read has been characterized as a series of stages (Chall, 1983). In each stage, the child masters new dimensions of the complex task of reading. Reading instruction programs often follow a sequence similar to Chall's stages.

In an initial prereading stage, from birth through kindergarten, children learn to speak and understand language and acquire a fund of knowledge about the world. Their knowledge and language skills are critical as they learn to utilize contextual cues in reading. During this period, children also learn that print is an important medium for communication; they begin to learn the purposes of reading and writing. They learn to expect written language and events in books to make sense. From this understanding, they eventually develop strategic use of context cues. Stahl and Miller (1989) suggest that whole language and/or language experience approaches to reading instruction may be especially effective at this stage.

Early instruction teaches children to use the simplest structural cues: They learn how to hold a book, to refer to words, to utilize pictures, and to turn pages. Children at this stage know some letter names and recognize certain salient words such as their own name and product logos. They have some knowledge about language (e.g., some words rhyme, word parts can be synthesized to make words).

Reading-disabled students generally do not have noticeable difficulty with most tasks of the prereading stage. The important exception is failure to acquire phonemic awareness. Reading instruction should begin with phonemic awareness training for reading-disabled students who are not yet able to attend to sounds in words. Lack of facility in phonemic awareness can be identified by asking students to give the initial sound in a spoken word or to identify spoken words with same or different sounds in the initial, medial, and final position.

Grades one and two have been characterized as a decoding stage; this is when students learn to use letter cues. As noted earlier, most reading-disabled children do not successfully complete this stage given traditional basal reading instruction. Difficulty with decoding may be identified by asking students to read phonetically regular words or nonsense words in isolation, or by asking students to read text and analyzing the types of errors they make. Students with inadequate decoding skills require additional direct instruction and practice.

A first task of the decoding stage is to learn that reading involves use of a code: Words are not written in arbitrary ways but according to an alphabetic principle, by which letters have a regular and predictable relationship with sounds. Children come to understand that the alphabetic principle simplifies the reading process and that it is crucial that they attend to all of the letters to read accurately. Vellutino and Scanlon (1986) characterize this as adopting an analytic attitude toward reading.

Of course, an analytic attitude is not sufficient; the reader must also know the specific correspondences between letters or letter patterns and sounds. Acquiring this knowledge is the primary task of the decoding stage. It is an especially difficult task in English, because letters and letter combinations may represent more than one sound.

Decoding programs vary somewhat in the scope and sequence of skills taught (Carnine *et al.*, 1990), but most begin with teaching consonants and short vowels. Students are taught to sound out letter by letter and to blend sounds so that consonant–vowel–consonant (CVC) words such as "cat" can be read. Consonant blends are taught so that longer words can be read. Some irregular words are introduced, and short sentences are read. Students are then taught to attend to larger letter groups (rather than sound out letter by letter) to produce the proper sound when reading words containing vowel digraphs (tr*ai*n), consonant digraphs (*ch*ain), r-controlled vowels (c*ar*), l-controlled vowels (c*all*), dipthongs (*ou*ch), and silent "e" words (pal*e*). Analysis of prefixes, suffixes, and compound words is taught.

For students who successfully negotiate the decoding stage, a next stage is "ungluing from print" (grade two and three). Here, students gain fluency in reading and learn to coordinate use of letter and context cues. Rather than laboriously decoding letter by letter, decoding becomes more automatic and requires less conscious attention. Students appear to recognize many words or word parts. Decoding is integrated with other word-attack strategies, such as using context to assist word recognition. Skills and strategies that were practiced in isolation are used in a coordinated, flexible fashion.

Less able readers lack fluency (Ehri and Wilce, 1983). Disabled readers need to build a repertoire of words they can read on sight, because proficient reading entails recognizing words accurately and rapidly (Stanovich *et al.*, 1984b). LaBerge and Samuels (1974) argue that poor decoders expend cognitive resources in decoding and, hence, reduce the resources available to facilate comprehension. Fluent readers, in contrast, have automatized decoding and word recognition so that these activities do not require mental effort; they can direct their attention toward comprehension.

IV. GENERAL INSTRUCTIONAL RECOMMENDATIONS

In summary, many children with or at risk for reading disability have not successfully negotiated the decoding stage and also lack the integration and automaticity that are the hallmark of ungluing from print. These skill deficits are a consequence of unusual difficulty with the phonological demands of learning to read; i.e., the phonemic segments of spoken language are not readily apparent to reading-disabled children, and they tend not to learn letter–sound correspondences as many children do, simply through exposure to letters in familiar words.

Instead, reading-disabled students require explicit, systematic intensive teaching, which involves a maximum amount of interaction with the teacher (Haring and Bateman, 1977), an approach termed direct instruction. Because of the importance of direct instruction techniques for disabled readers, a brief review of these techniques is provided here. The reading programs reviewed later in this chapter incorporate direct instruction techniques, some to a greater extent than others.

Direct instruction incorporates methods for gaining and maintaining pupil attention. These methods may be as simple as arranging seating to ensure teacher–student eye contact or as imaginative as using puppets to demonstrate concepts. Hand signals are used by some teachers to direct pupil responding and promote attending.

Teacher modeling is another critical feature of direct instruction. To be as explicit as possible, the teacher models exactly what students are expected to learn.

During guided practice, prompting techniques are often used to decrease potential errors. Such techniques include using pictures as memory aids for letter sounds and providing letter models for tracing and copying that have arrows to demonstrate directionality in letter formation. Erhi et al. (1984) found that mnemonics (e.g., a house in the shape of an "h") were especially useful prompts to help students to integrate letters with sounds. As students gain proficiency, prompts are faded and independent practice is provided.

Academic feedback is a crucial element of direct instruction. So that their errors are corrected and not practiced, students are told immediately whether or not their answers are right or their performance appropriate (Rosenshine and Stevens, 1984). Response feedback is most often provided by the teacher, at least at the early stages of learning to read; computer-assisted reading instruction can also be used to provided immediate response feedback. As students become more proficient, they are expected to take more responsibility for correcting their own errors.

In direct instruction, lessons are carefully paced to allow for extensive amounts of practice. Discrete skills are practiced to ensure student success. Lessons are carefully paced to avoid overwhelming students with too much information at one time (Bryant *et al.*, 1982).

Monitoring and evaluating student progress is another essential aspect of direct instruction. Monitoring serves two purposes: (1) providing the teacher with information on student progress to adjust the curriculum as necessary, and (2) informing students about their progress, which may serve to motivate them.

In direct instruction, reading skills are taught to a mastery level. Criteria for mastery are established for the different components of the reading curriculum and must be achieved before moving a student on to a higher level in the curriculum. Gaining automaticity at basic skills is another critical instructional goal, so that attention may be directed toward comprehension of what is read.

V. MORE SPECIFIC INSTRUCTIONAL RECOMMENDATIONS

A. Phonemic Awareness Training

Because the phonemes that make up spoken words are abstract, phonemic awareness training often includes activities to make phonemes more concrete—for example, teaching children that the phoneme \f\ is the sound that an angry cat makes (Venezky, 1976). Another approach is teaching students to attend to the shape of the mouth as particular sounds are produced (Lindamood and Lindamood, 1975). Elkonin (1963) developed a method in which phonemes are represented as a sequence of squares; as a word is spoken, the student moves a token to a new square with each new sound. Williams (1980) modified this approach for use with reading-disabled students. Each phoneme is represented with a block; segmentation training is integrated with instruction in blending sounds together. Eventually, letters are written on the blocks and decoding instruction begins.

Other programs encourage students to attend to phonemes by drawing attention to parts of the word. For example, in a program developed by Bradley and Bryant (1985), students are asked to attend to final sounds to select which of four words did not rhyme. Other word sets are used in which students are asked to select the word that has a different initial sound or a different middle sound. Another approach to developing phonemic awareness involves asking children to add, omit, substitute, and rearrange phonemes in words (Rosner and Simon, 1971).

Each of these programs was successful in teaching children to attend to sounds in words; in addition, a number of them demonstrated transfer effects to reading tasks (Bradley and Bryant, 1985; Williams, 1980). Use of letters to represent phonemes may enhance transfer of phonemic awareness training to reading (Bradley and Bryant, 1985; Hohn and Enri, 1983). However, letters may overload the reading-disabled student initially, and it is recommended that letters be introduced only as proficiency is gained (Williams, 1980).

B. Developing Phonics Skills

There are two approaches to teaching phonics. One approach, referred to most often as synthetic phonics instruction, first teaches the individual letter–sound correspondences, and after mastery, uses them in syllables and words. The other approach, known as analytic phonics instruction, introduces whole words first and encourages students to deduce the letter–sound correspondences as they appear in those words. Words are selected on the basis of their phonemic patterns, which are introduced systematically, rather than for their frequency in children's vocabularies, as are the words introduced in basal readers. Multisensory phonics instruction will be discussed as a third approach to teaching phonics, although it is essentially a variation of synthetic phonics instruction that incorporates multisensory teaching techniques.

1. Synthetic Phonics Instruction

The Direct Instructional System of Teaching Arithmetic and Reading (DISTAR), now known as *Reading Mastery* (Engelmann and Bruner, 1983), provides a good example of synthetic phonics instruction that is rigorous in its use of direct instruction techniques. DISTAR was designed to provide instruction to children at risk for reading failure in classroom settings. The reading curriculum comprises six levels, which extend from preschool through sixth grade.

The first level, *Reading Mastery I*, teaches letter sounds, strongly emphasizing the oral pronunciation of these sounds; letter names are not introduced until *Reading Mastery II*. Each letter sound is first said aloud by the teacher; students then imitate her pronunciation in unison. After oral presentation, the corresponding letter is shown in written form. A line diagram running from left to right underneath the letter helps pronunciation and demonstrates the difference between continuous sounds (e.g., /s/, /m/, certain digraphs, all vowels), for which students are instructed to move their finger slowly along the line as they pronounce the sound (e.g., *aaa*), and stop sounds (e.g., /d/, /t/), for which they are told to trace the line quickly and say the sound fast.

Letter sounds are introduced slowly with a great deal of review. Children learn to write the corresponding letter symbols from the very first lesson. Reading begins when six sounds have been learned. As words are introduced, the line diagram becomes a device to assist sound blending; children are instructed to sound out a word first, moving their fingers slowly along the line as they pronounce the phonemes in the word, and then to say the word fast. Irregular words (those that are not phonetically predictable such as "is" and "was") are also taught in this way rather than as whole words, to emphasize those parts of the word that are phonetically predictable. All the words studied become part of the children's reading vocabularies and are incorporated first in simple sentences and later in stories.

Two particular features distinguish DISTAR from other synthetic phonics programs. One is that all lessons follow scripts; teachers are told exactly what to say and do, including how to correct or to anticipate student errors. As instruction is designed for small groups and unison responses, teachers use had signals to direct the type and timing of responses required. The other special feature of DISTAR is its modified orthography, used in the early stages of the program but phased out by the middle of *Reading Mastery II*. The modification is intended to compensate for the fact that there are many more sounds than corresponding letter symbols in the English language, to help children read words that do not follow phonic rules, and to emphasize differences between visually similar letters. For example, silent letters are printed smaller, heavy macrons appear over letters representing long vowel sounds, and consonant blends are printed as joined letters.

Unlike some of the other synthetic phonics programs, DISTAR introduces comprehension activities from the very first lesson. Spelling instruction, which in many synthetic phonic programs is totally integrated with reading instruction, is a separate and optional curriculum in DISTAR, albeit strongly encouraged. The spelling curriculum follows the sequence of the reading curriculum. Although children are taught manuscript letter formations as part of the reading curriculum, neither handwriting nor written expression are emphasized in DISTAR.

DISTAR has been proven successful with children from disadvantaged socioeconomic backgrounds, for whom it was specifically designed (Becker, 1977; Meyer *et al.*, 1983). It has also been used with students with a variety of problems that may lead to academic underachievement, including learning disabilities. Primary grade learning disabled students who received DISTAR instruction had better reading achievement test scores than those who had another form of phonics instruction (Stein and Goldman, 1980). Although in several communities the program has been immensely popular with parents as well as teachers, some teachers find the scripts too restricting (Meyer *et al.*,

1983). Furthermore, some children may have difficulty making the transition from the modified to the traditional orthography.

Corrective Reading (Engelmann *et al.*, 1980) is a direct instruction program designed to provide remedial reading instruction to disabled readers in grades four through twelve. Word recognition and comprehension skills are stressed. Studies have documented the success of *Corrective Reading* in increasing learning disabled students' word recognition (Lloyd *et al.*, 1981; Polloway *et al.*, 1986).

2. Analytic Phonics Instruction

The *Merrill Linguistic Readers* (Fries *et al.*, 1966) exemplifies an analytic approach to phonics instruction; it teaches letter–sound correspondences within the context of words rather than as isolated units. The Merrill program emphasizes word endings with invariable spelling patterns ("man," "ran," "Dan"), applying the principal of "minimal contrasts," whereby children are taught to attend to the word ending and then to note the varying initial consonant. This has also been called the word family method. The high degree of consistency of spelling patterns among the words introduced enables children to read continuous text early on in this program (e.g., "The fat cat sat on a mat.").

The program, developed for use in first-grade classrooms, comprises six readers and six corresponding workbooks. All new "words in pattern" and any high-frequency words not belonging to that pattern are presented in a list at the beginning of each chapter in which they first appear as well as being introduced by the teacher on the chalkboard. Only words having the same spelling pattern appear together in the early books; at more advanced levels, increasing numbers of different spelling patterns are included in the same text. Pictures are excluded in all the Merrill books to prevent distraction from the printed words. Because of the highly controlled vocabulary, the semantic interest level of the text is necessarily low. Comprehension activities as well as writing activities are at a minimum in the program.

The Merrill program is one of more than 10 reading programs that use an analytic approach to phonics instruction; others worth noting are the SRA Basic Reading Program (Rasmussen and Goldberg, 1976), the Stern Structural Reading Series (Stern and Gould, 1965), and the Glass Analysis for Decoding Only method (Glass and Glass, 1976). Because these programs avoid sounding out individual letters, they may help children who lack blending skills. At the same time, because they do not provide explicit instruction in grapheme–phoneme correspondences, for most disabled readers they are best applied after sounds have been taught. As yet, no substantial research supports or negates the use of these programs with children at risk for reading difficulties.

3. Multisensory Phonics Instruction

The descriptor multisensory refers to the simultaneous engagement of two or more sensory modalities in the learning process (visual, auditory, kinesthetic, and tactile). The rationale for use of multisensory teaching techniques is the belief that kinesthetic involvement enhances learning of letter–sound correspondences (Orton, 1966). It has been proposed that these procedures help children attend to details within letters and words (Gates, 1927) as well as to retrieve words from long-term memory (Slingerland, 1971).

The prototype of multisensory phonics instruction is the Orton–Gillingham approach (Gillingham and Stillman, 1960). Designed for one-to-one remedial instruction, all instruction is direct and systematic. Letters or phonograms (digraphs and diphthongs) are treated as discrete elements and introduced in a prescribed sequence on individual cards. The letter name is taught first; the teacher says the name, and the child repeats. When the name is secure, the letter sound is taught in the same way. Auditory-to-auditory association is then established as the teacher gives the letter sound and asks for the letter name. For visual–kinesthetic association, the teacher writes the letter, explaining its formation and orientation; the student traces the letter, then copies it, then writes it from memory, and finally writes it from memory with eyes closed. For auditory–kinesthetic reinforcement, the teacher says the letter sound and asks the student to write the corresponding letter. When writing, the student always says the letter name, not the sound. To reinforce memory of letter sounds, each letter or phonogram is given a key word (e.g., "i"—Indian). In subsequent drill exercises, the student states the key word along with the letter name and sound.

The difference between vowels and consonants is emphasized by drawing attention to open or closed mouth positions in pronunciation and reinforced using different-colored cards for vowels and consonants. Reading only begins when eight consonants and two vowels have been learned. The teacher lays out letter cards to form CVC words (e.g., b-a-t) and has the student pronounce each letter sound in succession, repeating them with increasing speed until able to pronounce the word. To avoid the schwa sound when pronouncing consonants in isolation, the student is encouraged to pronounce the first two letters together (e.g., ba-t). As with letters, the student traces, copies, and writes the words from memory. In the Orton–Gillingham program as well as in all other multisensory phonics programs, spelling is taught concomitantly with reading and as reinforcement for word recognition.

Text reading does not begin until all CVC words and four letter words with consonant digraphs that have been studied can be read easily. Stories containing these words are printed in the instructor's manual. Nonphonetic sight words, which the student has not yet encountered, are underlined and told to the student before reading. The student reads silently first, asking for help if needed. In oral reading, the student is encouraged to read with inflection, although no attention is paid to word meaning or comprehension.

Syllabication practice begins with students reading words with syllables separated, followed by their rearranging jumbled syllables to form real words. They are taught to place stress marks on accented syllables. Knowledge of syllable patterns is linked to spelling rules and used to decode unfamiliar multisyllable words.

A number of reading programs have adapted Orton–Gillingham-based multisensory instruction for school settings. The Slingerland Program (Slingerland, 1971) was designed for use with whole classes of children at risk for reading disabilities. Project Read (Greene and Enfield, 1985) is used with groups of children within regular classrooms, while Alphabetic Phonics (Cox, 1984) is implemented by pulling small groups of children from the regular classroom. In these programs, the role of multisensory procedures has been expanded. Kinesthetic activities include having children write letters and words in the air (sky-writing), using their whole arm, while saying aloud each letter name as the letter is formed, and having them spell words by placing individual letter cards in pocket charts (for a more detailed description of these programs, see Clark, 1988).

Disabled readers given Orton–Gillingham-based multisensory phonics instruction had higher reading scores than those in traditional basal programs (McCulloch, 1985); however, whether or not multisensory techniques added to the effectiveness of phonics instruction is not known. Most multisensory reading programs require extensive teacher training.

C. Developing Whole-Word Recognition

In addition to phonics instruction, disabled readers often need help in building a repertoire of words they can recognize on sight. Word recognition is equally important for phonetically regular and irregular words, although these two types of words may be introduced differently.

Most reading programs that focus on phonics instruction teach irregular words as "sight words" to be studied as wholes. Students are taught that these words are different because they cannot be sounded out. Assorted drill and practice activities are used to enhance recall. Bryant *et al.* (1982) found a mastery learning approach to be more effective than traditional drill activities in teaching irregular words to disabled readers. Words were presented in groups of only four or five, with ample practice that included discriminating the words from other words similar in appearance. In multisensory programs, irregular words are taught as wholes using activities such as tracing, copying, and sky-writing, while saying the individual letter names.

In contrast to most programs, DISTAR advocates sounding out irregular words. The rationale is that in irregular words some correspondences are regular and provide assistance to the reader. Also, it is feared that presentation of a global whole-word strategy may lead students to guess instead of attending to letter cues. In DISTAR, the teacher states the irregular word, sounds it out as if it were regular, and then states the correct pronounciation. Students then copy the teacher model.

Recognition of sight words should be practiced in sentence context so that children learn to utilize context to check their accuracy. Bryant *et al.* (1982) suggest teaching words first in isolation, then practicing reading them in phrases, sentences, and finally paragraphs. Word recognition is greater when words are initially presented in isolation rather than in context (Singer *et al.*, 1973).

Because children at risk for reading disability tend to become glued to print and laboriously decode every word (Chall, 1983), they need to practice reading phonetically regular words quickly and accurately. DISTAR teaches explicitly the transition from sounding out to word recognition. The teacher models sounding out a word subvocally and then stating the word. Students then copy that model. Initially, the teacher allows the students 5 sec for subvocal sounding out a word; this is eventually reduced to 2 sec. This approach is used to read both words in isolation and sentences.

Most programs develop word recognition through drill and practice activities. One simple approach is to keep a word bank with learned words on cards that are periodically drilled. During drill, both rate and accuracy should be monitored; rate should gradually increase with high levels of accuracy maintained.

Computer-assisted instruction (CAI) has been demonstrated to enhance disabled readers' word-recognition skills. Learning disabled students made significant gains in their speed and accuracy with a list of single-syllable, phonetically regular words given practice with the computer (Jones *et al.*, 1987). The effects of this practice generalized to reading unpracticed words containing the same medial vowels with novel initial and final consonants. In another study, learning disabled students practiced two- and three-syllable words using a multiple-choice format. This practice transferred to oral reading of the words in print (Torgesen *et al.*, 1988).

Although still at a formative stage, CAI appears to offer certain advantages for word-recognition instruction with at-risk students. It affords extensive one-to-one practice within classrooms with a minimum teacher supervisory time (Torgesen *et al.*, 1988) and with protection from potential embarrassment in front of classmates. It provides immediate response feedback to students so that errors can be promptly corrected. Some programs can monitor both speed and accuracy of responses and pace instruction according to mastery requirements. By incorporating game formats, CAI can alleviate the boredom of traditional drill exercises.

D. Developing Reading Fluency

Children with reading difficulties are apt to read connected text in a halting manner, indicating a need for instruction to promote reading fluency. One commonly used technique is to have students practice reading words and phrases from a chalkboard before encountering them in stories.

Another approach to fluency practice is repeated reading, where the student reads short passages several times until a satisfactory level of fluency and accuracy has been reached. Samuels (1986) has suggested several techniques for implementing this approach. One is the use of audio support—having a student read silently while listening to a tape recording of the passage. Another technique is having the student read for 1 min and count the words read in that time and then record them on a graph. A third technique is paired reading— having students read alternatively in pairs, keeping word count records for each other.

Other variations on the repeated reading model include imitative reading, where first the teacher reads a passage aloud with the student following along silently and then the student reads the passage aloud imitating the teacher's intonation and phrasing (Henk *et al.*, 1986). The neurological impress model entails the teacher and student reading a passage aloud simultaneously, with the teacher controlling the pace with her voice and finger. CAI has also been adapted for repeated reading practice with reading-disabled children (Rashotte and Torgesen, 1985).

When the instructional focus is on increasing fluency so as to increase reading comprehension, students should be encouraged to take advantage of context. Pflaum and Pascarella (1980) presented taped examples to reading-disabled students to model decoding errors that interfered with comprehension. Students learned to identify and self-correct serious errors, using tapes to assist analysis. Practice using context was also provided with cloze tasks. Learning disabled students with at least third-grade reading skills increased reading fluency with this program.

The focus of this chapter is teaching phonemic awareness, phonics, and whole-word identification to children with, or at risk for, reading disability, as weakness in these critical skills distinguishes most disabled readers from normally developing readers. However, we do not mean to imply that they are the only reading skills children need to be taught or that any of the instructional programs or approaches we have described provide a comprehensive reading curriculum. In fact, most of these programs are notably deficient in providing instruction in two essential components of the language arts curriculum, reading comprehension and expressive writing, topics addressed in other chapters.

VI. IMPLEMENTING SPECIAL READING INSTRUCTION

Providing the instructional support for the child having difficulty learning is a complex process. Factors that may influence implementation will vary from case to case. Questions that should be addressed at the outset of the intervention process are discussed below.

A. Who Will be Working with the Student?

The professional providing special instruction may be the regular classroom teacher, an assistant teacher in the regular classroom, a specialist (e.g., resource room or remedial reading) teacher within the school, or a private tutor.

B. What Age is the Student?

Many of the reading programs described in this chapter were developed for children in the early elementary grades. However, some have also been used with older students (e.g., Orton–Gillingham). Others are designed for use with a range of ages, including older students (e.g., Project Read, Alphabetic Phonics, Corrective Reading). More importantly, many of the teaching methods described can be used with older students, without adopting the entire program. However, judicious selection is called for because activities such as unison responding and sky-writing may embarrass older students.

C. How Many Students Need Special Instruction?

A large elementary school may have sufficient numbers of young children at risk for reading failure to warrant a self-contained classroom providing DISTAR or multisensory phonics instruction. In a small school, on the other hand, there may be as few as one child in a class requiring special intervention. This instruction would most likely be provided in a resource room. Often there is sufficient need to provide special instruction to small groups of children either within the classroom or in a resource room.

D. What is the Severity of the Student's Reading Deficits?

More than any other factor, the severity of the reading difficulty dictates the type and amount of special instruction the student will require. It also influences the choice of instructional setting for the student. Group instruction is inefficient when there is too much disparity among students in terms of reading ability. Instead, special reading instruction may be provided within the classroom by a second teacher or in a resource room during the classroom reading period. For students with mild deficits, minor modification may make the classroom program acceptable. Classrooms that have more individualized reading instruction are more able to accommodate a range of student needs.

E. What is the School's Philosophy of Reading Instruction, and What is the Classroom Reading Program?

These questions are critical to the success of any instructional intervention program. The school's reading philosophy will affect the administration's willingness to accommodate individual pupil needs and influence the type of reading program used in the regular classroom. If the school supports a phonics approach to early reading instruction, there is greater likelihood that children at risk for reading failure will receive appropriate early reading instruction. Alternatively, it may be possible to adapt the classroom reading program to include disabled readers. For example, the basal reader can be used to develop whole-word recognition and reading fluency, with additional phonics instruction provided for those who require it.

F. What Placements Are Available for Special Reading Instruction?

All possible options for providing special instruction to a student or students are rarely available. The choice of placement will depend on the school's resources: the teacher–student ratio, the number of specialist teachers, the amount of classroom space, the money available for teacher training, etc. The following are among the possible options.

1. Resource Room Model
This setting can allow individualized instruction and maximize teacher freedom in planning the curriculum for the poor reader. Some of the programs described or cited in this chapter were designed specifically for one-to-one instruction (e.g., Orton–Gillingham, the Glass Analysis method); others can be adapted for this purpose. However, if children are pulled out of the regular classroom for special instruction, the specialist teacher must be in close

contact with the classroom teacher to coordinate the special curriculum with the class curriculum (Allington and Broikou, 1988).

2. Whole-Class Model

This approach is feasible when there are enough students in the school having similar instructional needs to make up a full class. It is usually cost-effective, although it may require additional teacher training (Ballestros and Royal, 1981). Both DISTAR and the Slingerland Program were designed for whole classes of children considered to be at risk for reading failure, and most analytic phonics programs can be used with whole classes. Risks in adopting a whole-class program are that children not needing special instruction may be included, and instruction may not be adequately individualized.

3. Small-Group Model

Almost all of the programs described in this paper can be used in teaching small groups. Small-group instruction may take place outside or inside the regular classroom. The latter approach allows greater opportunity for coordinating special instruction with the classroom curriculum and avoids the stigma attached to removal from the mainstream (Gelzheiser and Meyers, 1990). The specialist teacher can come to the regular classroom during scheduled reading periods to work with students having reading difficulty or assist the classroom teacher in modifying the curriculum for disabled readers. CAI and peer tutoring can be used to further individualize reading instruction.

VII. RECOMMENDATIONS FOR FURTHER RESEARCH

The teacher planning instruction for reading-disabled students can identify many questions that need further research. For example, research is needed to determine when specific indicators of phonemic awareness (e.g., counting syllables in words, counting phonemes, recognizing rhymes) are acquired by normally developing readers (Lewkowicz, 1980). Such information can then be used to develop screening measures to identify children needing special instruction (Stanovich et al., 1984a). Studies that compare the effectiveness of various approaches to teaching phonemic awareness are also needed.

Carefully designed studies that compare the effects of various approaches to phonics instruction on students with reading deficits are also needed. To date, much of the research in this area has been methodologically flawed, lacking random assignment of subjects to treatments or use of blocking to control for pre-existing group differences. Often, there is insufficient description of the method of reading instruction with which the experimental method is being compared.

Little research has been done on methods of developing whole-word recognition among disabled readers (Carnine et al., 1990). It is especially important to study the transfer effects of whole-word recognition training to reading connected text containing those words. Furthermore, it would be useful to know which of the various methods developed for increasing reading fluency are the most effective with reading-disabled students.

VIII. SUMMARY

This chapter provides an overview of the issues related to providing appropriate early reading instruction for children having difficulty learning to read. It views reading development as a series of stages of skill acquisition that build incrementally. Most children who become labeled as reading-disabled face problems in the beginning stages of reading development, at the point where they should be acquiring the alphabetic principle and learning the letter–sound correspondences that would allow them to decode words. Their decoding problems appear to reflect a less-than-facile grasp of the phonological aspects of written language. Specifically, they are not readily aware of discrete phonemes that make up words and, thus, have difficulty learning to map sounds to symbols. Because they have not mastered the basic skills of the decoding stage, reading-disabled children have trouble moving on to the next stage of reading acquisition, the development of speed and accuracy in word recognition, and fluency in reading connected text.

This chapter also reviews direct instruction approaches that are appropriately used with students with these specific reading deficits. It describes alternative instructional methods and programs for developing phonemic awareness, decoding skills, whole-word recognition, and fluency. Suggestions are outlined for implementing appropriate instruction for reading-disabled students in various situations.

References

Allington, R. L., and Broikou, K. A. (1988). Development of shared knowledge: A new role for classroom and special teachers. *Read. Teacher* **41**, 806–811.

Ballestros, D. A., and Royal, N. L. (1981). Slingerland-SLD instruction as a winning voluntary magnet program. *Bull. Orton Soc.* **31**, 199–211.

Becker, W. C. (1977). Teaching reading and language to the disadvantaged—What we have learned from field research. *Harv. Educ. Rev.* **47**, 518–543.

Bradley, L., and Bryant, P. E. (1985). "Rhyme and Reason in Reading and Spelling." University of Michigan Press, Ann Arbor.

Bryant, N. D., Payne, H. R., and Gettinger, M. (1982). Applying the mastery learning model to sight word instruction for disabled readers. *J. Exp. Educ.* **50**, 116–121.

Carnine, D., Silbert, J., and Kameenui, E. J. (1990). *"Direct Instruction Reading,"* 2nd ed. Merrill, Columbus, Ohio.

Chall, J. S. (1983). "Stages of Reading Development." McGraw-Hill, New York.

Clark, D. B. (1988). "Dyslexia: Theory and Practice of Remedial Instruction." York Press, Parkton, Maryland.

Cox, A. R. (1984). "Structures and Techniques." Educators Publishing Service, Cambridge.

Ehri, L. C., Deffner, N.D., and Wilce, L. S. (1984). Pictorial mnemonics for phonics. *J. Educ. Psychol.* **76**, 880–893.

Ehri, L. C., and Wilce, L. S. (1983). Development of word identification speed in skilled and less skilled beginning readers. *J. Psychol.* **75**, 3–18.

Elkonin, D. B. (1963). The psychology of mastering the elements of reading. *In* "Educational Psychology in the U.S.S.R." (B. Simon and J. Simon, eds.), pp. 164–179. Routledge & Kegan Paul, London.

Engelmann, S., and Bruner, E. C. (1983). "Reading Mastery I and II: DISTAR Reading." Science Research Associates, Chicago.

Engelmann, S., Becker, W. C., Hanner, S., and Johnson, G. (1980). "Corrective Reading Series Guide." Science Research Associates, Chicago.

Fries, C. C., Wilson, R. G., and Rudolph, M. K. (1966). "Merrill Linguistic Readers. Charles E. Merrill, Columbus, Ohio.

Gates, A. I. (1927). "The Improvement of Reading: A Program of Diagnostic and Remedial Methods." Macmillan, New York.

Gelzheiser, L. M., and Meyers, J. (1990). Special and remedial education in the classroom: Theme and variation. *J. Read. Writ. Learn. Disabil. Int.,* **6**, 419–436.

Gillingham, A., and Stillman , B. (1960). "Remedial Training for Children with Specific Disability in Reading, Writing, and Penmanship. Educators Publishing Service, Cambridge.

Glass, G. G., and Glass, E. W. (1976). "Glass Analysis for Decoding Only: Teachers Guide." Easier to Learn, Garden City, New York.

Gough, P. B., and Hillinger, M. L. (1980). Learning to read: An unnatural act. *Bull. Orton Soc.* **20**, 179–196.

Greene, V. E., and Enfield, M. L. (1985). "Project Read Reading Guide: Phase 1." Bloomington Public Schools, Bloomington, Minnesota.

Haring, N. G., and Bateman, B. (1977). "Teaching the Learning Disabled Child." Prentice-Hall, Englewood Cliffs, New Jersey.

Henk, W. A., Helfeldt, J. P., and Platt, J. M. (1986). Developing reading fluency in learning disabled students. *Teach. Excep. Children* **12**, 202–206.

Hohn, W. E., and Ehri, L. C. (1983). Do alphabet letters help prereaders acquire phonemic segmentation skills? *J. Educ. Psychol.* **75**, 752–762.

Jones, K. M., Torgesen, J. K., and Sexton, M. A. (1987). Using computer guided practice to increase decoding fluency in learning disabled children: A study using the Hint and Hunt I program. *J. Learn. Disabil.* **20(2)**, 122–128.

LaBerge, D., and Samuels, S. J. (1974). Toward a theory of automatic information processing. *Cog. Psychol.* **6**, 293–322.

Lewkowicz, N. K. (1980). Phonemic awareness training: What to teach and how to teach it. *J. Educ. Psychol.* **72**, 686–700.

Liberman, I. Y., Shankweiler, D., Fischer, F. W., and Carter, B. (1974). Explicit syllable and phoneme segmentation in the young child. *J. Exp. Child Psychol.* **18(2)**, 1–12.

Lindamood, C. H., and Lindamood, P. C. (1975). "The A.D.D. Program, Auditory Discrimination in Depth: Books 1 and 2." Teaching Resources, Hingham, Massachusetts.

Lloyd, J., Epstein, M. H., and Cullinan, D. (1981). Direct teaching for learning disabilities. *In* "Developmental Theory and Research in Learning Disabilities" (J. Gottleib and S. Strichart, eds.), pp. 278–309. University Park Press, Baltimore.

McCulloch, C. (1985). "The Slingerland Approach: Is It Effective in a Specific Language Disability Classroom? Unpublished Masters thesis, Seattle Pacific University, Seattle, Washington.

Meyer, L. A., Gersten, R. M., and Gutkin, J. (1983). Direct instruction: A project follow-through success story in an inner-city school. *Elem. School J.* **84**, 241–252.

Orton, J. (1966). The Orton–Gillingham approach. *In* "The Disabled Reader" (J. Money, ed.), pp. 119–146. The Johns Hopkins University Press, Baltimore.

Pflaum, S. W., and Pascarella, E. T. (1980). Interactive effects of prior reading achievement and training in context on the reading of learning disabled children. *Read. Res. Q.* **16**, 138–158.

Polloway, E., Epstein, M., Polloway, C., Patton, J., and Ball, D. (1986). Corrective reading program: An analysis of effectiveness with learning disabled and mentally retarded students. *Remed. Special Educ.* **7**, 41–47.

Rashotte, C. A., and Torgesen, J. K. (1985). Repeated reading and reading fluency in reading disabled children. *Read. Res. Q.* **20**, 180–188.

Rasmussen, D. E., and Goldberg, L. (1976). "SRA Basic Reading." Science Research Associates, Chicago.

Rosenshine, B., and Stevens, R. (1984). Classroom instruction in reading. *In* "Handbook of Reading Research" (P. D. Pearson, ed.), pp. 745–798. Longman, New York.

Rosner, J., and Simon, D. P. (1971). The auditory analysis test: An initial report. *J. Learn. Disabil.* **4**, 384–392.

Samuels, S. J. (1986). Automaticity and repeated readings. *In* "Reading Education: Foundations for a Literate America" (J. Osborn, P. T. Wilson, and R. C. Anderson, eds.), pp. 215–230. D. C. Heath, Lexington, Massachusetts.

Singer, H., Samuels, S. J., and Spiroff, J. (1973). The effects of pictures and contextual conditions on learning responses to printed words. *Read. Res. Q.* **9**, 555–567.

Slingerland, B. H. (1971). "A Multi-Sensory Approach to Language Arts for Specific Language Disability Children: A Guide for Primary Teachers, Books 1–3. Educators Publishing Service, Cambridge.

Stahl, S. A., and Miller, P. D. (1989). Whole language and language experience approaches for beginning reading: A quantitative research synthesis. *Rev. Educ. Res.* **59**, 87–116.

Stanovich, K. E., Cunningham, A. E., and Cramer, B. B. (1984a). Assessing phonological awareness in kindergarten children: Issues of task comparability. *J. Exp. Child Psychol.* **38**, 1090.

Stanovich, K. E., Cunningham, A. E., and Feeman, D. J. (1984b). Intelligence, cognitive skills, and early reading progress. *Read. Res. Q.* **29**, 278–303.

Stein, C., and Goldman, J. (1980). Beginning reading instruction for children with minimal brain dysfunction. *J. Learn. Disabil.* **13**, 52–55.

Stern, C., and Gould, T. (1965). "Children Discover Reading." Random House, New York.

Torgesen, J. K., Waters, M. D., Cohen, A. L., and Torgesen, J. L. (1988). Improving sight–word recognition skills in LD children: An evaluation of three computer program variations. *Learn. Disabil. Q.* **11(2)**, 125–133.

Vellutino, F. R., and Denkla, M. (1990). Cognitive and neuropsychological foundations of word identification. *In* R. Barr, M. Kamil, P. Mosenthal, and P. D. Pearson, (Eds.) "Handbook of reading research," Vol. 2, pp. 571–608. Longman, New York.

Vellutino, F. R., and Scanlon, D. M. (1986). Experimental evidence for the effects of instructional bias on word identification. *Excep. Children* **53**, 145–155.

Vellutino, F. R., and Scanlon, D. M. (in press). The preeminence of phonologically based skills in learning to read. *In* "Phonological Processes in Literacy: A Tribute to Isabelle Liberman" (S. Brady and D. Shankweiler, eds.). Lawrence Erlbaum, Hillsdale, New Jersey.

Venezky, R. L. (1976). Prequisites for learning to read. *In* "Cognitive Learning in Children: Theories and Strategies" (R. Levin and V. L. Allen, eds.), pp. 163–185. Academic Press, New York.

Williams, J. P. (1980). Teaching decoding with an emphasis on phoneme analysis and phoneme blending. *J. Exp. Psychol.* **72**, 1–15.

CHAPTER 10

Reading Comprehension Failure in Children

Ruth Garner, Patricia A. Alexander, and Victoria Chou Hare

Editor's Notes

In the preceding chapter, you read about the critical role of decoding skills in children learning to read and the various ways of teaching decoding. However, reading not only consists of decoding but also of comprehension skills. Hence we turn now to focus on them.

The present chapter has three themes. The first concerns the causes of reading comprehension failures. Here, Garner, Alexander, and Hare debunk the assumption that students' reading comprehension failures are entirely due to decoding problems, an assumption that appears to be tacitly embraced by learning disabilities researchers and professionals. Consequently, it is instructive to learn that additional alternatives can cause reading comprehension problems. These include confusion about task demands, insufficient domain knowledge, insufficient comprehension monitoring, low self-esteem, and low interest in task. Garner and her colleagues rightfully point out the interrelated nature of all the causes of comprehension failures.

The second theme concerns instruction to rectify students' problems in reading comprehension. Here Garner and her colleagues provide relevant, research-based information. They underscore the link between research and practice.

The third theme is unique and most refreshing in a chapter on reading comprehension failures. It is the authors' advocacy and platform on teaching students to become self-regulated learners who sustain both skill and will in reading to learn and reading for enjoyment. Readers should realize the importance of this theme and attend closely to the suggestions on how to foster self-regulation in reading in students.

I. INTRODUCTION

Comprehension is the successful outcome of reading. It results from a learner-regulated interaction of information stored in memory and information presented in text. It is supported by other processes. Though these other processes (e.g., eye fixation, lexical access) are necessary to comprehension, they are not sufficient to ensure that comprehension will occur. If children cannot either "find a mental home" for text information or modify existing information to accommodate new information (Anderson and Pearson, 1984), comprehension has failed (and, of course, so has reading). Comprehension failure occurs frequently (Pressley *et al.*, 1989b).

Children often fail to comprehend text for reasons that have little to do with what we might label "comprehension proficiency" itself. Some of those reasons are (1) decoding deficiencies, (2) confusion about task demands, (3) meager domain knowledge, (4) weak comprehension monitoring, (5) low self-esteem, and (6) low interest in topic or task. In the first section of this chapter, we examine each of these reasons for comprehension failure. In subsequent sections of the chapter, we present models of effective comprehension instruction and discuss what teachers can do to sustain effective reading comprehension performance.

II. COMPREHENSION FAILURE

A. Decoding Deficiencies

As letters, syllables, and words are recognized rapidly, accurately, and automatically, two important things happen. One is that all these sources of information are used simultaneously (Just and Carpenter, 1984); the other is that cognitive resources are released from code-breaking to comprehension (Perfetti and Lesgold, 1979). Researchers generally agree that time spent practicing decoding is the principal determinant of skilled, automatic behavior.

When children are not fluent at decoding, many cognitive resources are devoted to identifying language components. Perhaps of most importance, when decoding processes make demands on working memory, memory resources are unavailable for integrating meaning at the sentence and text level. Very unskilled readers may labor so strenously over identifying a word at the end of a sentence that the meaning of words at the beginning of the sentence is forgotten (Perfetti, 1985).

Anderson *et al.* (1985) gave the following example of this dilemma: A young child reads a sentence such as "When Mary arrive at the r, ruh, ruh, ruh-es-tah, oh! restaurant! When Mary arrived at the … rest … restaurant …," requiring several attempts to decode the difficult word "restaurant." By the time this word has been identified, the child's memory for the earlier part of the sentence has faded, and he or she must work very hard to make sense of the text. Children who are just learning to read engage in particularly effortful, inefficient decoding of this sort. Their comprehension is inevitably hampered.

It is important to remember that automatic decoding is a necessary, but not sufficient, condition for successful comprehension (Mayer, 1987). Rapid, accurate, and automatic decoding reduces memory demands for word iden- tification, releasing memory resources for construction of meaning; however, it does not ensure that meaning will be constructed successfully. Factors other than decoding deficiency also produce comprehension failure.

B. Confusion about Task Demands

A series of studies from about a decade ago suggested that young children and less-skilled readers are likely to be confused about the task demands of reading. For instance, Myers and Paris (1978) interviewed second- and sixth- grade children about reading. The younger children emphasized decoding, not comprehension, processes. They frequently mentioned "sounding out" unfamiliar words but seldom mentioned any strategies to remedy confusion about sentence meaning.

In similar fashion, Forrest and Waller (1980) interviewed third- and sixth- grade children of different skill levels about reading. They too found a decoding emphasis and deficient strategic repertoires for comprehension among younger and less-skilled readers.

Still another study (Paris and Myers, 1981) presented 25 positive, negative, or neutral reading strategies to skilled and less-skilled fourth-grade readers. Less-skilled readers were more likely than skilled readers to produce rating reversals (i.e., rating negative strategies as positive and vice versa). The number of reversed ratings was significantly negatively correlated with recall perfor- mance for a narrative text.

In all three of these studies (and others), we find some children demonstrat- ing little awareness that they must make sense of text (Baker and Brown, 1984). We see little evidence of rich, varied strategic repertoires for text comprehension.

Very recent studies provide much the same view of children's confusion about task demands. Moore and Zabrucky (1989) employed six separate measures of comprehension evaluation and found that younger and less-skilled readers had an illusion of comprehension if they could decode the words in a text. Wagner *et al.* (1989) read Moroccan children stories about the habits of a good reader, using pairs of pictures to accompany the stories. Children selected one of each pair of pictures as the "better reader" (e.g., a girl memorizing her lesson without understanding the words vs. a girl attempting to understand). Just as in earlier studies conducted in the United States, Wagner *et al.* (1989) found that younger and less-skilled readers were quite naive about strategies, goals, and plans used by good readers.

Baker's work (e.g., Baker, 1984a,b, 1985) gives us one explanation of why children might have an illusion of comprehension if they decode words successfully. She proposes that readers use at least three standards to evaluate their understanding of information in text: lexical, syntactic, and semantic. The lexical standard operates at the level of the individual word, and context can be completely ignored ("Do I know what 'hypotenuse' is?"). The syntactic standard requires sensitivity to grammatical constraints of language ("This sentence is scrambled!"). The semantic standard requires consideration of sentences and of the text as a whole ("This piece of information is inconsistent with what I read a few pages ago."). It is the semantic standard that requires the most thorough processing of text and that is most important to effective comprehension.

Baker has found that less-skilled readers often use the lexical standard of evaluation exclusively. In some of her work, she introduced nonsense words, conceptual errors, and logical inconsistencies into text. Among younger children and less-skilled readers, only the nonsense words were mentioned as comprehension impediments.

One source of this overreliance on the lexical standard may be comprehension instruction itself. Some teachers and some teacher manuals emphasize code-breaking at the expense of comprehension. Allington (1983) found disturbing differences in instructional time and emphasis among skill groups, with the poorest readers receiving the least amount of instruction, but the greatest proportion of oral reading, interruptions for corrections, and low-challenge questions about text content.

Some cause for optimism can be found in Baker and Zimlin's (1989) recent finding that children could be taught to evaluate their comprehension using several different standards (lexical, external consistency, propositional cohesiveness, structural cohesiveness, internal consistency, or informational completeness). Training effects generalized to noninstructed standards among these and were maintained over time.

C. Meager Domain Knowledge

Knowledge is often described in terms of an associative network (Glaser, 1984; Rabinowitz and Glaser, 1985; Voss, 1984). Concepts are represented as nodes, relations between concepts as associative links. Individuals are considered to vary in the number of concepts available (i.e., the number of nodes in memory), the organization of information (i.e., the pattern of associative links), and the accessibility of information (i.e., the strength of the associative links). When a word or group of words is encountered in text, the corresponding concept in memory is (or is not) activated. Activation spreads automatically from that concept to many (or few) related concepts in the network. Stronger associative links lead to stronger activations beyond the original node.

In domains where children have few concepts and few linkages, comprehension of text information can be very difficult. The children have few expectations driving their encoding of information and few conceptual pegs to which new information can be attached for eventual retrieval.

Minsky (1986: 261) provided a simple text for our analysis of the effects of domain knowledge:

> Mary was invited to Jack's party.
> She wondered if he would like a kite.

Minsky noted that a whole set of expectations arise from these two lines: The "party" is a birthday party, Jack and Mary are children, and the kite would be a gift from Mary to Jack. These expectations (alternatively, inferences) arise from our prior experiences with parties and gifts. If we live somewhere where birthday parties are not common, we do not have the requisite concepts to comprehend this short text.

Dictionary definitions are far from adequate in capturing the rich information abstracted from prior experience that we bring to texts. Minsky suggested that most children in contemporary North American culture would know (and expect to see in the text or would assume, nonetheless) all of the following elements for birthday parties: arrival (be well dressed), gift (present to the guest of honor), games (blindfold competitions?), decor (balloons are favored), party meal (little that is nutritious), cake (candles represent the host's age), ceremony (host makes a wish), and song (guests sing a birthday song and get to eat cake). Note the cultural specificity of this sort of knowledge. As experiences vary, so do concepts stored in memory.

Rumelhart (1980) noted some time ago that comprehension can fail in three ways: (1) the reader may not have the appropriate concepts, (2) textual cues may be insufficient to activate concepts that the reader has, or (3) the reader may find a consistent interpretation of text information that is not the one intended by the author. For a birthday party text, then, comprehension could fail in any of the following ways: (1) a reader might not know about birthday gifts or games, (2) a reader might know about birthday ceremony but might not recognize that a rambling description of a young boy's desire to own a horse represents a "birthday wish," or (3) a reader might interpret young children's devouring of cakes and cookies as bad behavior (an interpretation not intended by the author of the birthday party text) because dietary excesses are labeled as misbehavior in his or her home.

D. Weak Comprehension Monitoring

If children do not notice that they are not understanding text information, they are unlikely to seek a strategic remedy (Garner, 1987). They will not reread confusing segments, or consult a teacher or peer for clarification of an apparent discrepancy, or check the meaning of a much-repeated unknown word. Instead, they will continue reading and, presumably, will continue to fail to comprehend.

Ideal comprehension monitoring has been described by Brown (1980): A child proceeds through a text with rapid construction of meaning until comprehension failure occurs and is detected. This situation can be characterized as cognitive failure (understanding is impaired) but metacognitive success (the child notices the problem). The child takes action; if the problem is serious enough to disrupt comprehension, some strategic remedy is applied.

Flavell (1979) noted that, although paralyzing, incessant evaluation of any cognitive enterprise might be debilitating, there surely is far too little, rather than enough or too much, monitoring around. The research literature supports this assessment. Faulty monitoring occurs more among younger and less-skilled readers than among older, skilled readers, but it occurs quite frequently among readers of all ages and skill levels (for summaries of this research, see Brown *et al.*, 1986; Garner, 1987; Markman, 1981).

For young children, the notions that they have minds, that there are distinct mental states, and that they can "read" their own mental states are just developing (Wellman, 1985). Comprehension and production of labels for understanding—labels such as "guess," "know," "remember," and "forget"— are acquired with age and experience in examining language and thought as analyzable objects. Flavell (1981) noted that scholars and lawyers treat most problems and texts as analyzable cognitive objects, but most children (and many adults) do not.

For children and adults, certain situations are more likely to elicit comprehension monitoring than others. When a child needs to follow directions carefully to assemble a model tractor, he is likely to evaluate how well he understands each step before executing it; he may well reread multicomponent steps many times lest he make a mistake and misglue pieces. When a child has chosen to read a scary story that she will then read aloud to her classmates over the next few days, she is likely to evaluate whether or not a particular segment is really scary and where breaks in reading should occur to maintain maximum suspense. When children completing homework tasks are alert and undistracted by external noise, they are likely to have "ahas" when comprehension fails. On the other hand, when children need not act on text, when an imposed task is viewed as unimportant, or when children are not devoting conscious attention to a text or related tasks, comprehension monitoring is much less likely.

E. Low Self-Esteem

As Anderson *et al.* (1985) noted, failure is not fun. It is not surprising that unskilled readers have unfavorable attitudes toward reading. Unfortunately, the correlational design of most research studies on children's attitudes toward reading does not allow us to assess whether poor performance causes an unfavorable attitude or vice versa (Wigfield and Asher, 1984).

Paris and Cross (1983) proposed that both skill and will are necessary for learning to take place. In the context of reading, then, children must possess requisite skills *and* must want to read successfully. They must also believe that they can read.

A rich literature on children's and adults' attributions for cognitive success and failure makes clear just how important efficacy beliefs are. From their experiences, learners derive expectations about likelihood of success or failure that profoundly affect both the initiation and persistance of problem-solving behaviors. Without high self-esteem and the tendency to attribute success and failure to their level of effort (rather than to their ability), both children and adults are unlikely to employ strategies to learn (Borkowski *et al.*, 1987).

Imagine that comprehension failure has just occurred and has been noted. What a child makes of the failure is critical. Nicholls (1983) suggested that a learner who tends to attribute failure to effort might ask "What might I do differently to succeed?" On the other hand, a learner who tends to attribute failure to ability might ask a very different question, something along the lines of "Am I stupid?" Only the first question is likely to induce strategy use and improved comprehension. Children asking the ability question are likely to assume that comprehension success is not in their control.

In classrooms, competition supports ability attributions (Ames, 1984). As Covington (1985) noted, though teachers label students who appear indifferent to learning as "lazy" or "unmotivated," these students may be engaging in self-protective behaviors that emerge because of their feelings of failure in competitive settings. Even fairly capable students can resist the prospect of competitive challenge (Dweck, 1986).

F. Low Interest

Textbooks are vehicles for knowledge acquisition. When they are poorly organized and when they do not signal important information (i.e., when they are "inconsiderate"), they present comprehension obstacles to children (Armbruster, 1984). Temporal shifts, unclear reference, and topically irrelevant information all serve to confuse readers.

Perhaps the most serious obstacle of all for readers is that textbooks are almost universally boring (Garner *et al.*, in press). A line of inquiry to which we have contributed recently convinces us that when importance and interestingness in text diverge, what is recalled is highly interesting, if structurally unimportant, detail—what we have labeled "seductive detail" (Garner *et al.*, 1989). Abstract, general principles are forgotten. In an important sense, then, comprehension failure occurs, because important information conveyed in text does not capture the attention of readers.

Hidi *et al.* (1982) were among the first researchers to examine text interestingness as a factor in text comprehension and recall. They located texts that they were able to categorize reliably as narratives (stories found in language arts materials), expositions (material presenting facts, explanations, or instructions), or mixed texts (expositions with some narrative episodes or elements).

Adults rated important and interesting information in each text. In the narratives, the most interesting information was also the most important. In the expositions, very few ideas were rated as interesting. In the mixed texts, no relation was found between importance and interestingness.

An example of divergence between importance and interestingness in a mixed text is the following: The idea that ancient divers had to rely on their own lung power rather than using some form of breathing gear (very important, not particularly interesting) was interrupted by an anecdote about Alexander the Great's adventures in the sea (very interesting on grounds of novelty, activity, and concreteness, but not at all important here).

Fifth- and seventh-graders read and recalled information from this set of texts, both immediately and 4 days later. In delayed recall, at both grade levels, students recalled more adult-rated important information for narratives and for expositions, but not for mixed texts. In the mixed texts, fifth-graders recalled equal amounts of important and interesting information, and seventh-graders recalled more interesting information.

We designed an experiment along similar lines (Garner *et al.*, 1989). We asked seventh-graders to read a three-paragraph text on the topic of differences among insects. Information in the text had been rated for importance and interestingness by adults. Half the seventh-graders read the text with seductive details (one per paragraph), half without. Seductive details were propositions presenting interesting but unimportant information (as rated by the adults). The first paragraph of the text appears below in the seductive detail condition:

> Some insects live alone, and some live in large families. Wasps that live alone are called solitary wasps. A Mud Dauber Wasp is a solitary wasp. Click Beetles live alone. When a Click Beetle is on its back, it flips itself into the air and lands right side up while it makes a clicking noise. Ants live in large families.

Note that the sentence about click beetles flipping and clicking is irrelevant to a paragraph about solitary or communal living patterns of insects; however, it is novel, active, concrete, and apparently very interesting.

Seventh-graders who read the "Insect" text with this and other seductive details recalled far fewer important ideas than peers who read the text without these details. Seductive detail readers recalled a combination of important and interesting information, never recalling all important ideas and never failing to recall at least one (of three) interesting ideas.

The appropriate metaphor for attention to information in text may be a light switch, which is turned on and off repeatedly (for a related argument, see Anderson *et al.*, 1984). When both interesting details and important ideas appear in a text, it is the interesting details that capture children's attention. They "switch attention on" to a detail and then off to abstract principles, and then on again to the next detail, and so on. Comprehension and recall failure for structurally important ideas is the result.

G. Summary

So far, we have examined six reasons for children's reading comprehension failure. It should be noted that these factors seldom operate independently. When children are not fluent at decoding, they inevitably have unfavorable attitudes and low self-esteem about a process that is intensely frustrating for them. When children have few experiences from which to abstract conceptual information about a topic, they are likely to be only moderately interested in reading more about the topic; they are also likely to experience difficulty in sorting out important and unimportant information on the topic. When children do not understand that they must make sense of text, they are certainly unlikely to monitor and detect the absense of sense.

Because comprehension is the goal of the reading process, we turn our attention next to instruction that improves comprehension. The instructional suggestions made in the next section of this chapter are based on our assumption that teachers can structure and guide reading activities in the classroom in such a way that the effects of the six factors discussed so far are diminished.

III. EFFECTIVE COMPREHENSION INSTRUCTION

Dolores Durkin's (1978–1979) influential study of reading comprehension instruction gave rise in the 1980s to many research efforts to enhance reading comprehension through direct instruction. In her study, Durkin set out to describe the typical amounts and kinds of reading comprehension instruction observable in intermediate-grade classrooms. She and her fellow researchers observed children and their teachers during reading and social studies lessons for 300 hours and coded the activities they recorded as to whether they were comprehension instruction or something else. Durkin claimed to have found virtually no comprehension instruction in any of the classrooms studied. Instead, she maintained that teachers focused largely on comprehension assessment, referring to the practice of teacher questions and student answers around text selections.

Some researchers thought Durkin's criteria were overly stringent or her definition of comprehension instruction too narrow (e.g., Heap, 1982; Hodges, 1980). Hodges' (1980) reanalysis of Durkin's data using different criteria, however, effected only modest increases in the percentages of time devoted to comprehension instruction. Heap (1982), on the other hand, argued that Durkin discounted too much that was instructional in nature, including the multifunctional nature of single instructional events and the reality of instructional sequences around what is worth attending to in text.

These are certainly legitimate points, but undoubtedly Durkin's original study prompted a great deal of thinking about the nature of comprehension and, concomitantly, comprehension instruction. She alerted teachers and researchers to the prevalence of "repeated exposures" (unguided practice) as a methodology in reading comprehension instruction. She also heightened consciousness about the need for good, precise explanations (see, e.g., Duffy and Roehler, 1982). She sensitized the field to what constituted comprehension instruction and what did not.

And what does good comprehension instruction look like? According to recent literature, several components seem essential: (1) assessing what children know and do not know, (2) analyzing tasks for comprehending text, (3) providing direct, explicit instruction as appropriate, (4) providing extensive practice opportunities, and (5) ensuring that skills are practiced in a variety of domains. We review each component here.

A. Assessing What Children Know and Do Not Know

Children come to every school task with prior knowledge organized around sets of personal experiences. We know that their prior knowledge colors all subsequent learning (see, e.g., Pearson *et al.*, 1979). Indeed, our current conceptions of learning incorporate the notion that one learns by assimilating something *new* to something that is *already known*. It will be remembered that earlier in this chapter we considered domain knowledge deficiencies as one factor related to comprehension failure. The point was made that children who have few concepts and few associations within a particular domain are likely to have few expectations about text in that domain. Given the emphasis on linking new knowledge to that which is already known (an emphasis evident in both research and practice), it is important to consider how we can find out what children already know.

What do we mean by prior knowledge? Experts cannot seem to come to a consensus here. Alexander *et al.* (1989b) found many different conceptions of this seemingly all-encompassing construct and many different terms used to describe prior knowledge. Here, we simply delimit the term to mean the knowledge required to understand any given text, be it domain-specific, discourse-specific, or situation-specific knowledge.

How do teachers assess children's prior knowledge, or lack thereof? If one believes content or domain-specific knowledge is valuable to assess, Langer (1980) has developed one assessment tool. She asks children to free-associate about three key terms from a to-be-assigned text and then to categorize their responses as to whether they indicate much, some, or little knowledge. "Much" responses are the most sophisticated responses. They include definitions or analogies such as "The eye is like a camera." "Some" responses include examples, attributes, or defining characteristics such as "The elephant has a long trunk." "Little" responses include loose associations, sound-alikes, and first-hand experiences such as "My daddy played ball with the Harlem Globetrotters."

Apart from paper-and-pencil pretests or diagnoses, the dominant mode of learning what children already know seems to be to ask them. Beck *et al.*'s (1982) work suggests, however, that one must take care not to ask about superficial aspects of story characters and plot. Beck and her colleagues use the example of a story about raccoons, which turns on the knowledge that raccoons are creatures of habit who happen to resemble burglars in appearance. The basal reader from which the story was drawn encourages teachers, puzzlingly, to query children about the playful nature of raccoons. The lesson of this is to focus on "big ideas" in a story or article and avoid sidetracking children with questions about irrelevant or trivial information. Only in this way can teachers structure lessons to help children build meaningfully on prior knowledge.

One must also remember that some children know more than they can tell. Either lack of verbal fluency or variation in adult–child use of language can lead teachers to believe that children know very little about a topic, when in fact they just cannot explain what they know (Garner and Alexander, 1989). Pictorial stimuli can sometimes assist children, particularly young children, in explaining what they know.

B. Analyzing Tasks for Comprehending Text

Once teachers have a sense of children's starting points, they can begin to think about designing appropriate instruction. This requires a working knowledge of what it takes to understand a particular text. Teachers can refer to the literature for several exemplary task analyses of the reading comprehension process or subprocesses. Such examples range from broad efforts mounted at understanding text to efforts aimed at utilizing a single strategy. (We also discuss task analysis procedures more in Section IV of this chapter.)

Choices of strategies for intervention vary across studies, and we have difficulty finding a single common thread among researchers' definitions of "strategy" (cf. Alexander *et al.*, 1989b). However, there seems to be agreement about the importance of including declarative, procedural, and conditional information about any given strategy—information commonly referred to in the literature as knowing *that*, knowing *how*, and knowing *when and where* to employ strategies (cf. Paris *et al.*, 1983).

An example of a comprehensive intervention aimed at improving reading comprehension is Paris *et al.*'s (1984) training of a curriculum known as Informed Strategies for Learning, or ISL. This package, delivered to third- and fifth-graders, was designed to inform students about strategies related to three accomplishments: awareness of reading goals, plans, and strategies; comprehension; and evaluating and regulating reading. Strategies were intended to be comprehensive and included determining and summarizing main ideas, drawing inferences, making critical evaluations, and monitoring comprehension. Instruction for each strategy was elaborately designed and ensured that students received information about the value of the strategy and how and when to utilize the strategy.

Garner *et al.* (1984) performed a task analysis of a text reinspection strategy, prior to teaching students about the strategy. Results of the task analysis were couched in the form of "hints" to students. The first hint informed students of what "text lookbacks" are:

> Most people do not remember everything they read in an article. That is *why* it is a good idea to look back at the article to find information needed to answer some questions . . . .

Subsequent hints related to *how* and *when and where* to reinspect text.

C. Providing Direct, Explicit Instruction

Lately, in the name of direct instruction, there has been a broad-based call for clear and accurate explanations in instruction. This version of direct instruction contrasts with that originated by Rosenshine (1979). His definition referred to academically engaged minutes, or time on task; the newer version does not preclude time on task but, rather, includes clearer reference to the nature of the activities in which students engage. Practice is still a necessary part of the instructional package, but it is commonly acknowledged that practice alone is not sufficient. Of late, direct instruction often includes *direct explanations about processes* entailed in comprehension (Duffy *et al.*, 1986), to the extent that they are explainable.

Duffy, Roehler, and their colleagues have conducted a number of studies investigating the nature of excellent teachers' explanations (Duffy *et al.*, 1986). They discovered several factors that seem to exemplify good explanations, including the following: responsive information-giving, developing awareness as an outcome, providing precise and accurate information in a meaningful context, and providing assistance or scaffolding for students as needed.

Pressley *et al.* (1989b) discussed how strategies should be taught to children and advocated, on the basis of empirical work of the past decade, an emphasis on "direct explanation." They noted that extensive modeling is a key component of this emphasis (more on modeling later in this chapter). Just as we advocated earlier in discussing conditional knowledge, Pressley *et al.* (1989b) suggested that explicit information about *when* to use strategies is as important as explicit information about *how* to use them.

D. Providing Extensive Practice Opportunities

Practice is still an important component of good comprehension instruction. It has been established for some time that cognitive processing capacity is not boundless. Proficient reading comprehension depends on rapid, accurate, and automatic decoding. Similarly, strategic activity moved to a near-automatic state allows a variety of text-processing strategies to be engaged simultaneously without the processing capacity being overloaded (van Dijk and Kintsch, 1983). Children eventually use strategies efficiently through practice.

The focus lately has been on the nature of the practice and the feedback provided students about their practice. Simply put, and not surprisingly, practice opportunities must be pertinent and related to the explanations provided. A number of recent papers have described the meaninglessness for students of much of the practice in classrooms. Typically, students engaged in seatwork, when asked why they are doing what they are doing, respond, "To get it done." This suggests that special care be taken to ensure that work is meaningful and relevant. Students must be aware of the purpose for work, and work must be guided. Teachers can intersperse practice with more direct instruction as needed.

Sometimes, practice alone is sufficient—particularly when comprehension processes are not well understood and/or difficult to explain. Hansen's (1981) work illustrated that merely increasing the ratio of inferential questions to literal questions asked of students during questioning sessions enhanced inferential comprehension. Carver (1987) argued that students can improve reading comprehension by increasing the amount of time they spend reading texts (i.e., practicing reading skills).

The nature of feedback provided to students is important. We are all familiar with the stacks of assignments returned to students in classrooms with little more than a number right or a number wrong noted at the top of the work. A number of educational researchers have commented lately that children need to be provided with informative feedback, particularly for incorrect items or lines of reasoning. This, of course, echoes Duffy *et al.*'s (1986) exhortations to teachers to create helpful explanations.

E. Ensuring that Skills Are Practiced in a Variety of Domains

As teachers, we often confront the puzzle of students who can pass a test but who don't seem to be able to "hang onto" a strategy or who fail to generalize a strategy to new situations and settings. We have learned much about transfer in recent years, and chief among the lessons learned is that a strategy must be exercised across a variety of domains. In some ways, this implies teaching directly for transfer—showing students how to flexibly apply strategies in new situations.

Brown *et al.* (1981) suggested that only "self-control" training requires learners to be full participants in their own learning, and only this training (where students are instructed in the use of a strategy and in how to monitor and evaluate the success of their strategy implementation) enhances transfer of training to new situations. Strategies are welded to original instructional settings unless broader applications are explicitly mentioned by teachers.

Garner (1987) provided an example of teaching for transfer. A teacher working with an elementary class in a social studies class could say something on the order of "Today, I'm going to show you one way to handle the confusion that sometimes arises when you're reading your social studies textbook and you encounter a completely unfamiliar word that 'stops you in your tracks.' I'll talk you through a step-by-step routine for trying to figure out that word by using what you've already read rather than by interrupting your reading for a long time to come to ask me the meaning of the word or to stop to look up the meaning in a dictionary." The teacher then engages in a think-aloud exercise on this day with the social studies textbook and on another day with the science textbook. On the second occasion, she mentions the generality of contextual analysis routines. Perhaps on still another occasion, she can allude to the times when impoverished linguistic–pictorial contexts require alternative routines, perhaps requesting information from an external source.

F. Summary

Some children do not acquire strategies for reading comprehension spontaneously. They need to be taught how to read strategically. We have suggested that the research of the past decade is generally optimistic in providing examples of a number of strategies that can be taught and learned; the result is improved comprehension performance.

As Pressley et al. (1989b) noted (and these are very optimistic points), many of these teachable strategies involve relatively simple procedures for children to learn, are relatively easy to teach, and can be taught in 10 hours or less as part of ongoing instruction, with materials readily available in most classrooms.

We turn next to perhaps an even greater challenge than teaching non-strategic readers to be strategic about text comprehension: the challenge of sustaining effective, self-regulating reading behaviors in children.

IV. SUSTAINING EFFECTIVE READING

That comprehension performance can be improved by carefully planned, well-executed instruction is encouraging. However, failure of students to employ comprehension strategies once teacher control is diminished or when the context of learning is modified is common and discouraging.

Bransford (1979) described a scenario of a student studying for a statistics test. Working the problems on a study sheet, the student solves them with ease; however, when a friend cuts the problems out and randomly presents them for solution (minus the chapter cues that had prompted selection of formulas and principles), the student performs poorly. This example illustrates what teachers know well: Few students maintain and generalize strategy use beyond a subset of applications that they were taught explicitly (Perkins and Salomon, 1989).

We suggest that potential for comprehension success ultimately resides with students. They must have the skill and will to persist in good comprehension activities (i.e., maintenance) and the inclination to "decontextualize" their knowledge and skills for broader application (i.e., transfer). They must learn to be self-regulating about their reading (Brown *et al.*, 1981).

Teachers can assist students in learning self-regulation. Specifically, we suggest that they can do five things: (1) teach general control strategies, (2) relinquish instructional responsibility, (3) model self-interrogation, (4) encourage procedural creativity, and (5) exhibit the excitement of literacy activities. In this final section of the chapter, we discuss each of these forms of assistance.

A. Teaching General Control Strategies

Having a repertoire of heuristic routines is basic to executive control of reading processes. Heuristics are guiding principles or general strategies that differ from problem-solving algorithms used to solve specific classes of problems.

A number of theorists have further differentiated between specific and general strategies by labeling them "powerful" and "weak" strategies. Powerful strategies are those that have limited uses but that lead to problem solution when effectively implemented. For example, once a statistics student correctly determines which formula is appropriate for solution of her practice problems, and provided she executes the formula correctly, solution is virtually guaranteed.

These limited-use, powerful strategies have also been labeled domain-specific (Alexander *et al.*, 1989a), context-specific (Rabinowitz, 1988), or task-limited (Pressley *et al.*, 1989a). In reading, decoding procedures for words with regular sound-symbol correspondence are examples of powerful strategies.

Other strategies are very general in that they can be applied across many tasks and in varied domains (Alexander and Judy, 1988). In reading, examples of such general strategies are summarizing, rereading, and self-questioning. Whether reading a Shakespearean sonnet, studying a chapter on Newtonian physics, or following a written recipe, readers may find it helpful to summarize the important information in what they have read, reread particularly difficult or confusing segments, and ask themselves questions about material on which they are likely to be tested. Note that these general strategies are taught as *means* for learning content, not in lieu of content.

However, these general strategies have been described as "weak" (Newell, 1980) because their application does not, in and of itself, ensure problem solution. For instance, a child might prepare testlike questions from his textbook to prepare for a social studies test on crops of the Midwest; however, either he or his teacher might ask questions about trivial information, creating a mismatch between study questions and test questions. In this case, the student might not do well on the test despite having studied strategically.

One problem with dichotomizing strategies into powerful and weak categories is that this process ignores differences inherent in domains and in learners. Strategies weak in one domain may be powerful in another (Alexander and Judy, 1988), and deficits in one class of strategies may be particularly powerful for one group of learners. For instance, a strategy of selective attention to numerals in text may be effective for mathematics story problems or for history textbooks but very ineffective for most essays. Strategies that demand working memory may be particularly difficult for learning-disabled students who are generally characterized as having memory problems (Wong and Jones, 1982).

It is our impression that while repertoires of domain-specific strategies are basic to good academic performance, general strategies serve a particularly important role in moving children to comprehension independence. These strategies help children plan, monitor, and fix (i.e., regulate) their comprehension.

Brown's (1980) description of comprehension monitoring given earlier in this chapter is an excellent example of a general strategy such as we have in mind: A skilled reader proceeds merrily through a relatively easy reading task with rapid construction of meaning. Then, a comprehension failure occurs and it is detected. The child takes action. If the problem is serious enough to disrupt comprehension, some strategic remedy is applied. The reader may decide to continue reading in a more analytical style, hoping that the confusion will be resolved. On the other hand, the reader may opt to reread earlier material in an effort to resolve confusion. In cases of serious confusion, the reader may decide to consult an external source (peer, teacher, or alternate text) for assistance.

B. Relinquishing Instructional Responsibility

At what point in the instructional cycle are children capable of sustaining effective comprehension performance on their own? Alexander *et al.* (1989a) proposed an "optimal instructional range" when students' general strategy knowledge may be most susceptible to instructional intervention. They suggested that it is unreasonable to expect students to use, maintain, and transfer general comprehension strategy knowledge before they have an adequate understanding of the target strategies or before they have sufficient content knowledge to which they can apply the strategies. They also suggested that teacher control of students' learning for too long ensures dependency.

We suggest that what is needed is a sensible transfer of control of learning from teacher to student. The process might proceed from explicit training to guided practice of trained strategies to student-regulated practice and independent performance. Pearson and Gallagher (1983) discussed a similar model as "planned obsolescence."

Palincsar and Brown's (1984) "reciprocal teaching" method is a successful example of ceding control in this manner. Summarizing, questioning, clarifying, and predicting were taught to students by researchers, classroom teachers, and resource room teachers. Instruction involved an interactive learning game in which instructor and student took turns in leading a dialog about particular text segments. The "teacher" for each segment first asked a question and then summarized and offered predictions and clarification as appropriate. The role the student played was expanded over time from mostly respondent to mostly instruction-giver. Instruction proved to be a powerful method for improving comprehension performance in all settings.

C. Modeling Self-Interrogation

Skilled readers engage in dynamic evaluation of their comprehension. One means used is readers asking themselves questions about their performance prior to, during, and after completion of a particular reading task. Some skilled readers surely acquire the habit of self-interrogation spontaneously, but many readers need to have self-interrogation behaviors modeled for them.

Modeling of this sort requires task analysis. A teacher can refer to research on skilled reading, can introspect about personal reading strategies, or can ask colleagues to "think aloud" about reading behaviors.

Case (1978) suggested a procedure for generating a sufficiently detailed sequence of strategic operations to be used in modeling. He suggested that a teacher begin by breaking down a strategy into global steps (getting past mere labeling and into analysis of component activities). Next, each global step would be broken down into a sequence of substeps. At this point, adequacy of the description would be tested by asking a colleague to perform the task (perhaps reading two editorials presenting opposing views on reducing illiteracy and noting the distinctions). The colleague would be asked to follow the outlined substeps, doing only what he or she was told. If the colleague wanted to deviate from the step-by-step description, modification of the description might be in order.

Meichenbaum's work (see, e.g., Meichenbaum and Asarnow, 1979) makes clear that coping strategies can be an important part of this sort of modeling. For instance, imagine a child reading a text on the topic of "Endangered Species." A teacher decides to model self-interrogation while reading the text; he incorporates coping strategy information into the modeling in the following manner:

> Oh, endangered species, I saw a National Geographic program the other night. It said that some great apes were in danger of becoming extinct. I wonder if this article will talk about those apes (modeling retrieval of prior knowledge on the topic of the text, tying old information to new). Oh, headings about the animals discussed. That tells me what I'll read about. Yup, gorillas. And bald eagles, I saw a bald eagle on a camping trip; they're neat (modeling use of headings to structure information read, a general strategy; also, modeling of interest in a subtopic). Oh, I don't know this word, h-a-b-i-t-a-t. But, I can skip it for now and see if the meaning is clear from other sentences; I can always look it up if I can't figure it out myself (modeling an efficient word-identification strategy). I'm pretty good at most words, and I don't need to know every single one to understand what I'm reading (modeling a coping plan).

An effective idea is to encourage children to model effective strategies to other children. Both groups of children benefit.

D. Encouraging Procedural Creativity

Although schools regularly publish curriculum guides that announce support for creativity, school practices often discourage inventive heuristics that may be at the heart of effective reading in children (see Brown *et al.*, 1989). Though we suggest that "unapproved" (usually uninstructed) routines that enhance comprehension should be valued, we have each had numerous experiences with children who have the impression that they must disguise inventive tactics that assist them in comprehending.

Examples are children using pictorial cues to meaning in phonics-oriented classrooms, children using acronym elaborations to recall character names in a story in classrooms where "brute force" rehearsal is advocated, and children using electronic spelling checkers in classrooms where dictionary look-up skills are taught and practiced as exclusive editing tools. In each of these cases, the strategy employed can be effective in accomplishing a comprehension–composition goal; yet, the strategy may be at odds with instructed routines.

Skilled readers often modify and personalize instructed strategies. For instance, Adams *et al.* (1982) taught children an explicit routine for studying textbook material for 4 days. The day after training was completed and again 2 weeks later, children were asked to read textbook material, to retell the content, and to answer questions about the content. Trained students out-performed untrained students for question-answering in both immediate and delayed testing. The trained students also studied longer for the tests. However, in the finding of most interest to us here, only 50% of the trained students were observed using the instructed routine for the immediate test. This figure dropped to 20% for the delayed test. A large proportion of the trained students did use an observable study strategy, if not the instructed one. Adams *et al.* (1982) suggested that by the second test session many of the trained students had adopted more personalized study methods with which performance did not decrease.

Sometimes, of course, a child can alter an instructed strategy to suit himself or herself and it will not be effective. Perkins (1985) pointed out that even adults experience strategy "drift," or the sense that one is using the effective strategy adopted some days before, but discovering that the behavior has shifted substantially, often away from effective action. A number of inter-mediate steps may have been deleted, thus reducing cognitive load *and* effectiveness.

E. Exhibiting the Excitement of Literacy Activities

If we return to our earlier discussion of why some students fail to comprehend, and focus particularly on the role of low self-esteem, we remember that children must desire to read in order to read successfully. National assess-ments have consistently shown that children coming from homes where reading is valued are more likely to be successful readers than children coming from homes where it is not (Anderson *et al.*, 1985). Furthermore, in classrooms where a variety of reading materials are available, and where instructional time is set aside for uninterrupted, free-choice reading, students demonstrate a greater interest and ability in reading (Morrow and Weinstein, 1986).

Teachers can model their excitement about reading, they can create en-vironments for pleasurable reading, and they can use assessment procedures that allow for some reading performance to be evaluated solely on the grounds of enjoyment ("Want me to continue reading this book to the class?" "Which of the author's books do you like best?" "Can you recommend a book for us to read next?"). Interest in topic, task, and process is clearly a factor in sustaining effective comprehension performance (Asher, 1980).

F. Summary

Children fail to comprehend for a number of reasons, but they can be assisted instructionally. Teachers can provide explicit instruction and guided practice that improves comprehension among children with diverse needs.

The concern we have expressed in the last section of this chapter is that children's reading comprehension will improve under the watchful eye of the effective teacher but will falter in the absence of continued instruction. In other words, some children will not become self-regulating readers, able to monitor their own comprehension and to intervene strategically when necessary. We have suggested that teachers need to help children become self-regulating.

If teachers settle for teaching a few procedural recipes for text comprehension to children, they have not, in the long run, assisted them very much. Far better is teaching that provides procedural detail, motivational impetus, and models of self-regulation that sustain effective performance in the teacher's absence. Then, the likelihood of failure in this cognitively challenging and critical activity is diminished.

References

Adams, A., Carnine, D., and Gersten, R. (1982). Instructional strategies for studying content area texts in the intermediate grades. *Read. Res. Q.* **18**, 27–55.

Alexander, P. A., and Judy, J. E. (1988). The interaction of domain-specific and strategic knowledge in academic performance. *Rev. Educ. Res.* **58**, 375–404.

Alexander, P. A., Pate, E. P., Kulikowich, J. M., Farrell, D. M., and Wright, N. L. (1989a). Domain-specific and strategic knowledge: Effects of training on students of differing ages or competence levels. *Learn. Individ. Diff.* **1**, 283–325.

Alexander, P. A., Schallert, D. L., and Hare, V. C. (1989b). "Coming to Terms with the Terminology of Knowledge." Paper presented at the annual meeting of the National Reading Conference (December 1989), Austin, Texas.

Allington, R. L. (1983). The reading instruction provided readers of differing reading abilities. *Elem. School J.* **83**, 548–559.

Ames, C. (1984). Achievement attributions and self-instructions under competitive and individualistic goal structures. *J. Educ. Psychol.* **76**, 478–487.

Anderson, R. C., and Pearson, P. D. (1984). A schema-theoretic view of basic processes in reading comprehension. *In* "Handbook of Reading Research" (P. D. Pearson, ed.), pp. 255–291. Longman, New York.

Anderson, R. C., Mason, J., and Shirey, L. (1984). The reading group: An experimental investigation of a labyrinth. *Read. Res. Q.* **20**, 6–38.

Anderson, R. C., Hiebert, E. H., Scott, J. A., and Wilkinson, I. A. G. (1985). "Becoming a Nation of Readers." National Institute of Education, Washington, D. C.

Armbruster, B. B. (1984). The problem of "inconsiderate text." *In* "Comprehension Instruction" (G. G. Duffy, L. R. Roehler, and J. Mason, eds.), pp. 202–217. Longman, New York.

Asher, S. R. (1980). Topic interest and children's reading comprehension. *In* "Theoretical Issues in Reading Comprehension" (R. J. Spiro, B. C. Bruce, and W. F. Brewer, eds.), pp. 525–534. Lawrence Erlbaum, Hillsdale, New Jersey.

Baker, L. (1984a). Children's effective use of multiple standards for evaluating their comprehension. *J. Educ. Psychol.* **76**, 588–597.

Baker, L. (1984b). Spontaneous versus instructed use of multiple standards for evaluating comprehension: Effects of age, reading proficiency, and type of standard. *J. Exp. Child Psychol.* **38**, 289–311.

Baker, L. (1985). How do we know when we don't understand? Standards for evaluating text comprehension. *In* "Metacognition, Cognition, and Human Performance," Vol. 1 (D. L. Forrest-Pressley, G. E. MacKinnon, and T. G. Waller, eds.), pp. 155–205. Academic, Orlando, Florida.

Baker, L., and Brown, A. L. (1984). Metacognitive skills and reading. *In* "Handbook of Reading Research" (P. D. Pearson, ed.), pp. 353–394. Longman, New York.

Baker, L., and Zimlin, L. (1989). Instructional effects on children's use of two levels of standards for evaluating their comprehension. *J. Educ. Psychol.* **81**, 340–346.

Beck, I. L., Omanson, R. C., and McKeown, M. G. (1982). An instructional redesign of reading lessons: Effects on comprehension. *Read. Res. Q.* **17**, 462–481.

Borkowski, J. G., Carr, M., and Pressley, M. (1987). "Spontaneous" strategy use: Perspectives from metacognitive theory. *Intelligence* **11**, 61–75.

Bransford, J. D. (1979). "Human Cognition: Learning, Understanding, and Remembering." Wadsworth, Belmont, California.

Brown, A. L. (1980). Metacognitive development and reading. *In* "Theoretical Issues in Reading Comprehension" (R. J. Spiro, B. C. Bruce, and W. F. Brewer, eds.), pp. 453–481. Lawrence Erlbaum, Hillsdale, New Jersey.

Brown, A. L., Campione, J. C., and Day, J. D. (1981). Learning to learn: On training students to learn from texts. *Educ. Research.* **10**, 14–21.

Brown, A. L., Armbruster, B. B., and Baker, L. (1986). The role of metacognition in reading and studying. *In* "Reading Comprehension: From Research to Practice" (J. Orasanu, ed.), pp. 49–75. Lawrence Erlbaum, Hillsdale, New Jersey.

Brown, J. S., Collins, A., and Duguid, P. (1989). Situated cognition and the culture of learning. *Educ. Research.* **18**, 32–42.

Carver, R. P. (1987). Should reading comprehension skills be taught? *In* "Research in Literacy: Merging Perspectives" (J. E. Readence and R. S. Baldwin, eds.), pp. 115–126. National Reading Conference, Rochester, New York.

Case, R. (1978). A developmentally based theory and technology of instruction. *Rev. Educ. Res.* **48**, 439–463.

Covington, M. V. (1985). Strategic thinking and the fear of failure. *In* "Thinking and Learning Skills," Vol. 1 (J. W. Segal, S. F. Chipman, and R. Glaser, eds.), pp. 389–416. Lawrence Erlbaum, Hillsdale, New Jersey.

Duffy, G. G., and Roehler, L. R. (1982). The illusion of instruction. *Read. Res. Q.* **17**, 438–445.

Duffy, G. G., Roehler, L. R., Meloth, M. S., Vavrus, L. G., Book, C., Putnam, J., and Wesselman, R. (1986). The relationship between explicit verbal explanations during reading skill instruction and student awareness and achievement: A study of reading teacher effects. *Read. Res. Q.* **21**, 237–252.

Durkin, D. (1978–1979). What classroom observations reveal about reading comprehension instruction. *Read. Res. Q.* **14,** 481–533.

Dweck, C. S. (1986). Motivational processes affecting learning. *Am. Psycholog.* **41,** 1040–1048.

Flavell, J. H. (1979). Metacognition and cognitive monitoring: A new area of cognitive-developmental inquiry. *Am. Psycholog.* **34,** 906–911.

Flavell, J. H. (1981). Cognitive monitoring. *In* "Children's Oral Communication Skills" (W. P. Dickson, ed.), pp. 35–60. Academic, New York.

Forrest, D. L., and Waller, T. G. (1980). "What Do Children Know about Their Reading and Study Skills. Paper presented at the meeting of the American Educational Research Association (April 1980), Boston.

Garner, R. (1987). "Metacognition and Reading Comprehension." Ablex, Norwood, New Jersey.

Garner, R., and Alexander, P. A. (1989). Metacognition: Answered and unanswered questions. *Educ. Psycholog.* **24,** 143–158.

Garner, R., Hare, V., Alexander, P., Haynes, J., and Winograd, P. (1984). Inducing use of a text bookback strategy among unsuccessful readers. *Am. Educ. Res. J.* **21,** 789–798.

Garner, R., Gillingham, M. G., and White, C. S. (1989). Effects of "seductive details" on macroprocessing and microprocessing in adults and children. *Cognit. Instruct.* **6,** 41–57.

Garner, R., Brown, R., Sanders, S., and Menke, D. J. (in press). "Seductive details" and learning from text. *In* "The Role of Interest in Learning and Development" (K. A. Renninger, S. Hidi, and A. Krapp, eds.). Lawrence Erlbaum, Hillsdale.

Glaser, R. (1984). Education and thinking: The role of knowledge. *Am. Psycholog.* **39,** 93–104.

Hansen, J. (1981). The effects of inference training and practice on young children's reading comprehension. *Read. Res. Q.* **16,** 391–417.

Heap, J. L. (1982). Understanding classroom events: A critique of Durkin, with an alternative. *J. Read. Behav.* **14,** 391–411.

Hidi, S., Baird, W., and Hildyard, A. (1982). That's important but is it interesting? Two factors in text processing. *In* "Discourse Processing" (A. Flammer and W. Kintsch, eds.), pp. 63–75. North Holland, Amsterdam.

Hodges, C. A. (1980). Toward a broader definition of comprehension instruction. *Read. Res. Q.* **15,** 299–306.

Just, M. A., and Carpenter, P. A. (1984). Reading skills and skilled reading in the comprehension of text. *In* "Learning and Comprehension of Text" (H. Mandl, N. L. Stein, and T. Trabasso, eds.), pp. 307–329. Lawrence Erlbaum, Hillsdale, New Jersey.

Langer, J. A. (1980). Relation between levels of prior knowledge and the organization of recall. *In* "Perspectives on Reading Research and Instruction" (M. L. Kamil and A. J. Moe, eds.), pp. 28–33. National Reading Conference, Washington, D.C.

Markman, E. M. (1981). Comprehension monitoring. *In* "Children's Oral Communication Skills" (W. P. Dickson, ed.), pp. 61–84. Academic, New York.

Mayer, R. E. (1987). "Educational Psychology: A Cognitive Approach." Little, Brown and Company, Boston.

Meichenbaum, D., and Asarnow, J. (1979). Cognitive-behavioral modification and metacognitive development: Implications for the classroom. *In* "Cognitive Behavioral Interventions: Theory, Research, and Procedures" (P. C. Kendall and S. D. Hollon, eds.), pp. 11–35. Academic, New York.

Minsky, M. (1986). "The Society of Mind." Simon and Schuster, New York.

Moore, D., and Zabrucky, K. (1989). Verbal reports as measures of comprehension evaluation. *J. Read. Behav.* **21,** 295–307.

Morrow, L. M., and Weinstein, C. S. (1986). Encouraging voluntary reading: The impact of a literature program on children's use of library centers. *Read. Res. Q.* **21,** 330–346.

Myers, M., and Paris, S. G. (1978). Children's metacognitive knowledge about reading. *J. Educ. Psychol.* **70,** 680–690.

Newell, A. (1980). One final word. *In* "Problem Solving and Education: Issues in Teaching and Research" (D. T. Tuma and F. Reif, eds.), pp. 175–189. Lawrence Erlbaum, Hillsdale, New Jersey.

Nicholls, J. G. (1983). Conceptions of ability and achievement motivation: A theory and its implications for education. *In* "Learning and Motivation in the Classroom" (S. G. Paris, G. M. Olson, and H. W. Stevenson, eds.), pp. 211–237. Lawrence Erlbaum, Hillsdale, New Jersey.

Palincsar, A. S., and Brown, A. L. (1984). Reciprocal teaching of comprehension-fostering and monitoring activities. *Cognit. Instruct.* **1,** 117–175.

Paris, S. G., and Cross, D. R. (1983). Ordinary learning: Pragmatic connections among children's beliefs, motives, and actions. *In* "Learning in Children: Progress in Cognitive Development Research" (J. Bisanz, G. L. Bisanz, and R. Kail, eds.), pp. 137–169. Springer-Verlag, New York.

Paris, S. G., and Myers, M. (1981). Comprehension monitoring, memory, and study strategies of good and poor readers. *J. Read. Behav.* **13,** 5–22.

Paris, S. G., Lipson, M. Y., and Wixson, K. K. (1983). Becoming a strategic reader. *Contemp. Educ. Psychol.* **8,** 293–316.

Paris, S. G., Cross, D. R., and Lipson, M. Y. (1984). Informed strategies for learning: A program to improve children's reading awareness and comprehension. *J. Educ. Psychol.* **76,** 1239–1252.

Pearson, P. D., and Gallagher, M. C. (1983). The instruction of reading comprehension. *Contemp. Educ. Psychol.* **8,** 317–344.

Pearson, P. D., Hansen, J., and Gordon, C. (1979). The effect of background knowledge on young children's comprehension of explicit and implicit information. *J. Read. Behav.* **11,** 201–209.

Perfetti, C. A. (1985). Reading ability. *In* "Human Abilities: An Information-Processing Approach" (R. J. Sternberg, ed.), pp. 59–81. W. H. Freeman, New York.

Perfetti, C. A., and Lesgold, A. M. (1979). Coding and comprehension in skilled reading and implications for reading instruction. *In* "Theory and Practice of Early Reading," Vol. 1 (L. B. Resnick and P. A. Weaver, eds.), pp. 57–84. Lawrence Erlbaum, Hillsdale, New Jersey.

Perkins, D. N. (1985). General cognitive skills: Why not? In "Thinking and Learning Skills," Vol. 2 (S. F. Chipman, J. W. Segal, and R. Glaser, eds.), pp. 339–363. Lawrence Erlbaum, Hillsdale, New Jersey.

Perkins, D. N., and Salomon, G. (1989). Are cognitive skills context-bound? *Educ. Research.* **18**, 16–25.

Pressley, M., Goodchild, F., Fleet, J., Zajchowski, R., and Evans, E. D. (1989a). The challenges of classroom strategy instruction. *Elem. School J.* **89**, 301–342.

Pressley, M., Johnson, C. J., Symons, S., McGoldrick, J. A., and Kurita, J. A. (1989b). Strategies that improve children's memory and comprehension of text. *Elem. School J.* **90**, 3–32.

Rabinowitz, M. (1988). On teaching cognitive strategies: The influence of accessibility of conceptual knowledge. *Contemp. Educ. Psychol.* **13**, 229–235.

Rabinowitz, M., and Glaser, R. (1985). Cognitive structure and process in highly competent performance. *In* "The Gifted and the Talented: A Developmental Perspective" (F. D. Horowitz and M. O'Brien, eds.), pp. 75–98. American Psychological Association, Washington, D.C.

Rosenshine, B. V. (1979). Content, time, and direct instruction. *In* "Research on Teaching: Concepts, Findings, and Implications" (P. Peterson and H. Walberg, eds.), pp. 28–56. McCutchan, Berkeley, California.

Rumelhart, D. E. (1980). Schemata: The building blocks of cognition. *In* "Theoretical Issues in Reading Comprehension" (R. J. Spiro, B. C. Bruce, and W. F. Brewer, eds.), pp. 33–58. Lawrence Erlbaum, Hillsdale, New Jersey.

van Dijk, T. A., and Kintsch, W. (1983). "Strategies of Discourse Comprehension." Academic, New York.

Voss, J. F. (1984). On learning and learning from text. *In* "Learning and Comprehension of Text" (H. Mandl, N. L. Stein, and T. Trabasso, eds.), pp. 193–212. Lawrence Erlbaum, Hillsdale, New Jersey.

Wagner, D. A., Spratt, J. E., Gal, I., and Paris, S. G. (1989). Reading and believing: Beliefs, attributions, and reading achievement in Moroccan schoolchildren. *J. Educ. Psychol.* **81**, 283–293.

Wellman, H. M. (1985). The child's theory of mind: The development of conceptions of cognition. *In* "The Growth of Reflection in Children" (S. R. Yussen, ed.), pp. 169–206. Academic, Orlando, Florida.

Wigfield, A., and Asher, S. R. (1984). Social and motivational influences on reading. *In* "Handbook of Reading Research" (P. D. Pearson, ed.), pp. 423–452. Longman, New York.

Wong, B. Y. L., and Jones, W. (1982). Increasing metacomprehension in learning disabled and normally achieving students through self-questioning training. *Learn. Disabil. Q.* **5**, 228–240.

CHAPTER 11

Writing Instruction

Steve Graham, Karen R. Harris, Charles MacArthur, and Shirley Schwartz

Editor's Notes

In the preceding chapter, you learned about the various causes of children's failures in reading comprehension and ways of remediating those problems. Together with the earlier chapter on instruction in decoding, we wrapped up our examination of reading problems and various instructional methods in reading (decoding plus reading comprehension). We follow the topic of reading with that of writing. In the present chapter, we consider writing problems in students and ways of dealing with them.

Graham, Harris, MacArthur, and Schwartz's chapter is rich with information on writing instruction—their main theme. However, there are other important themes. The first is their succinct introduction to cognitive processes in writing and the social context for writing. The second is the writing problems of students with learning disabilities. The third theme concerns a process approach to writing. The fourth theme concerns two approaches that help learning-disabled students develop competence in cognitive processes of writing: (1) procedural facilitation and (2) strategy instruction. The fifth, and major, theme is instructional methods in writing. Here, there are three subthemes: (1) methods for improving text production skills, (2) use of technology, and (3) additional "dos" and "don'ts." The last theme consists of the authors' concluding comments.

I. INTRODUCTION

This chapter reviews what is known about teaching writing to learning-disabled (LD) students. We begin our review by briefly considering what is known about the nature of composing and LD students' writing. The remainder and bulk of the chapter concentrates on specific instructional recommendations based on recent conceptualizations of the cognitive and social nature of writing, current knowledge of LD students' writing abilities, and principles of effective writing instruction. Special care is taken to accentuate general instructional practices in writing that should be emphasized with all students. The material presented in this chapter goes beyond these general recommendations though, by highlighting procedures that should benefit particularly LD students. Whenever possible, recommendations are based on procedures empirically validated with LD students. We did not limit our discussion just to research-supported practices, however; promising practices are discussed as well. Moreover, issues and challenges that need to be considered in implementing these recommendations are noted.

II. THE NATURE OF WRITING

A. Cognitive Processes in Writing

Recent models of composing tend to emphasize the cognitive nature of the writing process. The influential model by Flower and Hayes (1980) provides a useful framework for describing the cognitive processes involved in *skilled* writing. The model includes three main processes: planning, text production, and reviewing.

Planning involves the three subprocesses of setting goals, generating content, and organizing or framing text. First, writers develop goals for their writing based on consideration of audience and topic. During the writing process, they may adjust or revise their goals as they discover more about the topic through gathering information or through writing itself. Second, skilled writers must generate content through systematic searching of their memories and through searching external sources for information. Third, writers draw on their knowledge of text structures to help them generate content and organize or frame their writing. For example, they know that stories are focused on a central problem that the main character attempts to resolve, or that a letter to the editor should clearly state a position, support the position with reasons, and refute opposing arguments.

Text production includes the physical process of writing, the production of correct sentences, and attention to mechanics. For experienced writers, these low-level skills are automatic, freeing them to devote all of their attention to the larger concerns of planning, revising, and crafting text.

Reviewing includes evaluation and revision both of the text already written down and of goals and ideas not yet written. Skilled writers have a rich repertoire of criteria for evaluation and strategies for revising text.

The processes involved in writing do not occur in a linear order; rather, the writer switches back and forth in the processes among planning, drafting, and reviewing. Skilled writers consider their audience in setting goals, access their memories and outside sources to find content, organize and sequence their ideas, compose sentences, and attend to the formal requirements of written language. All of these processes go on more or less simultaneously as writers continuously evaluate and revise their emerging text. As can be seen from this brief presentation, developing competence in writing is a formidable task for any student.

B. The Social Context for Writing

> "See, I'm writing this story about my trip to Florida. And I know my friends will like the part about the dolphins because it's funny. So I'm telling a lot about that and trying to make it funny." (Jason)

Jason's transcript shows that he understands that the purpose of writing is to communicate with others. He is telling a story about his experiences to his friends in his class. He has set some goals—to make the story funny and to focus on the dolphins—and is planning the content with those goals in mind. His thinking as he plans and writes is guided by social, communicative goals.

As the above example indicates, writing is not only a cognitive process, but a social process as well. We write to communicate our experiences, thoughts, feelings, and ideas to other people. We also write to make things happen—to make requests or persuade others to take action. Studies of the thinking of experienced writers as they compose show that they attempt to tailor their purposes, content, and language to their audience (Flower and Hayes, 1980).

III. WRITING PROBLEMS OF LD STUDENTS

The majority of students who receive services for learning disabilities (LDs) have severe writing problems that persist over time (for reviews, see Graham and Harris, 1989b, 1990). Examination of their written products reveals that their papers are often replete with spelling, punctuation, capitalization, handwriting, and other errors. In addition, their writing tends to be inordinately short, poorly organized, and impoverished in terms of ideation (often missing important parts such as an ending or a premise). Perhaps more importantly, they appear to have considerable difficulty executing the cognitive processes underlying effective writing, including content generation, text production, framing text, planning, and revising. In planning an essay, for example, they may simply convert the writing assignment into a question-answering task, paying little attention to the needs of the reader, telling whatever comes to mind, and terminating their response in short, choppy phrases (Thomas *et al.*, 1987). Their revising appears to be equally ineffective and can be characterized as a simplistic approach to detect and correct mechanical errors and to make changes in individual words; little attention is given to making substantive changes (MacArthur and Graham, 1987). Furthermore, LD students are not especially knowledgeable about the writing process (Englert *et al.*, 1988), and they often overestimate their writing capabilities (Schwartz *et al.*, 1989).

We believe that at least three factors may account for LD students' difficulties in writing (Graham and Harris, 1990). First, their problems in producing text may interfere with other important writing processes such as generating ideas. Second, their lack of knowledge about writing or their inability to access what they do know may impact on their ability to operate and deploy the cognitive process considered central to effective writing. Third, the cognitive moves or writing strategies employed by LD students may be immature or ineffective. In the remainder of this chapter, we examine instructional procedures that are responsive to the difficulties demonstrated by LD students.

IV. A PROCESS APPROACH TO WRITING

The process approach to writing is probably the most common method recommended by language experts for teaching writing today. We believe that the process approach can help LD students develop competence in the process of writing as well as an interest and desire to write. First, this instructional approach is based on the current view that writing is a problem-solving or cognitive process that is recursive and nonlinear, involving the processes of planning, drafting, revising, and editing (Graves, 1983). Second, a process approach places value on establishing authentic reasons for learning to write and emphasizes the communicative purpose of writing by creating a social context in which students write for real audiences. Third, a process approach to teaching writing provides for continuous, mutually responsive interactions between teachers and students. Personalized and explicit instruction, individually tailored, is used to promote the development of a variety of skills that are often difficult for LD students to acquire (Schwartz and MacArthur, 1990).

Despite the popularity of the process approach among experts, many classroom writing programs concentrate almost exclusively on practicing "basic" skills such as grammar, spelling, and handwriting. While instruction in some of these skills is an important part of helping students develop writing competence, we agree with Emig (1978) that these skills are not the real basics of writing. In contrast, the process approach stresses higher-order writing processes such as planning and revising and emphasizes the importance of writing to an audience. Students are perceived as having meaningful things to say and the teacher's role is to help students learn how to say them. This is, in large part, promoted through the use of writing conferences, peer collaboration, modeling, and dialogs among students and teachers. The teacher functions as a facilitator creating an atmosphere (both nonthreatening and supportive) in which the writer can flourish, providing individually tailored assistance to students who will be functioning at different levels and working on different writing projects. Finally, in the process approach to writing, meaning is seen as more important than form and, thus, communication receives greater emphasis than correct spelling, grammar, and so forth.

A. An Example of the Process Approach

Over the past several years we have been involved in implementing a process approach to writing with elementary and secondary students. The framework for operationalizing the process approach that we have used is the Writers' Workshop (Atwell, 1987; Calkins, 1986). This approach includes four necessary elements: time, ownership, response, and instruction (Graves, 1983). The rationale for each of these is described below.

1. Time

Students need to write frequently and regularly to become comfortable with writing and to develop their ideas. It is unrealistic to think that setting aside time once a week will help LD students develop meaningful composing skills. A more productive schedule for developing writers is to create time in each school day for composing. Opportunities for sustained writing allows students to work on the same piece of text over time and helps validate the idea that writing is a worthwhile activity.

2. Ownership

Permitting students to make decisions about their own work is a necessary condition to creating an environment where they will want to write. At least initially, this includes encouraging students to choose what to write about and deciding how they will revise their work. Self-selected topics often have an additional advantage for LD students in that they make fewer organizational and planning demands on students. Self-selected topics also increase the likelihood that students will write about subjects that interest and matter to them. By encouraging students to decide what they will write about, and what and how much they have to say about it, teachers increase the possibility that students will view themselves as being responsible for their own writing.

3. Response

A primary purpose in writing is to communicate. The Writers' Workshop accentuates this aspect of writing by having students constantly share their work with each other. This allows each student to have an audience respond to the meaning of what they have written. Receiving regular, frequent responses to their texts help students learn what works in their writing and what doesn't. Reactions or responses to students' text can occur during teacher–student conferences (Vukelich and Leverson, 1987), a class or group sharing time (DiPardo and Freedman, 1988), or student–peer editor conferences (MacArthur and Stoddard, 1990).

4. Instruction

Beyond structuring the classroom by providing regular time for writing and responses to writing, teachers using the Writers' Workshop can further facilitate competence in writing by structuring and directing what students do as they compose. The emphasis here is on providing support and instruction aimed at extending students' skills at carrying out the cognitive processes underlying effective writing. In essence, the teacher is a designer of the learning environment, capitalizing on "teachable moments" during conferencing, offering direct instruction in revising and evaluating text, and integrating assigned topics with self-selected topics to extend students' writing skills.

To illustrate one aspect of instruction during the Writers' Workshop, teachers may initially help students become comfortable with the basic processes involved in composing by creating a predictable routine for students to follow (Graham and Harris, 1988). First, students could be urged to concentrate on topic choice, planning, and content generation. Once a first draft is generated, students could then concentrate on revising their paper with an eye focused on content and organization. When students feel comfortable that their paper is complete, then editing for mechanical errors could take place. A routine of this nature focuses students' efforts on content and meaning. However, students do not forget that the paper will eventually need to be edited. Hence, they will not be needlessly distracted by errors of mechanics and usage. As students master such a routine, they should further be encouraged to see the various processes recursively.

It is not only critical that students become comfortable with the various stages involved in writing, they also need to develop effective strategies for executing these processes. Within the Writers' Workshop, one way teachers can help students develop these strategies is to model the pertinent strategies and the thought processes involved in executing them. For instance, a teacher may demonstrate how to gather raw material, mentally rehearse ideas and images to write about, talk to others to gain information, or use brainstorming and webbing activities to generate content for a topic. Modeling will not be enough for most LD students, however. They will need direct instruction in applying writing strategies. Current research on teaching and learning suggests that this type of contextualized and explicit instruction is highly effective in promoting the development of cognitive and self-regulation skills central to academic success (Duffy and Roehler, 1986).

B. Implementing a Writers' Workshop

Something that has been extremely striking to us in helping teachers implement the Writers' Workshop is that a process-centered classroom looks and sounds different than many traditional classrooms. First, the physical arrangement of the classroom varies considerably from the traditional set-up. In a process classroom, space needs to be physically arranged for mobility and flexible seating. Students need space to write alone and with their peers, as well as a place to hold peer planning and revising conferences. In addition, teachers need to have areas in the classroom for holding individual conferences and for teaching skills to small groups of students. At any given time during the writing period, some students will be busy writing and others will be conferring with the teacher, while others will be meeting with peers to plan or revise their work.

A second difference involves the level of social interaction. In a process approach, writing does not take place in a vacuum, and verbal discussion between participants is a central part of the process. It is assumed that talking with others encourages thinking and the discovery of new ideas. It is not unusual to find students talking in order to rehearse and expand their ideas, verbalize writing strategies and decisions, evaluate efforts, and affirm their membership in the writing community (Cox, 1988).

A third characteristic of the Writers' Workshop is the creation of a predictable set of routines that are designed to let students work with a minimum of teacher direction and at their own pace. The use of such a routine not only allows students to know what to expect during writing time, but makes it possible for teachers to conference with individual students and to offer instruction within a meaningful context—the student's own text.

Typically, in the Writers' Workshop writing time is divided into four components: status of the class, a mini-lesson, workshop proper, and closure (Atwell, 1987). Components can be thought of as modular (Calkins, 1986) and their sequencing flexible to accommodate the needs of the students and teacher.

1. Status of the Class

In a brief period at the beginning of writing time, the teacher quickly checks with each student on what they're doing and/or planning to do. Establishing the status of the class allows the teacher to keep track of where each student is in the writing process. Not only does this allow students to articulate and formalize their intentions, but it gives the teacher an estimate of what student needs will be and helps the teacher keep track of student progress.

2. Mini-Lessons

Mini-lessons are brief (usually 5 minutes) lessons that expose students to information about writing. The lesson may focus on process skills (e.g., brainstorming), mechanical skills (e.g., punctuation), types of writing (e.g., parts of an opinion essay), or classroom procedures (e.g., criteria for group sharing). Instruction during mini-lessons is conducted in close association with the real writing activities that are going on in the classroom and the teacher assumes an overt role, focusing the lesson on a particular aspect of writing. Thus, information is provided to students when they need it within the context of their current writing tasks.

3. Workshop Proper

Two-thirds of Writers' Workshop is devoted to actual writing. While the bulk of teachers' time is spent conferencing with individual students, teachers should spend some of this time writing themselves. By demonstrating that they are writers familiar with all the phases of the writing process, teachers can be an effective role model for their students. This also demonstrates they value the utility and importance of writing.

Conferencing with students is probably the teacher's most critical role during writing time. Conferences are usually brief, ranging from a 30-second check to see how things are going to a 5-minute conversation about a completed draft or a particular problem. They may occur at any given point in the composing process. The teacher's task during a conference is to help writers extend their control over the writing process. An essential characteristic of all teacher–student conferences, no matter what the purpose, is responsive listening (Sowers, 1986). During conferences, the teacher responds as a reader and a coach assisting the writer with the massive amount of decision-making that goes on during writing.

Conferences are used for a wide range of purposes including finding something to write about, generating content, editing a text, or reflecting on the writing process. Many times conferences are centered around content and begin with a brief "How's it going?" This allows the student to maintain ownership of the text and at the same time allows the teacher to asks clarifying questions and help the student articulate problems and attempt solutions. Vukelich and Leverson (1987) report a strong relationship between conference discussion and text clarifications. Their research indicates that when novice writers use the information they've gained in teacher conferences to guide their text revisions, they typically make additions to the text. Through repeated cycles of conferencing, teachers gain enormous amounts of information about students' strengths and weaknesses and students gain expertise and control over their writing. However, teachers must be careful to guard against the temptation to do too much of the work or to be dictatorial during conferences; this will only serve to make the student more (instead of less) dependent on the teacher.

4. Closure

Closure is a time for group sharing of work or discussion of what was accomplished during the writing period. It is important that much of what students write be shared, presented, or published so that students view writing as a meaningful way of telling others about their experiences and knowledge (MacArthur et al., 1989a). Through group sharing students learn what effect their words have on an audience. Similarly, during group dialogs students learn to critically assess their own and others' text and to respond effectively to their peers as writers. Nonetheless, teachers may need to give some consideration, at least initially, as to how to promote positive interchanges between students. The development of specific ground rules for providing feedback and the modeling of positive dialogs are two procedures that teachers should consider.

Publication projects can also be discussed during the closing part of the workshop. Students are motivated to communicate ideas and information by the knowledge that their writing will be shared with an audience, and they learn about their writing by predicting how the audience will respond. Publications can be as simple as an attractive bulletin board in the hallway or more elaborate such as a class magazine, a newsletter, or a book for the school library. Whatever method of publication is chosen, however, the emphasis should be on providing real and meaningful outlets for student writing.

C. Closing Comments

Using the procedures just described, we found that the quality of what LD students produce when writing can be improved (MacArthur *et al.*, 1989a). While other researchers have also found the process approach to be beneficial with LD students (Bos, 1988), a number of issues are pertinent to the use of this approach. First, it is not clear that a process approach to writing will adequately prepare students for many of the writing tasks students face in school; these often involve a quick display of knowledge under timed conditions. Second, the utility of this approach with students who have extremely severe problems with mechanics and text production skills has not yet been demonstrated. Three, some teachers and parents may be resistant to the approach because of its relatively limited emphasis on correct form. For example, parents have been known to become concerned when they look in their child's writing folder and find various drafts replete with mechanical errors. And finally, the process approach usually does not lead to rapid gains in students' writing skills. Gains in writing tend to be slow and incremental. Thus, some teachers, who are initially excited about using the approach because their students become more enthusiastic about writing, may become disappointed when rapid gains in quality are not realized and decide to abandon the approach prematurely. We would advise against this. The valve of the process approach lies not only in improving what and how students write, but in helping students develop confidence in their own capabilities as well as promoting a desire and love of writing.

V. PROCEDURAL FACILITATION AND STRATEGY INSTRUCTION

As we indicated earlier, LD students have difficulty with many of the cognitive processes considered central to effective writing, including generating, framing, planning, and revising text (Graham and Harris, 1989b, 1990). Two approaches that have been recommended for helping LD students develop competence and security with these sophisticated mental processes are procedural facilitation and strategy instruction (Harris *et al.*, in press).

A. Procedural Facilitation

With procedural facilitation, students receive help ". . . of a nonspecific sort, related to the student's cognitive processes, but not responsive to the actual substance of what the student is thinking or writing" (Scardamalia and Bereiter, 1986: 796). For instance, in a study by Graham (1990a), LD students were encouraged to continue the process of composing via a prompt to write more. Such a prompt reduces the executive demands of the writing task by reminding the student to continue the process of composing, but no help is given as to what to write. Procedural facilitation can be contrasted with substantive facilitation where an adult or a peer act as an active collaborator, shouldering some of the burden for completing the writing assignment (Scardamalia and Bereiter, 1985). For example, teacher comments on a paper identifying a problem with what has been said and suggesting a general solution relieve the student of this responsibility, requiring them only to decide on a specific action to remedy the problem.

Bereiter and Scardamalia (1982) have developed several routines based on the concept of procedural facilitation. For example, Scardamalia and Bereiter (1983) designed a revising routine (labeled CDO, for Compare-Diagnosis-Operate) in which cue cards were used to help students first evaluate a unit of text and then decide what, if any, changes should be made. Each card included a general directive, such as "People may not be believe this" for supporting evaluation or "I'd better leave this part out" to aid in deciding what type of change should be made. Bereiter and Scardamalia (1982) have reasoned that these or similar cues and routines should lessen the executive demands of writing, allowing students to make fuller use of the knowledge and skills they already posses. They further claim that procedural facilitators have the potential to act as "change inducing agents" that will promote the development of the cognitive system, especially cognitive strategies and self-regulatory mechanisms. In their research examining procedural facilitation, they have been successful in changing what students do during writing, but this has not, in many instances, had a corresponding effect on the quality of students' text. Their claims regarding broader cognitive change have not been tested empirically.

We know very little about the potential impact of procedural facilitation on what or how LD students write. Although Graham (1990a) found that a simple procedural facilitator to "write more" resulted in longer text, improvements in text quality, while statistically significant, were small and a considerable amount of repetitive and irrelevant information was generated, Graves et al. (1989) reported that directing LD students to use cue cards, each containing a specific story element (e.g., ending), to evaluate the completeness of their compositions resulted in improvements in writing quality. Finally, preliminary results from a study by Graham (1990b) showed that the CDO procedure described above did affect how LD students revised but did not affect the quality of their text.

We have several concerns related to the use of procedural facilitation. One, the impact of a procedural facilitator depends on what the student eventually internalizes as a result of using it. As Scardamalia and Bereiter (1986) have indicated, the value of procedural facilitation lies in the external support provided for a procedure that will ultimately be run autonomously. A road-weary veteran of the classroom scene will realize that it will be important to keep tabs on what students learn as a result of using the procedure and how the procedure is used once the external supports are removed (i.e., Will it be dropped or corrupted?). Second, if students do not possess the necessary prerequisite skills, the impact of procedural facilitation on students' writing behavior will undoubtably be minimized. For example, in the study by Graham (1990), some of the LD students using the CDO procedure did not appear to have the competence to take advantage of the support provided by this particular procedure. In some cases they made poor decisions as to what was wrong with the text or how to fix it; in other instances, they appeared to be unable to carry out the revision successfully, even when their prior evaluations appeared to be sound. This situation could probably have been avoided by providing students with more substantive support, as is often done in strategy training. More guidance and initial support coupled with corrective feedback in the use of the CDO procedure would conceivably improve not only their decisions, but also the resulting revisions made by LD students.

An example of how teachers can effectively help LD students internalize a procedural facilitator can be gained from Englert and her colleagues (Englert, *et al.*, in press). They used a procedural facilitator consisting of "think sheets" that involved prompts to direct students' actions during the following writing processes: planning, organizing information, writing, editing, and revising. To help students internalize the strategies and the framework incorporated in the think sheets, a variety of features common to effective strategy instruction were used, including an emphasis on teachers modeling an inner dialog on how to use the think sheets; assisted teaching in using the procedures until such coaching was no longer needed; and guiding students to understand what they were learning, why it was important, and when it could be used. Bearing in mind the caveat that their program was field-based and they were unable to randomly assign students to the experimental and control conditions, Englert *et al.* (1990) found that their approach had a positive impact on the expository writing of LD students.

B. Strategy Instruction

With strategy instruction, students receive help in internalizing, executing, appropriately modifying, and maintaining the use of specific strategies. While we have chosen in this chapter to discuss procedural facilitation and strategy instruction separately, the reader should realize that common strategies frequently involve the use of self-directed cues or executive routines that direct how students deploy their attention; thus, strategy instruction often involves procedural facilitation.

The writing strategies that have currently been field tested with LD students have focused on several areas, including self-monitoring of productivity, content generation, framing and planning of text, and editing and revising. In terms of monitoring output, there have been several anecdotal records of well known authors such as Hemmingway and Darwin who contingently reinforced themselves according to their daily literary output (Stone, 1978; Wallace and Pear, 1977). Such procedures also appear to be applicable with LD students. For instance, Harris and McElroy (1989) found that LD students wrote more when they monitored their productivity.

The area that has been investigated most thoroughly is the use of strategies to promote the deployment and development of processes considered central to the planning of text. Harris and Graham (1985) reported that the quality and length of LD students' stories could be improved by teaching them a self-directed routine for generating individual words (action verbs, adjectives, and adverbs) in advance and during writing to use in their compositions. The primary value of this routine was that it appears to have provided the participating LD students with a more effective means for searching memory for relevant information. The training procedures resulted in an increase not only in the target vocabulary items but in other story content as well. The planning of text has also been facilitated by teaching LD students strategies for generating and organizing ideas in advance and during writing by using self-directed prompts related to the basic elements included in the genre under consideration (Graham and Harris, 1989a,c; Sawyer et al., 1989). For example, Graham and Harris (1989a) improved the quality of LD students' compositions by teaching them to use a strategy centered around a series of questions ("What does the main character do?") designed to prompt the production of content relevant to each of the parts commonly found in stories. LD students' writing has further been improved by teaching them a strategy that involved first setting product goals for what the paper would accomplish and then articulating how the desired accomplishments would be achieved (Graham et al., in press). Wong et al. (1991) have developed a planning strategy for writing about personal events that includes two basic steps: the students first search their memory to identify the personal event they wish to write about, and then they review the event in their mind's eye while trying to rekindle the emotions associated with it. We were generally intrigued with their use of visualization; such a strategy could be used with other narrative assignments like story writing.

Researchers have further tested several strategies for editing and revising. Schumaker et al. (1982) improved the editing skills of LD adolescents via a strategy that provided a self-directed routine for correcting errors of capitalization, appearance, punctuation, and spelling. Graham and MacArthur (1988) reported that the quality of LD students' essays improved as a result of instruction in how to use a strategy involving self-directed prompts for improving clarity and cohesiveness, adding relevant textual material, and correcting errors. MacArthur and Stoddard (1990) indicated that LD adolescents' writing was improved by teaching them a peer-editing strategy involving two components: one for initially editing a peer's paper for content, and another for editing the same paper for mechanical and grammatical errors.

While strategy instruction has been presented as a curricular option in and of itself (Deshler and Schumaker, 1986), we believe that it is much more powerful when it is integrated as part of the regular program. In the area of writing, for example, teaching students a peer-planning strategy that can be used as an integral part of the process approach to writing provides an excellent means for promoting collaboration and improving students' planning skills.

C. Teaching Writing Strategies

The overall objective of teaching strategies, in all academic areas, is to help students become self-regulated learners (Harris and Pressley, in press). To meet this goal, strategy theorists and researchers suggest that strategy instruction include three important components: (1) teaching target strategies; (2) informing students about the use and the significance of the selected strategies; and (3) fostering the development of self-regulation skills critical to effective strategy deployment, independent strategy use, and generalization and maintenance of strategy effects (Brown *et al.*, 1981). Variations in the combination and operationalization of these components has lead to the development of several strategy instruction models (see Deshler and Schumaker, 1986; Graham and Harris, 1987; Palinscar, 1986). The model that researchers have most commonly used to teach writing strategies to LD students is explicit strategy instruction; the instructor provides students with explicit input and instruction about how to carry the strategy out, which is gradually faded as students become more competent in executing the strategy independently (Harris *et al.*, in press). An example of explicit strategy instruction is provided in Table 11.1. This table gives a brief summary of the procedures, developed by Karen Harris and Steve Graham and labeled Self-Instructional Strategy Development, which we have employed when teaching students strategies in writing and other academic areas (Graham and Harris, 1987, 1989b). This approach emphasizes the student's role as an active collaborator during strategy instruction. Strategies are explicitly and overtly modeled in context, and the goals and significance of the target strategies are made clear to the student. Principles of interactional scaffolding and Socratic dialog are used to help students develop independent mastery in using the

Table 11.1

Overview of Strategy Instruction Procedures

Preskill Development: Prior to the collection of baseline data, preskills considered necessary to the understanding, acquisition, or execution of the target strategy that were not already in the student's repertoire were developed.

Initial Conference: Instructional Goals and Significance: The instructor and student examined and discussed the student's current level of performance on baseline probes. The significance and potential benefits of the proposed training were then discussed. Commitment by the student to participate as a partner and to attempt to learn and use the strategy was established.

Discussion of the Strategy: The instructor explicitly described the strategy, emphasizing how and why each step of the strategy was used.

Modeling of the Strategy and Self-Instructions: The instructor modeled the use of the strategy and supportive self-instructions (including problem definition, self-evaluation, copying and error correction, and self-reinforcement). After discussing the model's performance, the student generated his or her own self-statements for each type of self-instruction.

Mastery of the Strategy: Strategy steps were memorized and the student practiced the self-instructions previously generated.

Collaborative Practice of the Strategy and Self Instruction: The Student and instructor cojointly practiced using the strategy and supporting self-instructional statements. The student was provided guidance and feedback as needed.

Independent Performance: The student independently used the strategy and supporting self-instructional statements. Teacher guidance and physical prompts (such as strategy charts) were faded over practice sessions as the student independently reached criterion.

Generalization and Maintenance: The student and instructor discussed opportunities to utilize the strategy and supporting self-instructions with other tasks and settings. In addition, throughout training students were encouraged to cooperatively involve their teachers, be prepared to use the strategy, and discuss opportunities for and instances of generalization with the instructor.

strategies. Instruction is criterion-based, and students do not progress to the next level of training until previous skills are mastered.

The reader should not interpret our emphasis on explicit strategy instructional models as an indication that other approaches such as reciprocal teaching (see Palinscar, 1986) are not an effective means for teaching writing strategies. There has been little investigation in using approaches such as reciprocal teaching in writing. It should further be noted that regardless of the model employed, and even when instruction includes the three components emphasized in the previous paragraph, well-taught and well-learned strategies may not be used regularly and effectively by LD students (Graham and Harris, in press). While students may posses the know-how, they may not posses the will. Aspects of motivation are seen by many researchers as critical in strategy instruction (Garner and Alexander, 1989). Consequently, teachers should consider students' goal orientations and attitudinal dispositions when developing and providing strategy instruction. It is equally important to monitor if students continue to use the strategy over time and if they adapt its use to new situations. While provisions for promoting maintenance and generalization should be a routine part of good strategy instruction, teachers may need to use booster sessions to promote continued and adaptive strategy use (Wong *et al.*, in press).

There are at least three other issues that we would like to consider (Graham and Harris, 1991). First, we would encourage teachers to be sensitive to individual differences in children. Some students will benefit more from a specific strategy than other students, and the amount of instructional assistance needed to learn a strategy will vary among students (Pressley *et al.*, 1989). Second, while it would be tempting to suggest that students be taught a single, universal writing strategy for all writing tasks, we are hard-pressed to identify a strategy that would be adequate to meet the wide variety of assignments and genres students are asked to write about. Instead, teaching different strategies for different purposes would appear to be more reasonable. However, teachers need to give careful thought as to what strategies should be taught as students will not be able to remember and execute an infinite number. Third, it is important to pay careful attention as to what students internalize as a result of strategy instruction. They may modify an inculcated strategy making it less effective; therefore, do not assume that students will use a strategy just as you planned.

VI. METHODS FOR IMPROVING TEXT PRODUCTION SKILLS

Schools place considerable emphasis on teaching students the lower-level skills of getting language onto paper. Failure to develop proficiency and fluency in such skills can impede the writing of students in several ways (Graham, 1990a; MacArthur and Graham, 1987). If students' rate of writing is not fast enough to keep up with their thoughts, intended content may be forgotten before it can be written. Furthermore, higher-order writing processes such as planning may be interfered with when a student is caught up in the details of producing text. For example, if a student is concentrating on a spelling problem in the middle of a sentence, the purpose that the sentence was intended to serve may be forgotten (Scardamalia *et al.*, 1982). Difficulties with the mechanical aspects of producing text may also lower students' motivation and persistence during composing, and they may use a more restricted vocabulary or syntax to avoid words they cannot spell or complex sentences that might become confused. In this section of the chapter, we concentrate on what is known about teaching text production skills to LD students.

A. Handwriting and Spelling

We recommend that the basic skills of handwriting and spelling be taught during a separate period, not during the writing period or Writers' Workshop if a process approach is used (Graham, 1982). It is important to stress, though, that such instruction should not be viewed as an end unto itself but, rather, as a means to an end. Students need to be explicitly encouraged to use their developing skills as they write, and teachers need to look for ways to reinforce their use. For those who are interested in more information on the teaching of handwriting or spelling after reading this section, we highly recommend two anthologies edited by Walter Barbe (Barbe *et al.*, 1982, 1984).

1. Handwriting

The basic goals of handwriting instruction are to help students develop writing that is legible and can be produced quickly with little conscious attention. In the early elementary grades, considerable attention is directed at teaching students to form accurately and quickly individual letters. To promote accuracy and fluency in context, students also receive considerable practice copying or composing words, sentences, or longer sections of connected discourse containing the target letters. At this point, teachers often emphasize the importance of the overall appearance of students' writing, because factors such as neatness can affect other person's judgments concerning the quality of a composition (Graham, 1982). It is equally important to help students, as soon as possible, develop a comfortable and effective pencil grip and posture for writing.

Ample research on effective conventional practices for teaching letter formation skills exists (Barbe *et al.*, 1984), and many of these practices along with a variety of traditional procedures that have not been empirically validated are appropriate for use with LD students. According to Graham and Miller (1980), these include teacher modeling of the formation of the letter; comparing and contrasting features of the target letter with other letters that share common formational characteristics; visual and sometimes even physical prompts and cues to help guide the student in forming the letter; considerable practice in tracing, copying, and writing the letter from memory; corrective feedback and praise from the teacher regarding the student's effort in forming the letter; student's correction of malformed letters through the assistance of a visual aid or under the direction of the instructor; encouraging students to self-evaluate their efforts; and visual dramatization of student's progress through the use of charts or graphs. Available research with LD students has shown that the astute use of a combination of these procedures is advantageous (Fauke *et al.*, 1973; Robin *et al.*, 1975). Moreover, a photo-electric pen can be profitably employed to help some LD students learn how to correctly form letters. Such a device provides students with immediate feedback when their attempts at copying go astray. In contrast, having students overtly verbalize the steps in forming a letter as they are learning how to write it does not appear to be a viable instructional practice (Graham, 1983b; Robin *et al.*, 1975).

For handwriting practice involving the copying of connected discourse, Hallahan and his colleagues have examined a variety of procedures designed to improve LD students' penmanship. They found that copying accuracy was improved by reviewing specific copying rules in advance of writing, circling correctly copied words or letters, or saying words and their component parts aloud before and during copying (Kosiewicz *et al.*, 1981, 1982). They further indicated that an inattentive LD student copied more letters and was on-task more often when cued to monitor his or her attentional behavior (Hallahan *et al.*, 1979). Additional promising practices for improving LD students' handwriting fluency include self-competition on timed exercises and increasing student motivation through the use of reinforcement. Attempts to increase students' speed, however, must be balanced against any possible decreases in legibility. Teachers must keep in mind that handwriting fluency develops gradually as a result of extended practice. In some instances, it may be possible to make more dramatic gains if the student's slow rate of production is due to some interfering factor such as off-task behavior.

It is also important that LD students develop the skills necessary to ensure that the papers they turn in for class assignments are acceptable in appearance. Anderson-Inman *et al.* (1984) improved the appearance of students' writing by providing direct instruction in skills involving neatness coupled with self-monitoring in the use of those skills. Similarly, Blandford and Lloyd (1987) found that the appearance of LD students' journal writing was improved through the use of self-directed procedures for guiding and evaluating their sitting position and the formation and spacing of letters.

Before concluding this section on handwriting, several additional considerations need to be addressed. First, instructors should be sensitive to the special needs of left-handed writers. Special instructional provisions, such as having left-handed writers turn their papers somewhat clockwise and hold the pencil slightly farther back than right-handers do, should be an integral part of the remedial program (see Graham and Miller, 1980). Second, only a few errors account for a large percentage of the illegibilities in children's writing (Horton, 1969). Once basic letter forms have been mastered, focusing remedial efforts on the most common types of errors (e.g., malforming the letters a, e, r, and t) can often yield a high rate of return for a small amount of effort. Third, despite the common stereotype that LD students are plagued by reversals, this proposition has not received much empirical support. If students are still making a considerable number of reversals after the age of 7 or 8 yr, teachers should consider direct instructional methods for eliminating them. Finally, conflicting claims regarding the effectiveness of various forms of script with LD students have been made in the literature (Early, 1973; Myklebust and Johnson, 1967). While manuscript appears to have a slight edge over cursive writing for the general population (Graham and Miller, 1980), a recommendation for LD students based on empirical evidence would be premature at this time.

2. Spelling

The basic goals of spelling instruction are to help students become proficient and fluent in spelling words they are likely to use in their writing, develop backup strategies for determining the spelling of unknown words, and instill in students a desire to spell words correctly (Graham, 1983a). As a result, the conventional spelling program includes teaching a basic spelling vocabulary, instruction in spelling rules and phonic skills, and (hopefully) tutelage in dictionary and proofreading skills. While a comprehensive body of research on effective conventional spelling practices exists (Cahen *et al.*, 1971), most of it has focused on how to teach spelling vocabulary. Similarly, almost all of the research conducted with LD students has concentrated on this area as well. Thus our discussion will focus on this aspect of the spelling program.

Many of the empirically supported conventional practices used in teaching spelling vocabulary to the general school population have also been recommended for use with LD students (Graham and Miller, 1979), including presenting words to be studied in a list or column form rather than in sentences, pretesting words to be learned and concentrating study only on the words missed, teaching students a systematic procedure for studying unknown words, having students correct their spelling tests under the direction of the teacher, concentrating spelling vocabulary instruction on words most likely needed in present and future writing endeavors, and using spelling games to promote student interest. While these recommendations provide a good starting point for providing vocabulary instruction, LD students would further benefit from the inclusion of additional instructional procedures geared to their unique needs. Graham and Voth (1990) have identified effective modifications that can be made in how spelling vocabulary is typically taught to LD students; their recommendations will form the focal point for the remainder of this section.

The typical approach to teaching spelling vocabulary is to have students learn 15–20 (often unrelated) words. On Monday, the spelling list is introduced, followed by a pretest on Tuesday. On Wednesday, students use the words in sentences, and on Thursday they practice phonic skills or the words missed on the pretest. On Friday, a post-test is administered (Rowell, 1972).

Three ways in which this common pattern can be made more effective for LD students is to decrease the number of words to be learned each week, daily presentation and practice of a few words each day, and daily testing of the words to be learned (Bryant *et al.*, 1981; Gettinger *et al.*, 1982; Rieth *et al.*, 1974). We would advise that the weekly spelling lists for LD students be limited to 6–12 words (preferably sharing a common element, such as the *ong* sound). Because such a recommendation likely means that LD students are exposed to fewer spelling words than their normal-achieving counterparts, it is critical that the words they study yield a high rate of return. Therefore, we suggest that the 1,000 most common words, supplemented by words that students misspell in their writing, comprise the basic core of the spelling vocabulary program for LD students; the 1,000 most common words account for 90% of the words that adults and children use when writing (Graham and Miller, 1979).

While it is generally agreed that students should be taught a systematic procedure for studying their spelling words, this axiom appears to be especially significant for LD students. Graham and Freman (1986), for example, found that when LD students were directed to study 15 spelling words in their usual manner, they learned the correct spelling of less than 20% of the words. A variety of word-study techniques are useful for both LD and normal-achieving students (for examples, (see Graham, 1983a). An effective word-study technique should focus students' concentration on the whole word, require pronunciation of the word, involve distributed practice in learning the word, and involve self-evaluation and correction of the practiced response. Forming a visual image of the word in addition to tracing or sounding out the word may be helpful for some LD students. Although it is essential that students learn how to spell common words correctly, it is just as critical that they can produce the correct spellings quickly and with little conscious attention. As a result, weekly spelling units need to include interesting practice activities (such as games) designed to promote fluency in producing the correct spelling.

It would further appear to be advantageous to teach LD students strategies for using the skills they already posses when trying to learn new spelling words or when trying to figure out the correct spelling of words they want to use in their writing. To illustrate, Englert *et al.* (1985) were successful in teaching LD students to use their knowledge of spelling patterns to spell new words. Not surprisingly, though, the impact of such strategies is diminished if the student has few skills (e.g., word analysis skills) to draw upon (Wong, 1986).

We also think that teachers need to help LD students develop the skills and disposition necessary to self-regulate their study of weekly spelling words. While teaching students to independently use a word-study procedure is a good first step in this direction, we would invite teachers to go beyond this basic step and encourage students to use a broader array of self-regulation skills. For instance, researchers have demonstrated that study behavior and/or spelling performance can be improved by having LD students monitor the number of times they practice spelling words (Harris, 1986), assess their accuracy during study followed by self-administration of reinforcement contingent upon performance (Kapadia and Fantuzzo, 1988), and set goals on the number of words to be spelled correctly on weekly tests (McLaughlin, 1982). We would further like to draw attention to an innovative procedure developed by Beck et al. (1983) that could profitably be used with LD students. They had students who had been hospitalized in a short-term psychiatric facility use a self-help manual to learn a specific study system (involving a variety of self-regulation skills) for learning new spelling words. Use of the self-help manual resulted in a sizable increase in the number of words students learned to spell correctly.

A classroom resource that is not often employed during traditional spelling instruction are the students themselves. Two potentially powerful means of using student resources are peer tutoring and cooperative study arrangements. LD students' spelling performance has been improved by providing them with a tutor or having them act as a tutor to other students (cf. Dineen et al., 1977). Class-wide peer tutoring arrangements may be particularly useful, especially in mainstreamed classrooms (see Maheady and Harper, 1987). In terms of cooperative group arrangements, Lew and Bryant (1984) found that placing each of the special-need children in a mainstreamed classroom into a different cooperative study group resulted in improved spelling performance for all students and the teacher felt more confident about meeting the spelling needs of the whole class.

Several other procedures are worthy of consideration. A variety of behavioral procedures, such as high-density reinforcement for effort and alternating a practice trial on unknown words with similar practice on a known word, have resulted in more rapid learning of spelling words for mentally retarded students (Neef et al., 1980); teachers may find these procedures equally effective with LD students. In contrast, teachers should avoid procedures that encourage students to purposefully produce misspellings for the purpose of making visual comparisons. Brown (1988) has shown that exposures to incorrect spellings interferes with subsequent spelling accuracy.

B. Sentence Production Skills

In addition to developing fluent handwriting and spelling skills, students need to develop proficiency in framing their text within a variety of sentence formats (e.g., expressing their thoughts within the context of a complex sentence). Sentence combining, the practice of building more complex sentences from simpler ones, has proven to be a highly effective technique for promoting such skills (Hillocks, 1984). Other traditional procedures for improving students' sentence-building skills include arranging and rearranging word cards to form sentences, completing sentences from which specific words or phrases have been deleted, and encouraging students to imitate the patterns in exemplary sentences. Despite the fact that these last three procedures are common staple in many writing programs, not much evidence supports their effectiveness, even with normal-achieving students (Graham, 1982).

The only systematic attempt that we are aware of in improving the sentence-writing skills of LD students was conducted by Schumaker and Sheldon (1985). They have developed a strategy designed to help students generate 14 different types of sentences. For each sentence type, students use a formula to guide the process of building the sentence and selecting words. In addition, students are taught to identify and define a host of grammatical structures that are relevant to the parts included in the various formulas. Unfortunately, we cannot recommend the use of this strategy for the majority of LD students (Graham and Harris, 1989b). First, very little evidence supports the use of the procedures. Second, because of the amount of memorization required in learning to use the strategy and the complicated nature of some of the formulas, students may be especially susceptible to corruption and misuse of the strategy over time. Third, current research suggests that some of the practices incorporated within the strategy (e.g., identifying and defining various parts of speech) are not a necessary prerequisite to sentence writing.

VII. USE OF TECHNOLOGY

Word-processing and related computer programs have considerable potential as tools to improve the writing of LD students. The ability to produce a neat, printed copy can increase motivation and encourage writing for a wider audience. The editing power makes revision possible without tedious recopying, thus freeing students and teachers to approach writing as a process involving repeated drafts. Extensions to word processing, such as spell and style checkers, special purpose publishing programs, prompting programs for planning, and telecommunications programs can provide additional support.

Despite the current enthusiasm about word processing, there is limited research on its effects on normal-achieving or LD students' writing. Research, to date, indicates that word processing by itself has little impact on LD students' writing. MacArthur and Graham (1987) found no differences between LD students' handwritten and word-processed stories even though students preferred using the computer. Morocco *et al.* (1989) found no consistent differences between computer and noncomputer classrooms in growth in writing over a year for LD or non-LD students. A few studies, however, have shown that word processing in combination with well-designed writing instruction can result in improvements in the quality of LD students' writing (Graham and MacArthur, 1988; Kerchner and Kistinger, 1984; MacArthur *et al.*, 1989b). This suggests that the value of computers in writing instruction depends on how well the instructional program takes advantage of the capabilities of the computer to support the writing process.

A. Revision

The most frequently mentioned capability of word processing is the flexibility it provides in editing and revising text. It supports the process of revision by easing the physical burden of recopying and the mess of erasing; text material can easily be moved, deleted, added, or substituted. A mechanism such as word processing that lessens the physical burden of revising can be a great boon to writers if they can take advantage of its capabilities. Word processors, however, are not a replacement for the writer's skill in evaluating text, diagnosing problems, and making changes that improve the text. Furthermore, for LD students whose basic outlook in revising is to correct mechanical errors and to make word substitutions (MacArthur and Graham, 1987), it is unlikely that they will be able to take full advantage of the capability of the word processor without instruction aimed at improving their revising skills.

One means for improving LD students' revising skills is the process approach; its emphasis on teacher conferences and peer response can motivate and guide students in what and how to revise. The revising skills of LD students can also be improved by directly teaching them strategies for directing the revising process. Several studies have combined word processing and strategy instruction in teaching revision, resulting in increases in the number of substantive and mechanical revisions made by LD students as well as improvement in the quality of their text (Graham and MacArthur, 1988; MacArthur and Stoddard, 1990; MacArthur *et al.*, 1989b). The cooperative revision strategy developed by MacArthur and *et al.* (1989b) provides an example of a revising strategy that can be used in conjunction with both word processors and the process approach to writing. In this study, students worked in pairs using the following strategy (expressed as directions to the peer editor):

1. LISTEN and READ along as the author reads the story.
2. TELL what it is about and what you like best.
3. READ it to yourself and make NOTES about:
    A. CLARITY? Is there anything you don't understand?
    B. DETAILS? What details could be added?
4. DISCUSS your suggestions with the author.
5. Author: Make changes on the computer.

Please note that the evaluation questions in step 3 can be tailored to the ability of the students and to ongoing instruction.

Spell checkers and other programs that analyze mechanical features of text can also be useful in the editing process. A spell checker integrated with a word processor will scan a document for errors and suggest possible spellings to the writer. Spell checkers will not, however, automatically result in error-free documents. If the writer's error is not reasonably close to the correct spelling, the program may be unable to provide a list of alternatives. Misspelled words that are spelled correctly as another word will not be identified. Furthermore, the student may be unable to recognize the correct spelling in the list of suggestions provided. As a result, students will need to learn to use traditional aides like the dictionary in combination with spell checkers. Finally, teachers should not see spell checkers as a replacement for conventional spelling instruction; what or how many words students learn to internalize through the use of these programs is not clear. Nonetheless, for some LD students a spell checker may become a lifetime compensatory aide.

B. Publishing

Publishing is a critical motivator in any writing program. Word processors give LD students the power to produce more easily neat, error-free copies of their work to share with a variety of audiences. Special purpose publishing programs can help students create newspapers, class magazines, and bulletin board displays that have a professional look. For classrooms that have just one or two computers, the best use of that equipment is probably publishing. Students can work together on a class newsletter or other publishing project, or they can each select their best writing for inclusion in a literary magazine.

Telecommunications programs offer other avenues for publication. For example, the *Computer Chronicles Newsletter* project (Riel, 1985), which included LD and average students, linked children from different countries via a telecommunications network. Students wrote articles about events and issues in their area and posted them on the network. At each site, students edited and published a newsletter of articles from around the world.

C. Other Applications

Several word-processing programs are available that provide synthesized speech output, pronouncing the letters, words, and sentences that students write. Prototype programs are also available that will take dictation, and it may not be too many years before they become a practical alternative for students with severe writing difficulties. Furthermore, computer programs designed to assist students with planning and organizing compositions are commercially available. To illustrate, prompting programs have been designed that guide and stimulate thinking in the prewriting stage through the use of interactive questions. Because these various programs have only been used sparingly with LD students, additional study is needed to establish their strengths and limitations.

D. Required Skills

To use computers for writing, students must develop some proficiency at typing and learn to operate the word processor. Although typing can be considerably easier than handwriting for many students, LD students cannot be expected to develop typing skills without instruction and regular practice. A variety of software is available to provide such practice. In addition, difficulties in operating a word processor are common for beginners and can discourage the struggling writer (MacArthur and Shneiderman, 1986); for instance, the loss of a text or incorrectly formatting a text can be very frustrating. It is important, therefore, that students receive systematic instruction in the operation of word-processing programs and other software.

VIII. WHAT ELSE CAN I DO?

In addition to the procedures already discussed, we believe that a number of other techniques have considerable potential for use with LD students. Many of these procedures have only been field tested with normal-achieving students. Thus, the challenge for teachers will be to adapt these techniques effectively for use with LD students.

In a recent review, Hillocks (1984) indicated that writing can be enhanced by having students study and emulate model pieces of writing and discourse, engage in free writing such as keeping a journal, apply specific criteria or questions to evaluate their own or others writing, and participate in structured problem-solving writing tasks (e.g., analyzing situations that contain ethical problems and then developing arguments about those situations). His review also clarified that the most effective writing programs were those in which the objectives were clear and specified.

Fitzgerald and her colleagues have reported that direct instruction in the parts of stories and their interactions (Fitzgerald and Teasley, 1986) and the process of revision (Fitzgerald and Markham, 1987) had a positive impact on students' writing. We feel that efforts such as Fitzgerald's that are aimed at increasing students' knowledge of writing are particularly appropriate for LD students who appear to have incomplete knowledge about writing and the writing process. A variety of behavioral methods have also been investigated as a means for improving specific features of children's writing; contingent reinforcement has been the primary behavioral technique of choice (Kerr and

Lambert, 1982). To illustrate, in a study by Bording *et al* (1984), the correct use of capitalization and punctuation in special education students' writing increased as a result of awarding free-time dependent on performance of these skills. We found the results from this study intriguing because they suggest that poor writers' difficulties with the conventions of writing may, in part, be due to motivational factors. LD students' error-prone papers may also be a result of monitoring difficulties. In a study by Espin and Sindelar (1988), the percent of grammatical errors that LD students identified increased (the percent of errors corrected did not) when they listened and viewed a passage in contrast to just reading it. In any case, both of these procedures provide viable means for reducing the number of mechanical errors in LD students' writing.

Other methods that *may* hold potential promise for improving LD students' writing include creativity training and systematic monitoring of student progress using curriculum-based assessment. While the current research on creativity training is flawed experimentally, several investigators have reported gains in story-writing performance as a result of such training (cf. Fortner, 1986). In terms of curriculum-based assessment (CBA), it is well established that handicapped students make greater achievement gains as a result of systematic monitoring of progress (Fuchs and Fuchs, 1986). While systematic studies investigating gains in students' writing performance as a consequence of CBA are not presently available, several researchers have been examining the technical adequacy of CBA writing measures (Deno *et al.*, 1982; Tindal and Parker, 1989). However, until such measures are validated and the effects of CBA are demonstrated, the promise of this approach remains unfulfilled.

A final instructional technique that teachers may wish to use with LD students is dictation. For very young children or poor writers who have very limited mechanical skills in writing, dictation provides an excellent method for starting the instructional program. Dictation also may be a useful means for helping some LD students generate content for more structured writing later (Graham, 1990a). Dictation may further be a viable alternative to writing for LD adolescents and adults who, after years of intensive instruction, have not been able to automatize and integrate basic writing skills. Gould (1980) found, for instance, that college students could learn to dictate effectively with only a small amount of practice.

IX. WHAT NOT TO DO

One of the most robust findings in the research literature is that the study of traditional school grammar (e.g., definition of parts of speech, diagramming of sentences) does not improve the quality of students' writing (Graham,

1982). Likewise, the study of capitalization and punctuation has little or no effect on what students write (Hillocks, 1984). Nonetheless, an analysis of four recent editions of a language arts textbook series revealed that these materials relied heavily on decontextualized, transcription activities centered around grammar, punctuation, and capitalization (Bridge and Hiebert, 1985). Many of the activities involved copying a sentence and supplying the correct verb tense or correcting capitalization and punctuation. Based on our current knowledge of what constitutes effective writing, the use of such materials cannot be recommended.

This should not be taken to imply that we believe that correct capitalization, punctuation, verb tense, the use of plurals, and so forth are not important. Rather, it is our opinion that these skills are best developed within the context of real writing tasks (Graham and Harris, 1988). When specific errors occur in the child's writing or when the child asks how to use a particular form, this is the point at which such instruction should occur, when it will be meaningful and useful to the child (see the earlier section on the process approach). It should further be stressed that teachers need to use some restraint in terms of the amount of emphasis that they place on students' writing errors. The available evidence indicates that intensive evaluation (marking every error) may make students more aware of their limitations and less willing to write, resulting in poorer writing performance (Graham, 1982). Thus, teachers would be well advised to pinpoint only one or two types of errors made by the student at any one time, giving priority to errors that occur frequently and have the largest effect on obstructing the reader's understanding of text. The feedback that students receive should be explanatory and specific and include suggestions for making corrections.

Because children's written-language skills tend to be related to their oral-language development, some authors have indicated that oral-language training should be an integral part of the writing program (cf. Golub, 1974). We have reservations about this recommendation, especially if written-language instruction is delayed in favor of an oral-language program. General language training has not been shown to result in improvements in students' writing, and after the elementary grades students do not write as they speak (for additional information, see Graham, 1982).

X. THE CHALLENGE

School's success in teaching writing should be judged not only in terms of how well students develop the skills necessary for meeting academic and occupational demands, but also in terms of students' desire and ability to use writing for the purpose of social communication and recreation. In our mad dash to improve education and hold our critics at bay (often translated as more emphasis on basic skill development), we do not want to lose sight of the critical goals of helping students learn to appreciate writing and to enjoy doing it. In this chapter, we presented a variety of procedures that, when applied in concert, should help students realize all of these goals. Foremost among these procedures are the process approach to writing, the application of computer technology, and the use of procedures for helping students develop basic text production skills as well as the higher-order writing skills involved in planning and revising.

The challenge that teachers face is to take these suggestions and to make them a reality. Unfortunately, many teachers who work with LD students will have received very little, if any, exposure to many of these procedures. As a result, a logical starting point would be to acquire the knowledge and experience that will make implementation possible; however, most teachers or future teachers will probably not be able to acquire all that they need from a single source. They can obtain what they need though by carefully selecting university coursework, attending relevant professional seminars (e.g., one of the many process approach to writing seminars offered each year throughout North America), advocating for pertinent inservice activities, asking researchers for copies of their lesson plans, identifying appropriate commercial materials, and observing teachers who are successfully doing some of these things already.

Furthermore, we would like to caution teachers from trying to do everything at once. Many of the procedures that we have mentioned require either considerable expertise or a different orientation to teaching. Trying to implement them all at once may not only overwhelm the students, but the teacher as well. We think that a good starting point is to initially concentrate on getting a process approach to writing in place. Once the teacher and the students are comfortable with this new setup, new elements such as supportive strategies for peer editing can be added.

It is also important to note that some teachers may have difficulty in adjusting to a new role when initially implementing the process approach or strategy instruction. Actualizing the process approach to writing, for example, will require some teachers to change profoundly their approach to working with students. Instead of directing and controlling each facet of student behavior, it becomes necessary to act as a facilitator and resource that students can draw on as they work toward actualizing their own goals. Clearly this is a much more egalitarian approach to teaching than we see in many classrooms. While we realize that this transition will be laborious for some, it is well worth the toil in our estimation; self-directed behavior must be our ultimate goal for the students we work with.

Finally, if we are to improve in any meaningful way how and what LD students write, we must be dedicated to the importance of writing. Too often teachers, both regular and special, have made writing instruction the stepchild to reading or math. In allocating time for instruction, it is not unusual to find teachers giving maximum priority to teaching reading with little emphasis on teaching writing (Leinhart *et al.*, 1980). Similarly, we have found through our own experiences in working with schools and teachers that they are often hesitant and sometimes resistant to allocate sufficient time for writing instruction. They often fear that making such a commitment will have negative consequence because students will get less of something *really important*, like reading. We would argue that writing is as important as reading, especially in terms of school performance. It is the primary means by which students demonstrate their knowledge and the primary instrument by which teachers evaluate performance (Graham, 1982). Therefore, we would like to encourage teachers to provide at least 4 days of writing instruction a week, look for ways of promoting increased writing across the curriculum, and attempt to engage students in meaningful and purposive writing activities (Graham and Harris, 1988).

References

Anderson-Inman, L., Paine, S., and Deutchman, L. 1984). Neatness counts: Effects of direct instruction and self-monitoring on the transfer of neat-paper skills to nontraining settings. *Anal. Interven. Dev. Disabil.* **4,** 137–155.

Atwell, N. (1987). "In the Middle: Reading, Writing, and Learning from Adolescents." Heinmann, Portsmith, New Hampshire.

Barbe, W., Francis, A., and Braun, L. (1982). "Spelling: Basic Skills for Effective Communication." Zaner-Bloser, Inc., Columbus, Ohio.

Barbe, W., Lucas, V., and Wasylyk, T. (1984). "Handwriting: Basic Skills for Effective Communication." Zaner-Bloser, Inc., Columbus, Ohio.

Beck, S., Matson, J., and Kazdin, A. (1983). An instructional package to enhance spelling performance in emotionally disturbed children. *Child Family Behav. Ther.* **4,** 69–77.

Bereiter, C., and Scardamalia, M. (1982). From conversation to composition: The role of instruction in a developmental process. *In* "Advances in Instructional Psychology," Vol. 2 (R. Glaser, ed.), pp.1–64. Lawrence Erlbaum, Hillsdale, New Jersey.

Blandford, B., and Lloyd, J. (1987). Effects of a self-instructional procedure on handwriting. *J. Learn. Disabil.* **20,** 342–346.

Bording, C., McLaughlin, T., and Williams, R. (1984). Effects of free time on grammar skills of adolescent handicapped students. *J. Educ. Res.* **77,** 312–318.

Bos, C. (1988). Process-oriented writing: Instructional implications for mildly handicapped students. *Excep. Children* **54,** 521–527.

Bridge, C., and Hiebert, E. (1985). A comparison of classroom writing practices, teachers' perceptions of their writing instruction, and textbook recommendations on writing practices. *Elem. School J.* **86,** 155–172.

Brown, A. L., Campione, J. C., and Day, J. D. (1981). Learning to learn: On training students to learn from tests. *Educ. Research.* **10,** 14–21.

Brown, A. S. (1988). Encountering misspellings and spelling performance: Why wrong isn't right. *J. Educ. Psychol.* **80,** 488–494.

Bryant, N. D., Drabin, I. R., and Gettinger, M. (1981). Effects of varying unit size on spelling achievement in learning disabled children. *J. Learn. Disabil.* **14,** 200–203.

Cahen, L., Craun, M., and Johnson, S. (1971). Spelling difficulty a survey of the research. *Rev. Educ. Res.* **41,** 281–301.

Calkins, L. M. (1986). "The Art of Teaching Writing." Heinemann, Portsmouth, New Hampshire.

Cox, C. (1988). "Teaching Language Arts." Allyn & Bacon, Inc., Boston.

Deno, S., Marston, D., and Mirkin, P. (1982). Valid measurement procedures for continuous evaluation of written expression. *Excep. Children* **48,** 368–371.

Deshler, D. D., and Schumaker, J. B. (1986). Learning strategies: An instructional alternative for low-achieving adolescents. *Excep. Children* **52,** 583–590.

Dineen, J. P., Clark, H. B., and Risley, T. R. (1977). Peer tutoring among elementary students: Educational benefits to the tutor. *J. Appl. Behav. Anal.* **10,** 231–238.

DiPardo, A., and Freedman, S. (1988). Peer response groups in the writing classroom: Theoretic foundations and new directions. *Rev. Educ. Res.* **58(2),** 119–149.

Duffy, G.G., and Roehler, L. R. (1986). "Improving Classroom Reading Instruction: A Decision-Making Approach. Random House, New York.

Early, G. (1973). The case for cursive writing. *Academic Ther.* **9,** 105–108.

Emig, J. (1978). Hand, eye, brain: Some "basics" in the writing process. *In* (C. R. Cooper and L. Odell, eds.). "Research on Composing" National Council on Teachers of English, Urbana, Illinois.

Englert, C., Raphael, T., Anderson, L., Anthony, H., Stevens, D., and Fear, K. (in press). Making Writing Strategies and Self-Talk Visible: Cognitive Strategy Instruction in Writing in Regular and Special Education Classrooms. *American Educational Research Journal.*

Englert, C., Raphael, T., Fear, K., and Anderson, L. (1988). Students' metacognitive knowledge about how to write informational texts. *Learn. Disabil. Q.* **11,** 18–46.

Englert, C. S., Hiebert, E. H., and Stewart, S. R. (1985). Spelling unfamiliar words by an analogy strategy. *J. Special Educ.* **19,** 291–306.

Espin, C., and Sindelar, P. (1988). Auditory feedback and writing: Learning disabled and nondisabled students. *Excep. Children* **55,** 45–51.

Fauke, J., Burnett, J., Poers, M., and Sulzer-Azeroff, R. (1973). Improvement of handwriting and letter recognition skills: A behavior modification procedure. *J. Learn. Disabil.* **6,** 25–29.

Fitzgerald, J., and Markham, L. (1987). Teaching children about revision in writing. *Cognit. Instruct.* **4,** 3–24.

Fitzgerald, J., and Teasley, A. (1986). Effects of instruction in narrative structure on children's writing. *J. Educ. Psychol.* **78,** 424–432.

Flower, L., and Hayes, J. (1980). The dynamics of composing: Making plans and juggling constraints. *In* "Cognitive Processes in Writing" (L. Gregg and E. Steinberg, eds.), pp. 31–50. Lawrence Erlbaum, Hillsdale, New Jersey.

Fortner, V. (1986). Generalization of creative productive-thinking training to LD students' written expression. *Learn. Disabil. Q.* **9**, 274–284.

Fuchs, L., and Fuchs, D. (1986). Effects of systematic formative evaluation: A meta-analysis. *Excep. Children* **53**, 199–208.

Garner, R., and Alexander, P. A. (1989). Metacognition: Answered and unanswered questions. *Educ. Psycholog.* **24**, 143–158.

Gettinger, M., Bryant, N. D., and Fayne, H. R. (1982). Designing spelling instruction for learning disabled children: An emphasis on unit size, distributed practice, and training for transfer. *J. Special Educ.* **16**, 439–448.

Golub, L. (1974). How American children learn to write. *Elem. School J.* **74**, 236–247.

Gould, J. (1980). Experiments on composing letters: Some facts, some myths, and some observations. *In* "Cognitive Processes in Writing" (L. Gregg and E. Steinberg, eds.). Lawrence Erlbaum, Hillsdale, New Jersey.

Graham, S. (1982). Composition research and practice. A unified approach. *Focus Excep. Children* **14**, 1–16.

Graham, S, (1983a). Effective spelling instruction. *Elem. School J.* **83**, 560–568.

Graham, S. (1983b). The effects of self-instructional procedures on LD students' handwriting performance. *Learn. Disabil. Q.* **6**, 231–234.

Graham, S. (1990a). The role of production factors in learning disabled students' compositions. *J. Educ. Psychol.* **82**, 781–791.

Graham, S. (1990b). [Procedural facilitation: The effectiveness of the compare-diagnosis-operate revision procedure with students with learning disabilities.] Unpublished raw data.

Graham, S., and Freeman, S. (1986). Strategy training and teacher vs. student-controlled study conditions: Effects on learning disabled students' spelling performance. *Learn. Disabil. Q.* **9**, 15–22.

Graham, S., and Harris, K. R. (1987). Improving composition skills of inefficient learners with self-instructional strategy training. *Top. Lang. Disorders* **7**, 66–77.

Graham, S., and Harris, K. R. (1988). Instructional recommendations for teaching writing to exceptional students. *Excep. Children* **54**, 506–512.

Graham, S., and Harris K. R. (1989a). A components analysis of cognitive strategy instruction: Effects on learning disabled students' compositions and self-efficacy. *J. Educ. Psychol.* **81**, 353–361.

Graham, S., and Harris, K. R. (1989b). Cognitive training: Implications for written language. *In* "Cognitive Behavioral Psychology in the Schools: A Comprehensive Handbook" (J. Hughes and R. Hall, eds.), pp. 247–279. Guilford Publishing Co., New York.

Graham, S., and Harris K. R. (1989c). Improving learning disabled students' skills at composing essays: Self-instructional strategy training. *Excep. Children* **56**, 201–214.

Graham, S., and Harris, K. R. (1990). "Cognitive Strategy Instruction in Written Language for Learning Disabled Students. Unpublished manuscript.

Graham, S., and Harris, K. R. (1991). Teaching writing strategies to students with learning disorders: Issues and recommendations. *In* "Strategy and Processing Deficits in Learning Disorders (L. Meltzer, ed.). College Hill Press, Boston.

Graham, S., and MacArthur, C. (1988). Improving learning disabled students' skills at revising essays produced on a word processor: Self-instructional strategy training. *J. Special Educ.* **22,** 133–152.

Graham, S., and Miller, L. (1979). Spelling research and practice: A unified approach. *Focus Excep. Children* **12,** 1–16.

Graham, S., and Miller, L. (1980). Handwriting research and practice: A unified approach. *Focus Excep. Children* **13,** 1–16.

Graham, S., and Voth, V. (1990). Spelling instruction: Making modifications for students with learning disabilities. *Academic Ther.* **25,** 447–458.

Graham, S., MacArthur, C., Schwartz, S., and Voth, T. (in press). Improving LD students' compositions using a strategy involving product and process goal-setting. *Excep. Children.*

Graves, A., Montague, M., and Wong, Y. (1989). "The Effects of Procedural Facilitation on Story Composition of Learning Disabled Students. Paper presented at the Annual Meeting of the American Educational Research Association, San Francisco.

Graves, D. H. (1983). "Writing: Teachers and Children at Work." Heinemann, Portsmouth, New Hampshire.

Hallahan, D.P., Lloyd, J. W., Kosiewicz, M., Kauffman, J. M., and Graves, A. (1979). Self-monitoring of attention as a treatment for a learning disabled boy's off-task behavior. *Learn. Disabil. Q.* **8,** 27–36.

Harris, K. (1986). Self-monitoring of attentional behavior vs. self-monitoring of productivity: Effects on on-task behavior and academic response rate among learning disabled children. *J. Appl. Behav. Anal.* **19,** 417–423.

Harris, K. R., and Graham, S. (1985). Improving learning disabled students' composition skills: Self-control strategy training. *Learn. Disabil. Q.* **8,** 27–36.

Harris, K. R., and McElroy, K. (1989). [A comparison of self-monitoring of attention and self-monitoring of productivity on the writing of students with LD.] Unpublished raw data.

Harris, K. R., and Pressley, M. (in press). The nature of cognitive strategy instruction: Interactive strategy construction. *Excep. Children.*

Harris, K. R., Graham, S., and Pressley, M. (in press). Cognitive behavioral approaches in reading and written language: Developing self-regulated learners. *In* "Current Perspectives in Learning Disabilities: Nature, Theory, and Treatment" (N. N. Singh and I. L. Beale, eds.). Springer-Verlag, New York.

Hillocks, G. (1984). What works in teaching composition: A meta analysis of experimental studies. *Am. J. Educ.* **93,** 133–170.

Horton, L. (1969). An analysis of illegibilities in the cursive writing of 1,000 selected sixth-grade students. Doctoral dissertation, Ohio State University, Columbus.

Kapadia, S., and Fantuzzo, J. (1988). Effects of teacher- and self administered procedures on the spelling performance of learning handicapped children. *J. School Psychol.* **26,** 49–58.

Kerchner, L., and Kistinger, B. (1984). Language processing/word processing: Written expression, computers, and learning disabled students. *Learn. Disabil. Q.* **7,** 329–335.

Kerr, M., and Lambert, D. (1982). Behavior modification of children's written language. *In* "Progress in Behavior Modification," (M. Hersen, R. Eisler, and P. Miller, eds.) Vol. 13, pp. 79–108. Academic Press, San Diego.

Kosiewicz, M., Hallahan, D., and Lloyd, J. (1981). The effects of an LD student's treatment choice on handwriting performance. *Learn. Disabil. Q.* **4,** 278–286.

Kosiewicz, M., Hallahan, D., Lloyd, J., and Graves, A. (1982). Effects of self-instruction and self-correction procedures on handwriting performance. *Learn. Disabil. Q.* **5,** 71–81.

Leinhart, G., Zigmond, N., and Cooley, W. (1980). "Reading Instruction and Its Effects." Paper presented at the Annual Meeting of the American Educational Research Association (April 1984), Boston.

Lew, M., and Bryant, R. (1984). The effects of cooperative groups on regular class spelling achievement of special needs learners. *Educ. Psychol.* **4,** 275–283.

MacArthur, C., and Graham, S. (1987). Learning disabled students' composing with three methods: Handwriting, dictation, and word processing. *J. Special Educ.* **21,** 22–42.

MacArthur, C., and Shneiderman, B. (1986). Learning disabled students' difficulties in learning to use a word processor: Implications for instruction and software evaluation. *J. Learn. Disabil.* **19,** 248–253.

MacArthur, C., and Stoddard, B. (1990). Teaching LD students to revise: A peer editor strategy. Paper presented at the Annual Meeting of the American Educational Research Association, Boston.

MacArthur, C., Schwartz, S., and Graham, S. (1989a). "The Computer and Writing Instruction Project: An Integrated Approach to Writing Instruction." The Eleventh International Conference for Learning Disabilities, Denver, Colorado.

MacArthur, C., Schwartz, S., and Graham, S. (1989b). [The effectiveness of a peer-editing strategy with LD students.] Unpublished raw data.

Maheady, L., and Harper, G. (1987). A class-wide peer tutoring program to improve the spelling test performance of low-income, third- and fourth-grade students. *Educ. Treatment Children* **10,** 120–133.

McLaughlin, T. (1982). Effects of self-determined and high performance standards on spelling performance. A multi-element baseline analysis. *Child Family Behav. Ther.* **4,** 55–61.

Morocco, C. C., Dalton, B., and Tivnan, T. (1989). "The Impact of Computer-Supported Writing Instruction on the Writing Quality of Learning-Disabled Students: Final Report." Education Development Center, Newton, Massachusetts.

Myklebust, H., and Johnson, D. (1967). "Learning Disabilities: Educational Principles and Practices. Grune & Stratton, New York.

Neef, N., Iwata, B., and Page, T. (1980). The effects of interpersonal training versus high-density reinforcement on spelling acquisition and retention. *J. Appl. Behav. Anal.* **13,** 153–158.

Palincsar, A. S. (1986). The role of dialogue in providing scaffolded instruction. *Educ. Psycholog.* **21(1&2),** 73–98.

Pressley, M., Goodchild, F., Fleet, J., Zajchowski, R., and Evans, E. (1989). The challenges of classroom strategy instruction. *Elem. School J.* **89,** 301–342.

Riel, M. M. (1985). The computer chronicles newswire: A functional learning environment for acquiring literacy skills. *J. Educ. Comput. Res.* **1,** 317–337.

Rieth, H. J., Axelrod, S., Anderson, R., Hathaway, F., Wood, K., and Fitzgerald, C. (1974). Influence of distributed practice and daily testing on weekly spelling tests. *J. Educ. Res.* **68,** 73–77.

Robin, A. L., Armel, S., and O'Leary, D. K. (1975). The effects of self instruction on writing deficiencies. *Behav. Ther.* **6,** 178–187.

Rowell, G. (1972). A prototype for an individualized spelling program. *Elem. English* **49,** 335–340.

Sawyer, R., Graham, S., and Harris, K. R. (1989). [Improving learning disabled students' composition skills with story grammar strategy training: A further components analysis of self-instructional strategy training.] Unpublished raw data.

Scardamalia, M., and Bereiter, C. (1983). The development of evaluative, diagnostic and remedial capabilities in children's composing. *In* "The Psychology of Written Language: Development and Educational Perspectives" (M. Martlew, ed.), pp. 67–95. John Wiley, London.

Scardamalia, M., and Bereiter, C. (1985). Fostering the development of self-regulation in children's knowledge processing. *In* "Thinking and Learning Skills: Current Research and Open Questions," Vol. 2 (S. Chipman, J. Segal, and R. Glaser, eds.), pp. 563–577. Lawrence Erlbaum, Hillsdale, New Jersey.

Scardamalia, M., and Bereiter, C. (1986). Written composition. *In* "Handbook of Research on Teaching," 3rd ed. (M. Wittrock, ed.), pp. 778–803. Macmillan, New York.

Scardamalia, M., Bereiter, C., and Goelman, H. (1982). The role of production factors in writing ability. *In* "What Writers Know: The Language, Process and Structure of Written Discourse" (M. Nystrand, ed.), pp. 173–210. Academic, New York.

Schumaker, J., and Sheldon, J. (1985). "The Sentence Writing Strategy." University of Kansas, Lawrence.

Schumaker, J., Deshler, D., Alley, G., Warner, M., Clark, F., and Nolan, S. (1982). Error monitoring: A learning strategy for improving adolescent performance. *In* "Best of ACLD," Vol. 3 (W. M. Cruickshank and J. Lerner, eds.), pp. 179–183. Syracuse University Press, Syracuse, New York.

Schwartz, S. S., and MacArthur, C. A. (1990). They all have something to say: Helping learning disabled students write. *Academic Ther.* **25,** 459–472.

Schwartz, S. S., Graham, S., and MacArthur, C. A. (1989). "Learning Disabled and Normally Achieving Students' Knowledge of the Writing Process." Paper presented at the Annual Convention of the Council for Learning Disabilities, Denver.

Sowers, S. (1986). Reflect, expand, select: Three responses in the writing conference. *In* "Understanding Writing: Ways of Observing, Learning and Teaching" (T. Newkirk and N. Atwell, eds.), pp. 123–129. Heinemann, Portsmouth, New Hampshire.

Stone, I. (1978). "The Origin." Doubleday, New York.

Thomas, C., Englert, C., and Gregg, S. (1987). An analysis of errors and strategies in the expository writing of learning disabled students. *Remed. Special Educ.* **8,** 21–30.

Tindal, G., and Parker, R. (1989). Assessment of written expression for students in compensatory and special education programs. *J. Special Educ.* **23,** 169–184.

Vukelich, C., and Leverson, L. D. (1987). Two young writers: The relationship between text revisions and teacher/student conferences. *In* "Research in Literacy: Merging Perspectives. Thirty-sixth Yearbook of the National Reading Conference" (J. E. Readence and R. S. Baldwin, eds.), (pp. 281–286). National Reading Conference, Rochester, New York.

Wallace, L., and Pear, J. (1977). Self-control techniques of famous novelists. *J. Appl. Behav. Anal.* **10,** 515–525.

Wong, B. Y. L. (1986). A cognitive approach to teaching spelling. *Excep. Children* **53,** 169–173.

Wong, B. Y. L., Wong, R., Darlington, D., and Jones, W. (1991). Interactive Teaching: An Effective Way to Teach Revision Skills to Adolescents with Learning Disabilities, *Learning Disabil. Res. Pract.*

Wong, B. Y. L., Harris, K. R., and Graham, S. (in press). Cognitive-behavioral procedures: Academic applicants with students with learning disabilities. *In* "Child and Adolescent Therapy: Cognitive-Behavioral Procedures" (P. C. Kendall, ed.). Guilford Press, New York.

CHAPTER 12

Mathematics

Deborah D. Smith and Diane P. Rivera

Editor's Notes

Following the topic of writing instruction, we turn to focus on mathematics instruction. The major theme in this chapter concerns instructional methods in mathematics, in particular, as they pertain to students with learning disabilities. However, there are other themes.

The first theme is the contextual framework of mathematical instruction for all students. Smith and Rivera aptly draw on the standards for curriculum and evaluation set by the National Council of Teachers of Mathematics as a framework for discussing instructional content in teaching mathematics.

The second theme is the nature of mathematical difficulties in students, especially those with learning disabilities. The third theme is formal and informal assessment of mathematics. The fourth, and major, theme is instructional methods, which Smith and Rivera categorize into generic interventions versus instructions specific to mathematics. Underlying these instructional methods is an important notion: stages of learning, which include initial and advanced acquisition, proficiency, maintenance, generalization, and adaptation. The authors emphasize the need for teachers to ascertain the student's particular learning stage and to match intervention to his or her learning stage. The last theme concerns research issues in mathematics instruction.

I. INTRODUCTION

This chapter begins with an examination of the contents of mathematics instruction as recommended by the National Council of Teachers of Mathematics (NCTM) and the National Council of Supervisors of Mathematics. Such an examination serves as a context for the discussion on trends in mathematics instruction in special education and the causes underlying difficulties in mathematics achievement. Subsequently, formal and informal assessments in mathematics are the foci of discussion, which lead logically into the final topic of the chapter, instructional methods. These are categorized into generic methods and methods specific to mathematics.

II. MATHEMATICS INSTRUCTION

Mathematics represents an important area of instruction for all students. All students must demonstrate proficiency in mathematical skills and concepts that will enable them to function successfully beyond the classroom. They must be able to reason and problem solve using mathematical knowledge and to generalize this knowledge to real-life situations. For many students with learning disabilities (LD), mastery of these important skills occurs only after considerable and concentrated direct instruction.

In recent years, special education researchers have devoted more attention to mathematics instruction due to the recognition that students with LD frequently demonstrate difficulties in mastering mathematical concepts and skills throughout their school years (McLeod and Armstrong, 1982). During the 1970s and 1980s, interest in how children learn mathematics prompted research that resulted in recommendations about effective teaching strategies and the development of assessment instruments and instructional materials (Mercer and Mercer, 1989). These recommendations greatly influence mathematics instruction for all students.

A. Trends in Mathematics Instruction

The NCTM, in an unprecedented move, published a set of Curriculum and Evaluation Standards for School Mathematics (NCTM, Commission on Standards for School Mathematics, 1989). This set of standards paves the way for the evaluation of and for the revision of mathematics basal series across grade levels. In addition, the NTCM urges the revision of local, state, and national assessment instruments to reflect students' knowledge of the curriculum recommended in the standards.

The standards set guidelines for instruction in a variety of areas sensitive to a changing society dominated by technological innovations. Specifically, more emphasis is put on identifying and developing thinking processes used by students to solve mathematical problems and less emphasis on mathematics instruction that relies solely on paper-and-pencil computation. The challenge for educators is to find an appropriate instructional balance so students attain mastery in mathematical skills and demonstrate an ability to reason and problem solve using mathematical skills and concepts.

The NCTM (1989) and the National Council of Supervisors of Mathematics (1989) recommend various topics for instruction reflecting the trend toward incorporating more problem-solving and technology into mathematics instruction and less paper-and-pencil computation as the basis for "covering" mathematics curriculum.

While computation clearly retains a position in the list of recommended topics, other areas for instruction (e.g., mathematical reasoning, estimation, statistics) reflect the acquisition and application of further mathematical concepts. In the following sections, discussion focuses on those skills generally found in most basal texts.

1. Numeration

To comprehend numeration, students must develop an understanding of number concepts, number usage, number sense, and place value. This understanding can be developed by having students: (1) manipulate physical objects and describe the represented numbers, (2) relate numbers to real-world experiences, and (3) experience numeration concepts in other areas of the curriculum, such as science and social studies (NCTM, 1989).

Students with LD may experience difficulties identifying a number for a group of objects, writing numbers correctly, recognizing patterns, skip-counting, recognizing numbers that are greater than or less than a designated number, or understanding the language associated with numeration such as before and after (Bley and Thornton, 1989). Thus, for many students with LD teachers will find it necessary to include activities that teach and reinforce numeration skills throughout the school years.

2. Problem-Solving

Problem-solving should be a major emphasis of any mathematics program. Through the use of problem-solving and reasoning, students apply skills and concepts in meaningful, everyday situations.

Problem-solving is often a difficult skill for students with LD to master. The language of the problem is at times made ambiguous by extraneous information that must be identified and sorted out from the actual problem.

For students with language delays, this task is a difficult one. Furthermore, students with abstract-reasoning deficiencies may find it difficult to identify useful strategies for working through complicated problems.

Students with LD should be given opportunities to explore a variety of strategies to assist them in learning how to solve problems. Some might learn best through the discovery approach, others might profit more through peer tutoring, and others might find teacher-directed instruction most efficient. Students should be encouraged to illustrate their reasoning of a particular problem with concrete objects, graphics, and symbols. Asking students to justify their solutions enables other students to learn from each other about such strategies. Through such methods, the teacher can determine how students are thinking and what instruction is necessary to promote more sophisticated or accurate reasoning and problem-solving skills.

3. Estimation

According to Reys (1986: 3), estimation is "the process of producing an answer that is sufficiently close to allow decisions to be made." The skill of estimating has received considerable attention and must be included in a total mathematics program. Numerous activities require an estimate because the exact number is not known or because an initial estimate will produce a more accurate answer. Estimates are also useful to judge the correctness of answers to problems solved on a calculator or answers computed on paper. Helping students realize the pervasiveness of estimation in everyday life and teaching them strategies in estimation should sharpen students' ability to use estimation wisely.

4. Computation

Successful computation requires a variety of skills. Students must be able to associate a symbol (e.g., $=$, $+$, $\times$) with a particular operation. They need to remember a sequence of steps to solve an algorithm. They must be able to retrieve automatically answers to basic facts embedded in process problems. Ability with estimating an answer before solving the problem and assessing one's answer as reasonable, based on the presented figures, are all skills that enhance computational success. Finally, students must be able to write their problems on paper by lining up numbers correctly (Bley and Thornton. 1989).

Computational skills include the accurate and proficient solution of problems in addition, subtraction, multiplication, and division. While computation of basic facts (e.g., $3 + 4$, 9×8, $12 - 7$) and process problems (e.g., 39×42, $400 - 173$) constitutes a basic functional skill of mathematics, it does not warrant the majority of mathematics instructional time. Numerous research-based teaching procedures for students with LD (see Section V) are available to expedite instruction in paper-and-pencil computation. While students need to understand the computational process, they must also have opportunities to apply computational skills and to develop other mathematical areas such as problem-solving, consumer math, measurement, and geometry.

5. Technology

The calculator and microcomputer are important aspects of any mathematics program and curriculum. Technology serves to enhance and expand instruction, problem-solving, and thinking. Numerous activity books for the calculator and software for the microcomputer make this technology instructionally appealing.

The calculator can be used to teach a variety of skills including statistics, estimation. computation, numeration, and number theory. Research has shown that the use of calculators serves as a powerful instructional tool and helps rather than hinders the acquisition of basic skills (Hembree and Dessart, 1986; Reys and Reys, 1987).

The microcomputer is commonly available in most schools either in the classroom or in a computer lab. Computer-assisted instruction, typically in the form of drill and practice, can be used to reinforce various skills. Instructional games such as Master of Mathematics (Educational Information Systems, 1988) turn tedious drills into a gamelike format (Smith, 1989).

For students with LD, who frequently require adaptations in instruction, drill and practice software is beneficial for several reasons. First, such software provides alternative ways to respond to information. Second, the teacher has the ability to adjust the level of difficulty of many software programs. Third, the rate of responding is usually presented at different levels, a slower response rate for students just learning the skill and a faster rate for students working on proficiency.

The microcomputer can be used to supplement mathematics instruction in other areas. Problem-solving software and computer programming packages, using either BASIC or Logo, offer alternative activities to expand and enrich the mathematics program (Smith, 1989).

6. Fractions and Decimals

The NCTM (1989) recommends that instruction in fractions and decimals be initiated in kindergarten and continue through fourth grade, with some additional instruction throughout the school years. Students should learn through concrete experiences about equivalent fractions and the relationship between fractions and decimals. Instruction should focus on incorporating fractions and decimals into problem-solving situations as well.

With the calculator and an interest in the metric system, which does not use fractions, complex operations (e.g., multiplying and dividing mixed fractions) with fractions, particularly for students with LD, is questionable. More instructional time should be devoted to fractions as they relate to life experiences, such as cooking, and to decimals and the relationship to money.

7. Measurement

Measurement skills are necessary for everyday situations. As such, the teaching of measurement represents an important part of the mathematics curriculum and deserves attention equal to other areas. According to the NCTM (1989), measurement instruction should include (1) recognition of standard units of measurement, (2) selection of the appropriate unit, (3) estimation, (4) application to everyday situations, and (5) development of formulas.

Measurement can be taught to students with LD as discrete skills until mastery is achieved. Simultaneous opportunities should exist for students to apply skills being learned to everyday situations and to other curriculum for generalization purposes. For example, students can be learning about the ruler and the inch while using the ruler and inches in a science lesson on plants to describe the length of various types of leaves.

Time, temperature, volume, height, distance, and weight are continuous measurements and are measured by standard instruments such as clocks, thermometers, rulers, and so forth. Numerous "hands-on" experiences are necessary to assist students with LD in developing a conceptualization of the various types of measurements and their measuring devices. Measurement activities should be integrated into other curricular areas to help students see the direct application of measurement.

Time is an area that is usually difficult to teach. Students with memory and language problems tend to find the telling of time and the use of time concepts somewhat baffling. The teaching of time requires direct and incidental instruction throughout the school day. Teachers should use terms to describe a variety of concepts relating to time. For example, reference can be made to morning, afternoon, the present, tomorrow, and the future. Activities can be related to the morning or after lunch.

Telling time should include digital as well as conventional clocks, and times for various activities should be posted. Calendar activities including the month, day, year, and holidays can be part of opening exercises. Additionally, students should be able to read the calendar telling, for example, how many Fridays are in a month, what date a particular day falls on, and how many days are in a month. Only through many opportunities of working with time and time concepts will students with LD develop proficiency in this area.

8. Geometry

Geometric principles surround us in daily living. Principles such as shape, patterns, theorems, geometric relationships, and properties of figures influence how we look at and interact with the world around us. Students discover these principles through informal and formal learning experiences, including manipulating objects, using geoboards, or engaging in computer activities.

A wide variety of geometric skills exist for students to learn. Certainly, developing an awareness of and appreciation for the pervasiveness of geometry in one's surroundings is one skill. Identifying and describing geometric figures, plus applying geometric properties to the solving of problems, represent other skills.

Studies have shown that some teachers do not demonstrate adequate conceptual knowledge regarding geometric principles (Hershkowitz *et al.* 1987). Without more preservice and inservice activities that provide teachers with a sound theoretical understanding of geometric concepts, it is doubtful that students will master these skills.

B. Trends in Mathematics Instruction in Special Education

One-third of instructional time in the resource room setting is now devoted to mathematics (Carpenter, 1985). As the field of mathematics, in general, undergoes philosophical shifts in curricular emphases, teachers of students with LD must assess not only how to teach but also what constitutes appropriate curriculum content.

Students with LD should have opportunities to master and apply many different mathematical skills. Students who receive mathematics instruction in the resource room should be placed in the regular education mathematics curriculum scope and sequence, where scope refers to topics and sequence refers to grade levels for introduction. For some students with LD however, instructional time should be devoted to skills necessary for adult life (Smith, 1989).

Lloyd and Keller (1989: 1) identified three major characteristics for effective mathematics instruction:

1. It is based on empirical evidence about development and use of the knowledge and skills that comprise the area to be taught.
2. It is delivered using instructional procedures that have been shown to have positive effects on pupil outcome.
3. It uses programs that have been empirically validated.

These characteristics warrant further examination, because whether or not they characterize mathematical instruction given by special education teachers is not clear. Cawley *et al.* (1979) present data suggesting that teachers of students with LD consider their training to be inadequate in mathematics. Hence, special education teachers must be better prepared to teach mathematics. In particular, preservice preparation programs must include more information about mathematics instruction to individuals preparing to become teachers of students with special needs, and more inservice workshops should be available on particular topics of mathematics instruction or instructional materials.

A strong data base substantiating various instructional procedures as effective for the teaching of mathematical skills does exist (Lovitt, 1989; Mastropieri and Scruggs, 1987; Smith, 1989). Some of these teaching procedures are modeling, reinforcement, corrections, feedback, and cognitive strategy training. (These procedures are described later in this chapter.) However, more research studying the effectiveness of instructional procedures on students' efficient learning of mathematics is needed as the curriculum is altered and expanded.

Special educators, just like regular educators, have struggled with the issue of what teacher variables constitute effective instruction for students. Researchers (e.g., Mastropieri and Scruggs, 1987) have identified factors that they believe to be indicative of sound instructional principles:

1. Engage students in tasks.
2. State instructional objectives.
3. Pace instruction.
4. Provide information.
5. Ask questions to determine student understanding.
6. Provide feedback.
7. Utilize guided and independent practice opportunities.
8. Conduct formative evaluation.

The following example illustrates the above steps. When teaching the skill of place value, the teacher informs students of the objective for that lesson. She introduces new vocabulary and models place value concepts by using a place value chart. Students use their own place value charts and imitate the modeled instruction. Students then practice the new skill while the teacher provides feedback regarding progress. Measurement of the skill or observation by the teacher may determine that additional instruction for some students is necessary. For other students, who can perform the skill successfully under teacher guidance, independent activities are assigned. Examples of independent activities are completing homework, working in a learning center, or working cooperatively with other students.

Special education teachers must consider other factors when planning instruction for their students. Depending on their needs, the curriculum may require adaptations emphasizing more of a life skills approach. While mastery of basic skills is necessary, the focus of instruction may be to prepare students for the demands of daily living.

The sequence of instruction is another area that may require modification. For students who need skills presented in small steps, a task analysis of the scope of instruction will produce additional steps to be incorporated into the instructional sequence. These incremental steps serve to provide students with successful experiences.

Language is a major factor to consider when teaching. According to Wiig and Semel (1980), the language of mathematics is "conceptually dense." Students must understand the meaning conveyed by symbols (e.g., $+, =, >$); there are no contextual clues, as in reading, to assist in comprehending the number sentence. Teachers need to be aware of their language (e.g., questions, directions, sentence structure), the language of the curriculum, and the language level of the student. Being cognizant of this information will assist teachers in structuring instruction carefully so students comprehend skills and concepts presented.

Finally, teachers must consider the individual needs of students based on their Individualized Education Programs (IEP). Mathematics curriculum and instruction should be tailored to those needs. The trend in mathematics instruction in special education classrooms should blend with general curricular trends in regular education where appropriate and with the individual needs of students.

III. DIFFICULTIES IN MATHEMATICS

Poor mathematics achievement may be due to a variety of reasons. Difficulties with abstract thinking, language, reading, motivation, and memory can impede the ability to learn mathematical skills and concepts (Hammill and Bartel, 1986; Mercer and Mercer, 1989; Bley and Thornton, 1989). Apparently, students who receive remedial instruction at the elementary level continue to struggle in junior and senior high school. Teachers at the secondary level indicated that students with LD require instruction with skills (e.g., fractions, decimals) associated with fourth- and fifth-grade mathematics curriculum (McLeod and Armstrong, 1982). Secondary level students with LD also experience difficulties due to the vocabulary used in mathematics instruction (e.g., binomial) and the reading level of the material (Woodward and Peters, 1983).

Ineffective instruction also has been identified as a factor that inteferes with successful mathematical learning. The inability of teachers to match the correct instructional technique with the skill and level of the student can hamper learning. Also, the tendency to move students too quickly through an instructional sequence can risk the attainment of mastery and generalization training (Cawley et al., 1979; Hammill and Bartel, 1986). The danger here is that skills will not be retained or applied.

Computational skills also often pose problems for students with LD. One reason for this is lack of mastery and attainment of proficiency with basic facts. The ability to compute basic facts represents a discrete skill and also is a prerequisite for many higher-level mathematical abilities. Thus, accuracy and proficiency with basic facts is critical. Researchers have found that students with LD are slower at computing basic facts and rely more on overt counting techniques (e.g., lines, marks) than their NLD peers (Fleischner et al., 1980; Fleischner and Garnett, 1980). Also, LD students' computation of basic facts is not at a level of automaticity comparable with that of regular education students (Kirby and Becker, 1988). These data suggest that mainstreamed students may have difficulty keeping pace with their peer groups and acquiring more advanced skills.

Other computational deficiencies may be attributed to lack of awareness of appropriate solution strategies (Pellegrino and Goldman, 1987). For example, NLD students learn a variety of strategies while solving problems, such as "counting on" and "doubling." As NLD students mature, they use more efficient strategies and recognize when to apply particular strategies (Lloyd and Keller, 1989), whereas students with LD may not use any strategies, may not choose the most appropriate computational strategy, or may require more time to use a strategy (Geary et al., 1987).

A number of studies have been conducted in the area of word problems. Montague and Bos (in press) found that students with LD had more difficulty than average- and high-ability students in determining the appropriate operation and algorithm when solving word problems. Identifying extraneous information (Cawley et al., 1987) and speed and accuracy (Englert et al., 1987) are also common difficulties for students with LD when they are compared with NLD students.

Thus, students with LD exhibit difficulties in mathematics for a variety of reasons. Their slower response rate, inefficient selection and utilization of solution strategies, and difficulty with basic skills (e.g., facts) constitute some factors that impede effective mathematics learning.

IV. ASSESSMENT

Formal and informal assessment procedures are used for many purposes. For example, assessments are used to determine a student's current level of academic performance for instructional planning purposes and to monitor and evaluate student progress on specific instructional skills through direct and daily measurement procedures. Together, these procedures provide a complete picture of student performance in mathematics.

A. Formal Assessment Measures

Formal assessment measures yield norm-referenced test scores. The results compare a student's performance with a representative sample. These scores tell how the student performed in relation to other students of comparable ages and grades. Norm-referenced tests may be administered to a group of students or individually. These tests may be part of the assessment battery given to a student prior to special education placement (i.e., administered by a school psychologist or regular classroom teacher) or may be given by the special education teacher as an initial step in determining the student's strengths and weaknesses. Because norm-referenced tests merely sample students' abilities in various mathematical skills, it is important to continue with assessments that are more in-depth and skill-specific (for an explanation of formal and informal assessment instruments, see Mercer and Mercer, 1989).

B. Informal Assessment Measures

Informal assessment measures provide some of the best information regarding students' abilities and progress with mathematical skills and concepts. This type of assessment may involve curriculum-based assessment (CBA), observations and interviews, and error analysis.

1. CBA

CBA usually involves teacher-constructed tests to measure student progress on curricular objectives that relate to a student's IEP objectives. The construction of a CBA instrument requires (1) identification of skills, (2) identification of objectives, (3) development of test items to sample each skill, and (4) development of criteria.

2. Observation and Interview

Observations and interviews are powerful diagnostic tools for teachers to use. By carefully observing the student's responses, the teacher can determine at what place faulty performance is occurring. Furthermore, when teachers take the time to have youngsters explain how they arrived at their answers, the teacher has a better understanding of the thinking process behind the response. Then, instructional remediation might be more efficient because it is highly likely to be on target.

3. Error Analysis

Error analysis is one area that has received a great deal of attention by researchers concerned with the remediation of mathematics (Cox, 1975;

Roberts, 1968). It entails observing the student solve the problem, asking the student to explain the solution strategy, and analyzing written products to determine if patterns exist. Error analysis is very important for effective and efficient instruction. It can help pinpoint areas in need of instruction, thus enabling the teacher to plan corrective instruction in a timely fashion. It is also important to determine whether or not an error pattern exists so the most appropriate intervention might be selected. In addition, instructional emphasis depends on the nature of identified error pattern. For example, teachers focus on systematic error patterns and ignore careless error patterns (Cox, 1975).

Enright (1983) identified seven error patterns. They are (1) regrouping, (2) process substitution, (3) omission, (4) directional, (5) placement, (6) attention to sign, and (7) guessing. These error patterns are listed in Table 12.1.

C. Direct and Daily Measurement

Identifying, through assessment procedures, individual skills in need of instruction, teaching those skills on a daily basis, and measuring progress daily constitute several major components of direct and daily measurement (Smith and Robinson, 1986). Take the case of Randy as an example. Randy needs instruction in telling time to the hour. He receives instruction and practices each day. The teacher evaluates his performance by using percentage correct scores as the measurement system to record Randy's daily progress. The teacher determines level of mastery, and Randy's progress is monitored daily to see whether or not the instructional technique is effective in teaching him to tell time. As another example, Melissa needs to become proficient in basic facts. The teacher selects an instructional technique and monitors her progress by counting how many facts Melissa computed correctly (correct rate) and incorrectly (error rate) in 1 minute each day. Again, daily progress is observed where the teacher expects Melissa's correct rate to increase and her error rate to decrease. Such a progress pattern confirms whether or not the instructional technique is effective.

Two types of measurement systems are most useful: percentage correct scores and correct and error rate scores. Percentage correct scores can be used when a skill is being introduced or practiced to mastery; i.e., the emphasis is on accurate responding. An example of when percentage correct is appropriate would be computation of process problems.

Correct and error rate data are useful to measure how quickly a skill is being performed. Examples of skills to be measured by rate data include computing basic facts, writing numbers, naming numbers, and counting change. One way to determine correct and error rate criteria for a particular skill is to have a student in the regular classroom perform the skill and use that student's

Table 12.1

Error Patterns

Regrouping

    This cluster of errors shows that the student has little understanding of place value or the arithmetic steps to show it.

$$
\begin{array}{r}
460 \\
-126 \\
\hline
340
\end{array}
$$

Does not regroup and writes zeros in the difference when zeros appear in the minuend.

Process substitution

    In this error cluster, the student changes the process of one or more of the computation steps and creates a different algorithm that results in an incorrect answer.

$$
\begin{array}{r}
123 \\
\times \quad 3 \\
\hline
129
\end{array}
$$

Multiplies ones column, but copies other digit(s) in multiplicand.

Omission

    This cluster of errors is indicated when a student leaves out a step in the process or leaves out a part of the answer. An omission error differs from a process substitution error by representing an incomplete rather than a different algorithm.

$$
\begin{array}{r}
4.75 \\
+ \ .62 \\
\hline
1.37
\end{array}
$$

Ignores whole number(s).

Directional

    In this error cluster, the computation is correct, but the steps are performed in the wrong direction and/or order.

$$
\begin{array}{r}
.55 \\
- \ .3 \\
\hline
.22
\end{array}
$$

Subtracts subtrahend from each digit of minuend.

Placement

    These errors are often computed accurately, but because the numbers are written in the wrong place, the answers will be incorrect.

$$
\begin{array}{r}
9 \\
+ \ 6 \\
\hline
51
\end{array}
$$

Reverses digits in sum.

Attention to Sign

    By ignoring the sign, the student performs the wrong operation. This generally occurs when the student uses the "shape" of the item as his or her sole clue to which operation to perform.

$$
\begin{array}{r}
6 \\
\times \ 4 \\
\hline
10
\end{array}
$$

Adds.

Guessing

    In this cluster, the errors often lack logical quality, indicating a lack of basic understanding of the processes or skills being assessed.

$$
\begin{array}{r}
6 \\
\times \ 4 \\
\hline
46
\end{array}
$$

Copies multiplicand and multiplier as product.

Source: From "Enright Diagnostic Inventory of Basic Arithmetic Skills," B. E. Enright. Copyright 1983 by Curriculum Associates. Reprinted by permission.

correct rate scores as the criteria. That way, students in the special education classroom can work toward achieving rates comparable with their peer group in the mainstream.

A variety of formal and informal assessment measures exist for the teacher to use to determine mathematical skills in need of instruction. Assessment that provides a clear picture of ongoing instructional progress ensures that students' time is not wasted on ineffective teaching techniques.

V. INSTRUCTIONAL METHODS

A variety of methods are recommended for teaching students with LD mathematical skills. The following sections are devoted to interventions that are effective from a research and practice standpoint when teaching students with LD. Additionally, promising methods that require further research are presented. Table 12.2 lists interventions described.

A. Stages of Learning and Instruction

Research has shown that students' progress through different stages of learning in the instructional process and that instructional tactics vary depending on the stage of learning in which the student is functioning (Hopkins, 1968; Smith and Lovitt, 1976). Students pass through these stages of learning at different rates and may enter the learning process at different stages depending on previous instruction and retention. The stages of learning are initial and advanced acquisition, proficiency, maintenance, generalization, and adaptation (Smith, 1989; Smith and Robinson, 1986). Teachers should identify through careful assessment the stage of learning in which the student is performing for a particular skill and match the intervention with the stage.

1. Acquisition

Student performance during the acquisition stage of learning ranges from learning how to perform a skill (initial acquisition) to practice the skill to become more accurate (advanced acquisition). The emphasis in this stage is on accuracy for skill development.

2. Proficiency

During the proficiency stage, instruction shifts to developing fluent responding while maintaining accuracy. Students must perform certain skills fluently and automatically to match performance ability of their mainstreamed peer

Table 12.2

Instructional Methods

Area	Stage of learning	Method
Numeration	Acquisition	Manipulatives
		Demonstration
		Shaping
		Modeling
	Proficiency	Drill and practice
		Rewards
Computation facts	Initial acquisition	Manipulatives
		Abacus
		Rods
		Number lines
		Time delay
		Cue sheets
		Verbalize problems
		Drill
		Language master
		Flashcards
		Computer games
		Reward for accuracy
		Tutoring
	Advanced acquisition	Error drill
		Instructions
		Rewards
		Self-correct calculators
		Tutoring
	Proficiency	Modeling
		Instructions: Work faster
		Feedback
		Benchmark pacing devices
		Computer games
		Competition
		Rewards
Processes and fractions	Initial acquisition	Demonstration plus permanent model
	Advanced acquisition	Instructions: Be more careful
		Reward for accuracy
	Proficiency	Drill facts
		Calculators
	Generalization	Sequence of instruction
Problem-solving	Acquisition	Demonstration
		Manipulatives
		Models
		Charts
		Diagrams
		Objects
		Pictures
		Graphs
		Strategies
		Questions

Source: From "Teaching Students with Learning and Behavior Problems," 2nd Edition, D. D. Smith. Copyright 1989 by Prentice-Hall. Used by permission.

group and to learn higher-level skills. For example, fluency in basic facts helps students focus instructional attention on computing process problems (e.g., $432 - 197 =$) rather than on retrieving answers to facts. If students must labor over recalling answers to basic facts while learning how to compute process problems, then the computational task becomes that much more difficult.

3. Maintenance

Once mastery is achieved for a particular skill, students enter the maintenance stage of learning. For many students with LD, mastery of a skill for 2 or 3 consecutive days at an established criterion does not ensure retention of that skill once instruction ceases. Therefore, it is important for teachers to probe or assess the mastered skill periodically. Probes can occur once a week, then biweekly, and then once a month depending on the individual student. Probes can be planned as activities in a learning center or as practice sheets during seatwork.

4. Generalization

Generalization is the ability to use a skill in different situations. Unfortunately, many students with LD do not automatically generalize a skill once it is mastered (Lovitt, 1977). It is necessary to identify techniques that promote the occurrence of generalization of the skill. Ellis *et al.* (1987) suggest beginning generalization training while students are in the acquisition or proficiency stages rather than waiting until mastery. This early training encourages students to think about other times, places, and situations in which the skill can be used. Research has shown that students with LD are capable of generalizing during the initial stages of instruction (Rivera, 1986). Teachers must make a conscious effort to discuss with students appropriate uses of the skill during *all* stages of instruction.

5. Adaptation

Adaptation is a stage of learning that requires much emphasis, much like the generalization stage. During adaptation, students extend their knowledge and skills through the process of problem-solving (Smith, 1989). For example, this may require a decision that a situation warrants an estimated rather than precise answer, or a determination through comparative shopping which product is the better buy.

Stages of learning is an important concept for teachers to consider when planning instruction to meet individual needs of students. CBA and direct and daily measurement can provide information about the stage of learning in which students are performing so teachers can select appropriate interventions.

B. Generic Interventions

Certain interventions are considered generic because they are effective in teaching skills in different subject areas. Generic interventions for mathematics instruction are described in this section.

1. Modeling

Modeling is a very powerful intervention as it involves one individual (teacher) showing another individual (learner) how to perform a skill, followed by the learner's imitation of the skill. The "teacher" could be the classroom teacher, a parent, a peer tutor, or an educational aide. Modeling involves a demonstration of the skill or a demonstration coupled with verbal instructions. It is an appropriate intervention during the initial acquisition stage of learning when students are learning how to perform a skill and in the proficiency stage to demonstrate fluent responding.

2. Shaping

This intervention is appropriate during the initial acquisition stage of learning. It involves reinforcing successive approximations of the desired skill. For example, when learning how to write numbers, a student may be rewarded for numbers that resemble the desired response. This ensures that students with LD receive reinforcement initially for attempting the response. Following further instruction in how to form numbers, reinforcement is delivered only for increasingly refined versions of the numbers. Finally, correctly written numbers are targeted for reinforcement (Skinner, 1968; Wolf et al., 1964).

3. Instructions

Telling a student how to perform a skill is common instructional practice (Lovitt and Smith, 1972); however, students with LD may not be able to follow the instructions due to lack of clarity on the part of the teacher or to lack of understanding on the part of the student. To promote students' understanding of instructions, teachers need to (1) state specifically what students need to do, (2) check to be sure that students understand the instructions, and (3) monitor progress.

Following are examples of instructions for different stages of learning. During initial acquisition, students can be told the steps to follow to perform the skill, while in advanced acquisition students can be told to work more carefully to achieve criterion. Instructing students to work quickly is effective during the proficiency stage of learning and telling students to use the skill in different settings, for example, enhances the probability for generalization (Kraetsch, 1981; Lovitt and Smith, 1972).

4. Drill

Drill is a common intervention when students are acquiring a skill, becoming more accurate, or learning to perform the skill with more proficiency. Drill is accomplished through a variety of techniques including computers, flash cards, peer tutoring, homework, verbal repetition, practice sheets, card reader machines, and so forth. The key is that the student with LD is practicing the skill correctly and frequently receiving feedback regarding process. When students are first learning a skill, the drill procedure needs to remain constant. In the advanced acquisition stage, students may require drill on specific error patterns that impede obtainment of the criterion. When students move to proficiency, different drill techniques can be used to maintain interest. For instance, a student learning math facts can practice daily using flash cards. As the student becomes more accurate, through error analysis the teacher can pinpoint specific facts requiring drill. Once criterion is achieved, fluency with facts can be accomplished by drilling on the computer or by working with a stopwatch (Haring *et al.*, 1978).

5. Reward for Accuracy

Students in the advanced acquisition stage of learning may exhibit errors that are random or careless; i.e., there does not seem to be a consistent error pattern that could be remediated through error drill. The teacher must use an intervention that will stop careless performance and help the student reach mastery. Reward for accuracy implies that a criterion level is established for a skill, and a reward for reaching this level is selected by the student and agreed upon by the teacher. The intent is that the reward will increase the probability that the student will work harder and not make careless errors, thus obtaining mastery quickly (Deitz and Repp, 1983; Smith and Lovitt, 1976).

6. Feedback

Providing students with information about the accuracy of their performance including both correct and error analysis is feedback. Corrective feedback assists students in understanding why errors were made and how to remediate these mistakes. Corrective feedback is far superior in terms of instructional time than telling students to go back to their desks and figure out where they made a mistake. Additionally, feedback needs to occur relatively soon following completion of a task. Feedback is appropriate in the advanced acquisition stage of learning, when students benefit from information about errors; during proficiency, when performance on correct and error rate is crucial to increase fluency; and during the maintenance and generalization stages, when students must know about skill retention and utilization, respectively (Blankenship, 1978; Gable and Hendrickson, 1979).

7. Strategy Instruction

It is well documented that students with LD respond favorably to instruction that focuses on specific strategic approaches to completing tasks (Wong *et al.*, 1986; Lloyd *et al.*, 1980; Swanson and Rhine, 1985). Goldman (1989: 43) identifies several cognitive and metacognitive steps utilized in performing mathematical problems. These steps include "(a) representing the problem, (b) planning a solution, (c) carrying out the operations entailed by the plan, and (d) monitoring the course of solution."

C. Instructions Specific to Mathematics

1. Basic Math Facts

Many interventions can promote mastery of basic facts in the acquisition stage of learning. Several interventions are applicable across the four operations: addition, subtraction, multiplication, and division.

 a. Manipulatives Most teachers are taught during their preservice training the importance of using manipulatives when introducing a skill. The reason is that students must manipulate physical objects to gain a true understanding of skills and concepts. While this seems to make sense, Baroody (1989) emphasizes that manipulatives must be carefully chosen to represent the skill being taught and that teacher direction is necessary. Also, manipulatives must be meaningful to the student and should challenge student thinking during the learning process.

Manipulatives such as rods, the abacus, unifex cubes, paper clips, and blocks are some examples of materials found in many special education classrooms that have proven effective to help students with LD acquire basic facts (Lovitt *et al.*, 1974). The important point is that the manipulative must have meaning for the student and relate conceptually to the skill being introduced (Dunlap and Brennan, 1979).

Many educators believe that students must progress through an instructional representation of skills first in the concrete (e.g., hands-on manipulatives), then in the representational (e.g., pictures, tallies), and finally in the abstract (e.g., numbers) mode. Some research supports this idea (Baroody, 1987; Mercer and Mercer, 1989; Peterson *et al.*, 1988/1989). However, further research is necessary to substantiate this sequence as necessary and to determine the length of instruction in each step in the sequence to ensure student understanding.

From the perspective of stages in learning, manipulatives are suggested when students are acquiring a skill. Teachers are cautioned to collect data regularly to monitor student progress and to change the intervention when necessary.

b. Time Delay   This is an effective technique to promote acquisition of math facts. The teacher shows the student a fact on a flashcard. The student has 5 seconds to say the answer. If time elapses, then the teacher provides the answer. The amount of time to say the answer is shortened until the student says the answer when the flashcard is first presented. Those facts that continue to pose problems for students can be drilled separately until criterion is reached (Stevens and Schuster, 1988).

c. Verbalize the Problem   This instructional procedure requires students to say the problem and the answer. Studies with students with LD demonstrated that verbalizing the problem helped students compute facts accurately even after the intervention was terminated (Lombardo and Drabman, 1985; Lovitt and Curtiss, 1968).

For addition facts, several interventions are effective for students with LD. Count Ons requires that students start with the bigger number, and then count the number of times as indicated by the smaller number (e.g., $9 + 3 = ?$, start with 9 then count on three numbers—10, 11, 12). Doubles $(5 + 5, 9 + 9)$ are usually the easiest facts for students to learn at first. The Doubles strategy represents a good starting point from which other strategies can be added to solve more difficult facts. Near Doubles requires students to think of the double nearest to the problem presented, and then to count on to find the answer (e.g., $6 + 7$, think $6 + 6$ then count on 1) (Thornton and Toohey, 1985).

Several interventions can be used to teach substraction facts. The Separating From strategy involves starting with the minuend, taking away the number represented in the subtrahend, and then counting the number of objects remaining. This is often done with various manipulatives. Counting Down requires students to say the first number and then count down the number in the subtrahend to arrive at the answer. Students with LD must have a lot of practice with counting backward to be successful with this intervention. Counting Up means starting with the smaller number and determining how many numbers it takes to count up to the number in the minuend (e.g., $9 - 6$, start with 6 count up to 9, it takes 3 to reach 9, the answer is 3) (Baroody, 1984).

Learning the Count Bys (e.g., count by 2s, by 3s) helps students acquire multiplication and division facts. Count Bys can be presented in chart format initially and then practiced from memory. Teachers can make cassette tapes of the Count Bys for independent practice, or peers can work in small groups tutoring each other. Two other strategies to teach multiplication and division facts are presented in Tables 12.3 (Cullinan *et al.*, 1981; Smith, 1989).

When students move on to the proficiency stage of learning, the emphasis becomes one of building fluent responding. Pacing Devices are very effective in building proficiency. Examples of such devices include cassette tapes with a

Table 12.3

Attack Strategy for Multiplication Facts

Attack Strategy
Count by one number the number of times indicated by the other number.

Steps in Attack Strategy	Example
1. Read the problem.	$2 \times 5 =$ _____
2. Point to a number that you know how to count by	Student points to 2
3. Make the number of marks indicated by the other number	$2 \times 5 =$ _____
4. Begin counting by the number you know how to count by and by one for each mark, touching each mark.	////// "2, 4, …"
5. Stop counting when you've touched the last mark	"… 6, 8, 10"
6. Write the last number you said in the answer space.	$2 \times 5 = 10$

Source: From D. Cullinan, J. Lloyd, M. H. Epstein (1981), Strategy training: A structured approach to arithmetic instruction. *Excep. Educ. Q.* **2(1)**, 44. Used by permission of Pro-Ed, Inc.

tone recorded at equal intervals (e.g., every 3 seconds) or a metronome. Students write the answer to the fact each time the pacing device tone sounds. Facts not known are skipped and then targeted for error drill (Smith, 1989). Benchmarks require the teacher to circle or star the fact that the student should reach during the 1-minute timing session. Students then have a visual goal. The benchmark is determined by moving ahead several facts from the last fact computed at the previous day's session (Smith, 1989).

Instruction in the maintenance and generalization stages of learning is easy to accomplish with basic math facts. Many mathematical skills require knowledge of facts, thus students have frequent opportunities to "practice" and apply their knowledge of facts. Students need to understand the importance of learning their basic facts as knowledge of them assists in solving higher-level skills.

2. Estimation

Research-proven interventions in estimation involving students with LD are lacking; however, much information on best practices borrowed from regular education research makes sense when working with LD students. The key is to use interventions, such as modeling, known to be effective with students with LD and to monitor instruction.

Teaching students how to estimate involves two primary approaches. First, the teacher must establish estimation as a legitimate activity. This can be accomplished throughout the day as situation arise. For example, estimating the length of time for an academic task, a numerical answer, temperature, measurement, and cost are situations familiar to students and where they can realize the value of this skill. Additionally, when estimating frequently, students become familiar with the language of estimation, such as "about," "between," "approximately," and "close to" (Trafton, 1986). This is particularly important for students with LD who may struggle with a compounding language disability. Use the newspaper to identify when an estimate is reported rather than an exact answer. Discuss why an estimate is more logical than exactness. Look at advertised sales items and estimate the savings. Have students estimate how much money they will need to buy a cart of groceries. Give students a list of figures and have them estimate the total. Show students how to produce a rough estimate, and then how to refine the answer. Provide activities using fractions and percentages for estimating purposes (Reys, 1986).

Second, students need to learn strategies for estimating and to discriminate when certain strategies are more effective than others (Trafton, 1986). Because of lack of previous instruction with the skill and poor development of number sense, many students with LD will enter estimation instruction in the acquisition stage of learning. Thus, teachers are advised to utilize several of the generic interventions listed above, such as modeling and feedback, to help students acquire sound estimating abilities. Also, much practice will be necessary to help students generalize and apply estimation skills to real-life situations.

Teachers can identify how they use estimation as part of daily living and then incorporate activities around those situations for instruction. Teach estimating strategies such as the front-end approach, clustering, rounding, and compatible numbers (Reys, 1986). Provide estimation examples and decide which strategy is more appropriate and why. Estimating activities can be accomplished in a cooperative learning situation, as homework, or as independent seatwork. (Refer to the 1986 *Yearbook* published by the NCTM entitled "Estimation and Mental Computation" for a wealth of practical activities to do with students of all ages.)

3. Process Problems

Computations involving the four operations—addition, subtraction, multiplication, and division—for regrouping and no regrouping require proficiency with basic facts and place value skills. Students who lack proficiency with basic facts can be given a facts table while they are performing the process problems (e.g., $39 + 68, 600 - 238$). Inability to answer basic facts automatically does not have to interfere with computations of process problems, because the two skills can be taught simultaneously.

Sound place value skills are necessary so students understand the relationships of the numbers they are manipulating. Several excellent special education texts provide many activities to teach place value skills to students with learning problems (Bley and Thornton, 1989; Mercer and Mercer, 1989).

Demonstration Plus Permanent Model is a well-researched, effective technique for the acquisition stage of learning to teach students with LD how to perform process problems. The intervention requires (1) the teacher to perform the first problem on a worksheet for the student, (2) the teacher to verbalize the steps while performing the problem, (3) the student to imitate the process, (4) the computed problem to remain on the worksheet as a permanent model, and (5) the student to complete the remaining problems independently. This intervention has been successfully used to teach addition, subtraction, and multiplication process problems (Blankenship, 1978; Rivera and Smith, 1987).

In long division, an additional step was added to the demonstration and permanent model. Some students were not able to refer back to their permanent model to determine what to do next in the process of dividing. In essence, they got "lost" in the many division steps locating where they were in reference to the permanent model. Thus, for these students the teacher would ask the following key questions. (1) What is the problem? (2) What are the steps? (3) What did you just do? (4) What do you do next? (Rivera, 1986). This set of questions proved effective in helping students get back on track to determine what step came next.

Another effective technique for long division is to have students memorize the steps involved in the process:

1. How many numbers are in the answer?
2. Divide.
3. Multiply.
4. Subtract.
5. Check: Is the subtraction answer smaller than the divisor?
6. Repeat.
7. Put up remainder.

Step (1) was important because it helped students to see how many numbers should be in the answer when they were finished dividing. This is particularly important when a 0 is in the answer (Rivera, 1986).

An interesting finding from the Demonstration Plus Permanent Model research was the ability of many students with LD to generalize the process to other untaught problems of the same operation. For example, researchers found that students who were taught a problem such as $43 + 86$ could generalize the computational process to a more difficult problem such as $634 + 47$. This was important information because of the implications for teaching according to a particular instructional sequence and for instructional time. While beginning with the easiest skill in a task analysis and teaching forward through the sequence make sense, these research findings suggest that for a task analysis of arithmetic skills (e.g., 32 + 14, 245 + 13, 576 + 120) some students can begin instruction further along in the sequence and that generalization of learning does occur to easier skills, thus saving instructional time for other higher-level math skills (Blankenship, 1978; Rivera, 1986; Rivera and Smith, 1987, 1988).

4. Problem-Solving

Problem-solving is an area that should receive high priority and instructional focus throughout the school day to ensure that students become more adept problem-solvers. Research has demonstrated that students with LD fail to measure up to their peer group in accuracy, rate, and comprehension of problem-solving (Englert, *et al.*, 1987). Furthermore, the ability to solve problems is hampered by an inability to distinguish irrelevant numerical information (Englert *et al.*, 1987), to compute successfully problems with varying syntactic complexity (Larsen *et al.*, 1978), to interpret the vocabulary, and to make decisions about which strategy and operation to use (Bley and Thornton, 1989).

Practical, general suggestions for teaching students to become better problem-solvers include (1) teaching a variety of strategies, (2) weaving problem-solving into other content areas, (3) having children write their own problems, (4) estimating answers first, (5) using the calculator to solve the computation, (6) using manipulatives, charts, and drawings to depict the problem, (7) teaching the language of problem-solving, (8) practicing writing mathematical sentences for problems, (9) determining if reading ability is interfering with comprehension, and (10) task analyzing problem-solving and teaching the component steps (Suydam, 1982).

Using effective teaching principles promotes successful acquisition of problem-solving strategies. These teaching principles include (1) assessing student problem-solving ability level and approach (Peterson *et al.*, 1988/1989), (2) teaching prerequisite skills (e.g., vocabulary), (3) providing motivation for learning the skill, (4) modeling the strategy and choice of strategy, (5) having students verbally rehearse the strategy, and (6) providing corrective feedback (Montague and Bos, 1986).

Montague and Bos (1986) investigated the effect of a problem-solving strategy. Adolescent students with LD were taught to solve word problems using eight steps:

1. Read the problem aloud and be sure all words are known.
2. Paraphrase the problem aloud, identifying the question being asked.
3. Visualize the problem graphically representing the data.
4. State the problem underlining any important information.

5. Hypothesize a solution strategy.
6. Estimate the answer.
7. Calculate the answer.
8. Self-check for accuracy.

Results showed that the majority of students learned the strategy to solve two-step math problems and generalized the use of the strategy to three-step problems. The researchers cautioned that behavioral and motivational characteristics must be considered when selecting a particular strategy for students.

Fleischner *et al.* (1987) identified a problem-solving strategy that focused on helping students identify information contained in the problem (e.g., What is the question being asked?), examine the mechanics of the problem (e.g., What operation should be used?), and determine how to solve the problem (e.g., What strategy should I use to solve this problem?). They taught students to (1) read and identify the question, (2) reread and identify the information in the problem, (3) think and decide what operation to use, (4) solve the problem by writing the equation and using a calculator, and (5) check the work by recalculating and comparing. Results indicated that students with LD were successful at learning this problem-solving procedure.

Teaching students questions to ask themselves as they work through problems can be useful. Questions to teach are as follows. What information is needed? What operation will solve the problem? How many steps are involved? How can I visualize this information? What is the problem? Is there unnecessary information? These types of questions help students focus their thinking and examine how to work through the steps in the problem-solving process (Smith, 1989).

VI. TEXTBOOKS

Typically, textbooks are the primary vehicle of instruction for mildly handicapped students and for students who are in the regular classroom yet attend the resource room part time for specific academic instruction. Textbooks tend to dictate the curriculum taught and the format for instruction. While the curriculum may be appropriate for students with LD, the format may pose problems. Some of these problems are (1) limited opportunities to practice the skill, (2) too many skills or concepts presented in one chapter or on one page, (3) insufficient task analysis of skills, (4) visual information that is too confusing, and (5) insufficient review of skills and concepts (Bley and Thornton, 1989).

Textbooks at the secondary level pose additional problems for adolescent students with LD. Frequently, the vocabulary introduced is complex, plus the skills introduced are abstract. Consequently, secondary-level students may not be able to comprehend mathematical concepts due to language difficulties, reading level, or abstract thinking ability (Woodward and Peters, 1983).

To address these problems, teachers can adapt instruction by adding additional problems for further practice opportunities. Teachers can break skills down into smaller instructional steps, thus providing students with incremental steps and more opportunities to achieve success. And frequent review sessions can help students retain information. Older students with LD should be taught how to underline key words, define these terms, and relate previous knowledge to the new vocabulary.

VII. ISSUES

Mathematics curriculum and instruction continue to be controversial areas to all educators. Certainly it is important for special education teachers to remain apprised of current thinking in content for mathematics curriculum and methodology for instructing special education students. Teachers must keep in mind the importance of incorporating consumer mathematics education into special education mathematics and providing instruction in a variety of skills rather than focusing primarily on arithmetic.

Continued research is necessary in several areas. Research is needed regarding the effectiveness of manipulatives to teach skills in acquisition and to determine how long manipulatives should be used to promote comprehension when introducing a skill. Generalization is another area requiring ongoing research. Techniques that promote the occurrence of generalization of skills to other areas, situations, and people need to be studied to provide teachers with suggestions for a technology of generalization training.

VIII. SUMMARY

Mathematics instruction is an area in which many students with LD require special education intervention. However, curriculum should be shaped by current thinking in mathematics instruction in the fields of both regular and special education, coupled with individual programming needs of students with LD. Based on sound assessment practices and research-proven methodology, mathematics instruction can be planned to prepare and enable students with LD to become astute consumers and problem-solvers using mathematical concepts and skills.

References

Baroody, A. J. (1984). Children's difficulties in subtraction: Some causes and questions. *J. Res. Math.* **15**, 203–213.

Baroody, A. J. (1987). "Children's Mathematical Thinking: A Developmental Framework for Preschool, Primary, and Special Education Teachers." Teachers College Press, New York.

Baroody, A. J. (1989). Manipulatives don't come with guarantees. *Arith. Teacher* **37**, 4–5.

Blankenship, C. S. (1978). Remediating systematic inversion errors in subtraction through the use of demonstration and feedback. *Learn. Disabil. Q.* **1**, 12–22.

Bley, N. S., and Thornton, C. A. (1989). "Teaching Mathematics to the Learning Disabled," 2nd ed. Pro-Ed, Austin, Texas.

Carpenter, R. L. (1985). Mathematics instruction in resource rooms: Instruction time and teacher competence. *Learn. Disabil. Q.* **8**, 95–100.

Cawley, J. F., Fitzmaurice, A. M., Shaw, R., Kahn, H., and Bates, H. (1979). LD youth and mathematics: A review of characteristics. *Learn. Disabil. Q.* **2**, 29–44.

Cawley, J. F., Miller, J. H., and School, B. A. (1987). A brief inquiry of arithmetic word-problem-solving among learning disabled secondary students. *Learn. Disabil. Focus* **2(2)**, 87–93.

Cox, L. S. (1975). Systematic errors in the four vertical algorithms in normal and handicapped populations. *J. Res. Math. Educ.* **6**, 202–220.

Cullinan, D., Lloyd, J., and Epstein, M. H. (1981). Strategy training: A structured approach to arithmetic instruction. *Excep. Educ. Q.* **2**, 41–49.

Deitz, D. E., and Repp, A. C. (1983). Reducing behavior through reinforcement. *Excep. Educ. Q.* **3**, 34–36.

Dunlap, W. P., and Brennan, A. H. (1979). Developing mental images of mathematical processes. *Learn. Disabil. Q.* **2**, 89–96.

Educational Information Systems. (1988). "Master of Mathematics." Developmental Learning Materials, Allen, Texas.

Ellis, E. E., Lenz, B. K., and Sabornie, E. J. (1987). Generalization and adaptation of learning strategies to natural environments: Part 2: Research into practice. *Remed. Special Educ.* **8(2)**, 6–23.

Englert, C. S., Culatta, B. E., and Horn, D. G. (1987). Influence of irrelevant information in addition word problems on problem solving. *Learn. Disabil. Q.* **10**, 29–36.

Enright, B. C. (1983). "Enright Diagnostic Inventory of Basic Arithmetic Skills." Curriculum Associates, North Billerica, Massachusetts.

Fleischner, J. E., and Garnett, K. (1980). "Arithmetic Learning Disabilities: A Literature Review," Research Review Series, Vol. 4). Research Institute for the Study of Learning Disabilities, Teachers College, Columbia University, New York.

Fleischner, J. E., Garnett, K., and Shepherd, M. J. (1980). "Proficiency in Arithmetic Basic Fact Computation of Learning Disabled and Nondisabled Children," Technical Rep. No. 9. Research Institute for the Study of Learning Disabilities, Teachers College, Columbia University, New York.

Fleischner, J. E., Nuzum, M. B., and Marzola, E. S. (1987). Devising an instructional program to teach arithmetic problem-solving skills to students with learning disabilities. *J. Learn. Disabil* **20**, 214–217.

Gable, R. A., and Hendrickson, J. M. (1979). Teacher feedback: Its use and impact on learner performance. *J. Special Educ. Technol.* **3**, 29–35.

Geary, D. C., Widaman, K. F., Little, T. D., and Cormier, P. (1987). Cognitive addition: Comparision of learning disabled and academically normal elementary school children. *Cog. Dev.* **2**, 249–269.

Goldman, S. R. (1989). Strategy instruction in mathematics. *Learn. Disabil. Q.* **12**, 43–55.

Hammill, D. D., and Bartel, N. R. (1986). "Teaching Students with Learning and Behavior Problems," 4th ed. Allyn and Bacon, Inc., Nedham Heights, Massachusetts.

Haring, H. G., Lovitt, T. C., Eaton, M. D., and Hansen, C. L. (1978). "The Fourth R: Research in the Classroom." Merrill Publishing Company, Columbus, Ohio.

Hembree, R., and Dessart, D. J. (1986). Effects of hand-held calculators in precollege mathematics education: A meta-analysis. *J. Res. Math. Educ.* **17**, 83–89.

Hershkowitz, R., Bruckheimer, M., and Vinner, S. (1987). Activities with teachers based on cognitive research. *In* "Learning and Teaching Geometry, K-12" (M. M. Lindquist and A. P. Shulte, eds.), pp. 222–235. National Council of Teachers of Mathematics, Reston, Virginia.

Hopkins, B. L. (1968). Effects of candy and social reinforcement, instructions, and reinforcement schedule learning on the modification and maintenance of smiling. *J. Appl. Behav. Anal.* **1**, 121–129.

Kirby, J. R., and Becker, L. D. (1988). Cognitive components of learning problems in arithmetic. *Remed. Special Educ.* **9(5)**, 7–16.

Kraetsch, G. (1981). The effects of oral instructions and training on the expansion of written language. *Learn. Disabil. Q.* **4**, 82–90.

Larsen, S. C., Parker, R. M., and Trenholme, B. (1978). The effects of syntactic complexity upon arithmetic performance. *Learn. Disabil. Q.* **12**, 80–85.

Lloyd, J. W., and Keller, C. E. (1989). Effective mathematics instruction: Development, instruction, and programs. *Focus Excep. Children* **21(7)**, 1–10.

Lloyd, J., Saltzman, N. J., and Kauffman, J. M. (1980). "Predictable Generalization in Academic Learning by Preskills and Strategy Training," Technical Rep. No. 23. University of Virginia Learning Disabilities Research Institute. Charlottesville, Virginia.

Lombardo, T. W., and Drabman, R. S. (1985). Teaching LD children multiplication tables. *Academic Ther.* **20**, 437–442.

Lovitt, T. C. (1977). "In Spite of My Resistance I've Learned from Children." Merrill Publishing Company, Columbus, Ohio.

Lovitt, T. C. (1989). "Introduction to Learning Disabilities." Allyn and Bacon, Inc., Needham Heights, Massachusetts.

Lovitt, T. C., and Curtiss, K. A. (1968). Effects of manipulating an antecedent event on mathematics response rate. *J. Appl. Behav. Anal.* **1**, 329–333.

Lovitt, T. C., and Smith, J. D. (1972). Effects of instructions on an individual's verbal behavior. *Excep. Children* **38**, 685–693.

Lovitt, T., Smith, D. D., Kidder, J., and Evison, R. (1974). Using arranged and programmed events to alter subtraction performance of children with learning disabilities. *In* "Behavior Modification: Applications to Education" (F. S. Keller and E. Ribes-Inesta, eds.), Academic Press, New York.

Mastropieri, M. A., and Scruggs, T. E. (1987). "Effective Instruction for Special Education." Little, Brown and Company, Boston.

McLeod, T. M., and Armstrong, S. W. (1982). Learning disabilities in mathematics— Skill deficits and remedial approaches at the intermediate and secondary level. *Learn. Disabil. Q.* **5,** 305–311.

Mercer, C. D., and Mercer, A. R. (1989). "Teaching Students with Learning Problems," 3rd ed. Merrill Publishing Company, Columbus, Ohio.

Montague, M., and Bos, C. S. (1986). The effect of cognitive strategy training on verbal math problem solving performance of learning disabled adolescents. *J. Learn. Disabil.* **19,** 26–33.

Montague, M., and Bos, C. S. (in press). Cognitive and metacognitive characteristics of eighth grade student's mathematical problem solving. *In* Cognitive-Based Methods for Teaching Mathematics to Special Education Students." (K. Scheid, ed.). LINC, Washington, DC.

National Council of Supervisors of Mathematics. (1989). Essential mathematics for the twenty-first century: The position of the National Council of Supervisors of Mathematics. *Arith. Teacher* **37(1),** 44–46.

National Council of Teachers of Mathematics. Commission on Standards for School Mathematics. (1989). "Curriculum and Evaluation Standards for School Mathematics." National Council of Teachers of Mathematics, Reston, Virginia.

Pellegrino, J. M., and Goldman, S. R. (1987). Information processing and elementary mathematics. *J. Learn. Disabil.* **20,** 23–32, 57.

Peterson, P. L., Fennema, E., and Carpenter, T. (1988/1989). Using knowledge of how students think about mathematics. *Educ. Leadership* **46(4),** 42–46.

Reys, B. J. (1986). Teaching computational estimation: Concepts and strategies. *In* "Estimation and mental computation: 1986 Yearbook" (H. L. Schoen and M. J. Zweng, eds.), pp. 31–44. National Council of Teachers of Mathematics, Reston, Virginia.

Reys, B. J., and Reys, R. E. (1987). Calculators in the classroom: How can we make it happen? *Arith. Teacher* **35,** 12–14.

Rivera, D. (1986). "The relationship among response generalization, modeling, and sequencing instruction when teaching long division to learning disabled students. Doctoral dissertation, University of New Mexico, Albuquerque.

Rivera, D., and Smith, D. D. (1987). Influence of modeling on acquisition and generalization of computational skills: A summary of research findings from three sites. *Learn. Disabil. Q.* **10,** 69–80.

Rivera, D., and Smith, D. D. (1988). Using a demonstration strategy to teach learning disabled midschool students how to compute long division. *J. Learn. Disabil.* **21,** 77–81.

Roberts, G. H. (1968). The failure strategies of third grade arithmetic pupils. *Arith. Teacher* **15,** 442–446.

Skinner, B. F. (1968). "The Technology of Teaching." Appleton-Century-Crofts, New York.

Smith, D. D. (1989). "Teaching Students with Learning and Behavior Problems," 2nd ed. Allyn and Bacon, Englewood Cliffs, New Jersey.

Smith, D. D., and Lovitt, T. C. (1976). The differential effects of reinforcement contingencies on arithmetic performance. *J. Learn. Disabil.* **9,** 11–19.

Smith, D. D., and Robinson, S. (1986). Educating the learning disabled. *In* "Special Education Research and Trends" (R. J. Morris and B. Blatt, eds.), pp. 222–248. Pergamon, Elmsford, New York.

Stevens, K. B., and Schuster, J. W. (1988). Time delay: Systematic instruction for academic tasks. *Remed. Special Educ.* **9(5),** 16–21.

Suydam, M. N. (1982). Update on research on problem solving: Implications for classroom teaching. *Arith. Teacher* **29(6),** 56–60.

Swanson, H. L., and Rhine, B. (1985). Strategy transformation in learning disabled children's math performance: Clues to the development of expertise. *J. Learn. Disabil.* **18,** 596–603.

Thornton, C. A., and Toohey, M. A. (1985). Basic math facts: Guidelines for teaching and learning. *Learn. Disabil. Focus* **1(1),** 44–57.

Trafton, P. R. (1986). Teaching computational estimation: Establishing an estimation mind set. *In* "Estimation and Mental Computation" (H. L. Schoen and M. J. Zweng, eds.) pp. 16–30. National Council of Teachers of Mathematics, Reston, Virginia.

Wiig, E. H., and Semel, E. M. (1980). "Language Assessment and Intervention." Merrill Publishing Company, Columbus, Ohio.

Wolf, M. M., Risley, T. R., and Mees, H. (1964). Application of operant conditioning procedures to the behavior problems of an autistic child. *Behav. Res. Ther.* **1,** 305–312.

Wong, B. Y. L., Wong, R., Perry, N., and Sawatsky, D. (1986). The efficacy of a self-questioning summarization strategy for use by underachievers and learning-disabled adolescents. *Learn. Disabil. Focus* **2,** 20–35.

Woodward, D. W., and Peters, D. J. (1983). "The Learning Disabled Adolescent." Aspen Publications, Rockville, New York.

CHAPTER 13

Neuropsychology and Learning Disabilities

G. Reid Lyon, Robert E. Newby, Donna Recht, and JoAnne Caldwell

---

Editor's Notes

Like the preceding chapters in Section II, this chapter deals with the assessment and remediation of learning disabilities. However, this chapter proceeds from a different perspective, namely, a neuropsychological perspective. This chapter by Lyon, Newby, Recht, and Caldwell contains two major themes. The first is their concise descriptions of the purposes, principles, and measurement properties of various neuropsychological assessment batteries and the equally concise summaries of recent developments in the use of neurodiagnostic technology to understanding learning disabilities in children. The second theme, nested within these descriptions and summaries, are accompanying caveats (cautionary statements). These caveats are very important, insightful observations about the limitations of the neuropsychological assessment batteries and neurodiagnostic technology. Readers should attend to them carefully.

Other themes include introducing readers to the field of neuropsychology and why it is relevant to learning disabilities. The last theme concerns neuropsychological subtype intervention research.

I. INTRODUCTION AND RATIONALE

To fully understand why learning disabilities (LDs) occur in some children, we need to turn to research in the basic neurosciences (neurophysiology, neuroanatomy, neuropsychology). This is primarily because answers to questions concerned with how humans learn, use language, and think involve an in-depth understanding of how our brains receive, analyze, and store information and plan, program, and execute behavior. In recent years, neuroscience has made remarkable advances in attempting to answer these questions. Some of these strides have taken place within the research specialties that study learning and development in children. For example, we have begun to develop a richer understanding of how the environment influences brain development in early life, how the chemistry of the central nervous system (CNS) governs activity level and emotion, and how "memories" are formed through the interactions of environmental stimulation, neurochemistry, and reward. Specific to the content of this discussion, a number of recent investigations have attempted to identify neuroanatomical, neurophysiological, and neuropsychological factors that shed light on the reasons why a number of children fail to learn in school commensurate with their scholastic potential.

In light of these advances in the application of findings from the basic neurosciences to the study of children's learning and development, a number of explicit cautionary statements need to be made. First, understanding how the brain functions poses a formidable challenge because true comprehension of its workings requires that we unravel the mysteries of its chemistry, its electricity, and its circuitry. For some questions, such as how does the brain listen, speak, or read, answers may be available to us in detailed form sometime in future decades. For other questions, such as are our brains and minds one in the same, answers may never be forthcoming.

Second, understanding the specifics of a particular brain–behavior relationship is not tantamount to altering the nature of that relationship. For example, while we may be able to identify some physiological and anatomical correlates of reading disability, changing the anatomy or physiology to help people read better may not be possible (or even desired).

Third, because of the recent attention given to advances and discoveries in the neurosciences and to the application of these advances to the study of LD, many professionals and parents will probably accept tentative "neurological" findings before they become validated facts. Because all of us who work with learning-disabled (LD) children want to help them as quickly as possible, we have a tendency to embrace promising preliminary information about diagnostic and remediation procedures before such procedures are actually proven effective. Unfortunately, as we have seen in the past, premature acceptance of assessment and teaching practices that were thought to have promise but did not ultimately survive educational validation can do LD youngsters (and their teachers) much more harm than good. For example, a significant amount of time and energy was misspent on perceptual–motor training programs with LD children.

II. SCOPE AND OBJECTIVES

Given these considerations, the primary objective of this chapter is to acquaint the reader with (1) neuropsychology as a field of study and its application to LDs, (2) the major purposes and measurement properties of neuropsychological assessment practices with LD children, (3) recent advances in the application of neurodiagnostic technology to the understanding of LDs, and (4) neuropsychological subtype-intervention research.

III. DEFINITIONAL ASPECTS

Neuropsychology is a field of study that attempts to relate what is known about the functioning of the brain to what is understood about the behavior of people. More specifically, neuropsychology seeks to define the role of the brain in thought and action by studying empirically the behavioral phenomena associated with the neural changes induced by injury, disease, or dysfunction of the nervous system in children and adults (Lyon and Flynn, 1990). Historically, the efficacy of neuropsychological diagnostic methods in identifying and explaining deficient brain functioning in humans is greatest when such methods are applied to adults who manifest brain damage or dysfunction and least powerful when applied to children with subtle, albeit debilitating, LDs.

The reasons for this are apparent and are related to the fact that the CNS of youngsters is quite different from that of adults, both in terms of physiological characteristics and functional capabilities. By definition, the developing nervous system is in a state of constant maturation, whereas, for the most part, the adult brain is relatively static. Thus, CNS dysfunction in the child is typically reflected in deficient development of cognitive, perceptual, linguistic, academic, and behavioral skills, whereas insult to the adult brain generally results in the loss of previously acquired skill. Moreover, because until recently so little has been understood regarding the cerebral status of children with LDs, neuropsychological studies have typically made inferences regarding brain–behavior relationships in the absence of direct information about the brain functioning of the youngsters under study. Only within the past decade, and particularly the past 5 years, have neuropsychological and neurophysiological investigations obtained data that suggest significant differences between the brain functioning of LD children and their normal-achieving counterparts.

IV. THE INCREASED DEMAND FOR NEUROPSYCHOLOGICAL KNOWLEDGE

Within the past decade, neuropsychological studies of children have been increasingly called upon to make relevant and informed contributions to the assessment and treatment of acquired (i.e., cerebral trauma) and putative (i.e., LDs) neurologically based developmental disorders. This increase in the application of neuropsychological principles to the understanding and remediation of developmental disorders can be attributed to several factors. First, as mentioned earlier, advances in the basic neurosciences have provided new technologies for investigating the means by which the brain develops and processes information and the differences among individuals with respect to information processing.

Second, the survival rates for youngsters who have received traumatic brain injuries have markedly increased. In addition, improvements in neonatal intensive care practice have decreased the mortality rate of infants who are born with significantly low birthweight ($< 1,500$ g) (Hynd and Obrzut, 1986). However, children recovering from such conditions frequently display persistent learning and behavioral difficulties associated with their neurological history. As such, assessment practices that are based on knowledge of brain development (and maldevelopment) and behavior are useful for documenting the nature of the disorder, monitoring the recovery and/or development of cognitive, linguistic, perceptual, and motor skills, and delineating treatment options.

Finally, there is growing awareness that some relatively subtle learning and behavioral difficulties frequently seen in school settings (i.e., dyslexia, attention-deficit-hyperactivity disorder) are referable to intrinsic neurological differences in brain structures or functions that are responsible for linguistic processing, alertness, motor activity, and arousal levels (Duane, 1986; Rourke *et al.*, 1986). Because a greater number of children are identified each year as manifesting neurodevelopmental learning and behavior disorders, one can expect that the need for specialists with expertise in neuropsychological assessment will also increase in the future.

Given that neuropsychological assessment of LD children may be more frequently requested in the future, it may be useful to examine neuropsychological assessment principles and techniques with an eye toward identifying the purposes for which they were developed, their measurement and content characteristics, and how the assessment data have been related to remediation.

V. STANDARDIZED NEUROPSYCHOLOGICAL ASSESSMENT: PURPOSES, TEST BATTERIES, AND LINKAGES TO TEACHING

In the main, prominent neuropsychological assessment batteries and diagnostic procedures have been developed and refined over the past 50 years to (1) describe the impact of brain damage or dysfunction on a range of human abilities, (2) reliably differentiate individuals who present with brain damage and dysfunction from those who do not, and (3) discern the specific behavioral effects of different types of neuropathology (e.g., tumor vs. stroke vs. head injury) (Lyon et al., 1988).

The neuropsychology literature frequently reports that these clinical outcomes are realized most effectively when (1) the assessment procedures consist of objective, standardized, and quantitative measures of an individual's structure of neuropsychological ability (Reitan, 1966; Reitan and Wolfson, 1985; Rourke, 1981; Rourke et al., 1986); (2) the assessment procedures include measures that are psychometrically scaled to measure abilities on a continuous scale rather than on an interval scale (Golden et al., 1978); (3) the assessment tasks and measures are valid and reliable reflections of cerebral dysfunction and are not confounded by the effects of age and education (Finlayson et al., 1977); and (4) the assessment tasks sample a broad range of abilities to include measures of general intellectual ability, the ability to retain verbal and nonverbal information, motor and psychomotor abilities, sensory–perceptual functions, receptive and expressive language skills, attentional skills, analytical reasoning, and concept formation, and personality, behavioral, and emotional status (Reitan and Wolfson, 1985).

A number of studies have shown that neuropsychological assessment batteries and allied procedures that have been developed according to these principles are valid for the purpose of identifying the presence of brain damage or dysfunction in both adults (Boll, 1981; Reitan and Davison, 1974) and children (Hynd and Obrzut, 1986; Rourke, 1981; Rourke et al., 1986; Teeter, 1986). Furthermore, some data indicate that widely used neuropsychological batteries (e.g., Halstead–Reitan, Luria–Nebraska) are capable of describing the nature of the neural insult (e.g., type of lesion, site of lesion), particularly when those batteries are applied to adult clinical populations and interpreted by skilled clinicians. Also, some evidence, albeit limited in scope, indicates that the information derived from adult neuropsychological assessment batteries can be useful in constructing some remediation and rehabilitation programs (Diller and Gordon, 1981a,b; Finlayson *et al.*, 1986; Luria, 1966b; Luria and Tzetkova, 1968; Rao and Bieliauskas, 1983).

A. Neuropsychological Models and Assessment Batteries for Children

In general, neuropsychological models of developmental disorders conceptualize a child's learning strengths and weaknesses as manifestations of efficient or inefficient brain regions and/or systems (Gaddes, 1980; Hartlage and Telzrow, 1983; Obrzut and Hynd, 1986; Rourke *et al.*, 1983). A variety of standard neuropsychological batteries as well as selected neuropsychological assessment procedures have been employed to identify patterns of strengths and weaknesses. Selected batteries will be discussed in this section. Emphasis is placed on elucidating the general properties and clinical contributions made by each battery, with respect to their diagnostic validity and ability to forge linkages to treatment. Space limitations preclude comprehensive descriptions of the tasks and tests employed in the batteries. For such details, readers are referred to Boll (1981), Golden *et al.* (1978), Reitan and Davison (1974), Rourke (1981), and Teeter (1986).

1. The Halstead–Reitan Neuropsychological Test Batteries

The Halstead–Reitan assessment procedures (Reitan, R. M., 1979, Reitan Neuropsychological Laboratory) (Boll, 1981; Teeter, 1986) are a mainstay of clinical neuropsychological practice with children. The Halstead–Reitan tests are reportedly sensitive to brain dysfunction in a number of developmental disorders, including asthma (Dunleavy and Baade, 1980), autism (Dawson, 1983), Gilles de la Tourette's syndrome (Bornstein *et al.*, 1983), and epilepsy (Herman, 1982). An abundance of data shows that the Halstead–Reitan batteries are valid for the differential diagnosis of brain damage in children (Boll and Reitan, 1972; Reed *et al.*, 1965). Furthermore, the batteries have been found useful for the neuropsychological classification of minimal brain dysfunction in young children ages 5–8 years (Reitan and Boll, 1973) and LDs in older children (Reitan, 1980; Selz and Reitan, 1979).

The tests and clinical interpretation methods within the Halstead–Reitan Battery for adults have now been extended downward for children between the ages of 5 and 8 years (Reitan, 1979) and ages 9 and 14 years (Reitan and Davison 1974). Hartlage and Hartlage (1977) concluded after review that the tasks designed by Ward Halstead and expanded and revised by Reitan, now form the best and most comprehensive neuropsychological batteries available. In the main, the development and use of the Halstead–Reitan tasks are predicated on the belief that neuropsychological batteries must include procedures that are sensitive to the full range of human adaptive abilities that are subserved by the brain and that are predictably impaired when brain systems are deficient.

A critical element in all phases of the neuropsychological examination, from test selection to clinical interpretation, is the use of several inferential methods. These methods include (1) comparing an individual's performance on the tasks with the performance of an appropriate comparison sample, criterion group, or an absolute standard of expectation; (2) evaluating variations in performance within and between components of a task (e.g., comparing Verbal and Performance IQs); (3) identifying pathognomonic signs that are highly predictive of brain impairment (e.g., aphasia); and (4) comparing the functional efficiency of the two sides of the body. Excellent discussions of these interpretive methods can be found in Boll (1981), Reitan and Davison (1974), and Rourke (1981).

In 1980, Reitan initiated formal attempts to explicitly relate neuropsychological assessment data to treatment, through the development of a program entitled Reitan Evaluation of Hemispheric Abilities and Brain Improvement Training (REHABIT). According to Reitan (1979, 1980), the efficacy of REHABIT for remediation depends on (1) a comprehensive neuropsychological evaluation (by use of the Halstead–Reitan procedures), which clearly identifies areas of brain-related strengths and weaknesses and (2) a determination from the assessment data as to whether the particular neuropsychological deficits reflect specific neural-cognitive deficiencies or generalized cognitive problems affecting several functional systems.

According to Reitan (1980), direct linkages between neurological assessment and treatment are forged by the training concepts inherent in the REHABIT model. For example, REHABIT proposes that the general area of neuropsychological deficit can be directly treated using alternate forms of neuropsychological tests as training sites. According to Alfano and Finlayson (1987), such an approach seems reasonable, because challenging the areas measured by neuropsychological tasks could provide direct stimulation of the wide range of neural functions that they assess. However, as Mann (1979) and Mann and Sabatino (1985) have pointed out, the measurement tools used to assess neuropsychological deficits in children are flawed in the necessary psychometric qualities of reliability and validity. As such, one does not know if the hypothesized underlying neurological processes are being measured appropriately. Moreover, no data exist that indicate that underlying the processes in Reitan's (1980) REHABIT model can be strengthened (even if they can be accurately measured).

Following this general form of deficit training remediation in five specific areas (tracts) uses previously developed educational materials and tasks. The tracts include (1) Tract A, materials to develop expressive and receptive language and verbal skills; (2) Tract B, materials to develop abstract language functions, to include verbal reasoning, verbal concept formation, and verbal organization; (3) Tract C, materials designed to enhance general reasoning capabilities; (4) Tract D, materials for developing abstract, visual–spatial and temporal–sequential concepts; and (5) Tract E, materials designed to promote understanding of basic visual–spatial and manipulation skills. Thus, tracts A and B are generally linked to left hemisphere functions, tracts D and E to right hemisphere functions, and Tract C to general logical analysis and reasoning functions subserved by all functional systems.

Data to support the REHABIT rehabilitation and remediation concepts are difficult to find (Lyon *et al.*, 1988). Reitan (1979, 1980) does report a few case studies, but the information provided in them cannot be construed as empirical validation for the REHABIT model. In fact, reviews of similar neuropsychological process remediation models (Lyon and Moats, 1988; Mann, 1979) have indicated that such practices suffer from a lack of both construct and ecological validity, particularly in their application to children who display academic achievement deficits but do not demonstrate brain injury. In the absence of empirical validation for the REHABIT model, the clinician is ultimately responsible for judging whether or not the time spent in assessment and training activities is in the best interest of the child.

2. Rourke's Neuropsychological Assessment and Treatment Model

Rourke and his colleagues (Rourke *et al.*, 1983, 1986) have argued convincingly that the aims, content, and style of neuropsychological assessments are improved significantly when a comprehensive battery of neuropsychological tasks is administered to children and the data interpreted according to several frames of reference (level of performance, pathognomonic signs, differential (pattern) score approach, pre- and postlesion comparisons of performance on two sides of the body. Rourke's (1975) orientation to assessment practices and the relationship between assessment data and treatment is influenced significantly by Reitan's concepts of neuropsychological measurement and modes of clinical interpretation (see previous discussion and Rourke, 1981).

Rourke *et al.* (1986) propose that linkages between assessment and remediation are best formed when a developmental, neuropsychological model is employed. Within the context of such a model, specific information related to the child's neuropsychological ability structure is collected and interpreted in relation to (1) the immediate demands in the environment (e.g., school and social demands); (2) hypothesized long-range demands (e.g., occupational and social functioning); (3) specific short- and long-term behavioral outcomes that best characterize the child with respect to developmental status, information-processing strengths and weaknesses, and neuropsychological status; (4) based on the above information, an ideal remediation program for the child; and (5) the development of a realistic remediation program, taking into account the child's characteristics and the actual availability of remedial sources for family, school, and child. Rourke's developmental neuropsychological remediation–rehabilitation model appears to have potential for linking assessment data to treatment, because it stresses a comprehensive analysis of the systematic interactions between child variables and environmental factors, and the pragmatics of clinical-service delivery (Lyon *et al.*, 1988).

3. The Luria–Nebraska Neuropsychological Test Batteries

A. R. Luria's (1973, 1980) seminal conceptualization of the human brain as composed of functional systems has led to the development of standardized, neuropsychological assessment batteries for use with both adults and children. The first attempt to organize Luria's clinical assessment methods into a formal test battery was carried out by Anne-Lise Christensen (Teeter, 1986). Charles Golden and his colleagues further refined Luria's procedures into standardized batteries for adults (Golden *et al.*, 1978) and children (Plaisted *et al.*, 1983).

The Luria–Nebraska Neuropsychological Battery for Children (Golden, C. J., 1987, Western Psychological Services) (Plaisted *et al.*, 1983) consists of 11 scales, which assess motor skills, acoustico–motor organization, cutaneous and kinesthetic functions, visual functions, receptive language, expressive language, reading, writing, arithmetic, memory, and intellectual processes. The battery has been found to be sensitive to detecting demonstrable neuroencephalopathy in children (Teeter, 1986). Several recent studies have also shown that the battery can discriminate between LD children and normal-achieving students (Geary and Gilger, 1984; Noland *et al.*, 1983).

To date, no formal attempts have been made to relate assessment data obtained from the Luria–Nebraska program to structure remediation programs for children. However, Luria's (1973) concepts of brain–behavior relationships can be clinically useful if applied to intervention practices in an informed manner. This conclusion may be a reasonable one for at least two reasons. First, Luria's model incorporates concepts related to both brain systems and their development. As such, a dynamic theoretical basis exists from which predictions about outcome and potential for remediation can be made. Second, Luria's model argues that disturbances in complex cognitive functions can be related to a wide variety of brain-related deficiencies. For example, failure to learn to write could be attributable to deficits in any of several brain systems engaged in the regulation of attention, the linking of sounds to symbols, fine motor coordination, and language processing and production. Thus, different children who display written-language deficits might not each respond equally well to the same remediation procedure.

One additional point is in order. Luria (1973, 1980) advocated the use of dynamic, nonstandardized assessment methods that could vary across patients, according to the nature of the clinical question. He supported the use of these procedures with substantial data from clinical case studies. Furthermore, Luria (1963, 1980) presented a rationale for the application of assessment procedures directly to the treatment and rehabilitation process and reported case-history data to substantiate his point of view. Attempts to standardize Luria's dynamic assessment methods may reduce their power in relating assessment findings to treatment-program planning.

However, Naglieri and Das (1988) have argued that Luria's brain–behavior concepts can be measured in a systematic fashion through standardized means. These authors have recently constructed a battery of experimental tests that more accurately assess the functional systems proposed by Luria. Factor analytic studies using these tests suggest that Luria's model can be used to describe children's cognitive competence, particularly in the ability to plan, to process information simultaneously, and to process information successively.

4. The Kaufman Assessment Battery for Children

Another standardized assessment tool that relies on neuropsychological constructs is the Kaufman Assessment Battery for Children (K-ABC; Kaufman, A. S., and Kaufman, N., 1983, American Guidance Service) (Kaufman and Kaufman, 1983). Emphasizing a dual processing model of cognition, the K-ABC test purports to measure simultaneous and successive information-processing strengths and weaknesses in children up to age 12 years. In addition to the Simultaneous and Successive Scales, a third Achievement Test Cluster is used to measure acquired knowledge and verbal learning ability. The test user is then encouraged to formulate hypotheses regarding remediation of academic deficiencies; these hypotheses should emphasize the subject's preferred processing mode. The specificity of these recommendations to academic domains—reading, arithmetic reasoning, and written language—and the well-elaborated models of intervention, which attempt to code both the learner's behavior and the task demands along the simultaneous–sequential dichotomy, is unique to the K-ABC remediation framework (Gunnison, 1984).

Unfortunately, the usefulness of the K-ABC, even for descriptive and classification purposes, has not been uniformly accepted (Lyon and Moats, 1988; Lyon *et al.*, 1988). For example, Sternberg (1984) argued that the test lacks construct validity, a problem that might be related to the author's misrepresentation or misreading of the evidence supporting a simultaneous–sequential processing dichotomy. Furthermore, in equating processing style with scores on selected tasks, the test fails to assess constructs that pertain to dynamic problem-solving. Selecting and conducting remediation on the basis of K-ABC results would thereby be a questionable practice.

Empirical support for remediation based on the K-ABC, as for other neuropsychological approaches reviewed in this chapter, is sparse. Although Gunnison and her colleagues (in press, cited *in* Gunnison, 1984) have shown that children taught with methods described as simultaneous or sequential in emphasis can make meaningful gains in reading, both the assumptions underlying the aptitude-treatment linkages and the data base supporting those assumptions are weak (Ayres and Cooley, 1986). The logical–intuitive classification of children's responses and teaching strategies appears to have most value in its provision of a conceptual framework for diagnostic teaching. The concept of dual processing modes might simply encourage the clinician to behave in a flexible manner when alternative representations of concepts are needed by the learner.

B. Some Conclusions

In summary, neuropsychological assessment may contribute some useful clinical information to an understanding of the learning and behavioral difficulties observed in exceptional children. These clinical contributions most likely will have an impact on the diagnosis and description of neuropathology in pediatric populations. This will be particularly true as additional advances are made in the development and application of neuroimaging procedures (see Section VI).

Unfortunately, the clinical utility and validity of clinical neuropsychological assessment procedures in the design of remediation programs for exceptional children remain sparse (Lyon and Moats, 1988). This limitation appears to exist for several reasons. First, a large portion of the assessment tasks that comprise the most widely used, standardized neuropsychological batteries for children are downward extensions of batteries initially developed and validated on adult clinical populations. This is particularly true of the Halstead Neuropsychological Test Battery for Children (Reitan and Davison, 1974), the Reitan–Indiana Neuropsychological Test Battery (Reitan, 1966), and the Standardized Luria–Nebraska Battery for Children—Revised (Plaisted *et al.*, 1983). Likewise, the type of stimuli (task content) used in tasks to assess specific brain–behavior relationships are downward extensions of stimulus items presented to adults.

These test development practices could seriously compromise a battery's power in predicting which treatment methods are most efficacious for particular children because (1) the tasks employed and their content are primarily based on models of adult brain function and dysfunction that occur following a period of normal development, (2) many tasks are designed to assess the effects of local neuropathology typically seen in adults (e.g., tumors, cerebral vascular accidents, penetrating head wounds) rather than the generalized neural disorders usually observed in children (e.g., closed head injury, anoxia, epilepsy, perinatal trauma), and (3) the neuropsychological tasks' content might have minimal relationship to the ecological demands that the child is facing in home and school environments. For example, even though many widely used children's batteries contain tasks assessing reading, mathematics, and writing skills, such tasks rarely possess adequate content validity. Consider that the Wide Range Achievement Test, a staple of many children's neuropsychological batteries and procedures, assesses only the oral reading of single words, mathematics calculation, and spelling, thus leaving abilities in reading comprehension, math reasoning, and written language open to question.

A second issue, related to the previous points, is that some neuropsychological assessment procedures employed with children use tasks that yield static measures of competence in neuropsychological ability structures. The data obtained from such measures reflect only a child's past and current declarative knowledge of perceptual, linguistic, cognitive, psychomotor, and academic skills, not how they use or do not use such abilities in their daily lives (Brown and Campione, 1986; Lyon *et al.*, 1988). A notable exception is the Category Test, known for its sensitivity to abstract concept formation, mental efficiency, and the ability to assess new learning (Boll, 1981).

Third, there is increasing concern that tasks making up neuropsychological assessment batteries for children primarily assess general cognitive ability, not distinct neuropsychological processes (Hynd and Obrzut, 1986; Seidenberg *et al.*, 1983; Tramontana *et al.*, 1984). If this possibility is true, administering time-consuming batteries beyond administration of a WISC-R (Wechsler intelligence scale for children-revised) can net redundant information. Furthermore, the consistent finding that the WISC-R is not particularly useful for the development of instructional or remediation programs (Ysseldyke and Algozzine, 1982; Ysseldyke and Mirkin, 1981) does not bode favorably for the use of redundant neuropsychological batteries for the same purpose.

Fourth, issues related to development and brain maturation might obscure any possible benefits that accrue from the administration of standard neuropsychological batteries to children for the purpose of treatment-program design. For instance, Hynd and Obrzut (1986) reported that a number of neuropsychological tasks are simply not age-appropriate and that no neuropsychological test battery has established adequate cross-sectioned norms. Furthermore, these authors concluded that without such norms, "it becomes nearly impossible to provide any accurate appraisal for the possible impairment of developing abilities" (Hynd and Obrzut, 1986: 10).

Finally, as Lyon and Flynn (1990) have stressed, describing brain–behavior relationships through the application of assessment procedures does not ensure successful remediation of brain-based deficiencies. For example, neuropsychological assessment can help to clarify the physiological correlates of dyslexia, but altering the underlying neuropathology or identifying alternate intact processing routes might not be possible.

VI. NEURODIAGNOSTIC ADVANCES AND THE STUDY OF LEARNING DISABILITIES

During the past decade, a number of advances have been made in the neurosciences that allow us to better understand how and why differences in brain structure and function are associated with learning abilities and disabilities. The neurodiagnostic procedures that have received the most attention with respect to the study of LDs are (1) topographic brain mapping of electroencephalogram (EEG) data and evoked potential (EP) data, (2) computed tomography (CT) of the head, (3) postmortem anatomical studies of the brain tissue of dyslexic individuals, and (4) magnetic resonance imaging (MRI). Each of these procedures are described below along with a review of findings and necessary caveats.

A. Brain Electrical Activity Mapping

Historically, the use of EEG data in the study of LDs has not yielded information that is reliable enough to be useful for basic research or diagnostic practice with LDs. Recently, however, Duffy and his associates at Harvard Medical School (Duffy et al., 1980) have developed procedures for converting standard EEG and EP data (spatial and temporal waveform data) into color-coded maps. By converting the massive amount of "squiggly" lines of the EEG record into easily read color formats, Duffy has developed an experimental procedure for detecting differences in brain electrical activity between normal readers and dyslexics, between normal subjects and schizo-phrenic patients, and among different forms of brain tumors. This procedure is called brain electrical activity mapping (BEAM).

In one investigation that used BEAM procedures to study neurophysiolog-ical differences between normal and disabled readers, spontaneous EEG and EP data were recorded from good readers and dyslexics as they were engaged in listening, speaking, and reading tasks. The electrophysiological data were then converted into colored map displays, which indicated differences between the normal readers and the dyslexics. The dyslexic subjects in this study were clearly different from their normal-reading counterparts in brain electrical activity associated with the left temporal region, the left parietal region, and the medial frontal area. On the basis of these findings, Duffy hypothesized that the brain electrical differences observed in dyslexics reflected relatively limited activity in the cortical regions usually at work during reading.

While the results of this preliminary study suggest that dyslexic children differ from their normal-reading counterparts on basic measures of neuro-physiological functioning, the data are not strong enough to indicate that this technology can be used to diagnose dyslexia or other forms of LDs. This is the case for several reasons.

First, the Duffy investigation was carried out using extremely small and possibly nonrepresentative samples of LD (dyslexic) and normal readers. Specifically, only eight LD youngsters, between the ages of 9 and 10 years, were included in the study and the diagnosis of dyslexia was based on a child having an IQ in the "normal" range and reading 1.5 years or more below grade level as measured by the Gray Oral Reading Test. The study did not specify what type of IQ measure was employed or whether Full Scale, Verbal, or Performance IQs were used. Furthermore, four of the LD children were identified as right-handed, two as left-handed, and two as ambidextrous. No information was presented indicating whether or not this sample was considered representative of the dyslexic population as a whole. Ten normal readers comprised the control group. While these youngsters were similar to the LD readers in age and socioeconomic status, no direct comparisons of intellectual functioning were carried out.

Second, it must be pointed out that the electrophysiological data base that was used to form the grahic displays and to compare subjects was predicated on the average performance of three LD readers (dyslexics) as compared with the average performance of three control children. At no point was a specific comparison made of the electrophysiological functioning of any individual dyslexic with that of an individual control (normal reader).

Third, to date, no direct replication studies have been reported by Duffy that could indicate whether or not the findings obtained from the children in this investigation continued to occur over time; therefore, verifying the consistency of BEAM data for individual children or, for diagnostic purposes, within LD and normal reading groups is impossible. Readers are referred to Duffy and McAnulty (1985) for continued work in this area.

Finally, as Duane (1986) has pointed out, while the statistical procedures underlying the BEAM technology are both powerful and complex, one cannot be certain at this time whether or not all the appropriate conditions necessary for the application of such statistics have been met. This is particularly the case given the very small sample size studied in the Duffy investigations.

In summary, while the application of BEAM technology to the study of

LDs has led to some exciting preliminary findings, the data are in no way robust enough to warrant conclusions about the brain functioning of LD children or the use of this technology as a standard diagnostic tool.

B. CT Studies

Since 1978, several studies have been carried out using CT scanning techniques to determine if the brains of dyslexic and other LD individuals differed from normal learners with respect to the size and configuration of the cerebral hemispheres. Before discussing these investigations, a brief description of CT scanning procedures is in order.

CT scanning is a radiological technique that painlessly and safely allows visualization of brain structures. The images produced by the CT scanner are generated in the following way. Following the placement of the patient's head into the scanner, an X-ray tube rotates along a circular path. With each sweep of the rotating scanner, X-ray beams are emitted that pass through the skull and brain. The brain tissue absorbs the radiation according to the density of its parts. For example, the gray matter of the brain (nerve cells) differs in density as compared with the white matter of the brain (nerve axons), and healthy tissue has a different density than diseased tissue. By varying the angles of the X-ray beam, it is possible to see layer angles. The reader should keep in mind that the CT scan can only visualize brain structures, not brain function or activity. As such, it produces a static rather than a dynamic image.

CT scanning procedures were applied to the study of dyslexia because of the consistent finding that oral-language deficits tend to accompany reading disorders in a majority of LD children (Johnson and Myklebust, 1967). Given this consistent association between poorly developed linguistic skills and reading ability, researchers hypothesized that LD children may not have adequately developed brain structures in the left hemisphere that are primarily responsible for oral- and written-language behavior. To test this hypothesis, Daniel Hier *et al.* (1978) carried out CT scanning with 24 individuals diagnosed as having developmental dyslexia. The sample of people studied consisted of 22 males and 2 females who ranged in age between 14 and 47 years (mean = 25 years). Their Verbal IQs ranged from 71 to 124 and their Performance IQs ranged from 75 to 120. The criterion for the diagnosis of developmental dyslexia was performance on the Gray Oral Reading Test below the fifth-grade level or a history of reading at least 2 years below grade level while in school.

On the basis of the CT scans, Hier *et al.* (1978) reported that 10 of the subjects showed a reversal of the typical pattern of brain structure asymmetry observed in normal right-handed individuals. Normals typically have a wider left than right parietal-occipital region, but these 10 patients had a wider parietal-occipital region in the right hemisphere than in the left hemisphere. Furthermore, the 10 dyslexics with this reversal of cerebral asymmetry had a lower mean Verbal IQ than the 14 other dyslexics in the study and a history of delay in speech. On the basis of these findings, Hier suggested that the visible reduction in volume in the left hemisphere may reflect a relative risk factor for the development of oral- and written-language skills in the left hemisphere.

Similar reversals of hemispheric assymmetries was reported in a second study of dyslexics carried out by Hier and his colleagues (Rosenberger and Hier, 1980). In this investigation, 53 individuals diagnosed as manifesting school achievements deficits in reading "some time during their school careers" were studied with CT scanning procedures. The CT scans indicated that 22 of the 53 subjects demonstrated reversed asymmetry, i.e., right parietal-occipital regions wider than left. In general, the dyslexic subjects who displayed the reversed asymmetry had a Performance IQ that was, on the average, 16 points higher than the Verbal IQ. As in the study reported earlier, Rosenberger and Hier (1980) concluded that atypical development of structures of the left hemisphere is present in a number of individuals who display reading deficits and, thus, can be considered a risk factor for language delay and later academic failure.

While these findings generated from the use of CT scanning procedures are intriguing, it is very difficult to reach any meaningful conclusions regarding a link between differences in brain structure (e.g., reversed asymmetry) and LDs. In no instance can reversed asymmetry be considered as diagnostic or prognostic of reading disability because a certain proportion of symmetries and reversed asymmetries can be observed in normal readers. Furthermore, the majority of studies using CT scanning procedures with LD individuals have not controlled adequately for age, sex, education, IQ, and socioeconomic status, making any findings literally impossible to replicate or generalize. Thus, any conclusions drawn relative to brain structure and LDs remain tentative at best. Further advances in CT techniques and the application of higher-resolution procedures (e.g., MRI) may clarify to what extent anatomical asymmetry correlates with language development and reading ability.

C. Postmortem Cytoarchitectonic Studies

Recently, a series of studies have been reported that indicates that dyslexic individuals manifest abnormalities in the nerve tissue of brain structures involved in oral and written language. In 1968, Drake presented the first postmortem report on the brain of a dyslexic individual. He reported excessive numbers of neurons within the subcortical white matter of the posterior left cortex of a child with a history of developmental reading disorder. Subsequently, Galaburda and Kemper (1979) performed a detailed gross and microscopic analysis of the cerebral nervous system of a 20-year-old dyslexic who died from an accidental fall. They noted two types of brain abnormality in this individual. First, there was an anomalous pattern of cerebral lateralization in that the white matter (nerve axons) of the left hemisphere was larger than the right from front to back, which differs from the pattern of normal asymmetrics. Second, the left hemisphere of this dyslexic was abnormal in the regions responsible for some language functions. Specifically, deficient neuronal migration and incomplete layering and abnormal folding of the cortex in the region of the left temporal lobe were noted.

It is very difficult to generalize the findings of these postmortem case studies to all individuals who have language and reading deficits. The findings do represent the possibility that a relationship exists between gross and microscopic neuroanatomy and human behavior (e.g., reading). Furthermore, additional studies carried out by Geschwind and Galaburda (1985) indicate that genetic and/or immunological factors underlie aberrant neural cell migration patterns in LD individuals. Needless to say, these neuroanatomical and neurophysiological findings of neurobiologic deviation in dyslexics remain only suggestive of brain–behavior relationships, which hopefully can be clarified with many decades of future research.

D. MRI Studies

MRI images, generated radio frequency pulses within a magnetic field, are visually similar to CT scans, but with superior resolution. Additionally, MRI procedures do not require X-irradiation and therefore would be preferable in pediatric studies. Disadvantages of MRI procedures include cost and closeness of the chamber, which youngsters may find frightening.

Because of the technical advantages of MRI technology over other neuroimaging procedures, a number of researchers have begun to use MRI scans in research with LD children. For example, Hynd and Semrund-Clikman (1989) reported that MRI studies of LD youngsters indicated that specific areas of dyslexics' brains are smaller than those of normal children. Hynd found that the size differences were primarily confined to brain regions implicated in language and the regulation of motor control and attention.

The MRI studies conducted by Hynd are the best-designed investigations carried out to date and are the first to include well-defined groups of reading-disabled children (dyslexics), children with attentional deficits, and normal youngsters. Unfortunately, at the present time it is not known how brain size (morphology) differences are related to learning and behavioral difficulties. It is also not clearly understood why the abnormal brain morphology is present in LD individuals. Some researchers argue that the brain size differences are due to genetic differences, while others report that environmental toxins or impairments in the immune system are the primary culprits.

What is clear is that the study of the neurological origins of learning and behavioral differences in children can ultimately help us understand why some youngsters are not able to attend, listen, speak, read, or write effectively. Once we have this knowledge, new possibilities for prevention, identification, and treatment emerge. Interested readers are referred to Hynd and Semrud-Clikman (1989) for a thorough review of neurodiagnostic studies with LD individuals.

VII. NEUROPSYCHOLOGICAL SUBTYPING RESEARCH AND RELATIONSHIPS TO INTERVENTION

It is widely recognized that there are many different types of LDs, rather than one global picture of neuropsychological strengths and weaknesses that applies to all LD children. Current space does not permit a thorough review of the wide variety of LDs subtypes that have been proposed in the LDs literature in recent years, and the interested reader is referred to several recent reviews (Hooper and Willis, 1989; Newby and Lyon, in press). One example of a subtype scheme that has been proposed is that children with specific reading disabilities can be divided into one of two categories, although this grouping is by no means universally accepted or thoroughly validated. One group has problems learning basic phonics rules or difficulties with other language-related aspects of the reading process; this type is often termed auditory–linguistic because of their weakness in linguistic areas. The other group has problems with visual aspects of reading, such as the development of an efficient sight-word vocabulary, and is called visuo–spatial (Hynd and Cohen, 1983; Pirozzolo, 1979).

One of the most important reasons for defining subgroups of children within the overall LD population is that children with different neuropsychological patterns would be presumed to benefit from different types of educational interventions. For instance, children who have problems applying phonics rules in reading may need very different teaching methods than children who have problems developing an efficient sight-word vocabulary. Unfortunately, relatively little research has been conducted on the effectiveness of different teaching methods with different types of LD children, in contrast with the more voluminous research attempting to describe these children's underlying mental processing deficits and behavioral characteristics. One reason for this lack of treatment outcome research is that carefully designed intervention studies require considerable time, organization, and effort to validly answer the question of which treatments work best for which types of children.

For purposes of illustration, three research programs that have examined the differential response of neuropsychologically relevant subtypes of LDs to different treatment programs will be described. All three programs have hypothesized and/or lent at least tentative support to an important concept that has become increasingly prevalent in LDs research in recent years. This concept is that LD children may be unlikely to benefit from direct remediation or attempts to correct their basic underlying areas of mental processing weakness (e.g., phonics in many auditory–linguistic reading-disabled children). Rather, they may need to be taught to use relatively more preserved areas of mental processing strength to *compensate* for the learning deficits (e.g., emphasizing sight-word development in children with phonics weaknesses). A review of these programs will also provide representative examples of subtype schemes that have been proposed in the recent literature.

A. Lovett and Colleagues' Investigations

Lovett (1984, 1987) proposed two subtypes of reading disability, building on the theory that word recognition develops in three successive phases. In the first phase, children learn to "sound out" words accurately. Next comes automatic recognition without the need to sound out words. Finally, experienced readers develop maximum speed as components of the reading process become consolidated in memory (Ehri and Wilce, 1983). Children who fail at the first phase are labeled accuracy-disabled, and those who achieved age-appropriate word recognition but are markedly deficient in phases two or three are called rate-disabled. In Lovett's research program, these two groups are carefully diagnosed using a large number of reading tests. Research on these two groups has indicated that reading comprehension is globally impaired for the accuracy-disabled group and is highly correlated with word-recognition skill, but the rate-disabled group is impaired on only some comprehension measures (Lovett, 1987).

In a well-designed, large intervention study ($n = 110$) (Lovett, 1988; Lovett *et al.*, 1988), the two subtypes responded differently to various treatment methods. The treatments consisted of (1) a decoding skills (DS) program, which emphasized single-word recognition for both phonetically regular and exception words; (2) an oral- and written-language skills (OWLS) program, which stressed contextual reading, listening, and reading comprehension, vocabulary development, syntactical elaboration, and written composition; and (3) a classroom survival skills (CSS) program, which involved social skills, organizational strategies, and other instruction unrelated to reading development. The CSS program served as a control condition for nonspecific treatment effects. Word recognition improved significantly for both (accuracy- and rate-disabled) groups in the DS program, but only the rate-disabled group benefited substantially from the OWLS program. These findings suggested that children need better-developed overall language disabilities to benefit from OWLS as compared with DS.

In an expanded study with a larger sample ($n = 178$) (Lovett *et al.*, 1989), the DS program yielded greater generalization of word-recognition skills than the OWLS program. However, this was not attributable to gains in knowledge of grapheme–phoneme correspondence rules, as the latter did not change. Thus, familiarity with orthographic patterns may have produced greater generalization. Vocabulary knowledge improvements in the OWLS program were limited to words that were directly trained, but these gains could not be detected on standardized tests of the same skills. Interestingly, the two subtypes did not respond very differently to the different treatment methods in this study.

Lovett's subtype scheme is based on a well-defined theory of reading development, but this scheme does not refer as directly to neuropsychological concepts as the next program to be described. One of the main strengths of her program is her carefully designed intervention studies. Support for the idea that different subtypes respond differently to disparate treatments is mixed with this program.

B. Lyon and Colleagues' Cluster and Educational Validation Studies

Lyon and coworkers defined six reading-disability subtypes with cluster analyses of neuropsychological tests on 150 11- and 12-year-olds (Lyon and Watson, 1981). Cluster analysis is a sophisticated statistical method that groups subjects with similar patterns of strengths and weaknesses on a battery of tests. The theoretical viewpoint guiding this subtype research was based on Luria's (1966, 1973) notion that reading ability is a complex behavior effected by means of a complex functional system of cooperating zones of the cerebral cortex and subcortical structures. Within the context of this theoretical framework, a deficit in any one or several zones of the functional system in the brain may impede the acquisition of fluent reading behavior. As such, one could hypothesize the existence of several subtypes of disabled readers, each characterized by different patterns of neuropsychological deficits in subskills relevant to reading acquisition (i.e., linguistic abilities, perceptual skills, attentional mechanisms). A brief description of the six subtypes' information-processing characteristics is provided here. Readers are referred to cited references for specific details.

Children who were assigned empirically to subtype 1 ($n = 10$) exhibited significant deficits in language comprehension, the ability to blend phonemes, visual–motor integration, visual–spatial skills, and visual–memory skills, with strengths in naming and auditory discrimination skills. Analysis of the reading and spelling errors made by members of subtype 1 indicated significant deficits in the development of both sight-word vocabulary and word-attack skills.

Children in subtype 2 ($n = 12$) also exhibited a pattern of mixed deficits but in a milder form than that observed in subtype 1. Specifically, significant problems in language comprehension, auditory memory span, and visual–motor integration were observed and may have been related to the reading problems of these subjects. No deficits were seen in these youngsters' performance on naming, auditory discrimination, sound blending, visual–spatial, and visual memory tasks. Subtype 2 members produced mixed orthographic and phonetic errors when reading but to a much milder degree than did subtype 1 children.

Members of subtype 3 ($n = 12$) manifested selective deficits in language comprehension and sound blending, with corresponding strengths in all other linguistic and visual–perceptual skills measured. The oral reading errors made by subtype 3 youngsters were primarily phonetic in nature, as would be expected from their diagnostic profile.

Children in subtype 4 ($n = 32$) displayed significant deficiencies on a visual–motor integration task and average performance on all other measures. These youngsters presented with an assorted sample of oral reading errors, although most errors were made when attempting to read phonetically irregular words.

Subtype 5 ($n = 12$) members displayed significant deficits in language comprehension, auditory memory span, and sound blending, with corresponding strengths in all measured visual–perceptual and visual–motor skills. These characteristics appeared related to the severity of their oral reading and written spelling errors. The major academic characteristic that distinguished subtype 5 youngsters from other children was their consistently poor application of word-attack (phonetic) skills to the reading and spelling process.

The pattern of scores obtained by members of subtype 6 ($n = 16$) indicated a normal diagnostic profile. These results were unexpected. It is quite possible that these children were reading poorly for reasons that were not detected by the assessment battery.

In a related program of research carried out with younger disabled readers (mean age = 8.1 years) (Lyon, 1985b; Lyon et al., 1982), five LD subtypes were identified and validated internally and externally by using different variable subtests, clustering algorithms, and subtype-by-teaching method interaction studies. Again, a brief description of each of the subtypes' information-processing characteristics is provided.

Children assigned to subtype 1 ($n = 18$) manifested significant deficits in visual perception, visual–spatial analysis and reasoning, and visual–motor integration. Visual memory was also below average, but not significantly so. All measured linguistic and verbal expressive skills were within the average range. The reading errors made by members of subtype 1 appeared to be related to their diagnostic profile. Frequent mispronunciations due to confusion of orthographically similar words were noted, as were reading errors involving medial vowels and vowel combinations.

Children in subtype 2 ($n = 10$) displayed selective deficits in morphosyntactic skills, sound blending, language comprehension, auditory memory span, auditory discrimination, and naming ability, with corresponding strengths in all measured visual–perceptual skills. These deficits across linguistic and verbal memory span domains appeared to seriously impede their ability to decode single words and to apply decoding principles to the pronunciation of nonsense words.

Members of subtype 3 ($n = 12$) scored in the normal range on all diagnostic measures and, thus, can be compared with subjects in the subtype identified by Lyon and Watson (1981) that scored significantly below normal on reading tasks without concomitant low performance on the diagnostic test battery. It is possible that members of subtype 3 read inefficiently for social or affective reasons rather than because of inherent oral-language or perceptual deficiencies. It is also quite possible that the diagnostic battery employed did not assess effectively all skills relevant to the developmental reading process. As was the case with Lyon and Watson's (1981) subtype 6 (normal diagnostic profile), members of subtype 3 scored higher than all other subgroups on the reading measures. These youngsters did have relatively more difficulties in comprehending reading passages than in the other measured reading skills. No systematic patterns of errors could be identified from analysis of their performance on word-recognition and word-attack measures.

Children in subtype 4 ($n = 15$) displayed significant deficiencies in sound blending, language comprehension, auditory memory span, naming ability, and some aspects of visual perception. The difficulties manifested by subtype 4 members in remembering, analyzing, synthesizing, and correctly sequencing verbal information appeared to have a significant effect on their ability to decode phonetically regular real and nonsense words.

Members of subtype 5 ($n = 9$) manifested significant mixed deficits in morphosyntactic skills, sound blending, visual perception, visual–motor integration, visual–spatial analysis, and visual memory. These youngsters committed primarily orthographic errors when reading single words (both real and nonsense), possibly reflecting the influence of deficiencies in visual–verbal analysis and memory.

Following the identification of subtypes of the older and younger LD readers, the Lyon group conducted a series of subtype intervention studies.

With the older LD group, Lyon (1983) matched samples of five children from each of six subtypes and then provided 1 hour per week of reading instruction in a phonics-based approach for 26 weeks. The subtypes with isolated visual–motor deficits and normal neuropsychological profiles were the only ones to show significant gains in individual word recognition after instruction. It was hypothesized that an absence of auditory–verbal deficits was associated with better response to linguistically–phonetically oriented intervention.

The intervention study with the younger LD readers (Lyon, 1985a) used only the subtype with selective linguistic and verbal expressive deficits, in the context of robust visual–perceptual–motor–memory strengths. Ten subjects were randomly assigned to one of two different 30-hour treatment programs over a 10-week period. The first program was phonics-oriented. The second combined rapid whole-word recognition, syntactic analysis of suffixes, and emphasis on metalinguistic awareness that reading is a meaningful language skill. Over the course of instruction, children in the combined method gained an average of 11 percentile points in word recognition versus 1 percentile point for the phonics group; these differences were statistically significant. Apparently, the auditory receptive and auditory expressive language deficits that characterized the children impeded response to a reading instructional method that required learning letter–sound correspondences in isolation followed by blending and contextual reading components. Whole-word reading may have placed less linguistic demand on these readers.

Several limitations of these outcome studies must be acknowledged. First, pragmatics of subject availability necessitated small sample sizes. Second, it is difficult to determine if the effects should be attributed to subtype characteristics, the instructional program, the interaction between the two, the teacher, the time spent in remediation, or previous or concomitant educational experience. Third, as with all battery-based subtype definitions, probably not all relevant mental-processing variables were tested and considered in defining the subtypes. For instance, Lyon's program focused much more on the underlying neuropsychological variables in defining subtype, in contrast with Lovett's focus on direct reading-related variables such as accuracy and rate of word recognition. Nonetheless, these studies represent an important beginning in the important task of determining the pragmatic instructional implications of LD subtype research.

C. The Milwaukee Dyslexia Instruction and Research Program

The Milwaukee Dyslexia Instruction and Research Program hypothesizes two main subtypes of disabled readers, conceptually similar to the auditory–linguistic versus visuo–spatial dichotomy mentioned above. The first subtype, termed phonological dyslexics, has predominant problems with phonics analysis. The second subtype, termed orthographic dyslexics, is relatively stronger in phonics but has problems developing an efficient sight-word vocabulary. In this context, and in most usage of the term in the current literature, *dyslexia* refers to a specific learning disability in the area of reading. Unfortunately, the term dyslexia has been too broadly applied to a wide range of problems in the past and is often misunderstood among both professionals and the public. It is acknowledged that mixed children with deficits in both areas also exist, but the children have not been studied directly to date in this program.

An instruction program was designed to emphasize the development of reading comprehension strategies. In an attempt to dedicate more attention to the critical higher-order reading processes that strengthen meaning acquisition, this program combines training in basic word recognition, comprehension, and strategies for reading. Training in word recognition alone has been painfully slow or limited in successfully remediating dyslexia in previous research. The question of how much higher-order instruction dyslexics can productively use has yet to be answered, although some of Lovett *et al.*'s (1988) findings have suggested that some type of dyslexics fail to benefit from a complex whole-language type of approach.

The Milwaukee program embodies several pragmatic assumptions and educational values. First, reading is thought to be ultimately a meaning-acquisition process, so both word recognition and comprehension should be crucial aspects of instruction programs. Second, teaching methods used were relevant and available to the typical LDs or reading specialist in schools. Third, diagnostic criteria were designed using established, reliable clinical instruments. This was done to maximize applicability and to take advantage of presently available normative data rather than relying on experimental tests.

In the first intervention study (Caldwell *et al.*, 1987; Newby *et al.*, 1989a, b; Recht *et al.*, 1988), two treatment methods were designed to match each subtype's presumed processing strengths. These methods were applied in twice-weekly 60-minute individual tutoring sessions with reading specialists. Certain general procedures were the same for both methods. Each session focused on one 200- to 800-word narrative story at the child's reading instructional level and on three to five vocabulary words that had been preselected to be among the most meaning-bearing unit in the story and that the child could not read in isolation. Reading comprehension was emphasized by teaching children "story grammar mapping." Story grammar (Bakker and Stein, 1978) describes the parts of a well-formed story: setting, characters, problem, events, and resolution of the problem. These parts are intuitively understood by adults (Stein, 1979) but not well understood or utilized by children (Spiegel and Fitzgerald, 1986). Explicit instruction and directed practice in selecting and recording the story grammar elements has enhanced the reading comprehension of average readers (Whaley, 1981) and generally poor readers (Fitzgerald and Spiegel, 1983) but has not been studied with a specific dyslexic population. Tutors placed an emphasis on teaching children to be strategic in their reading, to solve problem, to verbalize processes that have been efficient for them, and to use a meaning-vocabulary approach to new words. Their conscious recall of these metacognitive elements of the instruction was assessed periodically. In instruction for phonological dyslexics, children were taught to first focus on the main idea or gestalt of the story, then to visually image the story, and then to draw or outline the story on key cards in any order. Word instruction was a multisensory sight-word approach using visual–auditory and tracing elements. In instruction for orthographic dyslexics, children verbally rehearsed the story and mapped the essential elements in sequential order. Word instruction was a phonics approach emphasizing word sounds, roots, and blending. In both methods, teachers used the initial stories to illustrate each component and then gradually shifted responsibility for identification to the students.

An initial study (Caldwell *et al.*, 1987; Newby *et al.*, 1989a) demonstrated significant treatment gains in reading comprehension for four out of five subjects using a single-subject multiple baseline design (Barlow and Hersen, 1984). Subtype assignment at this stage of the project relied primarily on the Boder test (Boder and Jarrico, 1982), which has been supplemented with other measures in later stages of the project, as outlined below. Baseline treatment consisted of two to six 1-hour individual tutoring sessions with traditional remedial reading methods. Experimental treatment involved 8–12 sessions using only the treatment type matched to each subject's strength, thus whether treatment effects were attributable to a specific strength-matched method or to strategies instruction in general is unknown. It should also be noted that three of the four subjects who improved were in the orthographic subtype, suggesting that this group may be easier to help than those with core phonological problems. Another limitation of this study was that the small number of available subjects prevented the evaluation of more than one treatment method with children from each subtype.

A larger study currently in progress has the following parameters. Subjects are 92 children aged 8-11 years who meet historically conventional criteria for diagnosis of dyslexia. All have average intelligence and marked delay on a number of reading measures, including word recognition and passage comprehension. Children with primary emotional–behavioral disturbance, uncorrected vision or hearing problems, or inadequate educational opportunity were excluded.

Subtype was assigned on the basis of scores on tests of word attack (reading nonsense word), spelling errors, and the balance of phonetically regular words (looks like it sounds; e.g., "bat") versus irregular words (does not look like it sounds; e.g. "right") read correctly in list format. The two groups are not significantly different in age (mean age = 9.5 years; range = 7.4–11.3), sex (80% male), grade placement (mean grade = 3.2; range = 2–6), overall reading instructional level (mean level = second grade; range = preprimer to third grade), or socioeconomic status (mean status [Hollingshead 4-factor] = 44; range = 23–66). Several measures of phonological and orthographic processing skills, such as oral-word segmentation and reintegration, are being used to test the validity of the subtypes in reference to underlying neuropsychological processes. In addition, BEAM procedures during rest, reading, and orthographic and phonological nonword-identification tasks were being used to compare the two subtypes and two normal control groups (age-matched and reading-level matched) on EEG and EP-related measures.

Treatment outcome is investigated by randomly assigning subjects to one of three treatment conditions, i.e. 12 weeks of twice-weekly 1-hour individual tutoring sessions using the two different methods outlined above *or* a 12-week period of no intervention (control condition). Control for concurrent classroom instruction in school programs is not practical, and effects of ongoing classroom instruction are assumed to be randomly distributed across groups and conditions. Multiple tests of reading skills are taken before and after treatment, including standardized tests of word identification, word attack, and passage comprehension; reading accuracy, speed, and comprehension from full-length stories that were constructed specifically for this study; and analysis of the children's oral reading errors. Diagnostic stability over time is being assessed by re-administering all diagnostic instruments at program exit. In general, it is hypothesized that subjects will maintain their initial subtype status in spite of treatment interventions, although changes in reading level may move some subjects out of the initial diagnostic criteria range.

The Milwaukee program illustrates the use of commonly employed reading instruction methods with carefully defined and diagnosed subtypes of disabled readers. Program data will be analyzed in several ways, to test the validity of an increasingly popular notion in LDs subtype research, i.e., that LD children differ from each other along dimensions, rather than falling into discrete, clearly separated groups. Stanovich (Stanovich, 1988) has been among the most vocal proponents of this view and argues that children with specific reading disabilities or dyslexia differ from "garden-variety" poor readers primarily on the dimension of phonological processing skill. The Milwaukee program needs to be expanded to consider children with mixed phonologic–orthographic deficits, younger disabled readers, and group as well as individual instruction formats.

VIII. SUMMARY

The neuropsychological study of learning and attentional disorders can ultimately help us better understand the biobehavioral factors that impede school learning. Through neuropsychological studies, we are hopeful that the etiologies for LDs and learning disorders may be discovered. For instance, advances in neuroimaging technology now allow us to study brain development in exciting new ways. Moreover, some neuropsychological assessment models and frameworks are proving to have some practical benefits in guiding practitioners in the choice and application of remediation strategies, particularly in the area of reading disorders.

Despite these positive strides in the use of neuropsychological assessment models, treatment strategies, and neurodiagnostic technology, the development of a neuropsychology of LDs remains an experimental endeavor. A number of obstacles continue to limit the reliability, validity, and generalizability of neuropsychological studies. For example, clearly lacking in most neuropsychological studies of LDs are adequate descriptions of the sample under study. Thus, generalization and replicability of findings are problematic. In addition, the valid measurement of neuropsychological aptitudes is in an embryonic stage, making the prediction of response to various forms of teaching or treatment extremely difficult.

Neuropsychology also has to contend with other limitations when applied to the study of children with LDs. First, children and their nervous systems are constantly changing as they mature, making measurement of neuropsychological status a tenuous process at best. Moreover, the effects of neural disease or lesions on children vary greatly with age. As such, predicting which behavior will be most seriously affected and which abilities can be developed and/or rehabilitated is difficult. Additionally, we must remember that children develop within the everchanging context of their environment. Thus, two children with similar LDs at age 7 years may show significantly different neuropsychological profiles at 10 years of age due to different teaching programs and the intensity and duration of remediation. This range of available services and remediation efforts make generalizations to children even within a specific age group difficult.

In summary, the application of neuropsychological principles, assessment tools, remediation models, and basic neuroscientific technology can surely enhance our efforts to understand why LDs occur and what we can do to help LD children. At present, neuropsychology is having its greatest impact in developing an understanding of the biological factors involved in human learning. Some progress, albeit limited in nature, is being made in using neuropsychological assessment data to help construct effective teaching programs.

References

Alfano, D. P., and Finlayson, M. A. K. (1987). Clinical neuropsychology in rehabilitation. *Clin. Neuropsycholog.* **1,** 105–123.

Ayres, R. R., and Cooley, E. K. J. (1986). Sequential versus simultaneous processing on the K-ABC: Validity in predicting learning success. *J. Psychoeduc. Assess.* **4,** 211–220.

Bakker, L., and Stein, N. (1978). The development of prose comprehension skills. *In* "Children's Prose Comprehension: Research and Practice" pp. 230–257. (C. Santa and B. Hayes, eds.). International Reading Association, Newark, Delaware.

Barlow, D. H., and Hersen, M. (1984). "Single Case Experimental Designs: Strategies for Studying Behavior Change," 2nd ed. Permagon Press, New York.

Boder, E., and Jarrico, S. (1982). "The Boder Test of Reading–Spelling Patterns: A Diagnostic Screening Test for Subtypes of Reading Disability." Grune & Stratton, New York.

Boll, T. J. (1981). The Halstead–Reitan Neuropsychological Test Battery. *In* "Handbook of Clinical Neuropsychology" (S. B. Filskov and T. J. Boll, eds.), pp. 577–607. John Wiley & Sons, New York.

Boll, T. J., and Reitan, R. M. (1972). Comparative ability interrelationships in normal and brain-damaged children. *J. Clin. Psychol.* **28,** 152–156.

Bornstein, R. A., King, G., and Carroll, A. (1983). Neuropsychological abnormalities in Gille de la Tourette's syndrome. *J. Nerv. Ment. Dis.* **171,** 497–502.

Brown, A. L., and Campione, J. C. (1986). Psychological theory and the study of learning disabilities. *Am. Psycholog.* **14,** 1059–1068.

Caldwell, J., Recht, D. R., and Newby, R. F. (1987). Improving the reading comprehension of dysphonetic and dyseidetic dyslexics using story grammar. Paper presented at the Third World Congress on Dyslexia (June, 1987), Chania, Greece.

Dawson, G. (1983). Lateralized brain dysfunction in autism: Evidence from the Halstead–Reitan Neuropsychological Battery. *J. Autism Dev. Disorder* **13,** 269–286.

Diller, L., and Gordon, W. A. (1981a). Intervention for cognitive deficits in brain-injured adults. *J. Consult. Clin. Psychol.* **49,** 822–839.

Diller, L., and Gordon, W. A. (1981b). Rehabilitation and clinical neuropsychology. *In* "Handbook of Clinical Neuropsychology" (S. B. Filskov and T. J. Boll, eds.), pp. 702–733. John Wiley & Sons, New York.

Duane, D. (1986). Neurodiagnostic tools in dyslexic syndromes in children: Pitfalls and proposed comparative study of computed tomography, nuclear magnetic resonance and brain electrical activity mapping. *In* "Dyslexia: Its Neuropsychology and Treatment" (G. Pavlidis and D. Fisher, eds.), pp. 65–86. John Wiley & Sons, New York.

Duffy, F. H., and McAnulty, G. B. (1985). Brain electrical activity in mapping (BEAM): The search for a physiology signature of dyslexia. *In* "Dyslexia: A Neuroscientific

Approach to Clinical Evaluation" (F. H. Duffy and N. Geschwind, eds.), pp. 105–122. Little Brown and Co., Boston.

Duffy, F. H., Denckla, M. B., Bartell, R. H., and Sandini, G. (1980). Dyslexia: Regional differences in brain electrical activity by topographic mapping. *Ann. Neurol.* **5,** 412–420.

Dunleavy, R. A., and Baade, L. A. (1980). Neuropsychological correlates of severe asthma in children 9–14 years old. *J. Consult. Clin. Psychol.* **48,** 564–577.

Ehri, L. C., and Wilce, L. S. (1983). Development of word identification speed in skilled and less skilled beginning readers. *J. Educ. Psychol.* **75,** 3–18.

Finlayson, M. A. J., Johnson, K. A., and Reitan, R. M. (1977). Relationship of level of education to neuropsychological measures in brain-damaged and non brain-damaged adults. *J. Consult. Clin. Psychol.* **45,** 536–542.

Finlayson, M. A. J., Gowland, C., and Basmajian, J. V. (1986). Neuropsychological predictors of treatment response following stroke. *J. Clin. Exp. Neuropsychol.* **7,** 647. [Abstract.]

Fitzgerald, J., and Spiegel, D. (1983). Enhancing children's reading comprehension through instruction in narrative structure. *J. Read. Behav.* **15,** 1–17.

Gaddes, W. H. (1980). "Learning Disabilities and Brain Function: A Neuropsychological Approach." Springer-Verlag, New York.

Galaburda, A., and Kemper, T. L. (1979). Cytoarchitectonic abnormalities in developmental dyslexia: A case study. *Ann. Neurol.* **6,** 94–100.

Geary, D. C., and Gilger, J. W. (1984). The Luria Nebraska Neuropsychological Battery-Children's Revision: Comparison of learning disabled and normal children matched on Full Scale IQ. *Percep. Motor Skills* **58,** 115–118.

Geschwind, N., and Galaburda, A. (1985). Cerebral lateralization: Biological mechanisms, associations, and pathology: A hypothesis and a program for research. *Arch. Neurol.* **42,** 428–654.

Golden, C. J., Hammeke, T., and Purische, H. (1978). Diagnostic validity of a standardized neuropsychological battery derived from Luria's neuropsychological tests. *J. Consult. Clin. Psychol.* **46,** 1258–1265.

Gunnison, J. A. (1984). Developing educational intervention from assessments involving the K-ABC. *J. Special Educ.* **18,** 325–344.

Hartlage, C., and Hartlage, P. L. (1977). Application of neuropsychological principles in the diagnosis of learning disabilities. *In* "Brain Function and Reading Disabilities" (L. Tarnapol and M. Tarnapol, eds.), pp. 72–89. University Park Press, Baltimore.

Hartlage, L. C., and Telzrow, K. F. (1983). The neuropsychological basis of education intervention. *J. Learn. Disabil.* **16,** 521–526.

Herman, B. P. (1982). Neuropsychological function and psychopathology in children with epilepsy. *Epilepsia* **23,** 545–554.

Hier, D. B., LeMay, M., Rosenberger, P. B., and Perlo, V. P. (1978). Developmental dyslexia: Evidence for a subgroup with a reversal of cerebral asymmetry. *Arch. Neurol.* **35,** 90–92.

Hooper, S. R., and Willis, W. G. (1989). "Learning Disability Subtyping: Neuropsychological Foundations, Conceptual Models, and Issues in Clinical Differentiation." Springer-Verlag, New York.

Hynd, G. W., and Cohen, M. J. (1983). "Dyslexia: Neuropsychological Theory, Research, and Clinical Differentiation." Grune & Stratton, New York.

Hynd, G. W., and Obrzut, J. E. (1986). Clinical child neuropsychology: Issues and perspectives. *In* "Child Neuropsychology," Vol. 2 (J. E. Obrzut and G. W. Hynd, eds.), pp. 3–14. Academic Press, Orlando, Florida.

Hynd, G. W., and Semrud-Clikman, M. (1989). Dyslexia and brain morphology. *Psycholog. Bull.* **106**, 447–482.

Johnson, D. J., and Myklebust, H. R. (1967). "Learning Disabilities: Educational Principles and Practices." Grune & Stratton, New York.

Kaufman, A. S., and Kaufman, N. L. (1983). "Kaufman Assessment Battery for Children: Interpretive Manual." American Guidance Service, Circle Pines, Minnesota.

Lovett, M. W. (1984). A developmental perspective on reading dysfunction: Accuracy and rate criteria in the subtyping of dyslexic children. *Brain Lang.* **22**, 67–91.

Lovett, M. W. (1987). A developmental approach to reading disability: Accuracy and speed criteria of normal and deficient reading skill. *Child Dev.* **58**, 234–260.

Lovett, M. W. (1988). Subtypes of reading disabilities. Paper presented at the First Annual Conference on Research and Theory in Learning Disabilities (May 1988), University Park, Pennsylvania.

Lovett, M. W., Ransby, M. J., Hardwick, N., and Johnson, M. S. (1989). Can dyslexia be treated? Treatment-specific and generalized treatment effects in dyslexic children's response to remediation. *Brain Lang.* **37**, 90–121.

Luria, A. R. (1966). "Higher Cortical Functions in Man." Basic Books, New York.

Luria, A. R. (1973). "The Working Brain: An Introduction to Neuropsychology." Basic Book, New York.

Luria, A. R. (1980). "Higher Cortical Functions in Man," 2nd ed. Basic Books, New York.

Luria, A. R., and Tzetkova, L. S. (1968). The re-education of brain-damaged patients and its psychopedagogical application. *In* "Learning Disorders" (J. Hellmuth, ed.), pp. 139–154. Special Child Publications, Seattle, Washington.

Lyon, G. R. (1983). Subgroups of learning disabled readers: Clinical and empirical identification. *In* "Progress in Learning Disabilities," Vol. 5 (H. R. Myklebust, ed.), pp. 103–134. Grune & Stratton, New York.

Lyon, G. R. (1985a). Educational validation of learning disability subtypes. *In* "Neuropsychology of Learning Disabilities: Essentials of Subtype Analysis" (B. P. Rourke, ed.), pp. 228–256. Guilford Press, New York.

Lyon, G. R. (1985b). Identification and remediation of learning disability subtypes: Preliminary findings. *Learn. Disabil. Focus* **1**, 21–35.

Lyon, G. R., and Flynn, J. (1990). Assessing subtypes of learning abilities. *In* "Handbook on the Assessment of Learning Disabilities: Theory, Research, and Practice" (H. L. Swanson, ed.), pp. 59–74. College Hill Press, San Diego, California.

Lyon, G. R., and Moats, L. (1988). Critical issues in the instruction of the learning disabled. *J. Consult. Clin. Psychol.* **56**, 830–835.

Lyon, G. R., and Watson, B. L. (1981). Empirically derived subgroups of learning disabled readers: Diagnostic characteristics. *J. Learn. Disabil.* **14**, 256–261.

Lyon, G. R., Stewart, N., and Freedman, D. (1982). Neuropsychological characteristics of subgroups of learning disabled readers. *J. Clin. Neuropsychol.* **4**, 343–365.

Lyon, G. R., Moats, L. E., and Flynn, J. M. (1988). From assessment to treatment:

Linkage to interventions with children. *In* "Issues in Child Neuropsychology: From Assessment to Treatment" (M. Tramontana and S. Hooper, eds.), pp. 113–142. Plenum Press, New York.

Mann, L. (1979). "On the Trail or Process." Grune & Stratton, New York.

Mann, L., and Sabatino, D. A. (1985). "Foundations of Cognitive Process in Remedial and Special Education." Aspen, Rockville, Maryland.

Naglieri, J. A., and Das, J. P. (1988). Planning—arousal—simultaneous—successive (PASS): A model for assessment. *J. School Psychol.* **26,** 35–48.

Newby, R. F., and Lyon, G. R. (in press). Neuropsychological subtypes of learning disabilities. *In* "Advances in the Neuropsychology of Learning Disabilities: Issues, Methods and Practice" (J. E. Obrzut and G. W. Hynd, eds.). Academic Press, New York.

Newby, R. F., Caldwell, J., and Recht, D. R. (1989a). Improving the reading comprehension of children with dysphonetic and dyseidetic dyslexia using story grammar. *J. Learn. Disabil.* **22,** 373–380.

Newby, R. F., Recht, D. R., and Caldwell, J. (1989b). Phonological processing, verbal and nonverbal memory, and attention in dysphonetic and dyseidetic dyslexics. Paper presented at the Biannual Meeting of the Society for Research in Child Development (May 1989), Kansas City, Missouri. Also presented at the Joint Conference on Learning Disabilities (June 1989), Ann Arbor, Michigan.

Noland, D. R., Hammeke, T. A., and Barkley, R. A. (1983). A comparison of the neuropsychological performance in two groups of learning disabled children. *J. Clin. Child Psychol.* **12,** 13–21.

Obrzut, J. E., and Hynd, G. W. (1986). "Child Neuropsychology," Vol. 2. Academic Press, Orlando, Florida.

Pirozzolo, F. J. (1979). "The Neuropsychology of Developmental Reading Disorders." Praeger Press, New York.

Plaisted, J. R., Gustavson, J. L., Wilkening, G. N., and Golden, C. J. (1983). The Luria–Nebraska Neuropsychological Battery—Children's Revision: Theory and current research findings. *J. Clin. Child Psychol.* **12,** 13–21.

Rao, S. M., and Bieliauskas, L. A. (1983). Cognitive rehabilitation two and one-half years post right temporal lobectomy. *J. Clin. Neuropsychol.* **5,** 313–320.

Recht, D. R., Caldwell, J., and Newby, R. F. (1988). Improving the reading comprehension of dysphonetic and dyseidetic dyslexics using story grammar. Paper presented at the First Annual Conference on Research and Theory in Learning Disabilities (May 1988), University Park, Pennsylvania.

Reed, H. B. C., Reitan, R. M., and Klove, H. (1965). Influence of cerebral lesions in psychological test performance of older children. *J. Consult. Psychol.* **29,** 247–251.

Reitan, R. M. (1966). A research program on the psychological effects of brain lesions in human beings. *In* "International Review of Research in Mental Retardation (R. M. Ellis, ed.), pp. 153–218. Academic Press, New York.

Reitan, R. M. (1979). "Neuropsychology and Rehabilitation." Author, Tucson, Arizona.

Reitan, R. M. (1980). "REHABIT—Reitan Evaluation of Hemispheric Abilities and Brain Improvement Training." Reitan Neuropsychological Laboratory and University of Arizona, Tucson.

Reitan, R. M., and Boll, T. J. (1973). Neuropsychological correlates of minimal brain dysfunction. *Ann. N. Y. Acad. Sci.* **205,** 65–88.

Reitan, R. M., and Davison, L. A. (1974). "Clinical Neuropsychology: Current Status and Applications." V. H. Winston and Sons, Washington, D.C.

Reitan, R. M., and Wolfson, D. (1985). "The Halstead–Reitan Neuropsychological Test Battery: Theory and Clinical Interpretation." Neuropsychology Press, Tucson, Arizona.

Rosenberger, P., and Hier, D. (1980). Cerebral asymmetry and verbal intellectual deficits. *Ann. Neurol.* **8,** 300–304.

Rourke, B. P. (1975). Brain–behavior relationships in children with learning disabilities: A research program. *Am. Psycholog.* **30,** 911–920.

Rourke, B. P. (1981). Neuropsychological assessment of children with learning disabilities. *In* "Handbook of Clinical Neuropsychology" (S. B. Filskov and T. J. Boll, eds.), pp. 453–478. John Wiley & Son, New York.

Rourke, B. P., Bakker, D., Fisk, J. L., and Strang, J. D. (1983). "Child Neuropsychology: An Introduction to Theory, Research, and Clinical Practice." Guilford Press, New York.

Rourke, B. P., Bakker, D., Fisk, J. L., and Strang, J. D. (1986). "The Neuropsychological Assessment of Children: A Treatment-Oriented Approach." Guilford Press, New York.

Seidenberg, M., Giordini, B., Berent, S., and Boll, T. J. (1983). IQ level and performance on the Halstead–Reitan Neuropsychological Test Battery for older children. *J. Consult. Clin. Psychol.* **51,** 406–413.

Selz, M. J., and Reitan, R. M. (1979). Rules for neuropsychological diagnosis: Classification of brain function in older children. *J. Consult. Clin. Psychol.* **47,** 258–264.

Spiegel, D., and Fitzgerald, J. (1986). Improving reading comprehension through instruction about story parts. *Read. Teacher* **39,** 676–682.

Stanovich, K. E. (1988). Explaining the differences between the dyslexic and the garden-variety poor reader: The phonological-core variable-difference model. *J. Learn. Disabil.* **21,** 590–612.

Stein, N. (1979). How children understand stories: A developmental analysis. *In* "Current Topics in Early Childhood Education" (L. Katz, ed.). Ablex, Hillsdale, New Jersey.

Sternberg, R. J. (1984). An information processing analysis and critique. *J. Special Educ.* **18,** 269–279.

Teeter, P. A. (1986). Standard neuropsychological test batteries for children. *In* "Child Neuropsychology," Vol. 2 (J. E. Obrzut and G. W. Hynd, eds.), pp. 187–227. Academic Press, Orlando, Florida.

Tramontana, M. G., Klee, S. N., and Boyd, T. A. (1984). WISC-R interrelationships with the Halstead–Reitan and Children's Luria Neuropsychological batteries. *Clin. Neuropsychol.* **6,** 1–8.

Whaley, J. (1981). Story grammar and reading instruction. *Read. Teacher* **34,** 762–771.

Ysseldyke, J. E., and Algozzine, B. (1982). "Critical Issues in Special and Remediation Education." Houghton Mifflin, Boston.

Ysseldyke, J. E., and Mirkin, P. K. (1981). The use of assessment information to plan instructional interventions: A review of the research. *In* "A Handbook for School Psychology" (C. Reynolds and T. Gutkin, eds.), pp. 113–132. Wiley, New York.

CHAPTER 14

Social Skills Enhancement in Students with Learning Disabilities

Sharon Vaughn

Editor's Notes

In the preceding chapters within Section II, we have been focusing on assessment and remediation of academic problems in students with learning disabilities. We now shift our attention to a major source of nonacademic problems that some of these students have—social problems.

You will recall that in Section I, Bryan dealt with research on social problems in children and adolescents with learning disabilities. Here, Vaughn deals with teaching social skills to students with learning disabilities.

Vaughn's chapter contains four themes. The first theme concerns the rationale for teaching learning-disabled students social skills and explanations for why teachers shy away from social skills instruction. The second theme concerns a definition of social skills and a summary of models in social skills training. The third theme lies in a comprehensive discussion of instructional methods in social skills enhancement. This discussion is organized around three topics: (1) a detailed account of instructional procedures, (2) an assessment of the empirical status of the specific instructional method under discussion, and (3) comments on the instructional method. The last theme focuses on issues in social skills enhancement.

I. SCOPE AND OBJECTIVES

Procedures for enhancing the social skills and peer acceptance of students with learning disabilities (LDs) is the focus of this chapter. Students with LD, by definition, have learning problems that interfere with their academic success in the classroom. Recently, the link between LD and social skills difficulties has persuaded the Interagency Committee on Learning Disabilities (ICLD) to identify social skills as a possible deficit area for identifying students with LD. This agency was established by the Health Research Extension Act of 1985 (P.L. 99–158). The ICLD definition of LD illustrates the importance of social skills with students and suggests the need for social skills training for students with LD who have deficits in this area. The ICLD definition (as appears in Kavanagh and Truss, 1988: 550–551) made the following changes in the National Joint Committee for Learning Disabilities' 1981 definition (with changes underlined):

> Learning disabilities is a generic term that refers to a heterogeneous group of disorders manifested by significant difficulties in the acquisition and use of listening, speaking, reading, writing, reasoning, or mathematical abilities, or of social skills. These disorders are intrinsic to the individual and presumed to be due to central nervous system dysfunction. Even though a learning disability may occur concomitantly with other handicapping conditions (e.g., sensory impairment, mental retardation, social and emotional disturbance), with socioenvironmental influences (e.g., cultural differences, insufficient or inappropriate instruction, psychogenic factors), and especially with attention deficit disorder, all of which may cause learning problems, a learning disability is not the direct result of those conditions or influences.

This chapter provides an overview of social skills and models for teaching social skills. Specific interventions developed and evaluated with LD students are described as well as social skills interventions developed for other populations. Procedures for implementing these interventions and comments about their applicability and use are provided. The final section of the chapter discusses issues that are relevant to the teaching of social skills to LD youngsters.

After reading this chapter, students should be able to address each of the following objectives:

- explain why many students with LD may need to be taught social skills;

- explain why teachers may not emphasize the teaching of social skills in their curricula for students with LDs;
- define social skills;
- describe the cognitive-social learning model;
- describe the interpersonal cognitive problem-solving model;
- compare and contrast characteristics of contextualist and deficit models of social skills;
- summarize the procedures and critical comments regarding empirically substantiated social skills interventions with LD students: cooperative learning, mutual interest discovery, contextualist intervention, and a social skills program for adolescents;
- summarize procedures and critical comments regarding empirically substantiated social skills interventions with other special populations: peer social initiations, social decision-making, and structured learning; and
- explain several key issues about teaching social skills to students with LDs.

II. OVERVIEW OF SOCIAL SKILLS

A. Why Teach Social Skills?

Why should we teach social skills to LD students? Students with learning disabilities are less accepted and more frequently rejected than their non-learning-disabled (NLD) peers (for review, see Vaughn and LaGreca, 1988; Wiener, 1987). Rejection status is associated with many negative outcomes including later adjustment difficulties, school dropout, and loneliness (for review, see Parker and Asher, 1987). Also, the rejection of LD students is not solely a function of their academic difficulties. After a few minutes of observing students on videotapes, unaware of which students are LD and NLD, strangers are more likely to perceive LD students more negatively than NLD students (Bryan and Perlmutter, 1979; Bryan and Sherman, 1980). In a prospective study examining the social skills, peer acceptance, and self-perceptions of LD students prior to identification, LD students demonstrated low peer acceptance and high peer rejection even prior to their referral and identification as LD (Vaughn et al., 1990). Not only are LD students more at risk for low peer acceptance than their NLD peers, they display social behaviors that interfere with their social adjustment (LaGreca, 1981; Vaughn and LaGreca, 1988).

As Bryan informs us in her chapter on the social characteristics of LD students, LD students are not well liked by teachers and peers. Thus, one would expect that teachers would make social skills training a part of their intervention program. Resource room teachers perceive approximately 38% of their LD students as having deficits in social functioning, yet they do not see social skills training as having a high priority in the curriculum (Baum *et al.*, 1988). Of the students identified as having social deficits, only 37% had goal statements on their Individual Education Programs (IEPs) that related to social skills interventions (Baum *et al.*, 1988). Thus, while teachers feel that many students are in need of social skills training, they do not address this need in the goals or objectives on students' IEPs.

Because peer relationships are highly valued by our society and associated with many positive outcomes, why is it that few teachers directly teach interpersonal social skills? Teachers may be aware that LD students have social difficulties but do not *value* social skills as an important component of the curricula. Educators may be aware that many of their students are missing important social skills but do not feel that they should "take away" from the student's academic program by spending time teaching social skills. Perhaps too, some teachers feel that teaching social skills is important but do not feel that they receive support from the administration to justify teaching social skills. These teachers may highly value the importance of teaching social skills, but because social skills are not valued by the school system and/or parents they do not teach them.

Some teachers may also feel that social behaviors are important and wish that their students demonstrated more prosocial behaviors, but they do not feel that it is the school's responsibility to teach social skills. They may feel that social behaviors should be learned at home and that it is the responsibility of the family to assure that positive social behaviors are acquired and practiced. Also, some educators feel that social skills are something that is acquired just in the process of growing up. They think of social skills more as a "characteristic" of the child, rather than as behaviors that are amenable to change. Fortunately, many children learn appropriate social behaviors without direct, systematic instruction. However social skills can be enhanced through structured intervention programs

Finally, the rationale that perhaps represents the greatest number of educators is that social skills are not taught because teachers do not know how to teach them. Teachers take courses that focus on teaching language arts, reading, math, and the academic subjects for which they are responsible. Teachers even take courses on how to structure and manage behaviors in the classroom. Very few teachers take courses that provide opportunities for learning how to teach social skills to their students. Teaching social behaviors requires that the teacher understand the development and acquisition of social behavior. Few teachers have confidence that they understand the "scope and sequence" of social development and that they would be able to identify and teach the social skills needed by their students. Thus, part of the solution to providing social skills training for LD students is to require related courses and field experiences in teacher training programs.

B. What Are Social Skills?

The issue of defining social skills has been approached by many researchers and has proven to be a difficult one. According to Foster and Ritchey (1979: 626), social skills are "... those responses, which within a given situation prove effective, or in other words, maximize the probability of producing, maintaining, or enhancing positive effects for the interaction" and, it should be added, without harm to others. Ladd and Mize (1983: 127) define social skills as "children's ability to organize cognitions and behaviors into an integrated course of action directed toward culturally acceptable social or interpersonal goals." Their definition focuses on the importance of cognition, or what the person thinks, as well as their abilities to implement behaviors as part of social skills.

Vaughn and Hogan (1990) have stressed the need to look at social skills as part of a higher-order construct (social competence) that encompasses numerous individual components. Although the components are described separately, they are thought to combine for effective behavior. The four components included in their model are (1) positive relations with others (ability to get along with peers and adults), (2) accurate age-appropriate social cognition (ability to problem solve and recognize and monitor social situations), (3) absence of maladaptive behaviors (absence of noxious and serious behavior problems such as attention problems, acting out, and withdrawal), and (4) effective social skills (ability to initiate and respond appropriately with others). Within this model, social skills are one component of social competence. The model proposed by Vaughn and Hogan (1990) provides the structure for the contextualist intervention described in this chapter under the heading "Empirically Substantiated Interventions with LD Students."

C. Social Skills Models

1. Cognitive-Social Learning Model

Ladd and Mize (1983) propose a cognitive-social learning model for social skills training. Based primarily on the work of Bandura (e.g., 1978, 1982), this model assumes children form constructs about behaviors based on their observations and their interpretation of the consequences of implementing these behaviors. Three basic training objectives are enhance skill concepts, promote skillful performance, and foster skill maintenance and generalization.

Accomplishing these objectives requires specific training procedures referred to as training variables.

The first training variable, instruction, is defined as providing information that illustrates the desired behavior or the performance standard expected. Instruction can occur in two forms: modeled and verbal. When instruction is modeled, the behavior is represented through a role play, film, videotape, or vignette. When instruction is verbal, it relies on spoken language to communicate the concept or desired behavior.

A second training variable, rehearsal, is to act or practice a behavior until it reaches a standard or criteria. Rehearsal can be overt, when the individual practices the skill, or covert, when the individual thinks about or rehearses in his or her mind how they would perform a skill. The third training variable, feedback, is an opportunity to evaluate the extent to which the behavior exhibited corresponds with the target behavior. Feedback can be given by "self" or by "others."

In addition to training variables, the cognitive-social learning model provides specific training procedures for teaching social skills. The training procedures correspond directly to the training objectives, and the relationship between the training objectives and training procedures can be seen in Table 14.1.

The authors admit that the model is designed to provide a schema for developing social skills training and that no comprehensive studies have been conducted to support or falsify the model as a whole; however, considerable research relates to aspects of the model (for review, see Ladd and Mize, 1983). The procedures of modeling, role-playing, and rehearsal have been a central part of most social skills training programs.

2. Interpersonal Cognitive Problem-Solving Model

Having problems with others is an inevitable part of life. Learning to share, to handle teasing, and to cope with a bully are just a few of the myriad difficulties that face children from the time they are toddlers. Learning how to be a good problem-solver is thought to be related to present and later adjustment and to be a buffer against the negative effects of stressful life events (Dubow and Tisak, 1989).

The interpersonal cognitive problem-solving (ICPS) model (Shure and Spivack, 1979, 1980) focuses on teaching thought processes that are expected to mediate behavior. The assumption underlying this model is that if children learn how to think through problem situations it will influence how they act. The ICPS model has received perhaps its most extensive evaluation through the work of Shure, Spivack, and their colleagues (Spivack et al., 1976; Shure and Spivack, 1979, 1980) who taught an ICPS training program to inner-city preschoolers. The success of their work encouraged others to intervene with

Table 14.1
Cognitive-Social Learning Model of Social Skills Training

Training objective	Training procedure
Enhancing skill concepts	A. Establishing an intent to learn the skill concept Providing an advance organizer Stressing the functional relevance of the concept B. Defining the skill concept in terms of its attributes Conveying concept meaning Identifying relevant and irrelevant attributes C. Generating exemplars Identifying positive and negative examples D. Promoting rehearsal and recall of the skill concept Encouraging verbal rehearsal Establishing a memory code E. Refining and generalizing the concept Correcting misconceptions Identifying alternative applications
Promoting skill performance	A. Providing opportunities for guided rehearsal Requesting overt skill rehearsal Conducting rehearsals in a sheltered context B. Evaluation of performance by the instructor Communicating performance standards Providing feedback about the match between standards and performance C. Fostering skill refinement and elaboration Recommending corrective action including concept reformulation and skill modification
Fostering skill maintenance/generalization	A. Providing opportunities for self-directed rehearsal Skill rehearsal in a series of contexts that approximate real-life situations B. Promoting self-initiation of performance Encouraging skill usage while withdrawing performance cues or aids C. Fostering self-evaluation and skill adjustment Self-appraisals of skill performance Self-monitoring of skill outcomes Adoption of nondefeating self-attributes and affective states Use of information from self-monitoring of modify performance

Source: A cognitive-social learning model of social-skill training, by G. W. Ladd and J. Mize, 1983, *Psycholog. Rev.* **90(2)**, 127–157 (p. 131).

ICPS programs with a range of youngsters including elementary students (Elardo and Caldwell, 1979; McKim et al., 1982; Vaughn and Lancelotta, 1990), aggressive and submissive youngsters (Deluty, 1981; Vaughn et al., 1984), students identified as mentally retarded (Vaughn et al., 1983), and low-accepted LD students (Vaughn et al., 1988, in press). The ICPS model has been successful as a mediator for adjustment and effective in increasing skills in generating alternatives and evaluating consequences and in generalizing skills to relevant situations and persons (for review, see Denham and Almeida, 1987; Pellegrini and Urbain, 1985).

The key components of an ICPS model include goal identification, alternative thinking, and consequential thinking. Goal identification teaches children to identify what they want and what another person wants. In the case of a problem situation, children are taught to identify their goals as well as the goals of others involved in the problem. This process starts with recognizing one's own feelings, how to prevent these feelings from leading to undesirable behaviors, and recognizing and coping with the feelings of others. Children are encouraged to identify goals that meet their needs and the needs of others involved in the problem situation. Emphasis is on finding alternatives that are safe and fair and that are good choices in the "long run," not just the "short run."

A second key component of the ICPS model is alternative thinking. Alternative thinking teaches one to generate a range of potential alternatives to problem situations. When teaching this component, the emphasis is on generating as many different solutions as possible with little attempt at this point to evaluate the potential effectiveness of the solution. When children offer a number of aggressive solutions (e.g., hitting, kicking, beating up), the instructor indicates that they have many ideas for solutions that involve hurting others and encourages participants to suggest different alternatives, ones that do not focus on hurting.

The third component of the ICPS model is consequential thinking. Consequential thinking emphasizes the importance of predicting the likely outcome of each alternative before selecting an alternative to a problem situation. Emphasis within consequential thinking is on anticipating what they expect would happen next if they implemented a suggested alternative. There are several important aspects to consequential thinking. One is that students are asked to consider who is involved in the problem situation, with the understanding that some alternatives are effective with some people and not with others. Another important aspect is to consider whether the solution will be effective in the long run or just in the short run. And finally, students are asked whether or not the selected alternative is safe and fair. Thus, consideration for how the alternative will affect others is part of the intervention program. While the components are often taught separately, they are combined through role plays and applied practice.

3. Contextualist versus Deficit Models

Both the cognitive-social learning model and the ICPS model assume that the primary source of the social skills difficulties of LD students is within the child. Thus, teaching the child specific skills and behaviors solve the student's social skills problems. Forman (1987) argues that the most common model for remediating peer difficulties, the deficit model, takes a "fix-the-breakdown" approach. Forman argues that a contextualist model that emphasizes several principles for remediating the social difficulties of LD students is necessary. First, others from the child's context such as peers and family members should be involved. Second, their social difficulties need to be identified and, when possible, the source of the identification should be described. Third, target students need to be motivated to make necessary changes or learn skills. Fourth, the intervention needs to be implemented in such a way so as to respond to changes in the child's school, classroom, family, and friendships. Fifth, the classroom teacher must be involved in monitoring the desired change. The need for family involvement and support in providing intervention for LD students is critical. Involving the family puts the problems in context and allows for a complete intervention program (Wilchesky and Reynolds, 1986).

Gresham (1984) argues that social skills training that is based on behavioral principles holds the greatest promise for youngsters with handicaps because it is performance-based. He cites the following instructional techniques as stemming from a behavioral model: modeling, behavior rehearsal, direct reinforcement-based techniques, and peer interaction strategies. The assumption underlying deficit-based approaches is that children learn social skills that result in improved relations with peers and adults from social skills training. Research examining the effects of social skills interventions with LD students have demonstrated few if any effects on peer ratings of acceptance. Even when positive behavioral changes are documented by trained observers (Northcutt, 1987; Williams, 1983), teachers and peers do not perceive the positive change. Appropriate social behaviors are observed in controlled settings, such as during training; however, these changes do not generalize to more natural settings (Berler *et al.*, 1982). In summary, it may be effective to use behavioral principles in teaching social skills; however, social skills interventions need not be isolated skills training and should involve significant others in the child's life as well as demonstrate an awareness of the effects of the context on the child acquisition and use of social skills.

III. INSTRUCTIONAL METHODS

The basic assumption underlying most social skills training is that children with poor peer relations lack social skills. This assumption is particularly relevant to LD students, as this link between low peer relations and social skills deficits has provided the rationale for developing social skills interventions with LD students. The low peer acceptance of many LD children has been repeatedly documented. What has been significantly less well documented are explanations for why many LD students are poorly accepted. The number of LD students rejected by their peers is considerably greater than those in the NLD population who are rejected; however, fewer than 50% of LD students are rejected (Vaughn *et al.*, in press; Stone and LaGreca, 1990). Thus, many LD students are, on the average, accepted and some are even highly popular.

No single pattern of social difficulties represents LD children (Rourke, 1988). Thus, interventions must provide some form of assessment to assure the social skills interventions will be directed toward the child's problems. For example, some students who are not well accepted by their peers and have social skills problems may need specific training in one or more of the following skills: conversational skills, reducing inappropriate behaviors, interpersonal problem-solving, giving positive feedback, accepting negative feedback, and initiating contact with others.

Vaughn and her colleagues (Vaughn and Hogan, 1990; Vaughn *et al.*, 1990) are providing an examination of LD students prior to identification through a prospective longitudinal study. These studies identify the social and academic patterns of LD students as compared with their low-average-, and high-achieving peers. Initial results suggest that as early as 10 weeks into their kindergarten year, children later identified as LD are significantly different from even their low-achieving peers on measures of peer acceptance and attention problems.

Even with efforts at grouping LD children with NLD classmates to encourage and promote positive peer interaction, the acceptance ratings of LD students remained low or, in some cases, even lower than before intervention (for review, see McIntosh *et al.*, in press). How students feel about their classmates is not as susceptible to change as we might like. Even though students demonstrate improved social skills and these changes can be documented through behavioral observations, classmates either do not perceive the changes or the changes are not dramatic enough to alter their perceptions of the target student. In Section III. A. 4 of this chapter, an intervention that provides opportunities for LD students and their NLD classmates to spend structured time together getting to know each other better is described. This procedure resulted in increased ratings by the students who participated.

A. Empirically Substantiated Interventions with LD Students

Four interventions will be discussed in this section: a social skills program for adolescents, a contextualist intervention, cooperative learning, and mutual interest discovery. An introduction to each intervention will be provided as well as procedures for implementing the intervention and comments that relate to evaluating the intervention.

1. A Social Skills Program for Adolescents

A Social Skills Program for Adolescents (ASSET) is a social skills program developed for adolescents and evaluated with adjucated youth and LD adolescents (Hazel *et al.*, 1981). Eight social skills are considered within this program as fundamental to making and maintaining relationships with others. These eight social skills are the foundation of the ASSET program. The assumption of this program is that many children do not exhibit the kinds of behaviors we find desirable, not because they are not motivated to do so, but because they do not know how to perform them. This program has been developed to teach the social skills needed by adolescents to interact effectively with peers and adults. The teaching procedures used in the program are based on success, successive approximations, mastery, and multiple exemplars.

a. Procedures   1. Each lesson is taught in a small group and contains nine basic steps. Step one is to *review* previously learned skills including reviewing homework. Step two is to *explain* or describe the skill that is the focus of the lesson. Sometimes this is a review of the skill being taught and sometimes this is an overview of a new skill. Step three is to provide a *rationale* for the skill being taught. This step requires "hooking" the student into learning the skill by providing a convincing rationale for its importance. Step four is a discussion of *example* situations for the skill. When presenting examples of the situation, choose those that are specific and believable and that a teenager can relate to. Students can also provide examples. Step five is to *examine* the skill steps. Within the ASSET program, a skill sheet provides the step-by-step sequence of subskills needed to effectively implement the target skill. Step six is to *model* the skill. Videotapes that provide a "model" of a student implementing the skill are available with the program. Opportunities for students in the program to demonstrate and model specific skills are also provided. Step seven, *verbal rehearsal*, familiarizes the students with the sequence of steps and provides a procedure for memorizing the steps in the sequence. Step eight, *behavioral rehearsal* and criterion performance, is an opportunity for the students to practice the skills and demonstrate that they meet criterion for exhibiting each of the delineated skills. Step nine, assignment of *homework*, is a

Table 14.2

ASSET: Skill Sheet for Following Directions

1. Face the person.
2. Keep eye contact.
3. Keep a neutral facial expression.
4. Use a normal voice tone.
5. Keep a straight posture.
6. *Listen* closely to the instruction so that you will know what to do and remember to give feedback with head nods and by saying "mmm-hmmm" and "yeah."
7. *Acknowledge* the instruction.
8. *Ask for more information* if you don't understand the instruction ("But I don't understand …").
9. *Say* that you *will follow* the instruction ("I'll do it …").
10. *Follow* the instruction.
11. Throughout, *give* polite, pleasant responses.
12. *Do not argue* with the person about the instruction; go ahead and follow it and you can talk to the person later about problems.

Source: "ASSET: A Social Skills Program for Adolescents," by J. S. Hazel, J. B. Schumaker, J. A. Sherman, and J. Sheldon-Wildgen, 1981, Research Press, Champaign, Illinois (p. 113).

home note for recording how they practice and use skills outside of the training setting, particularly at home.

2. Within these nine steps, eight specific skills are taught. At least one session is needed to address each of the eight skills: giving positive feedback, giving negative feedback, accepting negative feedback, resisting peer pressure, problem-solving, negotiation, following directions, and conversation. A summary of the skill sequence for following directions is presented in Table 14.2.

b. Comments   In a study by Hazel *et al.* (1982), eight LD students were taught six skills: giving positive feedback, giving negative feedback, accepting negative feedback, resisting peer pressure, negotiation, and personal problem-solving. Using behavioral role-play situations, subjects were tested on each of the six skills. LD students involved in the intervention demonstrated increases in the use of social skills during role plays. When compared with two other groups, NLD and court-adjudicated youth, the LD students made only slight gains on cognitive problem-solving.

This model specifically delineates the subskills within each target social skills component, and thus it is useful to teachers who seek a structured curriculum for teaching social skills. Zigmond and Brownlee (1980: 82) remind us that when teaching social skills to LD adolescents we need to "apply the same careful systematic procedures used in teaching academic skills." The ASSET program provides the guidelines and curriculum for applying systematic procedures.

Further research with the ASSET program is needed to determine the extent to which skill acquisition demonstrated during role plays is also demonstrated in nonstructured situations. For example, do students who display increased social skills in a role-play "testing" situation apply those same social skills in real-life settings? Also, further information on how target students perceive the ASSET training is needed. It is likely that students who feel the intervention is effective and has made positive changes in their ability to interact with others are more likely to apply and generalize skills learned.

2. A Contextualist Intervention

A social strategy training program emphasizing a contextualist perspective has been developed and evaluated by Vaughn and her colleagues (Vaughn and Lancelotta, 1990; Vaughn et al., 1988, in press). The contextualist model suggests that social skills need to be considered in light of family, school, environment, classroom, peer, and other relevant issues. Teaching social skills in isolation is unlikely to provide significant and longlasting change.

  a. Procedures 1. A schoolwide sociometric assessment is performed and students are informed that social skills trainers for the school are being identified and will be selected through a lottery.

  2. Social skills trainers are selected from two groups: rejected LD students and highly accepted NLD students.

  3. Social skills trainers for each participating class include a rejected LD student and a highly accepted NLD classmate. Social skills trainers are announced by the school principal.

  4. Children selected as social skills trainers are removed from the classroom several times (2–3) each week for approximately 30 minutes each session to learn specific social skills strategies.

  5. The first social skills strategy taught is the FAST strategy. This four-step strategy follows:

a. Freeze! Don't act too quickly. Stop and think: What is the problem?
b. Alternatives. What are all my possible solutions?
c. Solution Evaluation. What are the likely consequences of each solution. What would happen next if I do ...? Select the best solutions for the long run and the short run.
d. Try it. What do I need to do to implement the solution? If it doesn't work, what else can I try?

  6. In addition to the FAST strategy, social skills trainers are taught to address solutions in terms of long-run and short-run consequences. Coaching and role-playing are used to promote understanding of the lessons and to practice skills.

7. While social skills trainers are learning the social strategies, a problem-solving box (decorated shoe box) is put into every classroom. The problem-solving box is used by all of the children in the classroom to write problems they have with other children, at home, on the playground, etc. The teacher and social skills trainers explain to the class that the purpose of the problem-solving box is to ask questions about problems they have in the classroom, on the playground, and at home. Problems submitted by children are used by social skills trainers and the entire class to practice their social problem-solving skills. Problems from the problem-solving box are used by trainers in their training outside the class as well as for in-class training and discussion.

8. After social skills trainers have learned the FAST strategy and rehearsed it using real-life problems that they provide or are taken from the problem-solving box, they prepare to present the FAST strategy to the class.

9. Social skills trainers present the FAST strategy to their classmates with backup and support from the researcher.

10. For subsequent weeks, social skills trainers leave the room for only one session per week and review the FAST strategy with classmates in the classroom at least once per week. These reviews include large group ex-planations and small group problem-solving exercises using the problems from the problem-solving box.

11. Awards are given to social skills trainers in front of their class or school by the school principal. Social skills trainers wear special buttons on the bus and on the playground, which indicate they are social skills trainers for the school. Students in the school are asked to consult the social skills trainers when they have difficulties.

b. Comments   The social strategy training program proposed by Vaughn and her colleagues has been conducted with a female LD student in a case study design as well as with a group of LD students identified by their peers as socially rejected. Many of the students who participated in the intervention demonstrated increases in peer acceptance following the intervention. In the case study, the female LD student was identified as rejected at pretest and as popular at post-test. In the group intervention, all 10 LD students were iden-tified as rejected at pretest with only 5 identified as rejected at post-test and follow-up. Students who participated in the intervention received signifi-cantly more positive nominations at post-test than at pretest. Future work needs to examine the characteristics of students with whom this inter-vention is successful and those with whom it is not successful. Initial eval-uations with LD students whose peer ratings were not improved following intervention suggests that LD students who have acting out and aggressive behavior problems are less likely to demonstrate changes in peer acceptance following intervention. Also, this intervention has been used with elementary-aged LD students. The extent to which the model could be adapted and used with older youngsters is unknown.

3. Cooperative Learning

Slavin *et al.* (1984) have used a combination of cooperative learning and individualized programming in an intervention called Team Assisted Individualization (TAI). While the primary purpose of this procedure is to increase academic skill levels, cooperative learning has also been used to integrate handicapped and nonhandicapped students and to increase the social acceptance of children in the group. Students work in heterogenous groups and assist each other with directions and tasks as well as check each others work. The cooperative atmosphere as well as the increased exposure to all students in the classroom is expected to increase peer acceptance.

a. Procedures 1. High-, average-, and low-achieving students are assigned to four- or five-member *teams*. Students who are identified as special education and receiving resource help were assigned randomly to teams.

2. Students are *pretested* on the academic area of focus. Students are placed in an individualized program based on their performance on this test.

3. Students complete the following steps to finish their individualized academic area work.

a. Students bring their work materials into pairs or triads within their teams.
b. Students exchange answer sheets with partners.
c. Students read instructions and begin work on skill sheets.
d. When a student completes the first four problems, a partner is asked to check the answers. If the first four are correct, the student goes on to the next skill sheet. If any are wrong, the student continues with the next problems. If the student needs assistance, the teacher will provide instructive feedback.
e. When students complete the final skill sheet, they take an exam scored by a teammate. If they pass the exam, they go to the next more difficult set of problems. If they do not pass, they are provided instruction from the teacher.

4. Teams that meet criteria are rewarded with certificates at the end of the week.

5. The teacher works with individuals or small groups of students on specific skills.

b. Comments   The peer acceptance of children who participate in the TAI program increases; however, it may not be in response to the cooperation element in the program. In a comparison study between TAI and individualized instruction, students in the individualized instruction group demonstrated increases in peer acceptance that exceeded the increases of the TAI group when both groups were compared with a control group (Slavin *et al.*, 1984). There were no differences between the TAI group and the individualized instruction group on either academic achievement or peer acceptance.

Johnson and Johnson (1984a,b) have also evaluated the effects of cooperative learning on the amount and type of interaction of students with learning and behavior problems in the regular classroom (Johnson *et al.*, 1986). This study did not, however, examine the effects on the social acceptance of handicapped youngsters. A further study conducted with students classified as mentally retarded examined the positive interactions between handicapped and nonhandicapped children during cooperative learning tasks (Putnam *et al.*, 1989). While results suggest more positive interactions and fewer negative interactions for students instructed in collaborative skills, this investigation did not include students with LDs. Johnson and Johnson (1986) suggest that classrooms can be organized so that children work together in small groups or pairs with the emphasis on helping each other to accomplish goals and learn material. The elements needed for cooperative learning are provided in Table 14.3.

4. Mutual Interest Discovery

Mutual interest discovery is an approach developed by Fox (1980) and evaluated with LD students (Fox, 1989). The central idea of the approach is that persons who have similar attitudes will be attracted to each other. Knowing the ways you are like another person increases the likelihood you will like each other. By providing structured activities for NLD and LD students to find out more about each other, LD students will be better accepted.

a. Procedures   The focus on mutual interest discovery is to get to know your partner by participating in structured activities to identify and illustrate things you have in common.

1. Pair low-accepted LD students with a high-accepted classmate.
2. Students interact for approximately 40 minutes once each week. They interview each other on preassigned topics such as entertainment, hobbies, and sports.
3. Following the interview, each person writes three items they discovered they had in common about the topic.

Table 14.3

Basic Elements for Enhancing Cooperative Learning[a]

1. Positive interdependence
   a. The goal of the group is to assure that all group members learn, often by producing a group product.
   b. Reward is linked to the overall achievement of the group, not the achievement of individuals within the group.
   c. For group members to achieve their goal, coordination of all group members is necessary.
2. Individual accountability
   a. To assure that students work together and each member of the group is responsible and learning, randomly select one student's work to represent the group.
   b. Ask students to select one student's work to represent the group.
3. Collaborative skills
   a. Teach students the skills they need to be successful at working cooperatively with others. These skills include decision-making, role-taking, trust-building, and conflict management.
   b. Teach students skills at being leaders and at being cooperative partners.
4. Group processing
   a. How well the group is functioning needs to be a focus of discussion. What aspects of the group are functioning well and what aspects are not should be delineated by group members.
   b. Group should identify their goals and assess whether or not they are making progress toward those goals.
5. Teacher's role during cooperative learning
   a. Monitor the students' behavior by making suggestions and asking questions that teach. Do not take over and solve their problems, but teach them to solve them.
   b. Provide task assistance. If students are having difficulty with an assignment or project, provide needed assistance and background information.
   c. Intervene to teach collaborative skills. Assist students in acquiring and practicing skills that enhance cooperation.
   d. Provide closure to the lesson by reviewing the progress of each group.
   e. Evaluate each individual student's learning and assess how well the group as a whole functions.

[a] Identified by Johnson and Johnson (1986).

4. Partners then complete a brief art activity, which is placed in a book about the partner.

5. At the bottom of the art exercise, each person writes two sentences they learned about their partner. All of these art exercises are kept in a book about their partner.

b. Comments Partners who participated in the mutual interest group demonstrated higher ratings of their partners over time than did partners in a control group. Females were more responsive to a mutual interest group as opposed to an academic task group than were males, who responded about equally well to both groups. LD students rated their partners significantly higher than their partners rated them over time. This intervention was not designed to teach social skills, so the effects of this intervention on the overall social skills of LD students is left unanswered. This initial study suggests LD acceptance can be increased through mutual interest activities. However, whether or not LD students are perceived differently by others in the class remains unanswered. LD students who participated in the study were in the lower half of the students in their class for peer acceptance prior to the intervention. The low peer acceptance of many LD students may be a result of their being less well known to their classmates. Because mutual interest discovery is a relatively easy intervention to implement, and it can be implemented in the regular classroom, providing mutual interest activities for all students paired with social skills training for target students may be an effective intervention.

B. Empirically Substantiated Interventions with Other Special Populations

1. Peer Social Initiations

Peer social initiations is an empirically validated approach to teaching social skills to young handicapped children (for review, see Strain and Odom, 1986). Although this approach was not developed and evaluated with LD youngsters, it demonstrates the application of a highly replicated social skills intervention that shows promise for young LD students.

  a. Procedures   The successful implementation of the intervention has four aspects. First, *selecting specific peer initiations* requires the interventionist to target those social initiations that are most likely to yield a positive response from the child. Behaviors such as sharing, affection, and assistance are likely to receive positive responses from peers (Strain, 1983). Second, *arranging the physical environment to promote interaction* requires that materials are available to increase interaction. For example, with preschoolers some materials such as wagons, cars, blocks, and house materials are likely to yield interactions with youngsters, whereas materials such as puzzles, crayons, and paints are more likely to produce solo play. Third, *training peers to implement the intervention* requires selecting peers (confederates) that are desirable playmates as well as willing to participate. Confederates practice and rehearse the initiation skills with the researcher prior to implementing them with a target peer. Confederates rehearse the intervention in multiple role plays to know what to do to encourage the child to respond as well as what to do when the child does not respond. Table 14.4 demonstrates a sample script provided

Table 14.4
Session 1: Introduction to System-Share Initiation-Persistence

TEACHER: "Today you are going to learn how to be a good teacher. Sometimes your friends in your class do not know how to play with other children. You are going to learn how to teach them to play. What are you going to do?"

CHILD RESPONSE: "Teach them to play."

TEACHER: "One way you can get your friend to play with you is to share. How do you get your friend to play with you?"

CHILD RESPONSE: "Share."

TEACHER: "Right! You share. When you share you look at your friend and say, 'Here,' and put a toy in his/her hand. What do you do?" (Repeat this exercise until the child can repeat these three steps.)

CHILD RESPONSE: "Look at friend and say, 'Here,' and put the toy in his/her hand."

ADULT MODEL WITH ROLE PLAYER: "Now, watch me. I am going to share with _____. Tell me if I do it right." (Demonstrate sharing.) "Did I share with _____? What did I do?"

CHILD RESPONSE: "Yea! _____ looked at _____, said 'here _____' and put a toy in his hand."

ADULT: "Right. I looked at _____ and said, 'here _____' and put a toy in his hand. Now watch me. See if I share with _____." (Move to the next activity in the classroom. This time prove a negative example of sharing by leaving out the "put in hand" component. Put the toy beside the role player). "Did I share?" (Correct if necessary and repeat this example if child got it wrong.) "Why not?"

CHILD RESPONSE: "No." "You did not put the toy in _____'s hand."

ADULT: "That's right. I did not put the toy in _____'s hand. When I have to look at _____ and say, 'here _____' and put the toy in his hand." (Give the child two more positive and two more negative examples of sharing. When they answer incorrectly about sharing, repeat the example. Vary the negative examples by leaving out different components: looking, saying 'here,' putting in hand.)

CHILD PRACTICE WITH ADULTS: "Now _____, I want you to get _____ to share with you. What do you do when you share?"

CHILD RESPONSE: "Look at _____ and say, 'here _____,' and put a toy in his hand."

ADULT: "Now, go get _____ to play with." (For these practice examples, the role playing adult should be responsive to the child's sharing.) (To the other confederates:) "Did _____ share with _____? What did she/he do?"

CHILD RESPONSE: "Yes/No. Looked at _____ and said, 'here _____' and put a toy in his hand."

ADULT: (Move to the next activity.) "Now, _____, I want you to share with _____."

Introduce Persistence

TEACHER: "Sometimes when I play with _____, he/she does not want to play back. I have to keep on trying. What do I have to do?"

CHILD RESPONSE: "Keep on trying."

TEACHER: "Right, I have to keep on trying. Watch me. I am going to share with _____. Now I want you to see if I keep on trying." (Role player will be initially unresponsive.) (Teacher should be persistent until child finally responds.) "Did I get _____ to play with me?" CHILD: "Yes." "Did he want to play?" CHILD: "No." "What did I do?" CHILD: "Keep on trying." "Right, I kept on trying. Watch. See if I can get _____ to play with me this time." (Again, the role player should be unresponsive at first. Repeat above questions and correct if necessary. Repeat the example until the child responds correctly.)

Source: Peer social initiations: Effective intervention for social skills development of exceptional children," by P. S. Strain and S. L. Odom, 1986, *Excep. Children* **52(6)**, 543–551 (p. 547).

by Strain and Odom (1986) for how to train confederates to implement the intervention. Fourth, conducting daily *intervention sessions* is the step-by-step process for structuring the interactions between the target child and the confederate. In a small group that includes a confederate and a target peer, the teacher describes the activities and materials available to conduct those activities. Children initiate the activity while the confederate is taken aside by the teacher and prompted as to what social initiations they should implement with the target child during the activity. The teacher prompts and reinforces the confederate and the target child for their interactions.

b. Comments   The peer social initiations intervention has been systematically implemented across numerous settings and populations. It has demonstrated positive impact on both the confederates and the target children. Populations who have successfully participated in the intervention include preschool-aged handicapped youngsters, elementary-aged mentally retarded and behavior-disordered youngsters, and visually impaired children. These positive outcomes include increases in positive social responses, responses to initiations, increased length of social exchanges, and cross-setting generalization of responses.

One concern about this intervention is the lack of generalization and maintenance of treatment effects. A likely explanation is that the environments to which the children were returned did not have socially responsive peers to initiate and maintain the target behaviors. When responsive peers are present, generalization and maintenance effects have been documented (Shafer *et al.*, 1984).

This intervention has been powerful and is applicable in a wide range of settings. One of the strengths of this intervention is that it does not require a special curriculum or teacher's guide. Because this intervention has not yet been systematically tested with LD students, further research is needed before its efficacy with this population is known.

2. Social Decision-Making

Social decision-making skills (Elias and Clabby, 1989) is a curriculum developed for elementary-aged students and has been used in both regular and special education classes to teach decision-making and interpersonal problem-solving skills.

a. Procedures   The curriculum provides for two readiness areas and eight steps for social decision-making and problem-solving. While the authors list the steps in a sequence, they acknowledge that decisions are not always made by strictly adhering to the sequence. The readiness area and eight steps are

Table 14.5

Social Decision-Making and Problem-Solving: Readiness Areas and Steps

Readiness area	
self-control	Does the child listen?
	Does the child follow directions?
	Does the child follow through on requests and assignments?
	Does the child calm him/herself down?
	Does the child have conversations without upsetting or provoking others?
Social decision-making area	
Feelings	Does the child recognize and respond to their own feelings?
	Does the child recognize and respond to the feelings of others?
	Can the child accurately describe a range of feelings?
Problems	Can the child clearly identify problems?
Goals	Can the child state realistic interpersonal goals?
Alternatives	Can the child think of several ways to reach goals or solve problems?
Consequences	Does the child consider the effects of a solution on self and on others?
	Does the child look at the short- and long-term effects of solutions as well as positive and negative possibilities?
Choose	Does the child choose carefully so solutions are likely to be effective and safe for self and others?
Plan and check	Does the child consider details like who, when, where, and with whom before implementing a solution?
	Does the child anticipate obstacles and respond appropriately when they occur?
Try and rethink	Does the child try his or her ideas?
	Does the child learn from experience and/or from others?

Source: "Social Decision-Making Skills: A Curriculum Guide for the Elementary Grades," by M. J. Elias and J. F. Clabby, 1989, Aspen, Rockville, Maryland (pp. 33–34).

described in Table 14.5. The curriculum guide is also complete with sample worksheets, directions for how to teach students to role-play, and many helpful teaching tips.

b. Comments The authors describe the readiness steps as ones developed because many of the children in special education classes could not use the social problem-solving steps without additional self-control and listening skills. They describe the program as being used in regular classes, special education classes, middle schools, and high schools. They have also taught these skills to parents (Clabby and Elias, 1987). The authors report high satisfaction indices for the children who participate and the adults who use the curriculum. For example, children say they use what they learn in all aspects of their life: with parents, siblings, and friends. Children entering middle school who did not participate in the problem-solving training identified such school stressors as peer pressure, academic demands, coping with authority figures, and becoming involved in substance abuse as significantly greater problems than did students who participated in the problem-solving training (Elias *et al.*, 1986).

3. Structured Learning

Structured learning is a procedure for teaching prosocial skills to elementary school children and adolescents (Goldstein *et al.*, 1980; McGinnis *et al.*, 1984). The approach is designed for both handicapped and nonhandicapped children who have not learned to interact with others in socially appropriate ways. The procedure is designed to be used by teachers, social workers, psychologists, and school counselors.

a. Prodecures Structured learning is a psychoeducational, behavioral approach for teaching prosocial skills and is based on four components: modeling, role-playing, performance feedback, and transfer of training. None of these components are considered sufficient alone, but the combination of these four provide effective procedures for teaching prosocial skills. During the first step, modeling, the teacher describes the skill and provides a behavioral description of the steps that compose the skill. The teacher then role-plays the steps in the skill. Other models provide a portrayal of implementing the skill. In the second step, role-playing, the teacher encourages the students to relate the skills modeled in step one to their own life. Use of the skill in specific situations both present and future are discussed. Students then participate in role plays that are coached and cued by the teacher. Observers are also encouraged to look for specific behaviors.

The third step, feedback, occurs after each role play and provides specific responses to the role play. The trainer provides feedback on what aspects of the role play were effective and provides encouragement. The trainer also models and role-plays skills that were not role-played effectively.

The fourth step, transfer of training, provides opportunities to practice the steps and skills in real-life settings. One procedure for implementing this is the Homework Report, which requests detailed information on the consequences of implementing a skill sequence outside of the training setting.

The structured learning program, designed for elementary students, contains 60 prosocial skills arranged in five groups: classroom survival skills, friendship-making skills, skills for dealing with feelings, skill alternatives to aggression, and skills for dealing with stress. The five groups and skills that relate to each group are provided in Table 14.6. The structure learning skills for adolescents contain 60 skills arranged in six groups. The six groups include

Table 14.6
Structured Learning: Prosocial Skills

Group I.   Classroom Survival Skills
 1. Listening
 2. Asking for help
 3. Saying "thank you"
 4. Bringing materials to class
 5. Following instructions
 6. Completing assignments
 7. Contributing to discussions
 8. Offering help to an adult
 9. Asking a question
10. Ignoring distractions
11. Making corrections
12. Deciding on something to do
13. Setting a goal

Group II.   Friendship-Making Skills
14. Introducing yourself
15. Beginning a conversation
16. Ending a conversation
17. Joining in
18. Playing a game
19. Asking a favor
20. Offering help to a classmate
21. Giving a compliment
22. Accepting a compliment
23. Suggesting an activity
24. Sharing
25. Apologizing

Group III.   Skills for Dealing with Feelings
26. Knowing your feelings
27. Expressing your feelings
28. Recognizing another's feelings
29. Showing understanding of another's feelings
30. Expressing concern for another
31. Dealing with your anger
32. Dealing with another's anger
33. Expressing affection
34. Dealing with fear
35. Rewarding yourself

Group IV.   Skill Alternatives to Aggression
36. Using self-control
37. Asking permission
38. Responding to teasing
39. Avoiding trouble

(continues)

Table 14.6 (*cont.*)

40. Staying out of fights
41. Problem-solving
42. Accepting consequences
43. Dealing with an accusation
44. Negotiating

Group V.   Skills for Dealing with Stress
45. Dealing with boredom
46. Deciding what caused a problem
47. Making a complaint
48. Answering a complaint
49. Dealing with losing
50. Showing sportsmanship
51. Dealing with being left out
52. Dealing with embarrassment
53. Reacting to failure
54. Accepting no
55. Saying no
56. Relaxing
57. Dealing with group pressure
58. Dealing with wanting something that isn't mine
59. Making a decision
60. Being honest

Source: "Skillstreaming the Elementary School Child," by E. McGinnis and A. P. Goldstein, R. P. Sprafkin, and N. J. Gershaw, 1984, Research Press, Champaign, Illinois (pp. 108–109).

beginning social skills (e.g., listening, saying "thank you," giving a compliment), advanced social social skills (e.g., asking for help, following instructions, convincing others), skills for dealing with feelings (e.g., knowing your feelings, dealing with someone's anger, dealing with fear), skill alternatives to aggression (e.g., asking permission, negotiating, using self-control, keeping out of fights), skills for dealing with stress (e.g., making a complaint, standing up for a friend, responding to failure and persuasion, getting ready for a difficult conversation), and planning skills (e.g., deciding on something to do, setting a goal, making a decision, concentrating on a task).

b. Comments   Steps for teaching each of the 60 skills are provided within a "lesson" format that includes steps for performing the skill, notes for discussion about each step in the skill, suggested situations for role-playing the skill, and comments about the skill. A sample lesson is provided in Table 14.7. The lesson format provided for teaching each of the social skills can be readily used by teachers and other professionals interested in teaching social skills. While the program appears to hold promise, empirical reports of the efficacy of applying the lessons with LD students have not been documented.

Table 14.7

Group I.   Classroom Survival Skills.

Skill 1:   Listening

Steps	Notes for Discussion
1. Look at the person who is talking.	Point out to students that sometimes others may think someone isn't listening, even though he/she really is. These steps are to show someone that you are really listening.
2. Remember to sit quietly.	Tell students to face the person and remember not to laugh, fidget, play with something, etc.
3. Think about what is being said.	
4. Say yes or nod your head.	
5. Ask a question about the topic to find out more.	Discuss relevant questions (i.e., those that do not change the topic).

Suggested situations

School: Your teacher explains an assignment.
Home: Your parents are talking with you about a problem.
Peer group: Another student tells of a TV program he/she watched or what he/she did over the weekend.

Source: "Skillstreaming the Elementary School Child," by E. McGinnis, A. Goldstein, R. P. Sprafkin, and N. J. Gershaw, 1984, Research Press, Champaign, Illinois (p. 110).

C. Other Social Skills Interventions

Social skills training procedures have also been developed and tested with low-accepted, nonspecial education students. In a study by Bierman et al. (1987), rejected males in grades one and two were assigned to one of four groups: social skills training, prohibition to reduce negative behavior, combination of social skills training and prohibition, and a no-treatment control group. Students in the prohibition group (response cost for inappropriate behavior) demonstrated a reduction from pretest to post-test and also, 6 weeks later, in the number of negative behaviors they initiated. Students who participated in the social skills training and prohibition intervention demonstrated decreases in negative initiations, negative peer responses, and stable peer interactions.

In Bierman's research (Bierman, 1986; Bierman and Furman, 1984), she emphasizes the importance of peer models and teaching conversational skills. Conversational skills focus on self-expression (sharing information about oneself and one's feelings), questioning (asking others about themselves and their feelings), and leadership bids (giving advice, invitations, and suggestions).

Teaching, Learning, and Caring (TLC): (Vaughn, 1987; Vaughn and McIntosh, 1989) is a social skills intervention program designed to teach

Table 14.8

Overview of the TLC Model Core Components[a]

Prerequisite skill (Communication mode)	Product outcome
Goal identification Recognizing goal of both self and others	
Empathy 1. Recognizing their own feelings 2. Recognizing the feelings of others	
Cue sensitivity 1. Awareness of verbal cues 2. Awareness of nonverbal cues 3. Awareness of environmental cues	Integration—combining skills to create an interpersonal problem-solving process that
Alternative thinking 1. Alternative points of view; context versus content 2. Alternative solutions to interpersonal problems	leads to successful interpersonal skills
Consequential thinking 1. Cognitive predicting 2. Role play/acting out	
Skills implementation 1. Describe steps 2. Role playing	

[a] From Vaughn, Sharon (1987). TLC—Teaching, learning, and caring: Teaching interpersonal problem-solving skills to behaviorally disordered adolescents. *The Pointer* **31(2)**, 27.

interpersonal problem-solving and social cognition to adolescents with behavior problems and LDs. An overview of the TLC model is provided in Table 14.8.

TLC was developed to teach the social behaviors frequently identified by parents, teachers, and counselors as problematic for many LD and behavior-disordered youngsters. These behaviors include impulsivity, inability to respond and identify the affective state of others, difficulty generating a range of responses to problem situations, ability to evaluate and identify the likely consequences in a problem situation, and problems initiating appropriate interactions and responding appropriately to the initiations of others. Procedures for teaching appropriate social behaviors include modeling, role-playing real-life problems, and applying learned skills. Members of the group give positive and negative feedback about how well target students complete the role play by applying the social skills. Systematic evaluation of the efficacy of this intervention with LD students has not been reported.

IV. ISSUES

Many children with low peer status also have poor academic performance. Because the correlation between low peer status and academic performance is not perfect, some children with low peer status are not low achievers and other children who are low achievers do not have low peer status. Coie and Krehbiel (1984) examined the effects of academic tutoring on the social adjustment of rejected peers who had academic problems. Rejected low-achieving students were assigned to one of four groups: academic tutoring, social skills training, academic tutoring and social skills, and a no-treatment control condition. The results of the intervention are somewhat surprising because children in the academic tutoring conditions improved both in academic achievement and in social adjustment and maintained these gains a year later. Social skills training had some effects on adjustment but the gains did not remain a year later.

Those programs that are most effective are the ones that are tailored to the specific needs of the identified population (Coie, 1985). This notion of fitting the intervention to the needs of the population must be further explored with LD youngsters. If the goal is to increase the social acceptance of youngsters, a model that solely emphasizes teaching social skills to the child in isolation is probably insufficient; rather, models that include academic tutoring, peer involvement, social skills instruction, and perhaps even teacher training are needed. We may need to develop specific interventions for children with social skills difficulties based on whether they do or not have behavior problems. Children with externalizing behavior problems may need interventions that include prohibitions as well as social skills training.

An important issue in social skills interventions with LD students is the use of NLD peers in the intervention. Sancilio (1987) reviews the literature on peer interaction as a method of intervention with children and concludes that peers can serve as effective change agents with other peers, but the interventions need to be highly structured and focused on improving the target child's social skills. Peer interactions that emphasize increased peer contact without a structured intervention are less likely to be successful. Structured peer interactions usually take one of two forms: peers as social reinforcers or peers as trained initiators. As social reinforcers, peers may provide positive reinforcement such as "good," and "I like playing with you when you share." Additionally, peers can be trained to ignore negative behaviors and reinforce positive behaviors (Solomon and Wahler, 1973). Social skills training with peer interaction is significantly more effective than merely providing opportunities for peer interaction. However, when social skills training alone was compared with social skills training with peer interaction, there were no significant differences although both groups demonstrated increases in peer acceptance and social problem-solving when compared with a contact control group (Vaughn and Lancelotta, 1990).

Social skills interventions need to be part of the curriculum rather than brief, one-shot interventions. LaGreca and Mesibov (1981: 238) discussed the results of their 6-week intervention with LD students who have low social skills. They cautioned us, "It is not reasonable to expect that longstanding social problems can be entirely remediated within the span of six weeks, although definite inroads can be made. Thus, it is suggested that future investigators consider issues such as examing the effects of longer and more comprehensive intervention programs, as well as exploring the possibility of including social-skills training in the school curriculum, so that training can be accomplished on a regular, ongoing basis."

Reviews of social skills interventions with LD students (McIntosh et al., 1990; Vaughn and LaGreca, 1988) have yielded several guidelines for teaching social skills.

A. Use Principles of Instruction

Procedure for teaching social skills are similar to those for effectively teaching other skills. First, the student needs to be motivated to learn the target skill. As with all instruction, it is difficult to teach students skills they are not interested in learning. Second, assess the student's social behaviors in a variety of settings and through several methods including observation. Before instruction is effective, it is important to know what social behaviors and in what settings the child is displaying the behaviors. Third, after selecting appropriate social skills, the steps for performing the social skill need to be analyzed and described to the students. Fourth, students need to demonstrate they know the steps in the social skill. Fifth, the student needs to role-play the skill in controlled and naturalistic settings. Feedback and rehearsal are important aspects of role-playing. Sixth, students are taught to self-monitor and self-evaluate their progress and to generalize their newly learned skills to a variety of settings.

B. Teachers Must Interact with All Students in Ways that Communicate Acceptance

How teachers feel about the students in their class is communicated to all of the students in the room. Teachers' perceptions are a powerful force in the classroom (Brophy, 1979, 1983) and influence the perceptions of the children in the classroom. It is quite unlikely that any teacher truly feels equally positive about all of the students they teach. It is possible, however, for teachers to communicate with all students in accepting ways. Most teachers do not realize the extent to which their tone, voice, expression, and manner convey to the child and to others in the room that the child is "OK" or "not OK."

Acceptance is communicated by the teacher through a classroom environment that supports all students. This classroom environment conveys a clear message that all students are valued. What occurs in classrooms in which all children are valued? Children work cooperatively and in heterogenous groups. Educational and social situations are planned that provide opportunities for all children to feel successful and valued. Neither teachers nor other students "put down" others. The teacher knows each student's area of expertise and capitalizes on what they can do and know. The teacher encourages children to appreciate the talents and abilities of their classmates.

C. Give All Students the Opportunity to Be "Knower"

Self-perception and the perception of others is strongly influenced by the extent to which a person is perceived as having something important to say or contribute. LD students are seldom placed in a role in which they demonstrate "knowing" or having something important to say or contribute. Because LD students are by definition demonstrating academic difficulties, it is not easy for teachers to find opportunities to allow them to be "knowers."

The writing process approach (Graves, 1983) emphasizes the student as "knower" by having students write about what they know. When LD students read their writing to others, the story they tell places them in the position of "knower." The teacher and classmates ask questions about the story that only the target child can answer. Reciprocal teaching (Palinscar and Brown, 1984) provides a model for teaching reading comprehension through small group instruction. Children are taught to lead groups, ask questions, and involve other children in the groups. Because group leadership is rotated among children in the group, all children are provided opportunities to serve in the role of the knower.

D. Involve Peers, School Personnel, and the Community in Social Skills Training

Whenever possible, the entire school should have a model for social skills training; thus, it is a priority for the entire school. This does not mean that all students in the school need to be involved in a social skills intervention, but that the school provides support for those students who are involved. This might include articles written about the social skills program in PTA or student papers, awards given to students who successfully complete the social skills program, notes sent home to parents, and certificates of merit.

Most social skills programs are effective in altering target social skills but are less effective in improving the peer acceptance of target youngsters. Systematic involvement of peers in social skills training is an effective strategy for increasing peer acceptance and providing interventions.

V. SUMMARY

This chapter provides an overview of social interventions designed to enhance the social skills and peer acceptance of LD students. Background on why students need social skills interventions and what barriers might exist that discourage or prevent teachers from teaching social skills were provided. Definitions of social skills and models that provide a background for applied social interventions were presented. Models for social intervention that were presented in this chapter included cognitive-social learning, interpersonal cognitive problem-solving, and a comparison between the contextualist and deficit models of social skills.

Several interventions that have been conducted with LD students were described in detail. These interventions included a social skills program for adolescents, a contextualist intervention, cooperative learning, and mutual interest discovery. Procedures for implemeting these interventions as well as comments that might assist in knowing when and with whom to use the interventions were provided. In addition to social interventions implemented with LD populations, social interventions that were evaluated with other populations were also presented.

Finally, the chapter provides an overview of issues relevant to teaching social skills to LD students. The following guidelines for teaching social skills were presented: use principles of effective instruction, interact with students in ways that communicate acceptance, give all students the opportunity to be "knower," and involve peers, school personnel, and the community in social skills training.

References

Bandura, A. (1978). The self system in reciprocal determinism. *Am. Psycholog.* **33,** 344–358.

Bandura, A. (1982). Self-efficacy mechanism in human agency. *Am. Psycholog.* **37,** 122–147.

Baum, D., Duffelmeyer F., and Geelan, M (1988). Resource teacher perceptions of the prevalence of social dysfunction among students with learning disabilities *J. Learn. Disabil.* **21(6),** 380–381.

Berler, E. G., Gross, A. M., and Drabner, R. S. (1982). Social skills training with children: Proceed with caution. *J. Appl. Behav. Anal.* **15,** 41–53.

Bierman, K. L. (1986). Process of change during social skills training with preadolescents and its relation to treatment outcome. *Child Dev.* **57**, 230–240.

Bierman, K. L., and Furman, W. (1984). The effects of social skills training and peer involvement on the social adjustment of preadolescents. *Child Dev.* **55**, 151–162.

Bierman, K. L., Miller, C. L., and Stabb, S. D. (1987). Improving the social behavior and peer acceptance of rejected boys: Effects of social skill training with instructions and prohibitions. *J. Consult. Clin. Psychol.* **55**, 194–200.

Brophy, J. (1979). Research on the self-fulfilling prophecy and teacher expectations. *J. Educ. Psychol.* **71**, 733–750.

Brophy, J. (1983). Research on the self-fulfilling prophecy and teacher expectations. *J. Educ. Psychol.* **75**, 631–661.

Bryan, T., and Perlmutter, B. (1979). Female adults' immediate impressions of learning disabled children. *Learn. Disabil. Q.* **2**, 80–88.

Bryan T., and Sherman, R. (1980). Immediate impressions of nonverbal ingratiation attempts by learning disabled boys. *Learn. Disabil. Q.* **3**, 19–28.

Clabby, J. F., and Elias, M. J. (1987). "Teach Your Child Decision Making." Doubleday, New York.

Coie, J. D. (1985). Fitting social skills intervention to the target group. *In* "Children's Peer Relations: Issues in Assessment and Intervention" (B. H. Schneider, K. H. Rubin, and J. E. Ledingham, eds.), pp. 141–156. Springer-Verlag, New York.

Coie, J. D., and Krehbiel, G. (1984). Effects of academic tutoring on the social status of low-achieving, socially rejected children. *Child Dev.* **55**, 1465–1478.

Deluty, R. H. (1981). Alternative thinking ability of aggressive, assertive, and submissive children. *Cog. Ther. Res.* **5**, 309–312.

Denham, S. A., and Almeida, M. C. (1987). Children's social problem-solving skills, behavioral adjustment, and interventions: A meta-analysis evaluating theory and practice. *J. Appl. Dev. Psychol.* **8**, 391–409.

Dubow, E. F., and Tisak, J. (1989). The relation between stressful life events and adjustment in elementary school children: The role of social support and social problem-solving skills. *Child Dev.* **60**, 1412–1423.

Elardo, P. T., and Caldwell, B. M. (1978). The effects of an experimental social development program on children in the middle childhood period. *Psychol. Schools* **16**, 93–100.

Elias, M. J., and Clabby, J. F. (1989). "Social Decision-Making Skills: A Curriculum Guide for the Elementary Grades." Aspen, Rockville, Maryland.

Elias, M. J., Gara, M., Ubriaco, M., Rothbaum, P., Clabby, J. F., and Schuyler, T. (1986). The impact of a preventive social problem solving intervention on children's coping with middle school stressors. *Am. J. Commun. Psychol.* **14**, 259–275.

Forman, E. A. (1987). Peer relationships of learning disabled children: A contextualist perspective. *Learn. Disabil. Res.* **2**, 80–89.

Foster, S. L., and Ritchey, W. C. (1979). Issues in the assessment of social competence in children. *J. Appl. Behav. Anal.* **12**, 625–631.

Fox, C. (1989). Peer acceptance of learning disabled children in the regular classroom. *Excep. Children* **56(1)**, 50–57.

Fox. C. L. (1980). "Communicating to Make Friends." B. L. Winch & Associates, Rolling Hills Estates, California.

Goldstein, A. P., Sprafkin, R. P., Gershaw, N. J., and Klein, P. (1980). "Skillstreaming the Adolescent." Research Press, Champaign, Illinois.

Graves, D. H. (1983). "Writing: Teachers and Children at Work." Heinemann Educational Books, Portsmouth, New Hampshire.

Gresham, F. M. (1984). Social skills and self-efficacy for exceptional children. *Excep. Children* **51(3)**, 253–261.

Hazel, J. S., Schumaker, J. B., Sherman, J. A., and Sheldon-Wildgen, J. (1981). "ASSET: A Social Skills Program for Adolescents." Research Press, Champaign, Illinois.

Hazel, J. S., Schumaker, J. B., Sherman, J. A., and Sheldon, J. (1982). Application of a group training program in social skills and problem solving to learning disabled and non-learning disabled youth. *Learn. Disabil. Q.* **5**, 398–408.

Johnson, D. W., and Johnson, R. (1984a). Building acceptance of differences between handicapped and nonhandicapped students: The effects of cooperative and individualistic problems. *J. Social Psychol.* **122**, 257–267.

Johnson, D. W., and Johnson, R. T. (1984b). "Cooperation in the Classroom." Interaction Book Co., Edina, Minnesota.

Johnson, D. W., and Johnson, R. T. (1986). Mainstreaming and cooperative learning strategies. *Excep. Children* **52**, 553–561.

Johnson, D. W., Johnson, R. T., Warring, D., and Maruyama, G. (1986). Different cooperative learning procedures and cross-handicap relationships. *Excep. Children* **53(3)**, 247–252.

Kavanagh, J. F., and Truss, T. J. (1988). "Learning Disabilities: Proceedings of the National Conference." York Press, Parkton, Maryland.

Ladd, G. W., and Mize, J. (1983). A cognitive-social learning model of social-skill training. *Psycholog. Rev.* **90(2)**, 127–157.

LaGreca, A. (1981). Social behavior and social perception in learning-disabled children: A review with implications for social skills training. *J. Pediatr. Psychol.* **6(4)**, 395–416.

LaGreca, A. M., and Mesibov, G. B. (1981). Facilitating interpersonal functioning with peers in learning-disabled children. *J. Learn. Disabil.* **14**, 197–199, 238.

McGinnis, E., Goldstein, A. P., Sprafkin, R. P., and Gershaw, N. J. (1984). "Skillstreaming the Elementary School Child: A Guide for Teaching Prosocial Skills." Research Press, Champaign, Illinois.

McIntosh, R., Vaughn, S., and Zaragoza, N. (in press). Social interventions for students with learning disabilities: An examination of the research. *J. Learn. Disab.*

McKim, B. J., Weissbar, R. Pl., Cowen, E. L., Gesten, E. L., and Rapkin, B. D. (1982). A comparison of the problem-solving ability and adjustment of suburban and urban third-grade children. *Am. J. Commun. Psychol.* **10**, 155–169.

Northcutt, T. E. (1987). The impact of a social skills training program on the teacher–student relationship. Doctoral dissertation, University of Maryland, College Park, *Diss. Abstr. Int.* **47**, 3712A.

Palinscar, A. S., and Brown, A. L. (1984). Reciprocal teaching of comprehension fostering and comprehension monitoring activities. *Cognit. Instruct.* **1(2)**, 117–175.

Parker, J. G., and Asher, S. R. (1987). Peer relations and later personal adjustment: Are low accepted children at risk? *Psycholog. Bull.* **102(3)**, 357–389.

Pellegrini, D. S., and Urbain, E. S. (1985). An evaluation of interpersonal cognitive problem solving training with children. *J. Child Psychol. Psych.* **26,** 17–41.

Putnam, J. W., Rynders, J. E., Johnson, R. T., and Johnson, D. W. (1989). Collaborative skill instruction for promoting positive interactions between mentally handicapped and nonhandicapped children. *Excep. Children* **55(6),** 550–557.

Rourke, B. P. (1988). Socioemotional disturbances of learning disabled children. *J. Consult. Clin. Psychol.* **56,** 801–810.

Sancilio, M. F. M. (1987). Peer interaction as a method of therapeutic intervention with children. *Clin. Psychol. Rev.* **7,** 475–500.

Shafer, H. S.,-Egel, A. L., and Neef, N. A. (1984). Training mildly handicapped peers to facilitate changes in the social interaction skills of autistic children. *J. Appl. Behav. Anal.* **17,** 461–476.

Shure, M. B., and Spivack, G. (1979). Interpersonal cognitive problem solving and primary prevention: Programming for preschool and kindergarten children. *J. Clin. Child Psychol.* **2,** 89–94.

Shure, M. B., and Spivack, G. (1980). Interpersonal problem solving as a mediator of behavioral adjustment in preschool and kindergarten children. *J. Appl. Dev. Psychol.* **1,** 29–44.

Spivack, G., Platt, J. J., and Shure, M. B. (1976). "The Problem-Solving Approach to Adjustment." Jossey-Bass, San Francisco.

Slavin, R. E., Madden, N. A., and Leavey, M. (1984). Effects of cooperative learning and individualized instruction on mainstreamed students. *Excep. Children* **50(5),** 434–443.

Solomon, R. W., and Wahler, R. G. (1973). Peer reinforcement control of classroom problem behavior. *J. Appl. Behav. Anal.* **17,** 461–476.

Stone, W. L., and LaGreca, A. M. (1990). The social status of children with learning disabilities: A reexamination. *J. Learn. Disabil.* **23(1),** 32–37.

Strain, P. S. (1983). Identification of peer social skills for preschool mentally retarded children in mainstreamed classes. *Appl. Res. Ment. Retard.* **4,** 369–382.

Strain, P. S., and Odom, S. L. (1986). Peer social initiations: Effective intervention for social skills development of exceptional children. *Excep. Children* **52,** 543–551.

Vaughn, S., and Hogan, A. (1990). Social competence and learning disabilities: A prospective study. *In* "Learning Disabilities: Theoretical and Research Issues" (H. L. Swanson and B. K. Keogh, eds.), pp. 175–191. Lawrence Erlbaum, Hillsdale, New Jersey.

Vaughn, S., Hogan, A., Kouzekanani, K., and Shapiro, S. (1990). Peer acceptance, self-perceptions, and social skills of LD students prior to identification. *J. Educ. Psychol.* **82(1),** 101–106.

Vaughn, S., and LaGreca, A. M. (1988). Social skills of LD students: Characteristics, behaviors, and guidelines for intervention. *In* "Handbook in Learning Disabilities", (K. Kavale, ed.) (pp. 123–140.) College Hill, San Diego.

Vaughn, S., and Lancelotta, G. X. (1990). Teaching interpersonal social skills to low accepted students: Peer-pairing versus no peer-pairing. *J. School Psychol.* **28(3),** 181–188.

Vaughn, S., Lancelotta, G. X., and Minnis, S. (1988). Social strategy training and peer involvement: Increasing peer acceptance of a female, LD student. *Learn. Disabil. Focus* **4,** 32–37.

Vaughn, S., and McIntosh, R. (1989). Interpersonal problem solving: A piece of the social competence puzzle for LD students. *J. Read. Writ. Learn. Disabil.* **4(4),** 321–334.

Vaughn, S., McIntosh, R., and Spencer-Rowe, J. (in press). Peer rejection is a stubborn thing: Increasing peer acceptance of rejected students with learning disabilities. *Learn. Disabil. Res.*

Vaughn, S. R. (1987). TLC—Teaching, learning, and caring: Teaching interpersonal problem solving skills to emotionally disturbed adolescents. *Pointer* **31,** 25–30.

Vaughn, S. R., Ridley, C. A., and Bullock, D. D. (1984). Interpersonal problem-solving skills training with aggressive young children. *J. Appl. Dev. Psychol.* **5,** 213–233.

Vaughn, S. R., Ridley, C. A., and Cox, J. (1983). Evaluating the efficacy of an interpersonal skills training program with children who are mentally retarded. *Educ. Train. Ment. Retard.* **18,** 191–196.

Wiener, J. (1987). Peer status of learning disabled children and adolescents: A review of the literature. *Learn. Disabil. Res.* **2(2),** 62–79.

Wilchesky, M., and Reynolds, T. (1986). The socially deficient LD child in context: A systems approach to assessment and treatment. *J. Learn. Disabil.* **19(7),** 411–415

Williams, V. R. (1983). The effects of a classroom social skills training program on socially maladaptive learning disabled elementary students. Doctoral dissertation, North Texas State University, Denton. *Diss. Abstr. Int.* **44,** 1424A.

Zigmond, N., and Brownlee, J. (1980). Social skills training for adolescents with learning disabilities. *Excep. Educ. Q.* **12,** 77–83.

CHAPTER 15

Collaborative Consultation

Suzanne M. Robinson

Editor's Notes

Having dealt with topics on assessment and remediation of academic and nonacademic problems in learning disabilities, we conclude Section II with two chapters that examine topics that relate importantly to how we can best service students with learning disabilities. These topics are collaborative consultation and issues in service delivery.

Robinson's chapter centers on collaborative consultation. Her first theme focuses on explaining why collaborative consultation currently assumes so much importance. Within this theme, there is a subtheme on the personal and structural barriers to effective collaborative consultation. Robinson then continues to the second theme, which is definition of the term "collaborative consultation." The third theme focuses on the skills and knowledge required for effective implementation of collaborative consultation. The fourth theme focuses on service delivery structures that allow for implementation of it. The last theme focuses on development of effective collaborative programs. Robinson closes her chapter with a cogent and instructive articulation of what constitutes collaborative consultation, and what does not.

I. INTRODUCTION

This chapter provides an overview of collaborative consultation. Collaborative consultation is a term used to describe an interactive and ongoing process where individuals with different expertise, knowledge, or experience voluntarily work together to create solutions to mutually agreed upon

Learning about Learning Disabilities
Copyright © 1991 by Academic Press, Inc. All rights of reproduction in any form reserved.

problems. It is characterized by mutual trust and respect and open communication. Underlying assumptions and beliefs of collaborative consultation include an assumption of parity among participants, belief that *all* educators can learn better ways to teach *all* students, and belief that educators should be actively involved in creating, as well as delivering, instructional innovations. The goal of collaborative consultation is to better meet the needs of diverse students, both handicapped and nonhandicapped, in as integrated an educational setting as possible.

Collaborative consultation, as defined here, is a *process*, rather than a service delivery *model*. As a process that entails collaborative team work, different service delivery structures could be used if the educators working together see them as in the best interest of individual students or a particular school. For example, given an extremely diverse group of students, teachers of differing expertise might choose to teach together, taking on different instructional responsibilities dependent on their individual strengths to facilitate learning by all the students in that one setting. Or, a classroom teacher may consult with a special education teacher about how to develop and implement a behavior management system, instructional modifications, or other practices with which he or she is not familiar. Or, teachers may learn about a new instructional technique (e.g., learning strategies, cooperative learning) and then decide to work together within a coaching structure or support group structure to assist one another in implementing the innovation at a high level. All of these relationships are collaborative when individuals mutually agree that working together has benefits that go beyond what one can accomplish working alone. In this chapter, I discuss the context in which this process of serving youngsters with handicaps is coming to the fore, skills and knowledge needed for effective collaborative consultation, service delivery structures in which collaborative consultation can occur, and the development of effective collaborative programs. While collaborative consultation has applications outside of special education (e.g., as a schoolwide process among a school's faculty for meeting unique needs and accessing resources within an individual school), I will emphasize its utility for serving students with learning disabilities.

II. WHY THE MOVEMENT TOWARD COLLABORATIVE CONSULTATION?

A. Historical Context of Collaborative Consultation

While considered "new" as an area of focus and currently receiving considerable attention in the professional journals (see *Journal of Educational and Psychological Consultation*, Vol. 1, No. 1, 1990; *Remedial and Special*

Education, Vol. 9, No. 6, 1988; and *Teacher Education and Special Education*, 1985), in fact, consultation in special education has a long history. During the 1960s, when dissatisfaction with segregated special education classes grew, many researchers (Adamson and Van Etten, 1972; Dunn, 1968; Lilly, 1970) called for an expansion of special education services to include consultative and resource services for mildly handicapped students who could be educated in regular education classes for part, or most, of the school day. This call for a continuum of services resulted in an increased emphasis on "mainstreaming" and provision of an appropriate educational program in the "least restrictive environment." Most special education professionals responded with the development of the resource room model (Wiederholt *et al.*, 1983), although some responded with fully realized consulting models. The Vermont Consulting Teacher Model (McKenzie *et al.*, 1970) is the most well-known example.

While the resource room model ensured that participating youngsters were educated more of the school day in the mainstream, actual coordination of special and regular education was limited. Consultation between special educators and classroom teachers was constrained by lack of time to consult as well as lack of knowledge about how to integrate special education services effectively with regular classroom expectations. Thus, implementation of the resource room model did not result necessarily in students who were mainstreamed successfully.

B. Collaborative Consultation — Why Now?

Special education programs were developed to meet unique needs of certain students. However, research findings confirming their effectiveness have been equivocal. There are many reasons for this, including the following: difficulty controlling all variables in a complex educational school program, lack of control groups, differences in how programs are implemented, differences in the characteristics of students who are identified as having learning disabilities, and poorly designed studies (Keogh, 1988).

The disjointed nature of pull-out programs and the inefficiency of having special education programs and other special programs competing for time and students are questioned by policy analysts as to their effectiveness and efficiency in meeting the demonstrated need of particular students (Reynolds and Wang, 1983; Will, 1986). Fractionalized programs create deficiencies that might not occur if all students received the same education (although *direct* support might be required, the same education does not have to be delivered to all children in the same way).

Other researchers (Edgar, 1987; Zigmond and Thornton, 1985) have examined the success with which adolescents with disabilities have exited school and entered the work force. Their findings are discouraging. Young adults with disabilities are unemployed and underemployed (in terms of making enough income to live independently) to a much greater degree than their nonhandicapped peers. While it is unknown what contribution existing special education programs have made to these outcomes, it is obvious that schooling (as currently conceived) is not adequately preparing these youngsters to live independent lives.

Within this context, many special educators are examining special education services and asking how we can educate youngsters with learning disabilities more successfully. Discussion and subsequent actions to Will's (1986) call for special and general education to share the responsibility for educating students with learning and behavior problems has resulted in the development of innovative service delivery programs. Concurrent with these special education restructuring efforts, general educators are also exploring school reform. The foci of concern are compatible to increased collaboration among all educators. They include the type of preservice and inservice education that teachers should receive and how it should be delivered, empowerment of teachers through site-based decision-making, and restructuring the way resources (teachers) are used in schools through innovative scheduling, mentorship programs, and identification of master teachers.

C. Barriers to Effective Collaboration

The demand to improve the way in which youngsters with learning disabilities are served is great, and increased collaboration between special and regular educators appears a viable means of accomplishing that. However, barriers that inhibit the development and effective implementation of collaborative structures among teachers currently exist in schools. Some of these barriers are *personal*: Change is difficult and individual teachers may find it hard to change the way in which they teach. Some teachers may lack skills in working collaboratively. Traditionally, teaching is an activity carried out by an individual teacher in a classroom with students. Collaborative problem-solving and cooperative planning are not approaches with which many teachers feel comfortable. Other teachers may lack knowledge about instructional strategies that can be employed to accommodate a very diverse group of students in a classroom and be unwilling to seek assistance. Also, some teachers do not feel ownership of the education for students with diabilities. They believe that the difficulties these students exhibit should be addressed outside of their classroom by someone else (Huefner, 1988).

Some barriers to collaboration are *structural*: Schools are not structured to facilitate teachers planning and working together. Lack of time to meet and plan is frequently cited as impeding collaborative efforts (Johnson *et al.*, 1988; Nevin *et al.*, 1990). Currently, teachers spend almost all their time working directly with students.

Competing priorities in how teachers and students are scheduled also interfere. Special programs such as physical education, music, and band need to be accommodated. At the high school level, sections of a class that are offered on a limited basis require scheduling priority. At the elementary level, schedules are designed to address the number of classes at any grade level, teachers who are in the building for only part of the week, and special programs. For collaborative programs to succeed, schools must be structured differently. However, existing practice exerts a powerful influence on how we picture school organization. Thus, prevailing practice is a barrier to our visualizing teachers' and students' time scheduled differently so that more collaboration can occur. To use only precious and limited planning time for collaboration, or time before and after the school day, is not acceptable. Collaboration under those conditions would be too burdensome to be truly successful over the long-term.

Also, *external* barriers to the teacher–student unit impede successful collaboration: Lack of funds for training teachers in new and needed skills (Huefner, 1988), state and federal regulations that are not responsive to changing programs (Idol, 1988), and lack of administrative support for change (Huefner, 1988) are all cited as barriers to collaborative program development. Thus, many factors currently interfere with successfully implementing collaborative teaching arrangements.

III. DEFINITION OF COLLABORATION AND CONSULTATION

Currently, the terms collaboration and consultation often are used interchangeably, or together (as collaborative consultation) in the special education literature, although various authors discuss distinctions among the terms. This has been the source of confusion among readers of this literature. These discussions reflect both the theoretical perspective to which particular authors adhere and the type of problem-solving relationship between educators they promote. In this chapter, *collaboration* is used as a generic term and is equivalent to the term collaborative consultation. The different problem-solving relationships will be described and subsumed under the term collaboration.

A. Collaboration

Collaboration (or collaborative consultation) was defined briefly at the beginning of the chapter as a term describing an interactive and ongoing process where individuals with different expertise, knowledge, or experience voluntarily work together to create solutions to mutually agreed upon problems. It is characterized by mutual trust and respect and open communication. Here we examine components of the definition in greater detail.

1. Interactive and Ongoing Process

Collaboration entails a relationship among individuals with shared responsibility in producing desired outcomes. The commitment to shared responsibility predicates an interactive and ongoing relationship because many solutions to problems require adaptation and adjustment as they are implemented and require attention over a period of time.

2. Individuals with Different Expertise, Knowledge, or Experience

Individuals engaging in collaborative problem-solving acknowledge that often the best solution will evolve from contributions from more than one individual. No one individual is considered "the expert"; it is not assumed that any one individual has (or must have) all the answers. While individuals are recognized for their expertise in particular areas, an assumption of parity exists. This means that all participants are valued equally for their contributions, although their contributions to a particular solution may not be equivalent.

3. Voluntarily Work Together

Collaboration requires that individuals willingly agree to work with one another and believe that working together will be mutually beneficial. However, working together can be embodied by a variety of problem-solving relationships. It can occur within a helping relationship, where one individual purchases the expertise of another (e.g., requesting information on how to set up a behavior management system, asking for materials that would be appropriate for a particular student), is often delivered in a consultative structure (teacher assistance teams, child study teams, or collaborative consultation between a special and general educator), and is characterized as indirect assistance to students. Working together can occur within a joint problem-solving relationship, where individuals share responsibility and committment to implementing a solution (e.g., teachers planning how they will teach together to meet previously unmet needs of students), is often delivered in a collaborative structure (teaching teams, grade-level teams, or collaborative consultation structure), and all parties have responsibility in directly implementing the plan. Finally, working together can occur within a supporting relationship, where teachers share information to assist one another in individually implementing a solution or procedure. Two teachers helping one another learn a new curriculum or talking through an instructional concern are examples of supporting relationships, and they often occur within the structures of peer coaching, study groups, peer collaboration, or support group structures.

4. Mutually Agreed Upon Problems

Inherent to collaboration is respect for individuals and the process of decision-making by consensus. This means that individuals must have effective communication and relationship-building skills. There must be a belief in parity among participants, even though differences in knowledge and experience may exist.

The assumptions that underlie collaboration—parity among participants, belief that *all* educators can learn better ways to teach *all* students, and educators should be actively involved in creating, as well as delivering, instructural innovations—must be kept in mind as one defines the interaction among individuals and the structures within which collaborative relationships operate. Under the generic term of collaboration, one finds specific problem-solving relationships defined by different authors. These are described below.

a. Consultation   Some authors discuss consultation as a collaborative problem-solving relationship (Huefner, 1988; Idol, 1988; Reisberg and Wolf, 1986). It is seen as primarily a special education service; thus, a special education teacher is almost always a member of the problem-solving relationship. Special education teachers spend all or part of the day providing indirect service to students by problem-solving with and providing resources to general educators with the goal of preventing or resolving student problems. However, it is different from an "expert" model of consultation in that the relationship is perceived as collaborative. In the expert model of consultation, equal status and parity of participants in the relationship are not assumed; instead, the expert typically is assigned higher status than those with whom he or she consults because of his or her expertise.

b. Peer Collaboration   Other authors discuss collaboration as a problem-solving relationship among any teachers (Friend and Cook, 1990; Pugach and Johnson, 1988). It is different from the consultation model discussed previously because collaboration is *not* described as a special education service. Indeed, these authors stated that when collaboration is initiated primarily by special educators, it violates the assumptions of parity and equality. The implicit message in such a relationship is that general education teachers do not possess knowledge of instructional strategies that can be used with disabled learners and that special education teachers can provide it. In peer collaboration, any teacher can assist another in solving problems through the use of problem-solving strategies in which they all have been trained.

    c. Collaborative Consultation   It is important to note that the assumptions that underly these different perspectives are the same. Thus, the term collaborative consultation is used frequently in the literature and apparently attempts to reconcile these two perspectives on collaboration. Tindall *et al.* (1990) concluded that the complex context of any school will dictate many different problem-solving relationships. In any given school, the unique needs of students, parents, and teachers, and the resources the environment can marshall to address a problem, will determine the nature of, and participants in, a problem-solving relationship. Sometimes expertise will be purchased from somebody, sometimes someone will facilitate another's solution-finding, and sometimes shared responsibility and accountability for implementation of solutions will dictate truly equal participation in problem identification and solution-finding. As more educators (Nevin *et al.*, 1990) begin to discuss the collaborative school as the emerging restructured school, where all teachers have knowledge and skills in collaboration, one can see where many collaborative relationships will coexist.

IV. SKILLS NEEDED FOR
EFFECTIVE COLLABORATION

For teachers to be effective in collaborative endeavors, they need knowledge and skills in the process of collaboration and knowledge and skills in effective teaching practices. Without both, collaboration will not necessarily result in better outcomes for students. Lippitt and Lippitt's (1978) description of the multiple roles of a consultant (advocate, information specialist, trainer–educator, joint problem-solver and identifier of potential solutions, linker to resources, fact finder) emphasized the importance of a slightly different knowledge base than teachers have developed traditionally. Furthermore, given that collaborative programs are relatively new, teachers will need knowledge about change and program development so that they can participate in developing collaborative programs that meet the needs of a specific school.

A. Knowledge about the Process of Collaboration

West and Cannon (1988) conducted an extensive review of the literature on consultation to determine which interpersonal and communication skills were considered necessary for effective consultation. Forty-seven skills were identified as essential by a panel of experts on school consultation. The skills were then categorized into eight general categories: (1) consultation theory models; (2) research on consultation theory, training, and practice; (3) personal characteristics; (4) interactive communication; (5) collaborative problem-solving; (6) systems change; (7) equity issues and values/belief systems; and (8) evaluation of consultation effectiveness. Table 15.1 includes a complete listing of the skills identified as essential by the expert panel.

Table 15.1
Essential Skills for the Process of Consultation

Consultation Theory Models
1. Practice reciprocity of roles between consultant and consultee in facilitating the consultation process.
2. Demonstrate knowledge of various stages/phases of the consultation process.
3. Assume joint responsibility for identifying each stage of the consultation process and adjusting behavior accordingly.
4. Match consultation approach(es) to specific consultation situation(s), setting(s), and need(s).

Research on Consultation Theory, Training, and Practice
5. Translate relevant consultation research findings into effective school-based consultation practice.

Personal Characteristics
6. Exhibit ability to be caring, respectful, empathic, congruent, and open in consultation interactions.
7. Establish and maintain rapport with all persons involved in the consultation process, in both formal and informal interactions.
8. Identify and implement appropriate responses to stage of professional development of all persons involved in the consultation process.
9. Maintain positive self-concept and enthusiastic attitude throughout the consultation process.
10. Demonstrate willingness to learn from others throughout the consultation process.
11. Facilitate progress in consultation situations by managing personal stress, maintaining calm in time of crisis, taking risks, and remaining flexible and resilient.
12. Respect divergent points of view, acknowledging the right to hold different views and to act in accordance with convictions.

Interactive Communication
13. Communicate clearly and effectively in oral and written form.
14. Utilize active, ongoing listening and responding skills to facilitate the consultation process (e.g., acknowledging, paraphrasing, reflecting, clarifying, elaborating, summarizing).
15. Determine own and others' willingness to enter consultative relationship.
16. Adjust consultation approach to the learning stage of individuals involved in the consultation process.
17. Exhibit ability to grasp and validate overt/covert meaning and affect in communications (perceptive).
18. Interpret nonverbal communications of self and others (e.g., eye contact, body language, personal boundaries in space) in appropriate context.
19. Interview effectively to elicit information, share information, explore problems, and set goals and objectives.

(continues)

Table 15.1 (*continued*)

20. Pursue issues with appropriate persistence once they arise in the consultation process.
21. Give and solicit continuous feedback that is specific, immediate, and objective.
22. Give credit to others for their ideas and accomplishments.
23. Manage conflict and confrontation skillfully throughout the consultation process to maintain collaborative relationships.
24. Manage timing of consultation activities to facilitate mutual decision-making at each stage of the consultation process.
25. Apply the principle of positive reinforcement to one another in the collaborative team situation.
26. Be willing and safe enough to say "I don't know...let's find out."

Collaborative Problem-Solving

27. Recognize that successful and lasting solutions require commonality of goals and collaboration throughout all phases of the problem solving process.
28. Develop a variety of data collection techniques for problem identification and clarification.
29. Generate viable alternatives through brainstorming techniques characterized by active listening, nonjudgmental responding, and appropriate reframing.
30. Evaluate alternatives to anticipate possible consequences, narrow and combine choices, and assign priorities.
31. Integrate solutions into a flexible, feasible, and easily implemented plan of action relevant to all persons affected by the problem.
32. Adopt a "pilot problem-solving" attitude, recognizing that adjustments to the plan of action are to be expected.
33. Remain available throughout implementation for support, modeling, and/or assistance in modification.
34. Redesign, maintain, or discontinue interventions using data-based evaluation.
35. Utilize observation, feedback, and interviewing skills to increase objectivity and mutuality throughout the problem-solving process.

Systems Change

36. Develop role as a change agent (e.g., implementing strategies for gaining support, overcoming resistance).
37. Identify benefits and negative effects that could result from change efforts.

Equity Issues and Values/Beliefs Systems

38. Facilitate equal learning opportunities by showing respect for individual differences in physical appearance, race, sex, handicap, ethnicity, religion, socioeconomic status, or ability.
39. Advocate for services that accommodate the educational, social, and vocational needs of all students, handicapped and nonhandicapped.
40. Encourage implementation of laws and regulations designed to provide appropriate education for all handicapped students.
41. Utilize principles of the least restrictive environment in all decisions regarding handicapped students.
42. Modify myths, beliefs, and attitudes that impede successful social and educational integration of handicapped students into the least restrictive environment.
43. Recognize, respect, and respond appropriately to the effects of personal values and belief systems of self and others in the consultation process.

Evaluation of Consultation Effectiveness

44. Ensure that persons involved in planning and implementing the consultation process are also involved in its evaluation.
45. Establish criteria for evaluating input, process, and outcome variables affected by the consultation process.
46. Engage in self-evaluation of strengths and weakneses to modify personal behaviors influencing the consultation process.
47. Utilize continuous evaluative feedback to maintain, revise, or terminate consultation activities.

Skills in effective communication are critical to collaboration. It will not matter what someone knows if others will not listen to him or her. In collaboration, developing and maintaining working relationships are crucial. Effective communication is the key to building working relationships. Therefore, teachers in collaborative relationships must be skilled in active listening, reflecting and responding, problem-solving, negotiating, conflict management, and cooperative planning.

B. Knowledge about Effective Instruction

Idol (1990: 5) noted the important distinction between knowledge about the process (or art) of consultation, which "is the way in which consultations interact and work with consultees," and the scientific knowledge about effective instructional practice, which is "the content or knowledge base the consultant brings to the consulting process ... and is usually the primary reason that a consultant is brought in to work with the consultee to help solve the problem." Both bodies of knowledge are essential to effective collaborative consultation.

Thus, knowledge of effective teaching practices and knowledge about how to match instructional tactics with the demands of general education settings are critical. In a recent study to determine what experts thought that knowledge base should encompass, 96 competencies were identified and organized into six categories (Cannon et al., 1989): (1) assessment and diagnosis, (2) instructional content, (3) instructional practices, (4) managing student behavior, (5) planning and managing the teaching and learning environment, and (6) monitoring and evaluation.

.Teacher trainers and researchers (Idol, 1990; Reisberg and Wolf, 1986; Robinson, 1987) in collaborative consultation have identified validated instructional practices that are effectively implemented in general education classrooms and successfully address diversity among students. They are included in existing training programs in collaboration. While some dif- ferences exist among training programs, there is considerable agreement in what constitutes the needed knowledge base in effective practices. These recommended strategies can be grouped into three categories: structuring and managing learning, teacher presentation and instructional tactics, and monitoring and evaluating instruction. While no attempt is made to include every validated practice, the discussion here will provide an overview of the range and depth of needed knowledge.

1. Structuring and Managing Learning

Researchers (Rosenshine, 1980; Rich and Ross, 1989; Thurlow et al., 1983) demonstrated the relationship between time on task and learning for both students with disabilities and their nondisabled peers. Thus, how teachers structure learning environments and manage ongoing activities will impact greatly on student time on task and achievement.

a. Cooperative learning Cooperative learning is characterized by peers learning from peers. This can be done in cooperative learning groups, which researchers demonstrated increased student achievement for both normal-achieving and underachieving students (Johnson *et al.*, 1981; Slavin, 1983, 1988). Cooperative learning groups emphasize interdependence among heterogeneous groups of students and discourage competition. Instructional arrangements where peers tutor peers or older students tutor younger students are other validated strategies that emphasize cooperation among heterogeneous groups of students and can be used to structure learning with the result of increased time on task (Jenkins and Jenkins, 1981, 1985).

b. Behavior management and applied behavior analysis Englert (1984) identified competencies that effective teachers need to manage instruction and noted that without effective management strategies, instructional tactics teachers use, no matter what their demonstrated effectiveness, are less so. Validated practices that increase competence in management include knowledge of behavioral principles, behavioral intervention tactics, and applied behavior analysis (Baer *et al.*, 1968; Smith, 1984). This body of knowledge provides teachers with skills in analyzing patterns of teacher and student responses through the analysis of antecedent and consequent events and in manipulating interventions until the desired response occurs.

2. Teacher Presentation and Instructional Tactics

For teachers to assist one another in improving learning environments so that a diverse group of students are successful, teachers must know how to present information to be learned in ways that facilitate learning by all students. The reseach literature on validated practices that are effective with *all* learners is growing. Thus, collaborative teachers should be knowledgeable about a range of effective teaching practices.

a. Effective presentation strategies Use of teaching practices with validated effectiveness in heterogeneous groups of students will enable students with disabilities to be successful in general education classrooms. These include the use of advance organizers (Lenz, 1983), cognitive mapping (Bulgren *et al.*, 1988), key word strategies (Mastropieri, 1988), structured lecture presentations emphasizing prior knowledge and essential learning objectives (Kasselman and Robinson, 1990), and use of effective questioning and feedback strategies (Robinson and Kasselman, 1990). All of these strategies proved to increase all student achievement or time on task in general education classrooms and are part of the needed knowledge base of collaborative teachers. While not inclusive of all validated practices, they are representative of a fairly new but growing body of research.

b. Learning and cognitive strategies Learning and cognitive strategies instruction emphasize teaching students *how* to learn. Learning strategies are procedures that enable students to more effectively acquire, store, and retrieve information (Alley and Deshler, 1979). They are based on principles of cognitive-behavior modification and are characterized by the use of meta-cognitive and cognitive strategies to increase independent and self-directed learning behavior. Cognitive instruction is defined as "any effort on the part of the teacher or the instructional materials to help students process information in meaningful ways and become independent learners" (Jones, 1986: 7). It encompasses attending to various dimensions of thinking. (For a more extensive discussion of cognitive instruction, see Jones and Idol, in press). Both approaches are related in their emphasis on increasing independent learning behavior and, when used by teachers and learned by students, increase the likelihood of success in mainstream settings.

c. Curriculum/material modifications Sometimes planned instruction will still not meet the needs of individual students, and modifying the curriculum or materials is the appropriate intervention. While it should not be the intervention of first choice (learning environments should be designed to accommodate diversity), curriculum/material modification can accommodate unique needs efficiently. Principles of effective modification encompass matching curriculum objectives to student characteristics using individualized teaching strategies. Many resources exist on effective strategies to modify curriculum and materials (see Deshler and Graham, 1980; Hoover, 1987; Kasselman, 1988; Wang and Walberg, 1985; Wiseman, 1980).

3. Monitoring and Evaluating Instruction
Teachers engaged in collaboration also should know how to monitor and evaluate instruction. Validated practices in evaluation include curriculum-based assessment, applied behavior analysis, and mastery learning. These evaluation strategies are a component of some previously described management or instructional strategies and incorporate measurement of curriculum learned, and rate of individual acquisition of curriculum, to determine appropriate instruction. Evaluation and monitoring occur simultaneously and are ongoing, and data are used to make formative instructional decisions (i.e., evaluation data are used to determine what instructional tactics teachers should use). These techniques have proved more powerful in enhancing student learning than traditional summative evaluation strategies.

C. Change and Program Development

Collaborative planning and teaching arrangements represent emerging service delivery options. Because they are relatively new, teachers engaged in collaboration find themselves designing and facilitating implementation of new educational services. Therefore, teachers trained in effective collaboration must understand the process of school change. They must also be knowledgeable about program development considerations and strategies. Finally, they must be able to contribute to the change effort by sharing the information they have. This can occur informally through working with others in collaborative relationships. At times, it also can be addressed efficiently through the provision of staff development activities. Thus, competence in providing staff development enables teachers to facilitate change.

D. Summary

While research has yet to validate the need for particular skill training, trainers and trainees agree on the importance of learning skills in communication, instructional evaluation, effective instructional practice, program evaluation, training other adults, and change and program development (Idol, 1990; Nevin *et al.*, 1990; Reisberg and Wolf, 1988; Robinson, 1988). Until such time that researchers validate essential skills, trainers and practitioners agree on the importance for educators engaged in collaboration to have a broader knowledge base than traditional teacher training provides (Friend and Cook, 1990). Traditional teacher training programs emphasize content expertise and teaching methodology. Without the additional skills to work effectively with their colleagues in dramatically different teaching structures with changed expectations for teachers and students, failure in effective collaboration is likely.

V. POTENTIAL COLLABORATIVE ROLES

The roles of teachers engaged in collaboration and the service delivery structures each school decides upon will vary depending on the strengths and needs of each school and on the needs of the students. Roles define collaborative activities, while structures define the organizational arrangement used to carry out the activity. Collaborative programs should be dynamic, changing as needs change. However, the elements and assumptions discussed within the definition section of this chapter will underlie any roles or service delivery structures educators within a school employ. The intended outcome of collaboration is to better serve students; however, the means to that end vary. Some collaborative activities are indirect means of serving students; collaborative consultation occurs between a teacher and a facilitator of problem-solving and solutions are implemented primarily by the teacher. Or, collaborative consultation can result in multiple teachers engaging in problem-solving and sharing responsibility in developing and implementing solutions, thus providing direct service to students. Collaborative consultation can entail teachers providing direct service to other teachers through sharing techniques or knowledge or can result in indirect service to the system through resulting solutions (e.g., curriculum modifications, reorganization of responsibilities across a school's faculty). Collaborative programs can emphasize one role or encompass many. While not an inclusive list of all collaborative activities, the following provides descriptions of common collaborative roles and structures.

A. Facilitator of Effective Problem-Solving

Problem-solving is the core skill of effective collaboration and a component of every other collaborative role. However, the role of collaborative consultant is one where problem-solving is the primary activity. In such a role, the special education teacher spends a portion of every day or every week in indirect service activities. The collaborative consultant might assist in determining alternative teaching strategies that may be more effective than those in use, observe in a classroom, provide coaching for a teacher colleague, demonstrate a teaching procedure, develop modified curriculum materials, assist in starting a new program, etc. This role has great flexibility; it is structured as a teacher-to-teacher service delivery model and incorporates many of the other roles on an as-needed basis (Huefner, 1988; West and Idol, 1990). Considerations to implementing this role include scheduling time to consult, determining feasible caseload numbers, and balancing direct and indirect service responsibilities (Idol, 1988). Concerns relative to implementing this role include the implication that the special education teacher is an "expert," that initiating collaboration is a special education function that is inconsistent with the premises of collaboration (Friend and Cook, 1990; Pugach and Johnson, 1988), and whether or not the special education teacher has the required knowledge base to be successful (Huefner, 1988).

B. Cooperative Teaching

Cooperative teaching refers to an educational structure in which special and regular educators jointly teach heterogeneous groups of students in general education classrooms. Heterogeneous classrooms mean that students represent the entire range of ability. Cooperative teaching is not a means of delivering remedial or basic track instruction. Responsibility for instruction and student achievement is shared, and both teachers are accountable for all students in the class (Bauwens *et al.*, 1989; Nevin *et al.*, 1990; Reynaud *et al.*, 1987). In cooperative teaching, both the general and special education teachers are present in the classroom, and instructional responsibilities are decided based on the unique skills of each teacher. Because responsibility for all students is shared, teacher roles are *not* determined by existing disability classifications or by student achievement levels.

Bauwens *et al.* (1989) described three instructional approaches that emerge in cooperatively taught classes. While discussed separately, often all three approaches are in effect simultaneously. Complementary instruction occurs when the special education teacher focuses on instruction in learning strategies or skills that will facilitate the acquisition of content presented primarily by the general education teacher. The complementary instruction can occur prior to content instruction, interspersed with the content instruction, and as a review. The intent is to closely tie the presentation of content to processes students can use to learn the content in efficient and effective ways. It removes concerns about the lack of generalization frequently seen when students are expected to generalize skills learned in a segregated setting to a general education classroom (Anderson-Inmann, 1986). Complementary instruction utilizes the different knowledge bases general educators and special educators typically have.

Another instructional approach used in cooperative teaching is team teaching or collaborative teaching. It differs from "turn teaching" in that teachers jointly plan and carry out content instruction. This instructional approach is based on the premise that "diagnostic, planning, and evaluative procedures developed by a team of teachers are generally superior to those developed by a single teacher" (Bauwens *et al.*, 1989: 19).

A third instructional approach used in cooperative teaching is the provision of supportive learning activities to supplement content instruction. Within this approach, the general educator might have primary responsibility for content presentation while the special educator develops and directs guided practice activities or supplemental instruction. Both teachers are present and monitor student progress during lesson progression.

In evaluations of cooperative teaching benefits and effectiveness, teachers report increased job satisfaction, reduced stress, enhanced stability, and increased teaching–learning potential (Bauwens *et al.*, 1989; F. Hudson, personal communication). Considerations in implementing cooperative teaching include scheduling time for teachers to plan together and providing training in collaborative skills prior to and during implementation of cooperative teaching arrangements. Potential concerns of cooperative teaching focus not on its effectiveness but on its efficiency. While two teachers may be better than one in a heterogeneous classroom, it is not often feasible to staff schools in this manner comprehensively.

C. Facilitating Instructional Innovation

Sharing information about effective instructional practices is one desired outcome of any collaborative endeavor. Therefore, teachers engaging in collaboration may assume a role that focuses on facilitating teacher adoption and implementation of effective teaching procedures. This role is oriented toward providing direct service to other teachers and indirectly providing services to students. This can occur within the structures of peer coaching support or study group participation (Showers, 1985), staff development provider (Leggett and Hoyle, 1986), or collaborative problem-solving (Reisberg and Wolf, 1986; West and Idol, 1990). The focus on facilitating teacher adoption and implementation of effective teaching practices also can result in teachers collaborating to develop alternative curriculum that is more responsive to the needs of heterogeneous classrooms (Wiseman, 1980; Wang and Walberg, 1985; Hudson, 1990). While facilitating instructional innovation is a component of the other roles discussed, it can become the primary focus of collaborative activities.

D. Organizational Structures that Can Facilitate Collaboration

Some organizational arrangements used in schools, supported by research, can facilitate collaboration. Teacher assistance teams, school-based resource teams, student support teams, child study teams, and middle school teams are structures that allow collaboration to take place (Chalfant *et al.*, 1979; Johnson and Markle, 1986; West and Idol, 1990). These organizational arrangements do not ensure collaboration; however, if participants on teams have skills in collaboration and believe in its benefits, these structures can facilitate it.

E. Summary

Collaborative programs may emphasize one role, one structure, or a combination of roles and structures. Given the complex nature of schools, the unique contextual variables one must address in any given setting, and the emergent character of collaborative programs, great diversity among programs is evident at this time. To be responsive to needs, collaborative programs will probably remain varied. Researchers and participants in program development support this site-specific approach to creating collaborative programs (Bauwens *et al.*, 1989; Nevin *et al.*, 1990; Tindall *et al.*, 1990; West and Idol, 1990). It is consistent with school reform recommendations (Friend and Cook, 1990) and reflects the initial stages that collaborative program development is in. Researchers will need to examine individual program effectiveness before definitive guidelines can be provided on how collaboration should best occur.

VI. COLLABORATIVE PROGRAM DEVELOPMENT

Research confirms that change is a difficult process and that educational change must be addressed systematically over time (Fullan, 1982; Guskey, 1986; Hord *et al.*, 1987). Thus, collaborative program development needs to take into account what we know about innovation adoption. Hord *et al.* (1987) as well as others (Fenstermacher and Berliner, 1985; 1982) addressed the developmental process of program development and innovation adoption. The Concerns Based Adoption Model developed by Hord *et al.* (1987) explicitly delineates stages of concern that must be considered. These include self concerns (Exactly what is the innovation? What does it mean to me? What will participation cost in terms of my time and effort? What will be benefits be?), task concerns (How is it supposed to work? What changes in organization will be required?), and impact concerns (Have my students improved as a result of this innovation? How do I improve the program? How do we expand the program?). If program development is not responsive to these stages of concern, it is unlikely to be successful.

Responding to what is known about educational change and incorporating what is currently known about collaboration, researchers proposed guidelines to follow in developing site-specific collaborative programs. Some examples from the literature follow:

1. Identify teachers interested in building collaborative relationships and alternative program delivery structures. Gain administrative support and commitment (at both the building and district levels) to long-range training and program development.
2. Deliver ongoing skill training in the processes of collaboration and effective instructional practices.
3. Develop a collaborative model that is site-specific. Considerations include organizational arrangements, training and preparation, how to provide ongoing support of implementation efforts, monitoring procedures, and communication about and dissemination of program

design and effectiveness. Comprehensive planning of this sort is ongoing, changing focus as the program develops.

4. Implement the program with technical assistance to ensure desired results (Robinson and McGuire, 1989).

While presented here in an abbreviated form, this program planning process addresses the difficulties that change creates.

Another example of a planning process focused on the development of special education consultation programs. The areas to be considered include:

1. financing consultation programs,
2. establishing prereferral and referral practices,
3. establishing performance standards for consulting teachers,
4. determining essential skills consulting teachers will need to meet these standards,
5. determining appropriate caseload for consulting teachers,
6. designing a scheduling system to provide time for consultation, and
7. designing and implementing an ongoing evaluation system (Idol, 1988: 50).

The knowledge base regarding effective collaborative programs is limited at this time. As an emerging service delivery system, researchers have examined components of collaboration. It is premature to assess the effectiveness of collaborative programs, or even to define what they should be. Therefore, practitioners must proceed slowly and with the full knowledge that much is not known about collaborative programs.

VII. CONCLUSION: WHAT COLLABORATIVE CONSULTATION IS AND WHAT IT IS NOT

Collaborative consultation is emerging as a viable means of addressing the learning and behavioral difficulties of students with learning disabilities in predominantly mainstream settings. As a process of accommodating diversity among students in general education classrooms and in its emerging service delivery forms, it is consistent with current thinking on the integration of special education and general education knowledge and programs. It is also consistent with more global school reform efforts. If our goal is to make the mainstream learning environment responsive to the needs of students with learning disabilities, indications are that collaborative consultation is a means to that end.

However, there are issues to consider. First, research has yet to prove that collaborative programs are more effective than more traditional special education programs. While preliminary research reports are generally positive, substantial research is needed to determine effective components of collaborative programs, evaluate the relative effectiveness of various collaborative structures, and determine the additive effect of multiple collaborative activities. Second, what skills are essential to effective collaboration are unknown. Researchers must determine what the critical knowledge base is to function successfully in teaching roles very different from those teachers traditionally have filled. Third, who the critical players are in collaborative training and program development are also unknown. Currently there is considerable discussion about whether collaborative consultation should be primarily a special education activity (which perpetuates the division between special education and general education systems) or is viable as a schoolwide structure (which requires monumental, coordinated training efforts and restructuring of the way teaching arrangements are currently organized). Thus, while a seemingly viable process for better meeting the needs of children with learning disabilities, many questions remain to be answered about collaborative consultation.

Collaborative consultation is an emerging process for serving youngsters with learning disabilities. If concerted efforts are made to coordinate that we know about effective instruction, building working relationships, teacher training, and the change process, there are indications we are on the right path to developing inclusive, responsive educational programs.

References

Adamson, G., and Van Etten, G. (1972). Zero reject model revisited: A workable alternative. *Excep. Children* **38**, 735–738.

Alley, G., and Deshler, D. (1979). "Teaching the Learning Disabled Adolescent: Strategies and Methods." Love Publishing, Denver, Colorado.

Anderson-Inmann, L. (1986). Bridging the gap: Student centered strategies for promoting the transfer of learning. *Excep. Children* **52**, 487–488.

Baer, D. M., Wolfe, M. M., and Risley, T. R. (1968). Some current dimensions of applied behavior analysis. *J. Appl. Behav. Anal.* **1**, 91–97.

Bauwens, J., Hourcade, J. J., and Friend, M. (1989). Cooperative teaching: A model for general and special education integration. *Remed. Special Educ.* **10(2)**, 17–22.

Bulgren, J. A., Schumaker, J. B. and Deshler, D. D. (1988). Effectiveness of a concept teaching routine in enhancing the performance of LD students in secondary-level mainstream classes. *Learning Disabil. Quart.* **11**, 3–17.

Cannon, G. S., Idol, L., and West, J. F. (1989). An investigation of essential teaching competencies for general and special educators collaborating to educate mildly handicapped students in general classrooms. Tech. Rep. No. 104, Research and

Training Project on School Consultation, Department of Special Education, University of Texas at Austin, Austin.

Chalfant, J. C., Pysh, M. V., and Moultrie, R. (1979). Teacher assistance teams: A model for within-building problem solving. *Learn. Disabil. Q.* **2,** 85–96.

Deshler, D. D., and Graham, S. (1980). Tape recording educational materials for secondary handicapped students. *Teach. Excep. Children* **12(2),** 52–54.

Dunn, L. M. (1968). Special education for the mildly retarded—Is much of it justifiable? *Excep. Children* **35(1),** 5–22.

Edgar, E. (1987). Secondary programs in special education: Are many of them justifiable? *Excep. Children* **53,** 555–561.

Englert, C. S. (1984). Measuring teacher effectiveness from the teacher's point of view. *Focus on Exceptional Children,* **17(2),** 1–14.

Fenstermacher, D. G. and Berliner, D. C. (1985). Determining the value of staff development. *Elem. Schl. J.* **8(3),** 281–314.

Friend, M., and Cook, L. (1990). Collaboration as a predictor for success in school reform. *J. Educ. Psycholog. Consult.* **1(1),** 69–86.

Fullan, M. (1982). "The Meaning of Educational Change." Teachers College Press, New York.

Guskey, T. (1986). Staff development and the process of change. *Ed. Res.* **15(5),** 5–15.

Hoover, J. J. (1987). Preparing special educators for mainstreaming: An emphasis upon curriculum. *Teacher Educ. Special Educ.* **10(2),** 58–64.

Hord, S. M., Rutherford, W. L., Huling-Austin, and Hall, G. E. (1987). "Taking Charge of Change." Association for Supervision and Curriculum Development, Alexandria, Virginia.

Hudson, F. (1990). CWC: Class within a class. Department of Special Education, University of Kansas, Kansas City.

Huefner, D. S. (1988). The consulting teacher model: Risks and opportunities. *Excep. Children* **54,** 403–414.

Idol, L. (1988). A rationale and guidelines for establishing special education consultation programs. *Remed. Special Educ.* **9(6),** 48–58.

Idol, L. (1990). The scientific art of classroom consultation. *J. Educ. Psycholog. Consult.* **1,** 3–22.

Jenkins, J. R., and Jenkins, L. M. (1981). "Cross Age and Peer Tutoring: Help for Children with Learning Problems." Council for Exceptional Children, Reston, Virginia.

Jenkins, J. R., and Jenkins, L. M. (1985). Peer tutoring in elementary and secondary programs. *Focus Excep. Children* **17,** 1–12.

Johnson, D. W., Maruyama, G., Johnson, R., Nelson, D., and Skon, L. (1981). The effects of cooperative, competitive, and individualistic goal structures on achievement: A meta-analysis. *Psycholog. Bull.* **81,** 47–62.

Johnson, J. H., and Markle, G. C. (1986). "What Research Says to the Middle Level Practitioner." National Middle School Association, Columbus, Ohio.

Johnson, L. J., Pugach, M. C., and Hammittee, D. J. (1988). Barriers to effective special education consultation. *Remed. Special Educ.* **9(6),** 41–47.

Jones, B. F. (1986). Quality and equality through cognitive instruction. *Educ. Leader.* **43(7),** 4–11.

Jones, B. F., and Idol, L. (in press). "Dimensions of Thinking and Cognitive Instruction." Lawrence Erlbaum, Hillsdale, New Jersey.

Kasselman, C. J. (1988). Curriculum modifications for secondary students with learning disabilites: Influencing change. *LD Forum* **13(2)**, 16–19.

Kasselman, C. J., and Robinson, S. M. (1990). FRAME implementation manual. Tech. Rep. No. 3, Department of Special Education, University of Kansas, Kansas City.

Keogh, B. K. (1988) Learning disability—Diversity in search of order. *In* "Handbook of Special Education: Research and Practice," Vol. 2, (M. C. Wang, M. C. Reynolds, and H. J. Walberg, eds.), pp. 225–251. Pergamon Press, Oxford.

Legget D., and Hoyle, S. (1986). Peer coaching: One district's experience in using teachers as staff developers. *J. Staff Dev.* 16–20.

Lenz, B. (1983). Using advance organizers. *Pointer* **27**, 11–13.

Lilly, M. S. (1970). Special education: A tempest in a teapot. *Excep. Children* **37**, 43–49.

Lippitt, G., and Lippitt, R. (1978). "The Consulting Process in Action." University Associates, La Jolla, California.

Mastropieri, M. A. (1988). Using the keyboard method. *Teach. Excep. Children* **20(2)**, 4–8.

McKenzie, H. S., Egner, A. N., Knight, M. F., Perelman, P. F., Schneider, B. M., and Garvin, J. S. (1970). Training consulting teachers in the management and education of handicapped children. *Excep. Children* **37**, 137–143.

Nevin, A., Thousand, J., Paolucci-Whitcomb, P., and Villa, R. (1990). Collaborative consultation: Empowering public school personnel to provide heterogeneous schooling for all—or, who rang the bell? *J. Educ. Psycholog. Consult.* **1**, 41–67.

Pugach, M. C., and Johnson, L. J. (1988). Rethinking the relationship between consultation and collaborative problem-solving. *Focus Excep. Children* **21(4)**, 1–8.

Reisberg, L., and Wolf, R. (1986). Developing a consulting program in special education: Implementation and interventions. *Focus Excep. Children* **19(3)**, 1–14.

Reisberg, L. and Wolf, R. (1988). Instructional strategies for special education consultants. *Remed. Spec. Ed.* **9(6)**, 29–40.

Reynaud, G., Pfannenstiel, T., and Hudson, F. G. (1987). Class within a class: Implementation manual. Park Hill R-V School District, Park Hill, Missouri.

Reynolds, M., and Wang, M. C. (1983). Restructuring "special" school programs. A position paper. *Policy Stud. Rev.* **2**, 189–212.

Rich, H. L., and Ross, S. M. (1989). Students; time on learning tasks in special education. *Excep. Children* **55**, 508–515.

Robinson, S. M. (1987). The collaborative consulting teacher training project. *Collab. Consult. Newslett.* **1**, 1–2.

Robinson, S. M. (1988). Collaborative consultation as part of special education services; Questions to consider. *Collab. Consult. Newslett.* **2**, 1–2.

Robinson, S. M., and Kasselman, C. J. (1990). Feedback implementation manual. Tech. Rep. No. 4, Department of Special Education, University of Kansas, Kansas City.

Robinson, S. M., and McGuire, M. (1989). Program planning in collaborative consultation. Unpublished staff development module, Department of Special Education, University of Kansas, Kansas City.

Rosenshine, B. (1980). How time is spent in elementary classrooms. *In* "Time to Learn"

(C. Denham and A. Lieberman, eds.), pp. 38–43. National Institute of Education, Washington, D.C.

Showers, B. (1985). Teachers coaching teachers. *Educ. Leader.* **42(7)**, 43–48.

Slavin, R. E. (1983). "Cooperative Learning." Longman Press, New York.

Slavin, R. E. (1988). Cooperative learning and student achievement. *Educ. Leader.* **46(2)**, 31–33.

Smith, D. D. (1984). *Effec. Discipl.* Pro-Ed, Austin, Texas.

Thurlow, M. L., Garden, J., Greener, J. W., and Ysseldyke, J. E. (1983). LD and non-LD students' opportunities to learn. *Learn. Disabil. Q.* **6**, 172–183.

Tindall, G., Shinn, M. R., and Rodden-Nord, K. (1990). Contextually based school consultation: Influential variables. *Excep. Children* **56**, 324–336.

Wang, M. C., and Walberg, J. (1985). "Adapting Instruction to Individual Differences." McCutchan Publishers, New York.

West, J. F., and Cannon, G. (1988). Essential collaborative consultation competencies for regular and special educators. *J. Learn. Disabil.* **21**, 56–63.

West, J. F., and Idol, L. (1990). Collaborative consultation in the education of mildly handicapped and at-risk students. *Remed. Special Educ.* **11**, 22–31.

Wiederholt L., Hammill, D., and Brown, L. (1983). "The Resource Teacher: A Guide to Effective Practices." Allyn and Bacon, Inc., Boston.

Will, M. C. (1986). Educating children with learning problems: A shared responsibility. *Excep. Children* **52**, 411–415.

Wiseman, D. E. (1980). The parallel alternative curriculum for secondary classroom. *In* "Mainstreaming at the Secondary Level: Seven Models that Work" (R. H. Riegel and J. P. Mathey, eds.). Wayne County Intermediate School District, Plymouth, Michigan.

Zigmond, N., and Thornton, H. (1985). Follow-up of post secondary age learning disabled graduates and drop outs. *Learn. Disabil. Res.* **1**, 50–55.

CHAPTER 16

Issues in Service Delivery for Students with Learning Disabilities

James M. Kauffman and Stanley C. Trent

Editor's Notes

Kauffman and Trent grapple head on with the current controversial issues in service delivery in learning disabilities. They organize the topics in their chapter around two underlying themes. The first is their critical examination of the assumptions of proponents of the Regular Education Initiative. These assumptions include (1) the appropriate location of instruction for exceptional students is the regular classroom, (2) the ineffectualness of special education, and (3) special education teachers reduce the competency of regular class teachers. Kauffman and Trent systematically demolish these assumptions. Moreover, they rightfully point out that we should focus on the interactions between teacher and student, and on increasing the instructional capacity of teachers of exceptional students, rather than focusing on where instruction should occur.

The second theme is Kauffman and Trent's analysis of professional myopia among special educators. They state that special educators move from one service delivery model to another with premature readiness, without sufficient assessment of its potential advantages and disadvantages. Consequently, service delivery models in special education rise and fall in popularity. Kauffman and Trent rightfully suggest that each model may fit particular students and that we should use each as a framework to develop effective instruction for the benefit of students. In this way, exceptional students may be better served through the availability of various special educational service delivery models.

I. INTRODUCTION

Delivery of services to students with disabilities is today fraught with controversy. Much of the controversy involves disagreements about how and by whom services should be provided within certain school structures, specifically where students with learning disabilities should be taught and who should teach them. Although "restructuring" special and general education to change service delivery has been recommended by advocates of the Regular Education Initiative (REI; for detailed description of this initiative, see Hallahan *et al.*, 1988a; Kauffman, 1989; Lloyd *et al.*, 1991), the range of structures at issue has seldom been clearly defined.

Moreover, some structures apparently have received a disproportionate amount of attention in advocacy for reforming special education. In particular, teaching certain children particular skills in locations other than the regular classroom (often called a "pull-out" structure, whether it involves a special self-contained class or a resource room) versus full-time mainstreaming, in which students are not removed from the regular classroom for any instruction, has become the focal point of concern. Proponents of the REI suggest restructuring a "dual system" of special and general education so that compensatory or "second system" programs (special education, bilingual education, and other programs designed to compensate for students' disadvantages) are merged into a single service delivery structure. In the single structure REI proponents envision, pull-out programming would be eliminated for all or very nearly all children now served under the category of learning disabilities, and most or all instruction would be provided by general educators (cf. Gartner and Lipsky, 1989; Wang *et al.*, 1988).

The REI has engendered much debate and, in the opinion of some scholars, has "inflicted a great deal of mischief on the special education community" (Hallahan, in press). As Hallahan notes, preoccupation with eliminating pull-out programs, under the assumption that the regular classroom is always the least restrictive environment, has obscured the more important analysis of what happens between teachers and pupils regardless of where teaching may occur or whether the teacher is a special or general educator. In discussing this issue as it affects individuals with mental retardation, Zigler (1987:14) stated:

> We've been spending so much time worrying about retarded people's addresses that we're forgetting about the everyday environ-

ments *within* those addresses. I share Urie Bronfenbrenner's concern that we need more than a person's "social address" in order to know about and help that person.

Zigler challenges special educators to consider more than the place in which services are provided. We believe his statement applies as much to students with learning disabilities as to those with mental retardation. Our discussion in this chapter, therefore, is organized around five major topics. First, we briefly review definitions of school structures, with the aim of clarifying the range of topics that might be addressed in consideration of reforming or restructuring education. Second, we summarize rhetoric and research related to place and personnel structures, with the purpose of clarifying points of view related to the current high interest in these structures. Third, we discuss programmatic issues, with the intention of focusing attention on what we consider equally important but neglected structures related to service delivery. Fourth, we discuss the critical role of collaboration and consultation between regular and special educators in serving students in the predominant service delivery mode—mainstreaming. Finally, we suggest basic considerations for selecting a mode of service delivery.

II. DEFINITIONS OF SCHOOL STRUCTURES

Epstein (1988) describes school structures as comprised of six elements: tasks set for students, authority to make choices, rewards for progress, grouping for instruction, evaluations of standards, and time or rate of learning. Cuban (1988:344) offers the following definition:

> The structure of schools includes the formal and informal goals used to guide funding and organizing activities, including such things as who has authority and responsibility for governing schools and classrooms; how time and space are alloted; how subject matter in the curriculum is determined; how students are assigned to classes; how those classes are organized; how the different roles of teachers, principals, and superintendents are defined; and how such formal processes as budgeting, hiring, and evaluating are determined and organized. To a large extent, these structures shape the roles, responsibilities, and relationships within schools.

These definitions of structure clearly include more than where and by whom a student is taught. They include consideration of the structures of instruction as well as the structures of personnel and space. Nevertheless, current controversies regarding service delivery have emphasized the structures of place and personnel more than what happens between teachers and children in particular places. Our view is that a more balanced treatment of service delivery issues will better advance the field.

The importance of considering more than place and personnel issues is underscored by recent discussions of school reform (e.g., Cuban, 1988, 1990). As Cuban (1990:11) noted, "The transaction among a teacher, students, and content is the basic reason for compelling parents to send their children to school." Yet this most basic reason for schooling is particularly difficult to monitor and control and receives little attention in efforts to reform education. However, through administrative policy-making for some structures, such as assignment of children to particular classrooms, reformers can achieve a high degree of control of the external appearances of education without substantial effects on instruction. Understandably, perhaps, these highly visible and more easily altered structures tend to become the primary focus of reform.

School reform is essentially cosmetic unless it effects change in what transpires during instruction. Unless sufficient attention is given to changing what teachers actually do with their students within the structures of place and personnel, efforts to reform schools simply set the stage for the next wave of cosmetic reforms. We suggest that more attention be given to developing the instructional capacity of teachers within existing place and personnel structures.

III. PLACE AND PERSONNEL ISSUES

A popular notion among advocates of the REI is that special education is ineffective whenever it occurs outside the regular classroom. Physical separation of students from their nonhandicapped peers, even if for part of the school day, is assumed to debase students and degrade their instruction. Effective instruction is therefore assumed to depend on the simultaneous presence in a given classroom of all students who would be assigned to that class, with no consideration given to their exceptionalities in the matter of placement.

Another idea popular with REI advocates is that the relationship between special and general education teachers is inappropriate and unproductive because it relieves regular classroom teachers of their responsibilities for students who are difficult to teach. That is, an aspect of service delivery assumed to render special education ineffective is instruction by special educators. Reliance on special teachers is assumed to subvert the competence of regular classroom teachers, leaving them without the skills they otherwise might have or acquire to deal with students who are particularly difficult to instruct or manage. Effective instruction is therefore assumed to depend on regular classroom teachers assuming responsibility for instructing all students, regardless of their exceptionalities.

That place and personnel are seen as overriding issues in service delivery is revealed in comments by advocates of radical restructuring of special and general education, as the following sampling illustrates:

> Even when all measures are taken to coordinate the pullout program with the work of the regular class, *students do not benefit from this special education....* The strongest case against special education outside the regular class for mildly handicapped students is that it does not work (Biklen and Zollers, 1986: 581–582). What is known about the education of students labelled as handicapped? First, separate special education does not work.... But it is recognized that integrated programs work, and that preparation for full lives can only occur in integrated settings (Gartner and Lipsky, 1989:26). There was no evidence in the past and there is no evidence now showing that removing disabled children from the mainstream and putting them into special classes or schools is an advantage for them (Reynolds, 1989:8). With unlimited success special educators have socialized their colleagues in general education classrooms to the belief that, as general classroom teachers, they do not possess the skills to handle the wide variations in student ability (Pugach, 1988:54).

The logical foundations and empirical bases of the conclusions of these writers might be questioned. In our opinion, these conclusions—that separate special education does not work, that integrated education does work, and that special educators create the need for their services by convincing general educators of their ineptitude with exceptional children—go beyond the data. Empirical evidence may indeed support the conclusion that special education has often been poorly practiced and ineffective. Nevertheless, research does not support the conclusion that special education has been ineffective because it has involved special teachers offering instruction outside the regular classroom, nor does research support the inference that changing the location in which special education is delivered or reducing instruction by special teachers will result in more effective instruction.

Some research studies (e.g., Marston, 1987–1988; O'Connor *et al.*, 1979) and at least one meta-analysis (Carlberg and Kavale, 1980) have yielded findings at odds with the conclusions of REI advocates. Moreover, alternative conclusions have been reached by others who have reviewed findings on special education's effects (e.g., Hallahan, *et al.*, 1988b; Robert Wood Johnson Foundation, 1988; Singer, 1988; Wiederholt and Chamberlain, 1989) or obtained a national sample of the opinions of parents, teachers, and children (Harris, 1989). Beyond the findings of academic researchers, it is difficult to reconcile conclusions like those of Biklen and Zollers (1986), Gartner and Lipsky (1989), and Reynolds (1989) with national survey findings that 94% of educators believe that education for children with handicapping conditions is better now than 12 years ago, that 77% of parents of handicapped children are satisfied with the special education system, and that 74% of parents feel that the current extent of integration of their children into regular classrooms is best for their children (Harris, 1989).

A. Pragmatic View: The Need for a Special Education Initiative

Even before the enactment of the Education for All Handicapped Children Act (EHCA), special educators sought to develop and implement special programs for children who had not been successful in regular education (Deno, 1970). An examination of the service delivery options established for children with learning disabilities reveals that programs have been implemented hastily and that evaluation of these programs has been conducted haphazardly (Leinhardt and Pallay, 1982; Hallahan et al., 1988b). Furthermore, a review of the literature reveals that little emphasis has been given to the instructional approaches currently used in programs for students who are learning-disabled. Lessen et al. (1989) determined that between the years 1978 and 1987, less than 4% of published articles in eight major special education journals dealt with instruction. Additionally, Lessen et al. (1989: 107) concluded that "academic intervention research is crucial so that systematic analyses of student performance, rather than superstition and hunch, dictate teaching procedure, methods, and materials that are used."

Herein lies one of the major problems that have plagued programming for students with learning disabilities: In our quest to provide appropriate services, it appears that we have drawn premature conclusions about service delivery options and have attempted to solve instructional problems by moving on to the next less developed, "least restrictive" option along the continuum of services. As each service delivery option has failed to meet our expectations, we have exaggerated its faults as well as overestimated the benefits to be obtained by the next popular option (Kauffman and Pullen, 1989).

Several decades prior to the enactment of the EHCA, self-contained programs were established for hard-to-teach, difficult-to-manage children (Ryan, 1928). Shortly after the EHCA became law, the resource room concept was considered to be the state-of-the-art educational practice for students with learning disabilities (cf. Wiederholt and Chamberlain, 1989). Now, as we move into the last decade of the twentieth century, many special educators have concluded that consultation or collaboration between special and regular education will create learning environments designed to meet the needs of all learners, including those with learning disabilities (Gartner and Lipsky, 1987; Pugach, 1988; Reynolds, 1989; Stainback and Stainback, 1985; Wang and Birch, 1984; Will, 1986).

B. Strengthening All Service Models

Our contention is that, while a need exists to establish and strengthen collaborative programs, they should not be assumed to replace other special education service delivery models in the cascade of services described by Deno (1970). Instead, special education should take the initiative in strengthening delivery of appropriate education in all of these service delivery models. As Carnine and Kameenui (1990) noted, the needs of students with learning disabilities and those at risk for school failure suggest reforms opposite many of those suggested by advocates of the REI. At this juncture, it may be more productive to launch a special education initiative to "extend the support provided special education teachers and students to other teachers who have a majority of at-risk students" for the purpose of increasing "the efficacy, power, and professional pride of educators who work with at-risk students and students with learning disabilities" (Carnine and Kameenui, 1990: 144).

In addition to consultation, attention must also be given to improving self-contained and resource programs. Otherwise, our continued practice of developing models and abandoning them prematurely will only produce again the same problems that special educators have grappled with for decades. We contend that the research regarding the efficacy of integrated settings is inconclusive (cf. Fuchs and Fuchs, 1988; Hallahan *et al.*, 1988b; Kulik and Kulik, 1982) and that the EHCA, still in its youth, provides a framework that will allow us to develop and implement more effective instructional practices within each level of a continuum of service delivery models.

IV. PROGRAMMATIC ISSUES

Effective instruction requires that differences among students be recognized and accommodated. Efficient instruction requires that students be grouped according to the type of instruction that will be effective. Thus, a single program of instruction will be neither effective nor efficient for all learners. If individual students' needs are to be met, different instructional options must be offered. It is impossible to offer all options at the same time and in the same place. Therefore, we need to consider the options needed by particular students and the feasibility of offering these in various service delivery models.

Instruction differs along more dimensions than we are able to consider here; however, several of the dimensions most critical to our discussion are explicitness, measurement (monitoring student progress), cognitive strategy development, and vocational relevance. We shall comment briefly on the importance of these dimensions for students with learning disabilities and the probability that students' needs in relation to each dimension will be accommodated in regular classrooms as suggested by proponents of the REI.

A. Explicitness

A feature of instruction that research clearly indicates is critical to the learning of many students with learning disabilities or other differences compared with the typical student is explicitness—the extent to which instruction is directly controlled by the teacher rather than more loosely controlled in strategies involving exploration. Instructional approaches low in explicitness are often called developmental or process approaches. These approaches emphasize starting with students' curiosity and encouraging exploration with relatively little direction from the teacher. Approaches high in explicitness, often called direct instruction, emphasize teaching skills and concepts in a much more highly structured, teacher-directed manner.

Many students with special needs are likely to fail in the typical classroom, where instruction is geared toward the characteristics of middle-class children and relies to a great extent on developmental or process approaches (Carnine and Kameenui, 1990; Delpit, 1988). Thus, we would not expect such students to benefit from the kind of instructional procedures they are most likely to encounter in regular classrooms. Indeed, the fact that less explicit instructional approaches have not been successful with many students with learning disabilities is obvious. Success with these students will require a different approach, one in which instruction is more explicit.

Proponents of the REI argue for integration of students with learning disabilities into regular classrooms, in which instruction is moving strongly toward increasing reliance on developmental or process approaches (Carnine and Kameenui, 1990). Indeed, regular classroom teachers have tended to resist the adoption of the direct instruction strategies that research suggests are most likely to be effective with students with special needs (Lloyd et al., 1988b). Unfortunately, some proponents of the REI appear not to be cognizant of the consequences of developmental approaches to instruction for many students with learning disabilities and to endorse the movement of general education toward less explicit, less direct instruction. Gartner and Lipsky (1989: 28), for example, suggest that teachers not waste time on teaching but use class time for student collaboration, encouraging students to share their knowledge and experience, and to focus on how students learn rather than thinking of education in terms of content. These suggestions are consistent with a developmental or process approach and are likely to compound the problems of many students who have learning disabilities.

Given the press of educational reformers for greater investment in developmental or process approaches, we see the movement toward inclusion of students with learning disabilities in general education's instructional programs as likely to be counterproductive. Pull-out programs are not likely to be effective without greater attention to the instruction offered in them. In our opinion, increasing the explicitness of instruction is more feasible within the structure of pull-out programs than within the structure of regular classrooms.

B. Measurement: Monitoring Student Progress

After instructional programs have been selected, teachers must establish criteria for judging mastery of instructional goals. Teachers must also monitor student performance systematically and continuously to assess the appropriateness of instruction as reflected in progress toward instructional goals. Finally, teachers must modify their instructional strategies as necessary, based on measurement of student progress (Truesdell, 1987). Current research suggests that curriculum-based assessment (CBA; the term curriculum-based measurement [CBM] is also used) is a tool for performing these teaching functions (Deno *et al.*, 1984; Fuchs, 1986; Fuchs *et al.*, 1990; Marston and Magnusson, 1985; Shinn, 1988).

According to Deno (1987: 41), "The term *curriculum-based assessment* generally refers to any approach that uses direct observation and recording of a student's performance in the local school curriculum as a basis for gathering information to make instructional decisions." If this definition is interpreted superficially, monitoring student performance might be thought to consist merely of teacher-made tests designed to obtain pre- and postinstruction measures of performance related to arbitrarily derived objectives in students' individualized education plans (IEPs). When CBA is implemented appropriately, however, it goes beyond the development of nonstandardized criterion-referenced pre- and post-tests. CBA must conform to standards of technical adequacy of measurement (e.g., reliability and validity) if the results are to be used for decision-making (Shinn, 1988; Fuchs *et al.*, 1990).

CBA allows teachers of students with learning disabilities to (1) judge the appropriateness of an instructional goal, (2) monitor the adequacy of student progress through analysis of the data base, and (3) determine effective and ineffective interventions by analyzing the graphed data base. Research suggests that CBA procedures can significantly increase the utility of the IEP (Fuchs *et al.*, 1990). Such procedures will also encourage teachers to alter instructional strategies and presentation formats systematically so that students will learn at an optimal level. Additionally, researchers have reported increased engagement time and increased academic gains among students with learning disabilities when their teachers used systematic monitoring procedures (Fuchs, 1986).

An important consideration in selecting a service delivery model is whether or not student progress is likely to be monitored closely and accurately in a manner that facilitates effective instruction. Given the demands on regular classroom teachers' time and the increasing press for less explicit instructional approaches, it seems unlikely to us that CBA will be employed systematically with students with learning disabilities unless they are pulled out of regular classrooms for instruction by special education teachers (see also Lloyd *et al.*, 1988b). Special educators must take steps to ensure that CBA procedures are employed in pull-out programs, however, if such programs are to be as effective as possible.

C. Cognitive Strategy Development

A frequent recommendation of researchers is that training in cognitive strategies be incorporated into the instruction of many students with learning disabilities (see Hallahan *et al.*, 1985; Harris *et al.*, 1985; Schumaker *et al.*, 1983; Schumaker and Deshler, 1984). Programs have been designed to strengthen skills in metacognition, self-instruction, self-monitoring, and study skills, for example. Although training in cognitive strategies designed to help students take a more active role in learning, control their own behavior, and learn how to approach tasks effectively is now commonly recommended for students with special needs, such training is not yet a predictable feature of special education practice. Moreover, the extent to which regular classroom teachers can be induced to provide such training is a matter for speculation.

D. Vocational Relevance

Studies of employment of students following high school indicate that secondary programs for students with learning disabilities and other handicapping conditions are not meeting these students' needs for preparation for work (Edgar, 1987). The current school reform movement, with its emphasis on competitive excellence, has resulted in increasing academic standards and the goal of preparing more students for higher education. As Edgar (1987: 559) has noted, "there is a tendency to recommend common-core academic experiences for all students, and these common-core classes tend to focus on advanced academic standards." Consequently, programs designed to prepare students for employment have languished.

Advocates of the REI and other school reformers have stressed the elimination of academic tracking and the placement of nearly all students in heterogeneous groups for instruction under the assumptions that tracking is discriminatory and students do not need radically different curricula (e.g., Gartner and Lipsky, 1989; Goodlad and Oakes, 1988). Different programs or tracks are thus seen as unacceptable solutions to the problem of preparing students for a vocation. Edgar (1987: 560) has described the dilemma we must face in designing programs and service delivery for students with learning disabilities and other special needs—"two *equally* appalling alternatives; integrated mainstreaming in a nonfunctional curriculum which results in horrendous outcomes (few jobs, high dropout rate) or separate, segregated programs for an already devalued group, a repugnant thought in our democratic society." Our view is that a vocationally relevant curriculum involving a separate track or pull-out program may be a lesser evil than an integrated but nonfunctional curriculum in which students are heterogeneously grouped.

V. THE IMPORTANCE OF CONSULTATION AND COLLABORATION

The majority of handicapped students receive most of their education in mainstreamed settings (U.S. Department of Education, 1989). Thus, it is imperative that attention be given to service delivery options for serving students effectively in regular classrooms through consultation or collaboration of regular and special education teachers. The role played by special educators in consultation is a key factor in the success of any collaborative model. According to Idol (1988: 49):

> The consultant should be viewed as a helping teacher, one who provides helping support to teachers who have mainstreamed exceptional students enrolled in their classes. As a means of prevention it is anticipated that the indirect services provided by this consultant teacher could and should be extended to include low

achieving students in the mainstream who have not been identified as being exceptional. These low achieving students can be served through teacher collaboration but would not be counted for special education purposes.

As described by Pugach and Johnson (1989), the staff person who takes on the role of the consultant is generally the special education teacher or the school psychologist. The consultant works either at the expert or the collaborative level. Within the expert consultation framework, the referring teacher shares a problem with the consultant, who in turn assesses the situation through informal evaluation and observation and then develops a plan designed to ameliorate the problem. In collaborative consultation (Idol *et al.*, 1986), both the consultant and the referring teacher are considered equal in the relationship and both work cooperatively to deal with the problem. In this relationship, it is assumed that the referring teacher possesses problem-solving skills and a knowledge of the curriculum that will add to the appropriateness and the effectiveness of the interventions that will be prescribed.

Consultation and collaboration are highly appealing service delivery models for students whose learning and behavior problems are not severe. However, relatively little is known about what makes these models successful. Much additional research is needed to clarify the most appropriate roles of teachers and the effects that can and cannot be achieved through consultation and collaboration (Lloyd *et al.*, 1988a; Polsgrove and McNeil, 1989).

Factors inhibiting effective consultation have been identified by graduates of a program in school consultation (Idol-Maestas and Ritter, 1985). The teachers surveyed concluded that prominent factors contributing to ineffectiveness of consultation included resistance from other teachers, personality traits of consultants that detracted from the consultative process, failure to promote the program, lack of administrative support, and, above all, lack of time for consultation. These findings are consistent with barriers to collaboration described by practicing regular and special education teachers (see Hallahan and Kauffman, 1991, "Collaboration: A Key to Success").

Additional constraints on consultation include ineffective caseload management, converting the model to a tutoring or aide model, unrealistic expectations, inadequate support from regular educators, inadequate funding mechanisms, and faulty assumptions regarding cost savings and program effectiveness (Huefner, 1988). Huefner notes that program and cost effectiveness are intertwined and that both aspects of the program should be continuously evaluated. Hence, while conceptually sound consultation models have been developed (West and Idol, 1987), logistical issues such as these must be addressed and resolved prior to program implementation.

VI. SELECTING THE APPROPRIATE SERVICE DELIVERY OPTION

Some students will benefit most from instruction in self-contained settings, some will make optimal progress in resource settings, and some will function best with a consultative approach. Students should be able to move from one service delivery model to another as necessary to meet their individual needs. Those who have underdeveloped skills in particular areas might require instruction in a pull-out setting. The complex sequence outlined by Deshler and Schumaker (1986) appears to yield the most promising results when students begin in pull-out settings where the teacher–pupil ratio is low. As students move to the stage of generalization, the services of a consultant will be necessary to help the students transfer skills to regular classroom situations. In situations where intensive precision teaching procedures are required with daily monitoring of progress and with continuous modification of instructional materials and/or instructional techniques, students will likely benefit most from services in a pull-out setting.

Planning for students with learning disabilities must include consideration of logistical issues. Consultation, for example, brings to bear several possible problems that must be addressed prior to implementation of a program. Consultation in special education is not a new idea. At least since the enactment of the EHCA, consultation has been considered a part of the special education service delivery model. Through the years, however, lack of sufficient time for teachers to consult has been one of the major problems associated with the implementation of a successful consultation program. In regular public school settings, special education teachers have always been expected to serve mainstreamed children through direct interaction with regular classroom teachers. Typically, as special education enrollments increase, consultation assumes last place on the resource teacher's priority list.

If the instruction in the regular classroom is appropriate and if the student possesses the prerequisite skills needed for success in the mainstream, maintenance in the regular classroom can be assured with relatively little assistance from the consultant. If, however, the mainstreamed student experiences difficulty in the regular classroom setting, the consultant may not be able to spend the time necessary to ameliorate the problem.

VII. CONCLUSION

In our quest to provide effective, appropriate services to students who have learning disabilities, we must preserve and strengthen the framework established to protect the rights of students who were once denied access to a free, appropriate public education. No single service delivery model will meet the needs of all students. The challenge is development and reliable implementation of effective, research-based interventions within the structure of each model. In fact, radical restructuring of special education to eliminate pull-out service delivery models will only re-create problems that developed prior to the implementation of the EHCA. As Meyen (1990: 13) commented:

> If instruction that is appropriate to the needs of learners who have exceptionalities is the purpose of special education, then the profession must discipline itself to invest in developing interventions that make a difference in how students learn. It does not require a revolution for this to occur.

References

Biklen, D., and Zollers, N. (1986). The focus of advocacy in the LD field. *J. Learn. Disabil.* **19**, 579–586.

Carlberg, C., and Kavale, K. (1980). The efficacy of special versus regular class placement for exceptional children: A meta-analysis. *J. Special Educ.* **14**, 295–309.

Carnine, D. W., and Kameenui, E. J. (1990). The general education initiative and children with special needs: A false dilemma in the fact of true problems. *J. Learn. Disabil.* **23**, 141–144, 148.

Cuban, L. (1988). A fundamental puzzle of school reform. *Phi Delta Kappan* **69**, 341–344.

Cuban, L. (1990). Reforming again, again, and again. *Educ. Research.* **19(1)**, 3–13.

Delpit, L. D. (1988). The silenced dialogue: Power and pedagogy in educating other people's children. *Harvard Ed. Rev.* **58**, 280–298.

Deno, E. (1970). Special education as developmental capital. *Excep. Children* **37**, 229–237.

Deno, S. (1987). Curriculum-based measurement. *Teach. Excep. Children* **20**, 41–42.

Deno, S. L., Mirkin, P. K., and Wesson, C. (1984). How to write effective data-based IEPs. *Teach. Excep. Children* **16**, 99–104.

Deshler, D. D., and Schumaker, J. B. (1986). Learning strategies: An instructional alternative for low-achieving adolescents. *Excep. Children* **52**, 583–590.

Edgar, E. (1987). Secondary programs in special education: Are many of them justifiable? *Excep. Children* **53**, 555–561.

Epstein, J. L. (1988). Effective schools or effective students: Dealing with diversity. *In* "Policies for America's Public Schools: Teachers, Equity, and Indicators" (R. Haskins and D. MacRae, eds.), pp. 89–126. Ablex, Norwood, New Jersey.

Fuchs, L. S. (1986). Monitoring progress among mildly handicapped pupils: Review of current practice and research. *Remed. Special Educ.* **7(5)**, 5–12.

Fuchs, D., and Fuchs, L. S. (1988). An evaluation of the Adaptive Learning Environments Model. *Exceptional Child.* **55**, 115–127.

Fuchs, L. S., Fuchs, D., and Hamlett, C. L. (1990). Curriculum-based measurement: A standardized, long-term goal approach to monitoring student progress. *Academic Ther.* **25(5)**, 615–632.

Gartner, A., and Lipsky, D. K. (1987). Beyond special education: Toward a quality system for all students. *Harv. Educ. Rev.* **57**, 367–395.

Gartner, A., and Lipsky, D. K. (1989). "The Yoke of Special Education: How to Break It." National Center on Education and the Economy, Rochester, New York.

Goodlad, J. I., and Oakes, J. (1988). We must offer equal access to knowledge. *Educ. Leader.* **45(5)**, 16–22.

Hallahan, D. P. (in press). Learning disabilities: Personal reflections. *In* "Futures in Special Education: Essays in Honor of William M. Cruickshank" (S. C. Russell, ed.). University of Michigan Press, Ann Arbor.

Hallahan, D. P., and Kauffman, J. M. (1991). "Exceptional Children: Introduction to Special Education," 5th ed. Prentice-Hall, Englewood Cliffs, New Jersey.

Hallahan, D. P., Kauffman, J. M., and Lloyd, J. W. (1985). "Introduction to Learning Disabilities," 2nd ed. Prentice-Hall, Englewood Cliffs, New Jersey.

Hallahan, D. P., Kauffman, J. M., Lloyd, J. W., and McKinney, J. D. (eds.) (1988a). *J. Learn. Disabil.* **21(1)**. [Special issue on the Regular Education Initiative.]

Hallahan, D. P., Keller, C. E., McKinney, J. D., Lloyd, J. W., and Bryan, T. (1988b). Examining the research base of the regular education initiative: Efficacy studies and the adaptive learning environments model. *J. Learn. Disabil.* **21**, 29–35.

Harris, K. R., Wong, B. Y. L., and Keogh, B. K. (eds.) (1985). *J. Abnorm. Child Psychol.* **13(3)**. [Special issue.]

Harris, L. (1989, June). *The ICD survey III: A report card on special education.* New York: Louis Harris & Associates.

Heufner, D. S. (1988). The consulting teacher model: Risks and opportunities. *Excep. Children* **54**, 403–414.

Idol, L. (1988). A rationale and guidelines for establishing special education consultation programs. *Remed. Special Educ.* **9(6)**, 48–58.

Idol, L., Paolucci-Whitcomb, P., and Nevin, A. (1986). "Collaborative Consultation." Aspen, Rockville, Maryland.

Idol-Maestas, L., and Ritter, S. (1985). A follow-up study of resource/consulting teachers: Factors that facilitate and inhibit teacher consultation. *Teacher Educ. Special Educ.* **8**, 121–131.

Kauffman, J. M. (1989). The regular education initiative as Reagan–Bush education policy: A trickle-down theory of education of the hard-to-teach. *J. Special Educ.* **23**, 256–278.

Kauffman, J. M., and Pullen, P. L. (1989). An historical perspective: A personal perspective on our history of service to mildly handicapped and at-risk students. *Remed. Special Educ.* **10(6)**, 12–14.

Kulik, C. C., and Kulik, J. A. (1982). Effects of ability grouping on secondary school students: A meta-analysis of evaluation findings. *Am. Educ. Res. J.* **19**, 415–428.

Leinhardt, G., and Pallay, A. (1982). Restrictive educational settings: Exile or haven? *Rev. Educ. Res.* **52(4)**, 557–578.

Lessen, E., Dudzinski, M., Karsh, K., and Van Aker, R. (1989). A survey of ten years of academic intervention research with learning disabled students: Implications for research and practice. *Learn. Disabil. Focus* **4**, 106–122.

Lloyd, J. W., Crowley, E. P., Kohler, F. W., and Strain, P. S. (1988a). Redefining the applied research agenda: Cooperative learning, prereferral, teacher consultation, and peer mediated interventions. *J. Learn. Disabil.* **21**, 43–52.

Lloyd, J. W., Keller, C. E., Kauffman, J. M., and Hallahan, D. P. (1988b). What will the regular education initiative require of general education teachers? Paper prepared for the Office of Special Education Programs (January 1988), U.S. Department of Education, Washington, D.C.

Lloyd, J. W., Singh, N. N., & Repp, A. C. (eds.) (1991). *The regular education initiative: Alternative perspectives on concepts, issues, and models.* DeKalb, Illinois: Sycamore.

Marston, D. (1987–88). The effectiveness of special education: A time series analysis of reading performance in regular and special education settings. *J. Spec. Ed.* **21(4)**, 13–26.

Marston, D., and Magnusson, D. (1985). Implementing curriculum-based measurement in special and regular education settings. *Excep. Children* **52**, 266–276.

Meyen, E. (1990). Quality instruction for students with disabilities. *Teach. Excep. Children* **22(2)**, 12–13.

O'Connor, P. D., Stuck, G. B., and Wyne, M. D. (1979). Effects of a short-term intervention resource-room program on task orientation and achievement. *J. Spec. Ed.* **13**, 375–385.

Polsgrove, L., and McNeil, M. (1989). The consultation process: Research and practice. *Remed. Special Educ.* **10(1)**, 6–13, 20.

Pugach, M. (1988). Special education as a constraint on teacher education reform. *J. Teacher Educ.* **39(3)**, 52–59.

Pugach, M. C., and Johnson, L. J. (1989). Prereferral interventions: Progress, problems, and challenges. *Excep. Children* **56**, 217–226.

Reynolds, M. C. (1989). An historical perspective: The delivery of special education to mildly disabled and at-risk students. *Remed. Special Educ.* **10(6)**, 7–11.

Robert Wood Johnson Foundation. (1988, December). *Serving handicapped children: A special report.* Princeton, New Jersey: Author.

Ryan, W. C. (1928). The preparation of teachers for dealing with behavior problem children. *Proc. Minneapolis Meet. Natl. Educ. Assoc.*, pp. 236–244. Minneapolis, Minnesota.

Schumaker, J. B., and Deshler, D. D. (1984). Setting demand variables: A major factor in program planning for the LD adolescent. *Top. Lang. Disorders* **4(2)**, 22–40.

Schumaker, J. B., Deshler, D. D., Alley, G. R., and Warner, M. M. (1983). Toward the development of an intervention model for learning disabled adolescents. *Excep. Educ. Q.* **3(4)**, 45–50.

Shinn, M. R. (1988). Development of curriculum-based local norms for use in special education decision making. *School Psychol. Rev.* **17**, 61–80.

Singer, J. D. (1988). Should special education merge with regular education? *Ed. Pol.* **2**, 409–424.

Stainback, S., and Stainback, W. (1985). The merger of special and regular education: Can it be done? A response to Lieberman and Mesinger. *Excep. Children* **51**, 517–521.

Truesdell, L. A. (1987). Curriculum-based assessment: Process and application. *Read. Writ. Learn. Disabil.* **3**, 281–289.

U.S. Department of Education. (1989). "Eleventh Annual Report to Congress on Implementation of Public Law 94–142. U.S. Government Printing Office, Washington, D.C.

Wang, M. C., and Birch, J. W. (1984). Comparison of a full-time mainstreaming program and a resource room approach. *Excep. Children* **51**, 33–40.

Wang, M. C., Reynolds, M. C., and Walberg, H. J. (1988). Integrating the children of the second system. *Phi Delta Kappan* **70**, 248–251.

West, J. F., and Idol, L. (1987). School consultation (part I): An interdisciplinary perspective on theory, models, and research. *J. Learn. Disabil.* **20**, 388–408.

Wiederholt, J. L., & Chamberlain, S. P. (1989). A critical analysis of resource programs. *J. Learn. Disabil.* **10(6),** 15–37.

Will, M. C. (1986). Educating children with learning problems: A shared responsibility. A report to the secretary. US Department of Education, Washington, D.C.

Zigler, E. (1987). "From Theory to Practice." The Edgar A. Doll address given at the annual meeting of the American Psychological Association.

SECTION III

Understanding Learning Disabilities through a Life-Span Approach

Learning Disabilities from a Developmental Perspective: Early Identification and Prediction

Barbara K. Keogh and Sue Sears

Editor's Notes

Section III begins with the present chapter. You will recall that this section has three chapters, focusing, respectively, on the learning-disabled child, the learning-disabled adolescent, and the learning-disabled adult. These chapters highlight the importance of a life-span approach to understanding learning disabilities.

The central theme in Keogh and Sears' chapter is to pose issues for consideration in early identification and prediction of learning disabilities in the context of findings from four research studies. Focusing on the striking commonalities in the findings, they draw attention to three clusters of risk predictors: biological conditions, child variables, and family conditions. They highlight the powerful role of social–environmental conditions in the future outcome of at-risk children.

A secondary theme is the consideration of conceptual and methodological issues in longitudinal research on at-risk conditions or problem conditions such as learning disabilities.

The authors end their chapter by showing how early identification and prediction can be approached from a developmental perspective. They use early identification of reading problems for illustration.

I. INTRODUCTION

The study of learning disabilities (LDs) from a developmental perspective holds promise for new insights and improved practices. Developmentalists are concerned with the emergence and meaning of behaviors in different developmental periods, with continuities and discontinuities in development over time and with the contributions and interactions of individual and social–environmental factors to development and behavior. From a developmental perspective, it is also necessary to consider problems in development, to identify and describe the conditions and the influences that result in negative outcomes. Interest in problem conditions has led to study of a range of at-risk conditions, to consideration of a broad range of variables in the study of development, and to increased interest in development over the life span. The result has been an expanding research literature directed at adults as well as at children and a keen interest in specifying the relationships that allow reliable prediction over time.

The developmental, life-span approach is pertinent to our concerns for LDs, as it is increasingly clear that LDs may not be limited to a particular age group or to a particular setting. LDs are no longer thought to be school-specific or to be the exclusive province of elementary-aged children. We have seen a proliferation of programs for secondary school pupils and for adults (Johnson, 1984; Schumaker *et al.*, 1983; Smith, 1988; Vogel, 1986; White, 1985), and recent federal legislation (P.L. 99–457) mandates special education services for handicapped children from birth to 3 years of age. In many states, LDs will be included in the problem conditions covered in that legislation. Recognition of the importance of early identification and intervention with young learning-disabled (LD) children has resulted in the implementation of numerous screening, diagnostic, and intervention programs and the publication of a plethora of early-identification tests and procedures (Mastropieri, 1988). The broadened scope is also reflected in the nature of professional and special interest groups. As example, the Association for Children with Learning Disabilities recently changed its name to the Learning Disabilities Association of America, and the organization actively advocates for services for LD individuals from the early years through adulthood.

While of obvious relevance, applying a developmental framework to LDs raises some interesting but troublesome questions. What are the developmental or educational implications of LDs over the life span? What is the diagnostic significance of particular behavioral signs or "symptoms" in the early years? How valid are early indicators for predicting subsequent problems? Are LDs modifiable within and across developmental periods? What are the contributions to or influences on change and stability? While interesting theoretically, such questions also have implications for practice, because decisions about program development, expenditure of funds, and the like are based on our views about these issues. Given limited resources, program developers are often faced with decisions about whether to focus on early identification and intervention programs or to target adolescent LD pupils and whether to support programs of parent involvement with preschool LD children or to stress academic remediation programs in the elementary school.

In this chapter, we focus particularly on issues of early identification and prediction of LDs, framing the issues within a developmental perspective. Rather than a detailed description of characteristics of LD children, we rely on findings from selected longitudinal studies and draw particularly from previous research on at-risk conditions. This volume of work provides a foundation for considering long-term outcomes of LDs. Before considering the predictive question, by way of background it is necessary to review briefly some of the conceptual and methodological issues that attend to longitudinal research on at-risk or problem conditions, including LDs.

II. CONCEPTUAL AND METHODOLOGICAL ISSUES

A fundamental issue relates to the definition of the problem. The nature of a problem and its expression may be relatively clear when the condition is biologically or genetically based (e.g., Down syndrome). However, where more subtle or equivocal conditions exist or when problem conditions are socially or educationally expressed, there is often definitional uncertainty. This is particularly true in the case of LDs, where disagreement about definition and about definitional boundaries continues (see Doris, 1986 for discussion). Definitional differences have resulted in research on LDs directed at a broad range of problems and conducted with heterogeneous samples. Not surprisingly, techniques for identification, diagnosis, and treatment or intervention also vary widely, as diagnosticians' choices of methods reflect their conceptualizations or definitions of the problem (Keogh, 1989). The result has been inconsistent, even controversial, findings and limited generalizations (Keogh et al., 1982). The inconsistencies have serious implications for research and practice and have resulted in challenges to the reality of LDs and to the need for specialized educational services for LD students (see Reynolds et al.,

1987; Stainback and Stainback, 1984). The inconsistencies underscore the need for specification of definitional boundaries and for adequate and comprehensive description of subject characteristics, especially when considering the course of LDs over time.

A related point in longitudinal approaches to LDs concerns the selection of predictor and outcome variables. In the case of LDs, end-point or outcome criteria might be educational achievement in basic school subjects, social skills, behavioral adjustment, vocational success, or absence of legal or psychiatric problems. Predictors might be scores on tests tapping broad developmental domains, specific linguistic skills, or noncognitive dimensions such as temperament. Predictors might also be extra-child conditions such as economic level of the family or the availability of services. It is reasonable that the importance of particular characteristics or conditions may vary according to developmental period or to the outcome targeted; thus, both must be taken into account when making predictive decisions. This point is elaborated further in a later section on early identification of reading problems.

Findings about predictive accuracy or validity are also affected by the timing of pre- and follow-up information. At what point in infancy or early childhood can we identify reliable and valid indicators of risk for LDs? What should be the end point for determining outcomes? Just as LDs are not a unitary condition, so the developmental course is not necessarily linear or incremental. Thus, our inferences about outcomes and about the predictive power of particular characteristics or conditions will vary as a function of when we gather entering and end-point information. We might, then, expect some differences in conclusions from longitudinal short-term studies and from studies in which the same individuals are followed over long periods of time.

The length of time and the beginning and end points clearly influence the nature of findings and interpretations about contributors to developmental risk. Aylward (1988) suggests, for example, that medical–biological conditions are powerful contributors to outcomes when follow-up is conducted when children are young, but that environmental conditions become increasingly influential as children grow older. He suggests also that the same variable may have different influences on motor or cognitive outcomes across developmental periods. The specification of entering and outcome criteria and data and the time of collection of information, thus, become questions of major importance in longitudinal and predictive research on LDs.

A final point about at-risk prediction and longitudinal strategies relates to the need to describe the course of development between prediction and outcome. A number of investigators have documented the consistency of findings over time for children with severe cognitive delays (Bernheimer and Keogh, 1988). Findings for LD individuals are not as clear-cut, however, suggesting that for some children, at least, risk status changes over time. Designation as at-risk for LDs early on does not necessarily mean that a child will remain at-risk; similarly, some apparently intact preschoolers may become at-risk during the school years. Thus, Gordon and Jens (1988) propose a Moving Risk Model, which allows for findings that children may move in and out of risk status. If we take seriously the transactional nature of development as proposed by Sameroff and Chandler (1975), we should expect changes in risk status related to children's experiences and social and educational environments. Our task is to identify what conditions or influences are related to these changes.

III. FOUR ILLUSTRATIVE LONGITUDINAL STUDIES

We have selected four longitudinal studies of risk for review. Although they are not specific to LDs, they provide insights into the nature of risk and, therefore, may help us understand LDs from a developmental perspective. Two studies were prospective in design but used somewhat different methods and covered different periods of time, the third is a retrospective study of LD youths, and the fourth is an 8-year follow-up of children in a regular school system. Despite differences in methods and subjects, the studies yield some common findings that deserve consideration in the study of LDs over time.

A. The National Institute of Neurological and Communicative Disorders and Stroke Study

In the National Institute of Neurological and Communicative Disorders and Stroke study (Nichols and Chen, 1981), a part of the National Collaborative Study begun in 1959, child and family demographic information was collected prenatally and at intervals over an 8-year period (initial sample of over 50,000). The median socioeconomic status (estimated from education, occupation, and income) of the sample as a whole was lower than the national average; ethnic representation was 45% White, 47% Black, and 7% Puerto Rican. The 7-year follow-up included 29,889 children and involved assessment in four primary categories of functioning: behavioral, cognitive and perceptual–motor, academic, and neurological. Selected from pre- and postnatal periods, 331 variables were used as predictors or antecedents. These tapped family, socioeconomic, and maternal characteristics, as well as child variables related to pregnancy, birth, infancy, preschool scores on developmental tests, and histories of development between 1 and 7 years. Children with identified neurological conditions (e.g., cerebral palsy) or known mental retardation (IQs below 80) were excluded from the follow-up analyses.

Analyses of follow-up data yielded four primary factors: hyperkinetic impulsive behavior, learning difficulties, neurological soft signs, and social immaturity. Children were identified as at-risk if their scores were in the lowest 8% of the distributions for each factor; children in the lowest 3% in each of the groups were considered as severe risks. Almost 79% of the children evidenced no abnormal scores, and fewer than 1% of the total sample evidenced problems in three areas of functioning (learning difficulties, hyperactive–impulsive, neurological signs). There were, however, clear differences in prevalence of problems according to gender, ethnicity, and socioeconomic status. Higher rates of problems were found for boys than for girls. While a number of characteristics (e.g., IQ, activity level, sibling status) were associated with problem–nonproblem status for the sample as a whole, they were not accurate for individual prediction within a discriminant function analysis. As example, family size and socioeconomic status were significantly correlated with learning problems, but most children from large families did not evidence learning problems. The Nichols and Chen findings underscore the major contribution of social and family conditions to children's learning and achievement. They also underscore the important distinction between group and individual predictions of risk. This point is also well illustrated in the longitudinal work of Werner and Smith (1982) in Hawaii.

B. The Kauai Studies

The Kauai studies (Werner and Smith, 1982) began in 1954. This prospective study was focused on a sample of 2,203 women on the Hawaiian island of Kauai, the women identified in the first trimester of pregnancy. Almost 2,000 infants were liveborn during the 1955–1957 period; the largest number were of Japanese background (35%) and 3% were Caucasian. As a whole, the families were of lower socioeconomic status. Almost 700 children were followed at intervals over an 18-year period; systematic assessments were made at birth, 1 year, 20 months, 10 years, and 18 years. Child, family, school, social, and legal information was gathered over time.

By age 10 years, approximately one-third of the children had or had experienced some learning or behavioral problems. During the second decade, approximately one-fifth had histories of serious delinquencies and/or had mental health problems. Pre- and perinatal conditions were related to risk or nonrisk status at age 20 months, but *only in association* with environmental conditions such as poverty and family disorganization. The influence of environmental conditions was stronger as the children grew older. Problems and/or adjustment varied by gender and age, with boys showing more signs of stress and difficulties in the first decade and girls showing an increased rate of problems in adolescence and young adulthood. Overall, girls were better "copers" than were boys in situations of chronic family stress and poverty.

Key variables that were strongly associated with negative outcomes were of three kinds: biological conditions such as severe perinatal stress or congenital defect; caregiving or environmental variables such as low level of mothers' education and high ratings of family instability; and child–behavioral characteristics such as extremes of infant activity levels and low developmental test scores. Separately or in combination these variables were found to predict subsequent problem–nonproblem status. Whereas almost all children evidenced some of the indicators at some time, the presence of four or more risk variables early on was strongly associated with subsequent serious problems in learning and/or behavior.

Of particular interest in the Kauai research was the finding that a subset of children (42 girls and 30 boys) who were predicted to be at-risk (four or more predictive signs before age 2 years) were well-functioning, competent individuals at age 18 years. These resilient children were described as "vulnerable but invincible." They had apparently coped successfully with a range of negative conditions that overwhelmed or had negative consequences for their peers. A number of variables differentiated the resilient children from their not-so-successful peers who were similar in age, sex, and socioeconomic status. Many were first-born and were described as having good recuperative powers in response to childhood illness or physical stress, as having positive temperament attributes as babies, as performing age-appropriately on pre-school developmental tests, and as androgynous, responsible, and achievement-oriented as adolescents (Werner, 1986).

As Werner (1986) clearly points out, although no child in the study developed without stresses, many of the problems identified early on improved "spontaneously." However, children whose problems persisted tended to have histories of moderate to severe early physical stress in tandem with chronic poverty and/or family disruption or parental psychopathology. While not specific to LDs, the Kauai findings clearly illustrate the high probability of negative developmental outcomes for the class of children at-risk because of poverty and social conditions. The findings also underscore that probability statements derived from groups may not be applied directly as probability statements about individual children.

C. Retrospective Study of Learning Disabilities

The Retrospective Study of Learning Disabilities (Hartzell and Compton, 1984) of 114 LD students covered information over a 10-year period. Children seen at a child diagnostic clinic between 1970 and 1973 were followed up

10 years later. Children were from primarily middle- or upper–middle-class intact families. Entering or predictive data included standardized measures of intelligence, visual–motor integrity, language, and achievement as well as projective personality measures and family and school information. Outcome information about educational, social, and vocational status was gathered from parents through questionnaires and interviews for the LD individuals and their non-learning-disabled (NLD) siblings.

At the time of follow-up, the mean age for the LD group was 19 years (range 15–27 years); the comparable mean for the NLD siblings was 21.5 years (range 15–36 years). 72% of the LD individuals were male, whereas 62% of the NLD siblings were female. At follow-up, the NLD individuals were superior to their LD siblings in educational attainment and achievement as measured by such indices as high school drop-out rate, continuing postsecondary education, and college graduation rate. The LD individuals were also reported to have significantly more problems in school. Only 23% experienced high academic success; the comparable figure for the siblings was 75%. Similarly, in the social area the LD subjects, having fewer friends and less adequate interpersonal relationships, were less successful than their NLD siblings. No statistically significant differences were found for vocational success, a finding due in part to the relatively young age of members of both groups.

Correlational and multiple regression techniques identified entry variables that were associated with outcomes 10 years later. Family functioning and full-scale IQ were the most powerful predicators of academic success; psychosocial functioning as children and IQ were the best predictors of social outcome. On the basis of their data, Hartzell and Compton concluded that the effect of LDs continues from childhood to adulthood and that successful outcomes are associated with intellectual, personality, and family factors.

D. Prospective Study of Reading

The Prospective Study of Reading (Badian, 1982, 1986, 1988) is a follow-up of 180 children administered a predictive test before kindergarten entry. The chidren lived in a predominantly white suburban community, and families were described as close to the national median in number of years of education and income. By grade eight, 116 of the original sample were attending school in the district; 58 were boys and 58 were girls. The screening measures included verbal items such as telling a story about a picture; selected subtests from a standard intelligence scale; visual–motor tasks such as name writing, copying forms, pencil use, and cutting; and readiness items such as ability to count and name colors, letters, and shapes. Information about the family and additional biographical data were also obtained at the time of screening. This included birth history, family history of LDs, socioeconomic status, birth order, and history of speech delay.

Reading subtests of a standard achievement test were used as follow-up criterion measures. Relationships between screening and reading performance at grades three and eight were significant ($r = 0.6-0.7$), and over 85% of the children were correctly classified as problem or nonproblem readers at outcome (Badian, 1982, 1988). The best single predictors of reading achievement were measures of language, specifically, selected verbal subtests of the intelligence scale given at kindergarten entry.

For the children as a group, reading performance was relatively stable from third to fifth grade; however, one-fourth of the poor readers at grade three were adequate readers at grade eight, thus supporting the notion that risk status may change over time. Furthermore, 55% of children identified as at-risk in kindergarten were average readers at grade eight; they were considered "false-positives" at early screening. The large number of false-positives may be attributed to the success of intervention initiated at school. However, Badian (1988) suggests that biographical variables may also have been important. In general, the false-positive children, those who were incorrectly identified as at-risk early on, came from families with a higher socioeconomic status and without histories of LDs. For these children, compensating factors, including family–home conditions and educational experience, may have positively influenced outcome status.

While the false-positive children are of concern because of possible negative effects of labeling, another set of children, the "false-negatives," are of concern in predicting LDs. These are children incorrectly identified as not at-risk in kindergarten but who subsequently develop problems. The consequence of the false-negative identification is, of course, that children who may be at-risk for learning problems do not receive needed help or services. Without proper remediation, their problems often become more serious. In Badian's study, the reading progress of the false-negative children, as well as those correctly identified as at-risk, increasingly lagged behind the gains of their peers. At grade eight, the average reading score for the poor readers was 4.1 grade years below expectancy and 6.9 years below the group mean.

Badian focused her longitudinal studies on reading problems, but her findings are consistent with studies of other risk conditions. As example, the children who became poor readers in Badian's study were less likely to be first-born and were more likely to come from families with less education and income. Badian, thus, has suggested the use of background data to improve the early identification of good and poor readers. She reports that by applying additional biographical information to screening test results, the correct identification of poor readers was increased from 43 to 93% (Badian,

1986). Badian's work supports the generalization that reading performance, like other developmental outcomes, is not determined by one factor, and that prediction is improved when scores on screening measures are combined with family histories of LDs, birth history and order, socioeconomic status, and language skills.

IV. GENERALIZATIONS FROM LONGITUDINAL STUDIES

The four longitudinal studies described were based on different cohorts or groups of children and were conducted in different geographic areas. However, they yield some common findings that are consistent with the work of other investigators and that may help us understand the long-term course of LDs. The findings from longitudinal research may also improve our ability to identify at-risk children early and accurately.

Two major sets of variables were identified as important contributors to risk. The first had to do with characteristics of the children themselves; the second addressed the social and familial environments in which the children were reared. Considering the child characteristics first, findings in all four studies documented that more boys than girls were problem learners. The reasons for the discrepancy in prevalence of problems are uncertain but include the possibility of sex-related biological vulnerability, differences in maturation rates, or differences in role expectations. The higher prevalence of learning problems for boys than for girls is clearly a matter of concern for educators and should be a topic of further research.

Despite the historical link between LDs and neurological dysfunction, these studies yielded little evidence that documented the validity of mild neurological signs as causes of learning problems. Indeed, in the Nichols and Chen and the Werner and Smith studies, "soft" neurological signs, presumably indices of minimal brain dysfunction, were found to be only weak to negligible predictors of subsequent LDs. Some evidence, however, indicated that individual characteristics of ethnicity, temperament, personal–social competencies, and language abilities were associated with problem–nonproblem status. In addition, both the Hartzell and Compton and the Badian studies documented the relationship between early cognitive measures and later academic outcomes. Taken as a whole, the findings suggest that a range of child characteristics contribute to risk for learning problems.

As a group, the studies also underscored the importance of social and family variables to the development of learning problems. Many of the risk factors identified in the Werner and Smith Kauai study (e.g., chronic family dysfunction or discord, frequent change of residence, poverty, poor education of parents) were replicated in the Nichols and Chen work. Indeed, poverty and the conditions associated with poverty appear to be major contributors to the development of problem conditions, including learning difficulties. The importance of family conditions and functioning was also emphasized by Hartzell and Compton and by Badian, although their samples were drawn from higher economic levels. In general, the impact of the social–familial environment in the development of at-risk children was striking. This point carries implications for intervention and treatment, as many environmental conditions, including poverty, are amenable to change.

Viewed from a developmental perspective, it is clear that understanding learning problems necessitates consideration of a range of variables. An important finding from the longitudinal work reviewed was the increasingly powerful influence of social–environmental conditions as children grew older. Werner and Smith emphasize, and the Nichols and Chen and the Badian findings confirm, that child vulnerability or risk *plus* environmental conditions lead to positive or negative developmental outcomes. This is a well-documented finding (for review, see Sameroff and Chandler, 1975) and, in part at least, explains the longitudinal results. It also allows for a more optimistic picture of LDs, suggesting that powerful positive experiences and opportunities early on may mitigate against the impact of at-risk biological conditions. Early identification and intervention, thus, have both preventive and ameliorative potential.

It should be noted that in most studies there was a subset of children who were identified early on who continued to evidence problems across developmental periods. They did not outgrow their problems but, rather, continued to evidence learning and sometimes social adjustment problems across developmental periods. These children tended to be those with extreme or severe biological–neurological conditions as neonates or in the early years and those with multiple indicators of problems. They were clearly at risk and needed intense and often continuing services.

Importantly, however, there were also many children predicted to be at-risk who developed well and who evidenced few signs of learning or adjustment problems. These "vulnerable but invincible" children, as described by Werner and Smith, are a particularly interesting group. They defied the odds based on the usual predictive variables. Such children could be found in each of the studies reviewed, despite the differences in study samples. A variety of characteristics and conditions appeared to differentiate the resilient children from their less successful peers. These were not necessarily cognitive attributes but, rather, appeared more related to personal characteristics contributing to positive and satisfying social interactions. As described in the Kauai study, resilient children were perceived as energetic, easy to deal with, and competent, and as using their capabilities well. Key factors in the development of resilient children were also found in their homes and families. Athough poor economically, there were strong affective ties among family members, informal and supportive kin networks, consistent and stable caretaking (not necessarily the mother), and appropriate and adequate role models. In short, both child and family characteristics contributed to positive outcome. The traditional approach to learning problems has been to focus on deficits and deficiencies. The notion of resilience and the identification of positive attributes of children and families adds substantially to our understanding of risk and points the direction for needed services and interventions.

Taken as a whole, the findings from these longitudinal studies underscore the differences between prediction for groups and prediction for individuals and argue for the need to include a range of variables as predictors and as outcomes. Hartzell and Compton found different strength of association between predictors and social and academic outcomes, and the other investigators reported differences in relationships depending on the variables included in the analyses. Werner and Smith also demonstrated that the nature of problems changes over time, so that it is necessary to consider developmental period and demands when assessing the predictive power of early indicators of risk. In sum, the findings from these studies infer the need for more differentiated and powerful analytic models if we are to understand the developmental nature of LDs.

V. EARLY IDENTIFICATION OF READING PROBLEMS

To illustrate the approach to early identification and prediction from a developmental perspective, we provide a more detailed discussion of reading. We have chosen reading because it is probably the most important subject taught in school and is often central to identification as LD. Indeed, reading problems and LDs are sometimes viewed as synonymous. Reading is a major goal of early instruction and the basis for later academic success. Yet many students do not learn to read adequately, and reading problems often persist beyond childhood into adolescence and adulthood. For these reasons, researchers have attempted to predict those students at-risk for reading failure, and the early identification of reading problems is an important part of the early identification or risk literature (for discussion, see Satz and Fletcher, 1988).

This literature is broad in scope and diverse in focus, making it difficult at times to integrate findings across studies. Screening instruments include a wide variety of tasks and tap a range of processing domains. Some assess "readiness" for learning and others attempt to identify deficit and dysfunctional performance. In general, the accuracy of prediction is determined by one of two methods. The first, the correlation coefficient, examines the relationship between early measures and subsequent achievement for groups of children; the second, a categorical method, determines the number and percentages of correctly identified individuals.

Numerous investigators report significant correlations between predictor and criterion measures, but variance in strength of association is considerable (Horn and Packard, 1985). From a practical perspective, the goal of early identification is to identify individual children for specialized interventions. While correlation coefficients inform on test validity based on group data, they do not inform on the accuracy of prediction for individual children. For this reason, some researchers report predictive accuracy in terms of a 2- × -2 prediction–performance matrix. Using this model (Meehl and Rosen, 1955), numbers of subjects predicted to be at-risk or not at-risk on screening are compared with numbers of subjects found to be poor or adequate readers. The percentages of true positives and true negatives yields an overall "hit rate."

In most studies, the majority of children are correctly identified, yet on an individual basis it is important to consider those children who are misidentified, i.e., the false-positives and false-negatives (Hinshaw *et al.*, 1986; Keogh *et al.*, 1987; Satz *et al.*, 1978). Overidentification, resulting in large numbers of false-positives, may result in incorrectly labeling children as at-risk; underidentification, or high numbers of false-negatives, may deny services to children in need of intervention. It should be noted that cut-off points for defining risk or nonrisk status are arbitrary and may change over time or according to particular studies or programs. As example, one investigator may define risk as the lowest 30% of scores on a given reading readiness test. Another investigator may set cut-off scores at 20% or even 10%. Clearly the number of children identified as at-risk will vary depending on the level of the cut-off score; many more children are considered at-risk when the criterion is 30% than when it is 10%. Similarly, the definition of adequate or good reading varies according to the operational criteria used. Is adequate reading performance above the 33nd, the 50th, or the 75th percentile?

The issue of cut-off scores becomes of practical importance in school programs where services are linked to identification as at-risk, because more children will be eligible for services in schools applying lenient criteria than in schools applying stringent ones. Decisions about criteria for classification and about cut-off points, thus, carry powerful practical consequences, as the provision of services may be determined by the findings of early-identification procedures.

Several problems have limited prediction to date. One concerns the definition of reading and of reading problems. According to one view, reading is decoding; i.e., it is the ability to recognize or sound out the printed word. Another view of reading emphasizes comprehension; i.e., reading is defined as the ability to obtain meaning from text. The emphasis on code or meaning is certainly not a new issue, as it reflects nearly a century of definitional and pedagogical debate. However, failure to clearly define and conceptualize the reading process renders the integration of results across studies problematic. For example, in some studies measures of word identification are reported (Blachman, 1983; Mann, 1984), whereas in others measures of word recognition and reading comprehension performance are combined (Bradley and Bryant, 1985; Jansky and deHirsch, 1972; Satz et al., 1978). For the most part, investigators refer to outcome performance simply as "reading." However, some research findings indicate that reading, more precisely understood, is a combination of word recognition and comprehension, and that individuals differ in their ability to execute each of these separate tasks. Therefore, failure to differentiate measures of reading outcome may confound predictive relationships.

Another problem relates to the choice of risk indicator or predictor variables. The content of early-identification measures varies according to the researcher's theoretical perspective about the nature of development, learning, and reading disabilities. Tests such as those represented in the work of Ilg and Ames (1972) and Ilg et al. (1980) are based on notions of development as maturationally based. These researchers suggest that successful reading depends on the attainment of age-related behavioral characteristics and competencies. In this view, children should not be expected to profit from reading instruction until they are maturationally ready. However, scales of developmental functioning have not been found to be powerful predictors of reading performance (Diamond, 1987; Lindquist, 1982).

A different approach is reflected in measures of readiness that emphasize specific reading subskills. Based on learning theory, reading is conceptualized as the acquisition of a predetermined sequence of discrete skills such as knowledge of letter sounds and blending. This view focuses on specific skills or abilities rather than on broad developmental domains thought to underlie readiness for instruction. However, this approach does not provide a framework for prediction of reading performance before the experience of failure.

Although emphases and representative tasks differ, nearly all predictive instruments include measures of verbal-language and visual–perceptual abilities. Overall, measures of verbal-language skills appear to be more powerful predictors of reading performance than are measures of visual–perceptual skills, although the latter measures also obtain significant correlations and make independent contributions to reading performance at particular age periods (Badian, 1982, 1988; Hinshaw et al., 1986; Horn and Packard, 1985; Jansky and deHirsch, 1972; Keogh et al., 1987).

Predictive relationships are also influenced by the "reading age" at the time of outcome. Developmental models of reading (Chall, 1983; Gibson and Levin, 1975; LaBerge and Samuels, 1974) conceptualize reading as changing with increasing reading proficiency. These reading theorists describe early reading as decoding; the task for the beginning reader is word identification. Attention is paid to the graphic features, phonological correspondences, and orthographic regularities of words. With practice, decoding becomes less difficult and the process of word recognition demands less and less attention. With less attention directed toward decoding, more attention can be allocated to the understanding of the text. It follows, then, that those processes implicated in comprehension would become increasingly more important influences on reading as word-identification skills become more automatic. Fletcher and Satz (1980) and Fletcher *et al.* (1981) provide evidence that the developmental correlates of reading change over time. Those investigators found that measures of linguistic skills such as verbal reasoning and fluency were more strongly related to reading performance in the upper than in the lower elementary school grades. In seperate research, Sears (1989) found that the strength of relationship between listening comprehension and reading performance increased with overall reading skill. These findings suggest that predictive relationships may change with the level of reading proficiency at outcome. Thus, it is necessary to consider both the skill being assessed and the developmental level of the individual. Specifically, short-term studies that report reading performace at first or second grade may yield different results from those using a longer follow-up period.

The findings from predictive studies of reading and reading problems are more narrowly focused than studies of LDs. Yet, as shown in this brief overview, the prediction of reading achievement is complex. Methodological issues of definition, choice of variables, and time of data collection influence the accuracy of prediction of reading and reading disabilities and must be taken into account when planning research and intervention programs.

VI. IMPLICATIONS FOR IDENTIFICATION AND PREDICTION

Studies of LDs from a developmental perspective suggest that we need to view prediction as a probability statement (Werner, 1986; Keogh, 1989). To date, the exact probabilities are uncertain, but we have an increasingly refined understanding of the conditions and the characteristics that influence the course of LDs over time. We can, therefore, put this knowledge to work in programs of identification and intervention. On the basis of the research reviewed in this chapter, we propose four major directions for practice.

First, it is clear that both child and social–environmental conditions contribute to outcomes for children identified as at-risk for LDs. While this seems obvious, it should be noted that most procedures for identification and diagnosis are focused exclusively on the child. Relatively little attention is paid to the powerful extra-child influences on development and on problems (e.g., on home and family, on intervention programs). Yet, LDs are, in part, a result of both child and situational characteristics, as findings from the four longitudinal studies reviewed attest. This suggests the need to consider a range of variables in analyzing LDs. For children in school, this implies analysis of the learning (i.e., classroom) setting as well as of the structure and demands of the curriculum and the learning tasks.

Second, the findings suggest that LDs may be expressed in a number of ways, that we are not dealing with a single, unitary condition. A given child may be at-risk in one developmental domain but not in another. Risk or problems in one domain do not necessarily imply problems in another. Thus, for predictive as well as for remedial or intervention purposes, global identification as at-risk for LDs is inadequate. It is important to specify the areas or domains of problems and nonproblems and to relate these characteristics to situational and instructional demands.

Third, from an interactional perspective, it is apparent that risk or disabilities are not always invariant or stable. Perinatal or neonatal risk does not necessarily lead to subsequent problems in learning and behavior. Sameroff and Chandler's (1975) insightful review of the consequences of early problem conditions demonstrates clearly that a range of variables and experiences affect developmental outcomes for children identified as at-risk in infancy. Their findings are corroborated by a number of clinical and educational studies leading to the generalization that many children identified as LD early on may move out of risk status. Specific problems in learning may not be evident in the preschool years but may appear as tasks and demands change. Thus, identification programs must include opportunities to document change.

Fourth, despite our preoccupation with problems and deficits in children's functioning, it is increasingly important to recognize that developmental outcomes are also affected by children's compensating abilities or strengths. Diagnostic case reports of LD children tend to be litanies of problems. Yet, many children with identified deficits or disabilities become well-functioning and healthy youths and adults. Werner and Smith (1982) described "resilient" children, and Anthony (1974) has identified "invulnerable" children. Rutter (1979) and Keogh (1989) emphasize the importance of protective factors in development. It is reasonable that a number of problem or risk conditions are compensated for by strengths in other developmental domains, or by positive and effective environments or instructional programs. These compensating variables need to be taken into account when making diagnostic and intervention decisions about children with LDs. For this reason, Keogh (1989) has proposed a compensatory model of identification and prediction that combines both risk and protective factors. In our view, consideration of protective factors and strengths when planning programs for LD children attenuates the impact of specific disabilities and maximizes the potential power of interventions.

Acknowledgment

Preparation of this chapter was supported in part by the National Institute of Child Health and Human Development under a grant to the UCLA Socio-Behavioral Group of the Mental Retardation Research Center.

References

Anthony, E. J. (1974). The syndrome of the psychology of the invulnerable child. *In* "The Child in His Family," Vol. III, "Children at Psychiatric Risk" (E. J. Anthony and C. Koupernik, eds.). Wiley, New York.

Aylward, G. P. (1988). Issues in prediction and developmental follow-up. *Dev. Behav. Pediatr.* **9(5)**, 307–309.

Badian, N. (1982). The prediction of good and poor reading before kindergarten entry: A four-year follow-up. *J. Special Educ.* **16(3)**, 309–318.

Badian, N. (1986). Improving the prediction of reading for the individual child: A four-year follow-up. *J. Learn. Disabil.* **21**, 98–103.

Badian, N. (1988). The prediction of good and poor reading before kindergarten entry; a nine-year follow-up. *J. Learn. Disabil.* **21(2)**, 98–103.

Bernheimer, L. T., and Keogh, B. K. (1988). The stability of cognitive performance of developmentally delayed children. *Am. J. Ment. Deficiency* **92(6)**, 539–542.

Blachman, B. (1983). Are we assessing the linguistic factors critical in early reading? *Ann. Dyslexia* **33**, 91–109.

Bradley, L., and Bryant, P. (1985). "Rhyme and Reason in Reading Spelling." University of Michigan Press, Ann Arbor.

Chall, J. (1983). "Stages of Reading Development." McGraw-Hill, New York.

Diamond, K. (1987). Predicting school problems from preschool development screening: A four-year follow-up of the revised Denver Developmental Screening Test and the role of parent report. *J. Div. Early Childhood* **11(3)**, 247–252.

Doris, J. (1986). Learning disabilities. *In* "Handbook of Cognitive, Social, and Neuropsychological Aspects of Learning Disabilities, Vol. 1. (S. J. Ceci, ed.) pp. 3–53. Lawrence Erlbaum, Hillsdale, New Jersey.

Fletcher, J., and Satz, P. (1980). Development changes in the neuropsychological correlates of reading achievement: A six-year longitudinal follow-up. *J. Clin. Neuropsychol.* **2(1)**, 23–37.

Fletcher, J., Satz, P., and Scholes, R. (1981). Developmental changes in the linguistic performance correlates of reading achievement. *Brain Lang.* **13**, 78–90.

Gibson, E., and Levin, H. (1975). "The Psychology of Reading." MIT Press, Cambridge.

Gordon, B. N., and Jens, K. G. (1988). A conceptual model for tracking high-risk infants and making early service decisions. *Dev. Behav. Pediatr.* **9(5)**, 279–286.

Hartzell, H. E., and Compton, C. (1984). Learning disability: A ten-year follow-up. *Pediatrics* **74(6)**, 1058–1064.

Hinshaw, S. P., Morrison, D., Carte, E., and Cornsweet, C. (1986). Factor composition of the SEARCH scanning instrument in kindergarten. *J. Psychoeduc. Assess.* **4**, 95–101.

Horn, W. F., and Packard, T. (1985). Early identification of learning problems: A meta-analysis. *J. Educ. Psychol.* **77**, 597–607.

Ilg, F., and Ames, L. B. (1972). "School Readiness: Behavior Tests Used at the Gesell Institute." Harper & Row, New York.

Ilg, F. L., Ames, L. B., Bates, L. B., Haines, J., and Gillespie, C. (1980). "Gesell School Readiness Test," 2nd ed. Programs for Education, Flemington, New Jersey.

Jansky, J., and deHirsch, K. (1972). "Preventing Reading Failure." Harper & Row, New York.

Johnson, C. L. (1984). The learning disabled adolescent and young adult: An overview and critique of current practices. *J. Learn. Disabil.* **17**, 386–391.

Keogh, B. K. (1989). Learning disability: Diversity in search of order. *In* "Handbook of Special Education: Research and Practice" (M. Wang, M. C. Reynolds, and H. J. Walberg, eds.). Pergamon Press, Oxford.

Keogh, B. K., Major-Kingsley, S., Omori-Gordon, H., and Reid, H. P. (1982). "A System of Marker Variables for the Field of Learning Disabilities. Syracuse University Press, Syracuse, New York.

Keogh, B. K., Sears, S., Daley, S., Pelland, M., and Royal, N. (1987). "The Factor Structure and Predictive Power of the Slingerland Pre-Reading Screening Procedures," tech. rep. University of California, Los Angeles.

LaBerge, D., and Samuels, S. J. (1974). Toward a theory of automatic information processing in reading. *Cog. Psychol.* **6**, 293–323.

Lindquist, G. (1982). Preschool screening as a means of predicting later reading achievement. *J. Learn. Disabil.* **15(6)**, 331–332.

Mann, V. A. (1984). Longitudinal prediction and prevention of early reading difficulty. *Ann. Dyslexia* **34**, 117–136.

Mastropieri, M. A. (1988). Learning disabilities in early childhood. *In* "Learning Disabilities: State of the Art and Practice" (K. Kavale, ed.). Little Brown College Hill Press, Boston.

Meehl, P. E., and Rosen, A. (1955). Antecedent probability and efficiency of psychometric signs, patterns, or cutting scores. *Psycholog. Bull.* **52**, 194–216.

Nichols, P. L., and Chen, T. C. (1981). "Minimal Brain Dysfunction." Lawrence Erlbaum, Hillsdale, New Jersey.

Reynolds, M. C., Wang, M. C., and Walberg, H. J. (1987). The necessary restructuring of special and regular education. *Excep. Children* **53(5)**, 392–398

Rutter, M. (1979). Protective factors in children's responses to stress and disadvantage. *In* "Primary Prevention of Psychopathology," Vol. III: "Social Competence in Children" (M. W. Kent and J. E. Rolf, eds.). University Press of New England, Hanover, Vermont.

Sameroff, A. J., and Chandler, M. J. (1975). Reproductive risk and the continuum of caretaking casualty. *In* "Review of Child Development Research," Vol. IV. (F. D. Horowitz, ed.). University of Chicago Press, Chicago.

Satz, P., and Fletcher, J. (1988). Early identification of learning disabled children: An old problem revisited. *J. Consult. Clin. Psychol.* **56(6)**, 824–829.

Satz, P., Taylor, G., Friel, J., and Fletcher, J. (1978). Some developmental and predictive precursors of reading disabilities: A six year follow-up. *In* "Dyslexia: An Appraisal of Current Knowledge" (A. L. Benton and D. Pearl, eds.). Oxford University Press, New York.

Schumaker, J. B., Deshler, D. D., Alley, G. R., and Warner, M. M. (1983). Toward the development of an interaction model for learning disabled adolescents *Excep. Educ. Q.* **4(1)**, 47–74.

Sears, S. P. (1989). "The differential prediction of word recognition and reading comprehension: A longitudinal study. Ph.D. dissertation, University of California, Los Angeles.

Smith, J. O. (1988). Social and vocational problems of adults with learning disabilities: A review of the literature. *Learn. Disabil. Focus* **4(1)**, 46–58.

Stainback, W., and Stainback, S. (1984). A rationale for the merger of special and regular education. *Excep. Children* **51(2)**, 102–111.

Vogel, S. A. (1986). Levels and patterns of intellectual functioning among learning disabled students: Clinical and educational implications. *J. Learn. Disabil.* **19**, 71–79.

Werner, E. E. (1986). The concept of risk from a developmental perspective. *In* "Advances in Special Education," Vol. 5: "Developmental Problems in Infancy and the Preschool Years" (B. K. Keogh, ed.) pp. 1–23. JAI Press, Greenwich Connecticut.

Werner, E. E., and Smith, R. (1982). "Vulnerable but Invincible: A Longitudinal Study of Resilient Children and Youth." McGraw-Hill, New York.

White, W. J. (1985). Perspectives on the education and training of learning disabled adults. *Learn. Disabil. Q.* **8**, 231–236.

CHAPTER 18

Adolescents with Learning Disabilities

Edwin S. Ellis and Patricia Friend

Editor's Notes

In this chapter, Ellis and Friend propose a perspective in understanding the problems of adolescents with learning disabilities that focuses on various setting demands that are faced by them and how well they meet such demands. This is the first theme of the chapter. Setting demands refer to the set of expectations that students must meet so as to experience success in any given setting. They fall into four categories: academic, social, motivational, and executive demands. Not surprisingly, adolescents with learning disabilities do not meet setting demands satisfactorily.

The second theme focuses on the reasons for learning-disabled adolescents' failures to meet the various setting demands well. The third is a comprehensive and in-depth discussion of intervention practices designed to help learning-disabled adolescents to better meet setting demands. Ellis and Friend spice up their discussion here with insightful pedagogic pointers.

Ellis and Friend close their chapter with comments on their own perception of the future direction of research with learning-disabled adolescents.

I. UNDERSTANDING ADOLESCENTS WITH LEARNING DISABILITIES

When considering the characteristics of adolescents with learning disabilities (LDs), the natural tendency is to focus on the limitations and problems of these individuals and then view these characteristics as if they were unique to the learning-disabled (LD) condition. A wealth of research has revealed little in the way of identifying, in an educationally relevant fashion, characteristics that are unique to adolescents labeled LD. In fact, students who are labeled LD tend to be those who are the "lowest of the low achievers" (Deshler *et al.*, 1982). Differences between LD and low-achieving students lie mostly in (1) the perceptions of others resulting from their reaction to the label "learning-disabled" and (2) how these youth are treated and the services they receive as a function of the label. The problems that individuals experience are basically a function of the interaction between the demands of the environment and the characteristics of the individual. It is therefore wrong to assume that their problems reflect merely their innate characteristics. A meaningful way to understand LD adolescents, therefore, is to examine the characteristics of the settings in relation to how those labeled as LD are meeting the expectations of these settings, as well as what can be done to enable these students to function more effectively in these settings. To address these issues, this chapter summarizes what research has shown about:

- How the characteristics of LD adolescents interact with the characteristics of their settings,
- How well LD adolescents are meeting academic, social, motivational, and executive expectations of their settings, and
- The effectiveness of various special education interventions in enabling LD adolescents to successfully and independently meet the expectations in their settings.

II. UNDERSTANDING SETTING DEMANDS

In considering the issues of becoming an adolescent, most people typically think of the changes brought on by hormones, emotional upheaval, and psycho-social development issues. Adolescents' bodies as well as their family structures and social climate are changing. In addition, young adolescents face a whole new scenario regarding the expectations of school and nonschool environments (Schumaker and Deshler, 1988). In elementary school, the primary emphasis is on instruction in basic skills (e.g., reading, writing, mathematics) in relatively protective environments. In secondary schools, however, teachers assume that most students have mastered basic skills, so instruction in content subject matter (e.g., science, social studies, literature) becomes the primary focus (Alley and Deshler, 1979; Robinson *et al.*, 1985), and students are expected to use their basic skills to master the content subject matter. Moreover, in the short time of a summer vacation, students move from being treated as children who require management and structure to epectations of behaving as independent young adults who effectively use self-management skills. Many students who have traditionally received the bulk of their educational experiences in self-contained settings must suddenly adjust to meeting the demands of multiple settings.

"Setting demands" encompass the set of expectations students must meet to experience success in a given setting. For example, because up to 44% of the information that students are responsible for learning is presented in textbooks (Zigmond *et al.*, 1985), textbook reading would be considered a major setting demand. Within a major setting demand, students are expected to meet numerous task demands. For example, task demands associated with textbook reading include identifying main ideas, monitoring comprehension, sorting out relevant from irrelevant information, interpreting visual aids, and so on. In most secondary settings, students are expected to meet these task demands while *independently* reading textbooks. Clearly, LD adolescents must face many setting demands as well as the many concomitant task demands within each.

Another dimension of setting demands is defined by the variables within the setting that influence students' abilities to meet expectations. There are three types of such variables: (1) nature of materials, (2) environmental factors, and (3) learner's characteristics. Within reading setting demands is the nature of material students are expected to independently read. Many secondary textbooks are poorly written. Armbruster and Anderson (1988) found that many texts are "inconsiderate" in that they do not incorporate features that help the reader learn. These features include introductory statements, adjunct questions, objectives, advance organizers, summaries, pointer words (i.e., first, second, third, etc.), and textual highlighting (e.g., italicized words, bold-faced print words). They found that the manner in which ideas and relationships are organized by most textbooks was illogical, that most textbooks often presented information in "list-like format which fails to convey the relationship inherent in the text" (Armbruster and Anderson, 1988: 49), that transitions between topics were often sudden, and that sequences presented in the text were often out of chronological order of occurrence in real time. In spite of the limitations of the textbooks, successful students must still meet setting demands associated with reading these books.

Likewise, students' abilities to meet other setting demands (e.g., gaining information from lectures) are influenced by environmental factors such as teachers' lectures that are poorly organized or tangential. Thus, the characteristics of the environment affects students' abilities to meet setting demand expectations.

The third variable in meeting a setting demand is the characteristics of the learner (e.g., acquired skills, ability to use effective strategies, motivation). Understanding a condition such as LDs, therefore, involves (1) understanding the expectations of a setting, (2) the characteristics of the setting that are conducive to meeting the expectations, and (3) the characteristics of persons who are expected to meet these expectations. Successfully gaining information from textbooks is just one of many setting demands students must meet in secondary schools settings. Nonschool environments also present various setting demands (e.g., the expectations of a particular job) that students must meet to function successfully.

Most setting demands in both school and nonschool environments can be categorized into four areas: academic expectations, social expectations, motivational expectations, and executive expectations (Lenz *et al.*, 1989). An explanation of these demands is presented below followed by research findings on how well LD adolescents meet these demands.

A. Academic Expectations

1. What Are the Academic Expectations of Adolescents?

Academic setting demands can be organized into three types. The first type, *acquisition of information*, involves expectations such as reading textbooks, listening to lectures, conducting library research, etc., to gain new knowledge. The second type, *storage of information*, involves what students are expected to do to store information either in the form of permanent products (e.g., note-taking, outlining, drawing figures to show relationships between various concepts and facts) or in memory (e.g., creating mnemonic devices to assist memory). The third type of setting demand concerns expectations of students with regard to *expression or demonstration of competence*. These expectations include writing tasks (e.g., writing essays, book reports, taking tests), oral tasks (e.g., making oral reports, participating in class discussions), and various performance tasks (e.g., completing a science experiment). Because most secondary students have different teachers, textbooks, etc., for different subjects, each course they take presents a set of unique setting demands. Similar academic expectations are found in nonschool environments. For example, employees are often expected to gain information independently from procedures manuals (e.g., manufacturer's instructions for replacing faulty valves in an engine) and learn difficult concepts (e.g., understanding the functional difference between a transducer valve and an intake-vacuum valve and recognize these values when they see them) as well as demonstrate competency (e.g., replace faulty intake-vacuum valves in engines in an efficient and effective manner and complete written reports so that the manufacturer's warranty can be activated).

2. How Well Are LD Adolescents Meeting Academic Expectations?

Students with LDs have a great deal of difficulty meeting traditional academic setting demands of both school and nonschool settings due to several factors. First, *many LD students lack the basic academic skills necessary to meet academic demands.* For example, a study examining the basic skills of 360 LD adolescents revealed that the average reading ability of seventh-graders, as measured by an individually administered achievement test, was in the low third-grade level. Those in the twelfth grade were only functioning on low fourth-grade levels (Warner *et al.*, 1980a).

Second, *many LD adolescents possess knowledge of a variety of basic skills but fail to systematically use them in problem-solving situations.* For example, when comparing the knowledge of decoding skills of tenth-grade students classified as LD with those considered normally achieving, Warner *et al.* (1980a) found no significant differences between these groups, yet the normal-achieving students were more successfully meeting the reading demands of school. In effect, normal-achieving students tended to apply what they knew about decoding to meet the reading expectations; those classified as LD did not. In another study, Schumaker *et al.* (1982a) demonstrated that LD students who knew basic conventions of print (e.g., knew rules of capitalization and punctuation) often failed to apply them when writing. LD adolescents, thus, often have skills that they do not effectively use.

Third, *many LD adolescents do not use effective or efficient learning/ performance strategies.* The approach one takes preparing for a test would be considered a learning strategy. The approach one takes for taking the test would be a different strategy. An effective learning strategy for meeting the setting demand of test preparation might be composed of a subset of important behaviors including: (1) making correct decisions about what needs to be learned (e.g., identifying important concepts and associated facts that will be evaluated on the test), (2) organizing this information into a more learnable format (e.g., drawing diagrams, creating mnemonic devices, creating study flash cards), (3) systematically interacting with the material to encode the information into memory (e.g., paraphrasing the relationship between concepts, memorizing lists), and (4) self-checking to determine what has been learned from that which requires more study. The strategy is effective because, if followed, it will have a high likelihood of producing success when taking the test. The strategy is also efficient because it includes only those behaviors that are essential to success, and use of the strategy produces the desired results in a timely manner. Many LD adolescents use learning strategies when studying for a test, but the strategies they employ are often not effective nor efficient (e.g., a strategy they could use to study for a test might be rereading the chapter while watching television—a procedure not likely to produce a high degree of success on the test).

Examinations of the study/performance strategies employed by LD adolescents reveal that *many simply do not know how to approach a task* (e.g., they do not know a systematic, effective, and efficient strategy for studying for a test). Many do not possess some of the subsets of skills vital to the use of a strategy (e.g., many do not know how to distinguish important from unimportant information and, thus, make poor decisions about what should be learned; many do not know how to organize information appropriately for study). Because many LD students lack this essential knowledge and these skills, they often experience difficulty completing assignments, taking tests, participating in school, etc. Other LD students know and can perform these strategies but fail to do so at opportune times (Lenz, in press; Lenz *et al.*, 1989).

LD students often experience similar problems in nonschool settings. For example, a fast-food employer might ask the youth to clean the kitchen. The LD youth may not possess some of the skills or knowledge necessary to complete the task (e.g., not know the appropriate cleaning agents nor the procedure for cleaning the walk-in refrigerator) nor possess the social skills necessary for seeking assistance.

Fourth, *many LD students do not have sufficient semantic knowledge to readily learn new content.* Lack of semantic knowledge (e.g., knowledge base of various concepts and associated facts) affects student learning of new content information in two ways. First, new information is more easily learned when it can be readily associated with something already known, or prior knowledge. For example, it is easier to learn about the reproduction cycle of a frog if students have semantic knowledge of other reproductive systems (i.e., they are already familiar with how reproduction works in mammals). Unfortunately, many LD students do not possess enough of the prerequisite knowledge of the subject matter to readily learn by association (Wong, 1985b). Lenz and Alley (1983) found that LD adolescents had significantly less background knowledge of social studies content than normal-achieving adolescents, yet they were both required to meet the same content classroom demands.

Second, lack of prerequisite semantic knowledge affects students' abilities to use study strategies for learning new content knowledge. In other words, the power of the strategy is limited by students' knowledge base. For example, a performance strategy for point-of-view writing is of limited value when attempting to state a position about the sources of racism in South Africa when students do not possess sufficient knowledge about racism or South

Africa. Clearly, an interdependence exists between ability to employ effective study/performance strategies and the knowledge base upon which the strategy is to be employed (Chi, 1981; Ellis and Lenz, 1990; Voss, 1982; Wong, 1985a).

Why do LD students often fail to acquire sufficient content knowledge? To paraphrase the prison guard in the movie *Hud*, "What we have here is a failure to *accumulate*." First, the nature of the learning disability may affect encoding and retention of knowledge (i.e., ineffective use of metacognition and cognitive strategies, memory deficits; see Chapter 8). Second, the nature of special education service delivery often reduces opportunities for students to acquire content knowledge. Ellis and Lenz (1991) noted that due to the nature of many special education pull-out programs in elementary and secondary schools, many LD students attend special education classes during times when their normal-achieving counterparts are attending social studies or science classes; thus, LD students are denied opportunities to acquire semantic knowledge. In other words, participating in resource room special education programs to work on remediating basic skills often requires many students to forego content-area lessons (i.e., science, geography), and thus the opportunities to acquire semantic knowledge are reduced.

Fifth, *many LD adolescents fail to take advantage of learning enhancers provided by the environment*. In many instances, a number of learning enhancers can be found in students' environments. For example, some of the better-written textbooks provide features that help the reader understand and remember information (e.g., introductory statements, headings, summaries, textual highlighting). Likewise, to enhance the learnability of their lectures, many of the more effective teachers provide advance organizers prior to lectures (e.g., review previous learning; identify topics, goals, and expectations). Many teachers employ learning enhancers during their lectures as well. For example, to make difficult concepts more understandable, analogies between new concepts and familiar ones (e.g., comparing a camera to the human eye when teaching how the eye works) are often made (Schumaker *et al.*, 1989). Although these learning enhancers are not always present in students' environments, many LD students virtually ignore them when they are present. Thus, although educators may be diligently working to incorporate use of various learning enhancers into their instructional strategies, LD adolescents do not necessarily benefit from them because they might not attend to them, recognize their value in facilitating the learning process, or know how to use them to make learning easier (Lenz *et al.*, 1987).

In sum, many LD adolescents are not effectively meeting the academic expectations of their environments. Many of the reasons for these difficulties are also applicable to understanding the difficulties they experience in the social domain.

B. Social Expectations

1. What Are the Social Expectations of Adolescents?

Like academic demands, the social demands adolescents must meet will vary among settings, and social demands are present in both school and nonschool settings. Expectations focus primarily on demonstrating effective and efficient social behaviors at appropriate times. These demands can be grouped into three main areas (Hazel *et al.*, 1981). The first area, *conversation and friendship*, concerns expectations related to day-to-day interactions with peers and adults. Expected behaviors include use of active listening, greeting others, saying goodbye, initiating conversations, interrupting others, asking questions, etc. The second area of social demand focuses on expectations related to *getting along with others*. Expected behaviors include accepting or saying thanks, giving and receiving compliments, giving and receiving criticism, apologizing, etc. The third area of social demands concerns *problem-solving*. Expectations include appropriate use of social behaviors related to following instructions, giving and receiving help, asking for feedback, giving rationales, solving problems, persuading others, negotiating, joining group activities, starting activities, etc.

These areas of social expectations are prevalent in nonschool as well as school environments. For example, Mathews *et al.* (1980) found that several social-interactional skills were validated as highly important for attaining and maintaining employment. These included both listening and oral-language social skills (e.g., accepting suggestions and criticism from an employer, telephoning to request an interview, interviewing, explaining a problem to an employer, complimenting others). It is important to remember that the social behaviors used to meet an expectation will differ, depending on the characteristics of the setting. For example, to meet a setting demand associated with accepting criticism, a student might use an entirely different set of social behaviors when receiving criticism from a teacher than when receiving it from a peer or a supervisor on a job. To meet social expectations, students must not only know how to perform key social skills, but they must also make effective decisions concerning when and where to use them.

Like academic setting demands, the variables within the social setting also influence students' abilities to meet social expectations. For example, some adolescent groups appear to consider it undesirable (i.e., "uncool," "geekish," "nerdish") to appear too friendly with teachers or to appear too knowledgeable in class. Adolescents, then, are often attempting to meet simultaneous, but different, sets of social expectations: those of teachers and those of peers. Adolescents have to learn to maintain a balance between these expectations to succeed socially. Moreover, the social expectations may be entirely different when interacting with different persons within the same age group.

For example, students are expected to act differently when interacting with teachers than when interacting with adults in nonschool environments (e.g., on the job when interacting with the supervisor). To further complicate the situation, different persons often react differently to the same set of social behaviors. Providing a warm, friendly greeting to one teacher may be welcomed and reinforced, whereas the same behavior might be punished by another teacher's interpretation of the behavior (i.e., "He's doing that to 'brown-nose' me ...") and reaction to it.

2. How Well Are LD Adolescents Meeting Social Expectations?

Although all students with LDs should *not* be considered socially incompetent, some have a great deal of difficulty meeting social expectations of school and nonschool settings. For example, a social setting demand common to almost every school setting is participation in class. Ellis (1989) noted that class participation is particularly important or LD students because, since most are poor textbook readers, the teacher's lectures and class discussions are perhaps two of the most important sources for attaining new information. Unfortunately, many LD students fail to take full advantage of these learning opportunities. Second, many do not *look* like they are interested in the subject matter during the teacher's lesson presentation. In other words, they display negative nonverbal participation behaviors. Teachers often respond in kind by giving less eye contact, smiling less at these students, and asking them to respond to a smaller extent. In short, educators have a tendency to focus less instruction at apparently disinterested students. Third, many LD students do not frequently participate *verbally* in class. Verbally responding to content serves as an important learning tool because, as a result of verbalizing, students more readily make associations between new and existing knowledge and personalize the new information. Verbalizing about content also provides an opportunity for students to check their own comprehension, and it communicates to teachers that they are trying. Because some LD adolescents infrequently participate in class discussions, they are not taking advantage of important learning opportunities.

Many LD students also have difficulty meeting nonacademic social expectations of school. Many are less socially active in school than their normal-achieving counterparts. For example, Deshler *et al.* (1981b) found that they participate in fewer extracurricular activities (e.g., school clubs, choir, band, sports), and they are less likely to be invited to join groups. The relatively dismal picture painted by this evidence may be attributable, in part, to their failure to display effective and efficient social skills when interacting with others, and a limited amount of evidence supports this hypothesis. Schumaker *et al.* (1982b) conducted a study that required students to role-play what they would do and say given various social scenarios (e.g., when peers are attempting to persuade the student to shoplift; when the student is asking a parent permission to use the car). Students' use of specific social skills related to the various scenarios were evaluated, and many LD students scored about the same as adjudicated delinquents. Parenthetically, because many LD youth and juveniles who have been adjudicated share many of the same characteristics, some people believe that LDs lead to juvenile delinquency. Although some LD youth participate in delinquent acts and subsequently become involved with the judicial system, little evidence supports a causal relationship between LDs and juvenile delinquency.

Research concerning the extent to which LD adolescents socially interact with others in nonschool environments also indicates that, for many, meeting social expectations is a problem. For example, Schumaker *et al.* (1980) reported that LD students "hang around with friends" less often and participate in after-school activities less than their normal-achieving counterparts. Once LD students leave school, social problems persist. For example, when compared with non-learning-disabled (NLD) peers, LD adolescents tend to participate in recreational and social activities as well as belong to community clubs and groups significantly less often (White *et al.*, 1980). Instead of participating in activities that require social interaction, LD adolescents report that they spend significantly more of their free time watching television (Vetter *et al.*, 1983).

Why do LD students experience difficulty meeting the social expectations of school? Many of the reasons why they experience difficulty meeting academic expectations of school are also applicable to understanding their difficulty meeting social expectations. *Many LD students lack the basic social skills* (e.g., do not know *how* to look at someone in a pleasant manner when having a conversation; do not know *how* to maintain voice control in tense situations) necessary to meet social expectations. Many possess a knowledge of a variety of basic social skills, but fail to incorporate them into *social strategies* for use in specific situations. For example, students may know how to give appropriate eye contact, maintain voice control, maintain a relaxed posture, etc., but not know how to systematically integrate these and other important social skills into a social strategy for asking adults for permission to do something.

Many LD students *may have knowledge of effective and efficient social strategies but fail to generalize them for a variety of possible reasons.* They may not recognize opportunities for social skills use nor recognize the advantages of using specific social strategies and, thus, are not motivated to do so at appropriate times. Some students may recognize the importance of using social strategies but poorly monitor the degree to which they should do so and, thus, infrequently use them. Some students may display inappropriate social behaviors as a *communicative function.* In other words, in their own way, they are displaying socially incompetent behavior in an attempt to communicate what they believe to be important messages (e.g., an adolescent interacting with her parent might fail to employ appropriate social skills in a given situation in an attempt to communicate to her parent, "I am more powerful than you. You can't *make* me behave the way you want. Therefore, I choose to behave in a manner in which you don't approve.").

For some students, lack of social competence may not be the primary reason they fail to act competently in social situations. Some students may be under *inappropriate stimulus control* (Kerr and Nelson, 1989: 215–217). In other words, it may be more reinforcing to act in a socially incompetent manner than to act competently. For example, some LD adolescents purposefully avoid opportunities for social interaction to avoid anticipated pain that might result. Ellis (1989) noted that some LD adolescents appear to avoid participating in class to avoid the risk of being humiliated for giving an inept answer.

To summarize, LD students often fail to meet the social expectations of school. These problems may be due to skill or strategy deficits, or they may be a function of personal needs and motivation.

C. Motivational Expectations

1. What Are the Motivational Expectations of Adolescents?

To perform successfully, students not only desire to succeed and put forth effort to do so, they must often do so *independently*. Motivation must be continuous and intrinsic. McCombs (1984: 200) described these motivation processes as "a dynamic, internally mediated set of metacognitive, cognitive, and affective processes that can influence a student's tendency to approach, engage in, expend effort in, and persist in learning tasks in a continuing, self-directed basis." In other words, students must know themselves as learners and realize that they are responsible for their own learning. In both school and nonschool settings, a number of expectations of students directly relate to independent motivation. For example, students must plan for timely task completions, as well as complete assignments without reminders and, when needed, request assistance (Schumaker *et al.*, 1983). They must demonstrate a proactive approach to life; set short-, intermediate-, and long-term goals; and reinforce themselves for attaining these goals. For many educators and employers, meeting motivational expectations appears to be more important than youths' abilities to meet academic expectations. Ellis *et al.* (1991) suggested that, in many cases, teachers value students' behaviors that reflect effort and motivation as much as they value students' learning outcomes. For example, analysis of the manner in which teachers scored students' test responses suggested that adolescents who attempted to answer essay test questions using complete sentences written in a paragraphlike format often receive partial to full credit for their answers *even when the content of their answers was not accurate* (Ellis *et al.*, 1991a). Similar results were found in nonschool settings. Crain (1984) reported that employers are often more concerned with motivation factors related to dependability, persistence, and proper attitudes than they are with grades and advanced basic skills of their employees.

Like academic and social setting demands, motivational expectations and students' abilities to meet these expectations are influenced by the variables within the environment. An important dimension to motivation concerns students' beliefs about the probability of future success in attaining goals. Students' perceptions of probability of attaining short-term goals can be effected by environments created by teachers. For example, many teachers create competitive situations (academic contests, grading on a curve, challenging students to "see who can have the highest grade") in their classrooms in an attempt to motivate students to put forth greater effort. Some studies examining the effects of using competition in the classroom suggest that competitive activities may effectively motivate those students who feel they have a high probability of winning the competition (e.g., the two or three brightest students in the classroom), but these procedures may have a reverse effect on those students who feel they have little chance of winning (see Ellis, 1986). Moreover, results of competitions tend to positively highlight the winners but negatively highlight the losers as well.

Beliefs about probability of future success also might affect students' willingness to make commitments to attain long-term goals. For example, students perceptions of the relative probability of attaining a high school diploma can have a marked impact on their willingness to stay in school. Variables within students' environments (e.g., requirements to pass standardized competency tests to receive high school diplomas; school officials requiring students to repeat a grade; difficulty of courses required for graduation) naturally have great influences on students' perceptions of probability for future success in attaining the long-term goal of graduating from school.

The perceptions of value that adolescents attribute to activities in which they are expected to participate naturally effects the degree to which they meet motivational expectations. In other words, if adolescents do not value factors such as the subject matter in which they are expected to learn, the assignments and instructional techniques employed by the teacher, the specific job responsibilities they are expected to perform, the feedback others provide, etc., then motivation is affected. In an era when adolescents are saturated by media messages related to attaining immediate, salient stimulation (e.g., rock video) and gratification (e.g., high frequency of commercials with the basic message of "get it now or you'll miss out"), and the desirability of being self-centered (e.g., "*I* want *my* M-tv"), school is a relatively boring environment and the curriculum has little relevancy.

2. How Well Are LD Adolescents Meeting Motivational Expectations?

LD adolescents often have difficulty meeting the motivational expectations of secondary school and nonschool environments. The variables that affect their motivation are many, complex, and multidimensional and could easily take an entire book to address. What follows, therefore, is an overview addressing some of the dimensions of this problem. As these dimensions are addressed, remember that these occur *in conjunction* with academic and social experiences.

One of the reasons LD students have difficulty meeting the motivational demands of secondary school concerns their purposes for attending school. For example, Adelman and Taylor (1983) identified several subgroups of students with varying levels of motivation for attending school. The first subgroup represents students who want "to attend school and learn some, but not all" (Adelman and Taylor, 1983: 385) of what is expected. The second subgroup also wishes to attend school and learn some or most of what is offered, but *do not expect to succeed* with the activities and tasks teachers employ when teaching. In addition, they may not value the techniques employed by their teachers. The third group is interested in attending school, but do not want to learn what is being taught. Some of these students are willing to discuss alternative learning opportunities, but some are not willing to discuss alternatives because they are primarily motivated to attend school to socialize with peers, or they "have such major fears regarding failure that they avoid all discussion of their problem" (Adelman and Taylor, 1983: 385). The fourth group is not interested in attending school. Though not unique to LD students, several factors play into students' motivation. These are discussed below.

Many LD adolescents seem to *fail to see the relationship between appropriate effort and success* (see Licht and Kistner, 1986). Such a conclusion is not surprising when one considers the limited degree of success many LD students have experienced in spite of their efforts. Countless parents of LD youth have conveyed stories of the hours spent laboriously working with their children to help them prepare for tests only to find their LD students subsequently fail the tests in spite of these efforts (see Osman, 1979).

Many LD adolescents experience difficulty in making a commitment to learn or perform. The majority of LD adolescents have several years of experience with special education, and many have little faith in the effectiveness of such services in helping them overcome their difficulties. A lack of faith might be due to two common types of experiences, and both are closely related to the students' difficulties perceiving the relationship between effort and success.

First, in spite of the effort of many LD students, those of their parents and teachers, and the promise of special education, the performance gap between LD students and normal-achieving students is continuously increasing. Students are often identified and begin special education services in the third grade, and a history of failure experiences has typically been well established by this point. To motivate their new students, many elementary special education teachers communicate messages similar to, "I know things have been tough for you, but now things should get better since we're going to provide you with special help. You try real hard, stick with it, and we'll overcome these problems." In other words, they try to instill in their students a sense of hope or belief in the "promise of special education"—a combination of hard work and special techniques will result in overcoming the disability. In a short time, students learn that, in reality, the disability is not overcome. Although students tend to demonstrate an initial growth spirt in achievement, the rate of achievement quickly and substantially diminishes (Warner *et al.*, 1980a). Students may be achieving substantially more than they did prior to entering special education, but the gap between their achievement and that of their normal-achieving peers continues to grow larger. Special education interventions designed to enable students to learn how to learn and perform, therefore, loose credibility. Naturally, students are, thus, less willing to commit energies to something that has little credibility from their perspective.

The second set of experiences that may contribute to LD adolescents' unwillingness to make commitments to learning and performing may be related, in part, to the nature of special education service that students have received in the past. Some special education programs are driven by a philosophy that the role of special education is to augment instruction that takes place in regular classrooms. Instead of viewing special education as a means for learning how to learn or perform to diminish the effects of a learning disability, many LD students learn to view it as a means of support to help them meet academic expectations of regular classrooms—in other words, as a way to wade though the many obstacles of school to meet *social* expectations related to passing courses and making higher grades. Commitments related to working to attain self-sufficiency are not necessarily sought, nor expected in many instances; in lieu of this, commitments that are often sought by teachers to work harder to "play the school game" are not uncommon.

Another feature of the nature of special education services received in the past can contribute to LD students' unwillingness to make commitments to learn and perform. In many programs, student participation in decisions regarding what they will learn or how they will be taught is rare. Many LD adolescents have extensive histories working with teachers who have dictated these decisions for students. They have been reinforced for complying with the direction provided by adults and, in many cases, punished for failing to comply. To summarize, commitments have not historically been sought from students; compliance is often the modus operandi. Thus, while setting demands often require commitments, LD students are often not willing to provide them.

Many LD adolescents experience difficulties related to setting goals or establishing plans for the future. Many LD adolescents do not perceive the benefits of staying in school as outweighing the benefits of dropping out. As a result, the drop-out rate among this population has been alarmingly high. Although the drop-out rates of the general population are exorbitant (around 35%), the drop-out rates of LD youth are typically around 50% (Levin *et al.*, 1985; Zigmond and Thornton, 1985). It appears that incidences of having students repeat grades in high school are effective predictors of drop-out. Zigmond and Thorton (1985) found that 90% of LD students who dropped out of school had been required to repeat a grade, and most repetitions occurred in the ninth grade. It is notable that LD students are more often required to repeat grades (35%) than NLD students (16%).

In summary, LD adolescents often experience trouble meeting the motivational expectations of their environment. Some have misperceptions about the relationship between appropriate effort and success. They are often reluctant to make commitments, and many have not established long-term goals.

D. Executive Expectations

1. What Are the Executive Expectations of Adolescents?

In the business world, executives are those persons who are responsible for organizing information and resources, making key decisions, solving problems, and evaluating effectiveness. Meeting these responsibilities requires executives to be knowledgeable and independent and to apply their skills and knowledge across a wide variety of problems. Executives must be effective managers of information and resources. Adolescents are essentially expected to act in a similar fashion. For example, students in secondary schools are typically expected to work independently with little feedback, to organize to-be-learned information and resources for learning, solve problems, and apply their knowledge across content areas. Evaluating the effectiveness of strategies used to meet these demands is left to individual students.

The characteristics of settings in which adolescents must function can influence the extent to which they are successful in meeting executive expectations. Because teachers are typically responsible for up to 150 students, and they are in contact with individual students for only a short time, their ability to assist individuals in becoming more effective executives is greatly limited (Robinson, *et al.*, 1985). In many instances, teachers in secondary schools are mandated to follow specific curriculum guides related to their content areas and are often under pressure "to finish the book" by the end of the semester (Schumaker and Deshler, 1988). Chronic failure of many LD and other students who fail to perform successfully in regular classes tends to place teachers "between a rock and a hard place." Teachers are encountering ever-increasing numbers of low achievers in their classes while also facing escalating pressures to be accountable. Much is being demanded of content teachers in spite of limited resources. Teachers are encouraged to supplement their instruction with microcomputers, tape recordings of textbooks, study guides, etc., or to modify their expectations of what is to be learned by using alternative textbooks. Sometimes they are urged to reduce the amount of content to be learned so that low-achieving students can experience more success. Many teachers who employ some of these recommendations experience little or no success, and their efforts to accommodate low achievers are often punished. Skepticism of special techniques and pessimism about teaching these students inevitably increases. This makes it more difficult to motivate teachers to try other alternatives that create instructional atmospheres more conducive to enabling students to meet executive expectations of school. In short, teachers are rarely afforded opportunities to teach students strategies for executive functioning.

2. How Well Are LD Adolescents Meeting Executive Expectations?

Although some LD adolescents effectively meet executive expectations most of the time, and some effectively meet them some of the time, many experience a great deal of difficulty in this area almost *all* of the time. Disabilities related to executive functioning were found in over 50% of the 318 LD adolescents studied by Warner, *et al.* (1980b). Few LD adolescents are able to work independently with little feedback, and they often rely on others to perform key executive tasks for them. For example, effective use of executive skills in a problem-solving situation such as studying for a test requires one to *think ahead, think during, and think back.* Many LD adolescents, however, often rely on peers, teachers, or their parents to think ahead for them (e.g., determining what needs to be learned for the test, estimating how much time will be needed, organizing information and resources, figuring out the best approach for learning material). They may rely on others to perform key "think during" executive tasks (e.g., monitoring what has been learned and how well, what still should be learned, how much time remains with regard to completing the task). Thinking back and reflecting about the effectiveness of strategies previously used is not a frequently used problem-solving behavior nor is it necessarily viewed by LD adolescents as important (Ellis *et al.*, 1989).

The difficulties many LD adolescents experience in meeting executive demands of settings is reflected in three key areas. First, many LD adolescents do not often invent appropriate strategies to complete tasks. Second, many LD adolescents do not often generalize knowledge and skills to new situations, settings, and problems. Third, LD adolescents often fail to take advantage of prior knowledge when facing new problems. A number of studies (for an indepth review see Alley *et al.*, 1983) have demonstrated that LD adolescents often maintain their ability to perform skills at or near mastery levels for at least moderate periods of time (2–8 weeks) following instruction, and they demonstrate an ability to generalize a skill to differing tasks demands (e.g., adapt a writing strategy for descriptive paragraphs for use when writing sequential paragraphs). What many LD students often fail to do, however, is generalize the skill to different settings to solve problems encountered in that setting (for a review, see Ellis *et al.*, 1987). For example, an LD student might master a strategy for writing paragraphs in a special education setting but rarely use the strategy to meet the writing demands in other classes. Implications are that simply enabling LD students to perform a new skill at mastery levels will likely prove to have minimal impact on the future success of these students. Not only must LD students learn to perform key skills, they must learn the executive skills necessary to generalize them.

In sum, examining the setting demands of secondary schools and LD adolescents' abilities to meet these expectations reveals three key factors. First, the demands of secondary schools are very different from those encountered during the elementary years—the most fundamental difference is the expectation of independent functioning in students. The expectations of nonschool environments have many of the same demands as those found in school environments. Second, although students are expected to independently meet the demands, many LD students often fail to do so because (1) they often lack basic academic, social, and motivational skills and knowledge; (2) they do not effectively use or generalize existing skills and knowledge when performing tasks; (3) they often do not know or use effective and efficient routines or strategies for learning and performing; (4) they tend to ignore various learning enhancers found in the environment; and (5) they often lack skills related to executive functioning. Third, the nature of the adolescents' settings often interacts with the nature of students to exacerbate the problem. Thus, when considering interventions for LD adolescents, it is important to consider intervening with students *and* their environments.

III. PROMISING INSTRUCTIONAL PRACTICES FOR LEARNING DISABLED ADOLESCENTS

Although the problems experienced by LD adolescents are often substantial and much needs to be learned about how to enable these youth to become more independent, there is reason for considerable optimism. In the past decade, a great deal has been learned about how to improve the effectiveness of interventions for these students. The discussion that follows reviews some key instructional techniques that hold great promise for teaching LD adolescents. These instructional principles are appropriate for teaching a wide range of subjects (e.g., science, social studies, social skills, vocational/technical skills, learning strategies, survival skills). Thus, these principles are applicable regardless of whether the special education program is based primarily on facilitating success in traditional curriculum formats (e.g., meeting the demands of regular classes) or facilitating success in alternative curriculum formats (e.g., teaching transitional skills).

A. Providing Explicit Instruction

Although a number of instructional models with growing popularity might be effective when teaching LD adolescents (e.g., whose language or holistic instruction, discovery learning, thematic instruction, reciprocal teaching), those that focus on making instruction as explicit as possible have received the most research scrutiny and have, by far, the greatest empirical support as a means of effectively teaching LD adolescents. While the relative effectiveness of less explicit instructional models is unknown due to lack of research in this area, the effectiveness of using explicit instruction is well documented. Deciding to employ less explicit instructional techniques should be a carefully deliberated and purposeful decision in light of insufficient evidence to warrant their use.

Explicit instruction means that the teacher ensures that students are well informed about what is expected, what is being learned, why it is being learned, and how it can be used. Students are also informed about the instructional techniques that will be used to help students learn and why these techniques are useful to students in helping them master what is being taught. For example, if the teacher were teaching a textbook reading strategy to students, the purpose for learning the strategy, when and where the strategy can be used, and the rationale and function of each strategy step as well as the behaviors that are expected to result from performing the step are explicitly explained to students. Clear explanations of the mental actions that are to take place when performing each of the strategy steps are provided. Students are not only taught how to perform the strategy, but also how to be in control of key cognitive processes when using the strategy. To explicitly model how the strategy is used, teachers "think out loud" while performing the strategy so that students can witness effective use of self-regulation processes. In addition, students are informed about what they will be doing during each stage of the learning process and how these activities will help them master the strategy and use it in their regular classes to be more successful. All of the specific instructional techniques reviewed below illustrate the concept of using explicit instruction.

B. Using Explicit Organizers

An area of instruction that appears particularly beneficial to LD adolescents is the use of devices that help these students recognize organizational patterns of instruction. In addition, showing students, as precisely as possible, the organizational pattern of effective problem-solving processes as well as organizational structures of content subject matters appear to help LD students more readily understand and remember them.

1. Instructional Organizers

Instructional organizers are teaching routines used to help students understand what is being learned and to integrate new information with that which is previously learned. They also help students distinguish between important and unimportant information during the lesson and help them store the new information for future recall. The power of instructional organizers is significant when used with LD adolescents. Research has demonstrated that when instructional organizers are used and teachers specifically instruct students to take advantage of them, LD students can correctly answer more questions about important information than unimportant information following the lesson; when not used, they tend to answer more questions correctly about unimportant information (Lenz, 1984; Lenz et al., 1987).

Three types of instructional organizers have been found highly beneficial when teaching LD adolescents (Lenz and Ellis, in press): the advance organizer, the lesson organizer, and the post organizer. The *advance organizer* is provided at the beginning of the lesson. With the advance organizer, the teacher gains students' attention and cues them that an organizer is being provided. Previous learning is reviewed, and then topic and goals of the current lesson are discussed. Next, the content of the lesson is defined for students. Here, the teacher informs students what they will be learning about the topic of the lesson followed by a discussion or review of key vocabulary that will be used during the lesson. Learning is then personalized by discussing "if–then" statements (e.g., *if* you learn to explain each of the steps of the writing strategy in your own words, *then* you will be better able to use the strategy because you can tell yourself what to do."). Finally, expectations are clearly identified by discussing how the goals of the lesson will be achieved. For example, the teacher informs students about the *way* the lesson will be taught and *how* the activities that may follow the lesson will be *useful* in helping them master the information. Ellis (1991) developed a simple procedure to facilitate implementation of advance organizers. Teachers use the "FORM" device (Figs. 18.1 and 18.2) to introduce content area lessons.

During the lesson, effective teachers provide various *lesson organizers*. For example, the teacher will cue students about the organization or structure of the lesson by using organizing words such as "first," "second," "third," etc.,

.........FORM *the BIG PICTURE of the lesson*........

Focus: *What will we be focusing on?*
    Students focused on teacher
    What will the focus of the lesson be about?
    What are the key points that will be addressed?
    What are some questions students want answered?

Organization: *How will we learn it?*
    Organizational devices to be used
        What learning enhancers will be used to make it easier?

    Organization of lesson
        What is the sequence of activities you will be using during this lesson?

Relationship: *How will it effect you?*
    Relationship to **past**
        What have you learned before that will help you now?

    Relationship to **future**
        If you master the material, **then** *how will you benefit?*

Most important goal: *What do you need to learn if you don't learn anything else?*

Figure 18.1 The FORM device, an advance organizer teaching procedure to introduce content area lessons.

as they teach (e.g., "There were *four* main results of the French/Indian War. *First,* ..."). They also provide importance cues to help students distinguish critical from superfluous information (e.g., "This is critical to understand; let's review it once more ..."). Relationships are also explicitly cued to help students integrate information by drawing students' attention to associations between new information and that which is familiar to students. Another type of lesson organizing device is *cueing expectations*. Although the expectations should have been explicitly communicated during the advance organizer, they are also cued throughout the lesson. As new information is presented, students are cued to how it relates to the instructional goals, mastery requirements, etc., of the lesson.

    The third type of instructional organizer is the use of a *post organizer* at the end of a lesson. During the post organizer, students are first cued that a post organizer is being provided (e.g., "Now I'm giving you a post organizer to review what we learned today."). To determine whether or not students have sufficiently acquired and integrated the new information, students are then evaluated (oral or written) and students are informed with regard to how well

Focus:

Focus of lesson *1920s Development of organized crime
gangsters & gangster "families"*

Focus of students' questions:

*Why did gangsters shoot people from cars?
Where did they get their machine guns?
What did gangsters do?*

Organization:

Organizational devices to be used: *Compare / contrast form*

Organization of lesson:

1st *discuss modern-day drug lords & cartels*

2nd *compare drug cartels with gangster families*

3rd *discuss how gangsters became so powerful*

4th *quiz*

Relationship:

Relationship to **past:**
*yesterday -- why people wanted prohibition
today -- what happened as a result*

Relationship to **future:**
If..... *you learn why gangsters became so powerful*

Then... *you 'll understand why some people want to legalize
drugs today*

Most important goal: *understand how gangsters get & keep power*

Figure 18.2   See Figure 18.1 legend.

they are attaining the goals of the lesson. If teaching a skill, generalization is forecasted by discussing how what is being learned can be used across settings and situations. The post organizer ends with a forecast of future learning by discussing the focus of the next lesson.

In addition to instructional organizers, *process and content organizers* can be used to help explicitly communicate to-be-learned information. Pressley *et al.* (1987b) noted that it is often necessary to restructure material into a form that is "more learnable." The characteristics of the more learnable material are that the material is presented in such a way (1) as to facilitate elaboration, (2) that it is rich with organizational structures and cues that facilitate learning, or (3) both. These characteristics are discussed in Section III.E. Both process and content organizers are designed to address this need.

2. Process Organizers

To meet academic expectations, LD students are frequently expected to master multistep processes (e.g., the process of conducting a lab experiment, the process of writing an essay, the process of evaluating a diet to determine whether it is healthy). To teach these processes, some teachers describe the processes in general terms as well as model them. Unfortunately, following instruction, many LD students are still unable to identify the specific processes they are expected to learn. Highly effective LD teachers, however, make these processes as explicit as possible by using process organizers. For example, when teaching students how to multiply two-digit numbers by two-digit numbers, effective teachers not only tell and describe the steps of the process, the steps are written on the chalkboard. As each step is modeled, the teacher points to the written step.

More sophisticated processes (e.g., learning strategies) are also communicated to students in a very explicit manner. For example, the writing process associated with point-of-view writing involves (1) prewriting activities (e.g., clarifying task, establishing a point-of-view, identifying reasons that can be used to tell why a position has been established, identifying supporting information to be used to elaborate on each reason, organizing these ideas), (2) production activities (communicating the point of view and then explaining it in writing), and (3) postwriting activities (editing for meaning and mechanics, revising). To help students recognize the structure of these processes, organizers can be used by making the steps explicit and communicating them to students in a form that is memorable (Ellis *et al.*, 1991a). Figure 18.3 illustrates how these writing processes have been made more explicit for students.

Process organizers can also be used to mediate specific processes during content-area instruction in mainstream classes in which LD students are enrolled. For example, teachers might use the "SNIPS" procedure (Ellis, 1991, illustrated in Fig. 18.4) to facilitate students' analysis of visual aides presented in textbook chapters or study guides.

3. Content Organizers

Effective LD teachers also make the organization of the content subject matter as explicit as possible for students. Various forms of graphics that provide visual displays of the subject matter's organization or structure (e.g., charts, diagrams, etc.) are an effective means of providing content organizers. Figure 18.5 is a sample graphic organizer. The graphic can be used to help students understand the relationship among kings, knights, and serfs in a

Decide on goals & theme

Decide who will read this & what you hope will happen when they do.
Decide what kind of information you need to communicate.
Decide what your theme will be about.
Note the theme on your planning form.

Estimate main ideas & details

Think of at least two main ideas that will explain your theme.
Make sure the main ideas are different.
Note the main ideas on your planning form.
Note at least 3 details that can be used to explain each main idea.

Figure best order of main ideas & details

Decide which main idea to write about first, second, etc., & note on the planning form.
For each main idea, note the best order for presenting the details on planning form.
Make sure the orders are logical.

Express the theme in the first sentence

The first sentence of your essay should state what the essay is about.

Note each main idea and supporting points

Note your first main idea using a complete sentence; explain this main idea using the details you ordered earlier.
Tell yourself positive statements about your writing and tell yourself to write more.
Repeat for each of the other main ideas.

Drive home the message in the last sentence

Restate what your theme was about in the last sentence.
Make sure you used wording different from the first sentence.

Search for errors and correct

Look for different kinds of errors in your essay and correct them.

Set editing goals.
Examine your essay to see if it makes sense.
Ask yourself whether your message will be clear to others.
Reveal picky errors (capitalization, punctuation, spelling, etc.)
Copy over neatly.
Have a last look for errors.

Figure 18.3   An expository writing strategy.

feudal society. The critical features of each of these persons are graphically organized so that students can more readily compare and contrast them.

Use of various forms of graphic organizers should be viewed not only as a means for teaching content, but also within an overall framework of providing LD students with explicit organizer devices to facilitate success. The "organizational function of pictures" has been used in various ways, including "semantic maps" (Johnson and Pearson, 1978), "networks" (Dansereau and Holley, 1982), and what Scruggs *et al.* (1985) referred to as "figural

Start with questions
Question to clarify *why* you are analyzing the visual aid.

Question to find out what is important to understand and remember about the visual aid.
   __Picture   *What is it a picture of? Is it something **important** to remember?*
   __Graph / Chart   *What is being **compared**? How?*
   __Map   *What **key areas** are important to see? Why are they key areas?*
   __Time-line   *Shows the **history** of what? From when to when?*

Note what you can learn from the hints.
Look for hints that signal answers to your question, and then identify what they tell you.

  __*Title says the visual is about* _____

  __*Print says* _____

  __*Lines are used to show* _____

  __*Numbers are used to show* _____

  __*Color is used as* __*decoration* __*to show* _____

  __*Other hints show* _____

Identify what is important.
*The **main thing** I need to remember about this visual is* _____

*A **fact** I can tell from this visual is* _____

*Another **fact** I can tell from this visual is* _____

Plug it into the chapter.
How does the visual relate to what the chapter or unit is about? _____

See if you can explain the visual to someone
Find someone to whom who you can explain the visual (explain it to yourself if nobody else is available).
Tell **what** you think the visual is about and **how** you think it relates to what the chapter is about.
Identify what you think are the best hints on the visual and tell **why** they are good hints.

Figure 18.4   The SNIPS procedure, a strategy for interpreting visual aides.

---

taxonomies," or graphics that display superordinate, coordinate, and subordinate relationships among concepts, facts, and/or details. Graphic representations can assist in making the material more learnable because LD students often lack the basic reading skills to extract the information from texts (Torgesen and Licht, 1983) and the texts themselves are often "inconsiderate" due to poor structure and organization (Anderson and Armbruster, 1984).

Several studies have demonstrated that learners (with poor reading ability, low verbal ability, and underdeveloped vocabulary) performed better when graphics were used to supplement regular content-area text chapters (Koran and Koran, 1980; Moyer *et al.*, 1984). Recent studies provide positive evidence that the use of graphics as supplements to textbook material can be an effective instructional technique with LD students. For instance, Bergerud

FEUDALISM

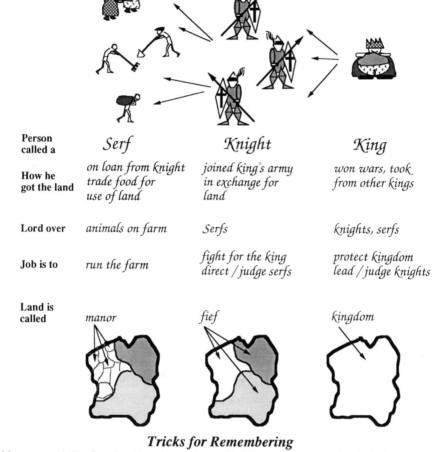

Person called a	*Serf*	*Knight*	*King*
How he got the land	*on loan from knight trade food for use of land*	*joined king's army in exchange for land*	*won wars, took from other kings*
Lord over	*animals on farm*	*Serfs*	*knights, serfs*
Job is to	*run the farm*	*fight for the king direct / judge serfs*	*protect kingdom lead / judge knights*
Land is called	*manor*	*fief*	*kingdom*

Tricks for Remembering

Manor: sounds like *"man"* -- think of *man's farm*
A manor is a man's farm

Serf: sounds like "servant" -- think of *slaves*
Serfs were basically servants or slaves

Fief: sounds like "life" -- think of *land for life*
A knight would promise to give his life in a fight for the king in exchange for a fief of land

Figure 18.5 Example of a graphic used as a content organizer.

et al. (1987) investigated the effectiveness of using graphics, as compared with study guides or self-study conditions with high school LD students. The students attended either a ninth-grade basic science class or one of three other study skills classes (grades nine through twelve) for students with LDs. Each class was exposed to each of the three treatments. Passages were taken from a life sciences textbook and 20-item multiple-choice tests were constructed for each passage. Graphics and study guides to be used in conjunction with the texts were also constructed. Results of the study indicated that the graphics treatment was the most effective in helping students attain the highest scores (60.5% of the students had scores above the minimal mastery level of 80% on the tests when graphics were used to facilitate the organization of the material). In the study guide condition, 42.1% of the students attained minimal mastery levels. When students were placed in the self-study condition, only 31.6% achieved mastery.

Concept diagrams (Fig. 18.6) can also be effectively used as organizer devices when teaching complex abstract concepts (e.g., "healthy life-style," "democracy," "sonnet," "metamorphosis"). Bulgren *et al.* (1988) found that when a diagram used to organize critical features of the concepts into categories of information (e.g., name and definition of concept; characteristics of the concept that are always, never, and sometimes present; examples and

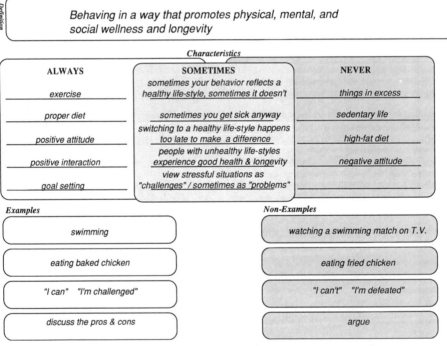

Figure 18.6 Example of a concept diagram used as a content organizer.

nonexamples of the concept), students' understanding and memory of the concept is significantly enhanced.

Another way teachers can provide explicit organizational cues is through the use of structured study guides consisting of sets of statements or questions designed to accompany reading assignments or teacher's lectures. Three common types are (1) multilevel guides, (2) concept guides, and (3) pattern guides (Horton and Lovitt, 1987). Multilevel guides are designed to address literal, interpretive, and applied levels of comprehension, whereas concept guides are designed to make new information more memorable by facilitating conceptual links or associations between the new information and that previously learned. Pattern guides are designed to enable the learner to recognize patterns of information (e.g., enumeration, sequence, compare–contrast, cause–effect).

To determine the relative effectiveness of multilevel study guides under teacher-mediated conditions (i.e., the teacher explicitly taught the content of the lesson using the study guide to provide structure to the lesson) relative to self-study conditions, Horton and Lovitt (1987) developed multilevel study guides to accompany two chapters from textbooks in science and social studies for middle school and high school classes. Tests containing 15 multiple-choice questions were also developed by the researchers to accompany the chapters. Results of the study indicated that almost half of the students in the self-study condition scored below minimal mastery levels (80%) in the self-study condition. However, when these same students were exposed to the teacher-mediated study guide condition, at least 90% of these students improved. More notable, 60% not only improved, but also scored at or above the minimal mastery levels with the teacher-mediated study guide condition.

The researchers conducted a similar study to examine the relative effects of student-directed study guides in which the student is provided the study guide but the teacher does not mediate the learning process by conducting a discussion of the study guide questions. In this study, the students independently completed the study guides at their desks, participated in a 5-minute feedback session to check their accuracy, followed by a 5-minute study session, and then took a 15-item test. Results indicated that about half the students scored below the minimal mastery level following the self-study condition. In the student-directed study guide condition, 63–74% of these same students scored above the minimal mastery levels.

Unfortunately, the small number of students classified as LD precluded a separate analysis of their performances, but the researchers did report that 13 out of 16 of the LD students improved with study guides, but only 7 of these improved to levels at or above the minimal mastery levels. In other words, the study guides helped considerably but were insufficient, in and of themselves, to facilitate mastery of the material. A possible explanation is that, although the learning process may be facilitated by the teacher providing organizational cues in the form of study guides and teacher-directed use of the guides, the learning process may continue to be impaired due to LD students' memory deficits or lack of cognitive learning strategies (e.g., students did not know *how* to use the guides to facilitate their learning). To summarize, LD students tend to greatly benefit from instruction embodied by explicit organizers.

C. Making Covert Processing More Explicit

To meet specific task demands (e.g., writing an essay, reading a textbook chapter), students must systematically apply problem-solving processes. While the results of performing some of these processes are readily observable, the processes themselves are often covert and not readily observable (e.g., many processes involve use of *cognitive* strategies such as visual imagery, prioritizing, hypothesis generating, relating new information to prior knowledge, or paraphrasing; and *metacognitive* strategies such as problem analysis, decision-making, goal setting, task analysis, and self-monitoring). An aspect of teaching that tends to be, perhaps, the least explicit is instruction in the covert processes that take place when performing tasks. For example, teachers may model and remodel the overt processes associated with writing a short essay and then prompt students to write their own essays. Often, students are required to *infer the mental processes that take place* when performing the task. They must infer what must be thought (1) prior to beginning the task (e.g., the thinking processes associated with analyzing the task requirements, reflecting on prior experiences with similar tasks, considering how best to approach the task, using self-motivation strategies), (2) while performing the task (e.g., monitoring the effectiveness of the strategy they are using, monitoring stress levels), and (3) after the task has been completed (e.g., reflecting on the effectiveness of the strategy employed, using self-reinforcement). Research has demonstrated that making covert processes more explicit for LD adolescents greatly increases effectiveness of instruction (Ellis *et al.*, 1991b). For example, when teaching a reading comprehension strategy that involves paraphrasing the main idea of a paragraph, an effective teacher will explain and demonstrate the cognitive processes one might use to find and state the main idea. This teacher would also coach students to enable them to perform these cognitive processes effectively and efficiently. Roehler and Duffy (1984: 265) have called instruction that emphasizes covert processing "direct explanation." In short, they argue that effective teachers focus not only on the mechanical aspects of learning and performing, but also on directly teaching students to understand and use the covert processes involved in the task. A less effective teacher, on the other hand, might simply instruct the student to perform the covert behavior while providing no explanation or demonstration of the covert behaviors and then provide feedback with regard to whether or not the desired outcome was attained. To summarize, LD adolescents seem to learn best when instruction is explicit; therefore, the covert processes they are expected to master must be explicitly explained.

D. Explicit Modeling of Procedures and Processes

Modeling important procedures and processes should be considered the "heart of instruction" (Schumaker, 1989). Unfortunately, when modeling, teachers tend to model more overt procedures and *tell* students what they are doing (e.g., "Now I'm going to find the main idea of this paragraph. Let's see, ... the main idea is ... traveling light—it's important to travel light when back packing.") as opposed to modeling overt procedures as well as "thinking out loud" to model more covert processes. The result is that LD students can witness how effective problem-solvers think. Thus, effective LD teachers not only need to thoroughly explain covert processes to LD adolescents, they need to explicitly model them as well. Schumaker (1989) identified three major phases of instruction involving modeling. In Phase I, teachers provide an organizer for the lesson that, among other things, alerts students to the fact that modeling will be provided and cues students to attend to the covert processes being modeled as they think aloud and ask students to imitate them. In Phase II, the teacher demonstrates the procedures and processes while thinking aloud and emphasizing the cognitive processes involved. The teacher demonstrates self-instruction and self-monitoring processes while performing the task. In Phase II, students are promoted to gradually perform more and more of the required thought processes and physical acts themselves; i.e., they become the demonstrators. Initially, students can be prompted to name the next step of the task. Once mastered, they should be prompted to say what they would say as they (1) check their progress, (2) evaluate their performance, (3) make adjustments, and (4) problem-solve. By involving students, the teacher can check their understanding of the procedures and processes involved in performing them. Ellis *et al.* (1991b) noted that forcing students to "think out loud" before they are ready can bog instruction down and make the task difficult. Students should participate in the modeling at a level that will prompt maximum involvement but still assure success.

E. Promoting Verbal Elaboration of To-Be-Learned Material

Pressley *et al.* (1987b) noted that facilitating students' elaboration of to-be-learned information is an excellent way to promote learning. Comprehension is enhanced and new information is more readily stored in long-term memory. Essentially, elaboration involves translating new information into one's own language structures by relating new information to that previously learned. Verbal elaboration can be promoted by LDs teachers when teaching both processes and content subject matter.

1. Verbal Elaboration of Processes

Ellis *et al.* (1991b) reported that LDs teachers must ensure that students comprehend the process involved in applying multistep procedures and processes. To effectively use self-instructional processes while performing a procedure, students need to be able to use their own language structures to communicate with themselves about the strategic process. Thus, instruction that focuses on having students describe, in their own words, key procedures and processes used when completing a task can facilitate students' understanding of the procedure and memory of what to do while performing it. Initially, the focus of instruction is on facilitating students' ability to elaborate on the "big picture" or intent of the overall strategy (what the strategy is designed to accomplish and generally what the process involves). Then the focus of instruction shifts to facilitating student elaboration of the specific steps in the procedure. Here, students describe what each step is designed to do and *why* it is an important component to the overall strategic process. Once students can accurately describe the strategy steps, they should be asked to discuss, in their own words, how self-instruction is used with regard to performing the strategy. Ellis *et al.* (1991b) also noted that LD students should memorize the steps to the procedure to an automatic level so that students can use self-instruction to prompt themselves on what to do next when performing the procedure.

2. Verbal Elaboration of Content Subject Matter

Ellis and Lenz (in press) noted that teachers can promote elaborative learning by prompting students to employ various cognitive processes (e.g., paraphrasing, summarizing, identifying main ideas and important details, predicting, generating questions, imagining, relating new information to personal experiences and interests) while interacting with the to-be-learned material. An example of an activity that promotes verbal elaboration of content subjects is the "instructional pause procedure" (Rowe, 1976, 1980, 1983). To use the procedure, the teacher provides direct instruction on the content subject matter for approximately 8–10 minutes and then initiates an activity that requires students to use various cognitive learning strategies (e.g., "Talk among the other members in your group and decide on what was the main idea and the two most important details of what I just taught," or "Talk among the other members in your group and make a prediction about what will happen when I add sulfur to this mixture. Then we'll see if your prediction is correct." or "Decide what would be a good way to remember ..."). The teacher then allows the students about 2 minutes to formulate their responses and then picks one group to express their response to the entire class. The other groups compare their response with the one expressed to class. Figure 18.7 shows sample tasks teachers can assign students to promote elaborative learning during instruction.

F. Providing Effective Practice Activities

Students who are learning to apply multistep processes or procedures (e.g., a procedure for determining whether or not someone has a healthy diet, a strategy for writing paragraphs, steps to replacing a faulty carburetor) should be provided with opportunities to practice the procedure in a context that has been carefully designed to assure that the student will correctly learn to use the procedure accurately, fluently, and strategically. There are two dimensions to effective practice. The first concerns processes for assuring that students will become effective mediators of the procedure. The second is designed to assure that students can apply the procedure to real-life situations and contexts.

1. Mediating Performance

Lenz and Ellis (in press) noted that mediation involves making decisions about when to use a procedure and determining how it should be used as well as regulating the process involved in applying the various steps of the procedure (e.g., deciding what to do next) and monitoring the whole process to assure that things are going as they should. Mastering the procedure, therefore, involves both learning how to perform overt behaviors (e.g., steps to the procedure) *and* learning how to perform critical covert behaviors associated with "mediation" or regulation of the problem-solving process (what one thinks while performing the steps). Ultimately, students will be able to take full responsibilities for the mediation process. When teaching a procedure, however, effective LDs teachers carefully structure practice activities so that the responsibilities for mediating correct use of the procedure gradually shift from the teacher to the student (Fig. 18.8).

When students first begin practicing use of the procedure, others who are more familiar with the process (e.g., teachers) assist with the mediation process involved with covert behaviors so that students can focus their attention on mastering the more overt behaviors associated with the procedure. During these early practice attempts, teacher mediation is *intensive*. Students receiving intensive teacher-mediated practice tend to be very dependent on teachers for direction and feedback, and if these students attempt to perform the procedure independently, there is a high probability of incorrect responses. During intensive teacher-mediated practice, effective LDs teachers frequently model and remodel specific behaviors associated with using the procedure, as well as

Preparing the lesson
Step 1: Generate an outline of the relevant information students need to master.
Step 2: Divide the information into 10–15-minute instructional modules.
Step 3: Identify specific tasks that will require students to employ elaboration strategies.

Teaching the lesson
Step 1: Divide the class into small groups (approximately 4 students per group).
Step 2: Provide an advance organizer of the lesson for the entire class.
Step 3: Teach the first module of the subject matter.
Step 4: Cue each group to perform the same cognitive strategy.
        *Be explicit in what they are being asked to do.
        *Be sure to inform students of the time allotment to activity.
Step 5: Allow students approximatley 3-5 minutes to perform the elaboration activity and
        discuss among themselves to formulate their response.
Step 6: Randomly select only one group to report their response to the entire class.
Step 7: Ask other groups to compare/critique their response to the one reported by the other
        group–use as a basis for discussing the subject matter.

Examples of tasks that require students to use cognitive elaboration strategies when interacting with the subject matter

Sample tasks that cue use of summarizing and prioritizing strategies
"Decide what was the main idea of the last module."
"Decide what was the main important piece of information ... ."
"Decide which of these details we've been discussing should be remembered."
"Write a telegraph message that states what happened. Each word will cost a dollar."

Sample tasks that cue use of questioning, predicting, and monitoring strageties
"Decide what you think happened next ... ."
"Tell me when you know the answer to the following question ... ."
"Tell me three things your group would like to find out about ... ."
"During the next instructional module, decide if _____ is what really happened."
"Tell me two things about what we just talked about that are confusing or difficult to under-stand."

Sample tasks that cue use of mnemonic strategies
"Figure out a good way to remember this list of key information."
"Generate a mini-story about these terms that will help you remember what they mean."

Sample tasks that cue use of activity prior to knowledge strategies
"You guys have three minutes to list everything you already know about ... ."
"How can what you already know about this topic help you remember this new information?"
"Look at this section of the block. Identify all the clues the book provides that help you identify important information."

Figure 18.7   Example of tasks used to promote elaborative learning.

Forms of mediated practice

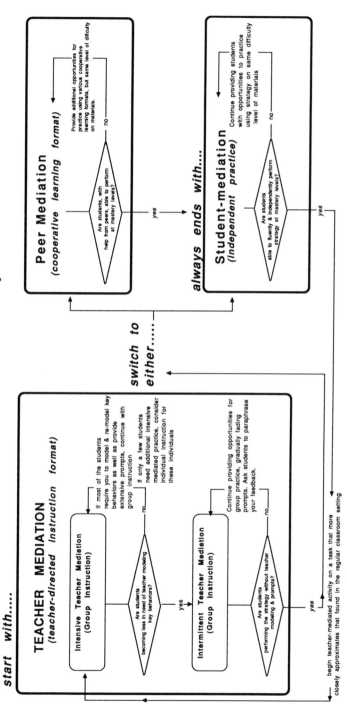

Figure 18.8 Forms of mediated practice that shift responsibility from the teacher to the students.

provide ample prompts and cues to mediate use of the procedure and to assure that the level of incorrect responses from students is very low. As students begin to assume more responsibility for mediating use of the procedure themselves, teacher mediation should become more *intermittent*. At this point in the learning process, students are generally familiar with how to perform the more overt behaviors associated with using the procedure. Now, the emphasis subtly shifts, so that the focus is more on mastering the covert, or mediation, processes associated with using the procedure independently. In other words, the prompts and cues extensively provided earlier are gradually faded until students can perform the procedure independently.

Peer-mediated practice can also be used to facilitate LD students' abilities to independently perform the procedure. Peer-mediated practice serves a slightly different, but equally important, purpose than teacher-mediated practice. Because LD students may learn as much from their peers as they do from teachers about how a procedure is performed, it is important to provide opportunities for students to interact among themselves when practicing the procedure as well as to use dialog among themselves about how the procedure is perceived and used (Lenz and Ellis, in press). Students participating in peer-mediated practice activities should be less in need of teachers for mediation and feedback but do require more opportunities to practice using the procedure to build fluency. Various cooperative learning group dynamics can be used to provide peer-mediated practice. *Student-mediated practice* is designed to provide students with opportunities to independently practice using the procedure to build fluency, so that both the overt and covert behaviors associated with using the procedure can be performed automatically and quickly.

2. Providing Appropriate Situations and Contexts for Practicing Use of Procedures or Processes

When students first begin learning to use a new procedure, they often are unfamiliar with "how it feels to use it," and they are not familiar enough with the procedure to apply it in a context filled with nuances that will make it difficult to apply. It is important, therefore, to select materials and design practice situations that will allow students to first become confident and competent at using a procedure in relatively trouble-free contexts. These types of practice activities are targeted at enabling students to use the procedure accurately and fluently. Once students have learned to mediate use of the procedure in these simple situations, then they will need to learn to apply it to problems more like those encountered in real life, so that students must learn to use the procedure strategically. In other words, they must learn to recognize situations to use the procedure and apply it as necessary. For example, if the procedure LD students were learning were a strategy for reading text chapters, the stimulus materials used as students initially begin practicing the strategy should be devoid of many of the demands of the regular class setting (e.g., complex vocabulary and concepts, lengthy reading selections) so that students can focus their attention on learning the technique and can build confidence and fluency in performing the strategy steps. As students become fluent in applying the strategy to these easier materials, increasingly more complex materials for practicing the strategy should be provided. Thus, students learn to use the strategy when interacting with materials that gradually approximate the difficulty of those found in their regular educational settings. Once students can perform the strategy when reading these easier materials, they are asked to apply the strategy to more challenging reading selections.

Although it is important to carefully design practice activities so that students gradually learn to apply the procedure to increasingly more complex tasks, it is equally important for students to understand why a particular type of practice activity is being provided. It is, therefore, important for teachers to orient students to the purpose of the specific practice activity and to inform them of how the activity fits into an overall plan for enabling them to apply the procedure to real-life tasks.

3. Providing Generalization Practice

If students will not likely need to use a procedure in real-life situations (e.g., one rarely, if ever, has to identify the parts of speech in real life), then investing considerable time and energy to teach LD students to use the procedure is a highly questionable practice. If, however, students are expected to use the procedure in real-life situations, it is often necessary to not only teach them how to perform the procedure, but also to teach them how to generalize it.

Unfortunately, because of the lack of teacher attention to the transition from the acquisition process to the generalization process, many LD students fail to generalize the recently learned procedure. Teachers must adopt an instructional philosophy in which the success of instruction is defined *only* by the degree to which the student uses the technique to meet demands of natural settings. In addition, this perspective must be transferred to students. When providing generalization practice, the teacher should assure that students are aware of the general goals of the generalization process, as well as the specific consequences related to focusing versus not focusing attention on the generalization process. Explicit commitments from students to generalize the skills should be sought.

For successful generalization to take place, Ellis *et al.* (1991b) noted that students must also be able to recognize naturally occurring cues across settings that signal appropriate opportunities for applying the skill. Therefore, the instructional processes for promoting generalization must focus on enabling the student to (1) discriminate when to use the procedure to meet everyday demands, (2) develop methods for remembering to use the procedure, (3) experiment with how the skill can be used across circumstances, (4) receive and use feedback to develop goals and plans to improve performance, (5) adapt the procedure to meet additional problems and demands, and (6) incorporate the procedure and various adaptations of it into the student's permanent system for approaching problems across settings and time. Practice activities should be specifically designed to target these goals.

G. Using Effective Feedback

Most teachers are aware that effective feedback is both positive and corrective. However, recent studies have demonstrated that some specific things can be done to enhance the effectiveness of feedback. The following outlines recent research concerning effective feedback for LD adolescents:

Feedback should focus on types of correct behavior as well as error types. Teachers often provide feedback that, regrettably, is often either too global for students to understand the problem clearly or is too specific (e.g., focuses on specific errors). Recent research with LD adolescents suggests feedback that focuses students' attention on the *types* of behaviors correctly performed as well as types of errors made and how to avoid these types of errors is more effective (Howell, 1986; Kea, 1987; Kline, 1989).

Feedback should focus on the effectiveness of strategic behaviors, as opposed to qualitative indices. Teachers often use qualitative descriptors when providing feedback (e.g., "This was a *good* use of the paraphasing strategy," or "That was *not a good* main idea statement."). Some educators have expressed concern that feedback based on qualitative indices may be counterproductive if used injudiciously (Ellis, 1986; Ellis *et al.*, 1987; Licht and Kistner, 1985). Its use may subtly encourage students to rely on others (reinforces external locus of control) for qualitative reinforcement. It also encourages the student to perform the learning task to impress others rather than to be successful in becoming self-sufficient. It also undermines the importance of effective use of those strategies that enable students to attain their goals. In lieu of using qualitative descriptors, feedback should focus on the effectiveness of behaviors (e.g., "That was an effective use of the paragraph writing strategy because you really explain yourself clearly ....").

Feedback on performance should be relative to an established mastery criteria. Students naturally perform better when (1) clear expectations have been communicated to them and (2) they know how well they need to perform the behaviors to be considered competent. Feedback, therefore, should be relative to a mastery criteria. In other words, students should understand both how well they need to be able to perform specific behaviors as well as how close they are to performing at this level. As an alternative to rewarding students with extrinsic reinforcers (e.g., points, prizes) for effective performance, providing students with charts that allow them to record their performance scores has been found to be an effective means of promoting intrinsic motivation in students (Lenz and Ellis, in press). The charts should have the mastery criteria indicated on them so that students can view their progress toward mastery and ascertain how close they are performing at mastery levels.

Effective feedback involves the students' elaboration on the feedback. Language deficits are a common characteristic of many students with mild learning handicaps. Because using language, or self-speech, can play an important role in the problem-solving process, providing students with opportunities to elaborate, using their own language, on the feedback can be an effective technique. For example, after explaining to students the types of errors they have been making when writing paragraphs, an effective teacher cues students to discuss the feedback. Students are asked to explain the feedback to the teacher by telling what they were doing that was less effective and what they need to do to improve the quality of their writing. The importance of encouraging LD students to elaborate on feedback is based on the work of Vygotsky (1978) and several other educators (Adelman and Taylor, 1983; Pressley *et al.*, 1987b).

Effective feedback includes establishing goals for improving specific behaviors in subsequent attempts. Many LD adolescents tend to depend on others for direction and perform academic tasks because others (e.g., teachers) expect them to. Having students establish goals, based on feedback, regarding future performance plays an important motivational role. The practice also places more responsibility on students for self-direction and assures that students understand the desired behavior. The importance of tying goal setting instruction to feedback is becoming increasingly more clear from recent research (see Bandura and Schunk, 1981; Seabaugh and Schumaker, 1981; Adelman and Taylor, 1983; Deshler *et al.*, 1984; Ellis, 1986; Ellis *et al.*, 1987).

Effective feedback is also provided just before a practice attempt. Although feedback is effective when it immediately follows a behavior, research has shown that it is also important that LD students receive feedback immediately *before* beginning the next practice attempt (Lenz, 1984). By reviewing the feedback on the previous performance and the goals established for the next attempt, the critical features of the correct behavior will more likely be incorporated into the student's upcoming practice attempt.

During the initial stages of practicing a skill, feedback should be directive. In other words, teachers should diagnose the type of error made by the students and provide explicit feedback regarding the error. Effective directive feedback is often composed of two components. First, the directive feedback focuses on examining the critical features of the behavior that need to be performed correctly, and, second, it often involves modeling the correct behavior (Lenz and Ellis, in press).

When students are building fluency, feedback should be mediative. Once students have mastered the basic behaviors associated with performing the strategy (e.g., teacher prompts are infrequently needed), the nature of feedback provided should shift from being directive (teacher diagnoses the problem and directs the desired behaviors) to being *mediative* (Ellis *et al.,* 1987; Stone and Wertsch, 1984; Vygotsky, 1978). Here, the teacher *cues* students to diagnose the problem and to generate their own solutions. In mediative feedback, the responsibility for monitoring and adjusting behaviors shifts from the teacher to the student. Mediative feedback structures opportunities for students to learn how to self-evaluate the effectiveness of their behaviors.

Feedback should be structured so that an awareness of where students have been and where they are going is facilitated. Sometimes the best feedback originates from students themselves. E. S. Ellis (1991) found that some effective LDs teachers facilitate self-evaluation in their students by having them maintain *journey logs,* which reflect an ongoing record of students' progress. Journey logs can be used in different ways. One approach is to have students record their perceptions of their ability to perform a specific task (e.g., how well the student writes paragraphs) just before teaching the strategy and then record brief, daily comments reflecting their perceptions of where they improved that day or other pertinent information about its use (e.g., information about attempts to use the strategy in a regular classroom, what they value about the strategy, recording attainment of a personal goal related to using the strategy, completing an instructional stage). Later, teachers can have students look back over their comments to review their "journey" mastering the strategy.

H. Requiring Mastery

An important principle underlying effective instruction of LD adolescents is to require student mastery of instructional objectives. Because concepts addressed in content-area classes often build upon each other, failure to master prerequisite concepts often assures difficulty mastering future, more complex concepts. Regrettably, many content-area teachers teach a unit, test students, and then move on to the next unit with little regard for how well students mastered concepts in the previous unit. Mastery of concepts means that students can *distinguish the critical features of the concept* that are always present from those that are never present or are only sometimes present, as well as *recognize examples and nonexamples* of the concept (Bulgren *et al.,* 1988). In addition, students must be able to *relate the new concept to previously learned concepts* in a meaningful way.

Mastering skill-based objectives is equally important. For example, research has shown that unless students can proficiently perform the skill at the specified mastery levels (Schmidt *et al.*, 1989), generalization is not likely to occur. Mastery of a skill involves three types of performance: (1) accuracy (student correctly performs the skill), (2) fluency (student performs the skill quickly and smoothly, and (3) strategically (student must independently use the skill at appropriate times when solving problems).

There are two implications of maintaining an "attain mastery" orientation to teaching LD students. The first is that the progress of students and their readiness for more complex instruction is the primary factor in instructional decisions. School climate factors (e.g., teachers' perception that school administrators expect them to "finish the book before the end of the year") become less important or less influential factors in determing future instruction. A second implication is that effective special education programs are "focused." In other words, effective programs focus on key areas and teach these areas intensively and extensively (i.e., Pressley *et al.*, 1987b). Less effective programs, on the other hand, bend to the many needs of LD students and often attempt to address all needs (e.g., attempt to provide tutoring services, basic skill remediation, counseling, transitional programming, social skills training, learning strategy instruction, etc.). Inevitably, the result of such practices is that too little instruction is provided in any one area, and, thus, the overall intervention program has minimal effectiveness. In short, the "spray and pray" approach (spray students with a little of everything—pray something has a positive effect on the students) to teaching LD adolescents is not effective because too little is ever mastered.

I. Incorporating Self-Control Techniques into Instruction

One of the highest priorities of the special education teacher should be creating an atmosphere in their instructional setting that reinforces in LD students the idea of taking responsibility for their lives, gaining independence, and being in control of their own destinies. Specific techniques for creating such an atmosphere include addressing the issue of who is in control, clarifying the role of a special education teacher, creating an atmosphere permeated by a student goal-setting and self-evaluation orientation, and communicating and teaching confidence.

1. Clarifying Who Is in Control and the Role of Special Education Services

Lenz and Ellis (in press) have noted that many LD students perceive themselves as passive recipients of "whatever life dishes out" and that they have little control over their own destinies. They reported that to address these debilitating beliefs, effective teachers invest considerable time counseling their students about who is in control of their lives to help them realize that they are already making adult decisions in their lives and to capitalize on this power to more actively take control. This concept of "who is in control" permeates the instructional atmosphere on a daily basis. The language used by effective LDs teachers consistently communicates this concept, and the manner in which instruction is delivered reinforces it.

Many LD students become dependent on their special education teachers to mediate their success in regular classrooms (Ellis, 1986). For example, many view behaviors related to finding out what assignments need to be completed in regular classes, determining how best to perform the assignments, "spoon feeding" the information, and checking to see that the assignment has been effectively performed in a timely fashion as the special education teachers' responsibility. Such beliefs are counterproductive to instructional goals related to facilitating independence in students. It is often necessary, therefore, to address counterproductive beliefs about the nature of the special education teacher's role. To change these beliefs, effective teachers frequently reiterate the role of special education in relation to facilitating independence over the long term (e.g., teaching skills which can be widely used now and in the future) as opposed to assuring short-lived success (e.g., tutoring a student so that he or she passes a test), and always relate what is being learned to how it will help LD students become more independent.

2. Facilitating Goal-Setting and Self-Reinforcement

Because many LD adolescents do not use effective self-motivation strategies such as making self-coping and affirmation statements, establishing their own goals, and providing themselves with reinforcement, these motivation strategies are explicitly taught to LD students. The overriding purpose of self-motivation training is to promote in students a perception of self-efficacy and personal control (McCombs, 1984). These perceptions underlie the ability of students to take positive self-control and change negative attitudes and orientations toward learning. Many teachers teach goal-setting both as a skill and as a philosophy. For example, they teach their students how to set annual goals for learning and how to present these goals at their Individual Education Program (IEP) conferences in such a way that the goals are included in their formal educational plans (Van Reusen et al., 1987, Van Reusen et al., 1989). Considerable time is spent with students discussing goals and teaching how to determine long-term (postsecondary, yearly, and semester), weekly, and even daily performance goals and how these goals relate to each other. For example, potential to-be-taught strategies are presented as a "vehicle to realize personal goals" (Lenz, in press: 17), and students subsequently participate in decisions regarding which strategies to learn. If students express their desire to learn a specific strategy, their subsequent commitment to the task is stronger and more enduring. Effective teachers help students write these commitments in the form of goal statements that reflect intended real-life future applications of the to-be-learned strategy (Ellis *et al.*, 1991b). Moreover, conversations between teachers and their LD students constantly reflect a goal-setting orientation. Students are encouraged to collaborate with teachers in the evaluation of the effectiveness of instruction as well as the effectiveness of the strategy in helping them meet specific tasks in their settings. Each week, specific time is alloted for discussing students' long-term goals, how they are being met, and progress toward meeting them. On a daily basis, students are encouraged to set performance goals and then provide time at the end of class for students to assess whether or not their goals were met. In short, student goals permeate the atmosphere of effective LDs classrooms (Lenz and Ellis, in press).

In addition to teaching goal-setting strategies, effective teachers also teach LD students to make positive affirmation and self-coping statements to motivate themselves as they work through a task, to evaluate their own performances, to use self-reinforcement and self-correction procedures, and to monitor progress toward their goals (Seabaugh and Schumaker, 1981). Thus, the instructional process in highly effective special education programs is driven by student goals, *not* teacher goals. For example, Ellis (1989) taught students, just prior to the beginning of a content lesson, to set goals for learning content by (1) writing a question about the content they hope will be answered in the upcoming lesson and (2) noting goals for participating in class. At the end of the content lesson, LD students were taught to think back and determine whether or not their question had been answered and whether or not they met their participation goals. Ellis reported that, as a result, the level of student participation significantly increased during the class and that teachers perceived LD students as more interested in the subject matter.

3. Communicating and Teaching Confidence

As noted earlier in this chapter, many LD students with a history of failure experiences have little confidence in their own abilities. They often attribute their successes to variables beyond their control (e.g., luck—"The teacher made the test easy this time.") and their failures to their own perceived ineptitudes (see Licht and Kistner, 1986). Many students also crucify themselves with negative self-statements (e.g., "I'm too dumb for this."). In a study examining the motivation techniques employed by expert master teachers, Ellis (1991) found that effective LD teachers frequently communicated a confidence in their students using such statements as "I know you can do it" or "Now you're ready for a more difficult problem because you'll be able to handle it." The expert teachers also taught students to communicate their confidence to peers. For example, some expert teachers employ cooperative learning techniques for group practice activities. One person in the group is designated the "encourager." During the activity, the encourager is responsible for encouraging and reinforcing others, as well as communicating confidence in others during difficult or frustrating circumstances.

J. Emphasizing Role of Personal Effort

Because many LD adolescents seem to believe that their successes are largely due to factors beyond their personal control (e.g., "I did well on the test because the test was easy"), the role of personal effort as a key factor in any formula for success should be continuously emphasized when teaching LD adolescents. Successful problem-solving, in the simplest terms, is related to one's choosing a strategy that can effectively address the demand of the setting and then trying as hard as possible to use the strategy in the correct way. Ellis *et al.* (1991b) noted that LD students should be taught that the key elements in the formula for successful problem-solving in an academic setting are the following:

Appropriately Chosen Learning Strategy + Personal Effort = Successful Problem-Solving

By frequently referring to this formula when discussing progress and providing feedback, students' understanding that personal effort must be exerted to ensure success is enhanced as well as their understanding of the learning process. Likewise, students are taught to attribute failure experiences to use of less effective or efficient strategies, or both. Emphasis is placed on encouraging students to try harder to use the *best* strategy (i.e., most effective and efficient strategy) for the task.

Frequently encouraging students to make positive attribution and affirmation statements can also, over time, help students use more effective motivation strategies (Lenz and Ellis, in press). Many LD students attribute failure experienced to their own personal attributes (e.g., "The reason I didn't do well on the test is because I'm dumb.") rather than on use of less effective strategies for the task. To facilitate more positive beliefs, teachers can employ a form of attribution retraining by requiring students to acknowledge the positive attributions (e.g., "You got a B on the test. One of the reasons you got a B instead of a lower grade was because you were really trying to use a good strategy for preparing for the test, *right*?") or to make the positive choice between negative and positive attributions (e.g., "You got a B on the test. Was it because the teacher made the test easy *or* because your studying hard made it easy?"), and then facilitate students' selection of the choice that reflects self-control. Because some LD students frequently use counterproductive negative self-talk (i.e., "I can't do this, I'm too dumb."), teachers can teach students to make positive affirmation statements prior to and during difficult tasks. For example, students can be taught to write at the top of the first page of their tests a positive affirmation statement (e.g., "I'm going to smoke this test.") before beginning the test (Hughes *et al.*, 1988). Although a number of studies have examined the effects of focusing students' attention on the importance of effort and attribution retraining on students with histories of failure experiences, only a few have specifically focused on students classified as LD (see Licht and Kistner, 1986; Anderson and Jennings, 1980; McNabb, 1984).

IV. OVERVIEW AND CRITIQUE OF INTERVENTION PRACTICES

In recent years, a number of intervention models and practices for teaching LD adolescents have emerged. Some of the most common interventions used with LD adolescents as well as some less common ones that hold great promise for enabling students to meet academic, social, motivational, and executive expectations of secondary and postsecondary environments are reviewed below. Issues associated with using these interventions are explored.

A. Basic Academic Skill Remediation

Considering that the average basic skills (reading, writing, spelling, mathematics) of LD adolescents are commensurate with those of fourth- or fifth-grade normal-achieving students, the decision to focus on remediating basic skills of adolescents would seem logical. In many cases, such a decision would be appropriate. Some LD students are not identified until they become adolescents and, thus, have not received intense remedial basic skills instruction in the past. Students who receive intense remedial instruction in basic skills for the first time as an adolescent often make marked improvement. In other words, for such students, basic skill remediation is often cost-effective because of the gains that are attained. The decision to continue to provide basic skills remediation for students who have long histories of this type of service, however, is not so clear-cut.

Several factors should be carefully considered before deciding to continue targeting intensive remediation of basic skills in adolescents. First, *how well has the student responded to previous attempts to remediate basic skills?* If students have demonstrated a steady growth in basic skills, then continuing to offer basic skill remediation might be appropriate, but if their growth in these areas appears to have plateaued in spite of intense efforts to remediate them, then continuing to offer this type of service, in lieu of other services that might be offered, might not be the best decision.

Before assuming that it is not desirable to continue teaching basic skills, however, it is important to also consider the manner in which basic skills have been taught in the past. For example, the *Corrective Reading Program*, published by Research Associates, Inc., can be a highly effective intervention for increasing reading skills of middle school students. If students have not previously received instruction using this or other similar programs based or *direct instruction* techniques, then it might be desirable to provide this form of instruction before abandoning basic skills remediation and looking to other curriculum options that might produce greater benefits for students.

Second, *how motivated are students to continue to work on remediating basic skills*? Many students have been "remediated to death" and see little value in continuing this form of instruction due to the limited success it may have produced in the past.

Third, *how critical is increasing students' basic skills to meeting the expectations of school and nonschool environments*? Since the amount of time allotted to special education services in secondary schools is usually limited, it is important to remember that the basic skills targeted for remediation should be those most critical to meeting expectations of school and nonschool environments. For example, basic skills related to writing complete sentences are critical to master because, to be successful, students are required to write complete sentences in almost all of their coursework as well as in employment settings. A basic skill that is not critical is the ability to compute long division problems, because there are very few instances in life where a person needs long-division skills. While the topic of increasing basic skills makes good rhetoric between school officials and politicians, this form of instruction may not necessarily enable students to meet life's expectations more effectively. Many students may have already reached a functional level in basic skills. Other forms of instruction may make more of an impact on facilitating students' independence.

Fourth, *how well are students using existing basic skills*? Many students are not using existing basic skills effectively in problem-solving contexts. It makes little sense to continue to teach basic skills when students are not using them. In lieu of teaching more basic skills, instruction targeting how to strategically use existing skills might be of more value for students.

Fifth, *how well have students mastered basic skills necessary for performing powerful learning strategies*? For learning strategies to be useful problem-solving tools for meeting setting demands, students must have mastered the basic skills that are used when performing the strategies. Students who have not mastered prerequisite basic skills for a specific strategy might greatly benefit from basic skill remediation that specifically targets those necessary for subsequent strategy instruction. For example, to successfully learn and use an error monitoring strategy for finding and correcting mechanical writing errors (e.g., spelling, capitalization, punctuation), students must know the rules of capitalization, how to look for a word in the dictionary, etc. Intensely targeting these specific basic skills for remediation just prior to instruction in the learning strategy may significantly affect how quickly students master the strategy as well as how much they subsequently use it to solve problems.

Finally, *to what extent do administrative mandates dictate decisions to provide basic skill remediation?* Many school districts are required to give students minimal competency tests (MCTs) and to attempt to remediate any deficiencies students display on such tests. In many school districts, graduating from high school or even passing on to another grade is contingent on passing MCTs. Because being forced to repeat a grade produces a high likelihood of school drop-out (Zigmond and Thornton, 1985) and the proposition of receiving a "certificate of attendance" as opposed to a diploma raises serious questions about the potential for future economic success, teachers have little choice but to provide basic skill remediation to LD students who did not perform well on MCTs. These decisions must often be made in spite of the questionable practice that teachers are expected to use in the hope that in the future LD students will correctly answer previously missed MCT test questions. The practice involves targeting isolated, unrelated skills thought to be represented by missed MCT test questions, and attempting to remediate them out-of-context from a meaningful curriculum.

B. Curriculum Reductions

Reducing the quantity or changing the emphasis of a curriculum represents an approach to teaching content-area subject matter to LD students that is commonly followed in schools (Weiderholt and McEntire, 1980). Reducing the breath of the curriculum to enhance the acquisition of appropriate secondary content can be a valuable strategy for teachers because the practice may relieve frustration and provide success for some individuals who have been unsuccessful in secondary content learning. Although this approach apparently is a common practice in schools (Schumaker and Deshler, 1984; Schumaker *et al.*, 1986), a review of the research literature suggests that evaluation of this practice has been practically nonexistent. In the absence of research in this area, educators often rely on speculation and personal perspectives with regard to its efficacy.

Reducing the breadth of what is to be learned may be problematic because, if curriculum content is reduced, the amount or kind of information that can be acquired is limited even before learning can begin, regardless of the quality of teaching (Ellis and Lenz, 1990). As noted earlier, many LD adolescents are already handicapped by their limited background information in certain content areas because they do not know enough about a topic to readily learn new information about the topic. Thus, the more curriculum reductions are used, the more handicapped LD students may become for future learning experiences.

C. Using Alternative Textbooks

Ideally, textbooks should be designed to help the reader understand and remember the content—not just present the content in print. Textbooks should include ample cues such as organizers, summaries, textual highlighting, etc., and the ideas presented in text should flow logically in an organized manner that makes sense to the reader. Visuals are most helpful to readers when they are tied directly to the text in specific ways (Schallert, 1980). The manner in which the text is written should match with the skills and knowledge of the reader (Armbruster and Anderson, 1988; Meyer, 1981). Because there is often a mismatch between the way textbooks are usually written and the reading skills of LD audiences, alternative textbooks that feature controlled reading levels, shorter chapters, and an increased number of visual aids are often sought by LDs teachers. Unfortunately, these special textbooks may be as problematic as those traditionally used in regular classrooms. Readability formulas based on word length, sentence length, word familiarity, and sentence complexity (Dupuis and Askov, 1982) are often used as a basis for determining how difficult the text is to read.

Alternative textbooks are often written in a manner that produces low readability scores when formulas are applied, so they will be attractive to teachers with students with low reading skills. To attain lower readability scores on their books, authors often use shorter words, sentences, and paragraphs, and they write shorter chapters. The practice may result in the text becoming more difficult for students to see contextual relationships, or how information, concepts, and ideas are related or form "the big picture." The information becomes too fragmented to be useful or meaningful to students. Alternative textbooks with these characteristics may actually be less useful than traditional textbooks because they are more difficult to understand.

To illustrate this concept, the above paragraph has been rewritten using shorter words, sentences, etc., to produce a considerably lower score when a readability formula is applied. Note, however, what happens to its comprehensibility:

> "Other textbooks are easy. Teachers will like them more. The books have short words and chapters. It is hard for students to understand all of it. They do not make sense. They may not be as good."

Authors of alternative textbooks also tend to include decorative or entertaining visuals (i.e., colorful pictures) and eliminate more informative visuals that may require studying (e.g., time lines, figures, charts, maps). The visuals also tended to supplant text rather than compliment text, thus forcing students to make their own contextual generalizations. Lenz *et al.* (1981) found that visuals used in alternative textbooks were harder for LD adolescents to interpret for meaning than visuals found in grade-level textbooks. LD adolescents were able to generate more statements relevant to the surrounding text from the visuals in grade-level texts than from those in alternative texts.

To summarize, results of these text-reduction practices are (1) considerably less information is conveyed by the alternative texts than traditional texts used in regular classrooms and (2) the limited amount of information that is conveyed is often difficult to understand because the elements that indicate important relationships tend to be eliminated in the process of achieving formula compatibility. It is possible for two texts to attain the same readability scores but be markedly different in their comprehensibility due to the nature of their organization, use of visual aids, sentence structure, and so forth (Ellis and Lenz, in press; Lovitt *et al.*, 1987). Armbruster and Anderson (1988) recommend the careful screening of textbooks so that the most "considerate" to the reader are selected for use.

D. Teaching Learning Strategies

Strategy instruction is different from basic skills instruction. A strategy is how an individual thinks and acts when planning, executing, and evaluating performance on a task and its outcomes—in short, a strategy is an individual's approach to a task (Lenz, in press: 4). Basic skills are often used when performing a strategy. The Strategies Intervention Model developed by colleagues associated with the University of Kansas Institute for Research in Learning Disabilities is perhaps the best example of an intervention model based on a strategies instructional approach. Specific learning strategies have been and continue to be designed and taught to students to enable them to meet academic demands related to knowledge acquisition, storage, and expression or demonstration of competence. Because some of the strategies LD students use do not always lead to success, specific strategies are designed that will be more optimally useful to them. For example, several knowledge acquisition strategies related to increasing students' abilities to meet reading expectations have proven promising.

Strategies that have proven to be the most beneficial to LD adolescents share a number of critical features, although a given strategy might not contain all of these features (Ellis and Lenz, 1987; Ellis and Lenz, 1991 Lenz, 1991). First and foremost, *the strategy is designed to be useful*. It must address a setting demand that is common in settings that students must face, and it should also be valuable for meeting future needs as well as being generalizable. Second, the steps of the strategy are designed to be an *efficient approach to the task for LD adolescents.* In other words, strategy steps are not just a sequenced set of "good things to do" but, rather, are a sequenced set of the "best mental and physical actions" organized into the "best sequence" resulting in the "best approach" for LD adolescents. It is important to note that what might be the best procedure for LD youth may not be the best approach for sophisticated learners. For example, the point-of-view writing strategy DEFENDS (see Fig. 18.3) is a very effective writing strategy for many LD youth because the thinking and writing processes are very structured, but sophisticated writers would not necessarily use it because it may be too structured.

To maximize efficiency, some strategy steps cue students to use effective thinking processes. Effective approaches to tasks often involve use of specific cognitive strategies (e.g., paraphrasing, imaging, predicting, setting priorities). Some steps cue students to use these cognitive strategies; others cue use of thinking behaviors related to reflecting on and evaluating the way a task is being approached and accomplished. The latter type of cues prompt students to use metacognitive processes involved in analyzing the task and setting goals, monitoring the problem-solving process during its implementation, and reviewing or checking to determine whether or not goals were met.

Finally, *the steps of effective learning strategies are designed to be memorable.* Strategy steps are often encapsulated into a remembering device, and the device is often representative of the strategic process reflected by the strategy or the type of task the strategy is designed to target. For example, a strategy for point-of-view writing uses the mnemonic device "DEFENDS" (as in defending a point of view). Although *implementing a strategies instructional approach* holds great potential for increasing students' abilities to meet setting demands, several factors should be considered before deciding to provide this type of service. First, is there sufficient opportunity to thoroughly teach the strategies? Second, is there a match between the needs of students and the strategies that can be offered? Third, is there a match between the skills and students and the strategies offered? Fourth, does the teacher possess the skills and knowledge to competently provide strategy instruction? These factors are discussed below.

Is there sufficient opportunity to teach strategies? For strategy instruction to have a sufficient impact on students, it must be intensive and extensive (Pressley *et al.,* 1987a). The intensity of instruction refers to the amount of work required of both teachers and students that is necessary for strategy instruction to have an impact. The more strategies students master, the more strategic they become. Thus, the extensiveness of instruction refers to the fact students must learn many strategies before a lasting, significant impact is made on their lives. The question is, therefore, are there sufficient opportunities for strategy instructors to do a credible job in providing strategies instruction? In many schools, services that many consumers have come to expect from special education teachers (e.g., tutoring in content areas; providing instruction in social skills, survival skills; vocational, career, and transitional skills) must be reduced to provide intensive and extensive strategy instruction. To implement a strategies-based intervention program successfully, teachers need support from their students, parents, mainstream teachers, and administrators. Gaining this support often means that consumers (e.g., students, regular teachers) must be willing to change their fundamental philosophy of the role of special education and the nature of services offered. Implications are that special education teachers must not only master knowledge and skills associated with becoming an effective teacher of strategies, they must also master knowledge and skills associated with becoming an effective "change agent" (Ellis, 1990b).

Is there a match between the needs of students and the strategies that can be offered? It is not always appropriate to invest large amounts of time and energy teaching learning strategies. Some students may have discovered or developed effective or efficient strategies on their own, and if students are successfully meeting setting demands using these strategies, substitute strategies should not be taught. For those adolescents who have very low-functioning skills, other types of services (i.e., interventions designed to enable students to make more successful transition into postsecondary environments) might be of greater benefit.

Is there a match between the skills and knowledge of students and the strategies offered? Of the many factors that could affect the ultimate success or failure of strategy training, students' knowledge of critical skills and information related to the strategy use, as well as students' motivation to learn and use strategies, are among the most important. In addition, strategies should not be taught if the need is not real and immediate. For example, a note-taking strategy would not be taught if note-taking is not a real, as opposed to perceived, setting demand in the student's school.

E. Teaching Social Skills

1. Should LD Adolescents Be Taught Social Skills?

Although social skills training procedures and issues have been addressed extensively by Vaughn in Chapter 14 of this book, some discussion of this intervention approach, with regard to LD *adolescents*, is warranted here. Clearly, most adolescents would benefit from some degree of social skills training. Because social skills instruction is typically not part of the traditional school program, the intervention must be added to the existing curriculum, or parts of the existing curriculum must be eliminated to make room for social skills instruction. Earlier, it was noted that for learning strategies instruction to be worthwhile, instruction had to be intensive and extensive. Essentially, the same principle holds true for social skills training. Providing only periodic instruction in social skills looks good on paper (e.g., parents like the fact that the IEP reflects that their LD student is receiving social skills training.), but, unfortunately, this approach will have little impact on the student; for the most part, intermittent, unsystematic social skills instruction will likely be a complete waste of time. Thus, effective training in social skills for adolescents is focused, intensive, extensive, and ongoing. Because social skills training requires a considerable commitment of time and energy, its implementation should be carefully weighed against other forms of interventions that might be offered to students. Rarely is there sufficient time to address *all* the LD students' needs by offering intensive social skills instruction, strategy instruction, tutoring in content areas, basic skills remediation, etc.

2. Teaching Students to Become Self-Advocates

Perhaps one of the most important social skills that LD adolescents should master is self-advocacy. Procedures for teaching LD adolescents self-advocacy strategies have received only limited attention from researchers, but results are promising. Van Reusen *et al.* (1987) developed an intervention specifically designed to facilitate LD students use of self-assessment, goal-setting, and self-advocacy procedures for partipating in IEP meetings. Results of the training indicated that during IEP meetings, LD students demonstrated significant increases in statements indicating what they perceived to be their strengths and weaknesses, their goals for their special education program, and their choices in learning. There is a great need for more research and development of interventions specifically designed to empower students to make decisions for themselves, to set goals, and to monitor progress based on their own analysis of abilities. Such strategies hold great promise for restoring self-esteem and imbuing students with a sense of control over their destinies.

V. CLOSING COMMENTS: THE GOOD NEWS AND THE BAD NEWS

Although many LD adolescents experience difficulty meeting the academic, social, motivational, and executive demands of their environments, research and development of interventions specifically designed to enable them to meet these demands independently has yielded some very promising results. The most promising interventions share some common characteristics. First, instructional techniques are designed to be as explicit as possible. Second, to help LD students meet academic and social demands of their settings, basic academic and social skills are taught, not as isolated parts of the curriculum that must be mastered but, rather, as integrated components of problem-solving strategies. Third, to help LD students meet the motivational demands of their settings, students are being explicitly taught to set goals, monitor their progress toward goals, and reinforce themselves. The philosophy of student goal-setting permeates the atmosphere of effective LD classrooms. Fourth, to help students meet executive demands, principles gained from basic research in cognitive psychology are becoming increasingly more integrated into practical instructional techniques for LD adolescents. Increasingly, key thinking processes involved in effective learning and performing are targeted for instruction. Students are explicitly informed, cued, and frequently reminded why a particular instructional procedure is being used to enhance their learning.

Teaching LD adolescents is a highly stimulating and worthwhile endeavor, and the effectiveness of interventions for enabling LD students to become more independent holds great promise. Unfortunately, many teachers of LD adolescents face complex decisions regarding the selection of interventions to be provided. The expectation placed on LD teachers to "be all things and teach all things to all LD students" is nothing short of impossible to meet. The greatest need for future research is not more clarification on what to teach these students or even how to teach them. Rather, how to integrate and implement what has already been learned is, perhaps, the single most pressing need for future research.

References

Adelman, H. S., and Taylor, L. (1983). Enhancing motivation for ovecoming learning and behavior problems. *J. Learn. Disabil.* **16,** 384–392.

Alley, G. R., and Deshler, D. D. (1979). "Teaching the Learning Disabled Adolescent: Strategies and Methods." Love Publishing, Denver, Colorado.

Alley, G. R., Deshler, D. D., Clark, F. L., Schumaker, J. B., and Warner, M. M. (1983). Learning disabilities in adolescent and young adult populations: Research implications (Part II). *Focus Excep. Children* **15(1),** 1–16.

Anderson, C. A., and Jennings, D. L. (1980). When experiences of failure promote expectations of success: The impact of attributing failure to ineffective strategies. *J. Person.* **48,** 393–407.

Anderson, T. H., and Armbruster, B. B. (1984). Studying. *In* "Handbook of Reading Research" pp. 657–744 (P. D. Pearson, ed.). Longman, New York.

Armbruster, B. B., and Anderson, T. H. (1988). On selecting "considerate" content area textbooks. *Remed. Special Educ.* **9,** 4–52.

Bandura, A., and Schunk, D. M. (1981). Cultivating competence, self-efficacy, and intrinsic interest through proximal self-motivation. *J. Person./Social Psychol.* **41**, 456–498.

Bergerud, D., Lovitt, T., and Horton, S. (1987). The effectiveness of textbook adaptations in life science for high school students with learning disabilities. University of Washington, Seattle.

Bulgren, J. A., Schumaker, J. B., and Deshler, D. D. (1988). Effectiveness of a concept teaching routine in enhancing the performance of LD students in secondary level mainstream classes. *Learn. Disabil. Q.* **11**, 3–17.

Chi, M. T. H. (1981). Interactive roles of knowledge and strategies in development. *In* "Thinking and Learning Skills: Current Research and Open Questions," Vol. 2 (S. Chipman, J. Segal, and R. Glaser, eds.), Lawrence Erlbaum, Hillsdale, New Jersey.

Crain, R. L. (1984). "The Quality of American High School Graduates: What Personnel Officers Say and Do about It," Rep. #354. Center for Social Organization of Schools, The Johns Hopkins University, Baltimore, Maryland.

Dansereau, D. F., and Holley, C. D. (1982). Development and evaluation of a text mapping strategy. *In* "Discourse Processing" (A. Flammer and W. Kintsch, eds.), 536–554. New York: Elsevier.

Deshler, D. D., Alley, G. R., Warner, M. M., and Schumaker, J. B. (1981a). Instructional practices for promoting skill acquisition and generalization in severely learning disabled adolescents. *Learn. Disabil. Q.* **4**, 415–421.

Deshler, D. D., Schumaker, J. B., Alley, G. R., Warner, M. M., and Clark, F. (1981b). Social interaction deficits in learning disabled adolescents—Another myth? *In* "Bridges to Tomorrow," Vol. 2. "The Best of ACLD" (M. C. Cruickshank and A. A. Silver, eds.), pp. 57–65. Syracuse University Press, Syracuse, New York.

Deshler, D. D., Schumaker, J. B., Alley, G. R., Warner, M. M., and Clark, F. L. (1982). Learning disabilities in adolescent and young adult populations: Research implications (Part I). *Focus Excep. Children* **15(1)**, 1–12.

Deshler, D. D., Schumaker, J. B., and Lenz, B. K. (1984). Academic and cognitive interventions for LD adolescents: Part I. *J. Learn. Disabil.* **17(2)**, 108–117.

Dupuis, N. M., and Askov, E. N. (1982). "Content Area Reading." Prentice-Hall, Englewood Cliffs, New Jersey.

Ellis, E. S. (1986). The role of motivation and pedagogy on the generalization of cognitive strategy training. *J. Learn. Disabil.* **19(2)**, 66–70.

Ellis, E. S. (1989). A metacognitive intervention for increasing class participation. *Learn. Disabil. Focus* **5(1)**, 36–46.

Ellis, E. S. (1990). What's so strategic about teaching teachers to teach strategies? *Teacher Educ. Special Educ.* **13(2)**, 1–5.

Ellis, E. S. (1991a). *Integrative Strategy Instruction in Content-Areas.* Cambridge, MA: Brookline Brooks, Inc. (in press).

Ellis, E. S. (1991b). "Perspectives from Expert Strategy Teachers: What They Do to Motivate Students to Learn and Use Strategies." University of South Carolina, Columbia. Columbia.

Ellis, E. S., and Lenz, B. K. (1987). An analysis of the critical features of effective learning strategies. *Focus Learn. Disabil.* **2(2)**, 94–107.

Ellis, E. S., and Lenz, B. K. (1990). Techniques for mediating content-area learning: Issues and research. *Focus Excep. Children.* **22(9)**, 1–16.

Ellis, E. S., and Lenz, B. K., (1991). The Development of Learning Strategy Interventions. Edge Enterprises, Lawrence, Kansas. (in press).

Ellis, E. S., and Sabornie, E. J. (1990). Strategy based adaptive instruction in content area classes: Social validity of six options and implications for designing instructional materials. *Teacher Educ. Special Educ.* **13(2),** 9–15.

Ellis, E. S., Lenz, B. K., and Sabornie, E. J. (1987). Generalization and adaptation of learning strategies to natural environments—Part 2: Research into practice. *Remed. Special Educ.* **8(2),** 6–23.

Ellis, E. S., Deshler, D. D., and Schumaker, J. B. (1989). Teaching learning disabled adolescents and executive strategy for generating task-specific strategies. *J. Learn. Disabil.* **22(2),** 108–119.

Ellis, E. S., Courtney, J., and Church, A. (1991a). A learning strategy for meeting the writing demands of secondary mainstream classrooms. *Teach. Excep. Children.* (in press).

Ellis, E. S., Deshler, D. D., Schumaker, J. B., Lenz, B. K., and Clark, F. L. (1991 b). An instructional model for teaching learning strategies. *Focus Excep. Children.* **23(1),** 1–22.

Hazel, J. S., Schumaker, J. B., Sherman, J. A., and Sheldon-Wildgen, J. (1981). "ASSET: A Social Skills Program Adolescents." Research Press, Champaign, Illinois.

Horton, S. V., and Lovitt, T. (1987). Information organization for secondary students: Study guides. University of Washington, Seattle.

Howell, S. B. (1986). A study of the effectiveness of TOWER: The theme writing strategy. Master's thesis, University of Kansas, Lawrence.

Hughes, C., Schumaker, J. B., Deshler, D. D., and Mercer, C. (1988). "The Test-Taking Strategy Instructor's Manual." Edge Enterprises, Lawrence, Kansas.

Johnson, D. D., and Pearson, P. D. (1978). "Teaching Reading Vocabulary." Holt & Co., New York.

Kea, C. D. (1987). "An Analysis of Critical Teaching Behaviors Employed by Teachers of Students with Learning Disabilities. Doctoral dissertation, University of Kansas, Lawrence.

Kerr, M. M., and Nelson, C. M. (1989). "Strategies for Managing Behavior Problems in the Classroom." Merrill, Columbus, Ohio.

Kline, F. M. (1989). "The Development and Validation of Feedback Routines for Use in Special Education Settings. Doctoral dissertation, University of Kansas, Lawrence.

Koran, M. L., and Koran, J. (1980). Interaction of learner characteristics with pictorial adjuncts in learning from science text. *J. Res. Sci. Teach.* **1,** 44–83.

Lenz, B. K. (1984). "The Effect of Advance Organizers on the Learning and Retention of Learning Disabled Adolescents within the Context of a Cooperative Planning Model." Final research report submitted to the U.S. Department of Education, Special Education Services. University of Kansas: Lawrence.

Lenz, B. K. (1991). In the spirit of strategies instruction: Cognitive and metacognitive aspects of the Strategies Intervention Model. *In* "Proceedings of the Second Annual Conference of the National Institute of Dyslexia" (S. Vogel, ed.). Longman, White Plains, New York. (in press).

Lenz, B. K., and Alley, G. R. (1983). "The Effects of Advance Organizers on the

Learning and Retention of Learning Disabled Adolescents within the Context of a Cooperative Planning Model." Final research report submitted to the U.S. Department of Education, Office of Special Education. University of Kansas: Lawrence.

Lenz, B. K., and Ellis, E. S. (in press). Effective Instruction for Learning Disabled Adolescents." College Hill Press, Boston.

Lenz, B. K., Alley, G. R., Beals, V. C., Schumaker, J. B., and Deshler, D. D. (1981). "Teaching LD Adolescents a Strategy for Interpreting Visual Aids." University of Kansas, Lawrence.

Lenz, B. K., Alley, G. R., and Schumaker, G. R. (1987). Activating the inactive learner: Advance organizers in the secondary content classroom. *Learn. Disabil. Q.* **10(1),** 53–67.

Lenz, B. K., Clark, F. L., Deshler, D. D., and Schumaker, J. B. (1989). "The Strategies Instructional Approach: A Training Package." University of Kansas Institute for Research in Learning Disabilities, Lawrence.

Levin, E., Zigmond, N., and Birch, J. (1985). A follow-up study of 52 learning disabled students. *J. Learn. Disabil.* **18,** 2–7.

Licht, B. C., and Kistner, J. A. (1986). Motivational problems of learning disabled children: Individual differences and their implications for treatment. *In* ((Psychological and Educational Perspectives on Learning Disabilities" (J. K. Torgesen and B. Y. K. Wong, eds.) pp. 225–255. Academic Press, New York.

Lovitt, T. C., Horton, S. V., and Bergerud, D. (1987). Matching students with textbooks: An alternative to readability formulas and standardized tests. *B. C. J. Special Educ.* **11(1),** 49–55.

Mathews, R. M., Whang, P., and Fawcett, S. B. (1980). "Behavioral-Assessment of Job Related Skills: Implications for Learning Disabled Young Adults," Research Report No. 6. University of Kansas Institute for Research in Learning Disabilities, Lawrence.

McCombs, B. L. (1984). Processes and skills underlying continuing intrinsic motivation to learn: Toward a definition of motivational skills training interventions. *Educ. Psycholog.* **19(4),** 199–218.

McNabb, T. (1984). A comparison of the affective consequences of ability, effort, and strategy attributions for academic failure. Paper presented at the Annual Convention of the American Psychological Association, Toronto, Canada.

Meyer, B. J. F. (1981). Basic research on prose comprehension: A critical review. *In* "Comprehension and the Competent Reader: Interspeciality Perspective." (D. F. Fisher and C. W. Peters, eds.). pp. 8–35. Praeger, New York.

Moyer, J. C., Sowder, L., Threadgill-Sowder, J., and Moyer, M. B. (1984). Story problem formats: Drawn versus telegraphic. *J. Res. Math. Educ.* **15,** 342–351.

Osman, B. B. (1979). "Learning Disabilities: A Family Affair." Random House, New York.

Pressley, M., Goodchild, F., Fleet, J., Zajchowski, R., and Evans, E. D. (1987a). "What Is Good Strategy Use and Why Is It Hard to Teach? An Optimistic Appraisal of the Challenges Associated with Strategy Instruction." Department of Psychology, University of Western Ontario, London, Ontario.

Pressley, M., Johnson, C. J., and Symons, S. (1987b). Elaborating to learn and learning to elaborate. *J. Learn. Disabil.* **20,** 76–91.

Pressley, M., Snyder, B. L., and Cariglia-Bull, T. (1987). How can good strategy use be taught to children?: Evaluation of six alternative approaches. *In* "Transfer of Learning: Contemporary Research and Applications" (S. Cormier and J. Hagman, eds.). pp. 81–120. Orlando, Fla.: Academic Press.

Robinson, S., Braxdale, C. T., and Colson, S. E. (1985). Preparing dysfunctional learners to enter high school: A transitional curriculum. *Focus Excep. Children.* **18(4),** 1–12.

Roehler, L. R., and Duffy, G. G. (1984). Direct explanation of comprehension processes. *In* "Comprehension Instruction: Perspectives and Suggestions" (G. G. Duffy, L. R. Roehler, and J. Mason, eds.), pp. 265–280. Longman, New York.

Rowe, M. B. (1976). The pausing principle: Two invitations to inquiry. *Res. Coll. Sci. Teach.* **5,** 258–259.

Rowe, M. B. (1980). Pausing principles and their effects on reasoning in science. *New Direc. Commun. Coll.* **31,** 27–34.

Rowe, M. B. (1983). Getting chemistry off the killer-course list. *J. Chem. Educ.* **60,** 954–956.

Schallert, D.L. (1980). The role of illustrations in reading comprehension. *In* "Theoretical Issues in Reading Comprehension: Perspectives from Cognitive Psychology, Linguistics, Artificial Intelligence, and Education" (R. J. Spiro, B. C. Bruce, and W. F. Brewer, eds.), pp. 503–524. Lawrence Erlbaum, Hillsdale, New Jersey.

Schmidt, J. L., Deshler, D. D., Schumaker, J. B., and Alley, G. R. (1989). Effects of generalization instruction on the written language performance of adolescents with learning disabilities in the mainstream classroom. *J. Read. Writ. Learn. Disabil.* **4(4),** 291–311.

Schumaker, J. B. (1989). The heart of strategies instruction: Effective modeling. *Strategram* **1(4),** 1–5.

Schumaker, J. B., and Deshler, D. D. (1984). Setting demand variables: A major factor in program planning for LD adolescents. *Top. Lang. Disorders* **4(2),** 22–40.

Schumaker, J. B., and Deshler, D. D. (1988). Implementing the Regular Education Initiative in secondary schools: A different ball game. *J. Learn. Disabil.* **21(1),** 36–41.

Schumaker, J. B., Warner, M. M., Deshler, D. D., and Alley, G. R. (1980). "An Epidemiological Study of Learning Disabled Adolescents in Secondary Schools: Details of the Methodoology," Research Report No. 12 University of Kansas Institute for Research in Learning Disabilities, Lawrence.

Schumaker, J. B., Deshler, D. D., Alley, G. R., Warner, M. M., Clark, F., and Nolan, S. (1982a). Error monitoring: A learning strategy for improving adolescent performance. *In* "Best of ACLD," Vol. 3 (W. M. Cruickshank and J. W. Lerner, eds.). pp. 170–183. Syracuse University Press, Syracuse, New York.

Schumaker, J. B., Hazel, S., Sherman, J. A., and Sheldon, J. (1982b). *Social Skill Performances of Learning Disabled, Non-Learning Disabled, and Delinquent Adolescents,* Research Report No. 60. University of Kansas Institute for Research in Learning Disabilities, Lawrence.

Schumaker, J. B., Deshler, D. D., Alley, G. R., and Warner, M. M. (1983). Toward the development of an intervention model for learning disabled adolescents: The University of Kansas. *Excep. Educ. Q.* **4,** 45–74.

Schumaker, J. B., Deshler, D. D., and Denton, P. (1984). "The Paraphrasing Strategy." University of Kansas, Lawrence.

Schumaker, J. B., Deshler, D. D., and Ellis, E. S. (1986). Intervention issues related to the education of learning disabled adolescents. *In* "Psychological and Educational Perspectives on Learning Disabilities" (J. Torgesen and B. Wong, eds.), pp. 329–364. Academic Press, New York.

Schumaker, J. B., Deshler, D. D., and McKnight, P. (1989). "Teaching Routines to Enhance the Mainstream Performance of Adolescents with Learning Disabilities." Final report submitted to the U.S. Office of Education, Special Education Services. University of Kansas: Lawrence.

Schumaker, J. B., Deshler, D. D., and McKnight, P. C. (in press). "Teaching Routines for Content Areas at the Secondary Level." National Association for School Psychologist, Washington, D. C.

Scruggs, T. E., Mastropieri, M. A., Levin, J. R., McLoone, B., Gaffney, J. S., and Prater, M. A. (1985). Increasing content-area learning: A comparison of mnemonic and visual–spatial direct instruction. *Learn. Disabil. Res.* **1,** 18–31.

Seabaugh, G. O., and Schumaker, J. B. (1981). "The Effects of Self-Regulation Training on the Academic productivity of LD and non-LD Adolescents," Research Report No. 37. University of Kansas Institute for Research in Learning Disabilities, Lawrence.

Stone, C. A., and Wertsch, J. V. (1984). A social interactional analysis of learning diabilities remediation. *J. Learn. Disabil.* **17,** 194–199.

Torgeson, J., and Licht, B. (1983). The learning diabled child as an inactive learner: Retrospect and prospects. *In* "Topics in Learning Disabilities," Vol. 1 (J. D. McKinny and L. Feagans, eds.). pp. 3–31 Aspen Press, Rockville, Maryland.

Van Reusen, A. K., Bos, C., Schumaker, J. B., and Deshler, D. D. (1987). "Motivation Strategies Curriculum: The Education Planning Strategy." Edge Enterprises, Lawrence, Kansas.

Van Reusen, A. K., Deshler, D. D., and Schumaker, J. B. (1989). Effects of a student participation strategy in facilitating the involvement of LD adolescents in the IEP process. *Learn. Disabil.* **1(2),** 23–34.

Vetter, A. A., Deshler, D. D., Alley, G. R., Schumaker, J. B., Warner, M. M., and Alley, G. R. (1983). "Post-Secondary Follow-Up Study of a Group of Learning Disabled and Low Achieving Young Adults," Research Report. University of Kansas Institute for Research in Learning Disabilities, Lawrence.

Voss, J. F. (1982). "Knowledge and Social Science Problem Solving." Paper presented at American Education Research Association meeting (March 1982), New York.

Vygotsky, L. S. (1978). "Mind in Society: The Development of Higher Psychological Processes." Harvard University Press, Cambridge.

Warner, M. M., Alley, G. R., Deshler, D. D., and Schumaker, J. B. (1980a). "An Epidemiological Study of Learning Disabled Adolescents in Secondary Schools: Classification and Discrimination of Learning Disabled and Low Achieving

Adolescents," Research Report No. 20. University of Kansas Institute for Research in Learning Disabilities, Lawrence.

Warner, M. M., Schumaker, J. B., Alley, G. R., and Deshler, D. D. (1980b). "An Epidemiological Study of Learning Disabled Adolescents in Secondary Schools: Performance on a Serial Recall Task and the Role of Executive Function," Research Report No. 55. University of Kansas Institute for Research in Learning Disabilities, Lawrenece.

Weiderholt, J. L., and McEntire, B. (1980). Educational options for handicapped adolescents. *Excep. Educ. Q.* **1(2)**, 1–11.

White, W. J., Schumaker, J. B., Warner, M. M., Alley, G. R., and Deshler, D. D. (1980). "The Current Status of Young Adults Identified as Learning Disabled during their School Career," Research Report No. 21. University of Kansas Institute for Research in Learning Disabilities, Lawrence.

Wong, B. Y. L. (1985a). Issues in cognitive-behavior interventions in academic skill areas. *J. Abnorm. Child Psychol.* **2,** 123–131.

Wong, B. Y. L. (1985b). Potential means of enhancing content skills acquisition in learning disabled adolescents. *Focus Excep. Children* **17,** 1–8.

Zigmond, N., and Thornton, H. (1985). Follow-up of postsecondary age learning disabled graduates and drop-outs. *Learn. Disabil. Res.* **1(1),** 50–55.

Zigmond, N., Levin, E., and Laurie, T. (1985). Managing the mainstream: An analysis of teacher attitudes and student performance in mainstream high school programs. *J. Learn. Disabil.* **18,** 535–541.

CHAPTER 19

The Learning-Disabled Adult

Pamela B. Adelman and Susan A. Vogel

Editor's Notes

Concluding the theme of the importance of a life-span approach to understanding learning disabilities, this chapter by Adelman and Vogel focuses on the adult with learning disabilities. It contains three themes. The first is research on the characteristics of the learning-disabled adult. Here the authors provide a most comprehensive report on extant research on the topic. They have covered eight areas: (1) academic achievement, (2) cognitive abilities, (3) personality and behavior traits, (4) psychological–emotional adjustment, (5) social–interpersonal abilities, (6) independent living skills, (7) educational achievement, and (8) employment attainment.

The second theme is a thorough critique of the research on characteristics of the learning-disabled adult. The authors identified and analyzed succinctly methodological problems in the research.

The third theme concerns very useful future research recommendations. The authors conclude their informative and instructive chapter by summarizing emergent themes and trends from the research findings and by considering the implications for education, psycho-social and employment needs for the learning-disabled adult.

I. INTRODUCTION

Currently, attention is directed to adults with learning disabilities (LDs), their characteristics and needs. Studies on adults have produced conflicting results. Whereas some studies report positive outcomes with respect to educational and occupational attainments, and emotional and social–interpersonal adjustment, other studies describe individuals who dropped out of high school, are unemployed or underemployed, and have significant social and emotional problems. This chapter focuses on the characteristics of learning-disabled (LD) adults in the following eight areas: (1) academic achievement, (2) cognitive abilities, (3) personality and behavior traits, (4) psychological–emotional adjustment, (5) social–interpersonal abilities, (6) independent living skills, (7) educational achievement, and (8) employment attainments.

II. ACADEMIC ACHIEVEMENT

The most consistent finding in the research literature concerning academic achievement of LD adults is continued difficulty in reading performance (Adelman and Vogel, 1990; Balow and Blomquist, 1965; Blalock, 1982; Frauenheim, 1978; Johnson 1987b; Rogan and Hartman, 1990). Johnson (1987b) reported on the varied reading problems of a group of 83 adults evaluated at the Learning Disabilities Center of Northwestern University who were classified as poor readers. Poor decoding and oral reading were noted including problems with phoneme segmentation and structural analysis, retrieval, and pronunciation. Johnson attributed these problems to difficulties with auditory analysis, linguistic awareness, and decoding.

With respect to reading comprehension abilities, Johnson (1987b) identified three patterns: (1) approximately one-half of the deficient readers' scores were at the same level on vocabulary and passage comprehension tests, indicating problems with decoding and word meanings; (2) approximately one-fourth scored higher on passage comprehension than on vocabulary, indicating good use of background information and context to aid comprehension, but also indicating inadequate and vague understanding of word meanings; and (3) the remaining one-fourth performed better on vocabulary than passage comprehension, indicating significant problems with comprehension, including the ability to read critically, reason, and infer information. A pervasive problem was reading rate, which affected all of the adults tested, and this problem was attributed to several reasons, including lack of automaticity, decoding problems, underlying language deficits, and anxiety.

There is also evidence of poor progress in mathematics, spelling, and written composition even among college students with LDs (Adelman and

Vogel, 1990; Blalock, 1982, 1987c; Bruck, 1985; Cordoni, 1979; Cowen, 1988; Dalke, 1988; Frauenheim, 1978; Hoffman *et al.*, 1987; Rogan and Hartman, 1990; Vogel and Moran, 1982; Vogel, 1985a; Vogel and Konrad, 1988). In several studies, math was the lowest or among the lowest scores in academic achievement (Adelman and Vogel, 1990; Bruck, 1985; Rogan and Hartman, 1990). Rogan and Hartman (1990) noted that individuals who were deficient in math avoided taking courses in math; this avoidance of the subject matter may explain the lower scores. Frauenheim (1978) tested 40 men who were diagnosed as dyslexic in childhood and found problems in remembering multiplication tables, understanding place value, and accurately recalling the procedures of basic operations. Mathematical problems affected daily living, which were evident from difficulties with checking change received, balancing checkbooks, and estimating or taking measurements (Blalock, 1987c; Bruck, 1985).

A major residual effect of having LDs, even for highly accomplished adults with LDs, is poor spelling. After reviewing 18 follow-up studies, Schonhaut and Satz (1983) concluded that even successful adults who were diagnosed as having a reading disability during childhood have life-long problems with using language, particularly evident from their difficulty with spelling. Underlying language deficits were often evident from analysis of spelling errors, which revealed problems with sound discrimination, memory, and understanding of linguistic patterns. Table 19.1 presents several studies that assessed reading, mathematics, and spelling achievement of LD adults. Included in the table are size of the sample, IQ, the time between initial evaluation and the age at follow-up (if applicable), the age at initial evaluation or at follow-up, the dependent measures, and a summary of the results.

There are other important aspects of written language in addition to spelling, and, although less easily quantified, these deficits are often significant. LDs may also affect development of basic writing skills, and these difficulties often persist even in LD students who enter postsecondary educational environments.

Vogel and Moran (1982) examined written-language abilities of LD college students. They compared writing samples of LD college students with those of their non-learning-disabled (NLD) peers. Their essays were compared on frequency, type, and accuracy of punctuation and capitalization marks, spelling accuracy, and usage. Not only did the LD writers use significantly fewer punctuation marks, but they used them only 69% correctly, while their NLD peers used them 85% correctly. In regard to spelling accuracy, the LD students made significantly more spelling errors than their NLD peers ($p < 0.008$). This difference occurred despite the fact that when writing essays, writers may avoid words that they do not know how to spell. Cordoni (1979) also reported that the lowest subtest score on the Peabody Individual

Table 19.1

Results of Studies Assessing Reading, Mathematics, and Spelling Achievement of LD Adults

Study	Sample Size	IQ $\bar{x}$ (SD)	Time between initial evaluation and follow-up	Age at initial evaluation or at follow-up	Dependent measures	Results (approximate grade equivalent (G.E.) percentile [or standard score (SS)])
Adelman and Vogel (1990)	36	WAIS Full Scale IQ 103.97 (9.81)	NA$_p$	$\bar{x} = 22$; 18–44 years	Reading comprehension:	
					SDRT	9.7
					PIAT	10.7
					W-J Passage Comprehension	11.0
					Spelling:	
					TOWL	8.4
					WRAT	8.3
					PIAT	10.4
					Math:	
					PIAT	9.6
					WRAT	6.9
					W-J	
					Quantitative concepts	10.0
					Calculation	9.0
					Applied problems	9.0
Bruck (1985)	101	WAIS Full Scale IQ 103 (11.22)	$\bar{x} = 13$ years	$\bar{x} = 21.1$ years	Reading comprehension:	
					SDRT	10.2
					Spelling:	
					WRAT	8.7
					Math:	
					WRAT	6.5
Blalock (1987c)	80	NA	NA$_p$		Math:	
					WRAT	6.68

Study	N	IQ	Age (identification)	Age (follow-up)	Measure	Result
Balow and Blomquist (1965)	32	WAIS FS IQ range 91–100; $\bar{x}$ = 100	10–15 years	20–26 years	Gates Reading Survey given to nine subjects:	
					Comprehension	10.2
					Vocabulary	10.9
					Speed	9.6
					Spelling	10.5
					PIAT:	
					Reading recognition	9.8
					Arithmetic	12.0
					WRAT	
					Reading	8.4
					Arithmetic	7.2
Cordoni (1979)	NA	NA	NA$_p$	NA		
Cordoni and Snyder (1981)	16	NA	NA$_p$	19 years, 4 mos.		
Cowen (1988)	25	W-J: Tests of cognitive ability 101.24	NA$_p$	NA	W-J Clusters:	
					Reading achievement	94.76
					Math	102.8
Dalke (1988)	36	W-J: Tests of cognitive ability 89.69	NA$_p$	NA	W-J Clusters:	
					Reading achievement	88.06
					Math	89.81
Frauenhein (1978)	40	WAIS Full Scale IQ range 80–112; $\bar{x}$ = 94	10–15 years	$\bar{x}$ = 21 years, 10 months; 18–31 years	Gate–McKillop Reading Diagnostic Test, oral reading; Gates Reading Test, vocabulary and comprehension Group Diagnostic Reading Aptitude and Achievement	$\bar{x}$ = 3.6 on oral reading, vocabulary, and comprehension; range 1.5–8.4
					Spelling	$\bar{x}$ = 2.9, range 1.3–6.6
					Math	$\bar{x}$ = 4.6, range 3.0–7.6

(continues)

567

Table 19.1 (*continued*)

Study	Sample Size	IQ x̄ (SD)	Time between initial evaluation and follow-up	Age at initial evaluation or at follow-up	Dependent measures	Results (approximate grade equivalent (G.E.) percentile [or standard score (SS)])
Rogan and Hartman (1990)	23	WAIS Full Scale IQ 113 (12)	20–30 years	30–40 years	WRAT:	
					Reading	12.3
					Spelling	10.3
					Math	9.6
					Nelson–Denny:	
					Vocabulary	14.4
					Comprehension	12.7
	28	98 (10)			WRAT:	
					Reading	10.9
					Spelling	8.6
					Math	5.6
					Nelson–Denny:	(n = 19)
					Vocabulary	13.0
					Comprehension	10.1
	17	79 (8)			WRAT:	
					Reading	7.2
					Spelling	5.5
					Math	4.3
					Monroe–Sherman paragraph comprehension	5.7

NA, not available. NA$_p$, not appropriate; SD, standard deviation.

Achievement Test (PIAT), (Dunn and Markwardt, 1970) for a group of LD college students was the spelling subtest (see Table 19.1).

Correct usage, another aspect of basic writing skills, was also found to discriminate between students with and without LDs (Vogel and Konrad, 1988). Characteristic usage and sentence construction errors in LD college students included sentence fragments, run-on sentences or comma splice errors, lack of subject–predicate agreement, and inappropriate coordination and/or subordination (Vogel and Konrad, 1988).

Dalke (1988) also studied written-language abilities in LD college students. She compared the performance of college freshmen with and without LDs on the Woodcock–Johnson Psycho-Educational Battery (W-J) (Woodcock and Johnson, 1977). Although significant differences existed between the two groups on all of the cognitive and achievement tests, the lowest mean standard score for the LD group was on the Written Language cluster, a measure of basic writing skills.

Research findings also suggest that written expression of LD students is poorer than that of their peers even in the college-able LD students. When Vogel and Moran (1982) compared holistically scored essays written in the compare–contrast mode of 226 NLD college students with those of LD college students, they found the LD writers' essays were significantly poorer on overall quality. When the essays were scored analytically on organization, development, style, and mechanics, Vogel and Moran found that LD writers' essays were most discrepant from their NLD peers on development of ideas and writing style.

Writing style is especially significant in mature writers and refers to variety, complexity, and accuracy of sentence structure. On visual examination, Vogel and Moran (1982) found that approximately 50% of the sentences written by LD students were simple sentence patterns, as compared with only 34% of the sentences written by their NLD peers. For each of the complex sentence types, the frequency counts were higher for the NLD writers. They concluded that LD students have less variety and complexity in sentence construction. This finding was confirmed and extended in another study by Vogel (1985a), which demonstrated that LD college students used fewer syntactically complex structures than NLD writers, as indicated by the number of subordinate clauses and main clause word length.

Given the considerable underachievement among LD college students, it is not surprising that these deficits exist in secondary school. Wagner and Shaver (1989) found that achievement in secondary school varies widely. Their research project, the National Longitudinal Transition Study (NLTS), identified a nationally representative sample of more than 8,000 youth between the ages of 13 and 23 years who were in special education during the 1985–1986 school year. In their study, Wagner and Shaver assessed academic achievement by looking at failing grades, promotion, and performance on competency tests. Of the 812 LD students in the sample, who were in specific grade levels or who were in ungraded programs but received a grade for at least one class in which they were enrolled, 34.8% received a failing grade in one or more courses in their most recent year in secondary school. These data were based on information taken from the students' records and/or from parents' reports. Wagner and Shaver (1989) also measured successful completion of the school year and whether or not the subjects were promoted to the next grade level by examining the most recent year posted on school records. For this measure of performance, students in twelfth grade and students who were in ungraded programs were not included. From a sample of 503 LD students, they found that 76.9% were promoted.

Meeting minimum competency requirements was the third measure of achievement assessed in the NLTS. With respect to performance on competency tests, 25% of 314 respondents who were in schools that required competency tests were exempted from taking the tests. Of those who were required to take the tests, 47.9% passed all of the tests, 31.7% passed some of the tests, and 23.6% did not pass any of the tests.

III. COGNITIVE ABILITIES

Several research studies attempted to determine characteristic cognitive abilities and profiles of adults with LDs by administration of the Wechsler Adult Intelligence Scale—Revised (WAIS-R) (Adelman and Vogel, 1990; Blalock, 1987b; Buchanan and Wolf, 1986; Cordoni et al., 1981; Salvia et al., 1988; Vogel, 1986). For example, Adelman and Vogel (1990) reported the cognitive abilities of 36 LD college graduates and found that the mean Verbal, Performance, and Full Scale IQs were average and quite even ($\bar{x}$ = approximately 103), with Similarities and Comprehension the two highest mean scaled scores (11.23 and 12.45, respectively) and the ACID (arithmetic, coding, information, digit span) subtests the four lowest. The pattern of grouped subtests according to the Bannatyne categories was similar to other samples of LD and NLD college students in the average IQ range, with Verbal Conceptualization the highest or next to highest and ACID the next to lowest (Cordoni et al., 1981; Vogel, 1986).

After reviewing several studies that assessed intellectual functioning by administering the Wechsler scales and the revised versions (WISC, WISC-R, WAIS, WAIS-R), Salvia et al. (1988: 633) concluded that "like children with learning disabilities, adults with learning disabilities may show VIQ-PIQ differences, considerable scatter on subtests, Bannatyne's hierarchy of category scores, and lower performance on the ACID cluster." Although no characteristic cognitive profile (i.e., VIQ-PIQ discrepancy) that can be used to diagnose LDs has emerged from these studies, significant variability in the subtest scores has been a pervasive finding (Blalock, 1987b; Buchanan and Wolf, 1986; Salvia et al., 1988; Vogel, 1986). Salvia et al. (1988) individually tested 74 LD and 74 NLD college students. Results of the WAIS-R indicated that no one profile characterized the LD sample, but the LD students had more variable profiles than the NLD students as measured by the range of WAIS-R verbal subtests, performance subtests, or on all subtests.

Further evidence of the range of cognitive abilities among LD adults was noted by Cowen (1988) and Stone (1987). Cowen (1988) administered the W-J to 25 college students previously identified as LD. She found that 22 of the 25 students had one of three profiles associated with LDs: six subjects had low verbal ability and high reasoning ability, five subjects had high verbal ability and low reasoning ability, and 11 subjects had high verbal ability and reasoning and low perceptual speed and memory. Stone (1987) also found considerable variability on a problem-solving strategy that assessed the ability for abstract reasoning.

Although considerable evidence indicates that Verbal – Peformance IQ discrepancy should not be used for diagnosing LD adults, this information has significance in understanding the manifestations of LDs and in planning remedial and support services (Vogel, 1986). Whereas nonverbal deficits have a significant impact upon social maturity and independence and may require extensive psychotherapy (Blalock, 1981, 1982; Johnson, 1987a; Vogel, 1986), verbal deficits are an indication of underlying problems in oral language (Blalock, 1981, 1982, 1987a; Vogel, 1986) and may require long-term support to improve basic skills.

Blalock (1987a) reported on the evaluation of 93 adults who were diagnosed as having LDs at the Learning Disabilities Center of Northwestern University. Seventy-eight percent were diagnosed as having some orallanguage, auditory processing, or metalinguistic problems. Deficits in all areas of language processing were noted, including problems with auditory perception, comprehension, and memory.

Johnson (1987a) reported that 18 of the 93 adults evaluated at the Learning Disabilities Center of Northwestern University had primary nonverbal disorders that significantly affected their daily functioning. Minor repairs and tasks requiring visual-motor skills such as changing license plates were extremely difficult. In addition to problems with visual-motor integration, these subjects also had significant deficits in visual analysis and synthesis. Blalock (1981, 1982) reported the effects of nonverbal LDs on interpersonal relationships. Problems with social perception prevented individuals from accurately assessing situations, facial expressions, or body language.

IV. PERSONALITY AND BEHAVIOR TRAITS

Little research exists on the personality and behavior traits of adults with LDs. Schonhaut and Satz (1983) concluded that the association between early learning problems and later antisocial behavior and emotional problems was unclear, and they noted the need for research to explore conduct disorders and emotional adjustment. Horn *et al.* (1983) identified self-concept as a neglected variable in determining adult outcomes. They suggested that gaining a better understanding of the importance of this variable may explain why some individuals are successful in employment, even though their basic skills are low, and why others, who have good educational and vocational attainment, have poor emotional and behavioral adjustments.

Buchanan and Wolf (1986) analyzed the personal and educational histories of 33 LD adults. In their study, subjects were asked to check behavioral characteristics that they perceived as strengths and those perceived as problem areas. The most common problems identified were shyness, self-consciousness, insecurity, passivity, and withdrawal.

Evidence of personal and emotional problems was also found by Hoffman *et al.* (1987), who conducted a needs assessment of 381 LD persons eligible for vocational rehabilitation by surveying the LD adults, providers of services to LD persons, and advocates for LD persons. All three groups identified impulsive social behavior as the major deficit. The findings from this study also point to personal problems ranging from frustration and low self-confidence to depression.

V. PSYCHOLOGICAL–EMOTIONAL PROBLEMS

Cohen (1985) compared 15 high school and college students with LDs ranging in age from 16 to 21 years with a similar group of 15 NLD students who were struggling with comparable types of issues related to work, school, and social activities. He concluded that the LD students were at risk for emotional problems even when they were diagnosed and received appropriate help.

Cohen identified a high propensity for distress and anxiety among the LD group, particularly in response to other people finding out about their weaknesses. They suffered from low levels of chronic depression, which was largely due to feeling "painfully damaged, inadequate, dumb, and vulnerable" (Cohen, 1985: 183).

From his evaluations, Cohen also suggested that LDs contribute to an individual's belief that frustration and failure are unpredictable and uncontrollable. He explains that "these repeated moments of frustration, failure, and helplessness seem to be accompanied by a painful lowering of self-esteem and negative self-representations. Gradually, these repeated moments (and the anxious anticipation of them) seem to result in trauma" (Cohen, 1985: 186).

The students seen by Cohen responded to their feelings of helplessness and inadequacy by developing compensatory strategies and rigid types of behaviors that often also had a negative psychological impact. For example, a student who compensated by working slowly on school work generalized this behavior to being "slow" in all areas of functioning. Cohen also found "that the adolescents' defensive and coping strategies were employed in a relatively rigid fashion" (Cohen, 1985: 190). Like the compensatory strategies, rigidity was also generalized and became part of the LD students' character. Cohen noted the negative impact that rigidity has on therapy; it is often a major obstacle to making therapeutic gains, because it undermines integration and educational and psychological development.

Cohen also found that the way others respond to LD individuals is extremely important in their psychological development. He found a strong relationship between feelings of how they think they are treated as adolescents and how they were treated as children.

Spekman *et al.* (1989) interviewed 50 young adults who had attended the Marianne Frostig Center of Educational Therapy for at least 1 academic year. After developing the criteria for identifying a subject as successful, former students were placed in either the successful or the unsuccessful group. Success was defined as achievement of certain accomplishments that are age-appropriate and socially acceptable, personal satisfaction with activities, accomplishments and relationships, and effective coping strategies. Major factors differentiating the successful and unsuccessful subjects were psychological and emotional traits, including self-awareness and acceptance of their LDs, the ability to plan and set realistic goals, participation in and enjoyment of social interactions, perseverance, and the ability to cope with stress and frustration.

VI. SOCIAL–INTERPERSONAL SKILLS

Several studies report problems with making and keeping friends (Blalock, 1981; Bruck, 1985; Fafard and Haubrich, 1981). In addition, the range of leisure activities in which some adults with LDs participate is limited, and many depend on family support for social activities (Blalock, 1981; Fafard and Haubrich, 1981; Haring *et al.*, 1990; Hoffman *et al.*, 1987). The ability of some LD adults to participate in specific social and recreational activities is affected by social perception problems, which manifest themselves in poor eye contact, saying the wrong thing, or interrupting behaviors. Some LD adults could not participate in activities such as word games, card games, or dances and sports because of problems with language and motor coordination (Blalock, 1981; Fafard and Haubrich, 1981).

The findings of Scuccimarra and Speece (1990) were more positive. Employment outcomes and social adjustment were examined in a study of 70 mildly handicapped students who participated in special education, 60 of whom were diagnosed as LD. Scuccimarra and Speece (1990) reported that the majority of participants were active and engaged in a variety of leisure activities with peers. However, they also found that a consistent number of respondents (24–29%) reported participating in only two or fewer activities, had no close friendships, and were generally dissatisfied with their social lives. The respondents who expressed the most satisfaction with their social lives were employed and active socially.

VII. EDUCATIONAL ATTAINMENTS

A. High School

The literature on educational attainment is inconsistent. Some studies found that there is a higher drop-out rate among LD youngsters (Levin *et al.*, 1985; Wagner, 1989a). From the results of the NLTS, Wagner (1989a) found that 61% of 533 LD students graduated, whereas the U.S. Department of Education "Wallchart" (U.S. Department of Education, 1987) estimates the graduation rate for the general student population to be 71%. Wagner (1989a) also reported the reasons most commonly cited by parents for youth dropping out of school: Students did not like school (30%) and/or they were not doing well in school (28%). However, other studies found more positive outcomes indicating that LD students graduated at the same rate as their NLD peers and also went on to postsecondary education (Bruck, 1985; Preston and Yarington, 1967). Studies that reported the same graduation rate for LD students pointed out that students often repeated grades and/or attended summer school to prevent grade repetition (Edgington, 1975; Preston and Yarington, 1967).

The most common reason cited for these inconsistent results is differences in socioeconomic status (SES) of the samples studied (Schonhaut and Satz, 1983; O'Connor and Spreen, 1988; Wagner, 1989a). O'Connor and Spreen (1988) found a significant correlation between the parents' SES, particularly the father's SES, and the educational achievement of the LD students. Wagner (1989b) also identified lower SES as a significant contributing factor to handicapped youths dropping out of school.

B. Postsecondary

A few studies reported on the percent of LD students who attended postsecondary institutions (Scuccimarra and Speece, 1990; Wagner and Shaver, 1989). Wagner and Shaver (1989) found that among a sample of 245 LD students, 10% attended vocational or trade schools, 7% attended 2-year colleges, and 1.8% attended 4-year colleges. They pointed out that these figures are significantly below the participation rate for NLD students in postsecondary education. Among the NLD students, 28% attended 4-year colleges and 28% attended 2-year colleges. For vocational or trade schools, the rate of participation (10%) was the same for LD and NLD students.

Considerable evidence indicates that some LD adults have attended and graduated from college, with some completing graduate degrees (Rawson, 1968; Rogan and Hartman, 1976; Silver and Hagin, 1985). Within the last 10 years, the number of LD students attending college has increased dramatically, attributable in large part to the passage of the Rehabilitation Act of 1973 and its implementing regulations (Mangrum and Strichart, 1988; Scheiber and Talpers, 1987). In view of how recently the number of LD students on college campuses has increased, little data, as yet, are available on graduation and attrition rate of LD students, not even at those colleges that provide support services specifically for students with LDs and that offer an environment of greater awareness and understanding of this handicap (Bursuck et al., 1989).

Bursuck et al. (1989) reported on the results of 197 surveys received from community colleges and 4-year colleges. Only 20 schools (10%) responded to the item asking for the number of students graduating or completing a course of study. Schools that responded reported a completion rate of approximately 30%, but whether this represents program completion or graduation rate is unclear Vogel and Adelman (1990) conducted an 8-year follow-up study on the 4-year degree completion and academic failure rate of 110 LD students. The LD students were compared with a random stratified sample of 153 peers attending the same college for at least one semester. They reported that the LD students graduated at the same rate and within the same time frame as their NLD peers. Moreover, their academic failure rate was no higher than that of the NLD students. Vogel and Adelman (1990) identified three factors that contributed to these positive outcomes: (1) the students with LDs self-referred at admissions; (2) they were screened for intellectual abilities, type and severity of LDs, and motivation and attitude toward the teaching–learning process; and (3) they requested and used comprehensive, highly coordinated support services and special academic advisors.

VIII. EMPLOYMENT ATTAINMENTS

A. Obtaining Employment

In a study by Fafard and Haubrich (1981), 21 young adults were interviewed regarding their adjustment as adults. With respect to obtaining employment, they found that these individuals were motivated to work but experienced considerable difficulty with finding employment. Subjects in the study conducted by Haring et al. (1990) reported that they were most successful finding employment when they had personal contacts.

B. Rate of Employment

There is evidence of considerable unemployment among LD individuals (Blalock, 1981, 1982; Haring et al., 1990; Scuccimarra and Speece, 1990); however, when compared with NLD individuals, some studies found that the unemployment rate is not significantly greater for LD individuals (Bruck, 1985; Preston and Yarington, 1967). Bruck (1985) found the unemployment rate for the LD students was the same as their NLD siblings in the control group. She reported that the LD individuals held a wide range of occupations and only a few were employed in unskilled jobs. Wagner and Shaver (1989) confirmed Bruck's findings and reported that the employment rate for the LD individuals 1 year after graduation was 58%, which approached the rate of 62% for NLD individuals.

Considerable evidence indicates that disabled women are unemployed at a significantly higher rate than disabled men (Buchanan and Wolf, 1986; Haring et al., 1990; Scuccimarra and Speece, 1990). In a study of 70 mildly handicapped students who participated in special education, 60 of whom were diagnosed as LD, Scuccimarra and Speece (1990) reported the unemployment rate for disabled women as 23.8% as compared with 6.8% for disabled men. Scuccimarra and Speece noted the importance of future research to determine the factors that contribute to the high rate of unemployment in women with LDs.

C. Underemployment

There is a common perception that many LD individuals are underemployed. Their specific deficit areas prevent them from obtaining certain jobs, accepting promotions, or succeeding when promoted (Blalock, 1981). As with the research on rate of employment, results of studies that have assessed unemployment are inconsistent. Whereas Scuccimarra and Speece (1990) found low levels of employment, with respondents in primarily unskilled and semiskilled positions such as clerical/sales and service positions, Bruck (1985) reported no underemployment. Respondents in her study held a wide range of occupations and only a few subjects were employed in unskilled jobs.

D. Job Success

Studies on LD adults' success in the work place have also produced conflicting results (Horn et al., 1983; O'Connor and Spreen, 1988). Whereas some studies on LD adults found significant problems with obtaining and maintaining jobs (Blalock, 1981, 1982; Hoffmann *et al.*, 1987), other studies reported successful employment of LD adults (Felton, 1986; Gerber, 1988; Preston and Yarington, 1967; Rawson, 1968; Silver and Hagin, 1985).

In recent research on LD adults who were not successfully employed, lack of self-understanding was cited as a pervasive characteristic (Blalock, 1981, 1982; Buchanan and Wolf, 1986; Hoffmann *et al.*, 1987). Although they knew they were having problems, these LD adults did not understand their specific deficits impacted on their difficulties. Consequently, they did not apply for jobs that capitalized upon their strengths, and they could not anticipate problems nor develop compensatory strategies when they were having trouble with meeting the demands of accurate and timely completion of their work responsibilities.

In contrast, the successful employment of LD individuals has been attributed to their choosing careers in their areas of strength. For example, those with strengths in the visual–perceptual and quantitative areas chose fields such as engineering, filmmaking, art history, medical illustration, accounting, and finance (Rogan and Hartman, 1976; Silver and Hagin, 1985). Those with reading disorders accepted jobs with relatively low dependence on reading, sometimes found in business, management, and administration (Felton, 1986). Silver and Hagin (1985) concluded that it is particularly important for LD individuals to receive career counseling and guidance during transition from school to employment and from one job to another to help them carefully select careers that will utilize strengths and de-emphasize weaknesses. Those individuals who failed to find the right match between career and personal strengths continued to experience frustration and disappointment.

Another factor in predicting success on the job relates to specific verbal strengths. In a recent study by Faas and D'Alonzo (1990), 86 LD adults, 18–59 years old, were evaluated clinically. They found that the comprehension cluster of the WAIS-R consisting of the Comprehension, Information, Vocabulary, and Similarities subtests was predictive of successful employment. Faas and D'Alonzo (1990) concluded that the verbal abilities of LD adults are very important as determinants of success in the work place.

E. Effect of LDs on Work

Little data exist on how specific LDs affect individuals on the job and how they compensate. Blalock (1981) described several ways LDs were manifested in the work place. For example, individuals with auditory processing deficits reported problems with telephone work and/or communicating in noisy environments. Some individuals turned in unfinished projects or forgot to complete tasks because of memory deficits and problems with organization.

Adelman and Vogel (1990) reported employment patterns for LD 4-year college graduates who participated in a highly coordinated, comprehensive support program for LD college students at a small, moderately selective, private college. Most graduates responded that their LDs do affect their work. Processing difficulties including their ability to retain information, the amount of time to complete work, and perception (particularly number and letter reversals) were the most common difficulties.

F. Compensatory Strategies

Even though the college graduates in the Adelman and Vogel (1990) study indicated that their LDs affected their work, an important finding was that the college graduates developed compensatory strategies. The most commonly used compensatory strategies included spending additional time to finish work, asking for additional help, and carefully monitoring work for errors. Adelman and Vogel suggest that these graduates' insight into how their LDs affected them on the job helped them to determine ways to compensate. This is consistent with the findings of other studies on LD adults who were successfully employed (Gerber, 1988; Rawson, 1968). For example, Rawson (1968) described a lawyer who compensated for his inability to remember large amounts of reading material by applying his analytical skills first to reason through a legal problem. As a result, his reading was more focused, and he could more effectively remember the information.

Although there is evidence of the creative ways LD adults have compensated for their LDs, Blalock (1981) pointed out that they devote a great deal of effort to hiding their LDs from employers and co-workers. For example, some describe taking reports home for spouses to write and calling upon friends for help with spelling.

G. Job Satisfaction

Very little data exist on job satisfaction of LD adults. Some of the individuals evaluated by Blalock (1982) considered their jobs temporary until they could improve their skills. Others were satisfied with their jobs but feared failure and were afraid to accept promotions. Schonhaut and Satz (1983), Scuccimarra and Speece (1990), and Rogan and Hartman (1990) reported high levels of job satisfaction. However, Schonhaut and Satz (1983) noted the need for further studies to assess occupational status.

H. Employer Perceptions

Some evidence indicates that employer awareness of LDs is increasing. For example, Blalock (1981) noted an increase in the number of referrals from the employers of individuals who were evaluated. Minskoff et al. (1987) surveyed 326 employers. Seventy-two percent of the employers responded that they would make special allowances for handicapped workers that they would not make for nonhandicapped workers. Special allowance identified included providing additional support and encouragement, providing extra time for training, providing more detailed directions, and helping handicapped workers find the right job. Employers reported that they would not reduce work demands or become involved in the worker's personal life. The pervasive attitude was one of support as long as the individual accomplished his or her responsibilities.

However, a discouraging finding of this study was that employers appeared to be more willing to make allowances for handicapped individuals in general than for LD workers in particular. Minskoff *et al.* (1987) suggested that employers may have a more positive attitude toward individuals with physical disabilities than cognitive disabilities, which may indicate a lack of understanding of LDs.

I. Effect of Educational – Vocational Training

Considerable evidence indicates that vocational training has been either ineffective or nonexistent for LD individuals (Fafard and Haubrich, 1981; Haring *et al.*, 1990; Hoffmann *et al.*, 1987; Scuccimarra and Speece, 1990). Haring *et al.* (1990) found that those who received training were less likely to be employed, and they suggested that this training "did not greatly enhance ... employability." After surveying service providers and LDs advocates, Hoffmann *et al.* (1987) found that most LD adults received little or no vocational or career training. In contrast, the results of Scuccimarra and Speece's (1990) study were more positive. Approximately an equal number of employed and unemployed respondents reported a high degree of satisfaction with their high school training. Scuccimarra and Speece also found a relationship between finding summer jobs in high school and obtaining employment after high school.

Geographic location appears to be a variable in whether or not dropping out of high school has an affect upon later employment. Whereas deBettencourt *et al.* (1989) found that in rural areas dropping out of school did not affect employment, Zigmond and Thornton (1989) reported that LD students who did not finish high school in urban areas experienced greater difficulty with finding employment than those who graduated.

IX. INDEPENDENT LIVING SKILLS

A consistent finding in the research literature is that most LD adults live with their parents (Fafard and Haubrich, 1981; Haring *et al.*, 1990; Menkes *et al.*, 1967; Scuccimarra and Speece, 1990; Spekman *et al.*, 1989; Wagner,

1989b). Scuccimarra and Speece (1990) surveyed students 2 years after graduating from high school and found that over 80% resided with their parents, which they attributed primarily to the cost of living independently. These findings were consistent with Wagner's (1989b) data in which only 22% of the LD youth lived independently 1–2 years after graduation and a study conducted by Haring et al. (1990), who found that wages earned were insufficient for self-support.

Scuccimarra and Speece (1990) concluded that given the low number of individuals who received additional training after high school, significant income increases that would enhance independence are unlikely unless opportunities exist for on-the-job training.

Although some LD individuals either did not apply or were not eligible for a driver's license and had orientation problems that inhibited their mobility (Blalock, 1981; Fafard and Haubrich, 1981), evidence also indicates that LD adults have no problems with accessing the communities in which they live (Haring et al., 1990). In a study by Haring et al. (1990), 64 students with LDs who had attended self-contained special education classes were sent questionnaires to assess vocational and community adjustment. Thirty-one percent did not have drivers' licenses, but they used city buses, asked friends or family to transport them, or rode their bicycles as their main methods of transportation.

X. CRITIQUE OF RESEARCH

As can be seen from the above review, the results of studies on LD adults have been inconsistent. Several reasons have been cited for these inconsistencies, including differences in intellectual ability and SES of the specific population sampled, the amount of family support, and the degree and quality of educational intervention (O'Connor and Spreen, 1988; Silver and Hagin, 1985). Considerable evidence regards the methodological factors that account for the conflicting results, including (1) choice of outcomes, (2) selection criteria, (3) severity of LDs, (4) sample size and subject attrition, (5) IQ level, (6) demographics, (7) educational opportunity and remediation–intervention, (8) comparison groups, and (9) instrumentation (Herjanic and Penick, 1972; Horn et al., 1983; O'Connor and Spreen, 1988; Schonhaut and Satz, 1983).

A. Choice of Outcomes

After reviewing 24 follow-up studies of persons with LDs, Horn et al. (1983) identified the choice of outcome measures as the most important methodological consideration in designing follow-up studies. They found that the dependent variables selected will generally determine the overall prognosis. When educational and vocational outcomes are the dependent variables, the outcomes are usually favorable. However, measurement of basic skills generally yields poor prognosis for LD adults.

The number of dependent variables in a study also has a significant effect on the outcomes. In past research studies, areas of investigation were mainly limited to academic and occupational achievement; therefore, little is know about adjustment in social and emotional domains (Herjanic and Penick, 1972; Horn *et al.*, 1983; Schonhaut and Satz, 1983). Herjanic and Penick (1972: 407) pointed out that "studies have generally ignored other kinds of intervening situational events, behavioral and personality characteristics, or personal experiences which could possibly augment or mitigate the effect of a childhood reading disorder upon adult functioning." Thus, both the type and number of outcome measures may determine not only the favorable or unfavorable prognosis but also the scope of the study.

Regardless of the choice of outcomes and prognosis, quantitative data analysis from grouped data should not be the only method for measuring outcomes (Horn *et al.*, 1983). Because significant differences often exist between subjects, Horn *et al.* (1983) suggested assessing individual achievements that may yield valuable information on the educational intervention or compensatory strategies that contributed to the success of some of the individuals.

B. Selection Criteria

Studies often do not clearly describe the criteria used in selecting LD subjects (Horn *et al.*, 1983). Some studies give criteria, but considerable variation among them precludes comparing results across studies. For example, in their review of follow-up studies, Horn *et al.* (1983) found that some studies define LDs as a discrepancy between reading level and grade placement or between reading level and chronological age, and they do not indicate whether or not a discrepancy exists between reading level and IQ. Furthermore, they also noted the importance of describing whether the LD sample was clinically referred or school-referred, because clinically referred subjects are more likely to have more severe LDs and confounding behavioral problems. Certainly, inconsistent results can be due to differences in diagnostic and sample selection criteria.

C. Severity of LDs

The severity of LDs is not always addressed in designing studies, and, yet, a commonly held perception is that the more severe the learning disability, the greater the possibility of a poor prognosis with respect to educational and employment attainments (Bruck, 1985; Herjanic and Penick, 1972; Horn *et al.*, 1983). Silver and Hagin (1985), for example, identified a subgroup of children whose performance on neurological exams indicated structural defects of the central nervous system. Silver and Hagin (1985) noted the importance of identifying this subgroup, which they termed "organic," because educational outcomes were less favorable and indicated the persistent effect of neuropsychological problems of adults.

Bruck (1985) believes her sample is well defined, because she only examined children with primary LDs and included in her sample students whose disabilities ranged in severity. Bruck suggested that her results are better able to be generalized to other samples because of the variability of the LDs sample examined.

D. Sample Size and Subject Attrition

A consistent problem cited in the critiques of studies on LD adults is inadequate sample size (Bruck, 1985; Haring *et al.*, 1990; Herjanic and Penick, 1972). For example, samples cited in Table 19.1 range from 9 to 101 subjects.

Subject attrition is another critical methodological variable. If attrition alters the sample size, the characteristics and the outcome results may also be altered. The outcome results are specific to the follow-up sample and not to the original LD sample (Haring *et al.*, 1990; Horn *et al.*, 1983). Not only is it often questionable as to whether or not the sample in the follow-up study is not representative, but the reduced sample itself may also bias the results. It is important to determine why individuals did not participate and whether or not their reasons for not participating will bias the outcomes. Whereas the omission of subjects who cannot be located may have neither a positive nor negative impact on the results, the lack of participation of reluctant subjects may decrease the number of negative outcomes and, therefore, bias the results.

E. IQ Level

Intelligence, like severity of the learning disability, is a very important variable in research studies of adults with LDs. A reasonable expectation is that the higher the IQ, the better the prognosis. Rawson's (1968) study on the educational and occupational achievement of 20 dyslexic men is often cited as an example of a study with extremely favorable outcomes. The mean childhood IQ of this sample was 130.

The effect of IQ upon outcomes is particularly evident from a follow-up study reported by Rogan and Hartman (1990). They presented data on 68 young adults who attended a private school. The sample of 68 participants was divided into three subgroups: college graduates, high school graduates, and students who were placed in self-contained special education classes. The mean Full Scale IQ scores differed significantly: college graduates, $\bar{x} = 113$; high school graduates, $\bar{x} = 98$; and those in self-contained special education classrooms, $\bar{x} = 79$.

Although participants in all groups continued to experience residual academic deficiencies, levels of academic achievement were also significantly disparate. However, Rogan and Hartman (1990) concluded that overall outcomes for most of the college and high school graduates and for several in the self-contained special education classrooms were favorable, which indicates that although intelligence is a significant factor, several other variables contribute to outcomes for LD adults. These variables include effective intervention during elementary and middle school years, appropriate course support in mainstreamed classes, supportive parents, counseling and therapy when necessary, and the absence of severe emotional and neurological problems.

F. Demographics

The demographic variables of the LD sample can also affect outcomes. These demographic factors include SES, age of onset, gender, and regional differences.

1. SES

Several reviews of follow-up studies emphasize the significance of SES of the LD sample (Horn et al., 1983; O'Connor and Spreen, 1988; Schonhaut and Satz, 1983; Silver and Hagin, 1985). After reviewing 18 follow-up studies, Schonhaut and Satz (1983) concluded that SES is a powerful variable that is related to the probability of developing learning problems and to academic prognosis. The SES of the dyslexic men in Rawson's (1968) study is also cited as a major reason for their excellent educational and occupational attainment (Herjanic and Penick, 1972; Schonhaut and Satz, 1983).

2. Age

Another demographic variable that affects outcomes is age (Horn et al., 1983). Age of diagnosis may be an indication of severity of the learning disability (Horn et al., 1983; Schonhaut and Satz, 1983). Because school districts do not typically screen for LDs, but rely on teacher referrals, it is reasonable to expect youngsters with more severe LDs to be identified earlier.

Because age of identification is often an indication of severity, it is also an indication of a poorer prognosis for educational and occupational attainments. However, Schonhaut and Satz (1983) also noted that SES can "attenuate this prediction." Youngsters from higher socioeconomic backgrounds often benefit from considerable family support and appropriate early identification and educational intervention. In addition, parental and teacher understanding is better, because these students are not perceived as stupid, lazy, and/ or emotionally disturbed. This information suggests the importance of describing age of onset, SES, and educational and family background.

Age at follow-up is also important, particularly because LD adults may continue to improve in academic achievements skills after completion of formal education as a result of greater motivation and access to remediation. Outcomes regarding the level of basic skills attainment are generally less favorable than occupational attainment in follow-up studies, which may be due to the subject's age at follow-up (Horn *et al.*, 1983). Based on their review of follow-up studies, Horn *et al.* (1983) suggest looking at outcomes at middle age and older.

3. Gender

Other important demographic information (not always provided) is the gender of the subjects and proportion of males and females in the sample. Because the ratio of LD males to females in the school-identified population is approximately four to one (Finucci and Childs, 1981), many research samples have been all male. Moreover, some have assumed that findings on male research samples generalize to all individuals with LDs, when in actuality we have very scant information regarding the nature of LDs in females.

When LD females are included in research samples, very few studies have reported data separately for males and females (Horn *et al.*, 1983). Moreover, even when this analysis has been conducted, there are significant methodological problems. In an extensive review of the literature, Vogel (1990) found that for LD females to be identified, they must be (1) significantly lower in intelligence, (2) more severely impaired in their language abilities and/or academic achievement, and (3) have a greater aptitude–achievement discrepancy than their male counterparts. The evidence suggests that LD females with the same level of intelligence and type, and severity of LDs as males, will not be as frequently identified.

Reasons for the underidentification of LD females include teacher-referral bias, lack of understanding of the nature of LDs in females, differences in psychometric profiles of females and males (Vogel and Walsh, 1987), and the differential incidence of attention deficit and hyperactivity in males and females (Vogel, 1990). As a result, gender differences found in longitudinal and follow-up studies on samples of school-identified males and females with LDs may be the result of bias of ascertainment and must be interpreted cautiously.

4. Regional Differences

Another important demographic factor is regional differences (deBettencourt *et al.*, 1989; Herjanic and Penick, 1972). In a study of LD youngsters who lived in a rural area, dropping out of high school did not affect employment opportunities (deBettencourt *et al.*, 1989), whereas in a study of LD students in an urban area, dropping out of high school affected succcesful employment. From their research, deBettencourt *et al.* (1989) emphasized the importance of noting regional differences as an important variable in determining outcomes.

G. Educational Opportunity and Remediation–Intervention

Evidence indicates that the length and quality of educational support and remedial help contribute to occupational and academic success (Blalock, 1981; Silver and Hagin, 1985). Yet, several reviews of follow-up studies found that in virtually none of the studies did the researchers focus on the quality of treatment as it affected outcomes (Schonhaut and Satz, 1983; Herjanic and Penick, 1972; Horn *et al.*, 1983). However, when samples have shared a common educational experience, for example, in Rawson's (1968), Rogan and Hartman's (1990), and Vogel and Adelman's (1990) studies, this experience provides an indirect measure of intervention effectiveness.

H. Comparison Groups

A major criticism of studies on adults with LDs is the absence of an appropriate control group (Bruck, 1985; Herjanic and Penick, 1972; Horn *et al.*, 1983). Without control or comparison groups, it is impossible to determine the effect of LDs upon adult adjustment and attainments. In addition, the absence of control groups also renders an inaccurate assessment of the long-term effects of remedial programs.

I. Instrumentation

Another limitation of studies on adults with LDs is the lack of valid and reliable measures for assessment (Herjanic and Penick, 1972; Vogel 1982). Only recently, diagnostic instruments such as the W-J–Revised (1989) have been developed and standardized on representative samples of the adult population (Cuenin, 1990). These new or revised instruments will not only enable more accurate and complete assessment immediately after high school, but they will also provide the means for ongoing evaluation through middle age and beyond.

XI. FUTURE RESEARCH RECOMMENDATIONS

Results of research on adults with LDs should be interpreted in light of the above critique. Overgeneralizing should be avoided when studies are flawed by use of nonrepresentative samples, bias of ascertainment, small sample size, lack of a comparison group, or attrition, to mention only a few. Moreover, the following recommendations are made for those planning descriptive, longitudinal, and/or follow-up studies of adults with LDs.

1. The definition and criteria for determining the presence of a learning disability and the selection criteria for the sample should be carefully delineated.

2. The subject pool from which the sample was drawn should be specified (e.g., a school-identified, clinic-identified, or research-identified sample) as well as the influence this may have on the results.

3. Demographic information should be delineated and used in interpretation of findings in light of the previous studies regarding the importance of age at first evaluation, retesting, or follow-up; gender; and SES.

4. Aptitude–achievement discrepancy as it reflects the severity of the learning disability of the sample studied should also be described at initial evaluation and at follow-up. Severity has been found to be one of several important variables influencing educational and occupational attainments and academic achievement levels in adulthood. The methods of quantification of severity should also be described as well as the rationale for selection of the specific model.

5. Etiology of the learning disability can have a significant impact on later achievement. Individuals whose learning disability is the result of known trauma to the brain comprise a distinct subgroup within the LD population and should be studied as a comparison group.

6. In conducting longitudinal and follow-up studies, researchers should determine whether or not the resultant sample has the same characteristics as the original sample as well as the reasons for nonparticipation. In the discussion of findings, researchers can then provide documentation as to whether or not the reasons for subject withdrawal have biased the results of the study.

7. Results must be interpreted in light of the sample studied. Descriptive data should be provided in all research studies on adults with LDs including:

a. cognitive abilities,
b. academic achievement,
c. age at first identification, and
d. educational history.

8. Selection of reliable and valid instrumentation appropriate to the age level of subjects is an important factor in designing research on LD adults. Recently, several measures have been revised that include adults in the standardization sample at various educational attainment levels. However, use of informal measures will still be required to supplement the available diagnostic tests. The importance of control and/or comparison groups will remain central in understanding and interpreting findings.

XII. CONCLUSIONS

As a result of methodological differences and weakness in the research studies to date, findings on adults with LDs are inconsistent. Nevertheless, some themes emerge. For example, considerable evidence indicates underachievement in the areas of reading, written language, and mathematics. With respect to cognitive abilities, the most consistent finding is that significant variability exists among subtest scores of both the WAIS-R and the W-J. Processing deficits are still present in LD adults as they continue to demonstrate problems with auditory perception, comprehension, and memory. Although not as prevalent as verbal deficits, particularly in the area of oral language, non-verbal abilities are also deficient in many LD adults, including problems with visual analysis and synthesis, visual–motor integration, orientation, and social perception. The persistent processing difficulties and resulting under-achievement have affected academic progress; considerable evidence indicates grade repetition, higher incidence of high school drop-out rate, and failure to go on to postsecondary programs.

The problems caused by LDs have also interfered with the psychological well-being of LD adults and have placed their emotional health at risk. Although there is much diversity with respect to the severity of personality and behavior traits, low self-esteem was repeatedly identified as a character-istic of individuals with LDs. Even as adults, they continued to struggle with feelings of helplessness, inadequacy, and stupidity.

Adults with LDs often depend on their families for financial and social sup-port. Many continue to live with their parents well past the traditional age of independence, and their social lives tend to revolve around family functions well beyond the norm. Problems with making friends and participating in social activities with peers continue into adulthood.

Although it cannot be gainsaid that some LD adults achieved success in the work place, they still experience disproportionate unemployment and under-employment. Using self-understanding of one's learning disability to select a career in which the individual's area of strength predominates is the major factor differentiating individuals who are successfully and unsuccessfully employed. Vocational training has essentially been either nonexistent or ineffective for LD individuals. Despite the fact that employers are becoming increasingly aware of how certain modifications in the work place could enable geater success for handicapped workers, it appears that employers are less understanding of individuals with cognitive disabilities and are focused on accommodating those with physical disabilities.

XIII. IMPLICATIONS

A. Educational Needs

Early identification of the disability is of primary importance to the future success of LD individuals. Although many schools have screening programs prior to kindergarten, screening after kindergarten is generally terminated; postkindergarten, schools rely almost exclusively on teacher referral. The benefits of early diagnosis (appropriate intervention, parent and teacher support, counseling and psychotherapy when necessary) have been documented and support the need to extend screening beyond kindergarten. Teacher-referral bias that has contributed to the underidentification of LD females also supports the need for extended screening.

A lack of understanding of LDs in general and the specific differences between LD males and females is pervasive. It is important to disseminate this information through the schools, medical professionals, and parent support groups. Parents must not just be aware of LDs; the opportunity to obtain a more thorough understanding must be made more accessible. Inferentially, the parents' lack of understanding has contributed to the limited and vague understanding that LD individuals have of their own strengths and weaknesses, even as adults. More extensive preservice and inservice training is important: (1) to ensure that teachers are properly prepared to accurately identify and refer students experiencing difficulties that may be due to a learning disability (2) to enable teachers to help LD students who are mainstreamed more effectively; and (3) to provide teachers with a framework for understanding the psychological concomitants of a learning disability.

Because the manifestations of LDs change with age, updated diagnostic information should be obtained prior to and during transitional periods (e.g., entering kindergarten, middle school, junior high, high school, postsecondary, and employment). There is a need to continually design and update intervention that addresses areas affected by processing deficits using individually prescribed strategies and remediation that target affected areas. Diagnostic reports should identify individual strengths and weaknesses and then provide remedial techniques and compensatory strategies that will specifically address problems caused by LDs in academic, social, and employment situations.

Whether or not LD students go on to postsecondary programs, there is a need for ongoing assistance with developing skills in reading, written language, and mathematics. Because evidence indicates that many LD students take longer to "catch up" academically and socially, some students might benefit from a fifth year of high school or a precollege program. This is particularly important for students who were in self-contained special education classes and/or in lower-track courses, where they never had the opportunity to take college-preparatory classes. Many of these students may be capable of attending 2 or 4-year college if they are first given the opportunity to take more challenging classes, particularly in English and mathematics in precollege programs.

Students who are qualified to attend college need to be aware of the range of available services for college students with LDs and how to access information not only about the programs, but also their individual rights to reasonable accommodations in the application process, program planning, and specific course work.

For those students who have either graduated from a postsecondary institution or for whom postsecondary education was not appropriate, there is need for ongoing assistance with improving reading, written language, math abilities, developing and using compensatory strategies, and interpersonal skills. Such assistance is vital for them to obtain appropriate jobs, maintain jobs, receive promotions, and improve the quality of their personal lives. Adult remediation centers that provide training in basic skills, personal and career counseling, job placement, and support groups would address these continuing needs of adults with LDs.

Of paramount importance is the need to educate employers about LDs. If employers do not understand the nature of LDs and how they may affect job performance, LD employees will be prevented from demonstrating their ability to successfully complete job responsibilities. Employers must also understand the rights and responsibilities of the employee and the employer with respect to reasonable accommodations; without tandem knowledge and cooperation, frustration and not progress is the likely result.

B. Psycho-Social Needs

The debilitating psycho-social effects of a learning disability certainly highlight the need for addressing emotional, behavioral, and social problems. There needs to be greater awareness of the importance of psychotherapy for individuals with LDs throughout their lives. During various transitions and/or periods of extreme stress, individual therapy might be necessary; at other times, it may be helpful for the LD individuals to participate in therapy with peers, family members, and spouses. During transitional times, support groups can be beneficial in addressing issues of adjustment and overcoming the feelings of fear and inadequacy that new situations tend to generate.

Some LD individuals need to acquire daily living skills that would enhance their ability to live independently and to have more active and fulfilling personal lives. A range of independent living facilities may address these issues. Some of these facilities might only provide support groups and the opportunity to participate in social activities, whereas other facilities might be designed to help individuals learn to cook, care for their apartments, and manage their finances.

C. Employment Needs

There is a need for vocational education and career counseling for individuals with LDs who must be assisted with identifying appropriate jobs, in the job search process, and in understanding their rights under federal and state civil rights law that entitle them to reasonable accommodations in connection with all aspects of employment. During enrollment in high school and in postsecondary educational programs, prework experiences should provide internships, job shadowing, and mentoring that would enhance future employability. Students with LDs need to experience first-hand how their learning disability may affect job performance and the compensatory skills required to accomplish job tasks. Some LD individuals would also benefit from ongoing mentoring to assist with solving problems that arise on the job and to help with working toward advancement. Services are needed that offer retraining and remediation to enhance basic skills, which will in turn lead to better wages, greater independence, and the likelihood of achieving a more satisfying life.

References

Adelman, P. (1988). An approach to meeting the needs of the learning disabled students in a four-year college setting. In "College and the Learning Disabled Student: Program Development, Implementation and Selection," 2nd ed., (C. T. Mangrum II and S. S. Strichart, eds.), pp. 237–249. Grune & Stratton, Philadelphia.

Adelman, P. B., and Vogel, S. A. (1990). College graduates with learning disabilities; Employment attainment and career patterns. Learn. Disabil. Q., 13(3), 154–166.

Balow, B., and Blomquist, M. (1965). Young adults ten to fifteen years after severe reading disability. Elem. School J. 66, 44–48.

Blalock, J. W. (1981). Persistent problems and concerns of young adults with learning disabilities. In "Bridges to Tomorrow," Vol. 2, "The Best of ACLD" (W. Cruickshank and A. Silver, eds.), pp. 35–55. Syracuse University Press, Syracuse, New York.

Blalock, J. W. (1982). Residual learning disabilities in young adults: Implications for rehabilitation. *J. Appl. Rehabil. Counsel.* **13(2),** 9–13.

Blalock, J. W. (1987a). Auditory language disorders. *In* "Young Adults with Learning Disabilities: Clinical Studies" (D. Johnson and J. Blalock, eds.), pp. 81–105. Grune & Stratton, Orlando, Florida.

Blalock, J. W. (1987b). Intellectual levels and patterns. *In* "Young Adults with Learning Disabilities: Clinical Studies" (D. Johnson and J. Blalock, eds.), pp. 47–65. Grune & Stratton, Orlando, Florida.

Blalock, J. W. (1987c). Problems in mathematics. *In* "Young Adults with Learning Disabilities: Clinical Studies" (D. Johnson and J. Blalock, eds.), pp. 205–217. Grune & Stratton, Orlando, Florida.

Bruck, M. (1985). The adult functioning of children with specific learning disabilities: A follow-up study. *In* "Advances in Applied Developmental Psychology," Vol. 1 (I. E. Sigel, ed.), pp. 91–129. Ablex, Norwood, New Jersey.

Buchanan, M., and Wolf, J. (1986). A comprehensive study of learning disabled adults. *J. Learn. Disabil.* **19(1),** 34–38.

Bursuck, W. D., Rose, E., Cowen, S., and Yahaya, M. A. (1989). Nationwide survey of postsecondary education services for students with learning disabilities. *Excep. Children* **56(3),** 236–245.

Cohen, J. (1985). Learning disabilities and adolescence: Developmental considerations. *In* "Adolescent Psychiatry: Developmental and Clinical Studies, Vol. 12 (M. Sugar, A. Esman, J. Looney, A. Schwartzberg and A. Sorosky, eds.), pp. 177–196. University of Chicago, Chicago.

Cordoni, B. (1979). Assisting dyslexic college students: An experimental program design at a unversity. *Bull. Orton Soc.* **29,** 263–268.

Cordoni, B., O'Donnell, J., Ramaniah, N., Kurtz, J., and Rosenshein, K. (1981). Wechsler Adult Intelligence score patterns for learning disabled young adults. *J. Learn. Disabil.* **14(7),** 404–407.

Cordoni, B. K., and Snyder, M. K. (1981). A comparison of learning disabled college students' achievement from WRAT and PIAT grade, standard, and subtest scores. *Psychol. Schools* **18,** 28–34.

Cowen, S. E. (1988). Coping strategies of university students with learning disabilities. *J. Learn. Disabil.* **21(3),** 161–164.

Cuenin, L. (1990). Use of the Woodcock–Johnson Psycho-Educational Battery with learning disabled adults. *Learn. Disabil. Focus* **5(2),** 119–123.

Dalke, C. (1988). Woodcock–Johnson Psycho-Educational Test Battery profiles: A comparative study of college freshmen with and without learning disabilities. *J. Learn. Disabil.* **21(9),** 567–570.

deBettencourt, L. U., Zigmond, N., and Thornton, H. (1989). Follow-up of postsecondary-age rural learning disabled graduates and dropouts. *Excep. Children* **56(1),** 40–49.

Dunn, L., and Markwardt, F. (1970). "Peabody Individual Achievement Test." American Guidance Service, Circle Pines, Minnesota.

Edgington, R. E. (1975). SLD children: A ten-year follow-up. *Academic Ther.* **11,** 53–64.

Educational Testing Service. (1977). "Sentence Structure Test, College Board Descriptive Tests of Language Skills." Author, Princeton, New Jersey.

Faas, L. A., and D'Alonzo, B. J. (1990). WAIS-R scores as predictors of employment success and failure among adults with learning disabilities. *J. Learn. Disabil.* **23(5),** 311–316.

Fafard, M.-B., and Haubrich, P. A. (1981). Vocational and social adjustment of learning disabled young adults: A followup study. *Learn. Disabil. Q.* **4,** 122–130.

Felton, R. (1986). Bowman–Gray follow-up study. Presented at the Orton Dyslexia National Conference, Philadelphia, Pennsylvania.

Finucci, J. M., and Childs, B. (1981). Are there really more dyslexic boys than girls? *In* "Sex Differences in Dyslexia" (A. Ansara, N. Geschwind, A. Galaburda, M. Albert, and N. Gartrell, eds.), pp. 1–10. Orton Dyslexia Society, Baltimore, Maryland.

Frauenheim, J. G. (1978). Academic achievement characteristics of adult males who were diagnosed as dyslexic in childhood. *J. Learn. Disabil.* **11,** 476–483.

Gerber, P. (1988). Highly successful learning disabled adults: Insights from case interviews. Presented at the Annual Association on Handicapped Student Service Programs in Postsecondary Education Conference, New Orleans, Louisiana.

Hammill, D., and Larsen, S. (1978). "Test of Written Language." Pro-Ed., Austin, Texas.

Haring, K. A., Lovett, D. L., and Smith, D. D. (1990). A follow-up study of recent special education graduates of learning disabilities programs. *J. Learn. Disabil.* **23,** 108–113.

Herjanic, B. M., and Penick, E. C. (1972). Adult outcomes of disabled child readers. *J. Special Educ.* **6,** 397–410.

Hoffmann, F. J., Sheldon, K. L., Minskoff, E. H., Sautter, S. W., Steidle, E. F. Baker, D. P., Bailey, M. B., and Echols, L. D. (1987). Needs of learning disabled adults. *J.Learn. Disabil.* **20(1),** 43–52.

Horn, W. F., O'Donnell, J. P., and Vitulano, L. A. (1983). Long-term follow-up studies of learning-disabled persons. *J. Learn. Disabil.* **16(9),** 542–555.

Jastak, J., and Jastak, S. (1978). "The Wide Range Achievement Test." Jastak Associates, Wilmington, Delaware.

Johnson, D. (1987a). Nonverbal disorders and related learning. *In* "Young Adults with Learning Disabilities: Clinical Studies" (D. Johnson and J. Blalock, eds.), pp. 219–232. Grune & Stratton, Orlando, Florida.

Johnson, D. (1987b). Reading disabilities. *In* "Young Adults with Learning Disabilities: Clinical Studies" (D. Johnson and J. Blalock, eds.), pp. 145–172. Grune & Stratton, Orlando, Florida.

Karlsen, B., Madden, R., and Gardner, E. (1977). "Stanford Diagnostic Reading Test" Blue Level. Harcourt-Brace-Jovanovich, Chicago.

Levin, E., Zigmond, N., and Birch, J. (1985). A follow-up study of 52 learning disabled students. *J. Learn. Disabil.* **13,** 542–547.

Mangrum, C. T., II, and Strichart, S. S. (1988). Peterson's Guide to Colleges with Programs for Learning Disabled Students." Peterson's Guides, Princeton, New Jersey.

Menkes, M. M., Rowe, J. S., and Menkes, J. H. (1967). A twenty-five year follow-up on the hyperactive child with MED. *Pediatrics* **39,** 393–399.

Minskoff, E. H., Sautter, S. W., Hoffmann, F. J., and Hawks, R. (1987). Employer attitudes toward hiring the learning disabled. *J. Learn. Disabil.* **20(1),** 53–57.

O'Connor, S. C., and Spreen, O. (1988). The relationship between parents' socioeconomic status and education level, and adult occupational and educational achievement of children with learning disabilities. *J. Learn. Disabil.* **21(3)**, 148–153.

Preston, R. C., and Yarington, D. J. (1967). Status of fifty retarded readers eight years after reading clinic diagnosis. *J. Read.* **11**, 122–129.

Rawson, M. R. (1968). "Developmental Language Disability: Adult Accomplishments of Dyslexic Boys." The Johns Hopkins Press, Baltimore.

Rogan, L., and Hartman, L. (1976). "A Follow-Up Study of Learning Disabled Children as Adults. Final report." ERIC Document Reproduction Service No. ED 163-728, Cove School, Evanston, Illinois.

Rogan, L. L., and Hartman, L. D. (1990). Adult outcome of learning disabled students ten years after initial follow-up. *Learn. Disabil. Focus* **5(2)**, 91–102.

Rudel, R. G. (1981). Residual effects of childhood reading disabilities. *Bull. Orton Soc.* **31**, 89–103.

Salvia, J., Gajar, A., Gajria, M., and Salvia, S. (1988). A comparison of WAIS-R profiles of nondisabled college freshmen and college students with learning disabilities. *J. Learn. Disabil.* **21(10)**, 632–641.

Scheiber, B., and Talpers, J. (1987). "Unlocking Potential: College and Other Choices for Learning Disabled People—A Step-by-Step Guide." Adler & Adler, Bethesda, Maryland.

Schonhaut, S., and Satz, P. (1983). Prognosis for children with learning disabilities: A review of follow-up studies. *In* "Developmental Neuropsychiatry" (M. Rutter, ed.), pp. 542–563. Guilford Press, New York.

Scuccimarra, D. J., and Speece, D. L. (1990). Employment outcomes and social integration of students with mild handicaps: The quality of life two years after high school. *J. Learn. Disabil.* **23(4)**, 213–218.

Silver, A. A., and Hagin, R. A. (1985). Outcomes of learning disabilities in adolescence. *In* "Adolescent Psychiatry: Developmental and Clinical Studies," Vol. 12, (M. Sugar, A. Esman, J. Looney, A. Schwartzberg and A. Sorosky, eds.), pp. 197–211, University of Chicago, Chicago.

Spekman, N. J., Oi, M. T., Goldberg, R. J., and Herman, K. (1989). LD children grow up: What can we expect for education, employment, and adjustment? Presented at the 40th Annual Conference of The Orton Dyslexia Society, Dallas, Texas.

Stone, C. A. (1987). Abstract reasoning and problem solving. *In* "Young Adults with Learning Disabilities: Clinical Studies" (D. Johnson and J. Blalock, eds.), pp. 67–79. Grune & Stratton, Orlando, Florida.

U.S. Department of Education (1987). "State Education Statistics Wallchart." U.S. Government Printing Office, Washington, D.C.

Vogel, S. A. (1982). On developing LD college programs. *J. Learn. Disabil.* **15**, 518–528.

Vogel, S. A. (1985a). Syntactic complexity in written expression of college writers. *Ann. Dyslexia* **35**, 137–157.

Vogel, S. A. (1985b). "The College Student with a Learning Disability: A Handbook for College LD Students, Admissions Officers, Faculty, and Administrators."Author, Lake Forest, Illinois.

Vogel, S. A. (1986). Levels and patterns of intellectual functioning among LD college students: Clinical and educational implications. *J. Learn. Disabil.* **19(2)**, 71–79.

Vogel, S. A. (1990). Gender differences in intelligence, language, visual–motor abilities, and academic achievement in students with learning disabilities: A review of the literature. *J. Learn. Disabil.* **23,** 44–52.

Vogel, S. A., and Adelman, P. (1981). Personnel development: College and university programs designed for learning disabled adults. *ICEC Q.* **1,** 12–18.

Vogel, S. A., and Adelman, P. B. (1990). Intervention effectiveness at the postsecondary level for the learning disabled. *In* "Intervention Research in Learning Disabilities" (T. Scruggs and B. Wong, eds.), Springer-Verlag, New York.

Vogel, S. A., and Konrad, D. (1988). Characteristic written expressive language deficits of the learning disabled: From general and specific intervention strategies. *J. Read. Writ. Learn. Disabil. Int.* **4,** 88–99.

Vogel, S., and Moran, M. (1982). Written language disorders in learning disabled college students; A preliminary report. *In* "Coming of Age: The Best of ACLD 1982," Vol. 3 (W. Cruickshank and J. Lerner, eds.), pp. 211–225. Syracuse University Press, Syracuse, New York.

Vogel, S. A., and Walsh, P. (1987). Gender differences in cognitive abilities in learning disabled females and males. *Ann. Dyslexia* **37,** 142–165.

Wagner, M. (1989a). The transition experiences of youth with disabilities: A report from The National Longitudinal Transition Study. Presented to the Division of Research, Council for Exceptional Children annual meetings, San Francisco.

Wagner, M. (1989b). Youth with disabilities during transition: An overview of descriptive findings from The National Longitudinal Transition Study. SRI International, Menlo Park, California.

Wagner, M., and Shaver, D. M. (1989). Educational programs and achievements of secondary special education students: Findings from The National Longitudinal Transition Study. Presented to the Special Education Special Interest Groups at the meetings of the American Educational Research Association, San Francisco.

Woodcock, R., and Johnson, M. B. (1977). "The Woodcock–Johnson Psycho-Educational Battery." DLM Teaching Resources, Allen, Texas.

Woodcock, R., and Johnson, M. B. (1989). "The Woodcock–Johnson Psycho-Educational Battery—Revised." DLM Teaching Resources, Allen, Texas.

Zigmond, N., and Thornton, H. (1989). Follow-up of postsecondary age learning disabled graduates and dropouts, *Learning Disabil. Res.* **1(1),** 50–55.

Author Index

Subject Index